HOLT Handbook
Grammar • Usage • Mechanics • Sentences

First Course
ANNOTATED TEACHER'S EDITION

Instructional Framework by

John E. Warriner

HOLT, RINEHART AND WINSTON
A Harcourt Education Company

Austin • Orlando • Chicago • New York • Toronto • London • San Diego

AUTHOR: JOHN E. WARRINER taught for thirty-two years in junior and senior high schools and in college. He was a high school English teacher when he developed the original organizational structure for his classic *English Grammar and Composition* series. The approach pioneered by Mr. Warriner was distinctive, and the editorial staff of Holt, Rinehart and Winston have worked diligently to retain the unique qualities of his pedagogy in the *Holt Handbook*. John Warriner also co-authored the *English Workshop* series and edited *Short Stories: Characters in Conflict*.

STAFF CREDITS

EDITORIAL

Executive Editor
Robert R. Hoyt

Program Editor
Marcia L. Kelley

Project Editor
Kathryn Rogers

Writing and Editing
David Bradford, Gabrielle Field, Karen H. Kolar, Theresa Reding, Suzi Hunn

Copyediting
Michael Neibergall, *Copyediting Manager;* Mary Malone, *Copyediting Supervisor;* Christine Altgelt, Joel Bourgeois, Elizabeth Dickson, Emily Force, Julie A. Hill, Julia Thomas Hu, Jennifer Kirkland, Millicent Ondras, Dennis Scharnberg, *Copyeditors*

Project Administration
Marie Price, *Managing Editor;* Lori De La Garza, *Editorial Operations Coordinator;* Heather Cheyne, Mark Holland, Marcus Johnson, Jennifer Renteria, Janet Riley, Kelly Tankersley, *Project Administration;* Ruth Hooker, Joie Pickett, Margaret Sanchez, *Word Processing*

Editorial Permissions
Janet Harrington, *Permissions Editor*

ART, DESIGN, AND PHOTO

Book Design
Diane Motz, *Senior Design Director;* Sally Bess, Tim Hovde, *Designers;* Charlie Taliaferro, *Design Associate*

Graphic Services
Kristen Darby, *Manager*

Image Acquisitions
Joe London, *Director;* Jeannie Taylor, *Photo Research Supervisor;* Rick Benavides, *Photo Researcher;* Sarah Hudgens, *Assistant Photo Researcher;* Elaine Tate, *Art Buyer Supervisor*

Cover Design
Bruce Bond, *Design Director*

PRODUCTION
Belinda Barbosa Lopez, *Senior Production Coordinator*
Carol Trammel, *Production Supervisor*
Beth Prevelige, *Senior Production Manager*

MANUFACTURING/INVENTORY
Shirley Cantrell, *Supervisor of Inventory and Manufacturing*
Wilonda Ieans, *Manufacturing Coordinator*
Mark McDonald, *Inventory Planner*

Copyright © 2003 by Holt, Rinehart and Winston

All rights reserved. No part of this publication may be reproduced or transmitted in any form or by any means, electronic or mechanical, including photocopy, recording, or any information storage and retrieval system, without permission in writing from the publisher.

Requests for permission to make copies of any part of the work should be mailed to the following address: Permissions Department, Holt, Rinehart and Winston, 10801 N. MoPac Expressway, Building 3, Austin, Texas 78759.

For acknowledgments, see page 520, which is an extension of the copyright page.

Printed in the United States of America

ISBN 0-03-066134-X

1 2 3 4 5 6 7 8 9   048   05 04 03 02

CONTENTS IN BRIEF

TEACHING RESOURCES

About This Book

John Warriner: In His Own Words T18
To Our Students T21
Teaching Strands: Connecting Grammar and Writing T24
Essays on Teaching Grammar T26
Overview of the Holt Handbook T48
Instructional Resources: Chapter by Chapter T60

PART 1

Grammar, Usage, and Mechanics

Grammar
1 The Parts of a Sentence 2
2 Parts of Speech Overview: Noun, Pronoun, Adjective 24
3 Parts of Speech Overview: Verb, Adverb, Preposition, Conjunction, Interjection 44
4 Complements 72
5 The Phrase 88
6 The Clause 112
7 Kinds of Sentence Structure 128

Usage
8 Agreement 146
9 Using Verbs Correctly 174
10 Using Pronouns Correctly 200
11 Using Modifiers Correctly 222
12 A Glossary of Usage 244

Mechanics
13 Capital Letters 264
14 Punctuation: End Marks, Commas, Semicolons, and Colons 288
15 Punctuation: Underlining (Italics), Quotation Marks, Apostrophes, Hyphens, Parentheses, Brackets, and Dashes 318
16 Spelling 346
17 Correcting Common Errors 376

PART 2

Sentences

18 Writing Effective Sentences 412
19 Sentence Diagramming 444

PART 3

Resources

▶ The History of English 466
▶ Test Smarts 470
▶ Grammar at a Glance 476

● Index 505
● Acknowledgments 520
● Photo and Illustration Credits 520

Contents **T3**

CONTENTS

Teaching Resources

About This Book **T18**
John Warriner: In His Own Words T18
To Our Students T21
Teaching Strands: Connecting Grammar and Writing T24
Essays on Teaching Grammar
    Dispelling the Myths about Grammar Instruction, by Amy Benjamin T26
    Grammar: Why Teach it? by Brock Haussamen T34
    Getting Down to Basics: Using What Students Already Know, by Rei Noguchi T41
    Raising Expectations: The Importance of Teaching Grammar to ESL Students,
        by Billy Boyar T45
Overview of the Holt Handbook T48
Instructional Resources: Chapter by Chapter T60

PART 1   Grammar, Usage, and Mechanics 1

The Parts of a Sentence

CHAPTER 1

Subject and Predicate, Kinds of Sentences 2

DIAGNOSTIC PREVIEW 2
    A. Identifying Sentences
    B. Identifying Subjects and Predicates
    C. Punctuating and Classifying Sentences

THE SENTENCE 4
    Sentence or Sentence Fragment? 4

SUBJECT AND PREDICATE 5
    The Subject 5
    Simple Subject and Complete Subject 6
    The Predicate 8
    Simple Predicate and Complete Predicate 10
    The Verb Phrase 11
    Finding the Subject 13
    Compound Subjects and Compound Verbs 13

KINDS OF SENTENCES 18

CHAPTER REVIEW 21
    A. Identifying Sentences
    B. Identifying Subjects
    C. Identifying Predicates
    D. Classifying and Punctuating Sentences

Writing Application: *Writing a Letter* 23

Parts of Speech Overview
Noun, Pronoun, Adjective 24

CHAPTER 2

DIAGNOSTIC PREVIEW: Identifying Nouns, Pronouns, and Adjectives 24

THE NOUN 25
Proper Nouns and Common Nouns 26
Concrete Nouns and Abstract Nouns 28
Collective Nouns 29

THE PRONOUN 30
Personal Pronouns 30
Reflexive and Intensive Pronouns 31
Demonstrative Pronouns 31
Interrogative Pronouns 32
Indefinite Pronouns 32
Relative Pronouns 32

THE ADJECTIVE 34
Articles 35
Nouns or Adjectives? 35
Demonstrative Adjectives 36
Proper Adjectives 37

DETERMINING PARTS OF SPEECH 39

CHAPTER REVIEW 41
  A. Identifying Types of Nouns
  B. Identifying Types of Pronouns
  C. Identifying Adjectives
  D. Identifying Nouns, Pronouns, and Adjectives

Writing Application: *Using Pronouns in a Report* 43

Parts of Speech Overview
Verb, Adverb, Preposition, Conjunction, Interjection 44

CHAPTER 3

DIAGNOSTIC PREVIEW: Identifying Verbs, Adverbs, Prepositions, Conjunctions, and Interjections 44

THE VERB 45
Action Verbs 45
Linking Verbs 46
Helping Verbs and Main Verbs 49
Transitive and Intransitive Verbs 52

Contents **T5**

THE ADVERB 54
    Adverb or Adjective? 55
    The Position of Adverbs 56

THE PREPOSITION 58
    The Prepositional Phrase 59
    Preposition or Adverb? 61

THE CONJUNCTION 62

THE INTERJECTION 65

DETERMINING PARTS OF SPEECH 67

CHAPTER REVIEW 69
    A. Identifying Types of Verbs
    B. Identifying Verb Phrases
    C. Identifying Adverbs
    D. Identifying Prepositions and Prepositional Phrases
    E. Identifying Conjunctions
    F. Identifying Verbs, Adverbs, Prepositions, Conjunctions, and Interjections

    Writing Application: *Using Prepositions in Directions* 71

Complements

CHAPTER 4

Direct and Indirect Objects, Subject Complements 72

DIAGNOSTIC PREVIEW: Identifying Complements 72

RECOGNIZING COMPLEMENTS 73

DIRECT OBJECTS 74

INDIRECT OBJECTS 76

SUBJECT COMPLEMENTS 79
    Predicate Nominatives 79
    Predicate Adjectives 81

CHAPTER REVIEW 85
    A. Classifying Complements
    B. Identifying Complements

    Writing Application: *Using Subject Complements to Write Riddles* 87

The Phrase

CHAPTER 5

Prepositional, Verbal, and Appositive Phrases 88

DIAGNOSTIC PREVIEW 88
   A. Identifying and Classifying Prepositional Phrases
   B. Identifying and Classifying Verbal Phrases and Appositives Phrases

WHAT IS A PHRASE? 89

PREPOSITIONAL PHRASES 90
   Adjective Phrases 92
   Adverb Phrases 94

VERBALS AND VERB PHRASES 98
   The Participle 98
   The Participial Phrase 100
   The Infinitive 102
   The Infinitive Phrase 103

APPOSITIVES AND APPOSITIVE PHRASES 106

CHAPTER REVIEW 109
   A. Identifying Prepositional Phrases
   B. Identifying Adjective and Adverb Phrases
   C. Classifying Verbal Phrases
   D. Identifying Verbal Phrases
   E. Identifying Appositive Phrases

   Writing Application: *Using Prepositional Phrases in a Note* 111

The Clause

CHAPTER 6

Independent and Subordinate Clauses 112

DIAGNOSTIC PREVIEW 112
   A. Identifying and Classifying Independent and Subordinate Clauses
   B. Identifying and Classifying Subordinate Clauses

WHAT IS A CLAUSE? 113

THE INDEPENDENT CLAUSE 114

THE SUBORDINATE CLAUSE 114
    The Adjective Clause 117
    The Adverb Clause 120

CHAPTER REVIEW 125
    A. Identifying Independent and Subordinate Clauses
    B. Identifying Adjective and Adverb Clauses
    C. Identifying Subordinate Clauses

    Writing Application: *Using Clauses in a Manual* 127

Kinds of Sentence Structure
Simple, Compound, Complex, and Compound-Complex Sentences 128

CHAPTER 7

DIAGNOSTIC PREVIEW 128
    A. Identifying and Classifying Clauses
    B. Identifying Simple, Compound, Complex, and Compound-Complex Sentences

THE SIMPLE SENTENCE 130

THE COMPOUND SENTENCE 131
    Simple Sentence or Compound Sentence? 133

THE COMPLEX SENTENCE 135

THE COMPOUND-COMPLEX SENTENCE 137

CHAPTER REVIEW 141
    A. Identifying Independent and Subordinate Clauses
    B. Identifying Simple and Compound Sentences
    C. Identifying Compound and Complex Sentences
    D. Classifying Compound, Complex, and Compound-Complex Sentences
    E. Classifying Sentences by Structure

    Writing Application: *Writing a Letter*... 144

CHAPTER 8

Agreement
Subject and Verb, Pronoun and Antecedent 146

DIAGNOSTIC PREVIEW 146
    A. Identifying Correct Subject-Verb Agreement and Pronoun-Antecedent Agreement
    B. Proofreading for Subject-Verb Agreement and Pronoun-Antecedent Agreement

NUMBER 147

AGREEMENT OF SUBJECT AND VERB 148

PROBLEMS IN AGREEMENT 150
    Phrases Between Subject and Verb 150
    Indefinite Pronouns 152
    Compound Subjects 155
    Other Problems in Subject-Verb Agreement 158

AGREEMENT OF PRONOUN AND ANTECEDENT 165

CHAPTER REVIEW 171
    A. Determining Subject and Verb Agreement
    B. Determining Pronoun and Antecedent Agreement
    Writing Application: *Using Agreement in a Composition* 172

CHAPTER 9

Using Verbs Correctly
Principal Parts, Regular and Irregular Verbs, Tense, Voice ... 174

DIAGNOSTIC PREVIEW: Proofreading Sentences for Correct Verb Forms 174

PRINCIPAL PARTS OF VERBS 175
    Regular Verbs 176
    Irregular Verbs 178

TENSE 186
    Consistency of Tense 188

ACTIVE AND PASSIVE VOICE 189

SIX TROUBLESOME VERBS 190
   Sit and *Set* 190
   Rise and *Raise* 191
   Lie and *Lay* 193

CHAPTER REVIEW 197
   A. Using Irregular Verbs
   B. Changing Tenses of Verbs
   C. Making Verb Tenses Consistent
   D. Identifying Active and Passive Voice

   Writing Application: *Using Verbs in a Story* 199

Using Pronouns Correctly

CHAPTER 10

Nominative and Objective Case Forms, Other Pronoun Problems 200

DIAGNOSTIC PREVIEW 200
   A. Correcting Errors in Pronoun Forms
   B. Revising for Clear Pronoun Reference

CASE 201
   The Nominative Case 203
   The Objective Case 206

SPECIAL PRONOUN PROBLEMS 211
   Who and *Whom* 211
   Pronouns with Appositives 213
   Reflexive Pronouns 214
   Clear Reference 216

CHAPTER REVIEW 219
   A. Identifying Correct Pronoun Forms
   B. Correcting Errors in Pronoun Forms
   C. Revising for Clear Pronoun Reference

   Writing Application: *Using Pronouns in a Letter* 221

CHAPTER 11

Using Modifiers Correctly
Comparison and Placement 222

DIAGNOSTIC PREVIEW: Revising Sentences by Correcting Errors in the
Use of Modifiers 222

WHAT IS A MODIFIER? 223
    One-Word Modifiers 223
    Phrases Used as Modifiers 224
    Clauses Used as Modifiers 224

COMPARISON OF ADJECTIVES AND ADVERBS 224
    Regular Comparison 225
    Irregular Comparison 227

SPECIAL PROBLEMS IN USING MODIFIERS 228

DOUBLE NEGATIVES 231

PLACEMENT OF MODIFIERS 232
    Prepositional Phrases 233
    Participial Phrases 236
    Adjective Clauses 238

CHAPTER REVIEW 241
    A. Using the Correct Modifier
    B. Writing Comparative and Superlative Forms of Modifiers
    C. Correcting Double Comparisons and Double Negatives
    D. Correcting Misplaced and Dangling Modifiers

    Writing Application: *Using Comparisons in a Letter* 243

CHAPTER 12

A Glossary of Usage
Common Usage Problems 244

DIAGNOSTIC PREVIEW: Correcting Errors in Usage 244

ABOUT THE GLOSSARY 245

CHAPTER REVIEW 261
    A. Identifying Correct Usage
    B. Proofreading for Correct Usage

    Writing Application: *Writing a Speech* 263

CHAPTER 13

Capital Letters
Rules for Capitalization **264**

DIAGNOSTIC PREVIEW: Proofreading Sentences for Correct Capitalization 264

USING CAPITAL LETTERS CORRECTLY 266

CHAPTER REVIEW 285
    A. Correcting Errors in Capitalization
    B. Proofreading Sentences for Correct Capitalization
    Writing Application: *Using Capital Letters in a Letter* 287

CHAPTER 14

Punctuation
End Marks, Commas, Semicolons, and Colons **288**

DIAGNOSTIC PREVIEW: Using End Marks, Commas, Semicolons, and Colons 288

END MARKS 290

COMMAS 294
    Compound Sentences 297
    Interrupters 299
    Introductory Words, Phrases, and Clauses 305
    Conventional Situations 306

SEMICOLONS 310

COLONS 311
    Conventional Situations 312

CHAPTER REVIEW 315
    A. Using End Marks, Commas, Semicolons, and Colons Correctly
    B. Proofreading a Business Letter
    C. Proofreading for Correct Punctuation
    Writing Application: *Using Punctuation in an Announcement* 317

CHAPTER 15

Punctuation
Underlining (Italics), Quotation Marks, Apostrophes, Hyphens, Parentheses, Brackets, and Dashes 318

DIAGNOSTIC PREVIEW 318
    A. Proofreading Sentences for the Correct Use of Underlining (Italics), Quotation Marks, Apostrophes, Hyphens, Parentheses, Brackets, and Dashes
    B. Punctuating Quotations Correctly

UNDERLINING (ITALICS) 320

QUOTATION MARKS 322

APOSTROPHES 330
    Possessive Case 330
    Contractions 333
    Plurals 337

HYPHENS 338

PARENTHESES 340

BRACKETS 341

DASHES 341

CHAPTER REVIEW 343
    A. Using Underlining (Italics), Quotation Marks, Dashes, Parentheses, and Brackets
    B. Proofreading for the Correct Use of Punctuation and Capitalization in Quotations
    C. Writing Dialogue Correctly
    D. Using Apostrophes and Hyphens

Writing Application: *Using Quotations in Reports* 345

CHAPTER 16

Spelling
Improving Your Spelling 346

DIAGNOSTIC PREVIEW: Proofreading Sentences for Correct Spelling 346

GOOD SPELLING HABITS 347

SPELLING RULES 348
    ie and *ei* 348
    –cede, *–ceed,* and *–sede* 350
    Prefixes and Suffixes 350
    Forming the Plurals of Nouns 355

WORDS OFTEN CONFUSED 358

CHAPTER REVIEW 371
    A. Identifying Misspelled Words
    B. Writing the Correct Plural Form
    C. Choosing Between Words Often Confused
    D. Identifying Misused Words

    Writing Application: *Using Correct Spelling in a Review* 373

SPELLING WORDS 374

CHAPTER 17

Correcting Common Errors
Key Language Skills Review 376

GRAMMAR AND USAGE 377
    Grammar and Usage Test: Section 1 396
    Grammar and Usage Test: Section 2 397

MECHANICS 400
    Mechanics Test: Section 1 406
    Mechanics Test: Section 2 407

Contents

PART 2 Sentences 410

CHAPTER 18 Writing Effective Sentences 412

DIAGNOSTIC PREVIEW 412
    A. Identifying Sentences, Sentence Fragments, and Run-on Sentences
    B. Combining Sentences
    C. Revising Stringy and Wordy Sentences
    D. Creating Sentence Variety and Using Transitions

WRITING COMPLETE SENTENCES 414
    Sentence Fragments 414
    Run-on Sentences 416

COMBINING SENTENCES 418
    Inserting Words 419
    Inserting Phrases 420
    Using *And, But,* or *Or* 423
    Using Subordinate Clauses 425

IMPROVING SENTENCE STYLE 428
    Revising Stringy Sentences 428
    Revising Wordy Sentences 430

BEYOND SENTENCE STYLE 431
    Varying Sentence Beginnings 432
    Varying Sentence Structure 434
    Using Transitions 437

CHAPTER REVIEW 441
    A. Identifying Sentences, Sentence Fragments, and Run-ons
    B. Combining Sentences
    C. Revising a Passage to Correct Errors and Improve Style

CHAPTER 19 Sentence Diagramming 444

THE SENTENCE DIAGRAM 444
    Subjects and Verbs.. 444
    Adjectives and Adverbs 448
    Objects.. 450
    Subject Complements 452
    Phrases... 454
    Verbals and Verbal Phrases 456
    Appositives and Appositive Phrases 457
    Subordinate Clauses 458
    The Kinds of Sentence Structure 460

PART 3 | **Resources** **464**

THE HISTORY OF ENGLISH 466
    Origins and Uses 466

TEST SMARTS 470
    Becoming "Test-Smart" 470

GRAMMAR AT A GLANCE 476

Index 505

Acknowledgments 520

Photo and Illustration Credits 520

John Warriner: In His Own Words

The name of John Warriner has long been associated with a rather formal style of teaching traditional school grammar. Interestingly, however, John Warriner did not consider himself primarily a grammarian but rather an English teacher. Also, he did not consider his books primarily grammar textbooks but rather reference handbooks for students and teachers of composition.

In his prefaces to *Handbook of English: Book One* and *Handbook of English: Book Two* (published in 1948 and 1951, respectively), Warriner articulated his vision of what his textbooks were intended to do and how they might best be used. What he had to say might surprise you.

First, Warriner's goal in preparing these books was to create "a completely flexible teaching tool adaptable to . . . any individual classroom." He did *not* design his books to be teaching texts in which the class moves sequentially from chapter to chapter, every student doing all the exercises along the way. In fact, he asserted just the opposite: "[A] book of this kind is not intended for methodical coverage from cover to cover. The book contains more material than any one class can handle in a single year. Teachers will teach those chapters that a particular class needs and will assign exercises in proportion to the need."

John Warriner: In His Own Words

In the 1940s and '50s, John Warriner (1907–1987) published his first grammar and composition textbooks. Mr. Warriner's goal as a teacher and as a writer was to help students learn to use English effectively in order to be successful in school and in life. Throughout the years that followed, Mr. Warriner revised his original books and wrote others, creating the series on which this textbook is based. Included in Mr. Warriner's books were a number of short essays to his students. In these essays, Mr. Warriner explored the role of language in human life, the importance of studying English, and the value of mastering the conventions of standard English.

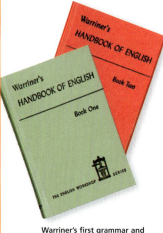

Warriner's first grammar and composition textbooks, published in the 1940s and '50s.

We could tell you what John Warriner thought about the study of English, but we'd rather let you read what he himself had to say.

Language Is Human

"Have you ever thought about how important language is? Can you imagine what living would be like without it?

"Of all creatures on earth, human beings alone have a fully developed language, which enables them to communicate their thoughts to others in words, and which they can record in writing for others to read. Other creatures, dogs, for example, have ways of communicating their feelings, but they are very simple ways and very simple feelings. Without words, they must resort to mere noises, like barking, and to physical actions, like tail wagging. The point is that one very important difference between human beings and other creatures is the way human beings can communicate with one another by means of this remarkable thing called language. When you stop to think about it, you realize that language is involved to some extent in almost everything you do."

(from *English Grammar and Composition: First Course*, 1986)

Why Study English?

"The reason English is a required subject in almost all schools is that nothing in your education is more important than learning how to express yourself well. You may know a vast amount about a subject, but if you are unable to communicate what you know, you are severely handicapped. No matter how valuable your ideas may be, they will not be very useful if you cannot express them clearly and convincingly. Language is the means by which people communicate. By learning how your language functions and by practicing language skills, you can acquire the competence necessary to express adequately what you know and what you think."

(from *English Grammar and Composition: Fourth Course*, 1977)

Why Study Grammar?

"Grammar is a description of the way a language works. It explains many things. For example, grammar tells us the order in which sentence parts must be arranged. It explains the work done by the various kinds of words—the work done by a noun is different from the work done by a verb. It explains how words change their form according to the way they are used. Grammar is useful because it enables us to make statements about how to use our language. These statements we usually call rules.

"The grammar rule that the normal order of an English sentence is subject-verb-object may not seem very important to us, because English is our native tongue and we naturally use this order without thinking. But the rule would be very helpful to people who are learning English as a second language. However, the rule that subjects and verbs 'agree' (when the subject is plural, the verb is plural), and the rule that some pronouns (*I, he, she, we, they*) are used as subjects while others (*me, him, her, us, them*) are used as objects—these are helpful rules even for native speakers of English.

"Such rules could not be understood—in fact, they could not be formed—without the vocabulary of grammar. Grammar, then, helps us to state how English is used and how we should use it."

(from *English Grammar and Composition: Third Course*, 1982)

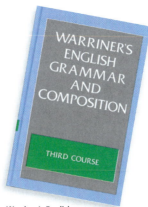

Warriner's English Grammar and Composition: Third Course, 1982

Warriner's English Grammar and Composition: Fourth Course, 1977

Warriner was also attuned to the needs of individual students within a class, acknowledging that "students arrive with greatly varying degrees of mastery of language essentials. One student may be weak in sentence sense, another in pronoun usage. But each student requires for his [or her] special weakness a full text explanation, a wealth of examples, and practice material," which Warriner endeavored to provide.

To organize his material, Warriner separated language instruction into sections, choosing to present grammar before usage. His rationale for doing so was that a working understanding of grammar terms and concepts would provide students and teachers a common vocabulary for discussing usage concepts. However, Warriner was not comfortable with the implications of such a separation: "This is not to imply that grammar can be separated from usage in practice. *The only valid reason for teaching grammar at all is to apply it to specific usage problems* [emphasis added]."

Finally, in spite of his reputation as a grammar curmudgeon, John Warriner had some rather modern ideas about language. He believed that English was an evolving language and that appropriate usage varied according to the situation. In fact, Warriner was adamant that a language arts textbook "must make clear to students that correctness in English is not fixed, but variable, that there are levels of usage, and that any living language suffers change."

Why Is Punctuation Important?

"The sole purpose of punctuation is to make clear the meaning of what you write. When you speak, the actual sound of your voice, the rhythmic rise and fall of your inflections, your pauses and hesitations, your stops to take breath—all supply a kind of 'punctuation' that serves to group your words and to indicate to your listener precisely what you mean. Indeed, even the body takes part in this unwritten punctuation. A raised eyebrow may express interrogation more eloquently than any question mark, and a knuckle rapped on the table shows stronger feeling than an exclamation point.

"In written English, however, where there are none of these hints to meaning, simple courtesy requires the writer to make up for the lack by careful punctuation."

(from *English Grammar and Composition: Fourth Course*, 1973)

Why Learn Standard English?

"Consider the following pair of sentences:

1. George don't know the answer.
2. George doesn't know the answer.

"Is one sentence clearer or more meaningful than the other? It's hard to see how. The speaker of sentence 1 and the speaker of sentence 2 both convey the same message about George and his lack of knowledge. If language only conveyed information about the people and events that a speaker is discussing, we would have to say that one sentence is just as good as the other. However, language often carries messages the speaker does not intend. The words he uses to tell us about events often tell us something about the speaker himself. The extra, unintended message conveyed by 'George don't know the answer' is that the speaker does not know or does not use one verb form that is universally preferred by educated users of English.

"Perhaps it is not fair to judge people by how they say things rather than by what they say, but to some extent everyone does it. It's hard to know what is in a person's head, but the language he uses is always open to inspection, and people draw conclusions from it. The people who give marks and recommendations, who hire employees or judge college applications, these and others who may be important in your life are speakers of educated English. You may not be able to impress them merely by speaking their language, but you are likely to impress them unfavorably if you don't. The language you use tells a lot about you. It is worth the trouble to make sure that it tells the story you want people to hear."

(from *English Grammar and Composition: Fourth Course*, 1973)

English Grammar and Composition: Fourth Course, 1973

John Warriner

TO OUR STUDENTS

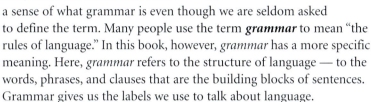

What is grammar?

That seems like a simple question, doesn't it? Most of us have a sense of what grammar is even though we are seldom asked to define the term. Many people use the term **grammar** to mean "the rules of language." In this book, however, *grammar* has a more specific meaning. Here, *grammar* refers to the structure of language — to the words, phrases, and clauses that are the building blocks of sentences. Grammar gives us the labels we use to talk about language.

What about the rules that govern how language is used in various social situations? In this book, these rules are called usage. Unlike grammar, **usage** determines what is considered standard ("isn't") or nonstandard ("ain't") and what is considered formal ("why") or informal ("how come"). Usage is a social convention, a behavior or rule that is customary among members of a group. As a result, what is considered acceptable usage can vary from group to group and from situation to situation.

To speak standard English requires a knowledge of grammar and of standard usage. To write standard English requires something more—a knowledge of mechanics. **Mechanics** refers to the rules for written, rather than spoken, language. Spelling, capitalization, and punctuation are concepts we don't even think about when we are speaking, but they are vital to writing effectively.

Why should I study grammar, usage, and mechanics?

Many people would say that you should study grammar to learn to root out errors in your speech and writing. Certainly, the *Holt Handbook* can help you learn to avoid making errors and to correct the errors you do make. More importantly, though, studying grammar, usage, and mechanics gives you the skills you need to take sentences and passages apart and to put them together, to learn which parts go together and which don't. Instead of writing sentences and passages that you hope sound good, you can craft your sentences to create just the meaning and style you want.

Knowing grammar, usage, and mechanics gives you the tools to understand and discuss your own language, to communicate clearly the things you want to communicate, and to develop your own communication style. Further, mastery of language skills can help you succeed in your other classes, in future classes, on standardized tests, and in the larger world — including, eventually, the workplace.

How do I use the *Holt Handbook*?

The skills taught in the *Holt Handbook* are important to your success in reading, writing, speaking, and listening.

Not only can you use this book as a complete grammar, usage, and mechanics textbook, but you can also use it as a reference guide when you work on any piece of writing. Whether you are writing a personal letter, a report for your social studies class, or some other piece of writing, you can use the *Holt Handbook* to answer your questions about grammar, usage, capitalization, punctuation, and spelling.

How is the *Holt Handbook* organized?

The *Holt Handbook* is divided into three main parts:

PART 1 The **Grammar, Usage, and Mechanics** chapters provide instruction on and practice using the building blocks of language—words, phrases, clauses, capitalization, punctuation, and spelling. Use these chapters to discover how to take sentences apart and analyze them. The last chapter, **Correcting Common Errors,** provides additional practice on key language skills as well as standardized test practice in grammar, usage, and mechanics.

PART 2 The **Sentences** chapters include Writing Effective Sentences and Sentence Diagramming. **Writing Effective Sentences** provides instruction on and practice with writing correct, clear, and interesting sentences. **Sentence Diagramming** teaches you to analyze and diagram sentences so you can see how the parts of a sentence relate to each other.

PART 3 The **Resources** section includes **The History of English,** a concise history of the English language; **Test Smarts,** a handy guide to taking standardized tests in grammar, usage, and mechanics; and **Grammar at a Glance,** a glossary of grammatical terms.

How are the chapters organized?

Each chapter begins with a Diagnostic Preview, a short test that covers the whole chapter and alerts you to skills that need improvement, and ends with a Chapter Review, another short test that tells you how well you have mastered that chapter. In between, you'll see rules, which are basic statements of grammar, usage, and mechanics principles. The rules are illustrated with examples and followed by exercises and reviews that help you practice what you have learned.

What are some other features of this textbook?

- **Oral Practice**—spoken practice and reinforcement of rules and concepts
- **Writing Applications**—activities that let you apply grammar, usage, and mechanics concepts in your writing
- **Tips & Tricks**—easy-to-use hints about grammar, usage, and mechanics
- **Meeting the Challenge**—questions or short activities that ask you to approach a concept from a new angle
- **Style Tips**—information about formal and informal uses of language
- **Help**—pointers to help you understand either key rules and concepts or exercise directions

Holt Handbook on the Internet

As you move through the *Holt Handbook,* you will find the best online resources at **go.hrw.com.**

Teaching Strands

Connecting Grammar and Writing
This teaching-strand chart shows you some ways to connect grammar instruction and writing instruction.

The *Holt Handbook* is designed to be a flexible teaching tool that accommodates many teaching philosophies and styles. For example, some teachers will prefer to use the handbook as a reference source, having students refer to it only as the need for explicit grammar instruction arises. Others will use the handbook as a teaching text, having their classes work through the instruction, examples, and exercises in a more methodical fashion. Your personal teaching style and the needs of your students will determine the best way for you to teach this material.

GO TO: go.hrw.com

Writing Assignments	Rationale
NARRATION	An effective short story should include proper pronoun use, strong verbs, vivid adjectives, precise adverbs, and correctly capitalized and punctuated supporting quotations.
RESPONSE TO LITERATURE	To describe a plot and offer an opinion when writing a book review, writers rely on carefully chosen positive and negative words, fresh descriptions, and words signaling order of events. Correct pronoun case must be used to show the author's point of view. Appositives are an easy way to provide additional information.
PERSUASION	An effective persuasive article makes skillful use of clear, exact adjectives and adverbs. Exclamatory sentences with strong active-voice verbs may be used to convey emotion; interrogative sentences may direct a line of thought.
RESEARCH	An effective research report depends on clear language and credible information correctly spelled, quoted, and cited. Showing relationships between main ideas and supporting information may require using compound and complex sentences and conjunctive adverbs.

Links to Grammar	Links to Usage	Links to Mechanics
▶ pronouns, adjectives (Ch. 2); adverbs (Ch. 3)	▶ pronoun-antecedent agreement (Ch. 8); pronoun case (Ch. 10); comparison (Ch. 11)	▶ quotation marks (Ch. 15)
▶ verbs (Ch. 3)	▶ verb tense, active voice (Ch. 9)	▶ commas in a series (Ch. 14)
▶ adjectives (Ch. 2); adverbs (Ch. 3)	▶ comparison of modifiers, double negatives (Ch. 11)	▶ capitalization of book titles (Ch. 13)
▶ pronouns (Ch. 2); complements (Ch. 4)	▶ pronoun-antecedent agreement (Ch. 8); pronoun case (Ch. 10)	▶ apostrophes with contractions and possessives (Ch. 15)
▶ phrases and clauses (Ch. 5 & Ch. 6)		▶ commas with interrupters (Ch. 14)
▶ adjectives (Ch. 2); adverbs (Ch. 3)	▶ comparison of adjectives and adverbs (Ch. 11)	▶ commas in a series (Ch. 14)
▶ kinds of sentences (Ch. 1)	▶ subject-verb agreement with indefinite pronouns (Ch. 8)	▶ question marks and exclamation marks (Ch. 14)
▶ verbs (Ch. 3)	▶ active voice (Ch. 9)	
▶ parts of speech (Ch. 2 & Ch. 3)	▶ common errors (Ch. 12)	▶ spelling words often confused (Ch. 16)
▶ clauses (Ch. 6); sentence structure (Ch. 7)	▶ correct placement of prepositional phrases and adjective clauses (Ch. 11)	▶ underlining (italics), quotation marks (Ch. 15)

ESSAYS ON TEACHING GRAMMAR

By Amy Benjamin

Dispelling the Myths about Grammar Instruction

I know an excellent English teacher whose students, many years after graduation, remember her for her grammar lessons. Unfortunately, instead of being proud of this, she is chagrined. . . . "*Grammar*!? Of all things in my class to remember! Why *grammar*? Why can't they remember me for all the wonderful literature I taught them? for what I taught them about composition? expression? creativity? Why just *grammar*? I don't even teach *grammar* anymore. I teach the *writing* process."

Perhaps these students remembered their grammar lessons because of the usefulness of those lessons or because of the satisfaction that they derived from learning challenging material. Perhaps they remembered because those lessons in syntax, placement, word classification, and the subtleties of style helped them to be better writers, more efficient readers, clearer thinkers.

It is not uncommon for English teachers as well as their trainers and supervisors to hold that the teaching of grammar is quaint and unnecessary at best, prejudicial and exclusionary at worst.

How lamentable it is that teaching writing through a process approach has become an orthodoxy in which the grammatical strand of English language arts is pitted against the literary strand, as if the two are not intertwined. Who set up this false dichotomy? The notion that grammar instruction is antithetical to the writing process is specious. My purpose in this essay is to debunk some of the myths about grammar instruction and to refurbish its tarnished reputation.

It is not uncommon for English teachers as well as their trainers and supervisors to hold that the teaching of grammar is quaint and unnecessary at best, prejudicial and exclusionary at worst. The problem begins with muddy terminology. Some people conflate the terms *grammar, usage,* and *mechanics,* as well as the terms *correct/incorrect* and *standard/ nonstandard.* Before I turn my fire extinguisher on the grammar myths, let me clarify my terms: By *grammar,* I refer to the rules which govern how words function in a sentence to make meaning. That *man bites dog* means something different from *dog bites man* is a function of grammar. By *usage,* I refer to the social conventions that determine what is considered standard. By *standard,* I do not mean *correct.* I mean that style of the English language which most educated people accept in formal circumstances. By *mechanics,* I refer to physical manifestations of language such as spelling, punctuation, capitalization and other conventions. In the case of *mechanics,* the terms *correct* and *incorrect* are more appropriate than they are when we are talking about matters of usage, but even spelling is not without gray areas.

Reasonable people can disagree over matters of content and methodology in teaching. However, I think everyone would agree that to understand a complicated system we need to know the names of its parts, their forms and functions, how the parts relate to the whole, and where these parts belong if the system is to operate at maximum efficiency. That said, here's what some people say about grammar instruction, and why I disagree with them.

Myth #1:

The explicit teaching of grammar does not improve writing ability, so time spent on grammar is time not spent on more worthy pursuits in the English classroom.

Think about it. Suppose my car is making a funny noise. Suppose I have no better understanding of what is going on under the hood than that. I take it to my mechanic, trusting his knowledge, integrity, and skill. He'll figure out what's wrong with my car and fix the problem. I'll pay the bill, and if all is not well, I'll get either another mechanic or another car. That is how many car owners (myself included) operate. We don't have the time or the inclination to learn the taxonomy, nomenclature, and anatomy of our cars.

When we don't speak explicitly to students about grammar, syntax, diction, and coherence, we have to resort to the "funny noise" method: We have to say "This part just doesn't sound right here," or "You're not saying this clearly." We may be able to help writers fix the sentence, but we haven't given them the generality that will allow them to apply what they've learned to similar circumstances.

On the other hand, I can know the names of all the tools in my toolbox, what each is for, and how they relate to one another; but if I don't use them to facilitate an actual job in progress, then my knowledge does not fulfill its intended purpose. For many of us, the grammar lessons that we learned in school were about "picking out." We'd "pick out" all kinds of structures: the parts of speech, subjects and predicates, simple subjects, helping verbs. Later, we'd hunt down adverbial clauses, subject complements, infinitives. We'd underline and double underline. We'd diagram. The trouble with our instruction was not that it was misguided, but that it was unfinished. Having learned to spot prepositional phrases, we may not have learned why doing so could improve our discourse.

How can we *use* our ability to identify grammatical structures such as prepositional phrases in our own reading and writing? We may have learned that the object of a preposition must be in the objective case, and that the object of a preposition is never the subject of the sentence. This knowledge helps us solve some usage problems, but that is not its main value. Knowing how to discern the subject and verb can help us read dense prose. When reading dense prose, the reader needs strategies. One such strategy is to reduce the sentence to its subject and verb. That done, the reader sees prepositional phrases for what they are: details. Beyond that, knowing about prepositions helps writers add sentence variety, as they learn not to begin sentence after sentence with the subject. Beginning a sentence with a prepositional phrase can set the stage for the action, but we have to be judicious: Sometimes, that prepositional phrase can be distracting or redundant. As modifiers, prepositional phrases can be movable, and their placement affects meaning, rhythm, and emphasis. Prepositional phrases, "time and place words," add detail and dimension. The novice writer who has difficulty fleshing out a topic can do well to consciously add more prepositional phrases. It is knowing what prepositional phrases can and can't do for you that makes being able to identify them worthwhile. Selecting standard pronoun case, creating purposeful variety in sentence structure, adding detail and dimension, and eliminating redundancy are some good reasons for being able to recognize prepositional phrases.

> It is knowing what prepositional phrases can and can't do for you that makes being able to identify them worthwhile.

Recognition of a grammatical structure is only the beginning. If we think of grammar instruction as building an awareness of language choices available to the careful writer, then we view such instruction in two phases: recognition and application. Too often, the application phase does not happen. When it does not, the recognition phase seems to lack practicality. Thus does grammar instruction fall out of favor.

Myth #2:

Grammar instruction applies only to the editing phase of the writing process.

When people operate under this myth, they are confusing grammar with usage and mechanics. Usage and mechanics may be seen as "touch-ups," part of the finishing-off of a written piece. As such, they are not essential to the real intellectual work of the process, although no one should minimize their importance. Usage and mechanics can determine the first and last impressions that the reader gets of the writer's work. The point is that we should not limit our understanding of grammar to the surface features of usage and mechanics.

Along with diction and rhetoric, grammar (unlike usage and mechanics) is *organic* to the crafting of sentences and text. Writers with an awareness of grammar can make informed choices about how word order affects meaning. Picture a carpenter. He doesn't just blindly reach into his toolbox, pull out a screwdriver, try to make it do the work of a wrench, and figure he'll just sand down the rough spots later. We can make our students better writers if we teach them to use grammatical knowledge consciously as they match their syntax to their intentions.

We understand the power of graphic organizers in both reading and writing for many learners. We teach students to map their ideas as a prewriting strategy. We teach them to make Venn diagrams to show similarities and differences, and flowcharts to express sequence. Sentence structures are patterns. We can think in terms of certain grammatical templates, containers, that work well for certain types of ideas. Parallel structure and compound sentences or simple sentences with compound constituents are good containers for *like* elements bearing equal importance. Complex sentences are good containers to use when we need to show the backgrounding and foregrounding of elements that do not bear equal importance. Sentence structure selections occur in the drafting and revision stages of the writing process, as the writer searches for the clearest, most efficient way to express thoughts.

Many writers have an intuitive sense of what kinds of containers work best with what kinds of ideas. When we bring this underlying awareness of grammar to the conscious level, we help students manage inchoate ideas in the same way

Essays on Teaching Grammar

that a graphic organizer, such as a Venn diagram, might. Indeed, there is much to be said for using one of the many versions of graphic organizers *along with* sentence structure templates. The writer can then look at a branch diagram or a cluster, decide how the ideas are related, and then consider an array of syntactical containers to suit them.

What I've described is a way of understanding the role of grammar in the writing process that is deeper than what is commonly thought, i.e., that grammatical thinking enters the picture only as the cleanup man. In fact, we already make intuitive grammatical choices as we compose our thoughts. Those intuitive choices may or may not be the best ones for the purpose. By building awareness of sentence and textual structure, we can increase our chances that our message is clear, efficient, and graceful.

Myth #3:
Grammar is boring.

There are many ways to make our classrooms boring. We can "cover material" in a perfunctory way, "going over" the exercises done for homework or as seatwork. We can convey to students that their language is "wrong" and ours is "right." We can be language prudes, fainting and blanching at every double negative or misplaced modifier that dares to show its face in our presence. We can insist that the answer key is always the authority and that grammar is a "no discussion" subject. We can isolate the study of grammar, treat it as something we "have to get through" before moving on to literature. We can fail to make any connection between grammar and journalism, grammar and advertising, grammar and novels, grammar and drama, grammar and music, grammar and poetry. These are ways to make grammar boring.

I've heard teachers claim that grammar instruction interferes with creativity.

I've heard teachers claim that grammar instruction interferes with creativity. "Grammar is boring," they say. "And writing should be fun and interesting." This is a misguided notion, because creativity thrives within structure. The sonneteer works within a strictly prescribed structure, choosing that structure because it is the best container for particular ideas. The sonnet form is not constraining but liberating: The format frees the writer from decisions about rhythm and rhyme scheme. Because of the structure, half the work is done. I can't think of any creative pursuit—music, fine arts, dance, photography, drama, writing—that does not demand mastery of technique. I can't think of any creative pursuit in which there is no terminology, no anatomy, no structure, no tradition, no rules. Why would learning any kind of writing, much less creative writing, be detached from the fundamentals? Knowledge of structure is not a hindrance, but a guide that enables, rather than impedes, creativity.

Sometimes, grammar instruction is thought of as "drill and kill." This pejorative implies that the instruction will consist of lower level thinking skills, mindless repetition, and lack of application to authentic language. We picture fill-in-the-blank workbook-type questions in which there is one right answer. The book that you have in your hands is an extremely useful, in fact indispensable, tool for the teaching of language. However, any grammar text is most effective when used *along with*, not in place of, literature and student writing. It might seem that students would naturally make the crossover from what they learn in grammar exercises to their own language use, but such is not necessarily the case. As teachers, we have to make that crossover happen very deliberately, pointing out structures that students have learned and how those structures are used to make meaning in authentic contexts. Thus does grammar instruction transcend the practice exercises that illustrate targeted concepts.

Everybody loves language; children and teenagers love it especially, because they are in the process of defining their own culture by laying claim to words and expressions all their own. When we invite students to analyze their own neologisms, grammatical idiosyncrasies, and dialectical styles, we enliven grammar lessons immeasurably. As English teachers, we embrace all forms of the English language even while we recognize that mastery of standard English is essential for success in certain precincts of society.

Another way to make grammar instruction interesting is to let students discover how language changes right before our eyes. Movies and novels set in various pockets of the English-speaking world are museums of linguistic anthropology. Compare the idioms of *To Kill A Mockingbird* to those of *The Color Purple*. Analyze the language of a movie set in New Orleans and compare it to the language of a movie set in Los Angeles.

There are many ways to make our classrooms interesting. Our love of the subject is contagious. Grammar is exciting and rewarding to learn not because we get the answers right, but because we've applied logic and found patterns, and because there may be more than one answer, depending on the circumstances, audience, and purpose. Contrary to myth, a good grammar lesson can invite a lively discussion about ambiguities in meaning and the best way to express thought in a particular context. It can even ignite a discussion about social power structures, prejudices, and immigration. This is not boring stuff.

Myth #4:
Grammar applies only to English classes.

For lack of a better term, we refer to subjects other than English as "content areas." Aside from the obvious expectation that we use standard English in school, how can students apply grammar to their content area classes?

Every teacher wants students to be better readers. A law student told me recently that she was glad that she knew something about grammar, because she needed it to read complex materials in her courses. She found that by mentally pulling out the subject and verb, she could follow the lines of technical text.

Needless to say, grammatical knowledge of the English language is essential for learning another language. Just as grammar has fallen out of favor in many English classes, it has suffered a similar blow in the pedagogy of learning other languages as well, where grammar instruction has been supplanted by "conversation." The predictable consequence has been much confusion and frustration for both teachers, who feel that their hands are tied, and students, many of whom are bewildered by the gymnastics of the French verb when they don't even know how English verbs behave.

What about science, math, social studies, the arts? All teachers love words. The biology teacher is fussy about the difference between *osmosis* and *diffusion*. Getting students to make fine distinctions is an important part of teaching students to think like scientists. Teachers want to give away the words of their subject areas the way grandmothers want to give away food. We want to invite our students into the professional conversation of our subject areas.

> Teachers want to give away the words of their subject areas the way grandmothers want to give away food.

As English teachers, we love words about words, language about language. To us, there is a vast difference between an action verb and a linking verb, a predicate nominative and a direct object, a transitive verb and an intransitive verb. In teaching students to talk the talk, we turn them into licensed operators, not just amateurs. A licensed operator can make the machinery run more efficiently, can anticipate potential problems, and can fix what is wrong. An amateur *hopes* that the sentence "sounds good."

Grammar should be the permeable membrane that allows knowledge learned in English class to transform into skill in the content area classes. Active voice may be preferable in English classes where the subject is often *people doing things* (S-V-O). In composing a lab report, however, passive voice may be the better choice. *The difference in pressure was recorded* might sound more scientific than *I recorded the difference in pressure.* In the language of lab reports, the fact that the technician did the action is

Essays on Teaching Grammar

irrelevant. A radiologist writes her report in the passive voice: *No abnormalities were found*, rather than *I found no abnormalities*. In English class, we show students the difference in tone between active and passive voice.

It is important to learn to think in action verbs in all subject areas. A student who is writing about the Reformation needs to focus on who did what: *Martin Luther <u>translated</u> the Bible into the German vernacular. His translation <u>enabled</u> more people to read the Bible.* The action verbs tell the story. They give students a starting point when writing and a focus when reading. All subject areas use this concept; it is we English teachers who actually teach it in our grammar lessons.

The social studies teacher and the science teacher may not know it, but the benefits of grammar instruction are carried through the student's entire day.

Myth #5:
Grammar instruction is ethnocentric and prejudicial.

As English teachers, we need to avoid giving the impression that we are the designated Keepers of the Language. We can teach the etiquette of standard English without denying a student the right to his or her own dialect.

An educated person has that social thermostat that linguists call code-switching. The metaphor of table manners is apt: What we are expected to do at an outdoor barbecue differs from what we're expected to do at Thanksgiving dinner. Those of us who can't tell the difference, who can't code-switch, are socially awkward. This is not to say that standard English is better than any particular dialect. Standard English is not more expressive, more poetic, or even more accurate. It is simply the expected currency of mainstream society in formal situations. We don't have to use it all of the time, but if we *can't* use it when it is expected, then we are at a cultural disadvantage that our education should remedy.

We are constantly making impressions that indicate our understanding of our social context. Those who are successful in their chosen fields, indeed, those for whom a chosen field is an option in the first place, know how to control the impression that others have of them. People judge our status and education levels not only through language, but also through dress, manners, and gesture.

Once we acknowledge that standard English is just another form of English that is appropriate for certain situations but not for all, then we are free to enjoy the dialects of English that we find in authentic literature, regional speech, song lyrics, and casual conversation. We can look at new coinages, popular metaphors, slang, and jargon with the interest of a linguist rather than the arrogance of a pedant.

We can teach the etiquette of Standard English without denying a student the right to his or her own dialect.

That language is a changing social contract is evidenced by grammar books of yore. Even in one generation, the *who/whom* distinction has attenuated, as has the use of the past perfect tense of verbs. Certain usages, such as the nominative case after a linking verb, sound stuffy. We have yet to solve the problem that exists because we lack a generic singular pronoun: *He,*

Essays on Teaching Grammar

once preferred, is thought to be sexist; *one* sounds stilted and British; *they* is a grammatical mismatch. That leaves *he or she*, which can seem awfully conspicuous. It's interesting to have students compare the style guides of various publications on sensitive points such as this.

Myth #6:
As native speakers, we don't have to learn grammar.

It is true that we already know grammar intuitively. Native speakers learn, quite naturally, how to put words together to make meaning. What we don't learn naturally is the metalanguage, that is, the language of language. Absent that, we can't explain what we mean about what we are trying to say, and others are at a loss to help us.

Terminology is powerful.

Recently, I worked with a group of elementary school teachers who were looking for teaching strategies that would improve their students' writing skills. When I suggested that they develop a scope and sequence in grammar skills, they were skeptical. "They already know how to use adjectives, nouns, and verbs," one teacher said. "Why do they have to know the *names* of these things?" "That just isn't the way we teach anymore," said another with a wave of her hand. "We don't want to interfere with the children's creativity. Teaching them grammar would interrupt their flow." A fourth-grade teacher added, "But that isn't on the state test, and we really don't have time for anything that doesn't get the scores up." Here's what I would answer:

Terminology is powerful. We can't improve our sentences until we understand the crucial role played by verbs. We certainly can't understand that role until we know how to identify verbs in context and that verbs come in various flavors: finite verbs, infinitives, participles, gerunds.

Further, creativity and "flow" are enhanced, not impeded, by knowledge of language structure and what certain kinds of phrases and sentences can and can't do. When the reader has to stumble over and re-read awkward, redundant, convoluted, or misplaced structures within sentences, does it matter how creative the writer was? Doesn't the logic of grammar *improve* the flow of prose?

To answer the last objection, the statewide tests may or may not have explicit questions regarding grammar. Some do; some don't, and the nature of those tests can and will change. What will not change is that a writer who knows where commas belong makes the job easier on the reader, as does the writer who understands subordination, agreement, and overall

Essays on Teaching Grammar

sentence management. If we acknowledge that the whole purpose of writing is to communicate, and that communication is accomplished by writing clearly, then we can see the application of grammar to writing. Of course, if grammar instruction never makes the leap from identification of a structure to its effective application, then these teachers are right to reject it as largely irrelevant.

What Knowing Grammar Can Do for Writers

Finally, here is a list of what you can do when you know a few things about grammar:

- If you know how to use parallel structure, you can make your message smoother, clearer, easier on the reader, more logical, and more memorable.

- If you know when to use active voice and when to use passive voice, you can control the directness or indirectness of your message. You control the power and impact of your words. You can also avoid the trouble that comes from being too direct or accusatory.

- If you know how to use verb tense consistently, you can guide your reader through the tangle of time in your narrative.

- If you know how to vary the grammatical constructs in your sentence structure, you can make your flow of sentences more musical, more nuanced, less choppy.

- If you know the difference between a phrase, a clause, and a sentence, you can guide your reader by using well-placed punctuation.

Like poetry, grammar is about the beauty of expressing exactly what we mean by placing the words just right.

Understanding how grammar works puts the writer on the right path. When writers begin a definition by saying "Osmosis is *when . . .*" they are failing to apply the concept that a subject complement, not an adverbial clause, must follow a linking verb. The "*is when . . .*" definition is going to fall on its face because the key term has not been handled properly in the sentence. Definitions call for classification. First, we must place the term in its proper realm: "Osmosis is a . . . process? means? phenomenon?" The writer must stop and think about what *kind* of thing osmosis is. Such categorical thinking is absolutely essential to the scientist, but it does not happen with the ungrammatical ". . . *is when*" structure. This example demonstrates the relationship between grammar and the logical progression of ideas.

Knowing grammar is useful, but even if it weren't, learning it would still be worthwhile because it is interesting. Like chess, grammar is about how power and proximity govern relationships and possibilities. Like engineering, grammar is about structure, balance, efficiency and strength. Like mathematics, grammar is about patterns and forms. Like geology, grammar is at once eternal and dynamic. Like poetry, grammar is about the beauty of expressing exactly what we mean by placing the words just right. ■

Amy Benjamin is an English teacher at Hendrick Hudson High School in Montrose, New York. In addition, she is a consultant to teachers, administrators, staff developers, and people in the business world. Amy specializes in showing people how to use clear, concise language. She has written several books about teaching literacy skills in all subject areas, as well as two plays (Romeo and Juliet Will Not Be Performed Tonight *and* Romeo and Juliet: Still Not Dead) *and a young adult novel* (Russell Kim: My Real Name). *Amy lives in Fishkill, New York, with her husband Howard and son Mitch.*

By Brock Haussamen

Grammar: Why Teach It?

Why should students learn—and teachers teach—grammar? Simply memorizing the parts of speech doesn't, by itself, make students better writers. Worrying about errors can quickly dampen student enthusiasm for a writing project. Over the past three decades, grammar's reputation has suffered. Is grammar useful? Why teach it?

I believe the central reason for teaching and learning grammar is that it gives all of us a language for talking about language, and certainly the ability to talk about language is a fundamental educational goal. It is difficult to discuss sentences without knowing basic grammar in the same way that it is difficult to talk about a sport or a science or politics without knowing the names of its elements and how they are organized. Knowing basic grammar is what enables students to discuss the sentences in a book they are reading or in a paper they are writing, and to discuss their native language or a second language.

> **T**hink of grammar as having two faces. One is its public face, which can be quite formal. The other face is private and more friendly.

The Two Faces of Grammar

To teach grammar effectively, we need to show students how to put it to use. The language of grammar—the names for the parts of speech and other sentence components that appear in the grammar section of this textbook—has two distinct kinds of uses. Think of grammar as having two faces. One is its public face, which can be quite formal. The other face is private and more friendly.

Public Grammar

The public face of grammar consists of all the rules we teach students to follow in their writing and all the errors we tell them to avoid making. In this textbook it is the material in the sections on usage and mechanics. I call usage and mechanics "public grammar" because they identify the conventions of the standard American dialect in which our society carries on its formal writing and speaking. There are many good reasons to teach these conventions. Such a standard dialect helps people from different places and different backgrounds to communicate clearly. The conventions of public grammar help sustain the uniformity of our writing system, on which our society depends utterly. Finally, they reflect the language of economic power. In general, people who can write and speak according to the standard conventions have a better chance at participating in the influential core of our society. People who do not master those conventions will likely face obstacles at every turn.

It is important for us to remember and to remind our students that public grammar is different from, not inherently better than, the language students normally use. The do's and don'ts of public grammar create an illusion that they are rigorously logical, like the rules of mathematics, and that they are permanent. Neither of these claims is true. The do's and don'ts are sometimes illogical, and they change. Just a few decades ago, grammar textbooks like this one would have insisted on the distinction between *will* and *shall*; today that distinction is all but gone. A few decades into the future, a book such as this will probably simplify and may even omit the distinction between *who* and *whom*, which is already fading in informal English.

T**he "right" clothes, like the "right" grammar, depend on what is appropriate or expected in a given situation.**

Try explaining to your students that their grammar is like the clothes they wear. The "right" clothes, like the "right" grammar, depend on what is appropriate or expected in a given situation. Around their friends, students talk and dress in particular ways. At formal occasions or in the workplace, they will be required to dress, to talk, and to write in other ways. This approach will less likely demean those students who do not routinely hear and use standard English. It also gives grammatical correctness a practical value and encourages your students to see language differences as an example of social diversity and opportunity.

Private Grammar

The other face of grammar is much more personal. By "private grammar," I mean the language structure that all of us already carry around in our heads and put to use when we communicate or think. In contrast to the study of public grammar, which has evolved over centuries, the description of our inherent language ability has grown from the work of linguists over the last several decades. Such grammar is private in the sense that it operates inside our heads, so quickly we are not even conscious of it. You won't find questions about private grammar on standardized tests; it is what students possess in order to read the tests in the first place.

If using public grammar can be compared to wearing socially acceptable formal clothes, private grammar can be compared to doing what comes naturally, to physical skills such as walking or running or throwing. Ask students to take a statement and turn it into a question in their native language. They can do it easily. They can fit new slang words into sentences fluidly. They know quickly when the language they hear or read sounds confusing or clear, choppy or smooth. They do all this with their private grammar.

Private grammar can be compared to doing what comes naturally, to physical skills such as walking or running or throwing.

If they can do all this already, how will studying grammar help them do more? The answer is that any skill that already comes somewhat naturally, like throwing a ball or making music, will improve if we learn about it and practice it. Students will be using the language of grammar to some degree when they revise and combine sentences in the section on "Writing Effective Sentences" in this textbook. They will do so to a greater degree whenever you show them how to improve the style of their writing by finding active verbs or expanding sentences with participles or prepositional phrases.

Putting Grammar to Use

As you can see from these descriptions of public and private faces, the language of basic grammar has many uses. Nonetheless, it is a difficult language for students to grow comfortable with; its vocabulary looks large and forbidding; many of the terms combine with each other in ways that seem strange to students ("adjective clause"); and because it is a language about language, it strains the verbal skills of many of its students, both children and adults. So, like any language it must be practiced often and put to use in a variety of contexts. Here are some general suggestions.

Use Private Grammar to Teach Public Grammar

As language users, we all have an intuitive sense that sentences are made up of sections. Give students a sentence and ask them to divide it into chunks and to group the words that go together. This approach can remain basic or can become more refined as students divide and cluster clauses and phrases.

This sort of activity easily leads to sentence diagramming. If you are not familiar with diagramming, see Chapter 19. I teach students not the whole of it but just the basic components; even elementary diagrams help many students see the subject-predicate core of a sentence more clearly. If you choose to teach diagramming more thoroughly, students will be able to analyze difficult sentences that they encounter in reading and will build their comprehension. Many students enjoy constructing the diagrams; the activity taps students' visual and spatial skills in addition to their verbal ones.

Another way to draw on students' private grammatical ability is to provide them with practical shortcuts for getting at the essential points of grammar. Grammarians over the years have assembled a number of these simple methods, and your students will love you for telling them about these methods. One good book on the subject is Rei Noguchi's *Grammar and the Teaching of Writing: Limits and Possibilities* (NCTE). Students find the shortcuts practical, and they also appreciate the positive reinforcement of their grammatical instincts.

Use Grammar for Reading

Although grammar is most closely associated with writing, students can put grammar to use when they read.

Knowing grammatical terminology gives students the tools they need to discuss a difficult sentence in a story or a poem. Ask students to pick out the main verb and then the simple subject; finding these can help them figure out the rest of the sentence. Poets bend sentences around a good deal, but most poetry consists of recognizable sentences and sentence parts. Often you can help students move beyond their perplexity about a poem by reminding them to look for the sentences and their basic parts.

In discussing with students what they enjoy or don't enjoy about a writer's style, look for the grammatical characteristics of the writer's sentences. What parts of speech stand out in the sentences? Some writers specialize in strong, active verbs, with few forms of the verb *be*. In other writers' texts, *is* and *are* abound, but the nouns stand out. In still others', the adjectives and adverbs catch the reader's attention.

Another approach is to ask students how long a writer's sentences are, on average. What characteristic sentence lengths do students notice among types of writers, or the writers of different periods? This approach can lead to a discussion of the different structures that make up a writer's sentences. Some writers like to add modifiers, phrases, and clauses; other writers keep sentences short to highlight the main nouns and verbs. Some start a sentence with long introductory word groups; others go right to the subject.

Bring grammar into the reading of advertisements, political language, and the World Wide Web. Advertisements provide good examples of sentence fragments, imperative verbs, and words that look like nouns but act like adjectives ("a Labor Day sofa sale"). Political speeches and slogans make interesting use of *we* and other personal pronouns. E-mail seems to encourage sentences that are variously clipped, casual, funny, skillful, and careless. Ask students to bring in examples for discussion.

Use Grammar for Revision

When students write, help them use grammar not just in the final editing stage, when they hunt out their violations of public grammar, but in the revising stage as well, when they can experiment with private grammar to develop their style as writers.

This textbook shows students how to combine sentences by inserting words or using conjunctions. Students can use some of the same methods to build a single sentence. They can build their sentences by adding participles (especially *–ing* participles that function half as an active verb, half as an adjective) and also by adding appositives. "A spider, **a repulsive, hairy creature, no bigger than a tarantula,** crawled into the room.... **Hands trembling, sweat dripping from his face,** he flung the magazine left and right, **trying to kill the spiders,** but there were too many." That example of an eighth-grader's work is from Harry Noden's *Image Grammar: Using Grammatical Structures to Teach Writing,* an excellent source for these and other techniques. Students can also add phrases, especially prepositional phrases, and clauses to a sentence, expanding the information about their main point, giving more details in order to paint a picture, building, and penetrating further into their topic. (The sentence that you just read is one example; you can find more—and better ones—in the work of most accomplished writers.) Students may think at first that they are merely making sentences longer, but they will quickly find that they are also saying more.

Conclusion

The suggestions in this essay are only a sample of the good ideas for using the language of grammar to help students become better readers and writers. The books I have mentioned will lead you to other ideas. And your colleagues in language arts can provide you with many other suggestions for using grammar in the classroom. If you think of grammar as a language for talking about language and you keep in mind the differences

Essays on Teaching Grammar

between public and private grammar, you can make grammar a valuable part of your students' language education.

For Further Reading

Assembly for the Teaching of English Grammar. www.ateg.org.

Berk, Lynn M. *English Syntax: From Word to Discourse*. New York: Oxford UP, 1999.

Haussamen, Brock. *Revising the Rules: Traditional Grammar and Modern Linguistics*. 2nd ed. Dubuque: Kendall/Hunt, 2000.

Kolln, Martha. *Rhetorical Grammar: Grammatical Choices, Rhetorical Effect*. 3rd ed. Boston: Allyn and Bacon, 1998.

Kolln, Martha, and Robert Funk (contributor). *Understanding English Grammar*. 5th ed. Needham: Allyn and Bacon, 1998.

Noden, Harry R. *Image Grammar: Using Grammatical Structures to Teach Writing*. Portsmouth: Heinemann/Boynton Cook, 1999.

Noguchi, Rei. *Grammar and the Teaching of Writing: Limits and Possibilities*. Urbana: NCTE, 1991.

Weaver, Constance. *Teaching Grammar in Context*. Portsmouth: Boynton/Cook, 1996.

William, Joseph M. Style: *The Lessons in Clarity and Grace*. 6th ed. New York: Longman, 2000. ■

Brock Haussamen has taught at Raritan Valley Community College in New Jersey since 1968. He is the author of Revising the Rules: Traditional Grammar and Modern Linguistics *(Kendall/Hunt) and also of a book on the history of the local New Jersey railroads. He began serving as president of the Assembly for the Teaching of English Grammar in 2000. His hobby and passion recently is playing ragtime piano.*

By Rei R. Noguchi

Getting Down to Basics:
Using What Students Already Know

> Like sentences, subjects and verbs are among the most basic elements of grammar and writing instruction.

Too often we struggle in teaching basic grammar to our students. Yet what really are the basics and how should we teach them? The most basic—the rock-bottom minimum—are sentence, verb, and subject. Surprisingly, we can teach these three basic elements by taking advantage of the unconscious linguistic knowledge that students already possess, their private grammar, so to speak. By tapping this unconscious knowledge, we can help students identify more easily the three basic elements, and, more important, help them better understand subsequent instruction in grammar, usage, and mechanics.

Why are the sentence, verb, and subject the very basics of grammar instruction? Take the notion of sentence. The sentence constitutes the most important unit in written texts, particularly in writing for school. A shaky grasp of what counts as a written sentence inevitably and unintentionally leads to distracting sentence fragments, fused sentences, and comma splices. Clearly, to master formal written English, students need to differentiate between a genuine sentence and an inappropriate nonsentence. Like sentences, subjects and verbs are among the most basic elements of grammar and writing instruction. Besides helping to define a sentence, subjects and verbs constitute elements on which a great deal of grammar and writing instruction builds. Without a reliable way of identifying subject and verb, students can almost certainly expect rough going.

Essays on Teaching Grammar

How can we teach the concepts of subject, verb, and sentence so that students can identify them easily? I would suggest that, rather than relying solely on semantic definitions, we take fuller advantage of what we often ignore or downplay in our teaching of grammar, namely, the tremendous unconscious knowledge that all fluent or near-fluent speakers of English bring to the classroom every day. Put more bluntly, our students know a great deal more about grammar than many of us think. This grammar is not school grammar but their "private grammar," the system of rules unconsciously learned and unconsciously used by all fluent speakers of English in everyday conversation. We cannot teach this personal underlying grammar for the simple reason that our students already know it. All we can do is bring this knowledge to the surface and exploit it to the fullest.

Identifying the Sentence

Exploiting the unconscious linguistic knowledge of students is the key to teaching the very basics of grammar. For students unaccustomed or resistant to working with abstract definitions, identifying sentences and fragments may prove difficult. To identify fragments, students must, at minimum, understand that a fragment is an "incomplete sentence"; to apply this definition, however, students must understand what a sentence is. To understand what a sentence is, students must understand such terms as subject, predicate, and independent clause. Each of these terms may require further definitions yet.

Exploiting the unconscious linguistic knowledge of students is the key to teaching the very basics of grammar.

To avoid the chain of seemingly endless definitions to identify sentences and fragments, teachers can take advantage of their students' unconscious knowledge of what constitutes a complete sentence. Teachers can, for example, use the following frame to help students tap what they already know.

Sentence Frame:
They liked the idea that
_____.

Many word groups will fit in the frame, but whatever they are, they will all be genuine declarative sentences. Students can try out fragments you provide, such as *Thinking of joining the team* or *Because he joined the team*, as well as any suspicious word groups they themselves may write. If students discover a fragment, they can add or delete words to make it fit into the frame and thereby change the fragment into a genuine sentence. There is no need to define a sentence formally at this stage. If students can perform the simple test given here, they already unconsciously know what a sentence is, and with that knowledge they can easily identify fragments, which are just parts of sentences. With a bit of guidance and exploration, students will discover that fused sentences and comma splices won't fit in the empty slot either.

Identifying Verbs

If we tap the private grammar of our students, we can also help them identify specific and important parts of the sentence. Below are two frames that will help students identify words that can serve as main verbs.

Main-Verb Frame 1:
They might _____ (it) now.

Main-Verb Frame 2:
They aren't _____-ing (it) now.

Any word that fits in the empty slots above will be the base form (infinitive) of the main verb, the form listed in the dictionary (e.g., *eat, collect, finish, sleep*). There is no need here to define *main verb*. If the word fits in the empty slot, it's a word that English speakers and writers can and do use as a main verb in sentences.

Because verbs don't always occur in the base form in actual sentences, students need other strategies to identify verbs, especially in the sentences they compose. Here again, we can take advantage of the unconscious linguistic knowledge of students, this time their uncanny ability to produce negative sentences

Essays on Teaching Grammar

and yes-no questions, to assist students in identifying helping verbs.

If we examine the following sentences, we see that a helping verb is a word that immediately precedes the negative element (*–n't* or *not*) in negated sentences or the word that gets fronted in yes-no questions.

EXAMPLES

1. Jim should go to the football game. *[Transform this into a negative sentence or a question.]*

   Jim **should**n't go to the football game.

   Should Jim go to the football game?

2. Jim went to the football game.

   Jim **did**n't go to the football game.

   Did Jim go to the football game?

If we have students transform declarative sentences into either negative sentences or yes-no questions, we can help them identify helping verbs. Again, there is no need to define *helping verb* formally. Though students may have never heard of the term *helping verb* (or *auxiliary verb*) before, they already unconsciously know what it is if they can produce a corresponding negative sentence or a corresponding yes-no question from a declarative sentence. Making such transformations requires complex linguistic knowledge. Yet, remarkably, we don't have to teach students how to do this. If students are fluent or near-fluent in spoken English, they already know it, as amply demonstrated in their daily speech. What we need to do, however, is to

take advantage of this knowledge in teaching the basics of grammar.

Main Verb *Be*

The main verb *be* (as in *They were friends*) is especially tricky because, unlike other main verbs, it moves to the front in yes-no questions (*Were they friends?*). It also takes the negative element in negative sentences (*They weren't friends*). The main verb *be* can thus masquerade as the helping verb *be* (compare *They were friends* to *They were running*). To make matters worse, the main verb *be* appears frequently in student writing. Indeed, when we complain that our students write with too many *be* verbs, we really mean the main verb *be*, not the helping verb *be*. This gives all the more reason for students to be able to identify the main verb *be*. Teaching students to use the main-verb frames and the helping-verb transformations can reduce confusion over the function of *be* in a sentence. Further, having students memorize the main-verb forms of *be* can reduce the confusion even more.

Identifying Subjects

Once students have identified the verb of a sentence, they can easily identify the subject. To identify the latter, they can insert the verb in the question frame below and then answer the question.

   Simple-Subject Frame:
   Who or what _____?

In most cases, the answer to the question will be the subject of the sentence.

Essays on Teaching Grammar   **T41**

Applying Knowledge of Subjects and Verbs

Being able to identify subjects and verbs brings considerable payoffs. It will help students understand *clause*, which, in turn, will help them understand *independent* (or *main*) *clause* and *subordinate* (or *dependent*) *clause*. Understanding these terms will help them better understand the notion of *sentence*, which, in turn, will help them better understand and correct any unintentional fragment or run-on sentence. (Think also of all the punctuation rules that directly or indirectly refer to these structures.) Being able to identify subjects and verbs will certainly help students identify errors in subject-verb agreement, errors in verb-tense consistency, and even the overuse of main verb *be*. This skill can also help students identify verbs in the passive voice and can help students choose the correct case of personal pronouns. In short, knowing how to identify subjects and verbs leads to an understanding of a host of other concepts.

Conclusion

For many language arts teachers, teaching grammar is both a labor of love and a love of labor. Many of us like the notion of grammar as a system, the wholes and parts fitting into place. Yet too often we struggle with difficult concepts and often with indifferent students. We can make the labor of teaching grammar less—and, hopefully, the love of grammar more for both teacher and student—if we take advantage of the prodigious private linguistic knowledge that all fluent speakers of English, native and non-native, bring to the language arts classroom every day.

Further References

DeBeaugrande, Robert. "Forward to the Basics: Getting Down to Grammar." *College Composition and Communication* 35 (1984): 358–67.

Noguchi, Rei R. *Grammar and the Teaching of Writing: Limits and Possibilities.* Urbana, IL: National Council of Teachers of English. 1991. ■

Rei R. Noguchi, Professor of English and Linguistics at California State University, Northridge, has taught courses in linguistics to practicing and prospective language arts teachers for over seventeen years. He is the author of Grammar and the Teaching of Writing: Limits and Possibilities *(NCTE). When not teaching or writing, he enjoys reading, bicycling, and following various kinds of sports, particularly baseball.*

By Billy T. Boyar, Ph.D.

Raising Expectations:
The Importance of Teaching Grammar to ESL Students

In the sixth grade, my class was taught sentence diagramming. Trying to superimpose our simple schoolbook diagrams on the infinity of language felt mysterious. Studying grammar in such a systematic way was like mapping the stars: We named unidentified words and charted their relationships. Words and phrases depended on other words like moons held to planets by gravity, and verbs sparkled like stars. I was not surprised, years later, to learn that the word *grammar* is etymologically related to *glamour* and *gramarye*,

> **S**tudying grammar in such a systematic way was like mapping the stars: We named unidentified words and charted their relationships.

suggesting magic. To me, the study of grammar has always been interesting and provocative in its own right. There are, however, important practical reasons for studying grammar and even more important practical reasons for ESL students to study it.

In the past, some people have disparaged the formal, systematic teaching of grammar to the ESL student. When people emphasize the importance of the natural way of learning language, beginning with hearing and mimicking, I agree with them. When they stress the necessity of creating a relaxed noncritical environment in which the ESL student feels free to practice speaking his or her new language, I agree with them. I agree that the study of literature and written composition is crucial. I even agree that grammar, if taught to young children or to ESL beginners of any age, should be fun and games, or should not be taught at all. However, when people advocate such approaches to the exclusion of a formal program of grammar for ESL students who are at least on an intermediate level and at least in the sixth grade, their argument is extreme, and I disagree with them.

Why is the study of grammar, usage, and mechanics important for appropriately mature and advanced ESL students?

Avoiding False Analogies

A study of English grammar, usage, and mechanics helps ESL students to avoid developing English language habits based on false analogies with the rules for their primary language. A comparative study of different languages shows that the basic patterns of grammar, conventions such as punctuation and capitalization, and the special uses of words can be vastly different. For example, a Spanish sentence doesn't necessarily need a subject (the subject can be implied by the verb); Spanish uses the present tense where English would sometimes use the past tense; question marks and exclamation points are placed both at the beginning and at the end of sentences; and a double negative is considered standard usage. English is even further from the grammatical expectations of Chinese and other non-Western ESL students.

In the past, some people have disparaged the formal, systematic teaching of grammar to the ESL student.

In my composition class, a Mexican American student submitted an essay that contained this sentence: "The Christmas party resulted well." The cognates *to result* (English) and *resultar* (Spanish) have confusingly similar meanings, yet their usage is distinctly different. Here, *resultar* could be translated *to turn out*. My student meant that the party turned out well, but she was basing her English usage on a false analogy with Spanish usage.

Not only does the ESL student tend to base English grammar rules on such false analogies, but also he or she often hears nonstandard usage repeated by friends and family. Being continually reinforced, the false analogy becomes an ingrained habit. Without the formal, systematic study of English grammar, usage, and mechanics, the ESL student may always have difficulty with standard English.

Promoting Academic Success

Teaching grammar to ESL students will help them succeed academically, especially if they plan to attend college. I have taught ESL and English at both high school and college. In composition classes, which also often contain ESL students, I frequently need to explain a point of grammar in order to help students understand why I am asking them to revise their papers. I want them to understand the principle so that they can avoid committing the same error over and over in future essays. For example, I ask them not to separate the subject and verb with only one comma (as in *Sara, who lives nearby is on my soccer team.*). This comment inevitably requires a further explanation: "Here you have inserted a nonessential clause between the subject and verb."

"But Mister," asks one ESL student, "what do you mean . . . *nonessential?*"

Essays on Teaching Grammar

"A nonessential clause is a clause that can be removed...."

"But what's a clause?"

"A clause contains a subject and a verb—it can be independent or subordinate. There are three kinds of subordinate..."

"What do you mean *subordinate*?"

"I mean that they have a subject and verb but that they cannot stand..."

"So what's a subject?"

"A subject is the noun or pronoun doing the..."

"Noun?"

> The problem is that trying to teach a little bit of grammar is like trying to paint a little bit of a wall: It doesn't work.

I encounter situations like this all the time—and of course, ESL students aren't the only ones who don't know formal English grammar. The problem is that trying to teach a little bit of grammar is like trying to paint a little bit of a wall: It doesn't work. In a college composition class, instructors typically explain points of grammar, usage, and mechanics as they are related to essays submitted by students. However, it would not be appropriate to stop the composition class in order to devote the rest of the course to the basics of grammar. The result is that the ESL student who knows no formal English grammar is poorly served because he or she cannot take full advantage of the instructor's explanations.

Like many a native English speaker's, the ESL student's grammar and usage may never be perfect. Rather than perfection, the goal is a workable compromise. If students can communicate effectively in English, does it matter that they speak with an accent? The lives of ESL students will not be destroyed, for example, if they do not master the subjunctive mood. As teachers, we must demand excellence, but at the same time, we should carefully consider what exactly we want students to master.

Supporting Career Success

Studying grammar will help ESL students succeed professionally. Recently, a city employee asked me to tutor him in English. He had started out as a garbage collector, but after a few years his bosses recognized his ability and promoted him, then promoted him again. He suddenly found himself having to write memos and job descriptions. Now, in order to keep the job, he was required to improve his English grammar, usage, and mechanics.

The reality is that proficiency in standard English is a badge required for acceptance in many careers and professions in the United States. Teachers, lawyers, doctors, and so forth may not be given the respect and trust they deserve if their use of language departs too far from the standard. Beyond this country, English has become the foremost international language. The dialect of the neighborhood, rightly cherished, will not succeed very well in commerce on the World Wide Web. The formal, systematic study of grammar, usage, and mechanics helps the ESL student separate neighborhood dialect from public language, in order to develop that public language in a clear and conscious way. Being truly bilingual, of

countless others, a refined bilingualism can open doors to wider possibilities.

Increasing Language Ownership

ESL students will benefit from the formal study of English because a better understanding of language patterns, a confidence in punctuation, and a command of the special uses of words will help them internalize English as a language of their own. Language ownership is an important topic. Language is a huge part of personal identity. It is a major reference point in our understanding of who we are. However, it should be emphasized that we can own more than one language; we can have two or more languages and dialects as expressions of our identity. It is helpful, healing, and sane for ESL students whose home is the United States to adopt English and care for it as their own. The problem is that immigrants have not always been welcomed with open arms, which is ironic in a land of immigrants. Our ESL students may therefore feel somewhat alien and sense that the English language is the language of others. One category of ESL students speaks English most of the time. They speak English in school; they speak it in their after-school jobs; and they even speak it most of the time at home: with brothers and sisters nearly all of the time, with parents some of the time, but with grandparents not at all. Even though these students speak English

> **The reality is that proficiency in standard English is a badge required for acceptance in many careers and professions in the United States.**

course, is more than merely owning a badge. Coupling a career or professional training with authentic bilingualism will broaden opportunities in ways that are numerous and unforeseen: as a police officer, nurse, doctor, lawyer, salesperson, diplomat, translator, flight attendant, psychotherapist, teacher, construction supervisor, municipal work supervisor, governor, or president. In any of these careers and professions and most of the time, they paradoxically still consider English their second language. In addition, since they use their "primary" (home) language less and less, it does not grow.

> The knowledge of grammar, usage, and mechanics is one tool in many, but we should not underestimate its importance.

These ESL students can be left in a world of little language indeed. A systematic study of grammar, usage, and mechanics in a friendly environment will tend to cut through the cycle of alienation. In the same way that we may feel better about our own cars when we learn how they work and can repair them ourselves, ESL students can learn how English works and can feel the pride of ownership.

Conclusion

Finally, ESL students are in the advantageous position of having a head start on bilingualism. If they continue to grow in their first language and if we give them the tools that they need for their second language, they will become truly bilingual. They need many tools in their language tool kits: the training to hear English phonemes, so that they can be good listeners; the skill of pronunciation, so that they can speak clearly; the knowledge of literature, so that they can contemplate the values of English-language cultures and the cultures of the rest of the world; and the art of writing compositions, so that they can express their own truths. The knowledge of grammar, usage, and mechanics is one tool in many, but we should not underestimate its importance. For ESL students, grammatical knowledge is a *sine qua non* of becoming bilingual on a professional level. On this level of bilingualism, the advantages are many, but it seems we and our students sometimes set our sights too low. Perhaps we have been guilty of not expecting our ESL students to accomplish as much as other students. They can aspire to the same—or better—careers and professions and can partake richly of the larger culture. Beyond these avenues, however, from the point of view of those of us who love language, ESL students will be able to look at language from a higher vantage point. From this aerial view, perhaps some will even rediscover the old meaning of grammar: magic. ■

Billy Boyar has taught composition, literature, and ESL in high schools and community colleges for twenty years. Billy lives in Austin, Texas, where he teaches at Austin Community College. He has worked with juvenile offenders, volunteered with Hospice, and mediated as an ombudsman in nursing homes. In his free time, he enjoys studying Spanish and reading philosophy and finds his garden rewarding and a great way to unwind. He believes that a formal, systematic study of grammar is an important part of an ESL program.

Holt Handbook

▶ Your **Road Map** to Grammar, Usage, and Mechanics Mastery

Now more than ever before, there is a demand for students at all grade levels to develop competence in the language arts and facility with the English language. Students need to be able to access information with ease, to appreciate the literary arts, and perhaps most importantly, to apply their language skills at levels demanded in the twenty-first century.

GIVING ALL STUDENTS ACCESS TO LANGUAGE SKILLS

Students in each classroom—including those at grade level, special education students, students with learning difficulties, advanced learners, and English-language learners—are at varying levels of preparation and have different strengths and needs. Giving these students all the tools they need to succeed is no easy task. That's where the *Holt Handbook* comes in.

The motivating force behind this program's organization and instructional delivery is the desire to offer teachers and students a method of focusing on written and oral language conventions and to provide a compelling and effective way to teach and learn grammar, usage, and mechanics skills. Based on John Warriner's time-tested model for instruction, the *Holt Handbook* can be an integral part of any balanced language arts program, or it can stand alone as a powerful tool for giving students access to the language skills they need most.

Covering All Your Students Need to Know About **Grammar, Usage,** and **Mechanics**

THREE MAIN PARTS COVER THE BASICS

PART I: GRAMMAR, USAGE, AND MECHANICS chapters help students use and practice using the building blocks of language—words, phrases, clauses, capitalization, punctuation, and spelling. The last chapter, **Correcting Common Errors,** gives students more practice building key language skills and taking tests in standardized formats.

PART II: The **SENTENCES** section covers the building blocks of constructing sentences, such as writing complete sentences, writing effective sentences, diagramming sentences, and improving sentence style.

PART III: The **RESOURCES** chapters include **The History of English,** a concise history of the English language; **Test Smarts,** a guide to taking standardized tests in grammar, usage, and mechanics; and **Grammar at a Glance,** a glossary of grammatical terms. In addition, grades 9–12 include **Manuscript Form,** a section that covers basic guidelines for preparing and presenting manuscripts and offers a sample research paper as a model.

Pupil's Edition

Instructional Delivery
That Keeps Students on Track

Each chapter in the **Holt Handbook** is carefully sequenced so that students are introduced to and taught new rules and skills at the right time. Each chapter includes an entry-level diagnostic preview; direct instruction of the rules followed immediately by examples and exercises; ongoing assessment; and application of new knowledge through writing. This direct and practical instructional approach allows you to keep track of your students' pace and progress.

CHAPTER 2
Parts of Speech Overview
Noun, Pronoun, Adjective

DIAGNOSTIC PREVIEW offers a short test that covers the whole chapter and lets you pretest for the most essential knowledge and skills.

Diagnostic Preview

A. Identifying Nouns, Pronouns, and A...

Tell whether each italicized word or word group in sentences is used as a *noun*, a *pronoun*, or an *adjecti...*

EXAMPLE 1. *Each* student is required to take a forei... *language*.
1. *Each*—adjective; *language*—noun

1. *That* drummer is the *best* performer.
2. That *German shepherd* puppy is a sweet-natured rascal.
3. *Everybody* says that *high school* will be more work but more fun, too.
4. *This* is the greatest year the junior varsity volleyball *team* has ever had.
5. *Who* can tell me whose bicycle *this* is?
6. *Jenna* prepared a special breakfast for her parents and *herself* this *morning*.
7. This is their fault because *they* ignored all the *danger* signals.
8. *We* received word that they aren't in *danger*.
9. *Each* of these clubs decorated a float for the Cinco de Mayo parade.
10. The runner *Carl Lewis* won several Olympic *medals*.

The Independent Clause

6b. An *independent* (or *main*) *clause* expresses a complete thought and can stand by itself as a complete sentence.

EXAMPLES
          S   V
The sun set an hour ago. [This entire sentence is an independent clause.]

          S   V
Jean Merrill wrote *The Pushcart War,* and

          S   V
Ronni Solbert illustrated the book. [This sentence contains two independent clauses.]

                       S   V
After I finish studying, **I will go to the** ... sentence contains one subordinate clau... independent clause.]

RULE, EXAMPLE, EXERCISE sequence introduces a new rule and follows it immediately with examples and exercises.

Exercise 1 Identifying Subjects and Verbs in Independent Clauses

Identify the subject and verb in each italicized independent clause in the following sentences.

EXAMPLE 1. Before she left for college, *my sister read the comics in the newspaper every day.*
1. sister—subject; read—verb

1. *She told me* that Jump Start was her favorite.
2. Since she liked it so much, *I made a point of reading it, too.*
3. *The comic strip was created by this young man,* Robb Armstrong, who lives and works in Philadelphia.
4. *Jump Start features a police officer named Joe* and his wife, Marcy, who is a nurse.

T50

Review B Proofreading for Words Often Confused

Identify and correct each error in words often confused in the following sentences.

EXAMPLE 1. Anne Shirley, here portrayed by actress Megan Follows, found a pieceful life and a loving family on Prince Edward Island.

1. pieceful—peaceful

1. Does the scenery shone in the picture on this page appeal to you?
2. My family enjoyed the green hillsides and rugged seashore during our two-weak vacation there last summer.
3. Prince Edward Island is quite a beautiful spot, and its Canada's smallest province.
4. Everyone who lives there calls the island PEI, and now I do, to.
5. During our visit, the weather was quite pleasant, so I lead my parents all over PEI on foot.
6. We walked to several places of interest in Charlottetown, the capitol.
7. I got to chose our first stop, and I selected the farmhouse that's the setting for the novel *Anne of Green Gables*.
8. That novel's main character, Anne Shirley, is someone who's ideas I admire.
9. Walking around "The Garden Province," we passed many farms; the principle crop is potatoes.
10. Take my advise and visit Prince Edward Island if you get the chance.

REVIEW EXERCISES offer both reinforcement of newly learned concepts and cumulative assessment.

Chapter Review

A. Using Irregular Verbs

Write the correct past or past participle form of the italicized irregular verb provided before each sentence.

1. *break* The thunder ____ the silence.
2. *ring* Who ____ the fire alarm so quickly?
3. *shrink* This shirt must have ____ in the dryer.
4. *throw* You've ____ the ball out of bounds!
5. *lead* Julio ____ the parade last year, so now it's my turn.
6. *rise* The sun ____ over the pyramids of Giza in Egypt.
7. *swim* We have ____ only three laps.
8. *choose* Vera was ____ as captain of the volleyball team.
9. *go* I have ____ to visit the Grand Canyon twice.
10. *sit* The tiny tree frog ____ motionless.
11. *write* Joan has ____ a story about aliens fr[om] Andromeda galaxy.
12. *do* During class, Jorge ____ the first five homework assignment.
13. *steal* Three runners ____ bases during the
14. *break* This summer's heat wave has ____ al
15. *drink* Have you ____ all of the tomato juic
16. *sink* The log had slowly ____ into the qui
17. *lie* The old postcards have ____ in the b
18. *drive* Have you ever ____ across the state o
19. *begin* Our local PBS station ____ its fund-r
20. *set* Have you ____ the paper plates and picnic table?
21. *throw* Who ____ the ball to first base?
22. *know* I have ____ some of my classmates fo
23. *take* Kadeem ____ the role of Frederick D
24. *tear* My mother ____ the paper to make c
25. *come* We ____ close to winning the tourna

CHAPTER REVIEWS provide additional practice and opportunities for ongoing assessment.

 Writing Application
Using Verbs in a Story

Verb Forms and Tenses A local writers' club is sponsoring a contest for the best "cliffhanger" opening of an adventure story. Write an exciting paragraph to enter in the contest. Your paragraph should leave readers wondering "What happens next?" In your paragraph, use at least five verbs from the lists of Common Irregular Verbs in this chapter.

Prewriting First, you will need to imagine a suspenseful situation to describe. Jot down several ideas for your story opening. Then, choose the one you like best. With that situation in mind, scan the lists of irregular verbs. Note at least ten verbs you can use. Include some lively action verbs like *burst, swing,* and *throw*.

Writing As you write your rough draft, think of your readers. Choose words that create a suspenseful, believable scene. Remember that you have only one paragraph to catch your readers' interest.

Revising Ask a friend to read your paragraph. Does your friend find it interesting? Can he or she picture the scene clearly? If not, you may want to add, delete, or revise some details.

Publishing Check your spelling, usage, punctuation, and grammar. Check to make sure the forms of verbs are correct and the tenses are consistent. You may want to exchange your cliffhanger with a partner, and complete each other's stories. With your teacher's permission, you can then read the completed stories aloud to the class.

WRITING APPLICATIONS guide students in applying new grammar, usage, and mechanics skills with end-of-chapter writing activities.

T51

Pupil's Edition

Instruction Based on Warriner's Model

An English teacher for thirty-two years, John Warriner developed the original instructional approach used throughout the grammar, usage, and mechanics chapters in the **Holt Handbook Pupil's Edition.** His logical model of instruction is based on a three-step process: Teach students the rule, show examples of the rule in writing, and provide immediate practice to reinforce the skill or concept. This model has been the authoritative standard for teaching grammar, usage, and mechanics skills for over fifty years.

RULE is always clearly stated and presented in red.

EXAMPLES illustrate the language skill or concept being taught in various student-friendly sentences.

Regular Verbs

9b. A *regular verb* forms its past and past participle by adding *–d* or *–ed* to the base form.

Base Form	Present Participle	Past	Past Participle
clean	[is] cleaning	cleaned	[have] cleaned
hope	[is] hoping	hoped	[have] hoped
inspect	[is] inspecting	inspected	[have] inspected
slip	[is] slipping	slipped	[have] slipped

One common error in forming the past or the past participle of a regular verb is to leave off the *–d* or *–ed* ending.

NONSTANDARD Our street use to be quieter.
STANDARD Our street **used** to be quieter.

Another common error is to add unnecessary letters.

NONSTANDARD The swimmer almost drownded in the riptide.
STANDARD The swimmer almost **drowned** in the riptide.

NONSTANDARD The kitten attackted that paper bag.
STANDARD The kitten **attacked** that paper bag.

—HELP—
Most regular verbs that end in e drop the e before adding *–ing*. Some regular verbs double the final consonant before adding *–ing* or *–ed*.

EXAMPLES
shake—shak**ing**
hug—hu**gged**

USAGE

Reference Note
For more about **spelling rules**, see Chapter 16. For information on **standard and nonstandard English**, see page 245.

Oral Practice 1 Using Regular Verbs

Read each of the following sentences aloud, stressing the italicized verbs.

1. We are *supposed* to meet at the track after school.
2. The twins *happened* to buy the same shirt.
3. They have already *called* me about the party.
4. Do you know who *used* to live in this house?
5. I had *hoped* they could go to the concert with us.

"The strongest motive in the preparation of the **Handbook of English** was the desire to create a book that would fit any course of study. The goal was a completely flexible teaching tool adaptable to any course of study or to any individual classroom."

—John Warriner
from Introduction to *Warriner's Handbook of English, Book One* © 1948

6. The chairs have been *moved* into the hall for the dance.
7. That salesclerk has *helped* my mother before.
8. Eli may not have *looked* under the table for the cat.

Exercise 1 Writing the Forms of Regular Verbs

Write the correct present participle, past, or past participle form of the italicized verb given before each of the following sentences.

EXAMPLES 1. *learn*   Many people today are ____ folk dances from a variety of countries.
1. learning

2. *hope*   Dad and I had ____ to take lessons in folk dancing this summer.
2. hoped

1. *practice* These Spanish folk dancers must have ____ for a long time.
2. *perform*   Notice that they are ____ in their colorful native costumes.
3. *wish*   Have you ever ____ that you knew how to do any folk dances?
4. *use*   Virginia reels ____ to be popular dances in the United States.
5. *promise*   Mrs. Stamos, who is from Greece, ____ to teach her daughter the Greek chain dance.
6. *lean*   The young Jamaican dancer ____ backward before he went under the pole during the limbo dance competition.
7. *start*   The group from Estonia is ____ a dance about a spinning wheel.
8. *request*   Someone in the audience has ____ an Irish square dance called "Sweets of May."
9. *dance*   During the Mexican hat dance, the woman ____ around the brim of the sombrero.
10. *fill*   The Jewish wedding dance ____ the room with both music and movement.

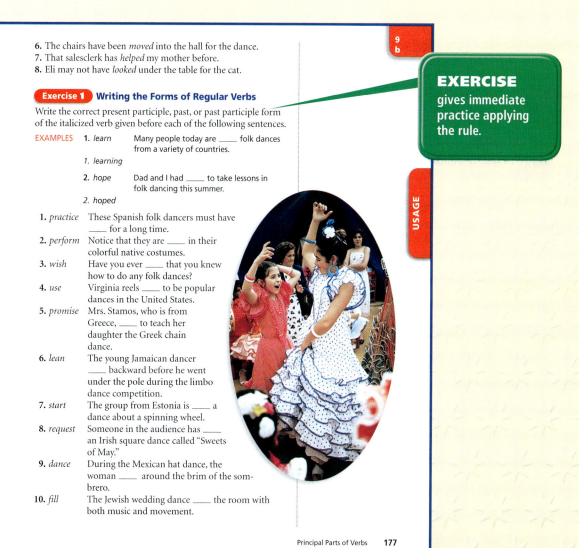

9b

EXERCISE gives immediate practice applying the rule.

USAGE

Principal Parts of Verbs   177

Pupil's Edition

Features That Help Students Along the Way

Oral Practice 5 Using Forms of *Rise* and *Raise* Correctly

Read the following sentences aloud, stressing the italicized verbs.

1. Mount Everest *rises* over 29,000 feet.
2. He *raises* the flag at sunrise.
3. The TV reporter *raised* her voice to be heard.
4. She *rose* from her seat and looked out the window.
5. The constellation Orion had not yet *risen* in the southern sky.
6. They had *raised* the piñata high in the tree.
7. I hope the bread is *rising*.
8. He will be *raising* the bucket from the well.

ORAL PRACTICE reinforces rules and concepts with spoken practice exercises.

TIPS & TRICKS

Sometimes a fragment is really a part of a nearby sentence. You can correct the fragment by attaching it to the sentence that comes before or after it.

SENTENCE WITH FRAGMENT
Mark is practicing his hook shot. Because he wants to try out for the basketball team.

SENTENCE
Mark is practicing his h...

TIPS & TRICKS offer easy-to-use hints that help students master language skills.

STYLE TIP

To avoid the awkward use of *his or her*, try to rephrase the sentence.

AWKWARD
Each of the actors had memorized **his or her** lines.

REVISED
All of the actors had memorized **their** lines.

STYLE TIPS guide students in making sound decisions about style and usage.

HELP

Some of the subjects and verbs in Review B are compound.

HELP gives pointers that help students understand key rules or exercise directions.

MEETING THE CHALLENGE

Write a poem, correctly using each of the six troublesome verbs, *sit, set, rise, raise, lie,* and *lay*. Be sure to check your poem for correct usage of the troublesome verbs.

MEETING THE CHALLENGE provides questions and short activities that ask students to approach a concept from a new angle.

Extend Grammar, Usage, and Mechanics Learning via the **Internet**!

GO.HRW.COM

Internet references throughout the *Pupil's Edition* direct students to **go.hrw.com**, a Web site that links students to resources related to concepts, rules, and assignments in the *Holt Handbook*.

HOW IT WORKS

When students see the **go.hrw.com** logo in the textbook, they can go to the **go.hrw.com** site to find resources that support the grammatical concept or rule they are studying.

INTERACTIVE EXERCISES IN GRAMMAR, USAGE, AND MECHANICS

Among the resources available to students on the **go.hrw.com** site are interactive exercises in grammar, usage, and mechanics. Students can practice skills with interactive exercises and then complete a chapter test that is scored immediately, giving students instant feedback on their progress.

Annotated Teacher's Edition

Unique Strategies That Make **Planning Lessons** Easy

The *Holt Handbook Annotated Teacher's Edition* helps you organize your lessons into manageable segments—preteaching, direct teaching, and reteaching, for example—so that students build skills in a systematic way. Suggestions for differentiating instruction are integrated with lessons to help you support students with special learning needs, including advanced learners, students with learning difficulties, and English-language learners. Features that direct you to program resources for each chapter and lesson are also there to help you along the way.

PRETEACHING

Lesson Starter

Prior Knowledge. Ask students to supply words that describe the similarities and differences between an orange and a baseball. Students might begin by saying that both objects are round. You might want to draw a Venn diagram on the chalkboard and ask students to suggest words that describe both items and words that

PRETEACHING offers strategies that help you identify prerequisite skills and build on the prior knowledge of your students.

DIRECT TEACHING

Modeling and Demonstration

Identifying Nouns. Model how to identify nouns by using the example *self-esteem*. First, ask whether the word names a person, place, thing, or idea. [idea] *Self-esteem* names an idea; therefore, *self-esteem* is a noun. Now, have a volunteer use another example from this chapter to demonstrate how to identify a noun.

DIRECT TEACHING helps you present content with strategies that include modeling and demonstrating new concepts.

RETEACHING

Pronouns

Activity. Ask students to write five descriptive sentences about a celebrity without ever mentioning the celebrity's name. Have two or three volunteers read their sentences, and let classmates try to guess the celebrity. Then, lead students to see that a common word in many of the sentences is *he* or *she*. Point out that pronouns like *he* and *she* are used in place of a noun, common or proper.

RETEACHING provides techniques to help you present material from a fresh perspective.

EXTENSION

Critical Thinking

Metacognition. Point out to students that there are probably too many pronouns to memorize all of them by type. Ask students what their strategies are for remembering the different types of pronouns. Have students describe and rate the effectiveness of their strategies. Students having trouble with pronouns should develop new strategies. Have students meet in groups to share and compare their ideas.

EXTENSION activities and strategies ask students to make new connections between what they are learning and what they already know.

DIFFERENTIATING INSTRUCTION

Advanced Learners

Have students read and discuss John Gardner's "Dragon, Dragon" or another folk tale that uses common nouns rather than proper names for its characters. Ask students to consider why the author uses common nouns rather than proper ones for the characters in the story. [*Students may say that there are so many characters in the story that it is easier for the reader to remember them with descriptive common nouns than with proper ones. Common nouns may also make the characters seem more universal.*]

DIFFERENTIATING INSTRUCTION helps you reinforce language skills with the wide variety of learners in your classroom, including advanced learners, on-level learners, learners having difficulty, special education students, and English-language learners.

CHAPTER RESOURCES

Internet
- Web resources: go.hrw.com

Practice & Review
- *Language & Sentence Skills Practice,* pp. 2–16; 17–20
- *Language & Sentence Skills Practice Answer Key,* pp. 1–7, 7–9

Application & Enrichment
- *Language & Sentence Skills Practice,* pp. 1, 21–22, 23
- *Language & Sentence Skills Practice Answer Key,* pp. 1, 9–10

CHAPTER RESOURCES BOXES list all materials that support each chapter lesson.

Teaching Suggestions and Resources

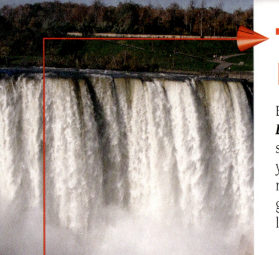

Teaching Suggestions That Help Students Make Connections

Because language arts skills are so interconnected, the **Annotated Teacher's Edition** provides a variety of extension and application strategies that help students make connections between the grammar, usage, and mechanics skills you're teaching them and the writing, science, and social studies skills they need to succeed in other classes. In addition, the **Annotated Teacher's Edition** gives you suggestions for facilitating an invaluable element of your students' learning experience—their families and communities.

> **MINI-LESSON Mechanics** Conti…
>
> **Punctuating Adjectives in a Series.** Often two or more adjectives are used before a noun to make its meaning more specific. Remind students of the rules regarding comma usage with series of adjectives.

MINI-LESSON helps students link various grammar, usage, and mechanics skills to one another through a variety of practical lessons.

> **Learning for Life**
>
> **Writing a Personal Profile.** For various reasons, adults are sometimes asked to write personal profiles, which require careful attention to verb tense. Ask your students to write profiles of themselves, including only material they are comfort-

LEARNING FOR LIFE offers real-world suggestions that help students relate grammar, usage, and mechanics skills to their own lives and to workplace skills they'll need in the future.

> **CONTENT-AREA CONNECTIONS**
>
> **Social Studies**
> **Places and Names.** To give students practice in naming proper nouns, have students complete a team race on a social studies topic that they are studying. Divide the class into groups of four. Give each group a social studies category, and have the groups write as many proper nouns as they can in five minutes. All group members are responsible for generating answers. (Possible categories include states and their capitals, continents, oceans, rivers, countries, presidents, and

CONTENT-AREA CONNECTIONS suggest a variety of extension activities that reinforce the relevance of language arts skills to other disciplines, such as science and social studies.

> **FAMILY/COMMUNITY ACTIVITY**
>
> **Introductions.** Most students have had or will have opportunities to introduce people to each other. In doing so, students will use complements. Provide the following examples:
>
> 1. Hi! I'm <u>Ms. King</u>. I teach <u>language arts</u> at Carson Middle School.
> 2. Maria, this is <u>Tom Jones</u>. Tom is <u>new</u> to our school. Tom, this is <u>Maria Gomez</u>. Maria is my best <u>friend</u>.

FAMILY/COMMUNITY ACTIVITY provides a real-world forum for students' language arts skills.

Additional **Practice** and **Strategies** to Help Students Succeed

LANGUAGE & SENTENCE SKILLS PRACTICE
These worksheets provide practice, reinforcement, and extension for topics covered in the *Holt Handbook*. Traditional worksheets offer additional practice for every rule taught in the *Pupil's Edition.* **Language in Context** worksheets let students apply and extend their study of grammar, usage, and mechanics to other areas in the language arts and to content in other disciplines. These worksheets include **Choices** worksheets, **Proofreading Application** worksheets, **Literary Model** worksheets, and **Writing Application** worksheets.

DEVELOPMENTAL LANGUAGE & SENTENCE SKILLS GUIDED PRACTICE
These worksheets provide developmental learners with instruction, practice, and reinforcement to supplement lessons in the *Holt Handbook* and in *Language & Sentence Skills Practice.* Targeted to those students who have not yet mastered specific concepts taught in the *Holt Handbook*, special features of this workbook include **Tips** that help students grasp abstract concepts with mnemonic devices, identification tests, and recognition strategies; **Points of Instruction** that explain how the rule applies to the examples provided; and **Guided Practice** that helps students with the first items of each exercise by asking guiding questions.

HOLT HANDBOOK CHAPTER TESTS
This booklet contains chapter tests in standardized test format for the grammar, usage, mechanics, and sentences chapters in the *Holt Handbook*. Presented in multiple-choice format, each test offers a sound means of assessing your students' grasp of key English-language conventions and, at the same time, offers students opportunities to practice their test-taking skills. The answer key provides useful references to specific rules that tie the answers to relevant instruction in the *Holt Handbook.* It also helps you pinpoint those skills and concepts students have mastered and those that need further attention.

Digital imagery® copyright 2003 PhotoDisc, Inc.

Instructional Resources: Chapter by Chapter

This chart outlines the chapters of the *Holt Handbook* and the resources available to help you teach these chapters. The chart lists materials appropriate for use with advanced students, on-level students, learners having difficulty, special education students, and English-language learners. Many of the resources listed are available at go.hrw.com.

Holt Handbook Chapter	Differentiating Instruction	
	Advanced Learners	On-Level Learners
1 The Parts of a Sentence	• Teacher's Edition, p. 7 • Language & Sentence Skills Practice, pp. 21–22, 23 • Language & Sentence Skills Practice Answer Key, pp. 9–10	• Teacher's Edition, pp. 2–23 • Language & Sentence Skills Practice, pp. 1–23 • Language & Sentence Skills Practice Answer Key, pp. 1–10
2 Parts of Speech Overview: Noun, Pronoun, Adjective	• Teacher's Edition, p. 39 • Language & Sentence Skills Practice, pp. 42–43, 44 • Language & Sentence Skills Practice Answer Key, pp. 19–20	• Teacher's Edition, pp. 24–43 • Language & Sentence Skills Practice, pp. 24–44 • Language & Sentence Skills Practice Answer Key, pp. 11–20
3 Parts of Speech Overview: Verb, Adverb, Preposition, Conjunction, Interjection	• Teacher's Edition, pp. 48, 56, 63 • Language & Sentence Skills Practice, pp. 65–66, 67 • Language & Sentence Skills Practice Answer Key, pp. 29–30	• Teacher's Edition, pp. 44–71 • Language & Sentence Skills Practice, pp. 45–67 • Language & Sentence Skills Practice Answer Key, pp. 21–30

Differentiating Instruction		Assessment
Learners Having Difficulty	**English-Language Learners & Special Education Students**	
• Teacher's Edition, p. 18 • Developmental Language & Sentence Skills Guided Practice, pp. 1–8 • Developmental Language & Sentence Skills Guided Practice Teacher's Notes and Answer Key, pp. 1–2	• Teacher's Edition, (English-Language Learners) pp. 9, 12, 19	• Holt Handbook Chapter Tests with Answer Key, pp. 1–2, 39, 46
• Teacher's Edition, p. 31 • Developmental Language & Sentence Skills Guided Practice, pp. 9–18 • Developmental Language & Sentence Skills Guided Practice Teacher's Notes and Answer Key, pp. 3–5	• Teacher's Edition, (English-Language Learners) pp. 27, 28, 31, 32, 33, 34, 35, 36, 37	• Holt Handbook Chapter Tests with Answer Key, pp. 3–4, 39, 46
• Teacher's Edition, p. 53 • Developmental Language & Sentence Skills Guided Practice, pp. 19–28 • Developmental Language & Sentence Skills Guided Practice Teacher's Notes and Answer Key, pp. 6–7	• Teacher's Edition, (English-Language Learners) pp. 47, 50, 52, 54, 55, 59, 60, 66, ; (Special Education Students) p. 46	• Holt Handbook Chapter Tests with Answer Key, pp. 5–6, 39, 46

(continued on next page)

Holt Handbook Chapter	Differentiating Instruction	
	Advanced Learners	On-Level Learners
4 **Complements**	• Teacher's Edition, p. 75 • Language & Sentence Skills Practice, pp. 82–83, 84 • Language & Sentence Skills Practice Answer Key, pp. 36–37	• Teacher's Edition, pp. 72–87 • Language & Sentence Skills Practice, pp. 68–84 • Language & Sentence Skills Practice Answer Key, pp. 31–39
5 **The Phrase**	• Teacher's Edition, p. 105 • Language & Sentence Skills Practice, pp. 107–108, 109 • Language & Sentence Skills Practice Answer Key, pp. 48–49	• Teacher's Edition, pp. 88–111 • Language & Sentence Skills Practice, pp. 85–109 • Language & Sentence Skills Practice Answer Key, pp. 38–49
6 **The Clause**	• Teacher's Edition, pp. 118, 121 • Language & Sentence Skills Practice, pp. 127–128, 129 • Language & Sentence Skills Practice Answer Key, pp. 58–59	• Teacher's Edition, pp. 112–127 • Language & Sentence Skills Practice, pp. 110–129 • Language & Sentence Skills Practice Answer Key, pp. 50–59
7 **Kinds of Sentence Structure**	• Teacher's Edition, p. 139 • Language & Sentence Skills Practice, pp. 141–142, 143 • Language & Sentence Skills Practice Answer Key, pp. 64–65	• Teacher's Edition, pp. 128–145 • Language & Sentence Skills Practice, pp. 130–143 • Language & Sentence Skills Practice Answer Key, pp. 60–65

Differentiating Instruction

Learners Having Difficulty	English-Language Learners & Special Education Students	Assessment
• Teacher's Edition, pp. 78, 80, 82, 85 • Developmental Language & Sentence Skills Guided Practice, pp. 29–36 • Developmental Language & Sentence Skills Guided Practice Teacher's Notes and Answer Key, pp. 8–9	• Teacher's Edition, (English-Language Learners) pp. 75, 78, 80	• Holt Handbook Chapter Tests with Answer Key, pp. 7–8, 39–40, 46
• Teacher's Edition, pp. 95, 99 • Developmental Language & Sentence Skills Guided Practice, pp. 37–46 • Developmental Language & Sentence Skills Guided Practice Teacher's Notes and Answer Key, pp. 10–12	• Teacher's Edition, (English-Language Learners) pp. 91, 95, 99, 103; (Special Education Students) p. 93	• Holt Handbook Chapter Tests with Answer Key, pp. 9–10, 40, 46
• Teacher's Edition, p. 116 • Developmental Language & Sentence Skills Guided Practice, pp. 47–52 • Developmental Language & Sentence Skills Guided Practice Teacher's Notes and Answer Key, p. 13	• Teacher's Edition, (English-Language Learners) p. 117	• Holt Handbook Chapter Tests with Answer Key, pp. 11–12, 40, 46
• Developmental Language & Sentence Skills Guided Practice, pp. 53–56 • Developmental Language & Sentence Skills Guided Practice Teacher's Notes and Answer Key, p. 14	• Teacher's Edition, (English-Language Learners) p. 132	• Holt Handbook Chapter Tests with Answer Key, pp. 13–14, 40–41, 46

(continued on next page)

Holt Handbook Chapter	Differentiating Instruction	
	Advanced Learners	On-Level Learners
8 Agreement	• Teacher's Edition, pp. 154, 158 • Language & Sentence Skills Practice, pp. 166, 167–168, 169 • Language & Sentence Skills Practice Answer Key, pp. 73–74	• Teacher's Edition, pp. 146–173 • Language & Sentence Skills Practice, pp. 144–169 • Language & Sentence Skills Practice Answer Key, pp. 66–74
9 Using Verbs Correctly	• Teacher's Edition, pp. 191, 195 • Language & Sentence Skills Practice, pp. 189, 190–191, 192 • Language & Sentence Skills Practice Answer Key, pp. 80–81	• Teacher's Edition, pp. 174–199 • Language & Sentence Skills Practice, pp. 170–192 • Language & Sentence Skills Practice Answer Key, pp. 75–81
10 Using Pronouns Correctly	• Teacher's Edition, p. 209 • Language & Sentence Skills Practice, pp. 210, 211–212, 213 • Language & Sentence Skills Practice Answer Key, pp. 87–88	• Teacher's Edition, pp. 200–221 • Language & Sentence Skills Practice, pp. 193–213 • Language & Sentence Skills Practice Answer Key, pp. 82–88
11 Using Modifiers Correctly	• Teacher's Edition, p. 234 • Language & Sentence Skills Practice, pp. 240, 241–242, 243 • Language & Sentence Skills Practice Answer Key, pp. 99–100	• Teacher's Edition, pp. 222–243 • Language & Sentence Skills Practice, pp. 214–243 • Language & Sentence Skills Practice Answer Key, pp. 89–100

Differentiating Instruction		Assessment
Learners Having Difficulty	**English-Language Learners & Special Education Students**	
• Teacher's Edition, pp. 157, 163, 169 • Developmental Language & Sentence Skills Guided Practice, pp. 57–66 • Developmental Language & Sentence Skills Guided Practice Teacher's Notes and Answer Key, pp. 15–16	• Teacher's Edition, (English-Language Learners) pp. 150, 151, 156, 159, 166	• Holt Handbook Chapter Tests with Answer Key, pp. 15–16, 41, 46
• Teacher's Edition, p. 191 • Developmental Language & Sentence Skills Guided Practice, pp. 67–72 • Developmental Language & Sentence Skills Guided Practice Teacher's Notes and Answer Key, p. 17	• Teacher's Edition, (English-Language Learners) pp. 176, 177, 179, 186, 187, 192	• Holt Handbook Chapter Tests with Answer Key, pp. 17–18, 41, 46
• Developmental Language & Sentence Skills Guided Practice, pp. 73–80 • Developmental Language & Sentence Skills Guided Practice Teacher's Notes and Answer Key, pp. 18–19	• Teacher's Edition, (English-Language Learners) pp. 202, 203, 212, 214; (Special Education Students) p. 219	• Holt Handbook Chapter Tests with Answer Key, pp. 19–20, 41–42, 46
• Developmental Language & Sentence Skills Guided Practice, pp. 81–90 • Developmental Language & Sentence Skills Guided Practice Teacher's Notes and Answer Key, pp. 20–21	• Teacher's Edition, (English-Language Learners) pp. 226, 227, 231, 233	• Holt Handbook Chapter Tests with Answer Key, pp. 21–22, 42, 46

(continued on next page)

Holt Handbook Chapter	Differentiating Instruction	
	Advanced Learners	**On-Level Learners**
12 **A Glossary of Usage**	• Teacher's Edition, p. 247 • Language & Sentence Skills Practice, pp. 253, 254–255, 256 • Language & Sentence Skills Practice Answer Key, pp. 104–105	• Teacher's Edition, pp. 244–263 • Language & Sentence Skills Practice, pp. 244–256 • Language & Sentence Skills Practice Answer Key, pp. 101–105
13 **Capital Letters**	• Teacher's Edition, pp. 273, 279, 283 • Language & Sentence Skills Practice, pp. 276, 277–278, 279 • Language & Sentence Skills Practice Answer Key, pp. 116–117	• Teacher's Edition, pp. 264–287 • Language & Sentence Skills Practice, pp. 257–279 • Language & Sentence Skills Practice Answer Key, pp. 106–117
14 **Punctuation: End Marks, Commas, Semicolons, and Colons**	• Teacher's Edition, pp. 292, 301 • Language & Sentence Skills Practice, pp. 301, 302–303, 304 • Language & Sentence Skills Practice Answer Key, pp. 127–128	• Teacher's Edition, pp. 288–317 • Language & Sentence Skills Practice, pp. 280–304 • Language & Sentence Skills Practice Answer Key, pp. 118–128
15 **Punctuation: Underlining (Italics), Quotation Marks, Apostrophes, Hyphens, Parentheses, Brackets, and Dashes**	• Teacher's Edition, p. 334 • Language & Sentence Skills Practice, pp. 326, 327–328, 329 • Language & Sentence Skills Practice Answer Key, pp. 138–139	• Teacher's Edition, pp. 318–345 • Language & Sentence Skills Practice, pp. 305–329 • Language & Sentence Skills Practice Answer Key, pp. 129–139

Differentiating Instruction

Learners Having Difficulty	English-Language Learners & Special Education Students	Assessment
• Developmental Language & Sentence Skills Guided Practice, pp. 91–96 • Developmental Language & Sentence Skills Guided Practice Teacher's Notes and Answer Key, p. 22	• Teacher's Edition, (English-Language Learners) pp. 250, 252, 259	• Holt Handbook Chapter Tests with Answer Key, pp. 23–24, 42–43, 46
• Teacher's Edition, pp. 270, 281, 285 • Developmental Language & Sentence Skills Guided Practice, pp. 97–108 • Developmental Language & Sentence Skills Guided Practice Teacher's Notes and Answer Key, pp. 23–25	• Teacher's Edition, (English-Language Learners) pp. 267, 277, 278	• Holt Handbook Chapter Tests with Answer Key, pp. 25–26, 43, 46
• Teacher's Edition, pp. 290, 305, 312 • Developmental Language & Sentence Skills Guided Practice, pp. 109–114 • Developmental Language & Sentence Skills Guided Practice Teacher's Notes and Answer Key, pp. 26–27	• Teacher's Edition, (English-Language Learners) pp. 292, 296, 312	• Holt Handbook Chapter Tests with Answer Key, pp. 27–28, 43, 46
• Teacher's Edition, p. 327 • Developmental Language & Sentence Skills Guided Practice, pp. 115–124 • Developmental Language & Sentence Skills Guided Practice Teacher's Notes and Answer Key, pp. 28–30	• Teacher's Edition, (English-Language Learners) pp. 324, 331; (Special Education Students) p. 325	• Holt Handbook Chapter Tests with Answer Key, pp. 29–30, 43–44, 46

(continued on next page)

Holt Handbook Chapter	Differentiating Instruction	
	Advanced Learners	**On-Level Learners**
16 Spelling	• Teacher's Edition, p. 367 • Language & Sentence Skills Practice, pp. 354, 355–356, 357 • Language & Sentence Skills Practice Answer Key, pp. 146–147	• Teacher's Edition, pp. 346–375 • Language & Sentence Skills Practice, pp. 330–357 • Language & Sentence Skills Practice Answer Key, pp. 140–147
17 Correcting Common Errors	• Language & Sentence Skills Practice, pp. 394, 395–396, 397 • Language & Sentence Skills Practice Answer Key, pp. 163–165	• Teacher's Edition, pp. 376–409 • Language & Sentence Skills Practice, pp. 358–398 • Language & Sentence Skills Practice Answer Key, pp. 148–165
18 Writing Effective Sentences	• Teacher's Edition, p. 417	• Teacher's Edition, pp. 412–443 • Language & Sentence Skills Practice, pp. 399–430 • Language & Sentence Skills Practice Answer Key, pp. 166–175
19 Sentence Diagramming	• Teacher's Edition, pp. 444–463	• Teacher's Edition, pp. 444–463

Differentiating Instruction		Assessment
Learners Having Difficulty	**English-Language Learners & Special Education Students**	
• Teacher's Edition, pp. 350, 361 • Developmental Language & Sentence Skills Guided Practice, pp. 125–136 • Developmental Language & Sentence Skills Guided Practice Teacher's Notes and Answer Key, pp. 31–32	• Teacher's Edition, (English-Language Learners) pp. 353, 355, 360, 368; (Special Education Students) p. 354	• Holt Handbook Chapter Tests with Answer Key, pp. 31–32, 44, 46
• Developmental Language & Sentence Skills Guided Practice, pp. 137–138 • Developmental Language & Sentence Skills Guided Practice Teacher's Notes and Answer Key, p. 33		• Holt Handbook Chapter Tests with Answer Key, pp. 33–34, 44, 44, 46
• Teacher's Edition, pp. 422, 425, 430, 436 • Developmental Language & Sentence Skills Guided Practice, pp. 139–156 • Developmental Language & Sentence Skills Guided Practice Teacher's Notes and Answer Key, pp. 34–38	• Teacher's Edition, (English-Language Learners) pp. 420, 433	• Holt Handbook Chapter Tests with Answer Key, pp. 35–38, 45, 45, 46
• Teacher's Edition, pp. 444–463	• Teacher's Edition, (English-Language Learners) pp. 444–463	

Instructional Resources

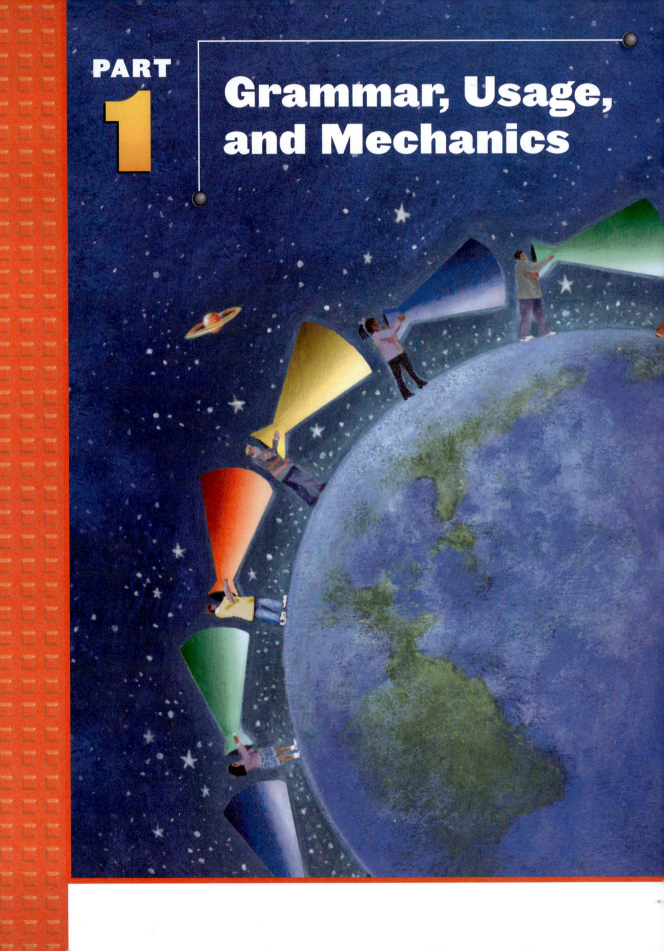

PART 1
Grammar, Usage, and Mechanics

Grammar

1. The Parts of a Sentence
2. Parts of Speech Overview: Noun, Pronoun, Adjective
3. Parts of Speech Overview: Verb, Adverb, Preposition, Conjunction, Interjection
4. Complements
5. The Phrase
6. The Clause
7. Kinds of Sentence Structure

Usage

8. Agreement
9. Using Verbs Correctly
10. Using Pronouns Correctly
11. Using Modifiers Correctly
12. A Glossary of Usage

Mechanics

13. Capital Letters
14. Punctuation: End Marks, Commas, Semicolons, Colons
15. Punctuation: Underlining (Italics), Quotation Marks, Apostrophes, Hyphens, Parentheses, Brackets, Dashes
16. Spelling
17. Correcting Common Errors

 GO TO: go.hrw.com

CHAPTER 1

The Parts of a Sentence
Subject and Predicate, Kinds of Sentences

INTRODUCING THE CHAPTER

- This chapter begins by contrasting complete sentences and sentence fragments. It identifies and explains the subject and the predicate and, following a discussion of complete and simple subjects and predicates, explores compound subjects, compound verbs, verb phrases, and sentence classification.

- The chapter closes with a **Chapter Review**, which includes a **Writing Application** feature that asks students to write a letter using complete sentences.

- For help in integrating this chapter with writing assignments, use the **Teaching Strands** chart on pp. T24–T25.

Numerals in brackets refer to rules tested by the items in the Diagnostic Preview.

Answers will vary. Sample responses are given.

1. frag.—, we'll brainstorm [1a]
2. sent. [1a]
3. sent. [1a]
4. frag.—I [1a]
5. sent. [1a]
6. frag.—This is the house [1a]
7. frag.—is [1a]
8. sent. [1a]
9. frag.—We enjoy [1a]
10. sent. [1a]

Diagnostic Preview

A. Identifying Sentences

Identify each of the following word groups as a *sentence* or a *sentence fragment*. If a word group is a sentence fragment, rewrite it to make a complete sentence.

EXAMPLES
1. Having forgotten their lunches.
1. sentence fragment—Having forgotten their lunches, the students bought sandwiches.
2. How strong the wind is!
2. sentence

1. After we visit the library and gather information for the research paper.
2. Are you ready for the big game next week?
3. Listen closely to our guest speaker.
4. Have written the first draft of my paper.
5. An excellent short story, "The Medicine Bag," is in that book.
6. That we helped Habitat for Humanity to build.
7. Mrs. Chin, our math teacher this year.
8. Be prepared to give your speech tomorrow.
9. Fishing, skiing, and swimming in the lake.
10. What a good idea you have, Amy!

Chapter 1 The Parts of a Sentence

CHAPTER RESOURCES

Internet
- Web resources: go.hrw.com

Practice & Review
- *Language & Sentence Skills Practice,* pp. 2–16; 17–20
- *Language & Sentence Skills Practice Answer Key,* pp. 1–7, 7–9

Application & Enrichment
- *Language & Sentence Skills Practice,* pp. 1, 21–22, 23
- *Language & Sentence Skills Practice Answer Key,* pp. 1, 9–10

B. Identifying Subjects and Predicates

Write the subject and the predicate in each of the following sentences. Then, underline the simple subject and the simple predicate.

EXAMPLE 1. A computer can be a wonderful tool for people with disabilities.

1. A computer; can be a wonderful tool for people with disabilities

11. Specially designed machines have been developed in the past several years.
12. Have you ever seen a talking computer?
13. It is used mainly by people with visual impairments.
14. Most computers display writing on a screen.
15. However, these special models can give information by voice.
16. Closed-captioned television is another interesting and fairly recent invention.
17. Subtitles appear on the television screens of many hearing-impaired viewers.
18. These viewers can read the subtitles and enjoy their favorite television shows.
19. With a teletypewriter (TTY), people can type messages over phone lines.
20. Many new inventions and devices make life easier.

11. [1b–e]
12. [1b–e]
13. [1b–e]
14. [1b–e]
15. [1b–e]
16. [1b–e]
17. [1b–e]
18. [1b–e, g]
19. [1b–e]
20. [1b–e, f]

C. Punctuating and Classifying Sentences

Copy the last word of each of the following sentences, and then punctuate each sentence with the correct end mark. Classify each sentence as *declarative*, *interrogative*, *imperative*, or *exclamatory*.

EXAMPLE 1. Flowers and insects depend on one another for life

1. life.—declarative

21. Have you ever watched a honeybee or a bumblebee in a garden?
22. The bee flies busily from one flower to another, drinking nectar.
23. Notice the yellow pollen that collects on the legs and body of the bee.
24. The bee carries pollen from flower to flower, helping the plants to make seeds.
25. What a remarkable insect the bee is!

21. int. [1j]
22. dec. [1h]
23. imp. [1i]
24. dec. [1h]
25. exc. [1k]

Diagnostic Preview   3

ASSESSING

Entry-Level Assessment

Diagnostic Preview. If students are writing sentence fragments or having other problems with sentence structure in their writing, you can use this informal **Diagnostic Preview** to pinpoint error patterns and specific strengths and weaknesses. **Part A** relates to the section in this chapter titled **The Sentence**; **Part B** relates to the material in the sections **Subject and Predicate** and **Compound Subjects and Compound Verbs**; and **Part C** relates to the material in **Kinds of Sentences**.

Differentiating Instruction

- *Developmental Language & Sentence Skills Guided Practice,* pp. 1–8
- *Developmental Language & Sentence Skills Guided Practice Teacher's Notes and Answer Key,* pp. 1–2

Assessment

- *Holt Handbook Chapter Tests with Answer Key,* pp. 1–2, 46

PRETEACHING

Lesson Starter

Motivating. Have students volunteer examples of verbs, and make a list of the suggestions on the board. Tell students they will write a four-line poem using at least two combinations of verbs from the list as compound verbs. To get started, have the class compose a poem together orally while you or a helper transcribes the work in progress on the chalkboard or a transparency.

The Sentence
Rule 1a *(pp. 4–5)*

OBJECTIVES

- To identify sentences and sentence fragments
- To use capital letters at the beginnings of sentences
- To use correct punctuation at the ends of sentences

DIRECT TEACHING

Modeling and Demonstration

The Sentence. Model how to identify a sentence by using the example *She won a prize for her book.* First, ask whether the example includes a subject. [yes—*She*] Then, ask whether the example includes a verb. [yes—*won*] Then, ask if the example expresses a complete thought. [yes] Point out that since the example includes both a subject and a verb and expresses a complete thought, it is a sentence. Now, have a volunteer use another example from this chapter to demonstrate how to identify a group of words as a sentence.

Reference Note
For information on the use of **capital letters,** see page 266. For information on **end marks,** see page 290.

Reference Note
For information on **the understood subject,** see page 19.

STYLE TIP
Sentence fragments are common and acceptable in informal situations. However, in formal writing, you should avoid using sentence fragments.

COMPUTER TIP
Many grammar-checking software programs can help you identify sentence fragments. If you have access to such a program, use it to help you evaluate your writing.

Reference Note
For information on **revising sentence fragments,** see pages 4 and 414.

4 **Chapter 1** The Parts of a Sentence

The Sentence

1a. A *sentence* is a word or word group that contains a subject and a verb and that expresses a complete thought.

A sentence begins with a capital letter and ends with a period, a question mark, or an exclamation point.

EXAMPLES   **S**he won a prize for her book**.**

            Why did you stop running**?**

            Wait**!** [The understood subject is *you*.]

Sentence or Sentence Fragment?

A *sentence fragment* is a group of words that looks like a sentence but does not contain both a subject and a verb or does not express a complete thought.

SENTENCE FRAGMENT	Sailing around the world. [The word group lacks a subject.]
SENTENCE	They are sailing around the world.
SENTENCE FRAGMENT	The hike through the Grand Canyon. [The word group lacks a verb.]
SENTENCE	The hike through the Grand Canyon was long and hard.
SENTENCE FRAGMENT	After they pitched the tent. [The word group contains a subject and a verb but does not express a complete thought.]
SENTENCE	After they pitched the tent, they rested.

Oral Practice   **Identifying Sentences**

Read each of the following word groups aloud. Then, say whether each word group is a *sentence* or a *sentence fragment*. If a word group is a sentence fragment, add words to make it a complete sentence.   Answers will vary. Sample responses are given.

EXAMPLES   1. During her vacation last summer.
                1. sentence fragment—During her vacation last summer, she hiked in the mountains.
                2. My friend Michelle visited Colorado.
                2. sentence

RESOURCES

The Sentence

Practice

- *Language & Sentence Skills Practice,* pp. 2–4, 17
- *Developmental Language & Sentence Skills,* pp. 1–2

1. Do you know what happened during Michelle's boat trip?
2. Down the rapids on the Colorado River.
3. At first her boat drifted calmly through the Grand Canyon.
4. Then the river dropped suddenly.
5. And became foaming rapids full of dangerous boulders.
6. Many of which can break a boat.
7. Michelle's boat was small.
8. With one guide and four passengers.
9. Some passengers prefer large inflatable boats with outboard motors.
10. Carrying eighteen people.

1. sent.
2. frag.—She rafted
3. sent.
4. sent.
5. frag.—The river swirled
6. frag.—Dangerous boulders,/, were spotted
7. sent.
8. frag.—Her boat was full
9. sent.
10. frag.—That boat,/, was big and roomy

Subject and Predicate

Sentences consist of two basic parts: subjects and predicates.

The Subject

1b. The *subject* tells *whom* or *what* the sentence is about.

EXAMPLES **Nicholasa Mohr** is a writer and an artist.

The girls on the team were all good students.

He shared his lunch with the boy on the other team.

Swimming is good exercise.

To find the subject, ask *who* or *what* is doing something or *whom* or *what* is being talked about. The subject may come at the beginning, middle, or end of a sentence.

EXAMPLES **The pitcher** struck Felicia out. [*Who* struck Felicia out? *The pitcher* struck Felicia out.]

After practicing for hours, **Tim** bowled five strikes. [*Who* bowled five strikes? *Tim* bowled five strikes.]

How kind **you** are! [*Who* is kind? *You* are kind.]

When will **the afternoon train** arrive? [*What* will arrive? *The afternoon train* will arrive.]

Hiding in the tall grass was **a baby rabbit**. [*What* was hiding? *A baby rabbit* was hiding.]

Reference Note

A compound noun, such as *Nicholasa Mohr*, is considered one noun. For information about **compound nouns,** see page 25.

Subject and Predicate 5

RESOURCES

Subject and Predicate
Practice
- *Language & Sentence Skills Practice*, pp. 5–9, 18–19
- *Developmental Language & Sentence Skills*, pp. 3–6

Subject and Predicate
Rules 1b–e *(pp. 5–13)*

OBJECTIVES

- To complete sentences by adding subjects
- To identify the subjects of sentences
- To identify simple and complete subjects in sentences
- To identify verbs, verb phrases, and complete predicates in sentences
- To complete sentences by adding predicates

DIRECT TEACHING

Modeling and Demonstration

The Subject. Model how to identify the subject of a sentence by using the example *He shared his lunch with the boy on the other team*. First, ask students to identify the verb of the sentence. [*shared*] Next, ask who shared. [*He*] Explain that *He* is the subject of the sentence. Now, have a volunteer use another example from this chapter to demonstrate how to identify the subject of a sentence.

PRACTICE

Guided and Independent

Exercise 1 You may want to use the first ten items in **Exercise 1** as guided practice. Then, have students complete the exercise as independent practice. **HOMEWORK**

DIRECT TEACHING

Correcting Misconceptions

Imperative Sentences. Because imperative sentences do not have stated subjects, students may incorrectly identify imperatives as sentence fragments. On the chalkboard, write an imperative sentence, such as "Please hand me the cassette." Then, ask who is expected to perform the action of the verb. [*you*] Ask students to explain in their own words how to tell whether a sentence is imperative or not. Then, remind them that even though its subject is understood rather than stated, an imperative sentence is considered a complete sentence.

Here is a test to find the simple subject of most sentences: If you leave out the simple subject, a sentence does not make sense.

EXAMPLE
The frisky cat chased its tail.
The frisky . . . chased its tail. [*Cat* is the simple subject.]

Exercise 1   Writing Subjects and Punctuating Sentences

Provide subjects to fill in the blanks in the following sentences. Use a different subject in each sentence.   Answers will vary. Sample responses are given.

EXAMPLE   1. ____ is very heavy.
          1. *That box is very heavy.*

1. ____ is an exciting game to play.   **1.** Soccer
2. ____ works in the post office.   **2.** Jack
3. Luckily for me, ____ was easy to repair.   **3.** this bike
4. Tied to the end of the rope was ____.   **4.** a calf
5. Did ____ help you?   **5.** anyone
6. ____ eventually became President of the United States.   **6.** He
7. Have ____ always wanted to visit Peru?   **7.** the Millers
8. Luis, ____ was the score?   **8.** what
9. Before the game, ____ will meet in the gym.   **9.** Jo and Han
10. ____ has always been one of my favorite books.   **10.** That
11. What a great basketball player ____ is!   **11.** Amber
12. Has ____ called you yet?   **12.** your mother
13. In the afternoon ____ takes a nap.   **13.** my cat
14. ____ is playing at the theater this weekend?   **14.** What
15. When did ____ start making that sound?   **15.** the car
16. In a minute ____ will feed you, Spot.   **16.** I
17. Under the pile of leaves in the front yard was ____.   **17.** the ball
18. ____ is the group's best-known song?   **18.** What
19. In my opinion, ____ is a better goalie than Alex.   **19.** she
20. Where in the world did ____ get that hat?   **20.** Michael

Simple Subject and Complete Subject

1c. The *simple subject* is the main word or word group that tells *whom* or *what* the sentence is about.

The *complete subject* consists of all the words that tell *whom* or *what* a sentence is about.

EXAMPLES   The four new students arrived early.
   Complete subject   The four new students
   Simple subject   students

Chapter 1   The Parts of a Sentence

MINI-LESSON   Mechanics

Spelling Compound Nouns. Explain to students that a simple subject could be composed of more than one word if the words are part of a compound noun. Some compound nouns are spelled as one word (*newspaper*); some are spelled as two or more words (*space station*); and some are hyphenated (*self-confidence*). Explain to students that a dictionary can be used to check the spelling of compound nouns.

Is the winner of the go-cart race present?

Complete subject	the winner of the go-cart race
Simple subject	winner

A round walnut table with five legs stood in the middle of the dining room.

Complete subject	A round walnut table with five legs
Simple subject	table

A simple subject may consist of one word or several words.

EXAMPLES **Jets** often break the sound barrier. [one word]

Does **Aunt Carmen** own a grocery store? [two words]

On the library shelf was **The Island of the Blue Dolphins.** [six words]

NOTE In this book, the simple subject is usually referred to as the *subject*.

Exercise 2 Identifying Subjects

Write the subject of each of the following sentences.

EXAMPLE 1. A book by N. Scott Momaday is on the table.
1. book

1. Born in 1934 in Oklahoma, Momaday lived on Navajo and Apache reservations in the Southwest.
2. Momaday's father was a Kiowa.
3. As a young man, Momaday attended the University of New Mexico and Stanford University.
4. In *The Way to Rainy Mountain*, he tells about the myths and history of the Kiowa people.
5. The book includes poems, an essay, and stories about the Kiowa people.
6. *The Way to Rainy Mountain* was published in 1969.
7. After Momaday's book came works by other modern American Indian writers.
8. William Least Heat-Moon traveled in a van across the United States and wrote about his journey.
9. Was he inspired to write by his travels?
10. Readers of this Osage writer enjoy his beautiful descriptions of nature.

Subject and Predicate   7

DIFFERENTIATING INSTRUCTION

Advanced Learners

Introducing sentence diagramming will help students—especially students with developed spatial and logical-mathematical skills—understand sentence structure.

The following examples can be displayed on poster board or a section of the chalkboard, as needed, as a helpful reminder. For more examples, see **Chapter 19: Sentence Diagramming.**

Simple Subject, Simple Predicate
Julia can sing.

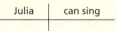

Compound Subject, Simple Predicate
Sharks and eels can swim.

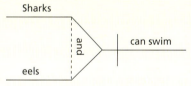

Simple Subject, Compound Predicate
Babies cry or sleep.

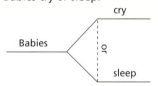

Compound Subject, Compound Predicate
Julia and Rose can sing and dance.

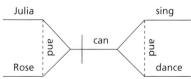

Read to students the following list of compound nouns, and ask them to offer possible spellings on the chalkboard:

nose dive   half-moon
backstage

Then, have students look up the correct spellings in a dictionary.

For more about compound nouns, see p. 25. For more about hyphens, see p. 338.

Subject and Predicate   7

RETEACHING

Complete Subjects and Predicates

To help students identify complete subjects and predicates, write complete subjects and complete predicates on separate strips of paper.

Divide the students into two equal groups, distributing complete-subject strips to one group and complete-predicate strips to the other. Make sure each student has a strip.

Have a student from the complete-subject group stand at the front of the class and display his or her strip. Then, have the complete-predicate group decide which of them holds a matching strip. After that student joins his or her counterpart at the front of the class, have the students arrange themselves to make a complete sentence.

As you continue, have the two groups take turns being the first in front of the class.

Exercise 3 Identifying Complete Subjects and Simple Subjects

Write the complete subject in each of the following sentences. Then, underline the simple subject.

EXAMPLES
1. Stories about time travel make exciting reading.
1. *Stories* about time travel
2. Samuel Delany writes great science fiction.
2. *Samuel Delany*

1. Ray Bradbury is also a writer of science fiction.
2. *The Golden Apples of the Sun* is a collection of Bradbury's short stories.
3. Is your favorite story in that book "A Sound of Thunder"?
4. The main character in the story is called Mr. Eckels.
5. For ten thousand dollars, Mr. Eckels joins Time Safari, Inc.
6. He is looking for the dinosaur *Tyrannosaurus rex*.
7. With four other men, Bradbury's hero travels more than sixty million years back in time.
8. On the safari, trouble develops.
9. Because of one mistake, the past is changed.
10. Do the results of that mistake affect the future?

The Predicate

1d. The ***predicate*** **of a sentence tells something about the subject.**

EXAMPLES   The phone **rang**.

Old Faithful **is a giant geyser in Yellowstone National Park.**

Jade Snow Wong **wrote about growing up in San Francisco's Chinatown.**

Like the subject, the predicate may be found anywhere in a sentence.

EXAMPLES   **Outside the tent was** a baby bear.

Late in the night we **heard a noise.** [The predicate in this sentence is divided by the subject, *we*.]

Chapter 1   The Parts of a Sentence

The Parts of a Sentence

Has the dough **risen enough**? [The predicate is divided by the subject, *the dough*.]

Stop right there! [The subject in this sentence is understood to be *you*.]

Exercise 4   Identifying Predicates

Write the predicate in each of the following sentences.

EXAMPLES
1. My favorite sports poster is this one of Roberto Clemente.
1. *is this one of Roberto Clemente*
2. Have you heard of this famous sports hero?
2. *Have heard of this famous sports hero*

1. Also among my baseball treasures is a book about Clemente's life and career.
2. Clemente played right field for the Pittsburgh Pirates, my favorite team.
3. During his amazing career, he won four National League batting titles.
4. In 1966, he was named the league's Most Valuable Player.
5. Twice Clemente helped lead the Pirates to World Series victories.
6. In fourteen World Series games, Clemente never went without a hit.
7. Roberto Clemente died in a plane crash off the coast of his homeland, Puerto Rico.
8. The plane crash occurred during a flight to Nicaragua to aid earthquake victims.
9. After his death, Clemente was elected to the National Baseball Hall of Fame.
10. In New York, a park has been named for this beloved ballplayer.

Subject and Predicate   9

Exercise 4

DISTRIBUTED REVIEW
After students have completed this exercise, have them identify the complete subject in sentences 1, 3, 5, and 10. [1. *a book about Clemente's life and career*; 3. *he*; 5. *Clemente*; 10. *a park*] Emphasize that any word not included in the complete subject is part of the complete predicate. Students can use this information to check their answers for the exercise.

DIFFERENTIATING INSTRUCTION

English-Language Learners

General Strategies. In many languages other than English, the meaning of a sentence does not depend on word order. Consequently, sentence structure is much less restrictive than it is in English. Point out to students that, in most cases, the simple subject comes before the simple predicate in English declarative sentences.

Japanese and Korean. In Japanese, the subject is always followed by *wa* or *ga*. In Korean, the subject is always followed by *i* (pronounced "ee") or *ga*. When identifying the subject of a sentence, Japanese and Korean speakers may benefit by finding which English word(s) would be followed by a subject particle in their native languages.

CONTENT-AREA CONNECTIONS

Science. Tell students that the simple subject and simple predicate of a sentence are sometimes called its *skeleton*. Like the body's skeleton, the subject and predicate form a framework—a base that supports everything else. Lead a discussion about how other parts of the sentence are like other body systems.

Subject and Predicate   9

Exercise 5   Writing Predicates

Make a sentence out of each of the following word groups by adding a predicate to fill the blank or blanks. **Answers will vary. Sample responses are given.**

EXAMPLES
1. A flock of geese ____
1. *A flock of geese flew high overhead.*

2. ____ a poster of Nelson Mandela.
2. *Over Kim's desk hung a poster of Nelson Mandela.*

1. My favorite food ____.   **1. is spinach**
2. A course in first aid ____.   **2. is offered here**
3. ____ our car ____?   **3. Does; look dirty**
4. Rock climbing ____.   **4. is fun**   **5. were looking for gold**
5. Spanish explorers in the Americas ____.
6. Several computers ____.   **6. were given to our school**
7. ____ a new pair of in-line skates.   **7. In the box was**
8. The skyscrapers of New York City ____.   **8. loomed above us**
9. Some dogs ____.   **9. chase cars**
10. ____ my family ____.   **10. In June; is going to Mexico**
11. Victory in the championship ____.   **11. is his dream**
12. ____ all sorts of birds ____.   **12. At night; roost there**
13. The new store at the mall ____.   **13. opened last week**
14. ____ a small, brown toad.   **14. There sat**
15. The flowers in Mr. Alvarez's garden ____.   **15. bloom in spring**
16. ____ my chores ____.   **16. Now; are finished**
17. Gerry's allowance ____.   **17. has been spent**
18. ____ we ____?   **18. Where are; going**
19. The cool of the morning ____.   **19. was soothing**
20. The tiny kittens ____.   **20. crawled out of the basket**

Simple Predicate and Complete Predicate

1e. The ***simple predicate,*** or ***verb,*** is the main word or word group that tells something about the subject.

The ***complete predicate*** consists of a verb and all the words that describe the verb and complete its meaning.

EXAMPLES   The pilot broke the sound barrier.

Complete predicate	broke the sound barrier
Simple predicate (verb)	broke

Learning for Life

Letters to the Editor. Clear writing relies on complete sentences. To show students examples of clear, complete sentences, bring to class some letters to the editor. Try to include a variety of sources: school, neighborhood, city, and national newspapers as well as various magazines.

Have students work in small groups to compile lists of guidelines for such a letter. As each group shares its guidelines with the rest of the class, write on the chalkboard the following list:

We should have visited the diamond field in Arkansas.
Complete predicate   should have visited the diamond field in Arkansas
Simple predicate (verb)   should have visited

The telephone on the table rang.
Complete predicate   rang
Simple predicate (verb)   rang

NOTE In this book, the simple predicate is usually referred to as the *verb*.

Exercise 6 Identifying Complete Predicates and Verbs

Write the complete predicate of each of the following sentences. Then, underline the verb.

EXAMPLE 1. Who created the U.S. flag?
1. <u>created</u> the U.S. flag

1. Many scholars are unsure about the history of the Stars and Stripes.
2. The Continental Congress approved a design for the flag.
3. The flag's design included thirteen red stripes and thirteen white stripes.
4. The top inner quarter of the flag was a blue field with thirteen white stars.
5. The name of the designer has remained a mystery.
6. During the American Revolution, the colonists needed a symbol of their independence.
7. George Washington wanted flags for the army.
8. Unfortunately, the flags did not arrive until the end of the Revolutionary War.
9. According to legend, Betsy Ross made the first flag.
10. However, most historians doubt the Betsy Ross story.

The Verb Phrase

Some simple predicates, or verbs, consist of more than one word. Such verbs are called **verb phrases** (verbs that include one or more helping verbs).

EXAMPLE   Kathy **is riding** the Ferris wheel.

Reference Note
For information about **helping verbs,** see page 49.

EXTENSION

Relating to Literature
If your literature textbook contains the Randall Jarrell poem "The Chipmunk's Day," have students read the poem and identify the simple predicate of each sentence. Then, ask what effect is created in the first three stanzas by placing the simple predicates at the ends of the lines where they appear. [*The placement emphasizes the chipmunk's rapid movements.*] Ask students what shift in emphasis is produced by placing the simple predicates in the last stanza at the beginning of the lines where they appear. [*The focus shifts from the chipmunk's quick activity to its burrow.*]

- is brief
- has a strong, clear opinion statement
- has supporting information that is organized logically
- has emotional appeal
- has a strong ending

Then, ask students to work individually to write letters to the editor. Encourage them to focus on issues about which they feel strongly and to target specific publications. Remind students to check their letters for sentence completeness.

Differentiating Instruction

English-Language Learners

General Strategies. In some languages, verbs always appear at the ends of sentences. Consequently, speakers of such languages might expect to find verbs at the ends of English sentences.

Make sure students know that verbs in English can appear anywhere in English sentences. You may want to share the following examples:

1. Beginning: *Listen to the rain.*
2. Middle: *Most of the players scored in last night's basketball game.*
3. End: *Please go.*

Reference Note
For information on **adverbs**, see page 54.

EXAMPLES The carnival **has been** in town for two weeks.

Should Imelda **have gotten** here sooner?

NOTE The words *not* and *never* are not verbs; they are adverbs. Adverbs are never part of a verb or verb phrase.

EXAMPLES She **has** not **written** to me recently.

I **will** never **forget** her.

They **do**n't **know** my cousins. [*Don't* is the contraction of *do* and *not*. The *n't* is not part of the verb phrase *do know*.]

Exercise 7 Identifying Verbs and Verb Phrases

Write the verb or verb phrase in each of the following sentences.

EXAMPLES 1. Look at these beautiful pictures of Hawaii.
1. *Look*

2. They were taken by our science teacher.
2. *were taken*

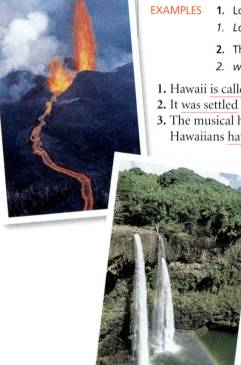

1. Hawaii is called the Aloha State.
2. It was settled by Polynesians about 2,000 years ago.
3. The musical heritage and rich culture of the original Hawaiians have contributed to the islands' popularity.
4. Have you ever seen a traditional Hawaiian dance, one with drums and chants?
5. The Hawaiian islands are also known for their lush, exotic scenery.
6. I can certainly not imagine anything more spectacular than an active volcano at night.
7. Would you like a helicopter ride over misty waterfalls like those in Hawaii?
8. What an incredible sight that surely is!
9. Those Hawaiian dancers must have been practicing for years.
10. Save me a place on the next flight!

Finding the Subject

To find the subject of a sentence, find the verb first. Then, ask *Who?* or *What?* before the verb.

EXAMPLES In high school we will have more homework. [The verb is *will have. Who* will have? *We* will have. *We* is the subject of the sentence.]

Can you untie this knot? [*Can untie* is the verb. *Who* can untie? *You* can untie. *You* is the subject of the sentence.]

The peak of Mount Everest was first reached by Sir Edmund Hillary and Tenzing Norgay. [The verb is *was reached. What* was reached? *Peak* was reached. *Peak* is the subject of the sentence.]

Ahead of the explorers lay a vast wilderness. [The verb is *lay. What* lay? *Wilderness* lay. *Wilderness* is the subject of the sentence.]

Where are the Canary Islands located? [*Are located* is the verb. *What* are located? *Canary Islands* are located. *Canary Islands* is the subject of the sentence.]

Pass the salad, please. [*Pass* is the verb. *Who* should pass? *You* pass. Understood *you* is the subject of the sentence.]

Compound Subjects and Compound Verbs

Compound Subjects

1f. A ***compound subject*** **consists of two or more subjects that are joined by a conjunction and that have the same verb.**

The conjunctions most commonly used to connect the words of a compound subject are *and* and *or*.

EXAMPLES **Paris** and **London** remain favorite tourist attractions. [The two parts of the compound subject have the same verb, *remain*.]

Nelson Mandela or **Archbishop Desmond Tutu** will speak at the conference. [The two parts of the compound subject have the same verb, *will speak*.]

Among my hobbies are **reading, snorkeling,** and **painting.** [The three parts of the compound subject have the same verb, *are*.]

HELP

When you are looking for the subject of a sentence, remember that the subject is never part of a prepositional phrase. Cross through any prepositional phrases; the subject will be one of the remaining words.

EXAMPLE
Several ~~of the puzzle pieces are under the sofa.~~

SUBJECT
Several

VERB
are

Reference Note
For information on **prepositional phrases,** see page 59.

Reference Note
For information on **conjunctions,** see page 62.

Compound Subjects and Compound Verbs

Rules 1f, g *(pp. 13–18)*

OBJECTIVES

- To identify compound subjects, compound verbs, and verb phrases in sentences
- To create sentences by adding compound subjects to predicates

---

RESOURCES

Compound Subjects and Compound Verbs
Practice
- *Language & Sentence Skills Practice,* pp. 10–14

DIRECT TEACHING

Modeling and Demonstration

Compound Subjects. Model how to identify compound subjects by using the example *Many rapids and waterfalls have also originated through the process of erosion.* First, ask students to identify the verb of the sentence. [*have originated*] Next, ask which subjects have that same verb and are connected by a conjunction. [*rapids, waterfalls*] Point out that these subjects make up the compound subject. Now, have a volunteer use another example from this chapter to demonstrate how to identify the compound subject of a sentence.

TIPS & TRICKS

In sentences with a compound subject joined by *or*, the verb agrees with the subject closest to it. Here is a quick test you can use. (1) Cover the part of the subject that is farther from the verb. (2) Decide whether the remaining part of the compound subject agrees with the verb.

EXAMPLE
The dog or the rabbits (*digs, dig*) holes in the garden. [*The rabbits digs or the rabbits dig? The rabbits dig is correct.*]

ANSWER
The dog or the rabbits **dig** holes in the garden.

Exercise 8 Identifying Compound Subjects

Write the compound subject in each of the following sentences.

EXAMPLE 1. The shapes and sizes of sand dunes are determined by the wind.
　　　　　1. shapes, sizes

1. The national parks and monuments of the United States include many of the world's most spectacular landforms.
2. The Grand Canyon and the waterfalls of Yosemite are examples of landforms shaped by erosion.
3. Water, wind, and other natural forces are continuing the age-old erosion of landforms.
4. On the Colorado Plateau, for example, natural bridges and arches, like the one in the photograph on the left, have been produced by erosion.
5. Likewise, Skyline Arch and Landscape Arch in Utah are two natural arches formed by erosion.
6. Underground, caves and immense caverns are created by rushing streams and waterfalls.
7. Stalagmites and stalactites, such as the ones in the photograph on the right, are formed by lime deposits from drops of water seeping into these caverns.

8. In river systems throughout the world, canyons and gorges are cut into the earth by erosion.
9. Many rapids and waterfalls have also originated through the process of erosion.
10. Do steep areas with heavy rainfall or dry regions with few trees suffer more from erosion?

14　Chapter 1　The Parts of a Sentence

Exercise 9 Writing Compound Subjects

Add a compound subject to each of the following predicates. Use *and* or *or* to join the parts of your compound subjects.

EXAMPLE 1. ____ were at the bottom of my locker.
1. *My bus pass and a pair of gym socks were at the bottom of my locker.*

1. Yesterday ____ arrived in the mail.
2. ____ make loyal pets.
3. On the beach ____ spotted a dolphin.
4. ____ will present their report on the adventures of Álvar Núñez Cabeza de Vaca.
5. In the attic were piled ____ .
6. Ever since first grade, ____ have been friends and neighbors.
7. Is ____ coaching the tennis team this year?
8. For Indian food, ____ always go to the Bombay Cafe in the shopping center nearby.
9. To our great surprise, out of my little brother's pockets spilled ____ .
10. Both ____ may be seen on the African plains.

Compound Verbs

1g. A *compound verb* consists of two or more verbs that are joined by a conjunction and that have the same subject.

The conjunctions most commonly used to connect the words of a compound verb are *and*, *or*, and *but*.

EXAMPLES The rain **has fallen** for days and **is** still **falling.**

The team **played** well but **lost** the game anyway.

Will Rolando **mop** the floor or **wash** the dishes?

A sentence may contain both a *compound subject* and a *compound verb*. Notice in the following example that both subjects carry out the action of both verbs.

EXAMPLE A few **vegetables** and many **flowers sprouted** and **grew** in the rich soil. [The vegetables sprouted and grew, and the flowers sprouted and grew.]

Answers
Exercise 9
Compound subjects will vary. Here are some possibilities:
1. four letters and a magazine
2. Dogs and birds
3. Daniel or Chandra
4. My sister and her friend
5. suitcases and picture albums
6. Kerry, Steven, and I
7. Hector or Alicia
8. Kimrey and I
9. a compass, six coins, and a toad
10. lions and zebras

STYLE TIP

Using compound subjects and verbs, you can combine ideas to make your writing less wordy. Compare the examples below.

WORDY
Orville and Wilbur Wright built one of the first airplanes. Orville and Wilbur Wright flew it near Kitty Hawk, North Carolina.

REVISED
Orville and Wilbur Wright **built** one of the first airplanes and **flew** it near Kitty Hawk, North Carolina.

Subject and Predicate   15

 Grammar   Continued on pp. 16–17

Compound Verb or Compound Sentence? Because of the punctuation needed in a compound sentence, students should distinguish between compound sentences and simple sentences with compounds verbs.

Write the following examples on the chalkboard:

Eric runs track and plays soccer.

Maurice writes poetry in his spare time, and Elayne paints portraits.

GRAMMAR

HELP
Be sure to include all parts of each verb phrase in Exercise 10.

MEETING THE CHALLENGE
You can use compound subjects and compound verbs to make your writing smoother—less repetitive and more concise. Find an interesting picture or photograph that shows several things or people. Then, write a paragraph describing the picture, making sure to use a compound subject or compound verb in at least four sentences.

ANSWER
Paragraphs will vary but should contain at least four compound subjects and/or verbs.

HELP
Some of the subjects and verbs in Exercise 11 are compound.

EXTENSION

Critical Thinking

Metacognition. After students have completed **Exercise 11,** ask the following questions:

- When identifying subjects and verbs, which do you look for first? Why? Does identifying one help you find the other?
- How do you know whether a subject or verb is compound?

Exercise 10 — Identifying Compound Verbs

Write each compound verb or verb phrase in the following sentences.

EXAMPLE 1. Have you heard of the game Serpent or learned the game Senet?
　　1. have heard, learned

1. Just like children today, children in ancient Egypt played games and enjoyed toys.
2. For the Egyptian board game Serpent, players found or carved a serpent-shaped stone.
3. Players placed the serpent in the center of the board and then began the game.
4. They used place markers and threw bones or sticks as dice.
5. The players took turns and competed with one another in a race to the center.
6. Senet was another ancient Egyptian board game and was played by children and adults alike.
7. Senet looked like an easy game but was actually difficult.
8. Players moved their playing pieces toward the ends of three rows of squares but sometimes were stopped by their opponents.
9. Senet boards were complex and had certain squares for good luck and bad luck.
10. These squares could help players or could block their pieces.

Exercise 11 — Identifying Subjects and Verbs

Identify the subject and verb in each of the following sentences.

EXAMPLE 1. American pioneers left their homes and traveled to the West.
　　1. pioneers—subject; left, traveled—verbs

1. Settlers faced and overcame many dangers.
2. Mount McKinley and Mount Whitney are two very high mountains.
3. Sacagawea of the Shoshone people helped open the West to explorers and settlers.
4. Every winter many skiers rush to the Grand Tetons.

16 Chapter 1 The Parts of a Sentence

MINI-LESSON Grammar *Continued from p. 15*

　　Explain that if a sentence is compound, a comma generally precedes a coordinating conjunction such as *and, but, or, nor, for, so,* or *yet.* No commas, however, are needed for compound verbs.
　　Ask students to write the following sentences and exchange their papers with partners to check for correct structure and punctuation:

- A simple sentence with one subject and one verb
- A simple sentence with one subject and a

5. Did all of the mountaineers successfully ascend and descend Mount Everest?
6. Valleys and dense forests cool and refresh travelers in the Appalachian Mountains.
7. On Beartooth Highway in Montana, excellent campgrounds and scenic overlooks provide many views of distant glaciers.
8. Mount Evans is west of Denver and can be reached by the highest paved road in the United States.
9. Is the view from the top slopes of Mount Evans breathtaking?
10. Thick forests cover the Great Smoky Mountains and help form the peaks' smoky mist.

Review A — Identifying Subjects and Predicates

Write the simple subject and the verb or verb phrase in each of the following sentences.

EXAMPLE   1. Even the ancient Incas and the Aztecs paid and collected taxes.
          1. *Incas, Aztecs; paid, collected*

HELP
Some of the subjects and verbs in Review A are compound.

1. Among the obligations of citizens in large cities is the prompt payment of taxes.
2. The ancient citizens of Mesoamerica were no exception to this rule.
3. Are some of these taxes also known today as "tribute"?
4. Bowls, blankets, honey, or even warriors' shields were given and accepted as tribute.
5. High officials and the sick did not, however, pay taxes.
6. In the interest of fairness, taxes must be counted and recorded in some way by accountants.
7. As a record, Incas knotted a string or cord and counted the number of knots.
8. The Codex Mendoza is a formal record of the Aztecs' taxes.
9. Both the Incas and the Aztecs used the number *20* as the base of their mathematics.
10. Might roads, buildings, or emergency supplies have been paid for with the tribute, or taxes?

HELP

Some of the subjects and verbs in Review B are compound.

Reference Note

For information about how **sentences can be classified according to their structure**, see Chapter 7.

Review B Identifying Subjects and Predicates

Write the following sentences. Underline the complete subjects once and the complete predicates twice. Then, circle each simple subject and each verb.

EXAMPLES
1. The entire continent of Australia is occupied by a single country.
1. The entire (continent) of Australia (is occupied) by a single country.

2. What do you know about this continent?
2. What (do) (you) (know) about this continent?

1. (It) (is located) within the Southern Hemisphere.
2. (Can) (you) (name) the capital of Australia?
3. (Australia) (is) a federation of six states and two territories.
4. The (continent) of Australia (was claimed) for Britain by Captain James Cook.
5. The native (people) of Australia (live) mainly in the desert regions and, traditionally, (have) a very close bond with their environment.
6. A large (number) of British colonists (settled) in cities and towns on the coast.
7. Many (ranchers) (raise) sheep and (export) wool.
8. In addition, large (quantities) of gold and uranium (are mined) in Australia.
9. The (country) (is) also highly industrialized and (produces) a variety of goods, ranging from shoes to airplanes.
10. Among Australia's most unusual animals (are) the (platypus) and the (anteater).

Kinds of Sentences

1h. A *declarative sentence* makes a statement and ends with a period.

EXAMPLES   Amy Tan was born in Oakland, California.

I couldn't hear what Jason said.

1i. An *imperative sentence* gives a command or makes a request. Most imperative sentences end with a period. A strong command ends with an exclamation point.

Chapter 1   The Parts of a Sentence

Kinds of Sentences

Rules 1h–k (pp. 18–20)

OBJECTIVE

- To classify sentences as declarative, imperative, interrogative, or exclamatory

DIFFERENTIATING INSTRUCTION

Learners Having Difficulty

Read the example sentences for **Rules 1h, 1i, 1j,** and **1k** aloud to students. Inflect your voice to indicate the purpose of each sentence.

RESOURCES

Kinds of Sentences

Practice

- *Language & Sentence Skills Practice*, pp. 15–17, 20
- *Developmental Language & Sentence Skills,* pp. 7–8

EXAMPLES   Be quiet during the play. [command]

Please give me another piece of melon. [request]

Stop! [strong command]

The subject of a command or a request is always *you*, even if *you* doesn't appear in the sentence. In such cases, *you* is called the **understood subject**.

EXAMPLES   (You) Be quiet during the play.

(You) Please give me another piece of melon.

(You) Stop!

The word *you* is the understood subject even when the person spoken to is addressed by name.

EXAMPLE   Miguel, (you) please answer the phone.

1j. An *interrogative sentence* asks a question and ends with a question mark.

EXAMPLES   When did you return from your camping trip?

Did the surfboard cost much?

1k. An *exclamatory sentence* shows excitement or expresses strong feeling and ends with an exclamation point.

EXAMPLES   Gabriella won the match!

How terrifying that movie was!

Exercise 12   Classifying Sentences by Purpose

Label each of the following sentences *declarative*, *imperative*, *interrogative*, or *exclamatory*.

EXAMPLE   1. Ask Yoshiko for the address.
          1. *imperative*

1. Will your grandfather compete in the Kansas City Marathon again this year?   1. int.
2. Our school's project, cleaning up the Silver River Nature Preserve, was a success.   2. dec.
3. Bring more sandbags over here now!   3. imp.
4. Is the Rig-Veda the oldest of the Hindu scriptures?   4. int.
5. Read this poem by Naomi Shihab Nye.   5. imp.

Kinds of Sentences   19

DIFFERENTIATING INSTRUCTION

English-Language Learners

Spanish. In Spanish, questions are preceded by an inverted question mark and followed by a regular question mark; exclamations are preceded by an inverted exclamation point and followed by a regular exclamation point. Explain to your Spanish-speaking students that a single question mark or exclamation point is used at the end of an English sentence and that neither is inverted.

DIRECT TEACHING

Modeling and Demonstration

Interrogative Sentences. Model how to identify an interrogative sentence by using the example *Did the surfboard cost much?* First, ask whether the sentence asks a question. [yes] Then, ask whether the sentence ends in a question mark. [yes] Ask students to explain in their own words how to tell whether a sentence is interrogative. Now, have a volunteer use another example from this chapter to demonstrate how to identify an interrogative sentence.

TEACHING TIP

Exercise 12 To help students recognize the differences between the types of sentences, give students a declarative sentence and ask them to convert it to the other three types of sentences. For example, *The test was hard* could become *Was the test hard?* (interrogative); *Please tell me whether the test was hard* (imperative); and *What a hard test that was!* (exclamatory).

6. How huge this library is! **6. exc.**
7. Origami is the fascinating Japanese folk art of folding paper into shapes. **7. dec.**
8. How did you make that paper crane? **8. int.**
9. Please line up alphabetically. **9. imp.**
10. After we eat supper, we're going to my aunt's house down the block. **10. dec.**

Review C Classifying and Punctuating Sentences

Write the last word of each of the following sentences, adding the correct end mark. Then, label each sentence as *declarative*, *imperative*, *interrogative*, or *exclamatory*.

EXAMPLE   1. Are prairie dogs social creatures
          1. creatures?—interrogative

1. dec. 1. Many of these small mammals live together in underground "towns" like the one shown below**.**
2. imp. 2. Look at how prairie dogs dig family burrows**. or !**
3. int. 3. How large are the burrows**?**
4. dec. 4. The burrows sometimes cover several acres**.**
5. dec. 5. These creatures can usually be seen at night or in the early morning**.**
6. exc. 6. What alert animals prairie dogs are**!**
7. dec. 7. At least one prairie dog always keeps a lookout for threats to the community**.**
8. imp. 8. Look at how it sits up to see better**. or !**
9. dec. 9. It then dives headfirst into the burrow and alerts the colony**.**
10. exc. 10. How shrill the prairie dog's whistle of alarm is**!**

20   Chapter 1   The Parts of a Sentence

CHAPTER 1

Chapter Review

A. Identifying Sentences

Identify each of the following groups of words as a *sentence* or a *sentence fragment*.

1. Trying a double somersault.
2. She barely caught her partner's hands!
3. As she began the triple.
4. She fell into the net.
5. The crowd gasped.
6. Even the clowns turned and looked.
7. Was she hurt?
8. Rolled off the net to the ground.
9. Smiling as she waved to the crowd.
10. She was fine!

B. Identifying Subjects

Identify the complete subject of the following sentences. Then, underline the simple subject. The simple subject may be compound.

11. Foods and beverages with large amounts of sugar can contribute to tooth decay.
12. The lava from a volcano hardens when it cools.
13. The earthquake survivors camped on blankets in the rubble.
14. In Beijing, bicyclists weave through the busy streets.
15. By 1899, many gold prospectors had rushed to Alaska.
16. The weather during an Alaskan summer can be hot.
17. Have you read this collection of Claude McKay's poems?
18. In the center of the table was a huge bowl of fruit.
19. Linked forever in legend are Paul Bunyan and Babe the Blue Ox.
20. Have many famous racehorses been trained in Kentucky?
21. The bright lights and the tall buildings amaze and delight most visitors to New York City.

Sidebar

Numerals in brackets refer to the rules tested by the items in the Chapter Review.

1. frag. [1a]
2. sent. [1a]
3. frag. [1a]
4. sent. [1a]
5. sent. [1b]
6. sent. [1a]
7. sent. [1a]
8. frag. [1a]
9. frag. [1a]
10. sent. [1a]

HELP
Remember that the subject may be the understood *you*.

11. [1b, c, f]
12. [1b, c]
13. [1b, c]
14. [1b, c]
15. [1b, c]
16. [1b, c]
17. [1b, c]
18. [1b, c]
19. [1b, c, f]
20. [1b, c]
21. [1b, c, f]

ASSESSING

Monitoring Progress

Chapter Review. To assess student progress, you may want to compare the types of items missed on the **Diagnostic Preview** to those missed on the **Chapter Review.** You could then work out specific goals for mastering essential information with individual students who are still having difficulty.

RESOURCES

The Parts of a Sentence

Review
- *Language & Sentence Skills Practice,* pp. 17–20

Assessment
- *Holt Handbook Chapter Tests with Answer Key,* pp. 1–2, 46

22. Are [Lita and Marisa] going to give their presentation?
23. After soccer practice tomorrow afternoon, please come to my house for dinner.
24. Inside the box were letters and postcards written around the turn of the century.
25. [The book *Come a Stranger*] was written by the award-winning author Cynthia Voigt.

C. Identifying Predicates

Identify the [complete predicate] of the following sentences. Then, underline the simple predicate (verb or verb phrase). The simple predicate may be compound.

26. Teenagers [need a balanced diet for good health].
27. A balanced diet [improves student performance in school].
28. Students [are sometimes in a hurry and skip breakfast].
29. [For a nutritious breakfast,] they [can eat cereal and fruit].
30. Cheese and juice [also provide good nutrition].
31. The cheese [contains calcium, an important mineral].
32. People [need protein as well].
33. Protein [builds body tissue].
34. Protein [can be supplied by eggs, dried beans, red meat, fish, and poultry].
35. Carbohydrates [include whole grains, vegetables, and fruits].
36. Junk foods [can ruin your appetite].
37. Sweets [cause tooth decay and contain many calories].
38. [According to nutritionists,] sweets [are low in nutrients and fill the body with "empty" calories].
39. Good eating habits [keep you healthy and make you stronger].
40. [Start eating right]!

D. Classifying and Punctuating Sentences

Classify each of the following sentences as *declarative, interrogative, imperative,* or *exclamatory*. Then, write each sentence with the correct end punctuation.

41. In ancient times, the Julian calendar was used.

42. Why was it called Julian?
43. It was named after the Roman leader Julius Caesar.
44. I thought so! *or* .
45. Because the Julian calendar was not perfect, the Gregorian calendar was invented.
46. In 1752, the calendar was changed in England.
47. Tell me the result.
48. Eleven days in September were lost.
49. That's the strangest thing I've ever heard! *or* .
50. Were those days lost forever?

Writing Application
Writing a Letter

Using Complete Sentences Think of a party or other interesting event you have attended. Write a letter describing the event to a friend or relative who lives far away. Include details about the activities you enjoyed and about the other people who were there. Use complete sentences to make sure your thoughts are clear.

Prewriting Make a list of the details that you would like to include in your letter. At this stage, you do not have to use complete sentences. Simply jot down your thoughts.

Writing Use your prewriting list of details as you write your rough draft. Choose details that would be interesting to your friend or relative. You might organize your letter chronologically (describing events in the order in which they occurred).

Revising Read your letter aloud. As you read, mark any parts of the letter that seem unclear. Add, cut, or rearrange details to make your letter clear and interesting to your reader.

Publishing Check your work to make sure you have used only complete sentences. Read your letter for any errors in spelling and punctuation. Then, send a copy of your letter to your friend or relative.

CHAPTER 2

INTRODUCING THE CHAPTER

- This chapter first explains nouns and classifies them as common or proper and concrete or abstract. The chapter next focuses on pronouns and their antecedents, discussing various types of pronouns—personal, reflexive, intensive, demonstrative, interrogative, indefinite, and relative. Finally, students are introduced to several types of adjectives: articles, demonstrative adjectives, and proper adjectives.

- The chapter closes with a **Chapter Review,** which includes a **Writing Application** feature that asks students to write a brief report using pronouns that refer clearly to their antecedents.

- For help in integrating this chapter with writing assignments, use the **Teaching Strands** chart on pp. T24–T25.

CHAPTER 2

Parts of Speech Overview
Noun, Pronoun, Adjective

Diagnostic Preview

Identifying Nouns, Pronouns, and Adjectives

Identify each italicized word in the following paragraphs as a *noun,* a *pronoun,* or an *adjective.*

EXAMPLES   The [1] *achievements* of the [2] *native* peoples of North America have sometimes been overlooked.

1. noun
2. adjective

Numerals in brackets refer to the rules tested by the items in the Diagnostic Preview.

1. [2a]	11. [2c]
2. [2a]	12. [2c]
3. [2a]	13. [2b]
4. [2a]	14. [2a]
5. [2c]	15. [2c]
6. [2c]	16. [2b]
7. [2a]	17. [2c]
8. [2c]	18. [2a]
9. [2a]	
10. [2c]	

Recent [1] *studies* show that the Winnebago people developed a [2] *calendar* based on careful observation of the [3] *heavens.* An [4] *archaeologist* has found that markings on an old [5] *calendar* stick are the precise records of a [6] *lunar* year and a solar year. These records are remarkably accurate, considering that at the time the [7] *Winnebagos* had neither a [8] *written* language nor a system of [9] *mathematics.*

[10] *The* calendar stick is a carved [11] *hickory* branch with [12] *four* sides. [13] *It* is worn along the [14] *edges* and shows other signs of frequent use. A [15] *similar* stick appears in a portrait of an early chief of the Winnebagos. In the portrait, the chief holds a calendar stick in [16] *his* right hand. [17] *One* current theory is that the chief went out at [18] *sunrise* and

---

CHAPTER RESOURCES

Internet
- Web resources: go.hrw.com

Practice & Review
- Language & Sentence Skills Practice, pp. 25–38; 39–41
- Language & Sentence Skills Practice Answer Key, pp. 11–19

Application & Enrichment
- Language & Sentence Skills Practice, pp. 24, 42–43, 44
- Language & Sentence Skills Practice Answer Key, pp. 11, 19–20

sunset to observe the sun and the moon. [19] He then marked on the stick what he saw. According to one researcher, this calendar is the [20] *oldest* indication we have that native North American peoples recorded the year day by day.

19. [2b]
20. [2c]

The Noun

2a. A ***noun*** **is a word or word group that is used to name a person, a place, a thing, or an idea.**

Persons	Jessye Norman, teacher, chef, Dr. Ling
Places	Grand Canyon, city, Namibia, kitchen
Things	lamp, granite, Nobel Prize, Golden Gate Bridge
Ideas	happiness, self-control, liberty, bravery

Notice that some nouns are made up of more than one word. A ***compound noun*** is a single noun made up of two or more words used together. The compound noun may be written as one word, as a hyphenated word, or as two or more words.

One Word	grandmother, basketball
Hyphenated Word	mother-in-law, light-year
Two Words	grand piano, jumping jack

TIPS & TRICKS
To find the correct spelling of a compound noun, look it up in a recent dictionary.

HELP
In Exercise 1, some nouns are used more than once.

Exercise 1   Identifying Nouns

Identify the nouns in the following sentences.

EXAMPLE
1. We have been reading about patriotic heroines in our textbook.
   1. heroines, textbook

1. Rebecca Motte was a great patriot.
2. During the Revolutionary War, British soldiers seized her mansion in South Carolina.
3. The American officer Henry Lee told Motte that the Americans would have to burn her home to smoke out the British.

The Noun   25

PRETEACHING

Lesson Starter

Motivating. Explain to students that grammar, just like various sports and hobbies, has special terminology that all participants must understand in order to communicate effectively. For example, if a soccer player were instructed by the coach to "dribble the ball to the penalty area," that player would need to be familiar with the terminology in order to complete the tasks.

Ask students to come up with examples of terminology from their activities or hobbies. On the chalkboard, list activities or hobbies and the corresponding terminology for each. Explain that if a peer reviewer or teacher suggests that a student use specific kinds of nouns or make sure that pronouns agree with their antecedents, the student must be familiar with the terminology in order to complete the tasks.

DIRECT TEACHING

Modeling and Demonstration

The Noun. Model how to identify a noun by using the example *intelligence*. First, ask whether the word names a person, place, thing, or idea. [yes—idea] *Intelligence* names an idea, so it is a noun. Now, have a volunteer use another example from this chapter to demonstrate how to identify a noun.

---

4. Motte supported the plan and was glad to help her country.
5. She even supplied flaming arrows and a bow for the attack.
6. Other people might not have been so generous or patriotic.
7. The house was saved after the enemy raised the white flag of surrender.
8. Afterward, Motte invited soldiers from both sides to dinner.
9. This gesture showed that Motte had a generous heart.
10. The colonies and all citizens of the United States are in her debt.

Proper Nouns and Common Nouns

A *proper noun* names a particular person, place, thing, or idea and begins with a capital letter. A *common noun* names any one of a group of persons, places, things, or ideas and is generally not capitalized.

Common Nouns	Proper Nouns
girl	Kay O'Neill
writer	Octavio Paz
country	Morocco
monument	Eiffel Tower
compact disc	*A Long Way Home*
book	*The Blue Sword*
religion	Buddhism
language	Arabic
city	Ottawa

Reference Note
For more information about **capitalizing proper nouns,** see page 266.

HELP
In Exercise 2, some nouns are used more than once.

Exercise 2 Identifying Common Nouns and Proper Nouns

Write the nouns in each of the following sentences. Then, identify each noun as a *common noun* or *proper noun*.

EXAMPLE 1. Mark visited an interesting museum in Colorado last month.
1. Mark—proper; museum—common; Colorado—proper; month—common

RESOURCES

The Noun
Practice
- *Language & Sentence Skills Practice,* pp. 25–28
- *Developmental Language & Sentence Skills,* pp. 9–10

1. Mark and his parents went to the Black American West Museum and Heritage Center in Denver.
2. The museum displays many items that cowboys used.
3. These items are from the collection of Paul Stewart, the man who founded the museum.
4. Mark saw saddles, knives, hats, and lariats.
5. He also saw many pictures of African American cowboys.
6. The museum is located in an old house that is listed in the National Register of Historic Places.
7. The house once belonged to Dr. Justina L. Ford.
8. She was the first black female physician in Colorado.
9. Mark was amazed by all of the old medical instruments in one display.
10. He said he was glad doctors don't use equipment like that anymore.

Exercise 3 Revising Sentences by Using Proper Nouns

Revise the following sentences by substituting a proper noun for each common noun. You might have to change some other words in each sentence. You may make up proper names.

EXAMPLE
1. An ambassador visited a local school and spoke about his country.
1. Ambassador Rios visited Jackson High School and spoke about Brazil.

1. That painting is in a famous museum.
2. The police officer cheerfully directed us to the building on that street.
3. My relatives, who are originally from a small town, now live in a large city.
4. The librarian asked my classmate to return the book as soon as possible.
5. That newspaper is published daily; this magazine is published weekly.
6. The girl read a poem for the teacher.
7. That state borders the ocean.
8. The owner of that store visited two countries during a spring month.
9. A man flew to a northern city one day.
10. Last week the mayor visited our school and talked about the history of our city.

The Noun   27

DIFFERENTIATING INSTRUCTION

English-Language Learners

Spanish. In Spanish, both concrete and abstract nouns are always accompanied by definite articles. Examples of abstract nouns include *la democracia* (democracy), *la justicia* (justice), and *la inflación* (inflation). Therefore, students might construct sentences such as "The freedom is our goal." Scan student writing for this type of construction, and offer extra practice if necessary.

RETEACHING

Abstract and Concrete Nouns

Activity. Students might understand the distinction between abstract nouns and concrete nouns more easily if they associate the terms with familiar words. Put the following charts on the chalkboard (without the sample answers). Then, ask students to supply words to fill in the charts.

CONCRETE NOUNS

PERSON	PLACE	THING
teacher	school	book

ABSTRACT NOUNS

IDEA	FEELING	CHARACTERISTIC
freedom	joy	courage

Students might need help filling in the abstract nouns.

Exercise 4 **Identifying and Classifying Nouns**

Identify the nouns in the following sentences, and label each noun as a *common noun* or a *proper noun*.

EXAMPLE [1] Lillian Evanti performed in Europe, Latin America, and Africa.

1. *Lillian Evanti*—proper noun; *Europe*—proper noun; *Latin America*—proper noun; *Africa*—proper noun

[1] Evanti was the first African American woman to sing opera professionally. [2] Her talent was recognized early; when she was a child, she gave a solo concert in Washington, D.C. [3] As an adult, she performed in a special concert at the White House for President Franklin Roosevelt and his wife, Eleanor. [4] Evanti also composed a musical piece titled "Himno Panamericano," which was a great success. [5] Her career inspired many other African American singers.

[6] A few years later Marian Anderson stepped into the limelight. [7] Always a champion of the arts, Mrs. Roosevelt again aided a great performer. [8] With the assistance and encouragement of the former First Lady, Anderson sang at a most appropriate site—the Lincoln Memorial. [9] Like Evanti, Anderson broke barriers, for before her, no other African American had sung at the famous Metropolitan Opera House in New York City. [10] One honor that Anderson earned was a place in the National Arts Hall of Fame.

Concrete Nouns and Abstract Nouns

A **concrete noun** names a person, place, or thing that can be perceived by one or more of the senses (sight, hearing, taste, touch, smell). An **abstract noun** names an idea, a feeling, a quality, or a characteristic.

Concrete Nouns	photograph, music, pears, filmmaker, sandpaper, rose, Brooklyn Bridge
Abstract Nouns	love, fun, freedom, self-esteem, beauty, honor, wisdom, Buddhism

---

MINI-LESSON **Mechanics**   Continued from p. 27

letters are not capitalized.

Write the following items on the chalkboard, and have students work in small groups to correct the capitalization.

For additional help or practice, refer students to p. 26.

1. winfield middle school
2. isle of pines
3. "madam and the rent man"
4. lost creek boulevard

Exercise 5 — Writing Sentences with Concrete and Abstract Nouns

Identify each noun in the following list as *concrete* or *abstract*. Then, use each noun in an original sentence.

EXAMPLE   1. truth
   1. abstract—People should always tell the truth.

1. soy sauce
2. brotherhood
3. laughter
4. ice
5. excitement
6. kindness
7. motor
8. health
9. pillow
10. honor

Collective Nouns

A *collective noun* is a word that names a group.

audience	committee	herd	quartet
batch	crew	jury	swarm
class	family	litter	team

Reference Note
For more information about **collective nouns,** see pages 158 and 167.

Review A — Using the Different Kinds of Nouns

Complete the following poem, which is based on this painting. Add common, proper, concrete, abstract, or collective nouns as directed. For proper nouns, you'll need to make up names of people and places. Be sure you capitalize all proper nouns.

Meet my [1] (*common*), the really amazing,
Truly tremendous [2] (*proper*), that's who.
You can see what [3] (*abstract*) he gives
The [4] (*collective*) of fans who hang on him
   like glue.

The walls of his gym on [5] (*proper*)
Are covered with [6] (*concrete*) that show
The muscled, tussled [7] (*common*) aplenty,
Who work out there, come rain or come snow.

Eduardo, [8] (*proper*), and I really enjoy
The [9] (*abstract*) of hanging on tight
Way above the [10] (*concrete*) and swinging,
Held up by the muscleman's might.

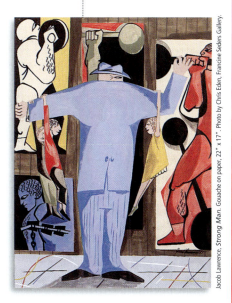

Jacob Lawrence, *Strong Man*. Gouache on paper, 22" x 17". Photo by Chris Eden, Francine Seders Gallery.

The Noun 29

---

5. thanksgiving day
6. washington monument
7. nobel prize
8. mayor gernhardt
9. *the wizard of oz*
10. *webster's new world dictionary*

Exercise 5 — Writing Sentences with Concrete and Abstract Nouns

ANSWERS
Sentences will vary. Here are some possibilities.

1. concrete—Do you want soy sauce on your rice?
2. abstract—A spirit of brotherhood among peoples of the earth might bring world peace.
3. concrete—Laughter is contagious.
4. concrete—I like to put ice in my water.
5. abstract—The crowd's excitement mounted as the players were introduced.
6. abstract—Her kindness is extraordinary.
7. concrete—The motor is electric.
8. abstract—His health is improving.
9. concrete—That pillow belongs on the sofa.
10. abstract—She served her country with honor.

Review A — Using the Different Kinds of Nouns

ANSWERS
Nouns will vary. Here are some possibilities.

1. friend
2. Lou
3. joy
4. group
5. Sycamore Street
6. posters
7. athletes
8. Jan
9. thrill
10. sidewalk

The Pronoun

Rule 2b (pp. 30–34)

OBJECTIVES

- To identify pronouns and classify them by type
- To revise sentences by replacing nouns with pronouns

DIRECT TEACHING

Modeling and Demonstration

Antecedents. Model how to identify antecedents by using the example *Ask Dan if he has done his homework.* First, identify the pronouns. (*he, his*) Then, list the information the pronouns provide. [*They both refer to one person who is male.*] Next, have students find the word to which the pronouns logically refer. [*The one male person in the sentence is Dan.*] *Dan* is the antecedent of *he* and *his*. Now, have a volunteer use another example from this chapter to demonstrate how to identify the antecedent of a pronoun.

Reference Note

For information about choosing **pronouns that agree with their antecedents**, see page 165.

HELP

Some authorities prefer to call possessive pronouns (such as *my, your,* and *their*) possessive adjectives. Follow your teacher's directions when you are labeling these words.

The Pronoun

2b. A *pronoun* is a word that is used in place of one or more nouns or pronouns.

EXAMPLES   Ask Dan if Dan has done Dan's homework.

Ask Dan if **he** has done **his** homework.

Both of Lois's friends said both would help Lois find Lois's missing books.

Both of Lois's friends said **they** would help **her** find **her** missing books.

The word or word group that a pronoun stands for (or refers to) is called its *antecedent.*

                   antecedent   pronoun   pronoun

EXAMPLES   **Frederick,** have **you** turned in **your** report?

                   antecedent   pronoun

Walking the dog is fun, and **it** is good exercise.

Sometimes the antecedent is not stated.

EXAMPLES   **Who** asked that question?

I did not understand what **you** said.

Someone will have to clean up the mess.

Personal Pronouns

A **personal pronoun** refers to the one speaking (*first person*), the one spoken to (*second person*), or the one spoken about (*third person*).

Personal Pronouns		
	Singular	**Plural**
First Person	I, me, my, mine	we, us, our, ours
Second Person	you, your, yours	you, your, yours
Third Person	he, him, his, she, her, hers, it, its	they, them, their, theirs

RESOURCES

The Pronoun

Practice

- *Language & Sentence Skills Practice,* pp. 29–33
- *Developmental Language & Sentence Skills,* pp. 11–16

Reflexive and Intensive Pronouns

A *reflexive pronoun* refers to the subject and is necessary to the meaning of the sentence. An *intensive pronoun* emphasizes a noun or another pronoun and is unnecessary to the meaning of the sentence.

Reflexive and Intensive Pronouns	
First Person	myself, ourselves
Second Person	yourself, yourselves
Third Person	himself, herself, itself, themselves

REFLEXIVE   Tara enjoyed **herself** at the party.
　　　　　　　The team prided **themselves** on their victory.

INTENSIVE   I **myself** cooked that delicious dinner.
　　　　　　　Did you redecorate the room **yourself**?

Demonstrative Pronouns

A *demonstrative pronoun* points out a person, a place, a thing, or an idea.

Demonstrative Pronouns			
this	that	these	those

EXAMPLES   **This** is the book I bought for my sister.
　　　　　　　Are **those** the kinds of plants that bloom at night?

NOTE *This, that, these,* and *those* can also be used as adjectives. When they are used in this way, they are called *demonstrative adjectives.*

DEMONSTRATIVE PRONOUN   **Those** are very sturdy shoes.
DEMONSTRATIVE ADJECTIVE **Those** shoes are very sturdy.

DEMONSTRATIVE PRONOUN   Did you order **this**?
DEMONSTRATIVE ADJECTIVE Did you order **this** salad?

HELP
If you are not sure whether a pronoun is reflexive or intensive, use this test: Read the sentence aloud, omitting the pronoun. If the basic meaning of the sentence stays the same, the pronoun is intensive. If the meaning changes, the pronoun is reflexive.

EXAMPLES
Mark repaired the car **himself**. [Without *himself,* the meaning stays the same. The pronoun is intensive.]

The children amused **themselves** all morning. [Without *themselves,* the sentence doesn't make sense. The pronoun is reflexive.]

Reference Note
For more about **demonstrative adjectives,** see page 36.

DIFFERENTIATING INSTRUCTION

English-Language Learners

Spanish. The English possessive pronouns *your, his, her, its,* and *their* all can be written in Spanish as *su* (or *sus* if more than one thing is possessed). *Yourself, himself, herself, itself,* and *themselves* can all be translated as *se.* Watch for any difficulties students may have distinguishing among these pronouns.

Asian Languages. Many Asian languages—such as Indonesian, Japanese, and Vietnamese—have a variety of possessive pronouns that mean *you.* Consequently, some English-language learners might avoid using *you* because it seems impolite or awkward to use the same word to address respected elders, peers, both men and women, and animals. Remind students that in English it is acceptable to use *you* in all of these situations.

Learners Having Difficulty

You may want to have the class perform exercises that require physically connecting pronouns with their antecedents. Having students circle pronouns and draw lines to their antecedents may help them understand the relationship between the two words.

Interrogative Pronouns

An *interrogative pronoun* introduces a question.

Interrogative Pronouns				
what	which	who	whom	whose

EXAMPLES **What** is the best brand of frozen yogurt?

Who wrote *Barrio Boy*?

Indefinite Pronouns

An *indefinite pronoun* refers to a person, a place, a thing, or an idea that may or may not be specifically named.

Common Indefinite Pronouns				
all	each	many	nobody	other
any	either	more	none	several
anyone	everything	most	no one	some
both	few	much	one	somebody

EXAMPLES **Both** of the girls forgot their lines.

I would like **some** of that chow mein.

NOTE Most indefinite pronouns can also be used as adjectives.

PRONOUN **Some** are bored by this movie.
ADJECTIVE **Some** people are bored by this movie.

Relative Pronouns

A *relative pronoun* introduces an adjective clause.

Common Relative Pronouns				
that	which	who	whom	whose

EXAMPLES Thomas Jefferson, **who** wrote the Declaration of Independence, was our country's third president.

Exercise is something **that** many people enjoy.

TIPS & TRICKS

The indefinite pronouns *some, any, none, all, more,* and *most* may be singular or plural. Look closely at any prepositional phrase that follows these pronouns. The object of the preposition determines whether the pronoun is singular or plural.

SINGULAR
None of the milk **is** sour.
[*Milk* is singular.]

PLURAL
None of the grapes **are** sweet. [*Grapes* is plural.]

Reference Note
For information on **indefinite pronouns and subject-verb agreement,** see page 153.

Reference Note
For information on **subordinate clauses,** see page 114.

GRAMMAR

DIFFERENTIATING INSTRUCTION

English-Language Learners

Spanish. Because the Spanish relative pronoun *que* can be translated as *that, which, who,* or *whom,* Spanish speakers may use *which* in cases where *who* would sound natural in English. Show students some sentences containing *that, who,* and *which* in adjective clauses, allowing them to investigate situations in which each is used. Once they seem to understand the distinctions, have them practice inserting the proper relative pronoun into sentences.

MINI-LESSON Usage

Subject-Verb Agreement. You may want to provide students with some instruction to help with subject-verb agreement when the subject of a sentence is an indefinite pronoun, as in <u>Neither</u> of the girls <u>wants</u> her ears pierced. Explain to students that the following pronouns are singular and need a singular verb: *each, either, neither, one, everyone, everybody, no one, nobody, anyone, anybody, someone,* and *somebody.* Point out that prepositional phrases following the singular indefinite pronoun may

Exercise 6 Identifying Pronouns

Identify each pronoun in the following sentences. Then, tell what type of pronoun each one is.

EXAMPLES
1. The drama coach said he would postpone the rehearsal.
1. he—personal
2. Does Pamela, who is traveling to Thailand, have her passport and ticket?
2. who—relative; her—personal

HELP
Some sentences in Exercise 6 have more than one pronoun.

1. "I want you to study," Ms. Gaines said to the class.
2. The firefighter carefully adjusted her oxygen mask.
3. The children made lunch themselves.
4. Jenny and Rosa decided they would get popcorn, but Amy didn't want any.
5. Who will be the next president of the school board?
6. Mr. Yoshira, this is Mrs. Volt, a neighbor of yours.
7. Ralph Bunche, who was awarded the Nobel Peace Prize, was a diplomat for his country at the United Nations.
8. Of all United States Olympic victories, perhaps none were more satisfying than Jesse Owens's 1936 triumphs in the 200-meter dash and broad jump.
9. Oh, yes, the puppy taught itself how to open the gate.
10. Only one of seventy-five qualified boys and girls will win the grand prize.

1. personal/personal
2. personal
3. intensive
4. personal/indefinite
5. interrogative
6. demonstrative/personal
7. relative/personal
8. indefinite
9. reflexive
10. indefinite

Oral Practice Adding Appropriate Pronouns to Sentences

Read each of the following sentences aloud. Then, re-read each sentence, replacing the italicized words with an appropriate pronoun.

EXAMPLE
1. The boy forgot *the boy's* homework.
1. The boy forgot his homework.

1. Put the flowers in water before *the flowers'* petals droop.
2. The canoe capsized as *the canoe* neared the shore.
3. The players convinced *the players* that *the players* would win the game.
4. Lori oiled the bike before *Lori* put *the bike* in the garage.
5. Tim said, "*Tim* answered all six questions on the quiz."
6. Ben folded the newspapers for Ms. Luke, and then *Ben* stuffed *the newspapers* in plastic bags for *Ms. Luke*.

1. their
2. it
3. themselves/they
4. she/it
5. I
6. he/them/her

The Pronoun 33

The Adjective

Rule 2c (pp. 34–39)

OBJECTIVES

- To identify adjectives and the words they modify in sentences
- To complete a story by inserting appropriate adjectives
- To identify common and proper adjectives in sentences
- To convert proper nouns into proper adjectives
- To identify articles and demonstrative adjectives

DIRECT TEACHING

Modeling and Demonstration

Adjectives. Model how to identify which words adjectives modify by using the example *A woman, kind and helpful, gave us directions.* First, ask *What kind or which woman?* [*A, kind, helpful*] The adjectives *A, kind,* and *helpful* modify the noun *woman.* Now, have a volunteer use another example from this chapter to demonstrate how to identify what word an adjective modifies.

DIFFERENTIATING INSTRUCTION

English-Language Learners

Vietnamese. Because Vietnamese adjectives follow nouns and pronouns, Vietnamese-speaking students may produce sentences with word order that is unusual in English. For example, a student may write "Mark saw birds beautiful" instead of "Mark saw beautiful birds." Remind students that in English, single-word modifiers usually precede the words they modify. Give students opportunities to describe people, things, and events in descriptive writing.

7. we
8. it
9. she
10. his/them

COMPUTER TIP

Using a software program's thesaurus can help you choose appropriate adjectives. To make sure that an adjective has exactly the connotation you intend, check the word in a dictionary.

Reference Note

For more about **predicate adjectives,** see page 81.

7. Sarah, Keith, and I arrived early so that *Sarah, Keith, and I* could get good seats.
8. Her wheelchair was amazingly fast, and *her wheelchair* was lightweight, too.
9. My sister just graduated from college, and *my sister* is now working as a computer programmer.
10. Because Japan fascinates Ron and *Ron's* brother, this film will interest *Ron and Ron's brother.*

The Adjective

2c. An *adjective* is a word that is used to modify a noun or a pronoun.

To *modify* a word means to describe the word or to make its meaning more definite. An adjective modifies a noun or a pronoun by telling *what kind, which one, how much,* or *how many.*

What Kind?	Which One or Ones?	How Much or How Many?
Korean children	**seventh** grade	**several** days
busy dentist	**these** countries	**five** dollars
braided hair	**any** book	**no** marbles

Sometimes an adjective comes after the word it modifies.

EXAMPLES A woman, **kind** and **helpful,** gave us directions. [The adjectives *kind* and *helpful* modify *woman.*]

The box is **empty.** [The predicate adjective *empty* modifies *box.*]

RESOURCES

The Adjective

Practice

- *Language & Sentence Skills Practice,* pp. 34–38
- *Developmental Language & Sentence Skills,* pp. 17–18

Articles

The most commonly used adjectives are *a*, *an*, and *the*. These adjectives are called **articles**. *A* and *an* are called **indefinite articles** because they refer to any member of a general group. *A* is used before a word beginning with a consonant sound. *An* is used before a word beginning with a vowel sound.

EXAMPLES **A** frog croaked.

An orange is **a** good source of vitamin C.

My cousin Jimmy wears **a** uniform to school. [Even though *u* is a vowel, the word *uniform* begins with a consonant sound.]

This is **an** honor. [Even though *h* is a consonant, the word *honor* begins with a vowel sound. The *h* is not pronounced.]

The is called the **definite article** because it refers to someone or something in particular.

EXAMPLES **The** frog croaked.

Where is **the** orange?

Nouns or Adjectives?

Many words that can stand alone as nouns can also be used as adjectives modifying nouns or pronouns.

Nouns	Adjectives
bean	**bean** soup
spring	**spring** weather
gold	**gold** coin
football	**football** game
Labor Day	**Labor Day** weekend
Super Bowl	**Super Bowl** party
Milan	**Milan** fashions
White House	**White House** security
Persian Gulf	**Persian Gulf** pearls

Reference Note
For more about **words used as different parts of speech,** see pages 39 and 67.

DIFFERENTIATING INSTRUCTION

English-Language Learners

Hmong. Because Hmong speakers are accustomed to a complex system of more than one hundred noun classifiers, each of which can be used only with nouns of the same class, shape, group, or form, English-language learners may be uncomfortable with the relative simplicity of English article use. Remind Hmong students that English relies on its indefinite articles, *a* and *an,* and its definite article, *the,* as its primary noun "classifiers."

DIRECT TEACHING

Correcting Misconceptions

Adjectives. Students may misidentify certain adjectives as nouns. When students are familiar with a word's use as a noun, they may automatically classify it as such without stopping to consider how the word functions in a specific context. Present students with phrases such as *leather jacket* and *feather pillow,* and ask them to identify the parts of speech of *leather* and *feather* (both are used as adjectives here). Remind students to first consider how a word is being used before they identify its part of speech.

The Adjective **35**

CONTENT-AREA CONNECTIONS

Social Studies
History. For extra practice with proper nouns and adjectives, tell students to write a paragraph about a famous historical figure. Have them go back through their paragraph and identify all the proper nouns and proper adjectives.

DIFFERENTIATING INSTRUCTION

English-Language Learners

Spanish. Spanish demonstrative adjectives and demonstrative pronouns are identical, except that demonstrative pronouns have a written accent (for example, *éste* from *este*). If your students have learned this accentuation rule, reminding them of it may help them distinguish between these two parts of speech.

TEACHING TIP

Exercise 7 If you have told students to classify possessive forms as adjectives, students will identify *my* in #6 and #7 as an adjective. For more information, see the Help on p. 30.

Demonstrative Adjectives

This, *that*, *these*, and *those* can be used both as adjectives and as pronouns. When they modify a noun or pronoun, they are called *demonstrative adjectives*. When they are used alone, they are called *demonstrative pronouns*.

Reference Note
For more about **demonstrative pronouns**, see page 31.

DEMONSTRATIVE ADJECTIVES	**This** drawing is mine, and **that** drawing is his. **These** soccer balls are much more expensive than **those** soccer balls are.
DEMONSTRATIVE PRONOUNS	**This** is mine and **that** is his. **These** are much more expensive than **those** are.

Exercise 7 Identifying Adjectives

Identify the adjectives in the following sentences, and give the noun or pronoun each modifies. Do not include the articles *a*, *an*, and *the*.

EXAMPLE 1. Why don't you take the local bus home from school on cold days?

1. local—bus; cold—days

1. On winter afternoons, I sometimes walk home after band practice rather than ride on a crowded, noisy bus.
2. I hardly even notice the heavy traffic that streams past me on the street.
3. The wet sidewalk glistens in the bright lights from the windows of stores.
4. The stoplights throw green, yellow, and red splashes on the pavement.
5. After I turn the corner away from the busy avenue, I am on a quiet street, where a jolly snowman often stands next to one of the neighborhood houses.
6. At last, I reach my peaceful home.
7. There I am often greeted by my older brother, Kenny, and my sister, Natalie.
8. I know they are glad to see me.
9. Delicious smells come from the kitchen where Mom and Dad are cooking dinner.
10. This quiet, private walk always makes me feel a little tired but also happy.

Learning for Life

Writing a Classified Ad. Explain to students that using vivid, descriptive language will enable them to communicate their ideas effectively. Tell students to choose an item— a bicycle, a baseball trading card, a music box, or something else—they might sell by using a classified ad. An accurate description will help potential buyers to get a clear picture of the object and also will help to ward off unnecessary phone calls that may result from misleading information.

First, ask students to describe in paragraph

Exercise 8   Writing Appropriate Adjectives

Complete the following story by writing an appropriate adjective to fill each blank.   Adjectives will vary. Sample responses are given.

EXAMPLES   [1] ____ parks have [2] ____ trails for hikers.
1. Many
2. wooded

The hikers went exploring in the [1] ____ forest. Sometimes they had difficulty getting through the [2] ____ undergrowth. On [3] ____ occasions they almost turned back. They kept going and were rewarded for their [4] ____ effort. During the [5] ____ hike through the woods, they discovered [6] ____ kinds of [7] ____ animals. In the afternoon the [8] ____ hikers pitched camp in a [9] ____ clearing. They were [10] ____ for supper and rest.

1. dark
2. thick
3. several
4. huge
5. long
6. ten
7. small
8. tired
9. beautiful
10. ready

Reference Note
For more information about **capitalizing proper adjectives,** see page 276.

Proper Adjectives

A *proper adjective* is formed from a proper noun.

Proper Nouns	Proper Adjectives
Thanksgiving	**Thanksgiving** dinner
Catholicism	**Catholic** priest
Middle East	**Middle Eastern** country
Africa	**African** continent

Notice that a proper adjective, like a proper noun, is capitalized. Common adjectives are generally not capitalized.

NOTE   Some proper nouns, such as *Thanksgiving,* do not change spelling when they are used as adjectives.

Exercise 9   Identifying Common and Proper Adjectives

Identify the adjectives in the sentences on the next page. Then, tell whether each is a *common* or *proper* adjective. Do not include the articles *a*, *an,* and *the.*

MEETING THE CHALLENGE

Make a list of at least five nouns and five adjectives that describe you. Use your list to write a short personal description. Underline the nouns and adjectives you picked.

ANSWER
Descriptions will vary but should contain five underlined nouns and five underlined adjectives.

The Adjective   37

GRAMMAR

DIFFERENTIATING INSTRUCTION

English-Language Learners

Spanish. Adjectives derived from names of languages, races, peoples, and nationalities are capitalized in English but not in Spanish. For example:

| español | Spanish |
| inglés | English |

EXTENSION

Critical Thinking

Evaluation. Tell students that well-chosen adjectives can make their writing more colorful and descriptive. Write the following phrases on the chalkboard:

<u>hot</u> sun   <u>nice</u> girl
<u>cute</u> monkeys   <u>pretty</u> day

Ask students to evaluate the adjectives in terms of their effectiveness, considering what sorts of images they bring to mind. [*Students may say the words are overused or not very descriptive.*] Add words to the expressions above to create the sentences below, and have students substitute adjectives that create a more vivid mental picture.

1. The <u>hot</u> sun had made us thirsty. [*blazing, scorching*]
2. We saw <u>cute</u> monkeys at the zoo. [*playful, active*]
3. Everybody thinks she is such a <u>nice</u> girl. [*polite, thoughtful*]
4. What a <u>pretty</u> day this is! [*glorious, splendid*]

---

form a real or imagined item for sale, including all necessary details. Explain that specific nouns and vivid adjectives will enhance their descriptions. Then, have students use classified ads in newspapers as models when they adapt their paragraphs to the abbreviated form used in advertisements.

If students wrote real ads, provide bulletin board space for students to post their ads (with their parents' permission).

The Adjective   37

Exercise 9

DISTRIBUTED REVIEW
Students who had trouble with **Exercise 7** (identifying adjectives and the nouns or pronouns they modify) might benefit from a reversal of the adjectives-first strategy. Have students identify the nouns in sentences 1, 4, and 8 of **Exercise 9**. [1. *animals, ways;* 4. *armor;* 8. *residents, citizens, creatures*] Point out that after identifying the nouns, students can more easily find the adjectives that modify them.

TEACHING TIP

Exercise 9 If you have told students to classify possessive forms as adjectives, students will identify *their* in #3, #4, and #10 as an adjective. For more information, see the Help on p. 30.

Also, in sentence 8 the word *these* functions as a demonstrative adjective. Remind students that *these* can also function as a demonstrative pronoun, depending on its use.

Exercise 10 Writing Proper Adjectives

ANSWERS
1. Roman
2. Victorian
3. Memorial Day (no change)
4. Korean
5. Congressional *or* congressional
6. New Year's Day (no change) *or* New Years'
7. Incan
8. Shakespearean
9. Jewish *or* Judaic *or* Judaistic
10. Celtic

EXAMPLE 1. We have been studying how various animals protect themselves.
 1. various—common

1. Many small animals defend themselves in unusual ways.
2. For example, South American armadillos wear suits of armor that consist of small, bony scales.
3. Armadillos seem delicate, with their narrow faces.
4. However, their tough armor protects them well.
5. Likewise, the Asian anteater has scales that overlap like the shingles on a roof.
6. Anteaters and armadillos have strong claws and long tongues.
7. *Armadillo* is a Spanish word that can be translated as "little armor."
8. Texas and Florida residents as well as Mexican citizens are familiar with these shy creatures.
9. At early twilight, look for armadillos, energetic and ready for a meal of unlucky spiders or insects.
10. Like tortoises, armadillos can pull in their noses and all four of their feet for better protection.

Exercise 10 Writing Proper Adjectives

Change the following proper nouns into proper adjectives.

EXAMPLE 1. Spain
 1. Spanish

1. Rome
2. Victoria
3. Memorial Day
4. Korea
5. Congress

6. New Year's Day
7. Inca
8. Shakespeare
9. Judaism
10. Celt

Review B Identifying Nouns, Pronouns, and Adjectives

Identify each italicized word in the following paragraph as a *noun,* a *pronoun,* or an *adjective.*

EXAMPLE Four [1] *forces* govern the flight of an aircraft.
 1. noun

―HELP―
Use a dictionary to help you spell the adjectives in Exercise 10.

MINI-LESSON Mechanics

Punctuating Adjectives Before Nouns.
Explain to students that a comma is used to separate two or more adjectives that come before a noun, as in *I rode a gentle, intelligent horse.* A comma should never be used between an adjective and the noun immediately following it.
 Sometimes, when the final adjective in a series is closely linked to the noun, a comma is not needed before the final adjective:

Lift and thrust must overcome [1] *drag* and weight. If an airplane is very [2] *heavy*, it cannot lift off unless it has great thrust or speed. If the craft is slow, [3] *it* may not have enough thrust to achieve lift. By 1783, the [4] *French* Montgolfiers had learned how to beat gravity and achieve lift in their hot-air balloon. However, it had little thrust and didn't steer well. Nevertheless, [5] *Parisians* didn't mind the unpredictability. In fact, everybody [6] *who* was anybody wanted to hitch a ride on a balloon. With a rudder and propellers, airships (also known as blimps, dirigibles, and Zeppelins) achieved enough thrust to be steered but became unpopular after the [7] *Hindenburg* met [8] *its* fiery fate. Not until Orville and [9] *Wilbur Wright* put an engine on their famous craft and made its wings slightly [10] *movable* was the quest for thrust and lift achieved. As you know, the rest is history.

Determining Parts of Speech

Remember, the way a word is used in a sentence determines what part of speech it is. Some words may be used as nouns or as adjectives.

NOUN   The helmet is made of **steel.**
ADJECTIVE   It is a **steel** helmet.

Some words may be used as pronouns or as adjectives.

PRONOUN   **That** is a surprise.
ADJECTIVE   **That** problem is difficult.

TEACHING TIP

Review B If you have told students to classify possessive forms as adjectives, students will identify *its* in # 8 as an adjective. For more information, see the Help on p. 30.

DIFFERENTIATING INSTRUCTION

Advanced Learners
A few words can be used as nouns, adjectives, *and* verbs. Challenge students to think of as many such words as possible (individually or in small groups) and to share their lists with the class. [Possibilities include *calm, cut, marble, quiet, silver, snap,* and *yellow.*]

Maya is a respected broadcast journalist.
If students aren't sure whether the final adjective and the noun form a compound, have them use this test. Insert the word *and* between the adjectives. If the use of *and* makes sense, students should use a comma.
For further instruction and practice, refer students to **Chapter 14: Punctuation.**

Review C Identifying Nouns, Pronouns, and Adjectives

Identify the nouns, pronouns, and adjectives in the following sentences. Do not include the articles *a*, *an*, and *the*.

EXAMPLE   1. We walked along the sandy beach at sundown.
   1. We—pronoun; sandy—adjective; beach—noun; sundown—noun

1. When the tide comes in, it brings a variety of interesting items from the sea.
2. When the tide ebbs, it leaves behind wonderful treasures for watchful beachcombers.
3. Few large creatures live here, but you almost certainly will find several small animals if you try.
4. Some live in shallow burrows under the wet sand and emerge in the cool evening to eat plants and other matter.
5. A number of different species of beetle like this part of the beach.
6. Around them you can find bristly flies and tiny worms.
7. You might also come across old pieces of wood with round holes and tunnels in them.
8. These holes are produced by shipworms.
9. If you watch the shoreline carefully, you will see many signs of life that casual strollers miss.
10. Low tide is a marvelous time to search along the shore.

CHAPTER 2

Numerals in brackets refer to the rules tested by the items in the Chapter Review.

1.–5. [2a]

Chapter Review

A. Identifying Types of Nouns

For each of the following sentences, identify the noun of the type indicated in parentheses. There may be more than one type of noun in each sentence.

1. No one understands why whales sometimes strand themselves. (*common*)
2. Since 1985, people in a group called Project Jonah have used an inflatable pontoon to rescue stranded whales and other marine mammals. (*proper*)
3. The people in Project Jonah find fulfillment in helping stranded mammals. (*abstract*)
4. More than two thousand marine mammals have been helped in recent years. (*concrete*)
5. The group has rescued mammals ranging in size from dolphins to whales. (*collective*)

B. Identifying Types of Pronouns

For each of the following sentences, identify the pronoun of the type indicated in parentheses. There may be more than one type of pronoun in each sentence.

6.–15. [2b]

6. Which of all the animals do you think has the worst reputation? (*interrogative*)
7. I believe the skunk is the animal that most people want to avoid. (*relative*)
8. The skunk can easily protect itself from others. (*reflexive*)
9. It can spray those nearby with a bad-smelling liquid. (*personal*)
10. This is a repellant that drives away predators. (*demonstrative*)
11. What do you think a skunk uses as its warning? (*interrogative*)
12. It warns possible predators by stamping its feet, which is intended to frighten the predator. (*relative*)
13. When the skunk needs to attack some other animal, it sprays in the direction of that animal. (*personal*)

ASSESSING

Monitoring Progress

Chapter Review To assess student progress, you may want to compare the types of items missed on the **Diagnostic Preview** to those missed on the **Chapter Review.** You may want to work out specific goals for mastering essential information with individual students who are still having difficulty.

RESOURCES

Parts of Speech Overview: Noun, Pronoun, Adjective

Review
- *Language & Sentence Skills Practice,* pp. 39–41

Assessment
- *Holt Handbook Chapter Tests with Answer Key,* pp. 3–4, 46

14. Anyone who has ever been sprayed by a skunk will never forget the smell. (*indefinite*)
15. I myself would prefer never to upset a skunk. (*intensive*)

C. Identifying Adjectives

Identify the adjectives in each of the following sentences. Then, write the word the adjective modifies. Do not include the articles *a*, *an*, and *the*. A sentence may have more than one adjective.

16. Chapultepec is the name of a historic castle on a hill in Mexico City.
17. This word means "hill of the grasshopper" in the language of the early Aztecs.
18. Aztec emperors used the park area for hunting and relaxation.
19. In 1783, the hilltop was chosen as the location for the castle of the Spanish viceroy.
20. Even though the castle was never finished, it was used as a fortress during the colonial period of Mexican history.
21. After several decades of neglect, the unfinished castle became the home of the National Military Academy in 1842.
22. In 1847, during a war against the United States, this castle was captured by invading troops.
23. Almost twenty years later, the emperor of Mexico, Maximilian, converted the castle into an imperial residence.
24. After the downfall of Maximilian in 1867, the castle became the summer residence of Mexican presidents.
25. In 1937, the property was converted into a national museum.

D. Identifying Nouns, Pronouns, and Adjectives

The following paragraph contains twenty numbered, italicized words. Identify each italicized word as a *noun*, a *pronoun*, or an *adjective*.

In [26] *this* country [27] *mangroves* grow along the coasts of [28] *Florida*. [29] *They* form a [30] *wonderland* where land, water, and [31] *sky* blend. [32] *The* lush, green [33] *mangrove* islands and [34] *shoreline* are both beautiful and valuable. Mangroves are important to [35] *our* [36] *environment*. They produce [37] *tons* of valuable [38] *vegetable* matter and are an [39] *essential* part of [40] *tropical* biology. So far as [41] we know, the [42] *first* reference to mangroves dates back to [43] *Egyptian* times. A [44] *South African* expert has also discovered evidence of mangrove islands along the [45] *Red Sea*.

37. [2a]	42. [2c]
38. [2c]	43. [2c]
39. [2c]	44. [2c]
40. [2c]	45. [2a]
41. [2b]	

Writing Application
Using Pronouns in a Report

Clear Pronoun Reference Your class is creating a bulletin board display to honor exceptional people. For the display, write a brief report about someone you know and admire. Be sure that the pronouns you use refer clearly to their antecedents.

Prewriting First, you will need to select your subject. Make a list of the different people you know. Which of these people do you find really remarkable? After you choose a subject, jot down notes about this person. Tell what this person has done to earn your respect and admiration.

Writing As you write your first draft, refer to your notes. Your thesis statement should briefly state what is exceptional about your subject. In the rest of your paragraphs, give specific examples that illustrate why the person is exceptional.

Revising Now, read through your report and imagine that you do not know the subject. What do you think about him or her? Does the person sound remarkable? If not, you may want to add or cut details or rearrange your report. Read your report aloud. Combine short, related sentences by inserting prepositional phrases or appositive phrases.

Publishing Look closely at your use of pronouns. Be sure that each pronoun has a clear antecedent. You may need to correct some sentences to make the antecedents clear. You and your classmates may want to use your reports to make a classroom bulletin board display. If possible, include pictures or drawings of your subjects. You may also wish to send a copy of your report to your exceptional subject.

Reference Note
For more about **combining sentences,** see page 418.

Chapter Review **43**

CHAPTER

INTRODUCING THE CHAPTER

- This chapter teaches students to recognize and understand the functions of verbs, adverbs, prepositions, conjunctions, and interjections.
- The chapter closes with a **Chapter Review** including a **Writing Application** feature that asks students to write a "how-to" composition that includes prepositional phrases.
- For help in integrating this chapter with writing assignments, use the **Teaching Strands** chart on pp. T24–T25.

Numerals in brackets refer to rules tested by the items in the Diagnostic Preview.

1. prep. [3h]
2. v. [3a]
3. prep. [3h]
4. conj. [3i(1)]
5. adv. [3g]
6. v. [3a]
7. prep. [3h]
8. adv. [3g]
9. adv. [3g]
10. adv. [3g]
11. adv. [3g]
12. v. [3a]

CHAPTER

3 Parts of Speech Overview

Verb, Adverb, Preposition, Conjunction, Interjection

Diagnostic Preview

Identifying Verbs, Adverbs, Prepositions, Conjunctions, and Interjections

Identify each italicized word or word group in the following paragraphs as a *verb*, an *adverb*, a *preposition*, a *conjunction*, or an *interjection*.

EXAMPLES Some [1] *very* unusual words [2] *are used* [3] *in* crossword puzzles.

1. adverb
2. verb
3. preposition

The first crossword puzzle was published [1] *in* 1913. It [2] *appeared* on the Fun Page [3] *of* a New York City newspaper, [4] *and* readers [5] *immediately* [6] *asked* the editors [7] *for* more. [8] *Almost* every daily newspaper in the United States [9] *now* publishes crossword puzzles.

Every day, millions of Americans [10] *faithfully* work crossword puzzles. Many people take puzzles [11] *quite* seriously. For many, solving puzzles [12] *is* a competitive game.

44 Chapter 3   Parts of Speech Overview

CHAPTER RESOURCES

Internet
- Web resources: go.hrw.com

Practice & Review
- *Language & Sentence Skills Practice,* pp. 46–61; 62–64
- *Language & Sentence Skills Practice Answer Key,* pp. 21–29

Application & Enrichment
- *Language & Sentence Skills Practice,* pp. 45, 65–66, 67
- *Language & Sentence Skills Practice Answer Key,* pp. 21, 29–30

I [13] *do* puzzles [14] *strictly* for fun. Best of all, I can work on them [15] *by* myself. That way, no one knows whether I succeed [16] *or* fail. I [17] *occasionally* [18] *brag* about my successes. [19] "*Aha*!" I exclaim. "That was a tough one, [20] *but* I filled in every space."

13. v. [3a]
14. adv. [3g]
15. prep. [3h]
16. conj. [3i]
17. adv. [3g]
18. v. [3a]
19. int. [3j]
20. conj. [3i(1)]

The Verb

3a. A *verb* is a word that expresses action or a state of being.

EXAMPLES We **celebrated** the Chinese New Year yesterday.

The holiday **is** usually in February.

NOTE In this book, verbs are classified as action or linking verbs, as helping or main verbs, and as transitive or intransitive verbs.

Action Verbs

3b. An *action verb* is a verb that expresses either physical or mental activity.

EXAMPLES The owls **hooted** all night. [physical action]

Gloria **plays** volleyball. [physical action]

She **thought** about the problem. [mental action]

I **believe** you. [mental action]

NOTE Action verbs may be transitive or intransitive.

Reference Note
For more information about **transitive and intransitive verbs**, see page 52.

Exercise 1 Classifying Verbs

Tell whether each of the following action verbs expresses physical or mental action.

EXAMPLE 1. visualize
1. mental

1. pounce 1. phy.
2. consider 2. men.
3. wish 3. men.
4. want 4. men.
5. rest 5. phy.
6. remember 6. men.
7. dash 7. phy.
8. anticipate 8. men.
9. shout 9. phy.
10. nibble 10. phy.

ASSESSING

Entry-Level Assessment

Diagnostic Preview. This informal **Diagnostic Preview** can help you gauge students' familiarity with verbs, adverbs, prepositions, conjunctions, and interjections. You may also want to evaluate students' writing to determine whether students are using these five parts of speech proficiently. If students are having difficulty using these parts of speech in their writing, you can use the **Diagnostic Preview** to pinpoint error patterns and specific strengths and weaknesses.

The Verb
Rules 3a–f *(pp. 45–53)*

OBJECTIVES

- To classify verbs according to physical or mental action
- To identify action verbs in sentences
- To identify linking verbs in sentences
- To identify verb phrases and helping verbs in sentences
- To identify verbs in sentences as transitive or intransitive
- To write sentences that use given verbs as both transitive and intransitive

---

Differentiating Instruction
- *Developmental Language & Sentence Skills Guided Practice*, pp. 19–28
- *Developmental Language & Sentence Skills Guided Practice Teacher's Notes and Answer Key*, pp. 6–7

Assessment
- *Holt Handbook Chapter Tests with Answer Key*, pp. 5–6, 46

GRAMMAR

PRETEACHING

Lesson Starter

Motivating. To introduce the concept of action verbs, have the class play a game of charades. In advance, prepare strips of paper with one action verb written on each strip. Have volunteers act out the words as the rest of the class tries to guess the action verb.

DIRECT TEACHING

Modeling and Demonstration

Action Verbs and Linking Verbs. Model how to identify a linking verb and an action verb by using the examples *We celebrated the Chinese New Year yesterday* and *The holiday is usually in February.* First, have students identify the verbs. [*celebrated, is*] Next, ask whether the verbs express an action or a state of being. [*celebrated*—action; *is*—state of being] Tell students that *celebrated* is an action verb, while *is* is a linking verb. Now, have a volunteer use another example from this chapter to demonstrate how to identify an action verb and a linking verb.

DIFFERENTIATING INSTRUCTION

Special Education Students

This chapter includes many terms. It might help students to have a helper review important ideas frequently with them. Students could benefit from beginning each lesson with a summary of material previously covered. This repetition will help students who have poor recall.

HELP

Sentences in Exercise 2 may contain more than one action verb.

Reference Note

For more information about **transitive and intransitive verbs,** see page 52.

Exercise 2 **Identifying Action Verbs**

Identify each action verb in the following sentences.

EXAMPLE 1. I saw that movie last week.
  1. saw

1. For a science project, Elena built a sundial.
2. Mr. Santos carefully explained the word problem to each of the students.
3. I enjoy soccer more than any other sport.
4. This waterfall drops two hundred feet.
5. Mike's bicycle suddenly skidded and fell hard on the wet pavement.
6. Mrs. Karras showed us the way to Johnson City.
7. Mix the ingredients slowly.
8. The heavy traffic delayed us.
9. For the Jewish holiday of Purim, Rachel and her sister Elizabeth gave a party.
10. The early Aztecs worshiped the sun.

Linking Verbs

3c. A ***linking verb*** is a verb that expresses a state of being. A linking verb connects, or links, the subject to a word or word group that identifies or describes the subject.

EXAMPLES Denzel Washington **is** an actor. [The verb *is* connects *actor* with the subject *Denzel Washington*.]

The children **remained** quiet. [The verb *remained* links *quiet* with the subject *children*.]

NOTE Linking verbs never have objects (words that tell who or what receives the action of the verb). Therefore, linking verbs are always intransitive.

Some Forms of the Verb *Be*			
am	were	will be	can be
is	has been	shall be	should be
are	have been	may be	would have been
was	had been	might be	

46 Chapter 3 Parts of Speech Overview

RESOURCES

The Verb

Practice

- *Language & Sentence Skills Practice,* pp. 46–51
- *Developmental Language & Sentence Skills,* pp. 19–22

46 Parts of Speech Overview

Other Linking Verbs			
appear	grow	seem	stay
become	look	smell	taste
feel	remain	sound	turn

NOTE *Be* is not always a linking verb. *Be* can express a state of being without having a complement (a word or word group that identifies or describes the subject). In the following sentences, forms of *be* are followed by words or word groups that tell *where*.

EXAMPLES We **will be** there.

The apples **are** in the bowl.

Some words may be either action verbs or linking verbs, depending on how they are used.

ACTION Amy **looked** through the telescope.
LINKING Amy **looked** pale. [The verb *looked* links *pale* with the subject *Amy*.]

ACTION **Stay** in your seats until the bell rings.
LINKING **Stay** calm. [The verb *stay* links *calm* with the understood subject *you*.]

Exercise 3 Identifying Linking Verbs

Identify the linking verb in each of the following sentences.

EXAMPLE 1. A radio station can be the voice of a community.
   1. can be

1. This is Roberto Martínez, your weather forecaster.
2. Unfortunately, the forecast looks bad today.
3. Outside the window here at Station WOLF, the skies appear cloudy.
4. It certainly felt rainy earlier this morning.
5. According to the latest information, it should be a damp, drizzly day with an 85 percent chance of rainfall.
6. Our sportscaster this morning is Marta Segal.
7. Things have been quiet here around Arlington for the past few days.

Reference Note
For information about **complements**, see Chapter 4.

Reference Note
For more about **understood subjects** in imperative sentences, see page 19.

MEETING THE CHALLENGE

A metaphor is an imaginative comparison that states directly that one thing is another thing. Metaphors often use linking verbs to connect two unlike things, as in "The stars **are** glittering jewels."

Write a descriptive paragraph that includes one or more metaphors. Then, underline all the linking verbs in your paragraph.

The Verb 47

DIFFERENTIATING INSTRUCTION

Advanced Learners

Point out that linking verbs are the language equivalent of equal signs. Any verb that can be replaced with *is, am, are, be, become,* or *becomes* to create a sentence with nearly the same meaning is a linking verb. ("The sky looks blue" passes this test, but "I walked home" does not.) If the replacement produces an unintelligible sentence or one with a substantially different meaning, then the original verb is an action verb.

DIRECT TEACHING

Linking Verbs

Point out that overusing the linking verb *be* can make writing seem dull and lifeless. Replacing overused *be* verbs with well-chosen action verbs can add life to writing.

Ask students to locate pieces of their own writing. Have them work in pairs to circle all forms of *be* that are used as linking verbs. Then, ask the pairs to determine which sentences would seem more lively using action verbs and to rewrite those sentences. Make sure students understand that there is nothing necessarily wrong with using forms of *be*. Have pairs of students share their changes with the rest of the class.

TECHNOLOGY TIP

Tell students that a computer's search function can help them locate and highlight forms of *be* in their writing. Then students can determine whether the highlighted verb should be replaced with an action verb for greater impact.

---

8. Stay alert for sports action tonight.
9. It should be an exciting game between our own Arlington Angels and the visiting Jackson City Dodgers.
10. The team looked great at practice today, and I predict a hometown victory.

HELP
Sentences in Review A may contain more than one verb.

Review A — Identifying Action Verbs and Linking Verbs

Identify the verbs in the following sentences. Then, label each verb as either an *action verb* or a *linking verb*.

EXAMPLE 1. I always enjoy field trips.
   1. enjoy—action verb

1. Last spring, our earth science class visited the Hayden Planetarium.
2. It is a wonderful place, full of fabulous sights.
3. We wandered slowly through the various displays and saw a collection of fine exhibits.
4. One space vehicle seemed like something from a science fiction movie.
5. Another display showed a thirty-four-ton meteorite.
6. When this meteorite fell to earth many years ago, it made a huge crater.
7. After a delicious lunch, we stayed for the show in the observatory.
8. As the room became darker, the picture of a galaxy appeared on the ceiling of the dome above us.
9. The lecturer said that the galaxy is so far away from here that its light reaches us centuries after its first appearance.
10. When we look at such stars, we actually see the ancient past!

SHOE © Tribune Media Services, Inc. All rights reserved. Reprinted with permission.

48   Chapter 3   Parts of Speech Overview

Exercise 4 **Identifying Action Verbs and Linking Verbs**

Identify the verb in each of the following sentences. Then, label each verb as either an *action verb* or a *linking verb*. If the verb is a linking verb, give the words that it connects.

EXAMPLES
1. We sent our dog to obedience school.
    1. sent—action verb
2. Some breeds are extremely nervous.
    2. are—linking verb; breeds, nervous

1. Everyone felt sorry about the misunderstanding.
2. In daylight, we looked for the lost ring.
3. The temperature plunged to ten degrees below zero.
4. The local museum exhibited beautiful Inuit sculptures.
5. Loretta felt her way carefully through the dark, quiet room.
6. The city almost always smells musty after a heavy summer thunderstorm.
7. Dakar is the capital of Senegal.
8. The firefighter cautiously smelled the burned rags.
9. Antonia Novello was the first female surgeon general of the United States.
10. They looked handsome in their party clothes.

1. l.v.
2. a.v.
3. a.v.
4. a.v.
5. a.v.
6. l.v.
7. l.v.
8. a.v.
9. l.v.
10. l.v.

Helping Verbs and Main Verbs

3d. A *helping verb* (*auxiliary verb*) helps the main verb express action or a state of being.

EXAMPLES **can** speak   **has been** named

were sent   **should have been** caught

A *verb phrase* contains one main verb and one or more helping verbs.

EXAMPLES Many people in Africa **can speak** more than one language.

The packages **were sent** to 401 Maple Street.

Kansas **has been named** the Sunflower State.

The ball **should have been caught** by the nearest player.

EXTENSION

Relating to Literature

Have students read Alfred Noyes's poem "The Highwayman" if it is available in your literature textbook. Ask students to identify action verbs and linking verbs in several stanzas of the poem. Then, ask students what effect the verb types have on the rhythm and meaning of the poem. [*For example, the repetitive use of the linking verb* was *in the first stanza creates rhythm and a sense of eerie stillness. The sharp onomatopoeic action verbs (*clattered, clashed, *and* creaked) *along with other action verbs (*tapped *and* whistled) *in the third and fourth stanzas break that stillness.*]

DIRECT TEACHING

Correcting Misconceptions

Helping Verbs. Students may confuse main verbs and helping verbs. To give students additional assistance with helping verbs, provide examples that can also be used as main verbs, either action or linking. Beginning with *am* in the **Commonly Used Helping Verbs** chart, write these sentence pairs on the chalkboard:

Main verb: I <u>am</u> a teacher.
Helping verb: I <u>am writing</u> a letter.

Main verb: We <u>are</u> hungry.
Helping verb: The girls <u>are playing</u> ball.

Have students volunteer sentences as you continue working through the chart. Make sure students realize that not all helping verbs can be used as main verbs.

DIFFERENTIATING INSTRUCTION

English-Language Learners

Spanish. In Spanish, helping verbs are not used as frequently as they are in English. Consequently, students might need extra help identifying and using helping verbs. You may want to have students write sentences using each of the helping verbs listed in the chart.

Commonly Used Helping Verbs			
Forms of *Be*	am are be	been being is	was were
Forms of *Do*	do	does	did
Forms of *Have*	have	has	had
Other Helping Verbs	can could may	might must will	would shall should

Some verbs can be used as either helping verbs or main verbs.

HELPING VERB **Do** you like green beans?
MAIN VERB Did you **do** this math problem?

HELPING VERB She **had** left early.
MAIN VERB She has **had** a cold.

HELPING VERB **Have** they arrived yet?
MAIN VERB They will **have** another chance.

HELPING VERB Where **can** he be?
MAIN VERB My grandparents will **can** green beans.

Sometimes a verb phrase is interrupted by another part of speech. Often the interrupter is an adverb. In a question, however, the subject often interrupts the verb phrase.

EXAMPLES Our school **has** always **held** a victory celebration when our team wins.

Did you **hear** Jimmy Smits's speech?

Should Anita **bring** her layout design to class?

Ken **does** not [or **does**n't] **have** a new desk.

Notice in the last example that the adverb *not* (or its contraction *–n't*) is not included in the verb phrase.

Exercise 5 Identifying Verb Phrases and Helping Verbs

Identify the verb phrases in the following sentences. Underline the helping verbs.

EXAMPLE 1. You can recognize redwoods and sequoias by their bark.
   1. can recognize

1. Have you ever visited Redwood National Park?
2. The giant trees there can be an awesome sight.
3. For centuries, these trees have been an important part of the environment of the northwest United States.
4. Surely, these rare trees must be saved for future generations.
5. More than 85 percent of the original redwood forest has been destroyed over the years.
6. Because of this destruction, the survival of the redwood forest is being threatened.
7. With better planning years ago, more of the forest might already have been saved.
8. Unfortunately, redwood forests are still shrinking rapidly.
9. According to some scientists, redwood forests outside the park will disappear within our lifetime.
10. However, according to other experts, the redwood forests can still be saved!

Review B Identifying Action Verbs and Linking Verbs

Identify the verbs in the following sentences. Then, label each verb as an *action verb* or a *linking verb*.

EXAMPLE 1. Have you ever seen a play in Spanish?
   1. Have seen—action verb

1. The Puerto Rican Traveling Theatre performs plays about Hispanic life in the United States.
2. Over the past twenty years, this group has grown into a famous Hispanic theater group.
3. Sometimes, a production has two casts—one that speaks in English and one that speaks in Spanish.
4. In this way, speakers of both languages can enjoy the play.
5. In recent years many young Hispanic playwrights, directors, and actors have begun their careers at the Traveling Theatre.

HELP
Some sentences in Review B contain more than one verb. Also, be sure to include all parts of each verb phrase.

GRAMMAR

RETEACHING

Verbs

Activity. To help students understand the different kinds of verbs, write the following story segment on the chalkboard.

> One bright, sunny day a frog (*intransitive*) onto a lily pad. "A frog's life (*linking*) so exciting!" he croaked. "I (*intransitive verb phrase*) all morning, and then I (*transitive*) tasty bugs for lunch."

Have the students supply the correct type of verb or verb phrase for each blank in the story. Then, divide the class into groups of three to continue the story or make up a segment of their own. They should supply only the verb labels instead of the verbs. Their choices are *transitive, transitive verb phrase, intransitive, intransitive verb phrase, linking,* and *linking verb phrase.* Then, ask groups to exchange papers and fill in the blanks. Circulate throughout the room to help students who are having problems.

Reference Note
For more about **objects** and their uses in **sentences,** see page 74.

6. Some became well-known at the Puerto Rican Traveling Theatre and then moved on to Broadway or Hollywood.
7. Others remain happy at the Traveling Theatre, where they enjoy the warm, supportive atmosphere.
8. Each production by the Traveling Theatre has its own style.
9. Some shows are musicals, full of song and dance, while other plays seem more serious.
10. Light or serious, Puerto Rican Traveling Theatre productions present a lively picture of Hispanic life today.

Transitive and Intransitive Verbs

3e. A ***transitive verb*** **is a verb that expresses an action directed toward a person, a place, a thing, or an idea.**

With transitive verbs, the action passes from the doer—the subject—to the receiver of the action. Words that receive the action of a transitive verb are called ***objects.***

EXAMPLES   Derrick **greeted** the visitors. [The action of the verb *greeted* is directed toward the object *visitors.*]

            When **will** Felicia **paint** her room? [The action of the verb *will paint* is directed toward the object *room.*]

3f. **An *intransitive verb* expresses action (or tells something about the subject) without the action passing to a receiver, or object.**

EXAMPLES   The train **stopped.**

            Last night we **ate** on the patio.

A verb may be transitive in one sentence and intransitive in another.

EXAMPLES   The children **play** checkers. [transitive]
            The children **play** quietly. [intransitive]

            Mr. Lopez **is baking** bread. [transitive]
            Mr. Lopez **is baking** this afternoon. [intransitive]

            Have Roland and Tracy **left** their coats? [transitive]
            Have Roland and Tracy **left** yet? [intransitive]

 Grammar

Prepositional Phrases. Recognizing and eliminating prepositional phrases from sentences should make finding objects easier for students. Write the following sentences on the chalkboard.

1. Ally swam across the pool.
2. He kicked the ball over the fence.
3. Will Tony go with us?

Explain that the receiver of the action of a transitive verb is almost always a noun or pronoun and will never be in a preposi-

Oral Practice **Identifying Transitive and Intransitive Verbs**

Read aloud each of the following sentences. Then, identify the italicized verb in each sentence as either *transitive* or *intransitive*.

EXAMPLE 1. She *runs* early in the morning.
1. runs—intransitive

1. If you do different kinds of exercises, you *are exercising* in the correct way.
2. When you exercise to improve endurance, flexibility, and strength, your body *develops*.
3. Aerobic exercise *builds* endurance and strengthens the heart and lungs.
4. When you *walk* quickly, you exercise aerobically.
5. Many active people in the United States *attend* classes in aerobics.
6. They *enjoy* the fun of exercising to popular music.
7. Exercises that *improve* flexibility require you to bend and stretch.
8. *Perform* these exercises slowly to gain the maximum benefit from them.
9. Through isometric and isotonic exercises, your muscle strength *increases*.
10. These exercises *contract* your muscles.

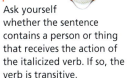

HELP
Ask yourself whether the sentence contains a person or thing that receives the action of the italicized verb. If so, the verb is transitive.

Exercise 6 **Writing Sentences with Transitive and Intransitive Verbs**

For each verb given below, write two sentences. In one sentence, use the verb as a *transitive* verb and underline its object. In the other sentence, use the verb as an *intransitive* verb. You may use different tenses of the verb.

EXAMPLE 1. write
1. Alex is writing a research <u>report</u>. (transitive)
   Alex writes in his journal every day. (intransitive)

1. fly	5. drive	9. climb	13. turn	17. skip
2. leave	6. jump	10. watch	14. pay	18. read
3. return	7. hear	11. visit	15. row	19. help
4. draw	8. answer	12. shout	16. run	20. sing

The Verb   53

The Adverb

Rule 3g (pp. 54–58)

OBJECTIVES

- To identify adverbs and the words they modify in sentences
- To supply adverbs to complete a paragraph

DIRECT TEACHING

Modeling and Demonstration

Identifying Adverbs. Model how to identify an adverb by using the example *The sprinter ran swiftly.* First, write the sentence on the chalkboard, along with the questions *Where? When? How? How often?* and *To what extent?* Next, ask students if any words in the sentence answer any of those questions. [*swiftly—how*] Tell students that *swiftly* is an adverb. Now, have a volunteer use another example from this chapter to demonstrate how to identify an adverb.

DIFFERENTIATING INSTRUCTION

English-Language Learners

General Strategies. Students may mistakenly use the adverbs *very* and *too* interchangeably. Explain that *very* means "extremely," whereas *too* means "excessively."

For extra practice, have students complete the following sentences by supplying either *very* + an adjective or *too* + an adjective.

1. Vegetarian pizza is _____.
2. I find English class _____.
3. My best friend is _____.
4. Rock music is _____.
5. Summer weather can be _____.

The Adverb

3g. An *adverb* is a word that modifies a verb, an adjective, or another adverb.

Just as an adjective makes the meaning of a noun or a pronoun more definite, an adverb makes the meaning of a verb, an adjective, or another adverb more definite.

Adverbs answer the following questions:

Where?	How often? *or* How long?
When?	To what extent?
How?	*or* How much?

EXAMPLES The sprinter ran **swiftly.** [The adverb *swiftly* modifies the verb *ran* and tells *how.*]

I read the funny pages **early** on Sunday morning. [The adverb *early* modifies the verb *read* and tells *when.*]

Jolene was comforting a **very** small child. [The adverb *very* modifies the adjective *small* and tells *to what extent.*]

The fire blazed **too wildly** for anyone to enter. [The adverb *too* modifies the adverb *wildly* and tells *to what extent.* The adverb *wildly* modifies the verb *blazed* and tells *how.*]

Dad will **sometimes** quote from Archbishop Desmond Tutu's speech. [The adverb *sometimes* modifies the verb *will quote* and tells *how often.*]

Put the apples **there,** and we will eat them **later.** [The adverb *there* modifies the verb *put* and tells *where.* The adverb *later* modifies the verb *will eat* and tells *when.*]

Words Often Used as Adverbs	
Where?	away, here, inside, there, up
When?	later, now, soon, then, tomorrow
How?	clearly, easily, quietly, slowly

RESOURCES

The Adverb

Practice

- *Language & Sentence Skills Practice,* pp. 52–54
- *Developmental Language & Sentence Skills,* pp. 23–24

Words Often Used as Adverbs	
How often? or *How long?*	always, usually, continuously, never, forever, briefly
To what extent? or *How much?*	almost, so, too, more, least, extremely, quite, very, not

NOTE The word *not* is nearly always used as an adverb modifying a verb. When *not* is part of a contraction, as in *hadn't, aren't,* and *didn't,* the *–n't* is still an adverb and is not part of the verb.

Adverb or Adjective?

Many adverbs end in *–ly*. These adverbs are generally formed by adding *–ly* to adjectives.

Adjective	+	–ly	=	Adverb
clear	+	–ly	=	clearly
quiet	+	–ly	=	quietly
convincing	+	–ly	=	convincingly

However, some words ending in *–ly* are used as adjectives.

Adjectives Ending in –ly		
daily	friendly	lonely
early	kindly	timely

NOTE The adverb *very* is often overused. In your writing, try to use adverbs other than *very* to modify adjectives. You can also revise sentences so that other words carry more of the descriptive meaning.

EXAMPLE Chloe is very tall.
REVISED Chloe is **amazingly** tall.
         or
         Chloe is **5'11"** tall and **is a guard on the varsity basketball team.**

Reference Note
For more about **contractions,** see page 333.

HELP
If you aren't sure whether a word is an adjective or an adverb, ask yourself what it modifies. If a word modifies a noun or a pronoun, it is an adjective.

EXAMPLE
She gave us a **friendly** hello. [*Friendly* modifies the noun *hello* and is used as an adjective.]

If a word modifies a verb, an adjective, or an adverb, then it is an adverb.

EXAMPLE
People from many nations have come to the United States **recently.** [The adverb *recently* modifies the verb *have come.*]

Reference Note
For more about **adjectives,** see page 34.

The Adverb 55

DIFFERENTIATING INSTRUCTION

English-Language Learners

Spanish. Point out to your Spanish-speaking students that the English *–ly* suffix is equivalent to the Spanish *–mente* suffix. Both convert adjectives to adverbs. (In Portuguese the suffix is also *–mente;* in French, it is *–ment.*)

DIRECT TEACHING

Adjectives and Adverbs

Explain to students that some words can be used either as adjectives or as adverbs. To reinforce the concept, divide students into groups of four, which will then split off into two pairs. Give each pair the following list of words: *close, next, far, late, more, most, low, light, deep,* and *first.* Have each pair work together to generate two sentences for each word—one using the word as an adjective [*That was a* close *call*] and one using the word as an adverb [*He cut the corner* close]. Then, ask the two pairs in each group to exchange sentences and label the words as adjectives or adverbs.

Use the **Mini-Lesson** that begins at the bottom of this page to help students who have difficulty distinguishing between adjectives and adverbs.

 Usage Continued on pp. 56–57

Adverb or Adjective? In their writing, students will often have to decide whether to use the adjective or the adverb form of a word. Write the following sentences on the chalkboard. Answers are underlined.

1. I am having a (*real,* <u>*really*</u>) good time.
2. Tim drove (*safe,* <u>*safely*</u>).
3. He spoke too (*quiet,* <u>*quietly*</u>).

   Ask volunteers to determine which of

The Adverb 55

PRACTICE
Guided and Independent

Exercises You may want to use the items in **Exercise 7** as guided practice. Then, have students complete the items in **Exercise 8** as independent practice.

HOMEWORK

DIFFERENTIATING INSTRUCTION

Advanced Learners

Some students may find sentence diagramming useful in understanding adverbs. Include the information about adjectives on p. 34 to help students differentiate between adjectives and adverbs.

You may want to use several example sentences from p. 54 to illustrate diagramming. For more information, see **Chapter 19: Sentence Diagramming**.

The sprinter ran swiftly.

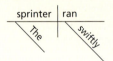

Jolene was comforting a very small child.

Statue of Cherokee mourning those who died on the Trail of Tears.

Exercise 7 Identifying Adverbs

Identify each adverb and the word or words it modifies in each of the following sentences.

EXAMPLE 1. Today, many Cherokee people make their homes in Oklahoma.

   1. *Today—make*

1. Oklahoma is not the Cherokees' original home.
2. The Cherokees once lived in Georgia, North Carolina, Alabama, and Tennessee.
3. A number of Cherokees still live in the Great Smoky Mountains of North Carolina.
4. Settlers often ignored the Cherokees' right to the land.
5. Feeling threatened by the settlers, the Cherokees readily supported the British during the Revolutionary War.
6. In 1829, people hurried excitedly to northern Georgia for the first gold rush in the United States.
7. Many white settlers of the region were extremely eager to find gold.
8. Later, the Cherokees were forced by the United States government to leave their land.
9. The Cherokee people were hardly given a chance to collect their belongings.
10. Many Cherokees will never forget the Trail of Tears, which led their ancestors to Oklahoma.

The Position of Adverbs

One of the characteristics of adverbs is that they may appear at various places in a sentence. Adverbs may come before, after, or between the words they modify.

EXAMPLES We **often** study together.

             We study together **often**.

             Often we study together.

When an adverb modifies a verb phrase, it frequently comes in the middle of the phrase.

EXAMPLE We have **often** studied together.

56 **Chapter 3** Parts of Speech Overview

 Usage *Continued from p. 55*

the answers are correct, and explain why. Remind students to ask themselves two questions:

- What does the word modify?

- What question does the word answer? (Refer students to p. 34 for a list of ways that adjectives modify nouns and pronouns and to p. 54 for a list of questions that adverbs answer.)

An adverb that introduces a question, however, appears at the beginning of a sentence.

EXAMPLES **When** does your school start? [The adverb *When* modifies the verb phrase *does start*.]

How did you spend your vacation? [The adverb *How* modifies the verb phrase *did spend*.]

Exercise 8 Identifying Adverbs

Identify the adverbs and the words they modify in the following sentences.

EXAMPLE 1. "To Build a Fire" is a dramatically suspenseful short story.
 1. *dramatically—suspenseful*

HELP— Some sentences in Exercise 8 contain more than one adverb.

1. In this story, a nameless character goes outdoors on a terribly cold day in the Yukon.
2. Except for a dog, he is traveling completely alone.
3. Soon both the dog's muzzle and the man's beard are frosted with ice.
4. Along the way, the man accidentally falls into a stream.
5. Soaked and chilled, he desperately builds a fire under a tree.
6. The flames slowly grow stronger.
7. Unfortunately, he has built his fire in the wrong place.
8. A pile of snow suddenly falls from a tree limb and kills the small fire.
9. Unable to relight the fire, the man again finds himself in serious trouble.
10. Based on what you now know about the story, what kind of ending would you write for "To Build a Fire"?

2. completely—alone
   alone—is traveling

Exercise 9 Writing Adverbs

Write ten different adverbs to fill the blanks in the following sentences.

EXAMPLE I have [1] _____ been a music lover.
 1. *always*

Every Friday I [1] _____ go to the record store. I can [2] _____ wait to see what new cassettes and CDs have arrived. As soon as

Exercise 9 Writing Adverbs

ANSWERS
Responses will vary. Only adverbs that answer certain questions can go in each blank.

1. how *or* how often
2. to what extent *or* how often

To extend the lesson, ask students to locate pieces of their own writing and circle all adjectives and adverbs to see whether the words have been used correctly.

Exercise 9   Writing Adverbs

ANSWERS continued

3. where *or* how
4. to what extent *or* how
5. how *or* when *or* how often
6. how *or* to what extent
7. how
8. how *or* when
9. where *or* how
10. how *or* to what extent

The Preposition
Rule 3h *(pp. 58–61)*

OBJECTIVES

- To supply prepositions in order to complete sentences
- To identify prepositional phrases in sentences
- To identify prepositions and their objects in prepositional phrases
- To identify words in sentences as adverbs or as prepositions

DIRECT TEACHING

Modeling and Demonstration

Identifying Prepositions. Model how to identify prepositions by using the example *The kite in the tree is mine.* First, ask which word shows the relationship between *kite* and *tree.* [*in*] Note that the preposition *in* shows where the kite is in relation to the tree. Then, read the example aloud, using different prepositions. Point out how the different prepositions change the relationship between the kite and the tree. Now, have a volunteer use another example from this chapter to demonstrate how to identify a preposition.

STYLE TIP

In formal writing, it is often considered best to avoid ending a sentence with a preposition. However, this usage is becoming more accepted in casual speech and informal writing. You should follow your teacher's instructions on sentences ending with prepositions.

---

school is out, I bicycle [3] _____ to the store and join the other [4] _____ enthusiastic customers. [5] _____ I stroll through the aisles and [6] _____ study the selections. I listen [7] _____ as the loudspeaker announces the day's specials. When I have decided what I want, I [8] _____ figure out which items I can afford. Then I walk [9] _____ to the cash register. I grin [10] _____ as I think of how much I will enjoy the music.

The Preposition

3h. A *preposition* is a word that shows the relationship of a noun or pronoun to another word.

Notice how changing the preposition in these sentences changes the relationship of *walked* to *door* and *kite* to *tree.*

The cat walked **through** the door.
The cat walked **toward** the door.
The cat walked **past** the door.

The kite **in** the tree is mine.
The kite **beside** the tree is mine.
The kite **in front of** the tree is mine. [Notice that a preposition may be made up of more than one word. Such a preposition is called a *compound preposition.*]

Commonly Used Prepositions				
aboard	before	for	off	toward
about	behind	from	on	under
above	below	in	out	underneath
across	beneath	in front of	out of	unlike
after	beside	inside	over	until
against	between	instead	past	up
along	beyond	into	since	up to
among	by	like	through	upon
around	down	near	throughout	with
as	during	next to	till	within
at	except	of	to	without

RESOURCES

The Preposition
Practice
- *Language & Sentence Skills Practice,* pp. 55–57
- *Developmental Language & Sentence Skills,* pp. 25–26

Exercise 10 Writing Prepositions

Write two prepositions for each blank in the following sentences. Be prepared to tell how the meanings of the two resulting sentences differ.

EXAMPLE 1. The car raced ____ the highway.
   1. *along, across*

1. We practiced karate ____ dinner.
2. She jumped up and ran ____ the park.
3. A boat with red sails sailed ____ the river.
4. The hungry dog crawled ____ the fence.
5. The marathon runner jogged easily ____ the track at the stadium.
6. Put the speakers ____ the stage, Cody.
7. Brightly colored confetti streamed ____ the piñata when it burst open.
8. Why does Roseanne always sit ____ the door?
9. Excuse me, but the blue fountain pen ____ your chair is mine, I believe.
10. Parrots ____ the South American jungle squawked all through the hot afternoon.

The Prepositional Phrase

A *prepositional phrase* includes a preposition, a noun or pronoun called the *object of the preposition,* and any modifiers of that object.

EXAMPLES You can press those leaves **under glass.** [The noun *glass* is the object of the preposition *under.*]

Fred stood **in front of us.** [The pronoun *us* is the object of the compound preposition *in front of.*]

The books **in my new pack** are heavy. [The noun *pack* is the object of the preposition *in.* The words *my* and *new* modify *pack.*]

A preposition may have more than one object.

EXAMPLE Thelma's letter to **Nina** and **Ralph** contained good news. [The preposition *to* relates its objects, *Nina* and *Ralph,* to *letter.*]

—HELP—
In the example for Exercise 10, in the first sentence, the car was on the highway. In the second sentence, the car crossed the highway.

OVERBOARD © 1993 Universal Press Syndicate. Reprinted with permission. All rights reserved.

The Preposition   59

Exercise 10 Writing Prepositions

ANSWERS
Responses will vary. Here are some possibilities:
1. before, after
2. by, to
3. down, along
4. under, through
5. around, near
6. above, on
7. from, out of
8. near, by
9. on, near
10. in, from

DIFFERENTIATING INSTRUCTION

English-Language Learners

General Strategies. There is no clear correspondence between English prepositions and prepositions in other languages. Using the list of **Commonly Used Prepositions,** pair English-language learners with native speakers to write down an example of each preposition used in a sentence and then to define the preposition.

Cantonese. Unlike English, Cantonese does not have a large range of prepositions. Since English preposition usage is unpredictable and idiomatic, Cantonese speakers may find prepositions difficult to master. Help students learn the patterns of preposition usage by teaching the prepositions along with the words they generally follow: *go to, come from.* Emphasize the preposition use when speaking to students.

*Tell us where that came **from**.*
*Will you walk **with** me?*

Learning for Life

Continued on pp. 60–61

Thank-you Notes. The instructions and exercises that help students identify parts of speech are simply stepping stones to the real objective: actually using the various parts of speech effectively in writing and speaking. Ask students to think of a reason to thank someone in their families or communities for taking the time, trouble, or expense to do something nice for them.

Before students write their rough drafts, explain that their notes should say more than simply "Thank you for the lovely

DIFFERENTIATING INSTRUCTION

English-Language Learners

Spanish. In Spanish, the preposition *a* can be used to denote *in, on,* and *at* (as well as other prepositions). To help students decide which of these three English prepositions is appropriate, define the prepositions and give examples of them that can be demonstrated in the classroom, such as *in the desk, on the desk,* and *at the chalkboard.*

Reference Note

For more about **infinitives,** see page 102.

HELP

Some sentences in Exercise 11 contain more than one prepositional phrase.

The objects of prepositions may have modifiers.

EXAMPLE   It happened during **the last** examination. [*The* and *last* are adjectives modifying *examination,* which is the object of the preposition *during.*]

NOTE   Be careful not to confuse a prepositional phrase beginning with *to* (*to the park, to him*) with an infinitive beginning with *to* (*to sing, to be heard*).

Exercise 11 Identifying Prepositional Phrases

Identify the prepositional phrases in the following sentences. Underline the preposition once and its object twice.

EXAMPLES   1. Commander Robert Peary claimed that he reached the North Pole in 1909.

1. in 1909

2. Peary and Matthew Henson searched for the North Pole for many years.

2. for the North Pole, for many years

1. Henson traveled with Peary on every expedition except the first one.
2. However, for a long time, Henson received no credit for his role.
3. Peary had hired Henson as an assistant on a trip Peary made to Nicaragua.
4. There, Peary discovered that Henson had sailing experience and could also chart a path through the jungle.
5. As a result, Peary asked Henson to join his Arctic expedition shown in the photograph on this page.
6. The two explorers became friends during their travels in the North.
7. On the last three miles to the North Pole, Henson did not go with Peary.
8. Because he was the leader of the trip, Peary received the credit for the achievement.
9. Finally, after many years, Henson was honored by Congress, Maryland's state government, and two U.S. presidents.
10. Both Peary and Henson wrote books about their experiences.

60   Chapter 3   Parts of Speech Overview

Learning for Life

sweater." Students should tell why the gift or gesture was special to them.

Upon completion, have students exchange papers and check for the appropriate use of the parts of speech. Peer

Continued from p. 59

reviewers might use the following questions:

1. Could any linking verbs be replaced with action verbs to make the writing more lively?

Preposition or Adverb?

Some words may be used either as prepositions or as adverbs. Remember that a preposition always has an object. An adverb never does. If you can't tell whether a word is used as an adverb or a preposition, look for an object.

ADVERB	I haven't seen him **since**.
PREPOSITION	I haven't seen him **since** Thursday. [*Thursday* is the object of the preposition *since*.]

ADVERBS	The bear walked **around** and then went **inside**.
PREPOSITIONS	The bear walked **around** the yard and then went **inside** the cabin. [*Yard* is the object of the preposition *around*. *Cabin* is the object of *inside*.]

TIPS & TRICKS

When you are looking for the object of a preposition, be careful. Sometimes the object comes before, not after, the preposition.

EXAMPLES
Here is the CD **that** I was looking for yesterday. [*That* is the object of the preposition *for*.]

She is the speaker **whom** we enjoyed listening to so much. [*Whom* is the object of the preposition *to*.]

Exercise 12   Identifying Adverbs and Prepositions

Identify the italicized word in each of the following sentences as either an *adverb* or a *preposition*.

EXAMPLE 1. He watches uneasily as the hunter slowly brings the pistol *up*.

1. up—adverb

1. "The Most Dangerous Game" is the story of Rainsford, a famous hunter who falls *off* a boat and comes ashore on a strange island.
2. Rainsford knows that this island is feared by every sailor who passes *by*.
3. In fact, *among* sailors, the place is known as Ship-Trap Island.
4. After looking *around* for several hours, Rainsford can't understand why the island is considered so dangerous.
5. Finally, he discovers a big house *on* a high bluff.
6. A man with a pistol *in* his hand answers the door.
7. Putting his pistol *down*, the man introduces Rainsford to the famous hunter General Zaroff.
8. Zaroff invites Rainsford *inside*.
9. Soon, however, Rainsford wishes he could get *out* and never see Zaroff again.
10. Rainsford has finally discovered the secret *about* the island—Zaroff likes to hunt human beings!

---

2. Would well-chosen adverbs add interest?
3. Could any subjects, verbs, or sentences be joined by conjunctions to improve the note?

Students may choose to mail or hand-deliver their thank-you notes.

The Conjunction

Rule 3i (pp. 62–65)

OBJECTIVES

- To identify conjunctions and the words they join in sentences
- To complete sentences by providing appropriate conjunctions
- To write sentences that contain conjunctions used in specified ways

DIRECT TEACHING

Modeling and Demonstration

Identifying Conjunctions. Model how to identify conjunctions by using the examples *Josie, Han, Jill, or Anna; across town, over the river, and through the woods;* and *Alice Walker wrote the book, yet she did not write the movie script.* [conjunctions joining words, joining phrases, and joining clauses]. First, explain to students that a *junction* is the place at which two roads join; a *conjunction* is a word that joins words, phrases, or clauses. Then, read the examples aloud, emphasizing the conjunctions. Now, have a volunteer demonstrate how to identify a conjunction by following the pattern of the examples and using the same conjunctions to join new words, phrases, and clauses. [*hit or miss; over the hill, under the bridge, and into the water; Daria shook his hand, yet he did not introduce himself.*] Last, have a volunteer use another example from this chapter to demonstrate how to identify a conjunction.

STYLE TIP

The conjunction *so* is often overused. In your writing, revise sentences as needed to avoid overusing *so*.

EXAMPLE
Traffic is bad, so we'll probably be late.

REVISED
Because traffic is bad, we'll probably be late.

TIPS & TRICKS

You can remember the seven coordinating conjunctions as FANBOYS:
For
And
Nor
But
Or
Yet
So

Reference Note

For more about **using commas between independent clauses,** see page 297.

The Conjunction

3i. A *conjunction* is a word that joins words or word groups.

(1) Coordinating conjunctions join words or word groups that are used in the same way.

Coordinating Conjunctions						
and	but	for	nor	or	so	yet

EXAMPLES Josie, Han, Jill, **or** Anna [*Or* joins four nouns.]

strict **but** fair [*But* joins two adjectives.]

across town, over the river, **and** through the woods [*And* joins three prepositional phrases.]

Alice Walker wrote the book, **yet** she did not write the movie script. [*Yet* joins two independent clauses.]

The word *for* may be used either as a conjunction or as a preposition. When *for* joins word groups that are independent clauses, it is used as a conjunction. Otherwise, *for* is used as a preposition.

CONJUNCTION   He waited patiently, **for** he knew his ride would be along soon.

PREPOSITION   He waited patiently **for** his ride.

NOTE Coordinating conjunctions that join independent clauses are almost always preceded by a comma. When *for* is used as a conjunction, there should always be a comma in front of it.

EXAMPLES She has read the book, **but** she has not seen the movie.

We can bathe the dog, **or** you can do it when you get home from school.

Did Nazir call her, **and** has she called him back?

We asked Jim to be on time, **yet** he isn't here.

I'll be home late, **for** I have basketball practice until 4:30 or 5:00 today.

RESOURCES

The Conjunction

Practice

- *Language & Sentence Skills Practice,* pp. 58–59
- *Developmental Language & Sentence Skills,* pp. 27–28

(2) *Correlative conjunctions* are pairs of conjunctions that join words or word groups that are used in the same way.

Correlative Conjunctions	
both . . . . and	not only . . . . but also
either . . . . or	whether . . . . or
neither . . . . nor	

EXAMPLES **Both** Bill Russell **and** Larry Bird played for the team. [The pair of conjunctions joins two nouns.]

She looked **neither** to the left **nor** to the right. [The pair of conjunctions joins two prepositional phrases.]

Not only did Wilma Rudolph overcome her illness, **but** she **also** became an Olympic athlete. [The pair of conjunctions joins two independent clauses.]

NOTE A third kind of conjunction—the *subordinating conjunction*—introduces an adverb clause.

EXAMPLES Meet me in the park **after** the bell chimes.

Before I washed the dishes, I let them soak in the sudsy water.

Reference Note
For more information about **subordinating conjunctions,** see page 121. For more on **adverb clauses,** see page 120.

Exercise 13 Identifying Conjunctions

Identify the conjunction or conjunctions in each of the following sentences. Be prepared to tell what words or word groups each conjunction or pair of conjunctions joins.

EXAMPLE 1. Both she and her mother enjoy sailing.
    1. Both . . . and

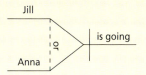

HELP
In the example in Exercise 13, the conjunction joins *she* and *her mother*.

1. I wanted to go to the beach, but it rained all weekend.
2. Our class is recycling not only newspapers but also glass bottles and aluminum cans.
3. He set the table with chopsticks and rice bowls.
4. Have you seen either LeAnn Rimes or George Strait in concert?

The Conjunction   63

RETEACHING

Diagramming

Conjunctions. To reinforce the concept of conjunctions as joining words, diagram some of the examples on p. 62, adding additional words to make complete sentences. Refer students to **Chapter 19: Sentence Diagramming** for more examples.

Jill or Anna is going.

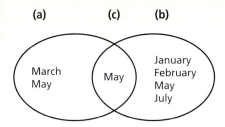

DIFFERENTIATING INSTRUCTION

Advanced Learners

Draw a Venn diagram on the chalkboard with the following labels: (a) months whose names start with *m*, (b) months whose names end with *y*, and (c) months whose names start with *m* and end with *y*:

(a)   (c)   (b)

March May | May | January February May July

The activity can be expanded to include other conjunctions besides *and*, such as *or* (months whose names start with *m* or end with *y*) and *neither . . . nor* (months whose names *neither* start with *m* nor end with *y*).

MINI-LESSON Usage   Continued on p. 64

Subject-Verb Agreement. Explain to students that subjects and verbs must agree in number. When a subject is compound, the conjunction that connects the subjects affects number. Write the following sentences on the chalkboard.

1. The train **and** the bus **leave** in five minutes.
2. **Neither** the train **nor** the bus **leaves** on time.
3. The conductor **or** the passengers **need** assistance.

GRAMMAR

Exercise 14 Writing Conjunctions

POSSIBLE ANSWERS

1. either...or *or* both...and
2. and
3. but
4. both...and *or* not only...but also
5. Either...or
6. so
7. or
8. whether...or
9. neither...nor
10. yet

PEANUTS reprinted by permission of United Feature Syndicate, Inc.

5. We learned to use neither too many adjectives nor too few in descriptive writing.
6. That diet is dangerous, for it does not adequately meet the body's needs.
7. Both the Mohawk and the Oneida are part of the famous Iroquois Confederacy.
8. It snowed most of the day, yet we still enjoyed cross-country skiing.
9. Shall we walk home or take the bus?
10. Revise your paper, and proofread it carefully.

Exercise 14 Writing Conjunctions

Provide an appropriate conjunction for each blank in the following sentences.

EXAMPLES
1. ____ solve the problem yourself, ____ ask your teacher for help.
1. Either . . . or

2. Would she prefer juice ____ iced tea?
2. or

1. We will visit ____ the Johnson Space Center ____ the Museum of Fine Arts in Houston, Texas.
2. Alaska ____ Hawaii were the last two states admitted to the Union.
3. Those two students are twin sisters, ____ they do not dress alike.
4. They were ____ hungry ____ thirsty.
5. ____ turn that radio down, ____ take it into your room while I'm studying.
6. These nails aren't long enough, ____ I'm going to buy some others.
7. You could put the chair in the living room, in your bedroom, ____ even in the dining room.
8. Their weather forecaster isn't sure ____ it will rain ____ not.
9. In the delicate ecosystem of the river, ____ motorboats ____ personal watercraft are allowed.
10. His bike is old, ____ it takes him anywhere he needs to go.

64 Chapter 3 Parts of Speech Overview

MINI-LESSON Usage *Continued from p. 63*

The first sentence shows that subjects joined by *and* usually take a plural verb. The second sentence illustrates that singular subjects joined by *or* or *nor* take a singular verb. When a singular subject and a plural subject are joined by *or* or *nor*, the verb agrees with the subject nearer the verb, as in the third sentence. For additional information and practice, refer students to p. 156.

Exercise 15 Writing Sentences with Conjunctions

Follow the directions given below to write sentences using conjunctions.

EXAMPLE 1. Use *and* to join two verbs.
1. The cast smiled at the audience and bowed.

1. Use *and* to join two adverbs.
2. Use *or* to join two prepositional phrases.
3. Use *for* to join word groups that are sentences.
4. Use *but* to join two linking verbs.
5. Use *either . . . or* in an imperative sentence.
6. Use *or* to join two nouns.
7. Use *both . . . and* to join two subjects.
8. Use *neither . . . nor* to join two adverbs.
9. Use *yet* to join two adjectives.
10. Use *whether . . . or* in an interrogative sentence.

The Interjection

3j. An *interjection* is a word that expresses emotion.

Commonly Used Interjections			
aha	my	ouch	wow
hey	oh	rats	yikes
hurray	oops	well	yippee

An interjection has no grammatical relationship to the rest of the sentence.

Usually an interjection is followed by an exclamation point.

EXAMPLES **Ouch!** That hurts!

Goodness! What a haircut!

Aha! I know the answer.

Sometimes an interjection is set off by a comma.

EXAMPLES **Oh,** I wish it were Friday.

Well, what have you been doing?

The Interjection   65

RESOURCES

The Interjection

Practice
- *Language & Sentence Skills Practice,* p. 60
- *Developmental Language & Sentence Skills,* pp. 27–28

DIRECT TEACHING

Modeling and Demonstration

Identifying Interjections. Model how to identify interjections by using the example *Goodness! What a haircut!* First, point out to the students that an interjection is a word that expresses emotion and that it does not modify any other word or have any grammatical relation to the rest of the sentence. Then, read the example aloud, emphasizing the interjection. Now, have a volunteer demonstrate how to identify an interjection by substituting a new interjection in the example. Last, have a volunteer use another example from this chapter to demonstrate how to identify an interjection.

Exercise 16 Writing Interjections

ANSWERS
Answers will vary.

DIFFERENTIATING INSTRUCTION

English-Language Learners

General Strategies. Most languages include interjections. Ask students who speak other languages to share appropriate interjections from their languages with the class. Often, interjections such as *ouch* are similar in many different languages.

STYLE TIP

Interjections are common in casual conversation. In writing, however, they're usually used only in dialogue meant to represent such conversation. When you use interjections in dialogue, use exclamation points to indicate strong emotion and commas to indicate mild emotion.

EXAMPLES
Hey! Watch out for that jogger!

I like that outfit, but, **wow,** it's really expensive.

Notice in the second example above that commas are used both before and after an interjection that interrupts a sentence.

1. int./adv.
2. adv./prep.
3. int./conj.
4. v./prep.
5. conj./adv.
6. v./conj.
7. v./prep.
8. conj./adv.
9. adv./prep.
10. int./adv.

Exercise 16 Writing Interjections

Choose an appropriate interjection for each blank in the following sentences. Use a variety of interjections.

EXAMPLE 1. _____ , I'd love to go to your party.
           1. Hey, I'd love to go to your party.

1. _____ ! The heel just fell off my shoe.
2. There's, _____ , about seven dollars in my wallet.
3. _____ , finally we're finished raking those leaves.
4. _____ ! You squirrels, stop eating the birds' food!
5. Young Eric, _____ , you certainly have grown!
6. _____ ! I sprained my ankle during the obstacle course!
7. Weren't the special effects in the movie amazing? _____ !
8. _____ , there's only one round left in the tournament.
9. _____ ! I knew you were planning a surprise!
10. _____ , what a relief it is to have that term paper finished.

Review C Identifying Parts of Speech

Label each *italicized* word or word group in the following sentences as a *verb*, an *adverb*, a *preposition*, a *conjunction*, or an *interjection*.

EXAMPLE 1. *Both* otters *and* owls hunt *from* dusk to dawn.
           1. Both . . . and—conjunction; from—preposition

1. *Oh*! I *just* spilled tomato soup on the new white tablecloth!
2. Luis Alvarez *closely* studied atomic particles *for* many years.
3. *Hey*, did Toni Morrison *or* Toni Cade Bambara write the book that you are reading?
4. The Inuit hunters *ate* their meal *inside* the igloo.
5. They were tired, *yet* they did *not* quit working.
6. I *like* Persian carpets, *for* they are beautiful and wear well.
7. The plane from Venezuela *nears* the terminal and taxis *down* the runway.
8. *Either* geraniums *or* daisies would grow *well* in that sunny corner of the garden.
9. Put your pencils *down*, class, *during* the instructions for this test.
10. Computers and, *oh*, all that electronic stuff seem *so* easy for you, Brittany.

---

66   Chapter 3   Parts of Speech Overview

CONTENT-AREA CONNECTIONS

Physical Science. In addition to its meaning in grammar, the word *conjunction* has a scientific meaning: the apparent meeting or passing of two or more celestial bodies. For example, the moon is in conjunction with the sun when the moon moves between the sun and the earth. In this way, the celestial bodies are "joined together" by the imaginary straight line that connects them. Have students research the meaning of *conjunction* in astronomy and present short reports to the class.

Determining Parts of Speech

3k. **The way a word is used in a sentence determines what part of speech the word is.**

The same word may be used as different parts of speech.

NOUN	The **play** had a happy ending.
VERB	The actors **play** their roles well.
NOUN	The **outside** of the house needs paint.
ADVERB	Let's go **outside** for a while.
PREPOSITION	I saw the birds' nest **outside** my window.
NOUN	The **well** has run dry.
ADVERB	Did you do **well** on the quiz?
ADJECTIVE	I don't feel **well** today.
INTERJECTION	**Well,** that's a relief.

Review D — Identifying Verbs, Adverbs, Prepositions, Conjunctions, and Interjections

For each of the following sentences, identify the italicized, numbered word or word group as a *verb*, an *adverb*, a *preposition*, a *conjunction*, or an *interjection*.

EXAMPLE   [1] *Hey,* I recognize that place!
          1. interjection

Though you might recognize the scene at right from the movies, it is [1] *not* a fake movie set. Khasneh al Faroun, or the "Pharaoh's Treasury," is the name of this magnificent structure, and it is [2] *quite* real. Located south of Jerusalem [3] *and* west of the Jordan River, the Pharaoh's Treasury is one of many sites in the ancient city of Petra. The word *Petra* [4] *means* "rock," and the city is carved out of solid sandstone. Petra served as a busy center of trade, and thousands of people strolled its streets [5] *or* sat in its outdoor theater. The theater seats [6] *about* four thousand people and is so old that the Romans had to repair it in A.D. 106. After a short occupation by Crusaders, the city was forbidden to Europeans [7] *for* about seven hundred years.

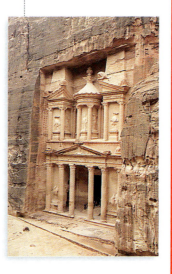

Determining Parts of Speech   67

Review D Identifying Verbs, Adverbs, Prepositions, Conjunctions, and Interjections

ANSWERS continued

8. int.
9. v.
10. v.

Review E Writing Sentences

ANSWERS
Sentences will vary. Here are some possibilities:

1. Don't *walk* on the grass.—verb
   The *walk* helped her headache.—noun
2. That smells *like* spaghetti.—preposition
   I *like* fresh vegetables.—verb
3. That *well* has been dry for years.—noun
   Are you feeling *well*?—adjective
4. I'm staying *inside*.—adverb
   He keeps his marbles *inside* a jar.—preposition
5. Who needs a *fast* car?—adjective
   He drives too *fast*.—adverb

---

[8] *Well,* you're probably wondering about the "treasury" part of the name. For many years, the large urn atop the dome over the statue [9] *was believed* to be full of gold. However, as Bedouin treasure hunters [10] *discovered* long ago, the urn is just rock.

Review E Writing Sentences

Write ten sentences, following the directions given below. Underline the given word in each sentence, and identify how it is used.

EXAMPLE 1. Use *yet* as an adverb and as a conjunction.
   1. Are we there yet?—adverb
      The sky grew somewhat brighter, yet the rain continued falling.—conjunction

1. Use *walk* as a verb and as a noun.
2. Use *like* as a preposition and as a verb.
3. Use *well* as a noun and as an adjective.
4. Use *inside* as an adverb and as a preposition.
5. Use *fast* as an adjective and as an adverb.

CHAPTER 3 Chapter Review

Numerals in brackets refer to the rules tested by the items in the Chapter Review.

1. l.v. [3c]
2. t.a.v. [3b, e]
3. l.v. [3c]
4. l.v. [3c]
5. t.a.v. [3b, e]
6. t.a.v. [3b, e]
7. i.a.v. [3b, f]
8. t.a.v. [3b, e]
9. i.a.v. [3b, f]
10. l.v. [3c]

11.–15. [3d]

HELP
There may be more than one adverb in each sentence in Chapter Review C.

16.–20. [3g]

A. Identifying Types of Verbs

Identify each italicized verb in the following sentences as a *linking verb*, a *transitive action verb*, or an *intransitive action verb*.

1. A land survey *is* a method of measuring land.
2. When he was cutting lumber, my father *used* a table saw.
3. Each concert in the series *was* an hour long.
4. The water *became* ice when the temperature dropped.
5. *Hang* the banner from the ceiling.
6. The astronomer *calculated* the distance to the galaxy.
7. Mr. Lurie and Ms. Modeski *stroll* in the park.
8. The cook *multiplied* the ingredients of the stew by three.
9. Substitute teachers *work* hard!
10. *Are* they weary at the end of the day?

B. Identifying Verb Phrases

Identify the verb phrase in each of the following sentences, and underline the helping verb.

11. Have you ever heard of a mongoose?
12. Do these small carnivores inhabit parts of Africa and Asia?
13. In captivity they have lived for more than twenty years.
14. They will attack even the largest snakes.
15. The mongoose was made famous by a Rudyard Kipling story.

C. Identifying Adverbs

Identify the adverb in each of the following sentences. Then, write the word it modifies.

16. The lonely boy looked longingly across the street.
17. "I'm going there after I've graduated," Rochelle said decisively, as she pointed to a map of Malaysia.
18. It is always easier for a child than for an adult to learn a second language.

ASSESSING

Monitoring Progress

Chapter Review. To assess student progress, you may want to compare the types of items missed on the **Diagnostic Preview** to those missed on the **Chapter Review.** You may want to work out specific goals with individual students who are still having difficulty mastering essential information.

RESOURCES

Parts of Speech Overview: Verb, Adverb, Preposition, Conjunction, Interjection

Review
- *Language & Sentence Skills Practice,* pp. 62–64

Assessment
- *Holt Handbook Chapter Tests with Answer Key,* pp. 5–6, 46

19. I unfailingly read the newspaper at breakfast.
20. Did Joni remember the details of the accident later?

D. Identifying Prepositions and Prepositional Phrases

Identify the prepositional phrases in each of the following sentences. Underline the preposition once and its object twice. A sentence may have more than one prepositional phrase.

21. Will I find the broom beside the refrigerator?
22. My cat Sam likes to sit upon the television.
23. Mr. Takei used tofu in the recipe instead of chicken.
24. My mom gets upset when people talk throughout the film.
25. During the storm the windowpane streamed with rain.

E. Identifying Conjunctions

Identify the conjunctions in each of the following sentences.

26. Are you coming to the party, or are you staying home?
27. Not only did he produce the film, but he also wrote it.
28. I didn't finish the *Odyssey*, but I enjoyed what I did read.
29. We will have red beans and rice for dinner.
30. Both Taj Mahal and B. B. King performed at the blues festival.

F. Identifying Verbs, Adverbs, Prepositions, Conjunctions, and Interjections

The following paragraphs contain twenty numbered, italicized words and word groups. Identify each of these italicized words as a *verb*, an *adverb*, a *preposition*, a *conjunction*, or an *interjection*.

Have you ever [31] *hiked* into the wilderness [32] *with* a pack on your back? Have you ever [33] *camped* under the stars? Backpacking [34] *was* once popular only with mountaineers, [35] *but* now almost anyone who loves the outdoors [36] *can become* a backpacker.

First, however, you [37] *must be* able to carry a heavy pack long distances [38] *over* mountain trails. To get in shape, start with short walks and [39] *gradually* increase them to several miles. Exercising [**40**] *and* going on practice hikes can [**41**] *further* build your strength. [**42**] *After* a few short hikes, you [**43**] *should* be ready for a longer one.

[**44**] *Oh*, you [**45**] *may be thinking*, what equipment and food should I take? Write [**46**] *to* the International Backpackers Association [**47**] *for* a checklist. The first item on the list will [**48**] *usually* be shoes with rubber [**49**] *or* synthetic soles. The second item on the list will [**50**] *certainly* be a sturdy backpack.

Writing Application
Using Prepositions in Directions

Prepositional Phrases   Your class has decided to provide a "how-to" manual for seventh-graders. The manual will have chapters on crafts and hobbies, personal skills, school skills, and other topics. Write an entry for the manual, telling someone how to do a particular activity. In your entry, be sure to use prepositional phrases to make your directions clear and complete. Underline the prepositional phrases that you use.

Prewriting   First, picture yourself doing the activity you are describing. As you imagine doing the activity, jot down each step. Then, put each step in the order it is done.

Writing   Refer to your prewriting notes as you write your first draft. You may find it necessary to add or rearrange steps to make your directions clear and complete.

Revising   Ask a friend or a classmate to read your paragraph. Then, have your reader repeat the directions in his or her own words. If any part of the directions is unclear, revise your work. Make sure you have used prepositional phrases correctly.

Publishing   Read your entry again to check your spelling, grammar, and punctuation. You may want to share your "how-to" hints with other students.

40. conj. [3i(1)]
41. adv. [3g]
42. prep. [3h]
43. v. [3a]
44. int. [3j]
45. v. [3a]
46. prep. [3h]
47. prep. [3h]
48. adv. [3g]
49. conj. [3i(1)]
50. adv. [3g]

Reference Note
See page 232 for more about the **correct placement of phrase modifiers.**

CHAPTER 4

INTRODUCING THE CHAPTER

- This chapter explains how complements can be added to the subject and verb of a sentence base to complete the meaning of a sentence. The first part of this chapter focuses on identifying direct and indirect objects in sentences. The second part of the chapter addresses predicate nominatives and predicate adjectives.

- The chapter closes with a **Chapter Review** including a **Writing Application** feature that asks students to write two riddles, using two subject complements in each.

- For help in integrating this chapter with writing assignments, use the **Teaching Strands** chart on pp. T24–T25.

Numerals in brackets refer to the rules tested by the items in the Diagnostic Preview.

1. d.o./d.o. [4a, b]
2. p.n. [4a, e]
3. i.o./d.o. [4a, c, b]
4. p.a. [4a, f]
5. d.o. [4a, b]
6. i.o./d.o. [4a, c, b]
7. p.a./p.a. [4a, f]
8. p.a. [4a, f]
9. i.o./d.o./d.o. [4a, c, b]
10. d.o. [4a, b]
11. d.o. [4a, b]
12. p.n. [4a, e]
13. d.o./d.o. [4a, b]

CHAPTER 4 Complements
Direct and Indirect Objects, Subject Complements

Diagnostic Preview

Identifying Complements

Identify the complement or complements in each of the following sentences. Then, label each complement as a *direct object*, an *indirect object*, a *predicate nominative*, or a *predicate adjective*.

EXAMPLE
1. I gave Marcy a tangerine.
1. *Marcy—indirect object; tangerine—direct object*

1. Our cat avoids skunks and raccoons.
2. Jim Thorpe was an American Indian athlete.
3. The teacher showed us a film about the Revolutionary War.
4. The television commercials for that new product sound silly.
5. Who put the tangerines in that basket?
6. I sent my grandparents a gift for their anniversary.
7. During her interview on television, Zina Garrison-Jackson appeared relaxed and confident.
8. At first the colt seemed frightened.
9. Mrs. Constantine offered us olives and grapes.
10. The DJ played songs by Will Smith, Shania Twain, and Paula Cole.
11. The newspaper story prompted an investigation by the mayor's office.
12. My sister has become a computer-repair technician.
13. Write your name and address on the envelope.

72 Chapter 4 Complements

CHAPTER RESOURCES

Internet
- Web resources: go.hrw.com

Practice & Review
- *Language & Sentence Skills Practice,* pp. 69–78; 79–81
- *Language & Sentence Skills Practice Answer Key,* pp. 31–36

Application & Enrichment
- *Language & Sentence Skills Practice,* pp. 68, 82–83, 84
- *Language & Sentence Skills Practice Answer Key,* pp. 31, 36–37

14. The weather forecasters haven't issued a tornado warning.
15. Before long, the mistake became obvious to nearly everyone.
16. The sky looked gray and stormy.
17. The Irish poet Seamus Heaney won the Nobel Prize in literature in 1995.
18. The consumer group wrote the senator a letter about this type of airbag.
19. *Red Azalea* is the autobiography of Anchee Min.
20. The presidential candidate and his running-mate seem ambitious and sincere.

14. d.o. [4a, b]
15. p.a. [4a, f]
16. p.a./p.a. [4a, f]
17. d.o. [4a, b]
18. i.o./d.o. [4a, c, b]
19. p.n. [4a, e]
20. p.a./p.a. [4a, f]

Recognizing Complements

4a. A *complement* is a word or word group that completes the meaning of a verb.

Every sentence has a subject and a verb. In addition, the verb often needs a complement to complete its meaning. A complement may be a noun, a pronoun, or an adjective.

INCOMPLETE	Dr. Charles Drew made [what?] S V
COMPLETE	Dr. Charles Drew made **advances** in the study of blood plasma. S V C
INCOMPLETE	Medical societies honored [whom?]
COMPLETE	Medical societies honored **him.**
INCOMPLETE	Dr. Drew's research was [what?]
COMPLETE	Dr. Drew's research was **important.**

An adverb is never a complement.

ADVERB	The package is **here.** [*Here* modifies the verb *is* by telling where the package is.]
COMPLEMENT	The package is **heavy.** [The adjective *heavy* modifies the subject *package* by telling what kind of package.]

Reference Note
For information on **adverbs,** see page 54.

PRETEACHING

Lesson Starter

Motivating. At the beginning of class, as students file in, casually pay compliments such as *I like your shirt; Your shoes look comfortable; Your outfit is so colorful; Your paragraph was exceptional.* (Make sure that each compliment contains an object, predicate nominative, or predicate adjective.)

Ask these individuals to write the compliments on the chalkboard. Then, write on the chalkboard the following words:

compliment
complement = completer

Explain to students that all of your *compliments* used *complements*—words that complete the meaning of the verb. In the compliments that students wrote on the chalkboard, underline the complements you used.

Direct Objects

Rule 4b *(pp. 74–76)*

OBJECTIVE

■ To identify direct objects in sentences

Reference Note

For information on **prepositional phrases,** see page 59.

Reference Note

For information on **transitive verbs,** see page 52.

Reference Note

For information on **linking verbs,** see page 46.

A complement is never in a prepositional phrase.

PREPOSITIONAL PHRASE	Erin is painting **in the garage.** [The prepositional phrase *in the garage* is an adverb phrase telling where Erin is painting.]
COMPLEMENT	Erin is painting her **room.** [The noun *room* completes the verb by telling what she is painting.]

Direct Objects

4b. A *direct object* is a noun, pronoun, or word group that tells *who* or *what* receives the action of the verb.

A direct object answers the question *Whom?* or *What?* after a transitive verb.

EXAMPLES I met **Dr. Mason.** [I met *whom*? I met *Dr. Mason. Dr. Mason* receives the action of the verb *met.*]

Did Bill hit a **home run**? [Bill did hit *what*? Bill did hit a *home run. Home run* receives the action of the verb *hit.*]

Please buy **fruit, bread,** and **milk.** [Please buy *what*? Please buy *fruit, bread,* and *milk. Fruit, bread,* and *milk* receive the action of the verb *buy.*]

My uncle repairs **engines** and sells **them.** [My uncle repairs *what*? My uncle repairs *engines. Engines* receives the action of the verb *repairs.* My uncle sells *what*? He sells *them. Them* receives the action of the verb *sells.*]

Because a linking verb does not express action, it cannot have a direct object.

LINKING VERB	Augusta Savage **was** a sculptor during the Harlem Renaissance. [The verb *was* does not express action; therefore, it has no direct object.]

A direct object is never in a prepositional phrase.

PREPOSITIONAL PHRASE	She worked **with clay.** [*Clay* is not the direct object of the verb *worked;* it is the object of the preposition *with.*]
DIRECT OBJECT	She worked the **clay** with her hands. [She worked *what*? She worked the *clay. Clay* receives the action of the verb *worked.*]

Chapter 4 Complements

RESOURCES

Direct Objects

Practice

■ *Language & Sentence Skills Practice,* p. 70
■ *Developmental Language & Sentence Skills,* pp. 31–32

Complements

A direct object may be a compound of two or more objects.

EXAMPLE We bought **ribbon, wrapping paper,** and **tape.** [The compound direct object *ribbon, wrapping paper,* and *tape* receives the action of the verb *bought.*]

Oral Practice Identifying Direct Objects

Say each of the following sentences aloud. Then, identify the direct object.

HELP
Remember, direct objects may be compound.

EXAMPLE 1. Many sports test an athlete's speed and agility.
 1. speed, agility

1. Long-distance, or marathon, swimming requires strength and endurance.
2. A swimmer in training may swim five or six miles every day.
3. Marathon swimmers smear grease on their legs and arms for protection against the cold water.
4. During a marathon, some swimmers may lose several pounds.
5. Fatigue, pain, and huge waves challenge marathon swimmers.
6. As they swim, they endure extreme isolation.
7. Toward the end of the marathon, swimmers hear the loud applause and shouts of encouragement from their fans.
8. Spectators generally watch only the finish of a marathon.
9. Nevertheless, they know the long distance traveled by the accomplished athletes.
10. Emerging from the cold water, the exhausted swimmers have successfully completed another marathon.

Direct Objects 75

  Grammar *Continued on p. 76*

Transitive or Intransitive? To help students understand the difference between transitive and intransitive verbs, write the following sentences on the chalkboard:

1. Eric plays the saxophone very well.
2. He practices for hours.

Explain to students that both sentences contain action verbs. In sentence 1, the verb is *transitive;* the action "goes over" from the doer (subject) to the receiver (direct object). In sentence 2, the verb is *intransitive* because it expresses action without passing the action to a receiver.

DIRECT TEACHING

Modeling and Demonstration

Identifying Direct Objects. Model how to identify direct objects by using the example *Many sports test an athlete's speed and agility.* First, ask which words are the subject and verb. [*sports*—subject; *test*—verb] Next, ask if the subject and verb express a complete thought by themselves. [*no*] Then, ask what sports test. [*speed, agility*] Explain that *speed* and *agility* are the direct objects of the sentence. Now, have a volunteer use another example from this chapter to demonstrate how to identify direct objects.

DIFFERENTIATING INSTRUCTION

English-Language Learners

General Strategies. You may want to give students extra practice using pronouns as direct objects. In some languages, a pronoun complement generally comes before the verb. For example, "Carlos told me" translates in Spanish as *Carlos me dijo.* To reinforce standard English syntax, ask students to read the following sentences aloud, stressing pronouns used as direct objects.

1. My friend likes me.
2. We know them.
3. I found it.
4. Manuel called her.
5. Lisa married him.

Advanced Learners

Some students may find sentence diagramming useful for understanding complements. As you address the different types of complements—direct objects, indirect objects, predicate nominatives, and predicate adjectives—refer students to **Chapter 19: Sentence Diagramming.**

Direct Objects 75

GRAMMAR

Indirect Objects
Rule 4c *(pp. 76–78)*

OBJECTIVE
- To identify direct objects and indirect objects in sentences

DIRECT TEACHING

Modeling and Demonstration

Identifying Indirect Objects. Model how to identify indirect objects by using the example *The waiter gave her the bill.* First, ask which words are the subject and verb. [*waiter—subject; gave—verb*] Next, ask if the subject and verb express a complete thought by themselves. [*no*] Then, ask to whom or what the bill is being given. [*her*] Explain that *her* is the indirect object of the sentence. Now, have a volunteer use another example from this chapter to demonstrate how to identify direct objects.

HELP
Remember, objects follow action verbs only. Also, direct objects in Exercise 1 may be compound.

HELP
Indirect objects almost always come between a verb and its direct object.

Exercise 1   Identifying Direct Objects

Identify each direct object in the following sentences. If a sentence does not contain a direct object, write *no direct object*.

EXAMPLES   1. Have you ever flown a hang glider?
1. hang glider

2. Hang gliding has become a popular sport.
2. no direct object

1. Many adventurous people enjoy the thrill of gliding through the air.
2. As you can see, a hang glider can carry a full-grown person in its harness.
3. The hang glider has a lightweight sail with a triangular control bar underneath.
4. At takeoff, the pilot lifts the glider shoulder-high and runs hard down a slope into the wind.
5. The wind lifts the hang glider and the pilot off the ground.
6. Because of wind currents, takeoffs from a hilltop or a cliff are the easiest.   6. no d.o.
7. Once airborne, the glider pilot directs the path of flight.
8. He or she also controls the glider's speed by either pushing or pulling on the control bar.
9. For example, a gentle pull increases speed.
10. To land, the pilot stalls the glider near the ground and drops lightly to his or her feet.

Indirect Objects

4c. An ***indirect object*** is a noun, pronoun, or word group that sometimes appears in sentences containing direct objects.

Indirect objects tell *to whom* or *to what*, or *for whom* or *for what*, the action of the verb is done. If a sentence has an indirect object, it always has a direct object also.

EXAMPLES   The waiter gave **her** the bill. [The pronoun *her* is the indirect object of the verb *gave*. It answers the question "To whom did the waiter give the bill?"]

76   Chapter 4   Complements

MINI-LESSON   Grammar   Continued from p. 75

For extra practice, write the following sentences on the chalkboard. Ask volunteers to locate each verb and draw an arrow from the subject to the direct object when the verb is transitive.

1. Swim team practice *starts* next week.
2. I *bought* new goggles.

Pam left the **waiter** a tip. [The noun *waiter* is the indirect object of the verb *left*. It answers the question "For whom did she leave a tip?"]

Did she tip **him** five dollars? [The pronoun *him* is the indirect object of the verb *Did tip*. It answers the question "For whom did she tip five dollars?"]

If the word *to* or *for* is used, the noun or pronoun following it is part of a prepositional phrase and cannot be an indirect object.

OBJECTS OF PREPOSITIONS	The ship's captain gave orders to the **crew**.
	Vinnie made some lasagna for **us**.
INDIRECT OBJECTS	The ship's captain gave the **crew** orders.
	Vinnie made **us** some lasagna.

Like a direct object, an indirect object can be a compound of two or more objects.

EXAMPLE Felicia threw **David, Jane,** and **Paula** slow curveballs. [The compound indirect object *David, Jane,* and *Paula* tells to whom Felicia threw curveballs.]

MOTHER GOOSE & GRIMM © Tribune Media Services, Inc. All rights reserved. Reprinted with permission.

Exercise 2 Identifying Direct Objects and Indirect Objects

Identify and label the direct objects and the indirect objects in the following sentences. Make sure that you include all parts of compound objects.

EXAMPLE 1. Did you buy Mom a calculator for her birthday?
1. *Mom*—indirect object; *calculator*—direct object

1. The usher found us seats near the stage.
2. I'll gladly lend you my new CD.

Reference Note
For information on **prepositional phrases** and **objects of prepositions**, see page 59.

HELP
In Exercise 2, you may find it easier to identify the direct object first and then to look for the indirect object.

DIRECT TEACHING

Correcting Misconceptions
Indirect Objects and Objects of Prepositions. Students may be confused by the difference between indirect objects and objects of prepositions. Write these two sentences on a chalkboard or transparency.

He gave her the letter.
He gave the letter to her.

Inform students that in the first sentence, *her* is an indirect object of the verb *gave*. Tell them that in the second sentence, *her* is part of the prepositional phrase *to her*. Remind students that if a noun or a pronoun is part of a prepositional phrase, that noun or pronoun cannot be an indirect object.

EXTENSION

Critical Thinking
Metacognition. Ask students to think about the processes they use to identify indirect objects in sentences. Do they first look for the verb or do they eliminate prepositional phrases? Do they always remind themselves that in order to have an indirect object, a sentence must have a direct object? What further steps do they follow? Suggest that students use a sequence chain like the one below to chart their steps.

SAMPLE

Encourage students to evaluate the effectiveness of their personal strategies and to consider more effective alternatives as needed.

RESOURCES

Indirect Objects
Practice
- *Language & Sentence Skills Practice,* pp. 71–73
- *Developmental Language & Sentence Skills,* pp. 31–32

DIFFERENTIATING INSTRUCTION

English-Language Learners

General Strategies. Because a pronoun used as a direct or indirect object comes before the verb in some languages, students might have difficulty positioning direct and indirect object pronouns within the sentence. For example, *Lalo gave me it* is translated in Spanish as *Lalo me lo dio* (Lalo me it gave). A small group activity can reinforce the sentence order used in English. Ask students to sit in a circle; next, hand a book to one student. Then, ask another "Did I give Delia the book?" The student should respond, "Yes, you gave her the book." Finally, hand the book to the student who just spoke and ask him or her "Did I give you the book?" He or she should respond "Yes, you gave me the book." Continue with other variations as needed.

Learners Having Difficulty

It might be easier for some students to hear direct and indirect objects than to recognize them visually. Have groups of students take turns reading aloud the example sentences and the sentences in the exercises, stressing the direct and indirect objects.

HELP—
Some sentences in Review A do not contain an indirect object.

3. The Nobel Foundation awarded Octavio Paz the Nobel Prize in literature.
4. Please show me your beaded moccasins.
5. They owe you and me an apology.
6. Our teacher taught us some English words of American Indian origin.
7. After the ride to Laramie, I fed the horse and the mule some hay and oats.
8. My secret pal sent me a birthday card.
9. Mai told the children stories about her family's escape from Vietnam.
10. Will you please save Ricardo a seat?

Review A   Identifying Objects of Verbs

Identify and label the direct objects and the indirect objects in the following sentences. Make sure that you include all parts of compound objects.

EXAMPLES 1. Did you bring the map?
1. map—direct object

2. My parents gave me a choice of places to go on our camping vacation.
2. me—indirect object; choice—direct object

1. I told them my answer quickly.
2. I had recently read a magazine article about the Flathead Reservation in Montana.
3. A Salishan people known as the Flatheads governs the huge reservation.
4. We spent five days of our vacation there.
5. We liked the friendly people and the rugged land.
6. I especially liked the beautiful mountains and twenty-eight-mile-long Flathead Lake.
7. My sister and I made camp beside the lake.
8. Someone gave my father a map and some directions to the National Bison Range, and we went there one day.
9. We also attended the Standing Arrow Pow Wow, which was the highlight of our stay.
10. The performers showed visitors traditional Flathead dances and games.

78   Chapter 4   Complements

CONTENT-AREA CONNECTIONS

Math. In mathematics, a complement is the number of degrees that must be added to an angle to make it equal 90 degrees. Ask students how this complement is similar to a grammatical complement. [*A mathematical complement completes a right angle, and a grammatical complement completes a predicate.*]

Subject Complements

4d. A *subject complement* is a word or word group in the predicate that identifies or describes the subject.

EXAMPLES Julio has been **president** of his class since October. [*President* identifies the subject *Julio.*]

Was the masked stranger **you**? [*You* identifies the subject *stranger.*]

The racetrack looks **slippery**. [*Slippery* describes the subject *racetrack.*]

A subject complement is connected to the subject by a linking verb.

Common Linking Verbs					
appear	become	grow	remain	smell	stay
be	feel	look	seem	sound	taste

There are two kinds of subject complements—*predicate nominatives* and *predicate adjectives*.

Predicate Nominatives

4e. A *predicate nominative* is a word or word group that is in the predicate and that identifies the subject.

A predicate nominative may be a noun, a pronoun, or a word group that functions as a noun. A predicate nominative is connected to its subject by a linking verb.

EXAMPLES A dictionary is a valuable **tool**. [*Tool* is a predicate nominative that identifies the subject *dictionary.*]

This piece of flint could be an old **arrowhead**. [*Arrowhead* is a predicate nominative that identifies the subject *piece.*]

The winner of the race was **she**. [*She* is a predicate nominative that identifies the subject *winner.*]

Is that **what you ordered**? [*What you ordered* is a predicate nominative that identifies the subject *that.*]

TIPS & TRICKS

To find a subject complement in a question, rearrange the sentence to make a statement.

EXAMPLE
Is Reagan the drummer in the band?

Reagan is the **drummer** in the band.

Reference Note
For more about **linking verbs,** see page 46.

STYLE TIP

Expressions such as *It is I* and *That was he* may sound awkward even though they are correct. In conversation, many people say *It's me* and *That was him.* Such expressions may one day become acceptable in formal writing and speaking as well as in informal situations. For now, however, it is best to follow the rules of standard, formal English, especially in your writing.

Subject Complements
Rules 4d–f *(pp. 79–84)*

OBJECTIVES

- To identify linking verbs and predicate nominatives in sentences
- To identify linking verbs and predicate adjectives in sentences

DIRECT TEACHING

Modeling and Demonstration

Identifying Subject Complements. Model how to identify a subject complement by using the example *The racetrack looks slippery.* First, ask which word is the subject. [*racetrack*] Next, ask which words are the predicate. [*looks slippery*] Then, ask if there is a word that identifies or describes *racetrack* in the predicate. [*slippery*] Explain that *slippery* is the subject complement. Now, have a volunteer use another example from this chapter to demonstrate how to identify subject complements.

RESOURCES

Subject Complements
Practice

- *Language & Sentence Skills Practice,* pp. 74–78
- *Developmental Language & Sentence Skills,* pp. 33–36

DIFFERENTIATING INSTRUCTION

Learners Having Difficulty
Students might need to review linking verbs before studying subject complements. Assign articles from provided newspapers, asking students to underline linking verbs. Have students write the sentences with linking verbs on the chalkboard. Using these examples, explain that any noun, pronoun, or adjective that follows a linking verb and identifies or describes the subject is a subject complement. Have volunteers circle the subject complements.

English-Language Learners
Vietnamese. Vietnamese rarely uses the equivalent of the English verb *be.* Vietnamese speakers of English sometimes drop forms of *be* in sentences having subject complements: *I very tired.*

Because the verb *be* is often contracted in conversation, it is especially difficult to hear. Model correct forms, and allow students time for quick drill and repetition.

Teacher: *I'm* hungry. *Are* you?
Student: Yes, *I'm* hungry, too.
Teacher: *Is* Emily hungry?
Student: Yes, she *is.*

Like other sentence complements, a predicate nominative may be compound.

EXAMPLES   The discoverers of radium were **Pierre Curie** and **Marie Sklodowska Curie.**

The yearbook editors will be **Maggie, Imelda,** and **Clay.**

Be careful not to confuse a predicate nominative with a direct object. A predicate nominative always completes a linking verb. A direct object always completes an action verb.

PREDICATE NOMINATIVE   We are the **delegates** from our school.

DIRECT OBJECT   We elected the **delegates** from our school.

A predicate nominative is never part of a prepositional phrase.

PREPOSITIONAL PHRASE   Bill Russell became famous **as a basketball player.**

PREDICATE NOMINATIVE   Bill Russell became a famous basketball **player.**

Reference Note
For more information about **prepositional phrases,** see page 59.

HELP
Sentences in Exercise 3 may contain a compound predicate nominative.

Exercise 3 Identifying Predicate Nominatives

Identify the linking verb and the predicate nominative in each of the following sentences.

EXAMPLE   1. Are whales mammals?
          1. Are—mammals

1. Kilimanjaro is the tallest mountain in Africa.
2. The kingdom of Siam became modern-day Thailand.
3. Dandelions can be a problem for gardeners.
4. Sue Mishima should be a lawyer or a stockbroker when she grows up.
5. When will a woman be president of the United States?
6. Reuben has become a fine pianist.
7. The team captains are Daniel, Mark, and Hannah.
8. At the moment, she remains our choice as candidate for mayor.
9. Is Alaska the largest state in the United States?
10. According to my teacher, *philately* is another name for stamp collecting.

80   Chapter 4   Complements

MINI-LESSON Grammar

Nominative Case Pronouns. To explain sentences such as *It is I* and *That was he*—which are standard English but probably not part of students' everyday speech—tell students that pronouns used as subjects or predicate nominatives should be in the nominative case. Use the following sentences to illustrate the rules:

1. He is the winner. (subject)

---

80   Complements

Predicate Adjectives

4f. A *predicate adjective* is an adjective that is in the predicate and that describes the subject.

A predicate adjective is connected to the subject by a linking verb.

EXAMPLES Cold milk tastes **good** on a hot day. [*Good* is a predicate adjective that describes the subject *milk*.]

    The pita bread was **light** and **delicious**. [*Light* and *delicious* form a compound predicate adjective that describes the subject *bread*.]

    How **kind** you are! [*Kind* is a predicate adjective that describes the subject *you*.]

Exercise 4   Identifying Predicate Adjectives

Identify the linking verbs and the predicate adjectives in the following sentences.

EXAMPLES 1. The crowd became restless.
    1. became—restless
    2. Do the waves seem high and rough today?
    2. Do seem—high, rough

1. Everyone felt good about the decision.
2. The milk in this container smells sour.
3. From my seat in the stadium, I thought the big bass drums sounded too loud.
4. The situation appears dangerous and complicated.
5. Everyone remained calm during the emergency.
6. Why does the water in that pond look green?
7. During Annie Dillard's speech, the audience grew thoughtful and then enthusiastic.
8. Jan stays cheerful most of the time.
9. She must be happy with her excellent results on the science midterm.
10. Don't the black beans mixed with rice and onions taste delicious?

MEETING THE CHALLENGE

As you review your writing, you may get the feeling that nothing is *happening*, that nobody is *doing* anything. That feeling is one sign that your writing may contain too many *be* verbs. In the following sentences, replace each dull *be* verb with a verb that expresses action.

1. Behind the door was a hideous monster.
2. What is under the bed?

POSSIBLE ANSWERS
1. Behind the door **lurked** a hideous monster.
2. What **hides** under the bed?

HELP——
Sentences in Exercise 4 may contain a compound predicate adjective.

EXTENSION

Relating to Writing

Point out to students that overusing vague predicate adjectives such as *nice, pretty,* and *neat* can deaden their writing. Give students the following sentence, and ask them to replace the vague adjective *good* with alternatives that are more precise.

The apples look good.
[*delicious, ripe, refreshing*]

Then, write the following sentences on the chalkboard. Have students work in pairs to think of vivid, precise adjectives to replace the underlined vague ones. Tell students to list as many vivid adjectives as they can for each sentence. Have them share their answers.

1. These drawings are neat.
[*eye-catching, colorful, marketable*]
2. Your dress is pretty.
[*fashionable, elegant, chic*]
3. The concert was bad.
[*boring, substandard, amateurish*]

To extend the activity, suggest that students check a piece of their own writing for overuse of vague predicate adjectives.

Subject Complements

---

2. The winner is he. (predicate nominative)

To extend the lesson, ask students to locate a piece of their own writing and to check for the correct use of pronouns as subjects and predicate nominatives. For additional instruction, refer students to p. 79.

DIFFERENTIATING INSTRUCTION

Learners Having Difficulty

To help students visualize the relationship of a predicate nominative or predicate adjective to the subject, write the following sentences on the chalkboard:

1. The two families were proud of their heritage.
2. The long road was hazardous.
3. She might be the winner.

Have students draw an arrow from each subject complement to the subject.

1. The two families were proud of their heritage.

2. The long road was hazardous.

3. She might be the winner.

HELP
Complements in Review B may be compound.

COMPUTER TIP
The overuse of *be* verbs is a problem that a computer can help you solve. Use the computer's search function to highlight each occurrence of *am, are, is, was, were, be, been,* and *being*. For each case, decide whether the *be* verb can be replaced with an action verb for greater variety.

Answers will vary. Possible answers are given.
1. sergeant—p.n.
2. doctor—p.n.
3. sweet—p.a.
4. difficult—p.a.
5. happy—p.a.
6. Mexico—p.n.
7. spring—p.n.
8. delicious—p.a.
9. surprised—p.a.
10. shark—p.n.

Review B — Identifying Predicate Nominatives and Predicate Adjectives

Identify each subject complement in the following sentences. Then, label each complement as a *predicate nominative* or a *predicate adjective*.

EXAMPLE 1. Are these your shoes, Janelle?
1. shoes—predicate nominative

1. This tasty eggplant dish is a favorite in Greece. — 1. p.n.
2. The twins are tired after the long flight. — 2. p.a.
3. How beautiful that kimono is, Keiko! — 3. p.a.
4. This perfume smells sweet and almost lemony. — 4. p.a./p.a.
5. When will the piñata be ready? — 5. p.a.
6. The winners of the race are Don, Shelby, and she. — 6. p.n./p.n./p.n.
7. Vijay Singh is a professional golfer. — 7. p.n.
8. What good dogs they are! — 8. p.n.
9. Why is your little brother acting so shy? — 9. p.a.
10. Loyal and true are the royal bodyguards. — 10. p.a./p.a.

Review C — Writing Predicate Nominatives and Predicate Adjectives

Choose an appropriate predicate nominative or predicate adjective for each blank in the following sentences. Then, label each answer as a *predicate adjective* or *predicate nominative*.

EXAMPLES 1. The currents looked _____ than they were.
1. slower—predicate adjective

2. Should I become a _____ ?
2. veterinarian—predicate nominative

1. He remained a _____ in the army for more than twenty years.
2. My sister became a _____ after many years of study.
3. In the night air, the jasmine smelled _____.
4. The Navajo way of life was sometimes _____.
5. Peggy seemed _____ with her new kitten.
6. For many travelers, a popular vacation spot is _____.
7. My favorite season has been _____ ever since I was five.
8. Don't these Japanese plums taste _____, Alex?
9. How _____ Grandpa will be to see us!
10. One of the most dangerous animals in the ocean is the _____.

FAMILY/COMMUNITY ACTIVITY

Introductions. Most students have had or will have opportunities to introduce people to each other. In doing so, students will use complements. Provide the following examples:

1. Hi! I'm Ms. King. I teach language arts at Carson Middle School.
2. Maria, this is Tom Jones. Tom is new to our school. Tom, this is Maria Gomez. Maria is my best friend.

Review D Identifying Complements

Identify the complement or complements in each of the following sentences. Then, label each complement as a *direct object*, an *indirect object*, a *predicate nominative*, or a *predicate adjective*.

EXAMPLES
1. Our teacher read us stories from *The Leather-Stocking Tales*.
   1. us—indirect object; stories—direct object
2. James Fenimore Cooper is the author of these tales.
   2. author—predicate nominative

1. Leather-Stocking is a fictional scout in Cooper's popular novels. 1. p.n. 2. p.n./p.n.
2. He is also a woodsman and a trapper.
3. He cannot read, but he understands the lore of the woods. 3. d.o.
4. To generations of readers, this character has been a hero. 4. p.n. 5. d.o.
5. He can face any emergency. 6. p.a./p.a.
6. He always remains faithful and fearless.
7. Leather-Stocking loves the forest and the open country. 7. d.o./d.o.
8. In later years he grows miserable. 8. p.a.
9. The destruction of the wilderness by settlers and others greatly disturbs him.
10. He tells no one his views and retreats from civilization.
   9. d.o. 10. i.o./d.o.

HELP
Complements in Review D may be compound.

Review E Identifying Complements

Identify the complement or complements in each of the following sentences. Then, label each complement as a *direct object*, an *indirect object*, a *predicate nominative*, or a *predicate adjective*.

EXAMPLES
1. Sean, my brother, won three medals at the Special Olympics.
   1. medals—direct object
2. Are the Special Olympics an annual event?
   2. event—predicate nominative

1. Sean was one of more than one hundred special-education students who competed in the regional Special Olympics.

HELP
Complements in Review E may be compound.

1. p.n.

Subject Complements   83

2. The games brought <u>students</u> from many schools to our city. **2.** d.o.
3. The highlights of the games included track <u>events</u> such as sprints and relay races.   **3.** d.o.
4. These were the closest <u>contests</u>.   **4.** p.n.
5. Sean's excellent performance in the relays gave <u>him</u> <u>confidence</u>.   **5.** i.o./d.o.
6. The softball throw and high jump were especially challenging <u>events</u>.   **6.** p.n.
7. Sean looked <u>relaxed</u> but <u>determined</u> as he prepared for the broad jump.   **7.** p.a./p.a.
8. He certainly felt <u>great</u> after his winning jump, shown in the top photograph.   **8.** p.a.
9. Mrs. Duffy, one of the coaches, told <u>us</u> the <u>history</u> of the Special Olympics.   **9.** i.o./d.o.
10. Eunice Kennedy Shriver founded the <u>program</u> in 1968.   **10.** d.o.
11. To begin with, the program was a five-week <u>camp</u>.   **11.** p.n.
12. Several years later, the camp became an international sports <u>event</u> with contestants from twenty-six states and Canada.   **12.** p.n.
13. Today, the organizers of the Special Olympics sponsor regional and international <u>games</u>.   **13.** d.o.
14. The Special Olympics are <u>exciting</u> and <u>inspiring</u>.   **14.** p.a./p.a.
15. Many of the contestants have physical <u>impairments</u>; some cannot walk or see.   **15.** d.o.
16. Teachers and volunteers train <u>contestants</u> in the different events.   **16.** d.o.
17. However, the young athletes themselves are the <u>force</u> behind the program.   **17.** p.n.
18. The pictures on the left give <u>you</u> a <u>glimpse</u> of the excitement at the Special Olympics.   **18.** i.o./d.o.   **19.** d.o.
19. In the middle photograph, a volunteer guides a <u>runner</u>.
20. In the photo on the left, this determined boy prepares <u>himself</u> for the wheelchair race.   **20.** d.o.

CHAPTER 4

Chapter Review

A. Classifying Complements

Classify each underlined complement in the following sentences as a *direct object*, an *indirect object*, a *predicate adjective*, or a *predicate nominative*.

1. Pamela was the <u>star</u> of the play.
2. The guidebook gave the lost <u>tourists</u> the wrong directions.
3. Monet is <u>famous</u> for the way his paintings captured light.
4. Manuel offered <u>Anita</u> some good advice.
5. Ms. Benton is our next-door <u>neighbor</u>.
6. Bring <u>me</u> the cutting board, please.
7. The box was <u>big</u> and awkward to handle.
8. The library receives many new <u>books</u> each week.
9. Mexico celebrates its <u>independence</u> on September 16.
10. The new president of the bank will be <u>Ms. Morales</u>.
11. Angel became a professional jai alai <u>player</u>.
12. Amelia Earhart flew her <u>plane</u> across the Atlantic in 1932.
13. The glow from the diamond is <u>dazzling</u>!
14. Thomas Edison provided <u>people</u> with electric light bulbs.
15. New York City was briefly the <u>capital</u> of the United States.
16. The Simpsons showed <u>him</u> slides of China.
17. My chair was hard and <u>uncomfortable</u>.
18. The machine can produce two <u>crates</u> a day.
19. Have you seen Akiho's yellow <u>sweater</u>?
20. The house appeared <u>empty</u>.

B. Identifying Complements

Write the <u>complement</u> or <u>complements</u> in each sentence. Then, identify each complement as a *direct object*, an *indirect object*, a *predicate adjective*, or a *predicate nominative*. Write *none* if the sentence does not contain a complement.

21. American Indian peoples taught the English <u>colonists</u> many useful <u>skills</u> for survival.

Numerals in brackets refer to the rules tested by the items in the Chapter Review.

1. p.n. [4e]
2. i.o. [4c]
3. p.a. [4f]
4. i.o. [4c]
5. p.n. [4e]
6. i.o. [4c]
7. p.a. [4f]
8. d.o. [4b]
9. d.o. [4b]
10. p.n. [4e]
11. p.n. [4e]
12. d.o. [4b]
13. p.a. [4f]
14. d.o. [4b]
15. p.n. [4e]
16. i.o. [4c]
17. p.a. [4f]
18. d.o. [4b]
19. d.o. [4b]
20. p.a. [4f]

21. i.o./d.o. [4a, c, b]

ASSESSING

Monitoring Progress

Chapter Review. The Chapter Review requires students to identify direct objects, indirect objects, predicate nominatives, and predicate adjectives in sentences. The results of this review can be compared to those of the **Diagnostic Preview** (p. 72) to assess student progress.

DIFFERENTIATING INSTRUCTION

Learners Having Difficulty

You may want to provide students with an organizational strategy for the **Chapter Review.** List the following steps on the chalkboard, and suggest that students follow this sequence to analyze each sentence in the exercise:

1. Bracket the prepositional phrases (as a reminder that essential parts of sentences cannot be within the brackets).
2. Find the verb.
3. Find the subject.
4. Find any complements that receive the action or identify or describe the subject.

RESOURCES

Complements

Review
- *Language & Sentence Skills Practice,* pp. 79–81

Assessment
- *Holt Handbook Chapter Tests with Answer Key,* pp. 7–8, 46

22. p.n./p.n. [4a, e]
23. d.o. [4a, b]
24. p.a. [4a, f]
25. p.a./p.a. [4a, f]
26. d.o. [4a, b]
27. d.o. [4a, b]
28. p.a./p.a./p.a. [4a, f]
29. none [4a]
30. p.a. [4a, f]
31. i.o./d.o. [4a, c, b]
32. d.o./d.o. [4a, b]
33. none [4a]
34. p.n. [4a, e]
35. p.n./p.n. [4a, e]
36. p.n. [4a, e]
37. p.a. [4a, f]
38. i.o./d.o. [4a, c, b]
39. d.o. [4a, b]
40. i.o./i.o./d.o. [4a, c, b]

22. Steven Spielberg is a famous director and producer of motion pictures.
23. A hurricane of immense power lashed the Florida coast a few years ago.
24. The fans became very anxious during the final minutes of the game.
25. This winter was colder and drier than most.
26. Nora sent postcards from Argentina to her friends.
27. The new homeowners found some rare photographs in the back of the attic.
28. Although many eggshells are white, others are brown, and still others are light green.
29. Lita and Trenell studied until seven o'clock.
30. During this month, Mars is too close to the sun to be seen easily from Earth.
31. Both the House and the Senate gave the President their support on the bill.
32. The movers carried the sofa and dining room table up the front stairs.
33. Armand worked all day with his grandfather.
34. That gigantic reflector may be the world's most powerful telescope.
35. Our dog Spike is both a good watchdog and an affectionate family pet.
36. *A Raisin in the Sun* was certainly Lorraine Hansberry's most successful play.
37. Why do some animals seem nervous during a storm?
38. The theater manager will pay each usher an extra five dollars this week.
39. Luis Alvarez won a Nobel Prize for his important research in nuclear power.
40. Our neighbor has offered my mother and father a good price for their car.

Writing Application
Using Subject Complements to Write Riddles

Predicate Nominatives and Predicate Adjectives

A magazine for young people is sponsoring a riddle-writing contest. Whoever writes the best riddle will win the most advanced computer game on the market. You are determined to write the best riddle and win. Write two riddles to enter in the contest. In each one, use at least two subject complements.

Prewriting The best way to make up a riddle is to begin with the answer. List some animals, places, and things that suggest funny or hidden meanings. For each animal, place, or thing, jot down a description based on the funny or hidden meaning. Then, choose the two topics that you think will make the best riddles.

Writing Use your prewriting notes as you write your first draft. In each riddle, make sure that your clues will help your audience guess the answer. Be sure that you use a subject complement (a predicate nominative or a predicate adjective) in the riddle.

Revising Ask a friend to read your riddles. If the riddles are too difficult or too simple, revise them. You may want to add details that appeal to the senses. Linking verbs such as *appear, feel, smell, sound,* and *taste* can help you add such details.

Publishing Read through your riddles again to check for errors in spelling, punctuation, and capitalization. Pay special attention to the capitalization of proper nouns. You and your classmates may want to publish a book of riddles. Collect your riddles, and draw or cut out pictures as illustrations. Make photocopies for all the members of the class.

Reference Note
For a longer **list of linking verbs,** see page 79.

APPLICATION

Writing Application

Prewriting Tip. You may want to stress the importance of brainstorming for riddle ideas before students begin jotting down descriptions. Explain to students that brainstorming is a necessary part of prewriting because it allows them to think of many ideas and to choose the best ones for their riddles.

Writing Tip. Students will be applying critical-thinking skills to create riddles. They must decide what characteristics of the persons, places, or things described by the riddles can be used cleverly to keep the audience guessing. You may want to discuss with students how riddles often rely on wordplay to divert the listeners. Encourage students to use plays on words to describe their subjects accurately but in such a way that the audience will have to think of all possible word meanings to solve the riddles.

Scoring Rubric. While you will want to pay particular attention to students' use of subject complements, you will also want to evaluate the students' overall writing performance. You may want to give a split score to indicate development and clarity of the composition as well as grammar skills.

CHAPTER 5

The Phrase
Prepositional, Verbal, and Appositive Phrases

INTRODUCING THE CHAPTER

- This chapter defines and explains prepositional, verbal, and appositive phrases. Prepositional phrases are classified as adjective or adverb phrases, and verbal phrases are classified as participial or infinitive phrases.

- The chapter closes with a **Chapter Review** including a **Writing Application** feature that asks students to write a note to a friend, explaining how to care for a pet while the owner is away. Students should use a combined total of ten adjective and adverb phrases in the note.

- For help in integrating this chapter with writing assignments, use the **Teaching Strands** chart on pp. T24–T25.

Diagnostic Preview

A. Identifying and Classifying Prepositional Phrases

Identify the prepositional phrase in each of the following sentences. Then, classify each phrase as an *adjective phrase* or an *adverb phrase*, and write the word that the phrase modifies.

EXAMPLE   1. The chairs in the kitchen need new cushions.
           1. in the kitchen—adjective phrase—chairs

1. I wish I were better at tennis.
2. The Rio Grande is the boundary between Texas and Mexico.
3. Those apples come from Washington State.
4. The most popular name for the United States flag is the Stars and Stripes.
5. The pony with a white forelock is Sally's.
6. Through the window crashed the baseball.
7. Cathy Guisewite is the creator of that comic strip.
8. During the last presidential election, we watched the national news often.
9. The first United States space shuttle was launched in 1981.
10. Outside the door the hungry cat waited patiently.

Numerals in brackets refer to the rules tested by the items in the Diagnostic Preview.

1. adv. [5a, b, d]
2. adj. [5a–c]
3. adv. [5a, b, d]
4. adj. [5a–c]
5. adj. [5a–c]
6. adv. [5a, b, d]
7. adj. [5a–c]
8. adv. [5a, b, d]
9. adv. [5a, b, d]
10. adv. [5a, b, d]

Chapter 5   The Phrase

CHAPTER RESOURCES

Internet
- Web resources: go.hrw.com

Practice & Review
- *Language & Sentence Skills Practice,* pp. 86–103; 104–106
- *Language & Sentence Skills Practice Answer Key,* pp. 38–48

Application & Enrichment
- *Language & Sentence Skills Practice,* pp. 85, 107–108, 109
- *Language & Sentence Skills Practice Answer Key,* pp. 38, 48–49

B. Identifying and Classifying Verbal Phrases and Appositive Phrases

Identify the verbal phrase or appositive phrase in each of the following sentences. Then, classify each phrase as a *participial phrase*, an *infinitive phrase*, or an *appositive phrase*.

EXAMPLE 1. The snow, falling steadily, formed huge drifts.
 1. falling steadily—participial phrase

11. Kevin, my cousin, was born in May.
12. The bus, slowed by heavy traffic, arrived at our stop later than it usually does.
13. Breaking the eggs into the wok, he made egg foo yong.
14. To remain calm is not always easy.
15. She wants to study Japanese in high school.
16. Maggie's favorite time of year, late spring, soon arrived.
17. Chilled to the bone, the children finally went inside.
18. Who are the candidates that they plan to support in the election?
19. Bethune-Cookman College, founded by Mary McLeod Bethune, is in Daytona Beach, Florida.
20. Teresa called Kam, her best friend, to ask about the assignment.

11. app. [5a, i, j]
12. part. [5a, e, f]
13. part. [5a, e, f]
14. inf. [5a, g, h]
15. inf. [5a, g, h]
16. app. [5a, i, j]
17. part. [5a, e, f]
18. inf. [5a, g, h]
19. part. [5a, e, f]
20. app. [5a, i, j]

What Is a Phrase?

5a. A *phrase* is a group of related words that is used as a single part of speech and that does not contain both a verb and its subject.

VERB PHRASE	could have been hiding [no subject]
PREPOSITIONAL PHRASE	in the kitchen [no subject or verb]
INFINITIVE PHRASE	to go with them [no subject or verb]

NOTE If a word group has both a subject and a verb, it is called a **clause.**

EXAMPLES   The wind howled. [*Wind* is the subject of the verb *howled.*]

when the Wilsons left [*Wilsons* is the subject of the verb *left.*]

Reference Note
For information on **clauses,** see Chapter 6.

PRETEACHING

Lesson Starter

Motivating. To show students the important role that prepositions play in our language, write on a transparency or on the chalkboard a "What am I?" riddle that describes an object in your classroom. Use as many prepositional phrases as possible, and underline them. For example: "I hang <u>above the chalkboard</u> <u>in the center</u> <u>of the front wall</u>. Students glance <u>at me</u> <u>throughout class</u>. My hands move <u>in a circle</u>. What am I?" Ask students to guess the answer to the riddle. [a clock]

Then, have students take turns creating similar riddles for the rest of the class to answer. Refer students to the list of prepositions on p. 58.

DIRECT TEACHING

Modeling and Demonstration

Identifying Phrases. Model how to identify a group of words as a phrase or a sentence by using the example *could have been hiding*. First, ask if the example *could have been hiding* has a subject. [no] Next, ask if the example has a verb. [yes] Then, ask if the example is used as a single part of speech. [yes, it is used as a verb] Point out that since the definition of a phrase is a group of related words that is used as a single part of speech and that does not contain both a verb and its subject, the example is a phrase. Now, have a volunteer use another example from this chapter to demonstrate how to identify a group of words as a phrase or a sentence.

Reference Note

For a list of commonly used **prepositions,** see page 58.

Reference Note

For more about the **object of a preposition,** see page 59.

Exercise 1 Identifying Phrases

Identify each of the following word groups as a *phrase* or *not a phrase*.

EXAMPLES 1. on the paper   2. after we eat
          1. *phrase*   2. *not a phrase*

1. when you know   **1. not phr.**   6. smiling brightly   **6. phr.**
2. as they walked in   **2. not phr.**   7. to the supermarket   **7. phr.**
3. in the garden   **3. phr.**   8. where the car is   **8. not phr.**
4. is sleeping   **4. phr.**   9. to laugh at myself   **9. phr.**
5. how she remembered   10. if he says so   **10. not phr.**
   5. not phr.

Prepositional Phrases

5b. A *prepositional phrase* includes a preposition, the object of the preposition, and any modifiers of that object.

EXAMPLES   under the umbrella   for ourselves
           among good friends   next to them

Notice that an article or another modifier may appear in a prepositional phrase. The first example above contains the article *the*. In the second example, *good* modifies *friends*.

The noun or pronoun that completes a prepositional phrase is called the **object of the preposition.**

EXAMPLES   Linh Phan has the lead in the school **play.** [The noun *play* is the object of the preposition *in*.]

           Standing between **them** was the Russian chess champion. [The pronoun *them* is the object of the preposition *between*.]

Any modifier that comes between the preposition and its object is part of the prepositional phrase.

EXAMPLE   **Into the thick mist** vanished the carriage. [The adjectives *the* and *thick* modify the object *mist*.]

An object of a preposition may be compound.

EXAMPLE   Come with **Rick** and **me** to the concert. [Both *Rick* and *me* are objects of the preposition *with*.]

RESOURCES

What Is a Phrase?
Practice

- *Language & Sentence Skills Practice,* p. 86
- *Developmental Language & Sentence Skills,* pp. 37–38

NOTE Be careful not to confuse an infinitive with a prepositional phrase beginning with *to*. A prepositional phrase always has an object that is a noun or a pronoun. An infinitive is a verbal that usually begins with *to*.

PREPOSITIONAL PHRASE Send the package **to them.**
INFINITIVE Are you ready **to go**?

Reference Note
For more information about **infinitives,** see page 102.

Exercise 2 Identifying Prepositional Phrases

Identify the prepositional phrases in each of the following sentences.

EXAMPLE 1. Many soldiers fought bravely during the Vietnam War.
1. during the Vietnam War

HELP
The sentences in Exercise 2 may contain more than one prepositional phrase apiece.

1. One of these soldiers was Jan C. Scruggs.
2. When the war was over, he and other veterans wondered why there was no national memorial honoring those who had served in Vietnam.
3. Scruggs decided he would raise funds for a Vietnam Veterans Memorial.
4. The memorial would include the names of all American men and women who were missing in action or who had died.
5. Organizing the project took years of great effort.
6. Many different people contributed their talents to the project.
7. Maya Ying Lin, a college student, designed the memorial that now stands in Washington, D.C.
8. This picture shows the V-shaped, black granite wall that was built from Lin's design.
9. A glass company from Memphis, Tennessee, engraved each name on the shiny granite.
10. Now the names of those who died in Vietnam will never be forgotten by the American people.

Adjective Phrases

Rule 5c (pp. 92–94)

OBJECTIVES

- To identify adjective phrases and the words they modify
- To complete sentences by supplying adjective phrases

DIRECT TEACHING

Modeling and Demonstration

Adjective Phrases. Model how to identify the word modified by an adjective phrase by using the example *Rosa chose the one with blue stripes.* First, ask students to identify the adjective phrase. [*with blue stripes*] Next, ask *which one with blue stripes.* [*one*] Then, point out that *with blue stripes* modifies *one.* Now, have a volunteer use another example from this chapter to demonstrate how to identify the word modified by an adjective phrase.

DIRECT TEACHING

Prepositional Phrases

Point out to students that using too many short, choppy sentences can make their writing seem dull. Use the following example to show students how prepositional phrases can be used to combine sentences.

> **Two sentences:** Put your bottle in the recycle bin. The recycle bin is behind the garage.
> **Revision:** Put your bottle in the recycle bin <u>behind the garage</u>.

Suggest that students examine their own writing for opportunities to use prepositional phrases to combine sentences.

Adjective Phrases

A prepositional phrase used as an adjective is called an ***adjective phrase.***

ADJECTIVE	Rosa chose the **blue** one.
ADJECTIVE PHRASE	Rosa chose the one **with blue stripes.**

5c. An ***adjective phrase*** modifies a noun or a pronoun.

Adjective phrases generally come after the words they modify and answer the same questions that single-word adjectives answer.

> What kind? Which one?
> How many? How much?

EXAMPLES The store **with the neon sign** is open. [The prepositional phrase *with the neon sign* is used as an adjective modifying the noun *store.* The phrase answers the question *Which one?*]

We bought a CD **by Janet Jackson.** [*By Janet Jackson* is used as an adjective modifying the noun *CD.* The phrase answers the question *What kind?*]

More than one adjective phrase may modify the same noun or pronoun.

EXAMPLE Here's a gift **for you from Uncle Steve.** [The prepositional phrases *for you* and *from Uncle Steve* both modify the noun *gift.*]

An adjective phrase may also modify the object in another adjective phrase.

EXAMPLE A majority **of the mammals in the world** sleep during the day. [The adjective phrase *of the mammals* modifies the noun *majority.* The adjective phrase *in the world* modifies the noun *mammals,* which is the object of the preposition in the first phrase.]

Exercise 3 Identifying Adjective Phrases

Identify the <u>adjective phrase</u> in each of the following sentences, and write the <u>word that each phrase modifies</u>.

Chapter 5 The Phrase

RESOURCES

Adjective Phrase

Practice

- *Language & Sentence Skills Practice,* p. 88

The Phrase

EXAMPLE   1. Marie Sklodowska Curie, a scientist from Poland, was awarded the Nobel Prize in 1911.
      1. from Poland—scientist

1. While she was a student in France, Marie met Pierre Curie.
2. Pierre had already gained fame as a scientist.
3. Paris was where the two of them became friends.
4. Their enthusiasm for science brought them together.
5. The marriage between the two scientists was a true partnership.
6. The year after their marriage another scientist discovered natural radioactivity.
7. The Curies began researching the radioactivity of certain substances.
8. Their theories about a new element were proved to be true.
9. Their research on the mineral pitchblende uncovered a new radioactive element, radium.
10. In 1903, the Curies and another scientist shared a Nobel Prize for their discovery.

HELP
Remember, an adjective phrase must modify a noun or a pronoun.

Exercise 4 Identifying Adjective Phrases

Identify the adjective phrases in the following sentences. Then, write the word that each phrase modifies.

EXAMPLE   1. R.I.C.E. is the recommended treatment for minor sports injuries.
      1. for minor sports injuries—treatment

1. The first letters of the words *Rest, Ice, Compression,* and *Elevation* form the abbreviation *R.I.C.E.*
2. Total bed rest is not necessary, just rest for the injured part of the body.
3. Ice helps because it deadens pain and slows the loss of blood.
4. Ice also reduces swelling of the injured area.
5. Compression with a tight bandage of elastic cloth prevents further strain on the injury.
6. This photograph shows an ice pack treating the injured knee of the athlete Robert Horry.
7. The last step in the treatment is elevation of the injured area.
8. The effect of gravity helps fluid drain away.

HELP
The sentences in Exercise 4 may contain more than one adjective phrase apiece.

Prepositional Phrases   93

5 d

Oral Practice Using Adjective Phrases

ANSWERS

Phrases will vary. Here are some possibilities:

1. from the stereo—sound
2. across the street—theater
3. of the bagels—more
4. in the Blue Ridge Mountains—vacation
5. of a blue whale—photograph
6. to her question—answer
7. on the table—vase
8. in a serape—boy
9. of the old oak tree—branch
10. in the front—Someone

Adverb Phrases

Rule 5d (pp. 94–97)

OBJECTIVES

- To identify adverb phrases and the words they modify
- To distinguish between adverb phrases and adjective phrases

DIRECT TEACHING

Modeling and Demonstration

Adverb Phrases. Model how to identify an adverb phrase by using the example *The cavalry will reach the fort by noon.* First, ask students to identify the prepositional phrase. [*by noon*] Next, ask whether the phrase modifies a verb, adjective, or adverb. [*yes—verb*] Then, point out that since the phrase modifies a verb, it is an adverb phrase. Now, have a volunteer, using another example from this chapter, demonstrate how to identify an adverb phrase.

9. If pain continues, someone with medical training should be called to examine the injured person.
10. Even injuries of a minor nature need proper attention.

Oral Practice Using Adjective Phrases

Read each of the following sentences aloud, providing an adjective phrase for the blank. Then, say which word the phrase modifies.

EXAMPLE 1. A flock _____ flew overhead.
         1. *A flock of small gray birds flew overhead.—flock*

1. The sound _____ suddenly filled the air.
2. The theater _____ often shows kung-fu movies.
3. May I have some more _____?
4. Our vacation _____ was relaxing.
5. Her photograph _____ looks like a prizewinner.
6. Andrea found the answer _____.
7. He put the flowers in a vase _____.
8. A boy _____ hung a piñata in the tree.
9. The nest is in the top branch _____.
10. Someone _____ shouted for quiet.

Adverb Phrases

A prepositional phrase used as an adverb is called an *adverb phrase.*

ADVERB   The cavalry will reach the fort **soon.**
ADVERB PHRASE The cavalry will reach the fort **by noon.**

5d. An *adverb phrase* modifies a verb, an adjective, or an adverb.

Adverb phrases answer the same questions that single-word adverbs answer: *When? Where? How? Why? How often? How long? To what extent?*

EXAMPLES   We got our new puppy **at the animal shelter.** [The adverb phrase *at the animal shelter* modifies the verb *got,* telling *where.*]

A puppy is always ready **for a game.** [The adverb phrase *for a game* modifies the adjective *ready,* telling *how.*]

He barks loudly **for a puppy.** [The adverb phrase *for a puppy* modifies the adverb *loudly,* telling *to what extent.*]

HELP

Remember, an adjective phrase must modify a noun or a pronoun.

RESOURCES

Adverb Phrases

Practice

- *Language & Sentence Skills Practice,* pp. 89–91

Unlike adjective phrases, which generally follow the word or words they modify, adverb phrases may appear at various places in sentences.

EXAMPLES **At dusk,** we went inside to eat dinner.

We went inside **at dusk** to eat dinner.

We went inside to eat dinner **at dusk.**

Like adjective phrases, more than one adverb phrase may modify the same word.

EXAMPLES She drove **for hours through the storm.** [Both adverb phrases, *for hours* and *through the storm,* modify the verb *drove.*]

The library is open **during the day on weekends.** [Both adverb phrases, *during the day* and *on weekends,* modify the adjective *open.*]

On Saturday we will rehearse our drill routine **before the game.** [Both adverb phrases, *On Saturday* and *before the game,* modify the verb phrase *will rehearse.*]

NOTE An adverb phrase may be followed by an adjective phrase that modifies the object in the adverb phrase.

EXAMPLE The boat landed **on an island near the coast.** [The adverb phrase *on an island* modifies the verb *landed.* The adjective phrase *near the coast* modifies the noun *island.*]

Exercise 5 Identifying Adverb Phrases

Identify the adverb phrase in each of the following sentences. Then, write the word that each phrase modifies. Do not list adjective phrases.

EXAMPLE 1. Pecos Bill will live forever in the many legends about him.

1. in the many legends—will live

1. When he was only a baby, Pecos Bill fell into the Pecos River.
2. His parents searched for him but couldn't find him.
3. He was saved by coyotes, who raised him.
4. He thought for many years that he was a coyote.
5. After a long argument, a cowboy convinced Bill that he was not a coyote.

TIPS & TRICKS

If you are not sure whether a prepositional phrase is an adjective phrase or an adverb phrase, remember that an adjective phrase almost always follows the word it modifies. If you can move the phrase without changing the meaning of the sentence, the phrase is probably an adverb phrase.

DIFFERENTIATING INSTRUCTION

English-Language Learners

Cantonese. Adverbs usually come before verbs and adjectives in Cantonese, so a Cantonese-speaking student may tend to place all adverb phrases at the front of the sentence: *This weekend on Saturday, I played soccer.* Have students practice sentence variety by placing adverbs and adverb phrases at the beginning and at the end of sentences, and discuss differences in emphasis and meaning.

This weekend I played soccer on Saturday.

Learners Having Difficulty

It might be easier for students to understand how placement of adverb phrases can be varied if they see two versions of the same sentence with an adverb phrase placed differently in each. Copy sentences 5, 6, and 7 of **Exercise 5** onto the chalkboard. Have student volunteers rewrite the sentences on the chalkboard by moving each adverb phrase to a new location. Point out that adverb phrases, unlike adjective phrases, do not always need to be next to the words they modify to be clear.

GRAMMAR

Prepositional Phrases **95**

CONTENT-AREA CONNECTIONS

Mathematics
Prepositional phrases. To show students that concepts learned in language arts apply to other subjects as well, discuss the use of prepositional phrases in mathematical language. For example, *six divided by two equals three; ten percent of sixty is six; two into eight is four.* Ask students to volunteer other examples. [*One half of ten is five; four goes into forty ten times; the circumference of the circle is fifteen inches; two multiplied by four equals eight.*]

Prepositional Phrases **95**

6. During a drought, Bill dug the bed of the Rio Grande.
7. On one occasion he rode a cyclone.
8. A mountain lion once leaped from a ledge above Bill's head.
9. Bill was always ready for trouble and soon had the mountain lion tamed.
10. Stories like these about Pecos Bill are common in the West.

Exercise 6 Identifying Adverb Phrases

Identify the adverb phrases in the following sentences. Then, write the word or words that each phrase modifies. Do not list adjective phrases.

EXAMPLE
1. Never before had a blizzard struck the coastal area with such force.
1. with such force—had struck

HELP
The sentences in Exercise 6 may contain more than one adverb phrase apiece.

1. Andrea saw the dark clouds and turned toward home.
2. The raging wind blew the eleven-year-old over a sea wall near the shore.
3. She found herself trapped in a deep snowdrift.
4. No one could hear her shouts over the howling wind.
5. Andrea's dog charged through the snow toward the beach.
6. He plunged into the snow around Andrea and licked her face, warming the skin.
7. Then the huge dog walked around Andrea until the snow was packed down.
8. The dog pulled her to an open area on the beach.
9. With great effort, Andrea and her dog made their way home.
10. Grateful to their dog, Andrea's family served him a special steak dinner.

Review A Identifying and Classifying Prepositional Phrases

Identify the prepositional phrase in each of the following sentences, and classify it as an *adjective phrase* or an *adverb phrase*. Then, write the word or words the phrase modifies.

EXAMPLE
1. Here is some information about sharks.
1. about sharks—adjective phrase; information

MINI-LESSON Usage

Misplaced Modifiers. To illustrate the confusion caused by misplaced modifiers, write the following sentences on the chalkboard:

1. I borrowed a radio from my sister with a weather band.

2. We read about the thieves who were captured in today's paper.

Ask volunteers to revise the sentences by repositioning the misplaced prepositional phrases. [*From my sister I borrowed a radio*

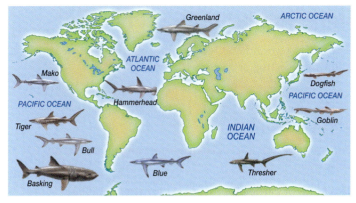

1. Did you know that there are hundreds of shark species?
2. Scientists group these species into twenty-eight families.
3. Sharks within the same family share many traits.
4. The body shape, tail shape, and teeth determine the differences among families.
5. Sharks are found throughout the world's oceans.
6. As the map shows, some sharks prefer cold waters, and others live mostly in warm tropical oceans.
7. Only thirty kinds of sharks are dangerous.
8. The huge whale shark, however, falls under the "not dangerous" category.
9. Divers can even hitch a ride on its fins.
10. Beautiful yet frightening to most people, sharks are perhaps the world's most awesome creatures.

1. adj.
2. adv.
3. adj.
4. adj.
5. adv.
6. adv.
7. adj.
8. adv.
9. adj.
10. adv.

Review B Writing Sentences with Prepositional Phrases

For each of the following items, write a sentence using the given prepositional phrase. Then, tell whether you have used each phrase as an *adjective phrase* or an *adverb phrase*.

EXAMPLE 1. through the tollbooth
1. A car passed through the tollbooth.—adverb phrase

1. in the movie theater
2. for the party
3. along the water's edge
4. about Madeleine
5. into the department store
6. underneath the bed
7. with chopsticks
8. of the equipment
9. in front of city hall
10. at the campsite

GRAMMAR

The Participle
Rules 5e, f *(pp. 98–102)*

OBJECTIVES

- To identify present and past participles and the words they modify
- To identify participial phrases and the words they modify
- To write sentences containing given participial phrases

DIRECT TEACHING

Modeling and Demonstration

Identifying Participles. Model how to identify a participle by using the example *Mr. Sanchez rescued three people from the burning building.* First, ask students to identify the adjectives. [*three, the, burning*] Next, ask whether one of the adjectives could also be used as a verb. [*yes—burning*] Then, explain that *burning* is a participle. Now, have a volunteer use another example from this chapter to demonstrate how to identify a participle.

Verbals and Verbal Phrases

A *verbal* is a word that is formed from a verb but is used as a noun, an adjective, or an adverb.

The Participle

5e. A *participle* is a verb form that can be used as an adjective.

Two kinds of participles are *present participles* and *past participles*.

(1) Present participles end in –ing.

EXAMPLES   Mr. Sanchez rescued three people from the **burning** building. [*Burning* is the present participle of the verb *burn*. The participle modifies the noun *building*.]

Chasing the cat, the dog ran down the street. [*Chasing* is the present participle of the verb *chase*. The participle modifies the noun *dog*.]

(2) Past participles usually end in –d or –ed. Some past participles are formed irregularly.

EXAMPLES   Well **trained,** the soldier successfully carried out her mission. [The past participle *trained* modifies the noun *soldier*.]

We skated on the **frozen** pond. [The irregular past participle *frozen* modifies the noun *pond*.]

> **NOTE** Be careful not to confuse participles used as adjectives with participles used in verb phrases. Remember that the participle in a verb phrase is part of the verb.
>
> ADJECTIVE   **Discouraged,** the fans went home.
> VERB PHRASE   The fans **were discouraged** by the string of losses.
>
> ADJECTIVE   **Singing** cheerfully, the birds perched among the branches of the trees.
> VERB PHRASE   The birds **were singing** cheerfully among the branches of the trees.

Reference Note
For a list of **irregular past participles,** see page 179.

RESOURCES

The Participle

Practice

- *Language & Sentence Skills Practice,* pp. 92–95
- *Developmental Language & Sentence Skills,* pp. 41–42

Exercise 7 **Identifying Participles and the Nouns They Modify**

Identify the participles used as adjectives in the following sentences. Then, write the noun that each participle modifies.

EXAMPLE 1. The deserted cities of the Anasazi are found in the Four Corners area of the United States.
1. deserted—cities

1. Utah, Colorado, New Mexico, and Arizona are the bordering states that make up the Four Corners.
2. Because of its natural beauty, Chaco Canyon is one of the most visited sights in this region of the Southwest.
3. Among the remaining ruins in Chaco Canyon are the houses, public buildings, and plazas of the Anasazi.
4. What alarming event may have caused these people to leave their valley?
5. Historians are studying the scattered remains of the Anasazi culture to learn more about these mysterious people.
6. Woven baskets were important to the earliest Anasazi people, who were excellent basket weavers.
7. On the floors of some caves are pits for stored food and other vital supplies.
8. Surviving descendants of the Anasazi include today's Zuni, Hopi, and some of the Pueblo peoples.
9. Programs protecting archaeological sites help ensure the preservation of our nation's heritage.
10. There are several national parks and monuments commemorating the Pueblo's past.

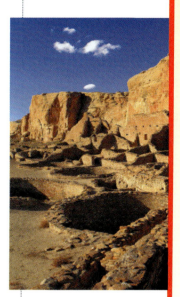

Exercise 8 **Identifying Participles and the Words They Modify**

Identify the participles used as adjectives in the following sentences. Then, write the noun or pronoun each participle modifies.

EXAMPLE 1. Buzzing mosquitoes swarmed around me.
1. Buzzing—mosquitoes

1. Annoyed, I went inside to watch TV.
2. I woke my sleeping father to ask about mosquitoes.
3. Irritated, he directed me to an encyclopedia.

Verbals and Verbal Phrases

DIFFERENTIATING INSTRUCTION

English-Language Learners

Spanish. The English present participle suffix –*ing* is equivalent to the Spanish –*ando* and –*iendo* (e.g., *hablando,* "speaking," from *hablar,* "to speak," and *comiendo,* "eating," from *comer,* "to eat"). The English past participle suffix –*(e)d* is equivalent to the Spanish –*ado* and –*ido* (e.g., *marcado,* "marked," and *adquirido,* "acquired"). In English and in Spanish, past participles can be used as adjectives.

Portuguese and French. The English –*ing* suffix corresponds to –*ando,* –*endo,* and –*indo* in Portuguese and –*ant* in French; the English –*(e)d* suffix corresponds to –*ado* and –*ido* in Portuguese and –*é(e)* in French.

Learners Having Difficulty

The following activity may help students who are having difficulty identifying and using participles.

First, list the verbs *jump, howl, march, polish, iron,* and *trust* on the chalkboard. Ask students to add *ing* to the first three verbs and *ed* to the last three verbs and to use these newly formed participles to modify nouns of their own choosing. [*jumping frogs, howling dogs, marching band, polished floor, ironed shirt, trusted friend*]

GRAMMAR

RETEACHING

Participles

To help students learn participles, pair students for this flashcard game. Make three signs: one saying *participle used in verb phrase,* one saying *participle used as adjective,* and one saying *participial phrase used as adjective.* Then, write the word *missing* on the chalkboard, and ask each pair to write a sentence using the word as instructed by the sign you hold up. For example, if you show the *participle used as adjective* sign, students might write *The missing photo is mine.*

Give students time to discuss their sentence while they are writing; then, call upon pairs at random to share their sentences. Continue with such words as *locked, running, dancing, broken,* and *startled.*

DIRECT TEACHING

Correcting Misconceptions

Participles in Sentence Fragments. Students might create sentence fragments by mistaking a participle for a verb. Write the following groups of words on the chalkboard, and ask students to explain why the word groups are not complete sentences. [*Each needs a helping verb.*]

1. The bird singing cheerfully

2. The game scheduled for tonight

3. Branches tapping on the roof

Explain to students that the word groups above can become sentences if a helping verb is added to the participle to complete the thought. [*The bird was singing cheerfully. The game is scheduled for tonight. Branches are tapping on the roof.*]

Reference Note

For information on **modifiers,** see Chapter 11. For information on **complements,** see Chapter 4.

Reference Note

For information on **how to place participial phrases correctly,** see page 236.

4. I learned that some flying insects carry diseases.
5. Biting mosquitoes can spread malaria.
6. Bites make the skin swell, and the swollen skin itches.
7. Sucking blood for food, mosquitoes survive in many different climates.
8. Sometimes you can hear mosquitoes buzzing.
9. Their beating wings make the sound.
10. Mosquitoes, living only a few weeks, may go through as many as twelve generations in a year.

The Participial Phrase

5f. A ***participial phrase*** **consists of a participle together with its modifiers and complements. The entire phrase is used as an adjective.**

EXAMPLES   **Stretching slowly,** the cat jumped down from the windowsill. [The participle *Stretching* is modified by the adverb *slowly.* The phrase modifies *cat.*]

The tornado **predicted by the meteorologist** did not hit our area. [The participle *predicted* is modified by the prepositional phrase *by the meteorologist.* The whole participial phrase modifies *tornado.*]

Reading the assignment, she took notes carefully. [The participle *Reading* has the direct object *assignment.* The phrase modifies *she.*]

A participial phrase should be placed close to the word it modifies. Otherwise, the phrase may appear to modify another word, and the sentence may not make sense.

MISPLACED	Hopping along the fence, I saw a rabbit. [Was *I* hopping along the fence?]
CORRECTED	I saw a rabbit **hopping along the fence.**

Exercise 9   Identifying Participial Phrases and the Words They Modify

Identify the participial phrases in the following sentences. Then, write the word or words each phrase modifies.

EXAMPLE 1. Living over four hundred years ago, Leonardo da Vinci kept journals of his ideas and inventions.
   1. Living over four hundred years ago—Leonardo da Vinci

1. The journals, written backwards in "mirror writing," are more than five thousand pages long.
2. Leonardo drew many pictures showing birds in flight.
3. He hoped that machines based on his sketches of birds would enable humans to fly.
4. Shown here, his design for a helicopter was the first one in history.
5. Studying the eye, Leonardo understood the sense of sight.
6. He worked hard, filling his journals with sketches like the ones on this page for a movable bridge.
7. The solutions reached in his journals often helped Leonardo when he created his artworks.
8. He used the hands sketched in the journals as models when he painted the hands in the *Mona Lisa*.
9. Painting on a large wall, Leonardo created *The Last Supper*.
10. Leonardo, experimenting continually, had little time to paint in his later years.

The Granger Collection, New York.

Exercise 10 Writing Sentences with Participial Phrases

For each of the following items, write a sentence using the given participial phrase. Make sure the participial phrase modifies a noun or pronoun.

EXAMPLE 1. cheering for the team
   1. Cheering for the team, we celebrated the victory.

1. confused by the directions
2. gathering information on the Hopi
3. practicing my part in the play
4. followed closely by my younger brother

HELP
In Exercise 10, place a comma after a participial phrase that begins a sentence.

Reference Note
For more information about **punctuating participial phrases,** see pages 299 and 305.

5 g, h

| Exercise 10 | Writing Sentences with Participial Phrases |

ANSWERS continued

5. The drummer, searching through the crowd, located the singer.
6. Shaped by wind and water, the sandbar changes daily.
7. Your car, freshly painted at the shop, will be ready tomorrow.
8. Born in Tahiti, she moved here last year.
9. Reading a book by the window, I saw my carpool arrive.
10. The mover holding the Ming vase walked carefully across the room.

The Infinitive
Rules 5g, h *(pp. 102–105)*

OBJECTIVES
- To identify infinitives and infinitive phrases in sentences
- To write sentences using given infinitive phrases

EXTENSION

Relating to Literature

If your literature textbook contains Charles Dickens's *A Christmas Carol*, select several paragraphs that illustrate how extensively Dickens uses descriptive phrases. Explain to students that many nineteenth-century writers used elaborate descriptions containing many phrases. The more descriptive the passages were, the more easily readers could visualize the scenes. Literature was the television of their day.

Ask students to analyze other paragraphs in *A Christmas Carol* for the author's use of descriptive phrases. Tell them to find at least one adjective prepositional phrase, one adverb prepositional phrase, one participial phrase, and one infinitive phrase.

---

5. searching through the crowd
6. shaped by wind and water
7. freshly painted at the shop
8. born in Tahiti
9. reading a book by the window
10. holding the Ming vase

The Infinitive

5g. An *infinitive* is a verb form that can be used as a noun, an adjective, or an adverb. Most infinitives begin with *to*.

Infinitives	
Used as	**Examples**
Nouns	**To succeed** is my goal. [*To succeed* is the subject of the sentence.] My ambition is **to teach** Spanish. [*To teach* is a predicate nominative.] She tried **to win**. [*To win* is the direct object of the verb *tried*.]
Adjectives	The place **to meet** tomorrow is the library. [*To meet* modifies the noun *place*.] She is the one **to call**. [*To call* modifies the pronoun *one*.]
Adverbs	Tamara claims she was born **to surf**. [*To surf* modifies the verb *was born*.] This math problem will be hard **to solve** without a calculator. [*To solve* modifies the adjective *hard*.]

Reference Note
For more information about **prepositional phrases,** see page 90.

NOTE *To* plus a noun or a pronoun (*to* Washington, *to* her) is a prepositional phrase, not an infinitive.

PREPOSITIONAL PHRASE I am going **to the mall** today.
INFINITIVE I am going **to shop** for new shoes.

Chapter 5 The Phrase

RESOURCES
The Infinitive
Practice
- *Language & Sentence Skills Practice,* pp. 96–101
- *Developmental Language & Sentence Skills,* 43–44

Exercise 11 Identifying Infinitives

Identify the infinitives in the following sentences. If a sentence does not contain an infinitive, write *none*.

EXAMPLE 1. I would like to go to New York City someday.
  1. to go

1. My first stop would be to visit the Statue of Liberty.
2. Thousands of people go to see the statue every day.
3. They take a boat to Liberty Island.   3. none
4. The statue holds a torch to symbolize freedom.
5. The idea of a statue to represent freedom came from a French historian.
6. France gave the statue to the United States in 1884.   6. none
7. The statue was shipped to this country in 214 cases.   7. none
8. It was a gift to express the friendship between the two nations.
9. In the 1980s, many people helped to raise money for repairs to the statue.
10. The repairs were completed in time to celebrate the statue's hundredth anniversary on October 28, 1986.

The Infinitive Phrase

5h. An *infinitive phrase* consists of an infinitive together with its modifiers and complements. The entire phrase may be used as a noun, an adjective, or an adverb.

EXAMPLES **To be a good gymnast** takes hard work. [The infinitive phrase is used as a noun. The infinitive *To be* has a complement, *a good gymnast*.]

The first person **to fly over both the North Pole and the South Pole** was Richard Byrd. [The infinitive phrase is used as an adjective modifying the noun *person*. The infinitive *to fly* is modified by the prepositional phrase *over both the North Pole and the South Pole*.]

Are you ready **to go to the gym now**? [The infinitive phrase is used as an adverb modifying the adjective *ready*. The infinitive *to go* is modified by the prepositional phrase *to the gym* and by the adverb *now*.]

Reference Note
For information on **modifiers,** see Chapter 11. For information on **complements,** see Chapter 4.

DIRECT TEACHING

Infinitive Phrases

Activity. To emphasize the different uses of infinitive phrases, use the same infinitive in three different ways—as a noun, adjective, and adverb—in three different sentences. Write the sentences on the chalkboard, and ask students to pick out the infinitive phrases. Then, discuss whether these phrases are used as nouns, adjectives, or adverbs. Here are some examples using the infinitive *to finish:*

1. I would like to finish early. [noun]
2. The first one to finish early already left. [adjective]
3. They hurried to finish early. [adverb]

Exercise 13 Writing Sentences with Infinitive Phrases

POSSIBLE ANSWERS

1. His goal is to sing with the Boys Choir of Harlem.
2. She wants to ask a question about the test.
3. Rusty is too shy to write a poem to his girlfriend.
4. It was important to understand the assignment before starting it.
5. To give a report on the Spanish exploration of California will take some research.
6. To learn a little Japanese over the summer, she traveled to Tokyo.
7. My grandmother is able to predict accurately the weather patterns for our area.
8. It would be better to develop your own ideas than to imitate that style.
9. It is impossible to be the best at everything.
10. We left our beach towels to dry in the sun.

Exercise 12 Identifying Infinitive Phrases

Identify the infinitive phrase in each of the following sentences.

EXAMPLE   1. We went to the park to watch birds.
           1. *to watch birds*

1. A bird is able to control many of its feathers individually.
2. Birds use their feathers to push their bodies through the air.
3. Human beings learned to build aircraft by carefully studying the way birds fly.
4. A bird sings to claim its territory.
5. To recognize the songs of different birds takes many hours of practice.
6. By molting (or gradual shedding), birds are able to replace their feathers.
7. Eagles use their feet to catch small animals.
8. Since they have no teeth, many birds have to swallow their food whole.
9. In many cases both parents help to build a nest.
10. Most birds feed their young until the young are ready to fly from the nest.

Exercise 13 Writing Sentences with Infinitive Phrases

For each of the following items, write a sentence using the given infinitive phrase. Try to vary your sentences as much as possible.

EXAMPLE   1. to see the carved masks of the Haida people
           1. *Terry wants to see the carved masks of the Haida people.*

1. to sing with the Boys Choir of Harlem
2. to ask a question about the test
3. to write a poem to his girlfriend
4. to understand the assignment
5. to give a report on the Spanish exploration of California
6. to learn a little Japanese over the summer
7. to predict accurately the weather patterns
8. to imitate that style
9. to be the best at everything
10. to dry in the sun

Learning for Life

Giving Directions. To review the various types of phrases in **Chapter 5**, write the following directions on a transparency or on the chalkboard. You may want to adapt the example to apply to your school. The prepositional phrases are underlined once, the participial phrases are bracketed, and the infinitive phrases are underlined twice.

To find the principal's office, go out the door and turn to your left. Walk down the hall until you see an orange banner [hanging above the lockers on your

Review C **Identifying and Classifying Participial Phrases and Infinitive Phrases**

Identify the participial phrase or the infinitive phrase in each sentence of the following paragraph. Classify each phrase as a *participial phrase* or an *infinitive phrase*.

EXAMPLES
[1] My family is proud to celebrate our Jewish holidays.
1. to celebrate our Jewish holidays—infinitive phrase

[2] Observing Jewish traditions, we celebrate each holiday in a special way.
2. Observing Jewish traditions—participial phrase

[1] During Rosh Hashana we hear writings from the Torah read in our synagogue. [2] Celebrated in September or October, Rosh Hashana is the Jewish New Year. [3] On this holiday, our rabbi chooses to wear white robes instead of the usual black robes. [4] Representing newness and purity, the white robes symbolize the new year. [5] My favorite food of Rosh Hashana is the honey cake baked by my grandmother. [6] During this holiday everyone eats a lot, knowing that Yom Kippur, a day of fasting, is only ten days away. [7] Yom Kippur, considered the holiest day of the Jewish year, is a serious holiday. [8] To attend services like the one you see here is part of my family's Yom Kippur tradition. [9] I am always pleased to see many of my friends and neighbors there. [10] Sunset, marking the end of the day, brings Yom Kippur to a peaceful close.

1. part.
2. part.
3. inf.
4. part.
5. part.
6. part.
7. part.
8. inf.
9. inf.
10. part.

DIFFERENTIATING INSTRUCTION

Advanced Learners

For a round-robin learning game, divide the class into teams of three. The first member of each team writes an infinitive on a sheet of paper and then passes it along to the second member of the team, who turns the infinitive into a phrase. Then, the paper is passed to the third member of the team, who uses the phrase in a complete sentence. Finally, the third team member passes the paper back to the first member, who checks the sentence's correctness with the other team members and writes the completed sentence on the chalkboard. Here is an example:

1. to be
2. to be happy
3. My goal is to be happy with my performance.

Ask students to complete the exercise three times, changing roles each time.

right]. Turn right into the next hallway. The principal's office is the third door on the right.

Next, ask students to write directions for a location of their choice in or around the school. Suggest that they try to use at least one example of each kind of phrase covered in this chapter. Then, ask students to read their directions aloud while the rest of the class guesses the destinations.

GRAMMAR

Appositives and Appositive Phrases

Rules 5i, j *(pp. 106–108)*

OBJECTIVE

- To identify appositives and appositive phrases in sentences

DIRECT TEACHING

Modeling and Demonstration

Identifying Appositives. Model how to identify appositives by using the example *My teacher Mr. Craig enjoys books by Jane Austen.* First, identify the nouns and pronouns. [*teacher, Mr. Craig, books, Jane Austen*] Next, ask if any of the nouns are next to each other. [*teacher and Mr. Craig*] Then, ask if *teacher* and *Mr. Craig* refer to the same thing. [*yes*] Explain to students that *Mr. Craig* is an appositive identifying *teacher*. Now, have a volunteer use another example in this chapter to demonstrate how to identify an appositive.

---

5 i, j

HELP

You can use phrases to combine sentences. Often, you can take a phrase from one sentence and insert it unchanged into another sentence.

EXAMPLE
She left the stable. She was in a hurry.
COMBINED
She left the stable **in a hurry.**

Other times you can turn one sentence into a phrase and combine it with another sentence.

EXAMPLE
In the pasture was her horse. It cantered along the fence.
COMBINED
In the pasture was her horse, **cantering along the fence.**

Reference Note

For more information on **sentence combining,** see page 418.

106 Chapter 5 The Phrase

Appositives and Appositive Phrases

5i. An *appositive* is a noun or pronoun placed beside another noun or pronoun to identify or describe it.

EXAMPLES My teacher **Mr. Craig** enjoys books by Jane Austen. [The appositive *Mr. Craig* identifies the noun *teacher*.]

Mr. Craig wishes he could go back in time to talk to one author, **her.** [The appositive *her* identifies the noun *author*.]

5j. An *appositive phrase* consists of an appositive and its modifiers.

EXAMPLES I recently saw the movie version of *Persuasion,* **a novel by Jane Austen.** [The noun *novel* is the appositive; *a* and *by Jane Austen* modify *novel*.]

Amanda Root, **the female lead in the movie,** plays Anne Elliot. [The noun *lead* is the appositive; *the, female,* and *in the movie* modify *lead*.]

Appositives and appositive phrases that are not essential to the meaning of a sentence are set off by commas. If the appositive is essential to the meaning, it is generally not set off by commas.

EXAMPLES Anne, **a goodhearted and intelligent woman,** must learn not to be too easily persuaded by others. [The appositive phrase *a goodhearted and intelligent woman* adds descriptive information that is unnecessary to the sentence's basic meaning, so it is set off by commas.]

Anne's friend **Lady Russell** sometimes gives Anne poor advice. [Anne has more than one friend. The appositive *Lady Russell* tells you which friend is meant, so it is not set off by commas.]

Exercise 14 Identifying Appositives and Appositive Phrases

Identify the appositives and appositive phrases in the following sentences. Then, give the word or words each appositive or appositive phrase identifies or describes.

EXAMPLE   1. My sister Roseanne is a software support specialist.
           1. Roseanne—sister

RESOURCES

Appositives and Appositive Phrases
Practice
- Language & Sentence Skills Practice, pp. 102–103
- Developmental Language & Sentence Skills, pp. 45–46

106 The Phrase

1. (John), a carpenter, lives across the street from us.
2. Will your (cousin) Charlene visit you this fall?
3. That (book), *The White Mountains*, is my favorite.
4. Janey is playing with her favorite (toy), a stuffed horse named Dapples.
5. I asked for a (volunteer), anyone, to lead the program.
6. (Al), the security guard at Mom's office, always says hello to me.
7. Noel sent Tony's (son) Ethan a birthday present.
8. The (shortstop) on our softball team, Deanna, broke her toe last Wednesday.
9. (Jackson Square), a landmark in New Orleans, has a statue of Andrew Jackson in it.
10. The beach was covered with (sargassum), a seaweed that is made up of brown algae.

Review D — Identifying Verbal Phrases and Appositive Phrases

Write the verbal phrase or appositive phrase in each of the following sentences. Then, label it as a *participial phrase*, an *infinitive phrase*, or an *appositive phrase*.

EXAMPLE 1. Startled by the noise, I looked up.
1. *Startled by the noise*—participial phrase

1. Josie wants to visit Thailand someday. **1.** inf.
2. I found Clive, my cat, on top of the refrigerator. **2.** app.
3. A job baby-sitting for a nice family is what I want. **3.** part.
4. The newspaper, an unreadable blob of wet paper, had been outside in the gutter during the storm. **4.** app.
5. A boy playing basketball asked Chris and Laney whether you rode our bus. **5.** part.
6. Monique would like that sweater, the green one. **6.** app.
7. Launched into the atmosphere, the spaceship turned in the direction of the moon. **7.** part.
8. To leave the place neat and clean was our goal. **8.** inf.
9. Do you want to play kickball, Jason? **9.** inf.
10. Laughing hard, Derrick could barely catch his breath. **10.** part.

MEETING THE CHALLENGE

To make your writing more interesting, you can vary your sentence beginnings. Rather than beginning each sentence with the subject of a clause, you can begin with a prepositional, verbal, or appositive phrase.

Rearrange the following sentences so that they begin with a phrase.

1. The daisies bloomed in the window box.
2. I will need a calculator to work those problems.
3. The children gasped, frightened by the noise.
4. Mr. Jaenz, a clever inventor, has several patents.

POSSIBLE ANSWERS
1. In the window box, the daisies bloomed.
2. To work those problems, I will need a calculator.
3. Frightened by the noise, the children gasped.
4. A clever inventor, Mr. Jaenz has several patents.

Reference Note
For more information on **varying sentence beginnings,** see page 432.

Review E **Writing Phrases for Sentences**

For each of the following sentences, write the kind of phrase that is called for in parentheses. *Answers will vary.*

EXAMPLE 1. ____, the audience cheered Yo-Yo Ma's performance. (participial phrase)

1. *Clapping loudly,* the audience cheered Yo-Yo Ma's performance.

1. toward the car
2. in the auditorium
3. my little brother
4. from the faucet
5. On our trip
6. Trying to catch his breath
7. using all his strength
8. to go to the movies
9. To help end world hunger
10. a copy of my favorite CD

1. We walked slowly ____. (adverb phrase)
2. The people ____ applauded Mayor Garza's speech. (adjective phrase)
3. Dennis, ____, is afraid of fire ants. (appositive phrase)
4. The water ____ dripped steadily. (adjective phrase)
5. ____ we saw many beautiful Navajo rugs. (adverb phrase)
6. ____, the principal entered the classroom. (participial phrase)
7. Suddenly, ____, the lion pounced. (participial phrase)
8. My friends and I like ____. (infinitive phrase)
9. ____ is my greatest ambition. (infinitive phrase)
10. I gave Stephen a present, ____, for his birthday. (appositive phrase)

CHAPTER 5

Numerals in brackets refer to the rules tested by the items in the Chapter Review.

1–10. [5a, b]

Chapter Review

A. Identifying Prepositional Phrases

Identify each prepositional phrase in the following sentences. Then, write the word or words each phrase modifies. There may be more than one prepositional phrase in a sentence.

1. The view from Mount Fuji is spectacular.
2. Boulder Dam was the original name of Hoover Dam.
3. Eat something before the game.
4. We heard stories about our Cherokee ancestors.
5. The coach paced nervously on the sidelines.
6. The second-longest river in Africa is the Congo.
7. For the costume party, Jody dressed as a lion tamer.
8. Has the hiking party returned to the campsite?
9. The Hudson River was once the chief trading route for the western frontier.
10. Hearing a loud noise, Rita stopped the car and looked underneath it.

B. Identifying Adjective and Adverb Phrases

Classify each italicized prepositional phrase in the following sentences as an *adjective phrase* or an *adverb phrase*. Then, write the word or words the phrase modifies.

11. adj. [5c]
12. adj. [5c]
13. adv. [5d]
14. adj. [5c]
15. adj. [5c]
16. adv. [5d]
17. adv. [5d]
18. adv. [5d]
19. adj. [5c]
20. adv. [5d]

11. The jacket *with the gray stripes* is mine.
12. The man *across the aisle* is sleeping.
13. Mai spoke *with confidence* at the leadership conference.
14. A young woman *in a blue uniform* answered the phone.
15. Nobody *except Alicia* was amazed at the sudden downpour.
16. Were you upset *about the delay*?
17. Does your doctor work *at Emerson Hospital*?
18. *Along the Appalachian National Scenic Trail*, you will find painted rocks that indicate the route.
19. Masud's friends *from New Jersey* are coming to visit.
20. He is tall *for his age*.

ASSESSING

Monitoring Progress

Chapter Review To assess student progress, you may want to compare the types of items missed on the **Diagnostic Preview** to those missed on the **Chapter Review**. You may want to work out specific goals with individual students who are still having difficulty mastering essential information.

RESOURCES

The Phrase

Review
- *Language & Sentence Skills Practice,* pp. 104–106

Assessment
- *Holt Handbook Chapter Tests with Answer Key,* pp. 9–10, 46

C. Classifying Verbal Phrases

Identify each italicized verbal phrase in the following sentences as an *infinitive phrase* or a *participial phrase*.

21. *Returning her library books*, Janelle chose two more.
22. Scott, *chilled by the brisk wind*, pulled on his gloves.
23. *To become a park ranger* is Keisha's dream.
24. The awards dinner *planned for this evening* was canceled.
25. A soufflé can be difficult *to prepare properly*.
26. *Organized in 1884*, the first African American professional baseball team was the Cuban Giants.
27. Guillermo hopes *to visit us soon*.
28. My brother was the first person *to see a meteor* last evening.
29. Stella did not disturb the cat *sleeping in the window*.
30. How do you plan *to tell the story*?

D. Identifying Verbal Phrases

Identify the verbal phrase in each of the following sentences. Then, classify each phrase as an *infinitive phrase* or a *participial phrase*.

31. To skate around the neighborhood was Lee's favorite pastime.
32. Racing around on his in-line skates, he felt as if he were flying.
33. Then one afternoon, prevented from skating by the rain, Lee wondered about the history of skates.
34. He decided to search the Internet for information.
35. Lee learned that Joseph Merlin, an eighteenth-century Dutchman, was the first person to adapt ice skates for use on dry land.
36. Merlin's idea was to attach wooden spools to a plate that supported them.
37. First fashioned in 1763, skates with metal wheels were in use for a century.
38. Appearing in 1863, the first modern skates were invented by an American.
39. Skates with more durable ball-bearing wheels, introduced later in the nineteenth century, popularized roller skating.
40. At the end of the afternoon, Lee exclaimed, "It's fun to know the history of skates!"

E. Identifying Appositive Phrases

Identify the appositive phrase in each of the following sentences.

41. Bamboo, a kind of grass, may reach a height of 120 feet.
42. My favorite author is Truman Capote, an American writer.
43. The capybara, the world's largest rodent, can grow to 4 feet in length.
44. *Centigrade*, another word for *Celsius*, comes from the Latin for *100 degrees*.
45. Mom, an avid bird watcher, enjoyed visiting the state park.
46. Are you familiar with okra, a vegetable used in gumbo?
47. I bought a protractor, an instrument for measuring and plotting angles.
48. Provence, a region of France, is on the Mediterranean.
49. His best move, the jump shot, earned the team twenty points.
50. Spaghetti, my favorite dish, is on the menu.

41–50. [5a, i, j]

Writing Application
Using Prepositional Phrases in a Note

Adjective and Adverb Phrases Write a note to a friend to explain how to care for your pet while you are away. In your note, use a combined total of at least ten adjective phrases and adverb phrases to give detailed instructions to your friend.

Prewriting Begin by thinking about a pet you have or would like to have. Then, make a chart or list of the pet's needs. If you need more information about a particular kind of pet, ask a friend or someone else who owns such a pet.

Writing As you write your first draft, focus on giving information about each of your pet's needs. Tell your friend everything he or she needs to know to care for your pet properly.

Revising Ask a family member or friend to read your note. Add any missing information and take out any unnecessary instructions. Be sure that you have used at least ten adjective and adverb phrases.

Publishing Check the grammar, punctuation, and spelling of your note. You and your classmates may wish to create a pet care guide by organizing your notes in a three-ring binder.

APPLICATION

Writing Application

Prewriting Tip. Tell students to visualize themselves going through the procedure. They should stop after each imagined action and write exactly what they did. Then, before they begin writing, they should look at their lists of steps to make sure that all steps are in the correct sequence.

Writing Tip. In prewriting, students might include more information than is necessary for writing the instructions. Tell students that in the writing stage, they should omit any procedures not essential to accomplishing the task. For example, while they will need to tell where to find can openers or food and water dishes, it is not necessary to include instructions for opening the can or placing the contents in a dish.

Tell students to keep in mind what information their friends will need and what knowledge a person would already have.

Scoring Rubric. While you will want to pay particular attention to students' uses of adjective and adverb phrases, you may also want to evaluate the students' overall writing performance. You may want to give a split score to indicate development and clarity of the composition as well as grammar skills.

6 The Clause
Independent and Subordinate Clauses

Diagnostic Preview

A. Identifying and Classifying Independent and Subordinate Clauses

Identify each of the following clauses as either *independent* or *subordinate*.

EXAMPLE 1. when I was eleven years old
              1. *subordinate*

1. because I have lived in Chile and Ecuador
2. his writing has improved
3. although Gullah is still spoken on South Carolina's Sea Islands
4. when that baseball team won the National League pennant
5. she served as secretary of labor
6. which we brought to the Juneteenth picnic
7. everyone laughed
8. whose mother you met yesterday
9. during the storm the power failed
10. to whom his mother explained the reason for the delay

B. Identifying and Classifying Subordinate Clauses

Identify the subordinate clause in each of the following sentences. Then, classify each as either an *adjective clause* or an *adverb clause*.

EXAMPLES
1. Today is the day that you are eating at my house.
   1. *that you are eating at my house—adjective clause*

2. I will give you a map so that you can find my house.
   2. *so that you can find my house—adverb clause*

11. If you have never had Caribbean food, you are in for a treat.
12. My mother, who was born and raised in Jamaica, really knows how to cook.
13. Whenever I have a chance, I try to learn her secrets.
14. My grandmother, whose cooking is spectacular, is making her special sweet potato pone for dessert.
15. Some of the fruits and vegetables that grow in Jamaica are hard to find in the markets around here.
16. Today we are shopping for coconuts, avocados, and callaloo greens, which were introduced to the Caribbean by Africans.
17. We must also remember to buy the fresh hot peppers, onions, and spices that are needed for seasoning the meat.
18. Although my mother never uses measuring spoons, she seems to know just how much of each spice to add.
19. As soon as we pay for these items, let's take them home.
20. Part of your treat will be to smell the delicious aroma from the kitchen before you even begin eating.

11. adv. [6c, e]
12. adj. [6c, d]
13. adv. [6c, e]
14. adj. [6c, d]
15. adj. [6c, d]
16. adj. [6c, d]
17. adj. [6c, d]
18. adv. [6c, e]
19. adv. [6c, e]
20. adv. [6c, e]

What Is a Clause?

6a. A *clause* is a word group that contains a verb and its subject and that is used as a sentence or as part of a sentence.

Every clause contains a subject and a verb. However, not all clauses express complete thoughts. A clause that does express a complete thought is called an *independent clause*. A clause that does not express a complete thought is called a *subordinate clause*.

NOTE A subordinate clause that is capitalized and punctuated as if it were a sentence is a *sentence fragment*.

Reference Note
For information about **correcting sentence fragments,** see page 414.

ASSESSING

Entry-Level Assessment
Diagnostic Preview. You may want to use this informal **Diagnostic Preview** to determine students' understanding of clauses, especially if you are working on combining sentences in the revision stage of compositions. You also will be able to assess students' comprehension of adjective and adverb clauses.

Differentiating Instruction
- *Developmental Language & Sentence Skills Guided Practice,* pp. 47–52
- *Developmental Language & Sentence Skills Guided Practice Teacher's Notes and Answer Key,* p. 13

Assessment
- *Holt Handbook Chapter Tests with Answer Key,* pp. 11–12, 46

PRETEACHING

Lesson Starter

Motivating. Show the class a set of sentence strips based on the following paragraph—five strips of one color that contain the independent clauses and five strips of another color that contain the subordinate clauses. (Independent clauses have a single underline; subordinate clauses have a double underline.) Ask students to combine the sentence strips to form a complete paragraph. By eliminating punctuation and capitalization, you will show students that some independent and subordinate clauses can be reversed within sentences.

Today was Dad's surprise birthday party, which we had been planning for weeks. Before the guests arrived, my sisters and I decorated the house with balloons and colorful streamers. I am the one who made the fantastic birthday cake. Mother signaled when it was time to hide. As soon as Dad walked through the door, we yelled, "Surprise!"

Independent and Subordinate Clauses

Rules 6a–c *(pp. 113–117)*

OBJECTIVES

- To identify independent and subordinate clauses in sentences
- To complete sentences by adding independent clauses to subordinate clauses

Reference Note

For information on using **commas and coordinating conjunctions to join two independent clauses,** see page 297. For information about **using commas to join independent and subordinate clauses,** see page 299.

COMPUTER TIP

A computer can help you proofread your writing for subordinate clauses that are sentence fragments. Most grammar checkers point out sentences that seem incomplete. Grammar checkers are not perfect, though. Be sure to check your work for fragments yourself, and double-check any word group that the computer says is incomplete.

The Independent Clause

6b. An *independent* (or *main*) *clause* expresses a complete thought and can stand by itself as a sentence.

EXAMPLES   I woke up late this morning.

Do you know Joseph?

When an independent clause stands alone, it is called a sentence. Usually, the term *independent clause* is used only when such a clause is joined with another clause.

EXAMPLES   **My mother drove me to school.** [This entire sentence is an independent clause.]

My mother drove me to school, but **my brother rode his bicycle.** [This sentence contains two independent clauses.]

Since I missed the bus, **my mother drove me to school.** [This sentence contains one subordinate clause and one independent clause.]

The Subordinate Clause

6c. A *subordinate* (or *dependent*) *clause* does not express a complete thought and cannot stand by itself as a complete sentence.

Words such as *because, if, since, that, until, which,* and *whom* signal that the clauses following them may be subordinate. *Subordinate* means "lesser in rank or importance." A subordinate clause must be joined with at least one independent clause to make a sentence and express a complete thought.

SUBORDINATE CLAUSES	**if** the dress is too long
	that the veterinarian recommended
SENTENCES	**If the dress is too long,** we will hem it.
	The new food **that the veterinarian recommended** is good for our hamster.

Subordinate clauses may appear at the beginning, in the middle, or at the end of a sentence.

RESOURCES

Independent and Subordinate Clauses
Practice

- *Language & Sentence Skills Practice,* pp. 111–115
- *Developmental Language & Sentence Skills,* pp. 47–48

Exercise 1 **Identifying Independent and Subordinate Clauses**

Identify the italicized clause in each of the following sentences as <u>independent</u> or <u>subordinate</u>.

EXAMPLE 1. *If you know any modern music history,* then you are probably familiar with the Motown sound.
   1. subordinate

1. Do you recognize the entertainers *who are shown in the photographs on this page and the next*?
2. These performers had hit records in the 1950s and 1960s *when the music business in Detroit (the Motor City, or "Motown") was booming.*
3. Berry Gordy, *who founded the Motown record label,* began his business in a small office in Detroit.
4. He was a songwriter and producer, and *he was able to spot talent.*
5. Gordy went to clubs to hear local groups *whose sound he liked.*
6. The Miracles, *which was the first group discovered by Gordy,* had a lead singer named Smokey Robinson.
7. *Robinson was also a songwriter,* and Gordy included him in the Motown team of writers and musicians.

The Subordinate Clause **115**

DIRECT TEACHING

Modeling and Demonstration

The Clause. Model how to identify independent and subordinate clauses by using the examples *I woke up late this morning* and *if the dress is too long*. First, ask which word is the subject of the first example. (*I*) Next, ask which word or words are the verb. (*woke*) Then, ask if the clause expresses a complete thought and can stand by itself. (*yes*) Explain that this means the clause is an independent clause. Next, repeat the procedure with the second clause. Although the clause has a subject (*dress*) and a verb (*is*), it does not express a complete thought and cannot stand by itself; therefore, it is a subordinate clause. Now, have a volunteer, using another example from this chapter, demonstrate how to identify independent and subordinate clauses.

RETEACHING

Independent and Subordinate Clauses

Remind students about the meanings of the prefixes *in–* ("not") and *sub–* ("below" or "under"). *Independent*, or "not dependent," clauses can stand by themselves as sentences; *subordinate*, or "ranked below," clauses must be accompanied in sentences by an independent clause. Knowing these prefixes can help students distinguish between the two types of clauses.

DIRECT TEACHING

Phrases and Clauses

To help students distinguish between phrases, subordinate clauses, and independent clauses, divide the class into small groups. Provide each group with three signs: one that says *phrase,* one that says *independent clause,* and one that says *subordinate clause.* Then, write on the chalkboard or on a transparency the following group of words: *because I lost my book.*

Ask group members to confer and then to hold up the sign that correctly identifies the word group. Check to see that all groups have the right answer. [*subordinate clause*] Continue the activity with the following word groups. Then, have the members of each group take turns adding words to the phrases and subordinate clauses to make complete sentences.

1. around the beautiful, fragrant garden [*phrase*]
2. that I really want [*subordinate clause*]
3. any student can join [*independent clause*]
4. thinking about tonight's game [*phrase*]
5. as soon as the bell rings [*subordinate clause*]

DIFFERENTIATING INSTRUCTION

Learners Having Difficulty

Some students may find it easier to hear the difference between a complete and an incomplete thought than to recognize the difference visually. You or a student helper could read aloud the examples in this lesson.

MEETING THE CHALLENGE

To make your writing smoother, you can combine short, choppy sentences by changing some into subordinate clauses.
  Combine the following sentences.

  Our dog, Skippy, is five years old. He is a Yorkshire terrier.

  I visit my aunt in June. I will get to swim in a nearby lake.

POSSIBLE ANSWERS
Our dog, Skippy, who is five years old, is a Yorkshire terrier.
When I visit my aunt in June, I will get to swim in a nearby lake.

Reference Note
For information about **using subordinate clauses to combine sentences,** see page 425.

8. Gordy carefully managed all aspects of the Motown sound, *which is a special combination of rhythm and blues and soul.*
9. Diana Ross and the Supremes, Stevie Wonder, Marvin Gaye, the Four Tops, the Temptations, Gladys Knight and the Pips, and Michael Jackson are just some of the performers *that Gordy discovered.*
10. As you look carefully at the photographs again, *can you and your classmates recognize these music legends*?

Exercise 2 Identifying Subordinate Clauses

Identify the subordinate clause in each of the following sentences.

EXAMPLE 1. When you get up in the morning, do you look at your sleepy face in a mirror?
    1. When you get up in the morning

1. A mirror is a piece of polished metal or glass that is coated with a substance such as silver.
2. The most common type of mirror is the plane mirror, which is flat.
3. The image that is reflected in a plane mirror is reversed.
4. As you look into a mirror, your left hand seems to be the image's right hand.
5. When an image is reversed, it is called a mirror image.
6. A sailor who looks through the periscope of a submarine is using a system of lenses and mirrors in a tube to see above the water's surface.
7. Right-hand rearview mirrors on cars, which show a wide area of the road behind, are usually convex, or curved outward.
8. Drivers must be careful because convex mirrors make reflected objects appear far away.
9. Because the mirror in a flashlight is concave, or curved inward, it strengthens the light from a small lightbulb.
10. When you look in a concave mirror, you sometimes see a magnified reflection of yourself.

Oral Practice Writing Sentences with Subordinate Clauses

Read each of the following subordinate clauses aloud. Then, add an independent clause to make a complete sentence. Make your sentences interesting by using a variety of independent clauses.

EXAMPLES
1. who lives next door to us
1. *Have you or Peggy met the woman who lives next door to us?*
2. that Alexander bought
2. *The sleeping bag that Alexander bought was on sale.*

1. when I bought the CD
2. who won the contest
3. if my parents agree
4. as Jessye Norman began to sing
5. because we are going to a concert
6. that you made
7. who built the pyramids
8. for which this musician is famous
9. since the telephone was invented
10. whose paintings are now in the museum

The Adjective Clause

6d. An *adjective clause* is a subordinate clause that modifies a noun or a pronoun.

Like an adjective or an adjective phrase, an adjective clause may modify a noun or a pronoun. Unlike an adjective phrase, an adjective clause contains both a verb and its subject.

ADJECTIVE	a **blue** flower
ADJECTIVE PHRASE	a flower **with blue petals** [The phrase does not have a verb and its subject.]
ADJECTIVE CLAUSE	a flower **that has blue petals** [The clause does have a verb, *has,* and its subject, *that.*]

An adjective clause usually follows the word or words it modifies and tells *which one* or *what kind.*

The Subordinate Clause   **117**

RESOURCES
The Adjective Clause
Practice
- *Language & Sentence Skills Practice,* pp. 116–118
- *Developmental Language & Sentence Skills,* pp. 49–50

6d

Oral Practice Writing Sentences with Subordinate Clauses

ANSWERS
Sentences will vary. You may want to require that students vary the position of the subordinate clauses in their sentences.

The Adjective Clause
Rule 6d *(pp. 117–119)*

OBJECTIVES
- To identify adjective clauses and relative pronouns in sentences
- To complete sentences by supplying appropriate adjective clauses

DIFFERENTIATING INSTRUCTION

English-Language Learners
General Strategies. Students may have difficulty with adjective clauses that end with a verb, such as "I like the book *that Maria is reading.*" In some languages, it is considered awkward to end a clause with a verb. For instance, a Spanish speaker will invert the subject and the verb, as in the following sentence: "Me gusta el libro *que lee Maria."* English-language learners may invert the word order in this manner when writing in English.

APPLICATION

Relating to Writing

Discuss with students how unnecessary adjective clauses can contribute to wordiness in their writing. Use the following examples to show students how sentences can be revised to eliminate unnecessary adjective clauses.

1. This is the car <u>that I want</u>.
   Revision: I want this car.
2. My house has a door <u>that is red</u>.
   Revision: My house has a red door.
3. She wore a floral dress, <u>which was lovely</u>.
   Revision: She wore a lovely floral dress.

Ask students to highlight any adjective clauses in a piece of their own writing. Have students decide whether any of the sentences containing adjective clauses could be revised to reduce wordiness. Check students' revisions.

DIFFERENTIATING INSTRUCTION

Advanced Learners

A relative pronoun can perform various functions within the adjective clause it introduces. Write the following examples on the chalkboard, and ask students to give additional examples.

1. **Subject:** Elsa is a good friend <u>who</u> listens to my problems.
2. **Direct Object:** Have you read the story <u>that</u> I wrote?
3. **Object of a Preposition:** She is the woman from <u>whom</u> we bought the car.
4. **Modifier:** She is the artist <u>whose</u> painting took first place.

HELP

The relative pronoun *that* is used to refer both to people and to things. The relative pronoun *which* is used to refer to things.

EXAMPLES
She is the person **that** I met yesterday.

This is the CD **that** you should buy.

The bus, **which** is behind schedule, stops at the next corner.

Reference Note

For information about **when to use commas to set off adjective clauses,** see page 299.

EXAMPLES Emma Willard was the one **who founded the first women's college in the United States.** [The adjective clause modifies the pronoun *one*, telling *which one*.]

I want a bicycle **that I can ride over rough ground.** [The adjective clause modifies the noun *bicycle*, telling *what kind*.]

The Relative Pronoun

An adjective clause is usually introduced by a *relative pronoun*.

Commonly Used Relative Pronouns				
that	which	who	whom	whose

These words are called **relative pronouns** because they *relate* an adjective clause to the noun or pronoun that the clause modifies.

EXAMPLES A snorkel is a hollow tube **that lets a diver breathe underwater.** [The relative pronoun *that* begins the adjective clause and relates it to the noun *tube*.]

The team's mascot, **which is a horse,** is called Renegade. [The relative pronoun *which* begins the adjective clause and relates it to the noun *mascot*.]

Gwendolyn Brooks is the writer **who wrote *Annie Allen*.** [The relative pronoun *who* begins the adjective clause and relates it to the noun *writer*.]

Those **whose library books are overdue** must pay fines. [The relative pronoun *whose* begins the adjective clause and relates it to the pronoun *Those*.]

NOTE In some cases, the relative pronoun can be omitted.

EXAMPLE The person [**that** *or* **whom**] we met at the market was Mrs. Herrera.

Exercise 3 Identifying Adjective Clauses

Identify the adjective clause in each of the sentences on the next page. Underline the relative pronoun that begins the clause.

Chapter 6 The Clause

MINI-LESSON Grammar

Sentence Structure. Sentences can be classified by the kinds of clauses they contain.

- A simple sentence has one independent clause and no subordinate clauses.

   The **girls** on our team **want** new uniforms.

- A compound sentence has more than one independent clause and no subordinate clauses.

   We ordered new uniforms last year, but **they were** the wrong colors.

The Clause

EXAMPLE 1. The person who wrote the Declaration of Independence was Thomas Jefferson.
   1. *who wrote the Declaration of Independence*

1. In his later years, Jefferson lived at his home, Monticello, which he designed.
2. Jefferson planned a daily schedule that kept him busy all day.
3. He began each day by writing himself a note that recorded the morning temperature.
4. Then he did his writing, which included letters to friends and businesspeople.
5. Afterward, he ate breakfast, which was served around 9:00 A.M.
6. Jefferson, whose property included stables as well as farm fields, went horseback riding at noon.
7. Dinner, which began about 4:00 P.M., was a big meal.
8. From dinner until dark, he talked to friends and neighbors who came to visit.
9. His large family, whom he often spent time with, included twelve grandchildren.
10. Jefferson, whose interests ranged from art and architecture to biology and mathematics, read each night.

Exercise 4 Writing Appropriate Adjective Clauses

Complete each of the following sentences with an adjective clause. Then, underline the relative pronoun.

EXAMPLE 1. We read the Greek legend ____.
   1. *We read the Greek legend that tells the story of the Trojan horse.*

1. You should proofread every composition ____.
2. My best friend, ____, is a good student.
3. Mrs. Rivera, ____, was my fifth-grade teacher.
4. We heard a sound ____.
5. Our neighbors ____ are from Fez, Morocco.
6. The ship, ____, carried bananas.
7. Anyone ____ is excused from the final exam.
8. Carmen, can you tell us about the scientist ____?
9. Is Victor Hugo the author ____?
10. Wow! I didn't know you had a dog ____.

HELP
Remember, to be a clause, a word group must contain both a verb and its subject.

GRAMMAR

The Adverb Clause
Rule 6e (pp. 120–124)

OBJECTIVES
- To identify adverb clauses in sentences
- To complete sentences by writing adverb clauses

DIRECT TEACHING

Modeling and Demonstration

The Adverb Clause. Model how to identify an adverb clause by using the example *Because Jason was brave, he battled the fierce dragon.* First, ask students to identify the subordinate clause. [*Because Jason was brave*] Next, ask what question the clause answers. [*why*] Then, tell students that because the clause answers the question *why*, it is an adverb clause. Now, have a volunteer use another example from this chapter to demonstrate how to identify an adverb clause.

STYLE TIP

In most cases, deciding where to place an adverb clause is a matter of style, not correctness.

As he leapt across the gorge, Rex glanced back at his alien pursuers.

Rex glanced back at his alien pursuers **as he leapt across the gorge.**

Which sentence might you use in a science fiction story? The sentence to choose would be the one that looks and sounds better in context—the rest of the paragraph to which the sentence belongs.

Reference Note

For more information on **punctuating introductory adverb clauses,** see page 305.

The Adverb Clause

6e. An ***adverb clause*** is a subordinate clause that modifies a verb, an adjective, or an adverb.

Like an adverb or an adverb phrase, an adverb clause can modify a verb, an adjective, or an adverb. Unlike an adverb phrase, an adverb clause contains both a verb and its subject.

ADVERB	**Bravely,** Jason battled the fierce dragon.
ADVERB PHRASE	**With great bravery,** Jason battled the fierce dragon. [The phrase does not have both a verb and its subject.]
ADVERB CLAUSE	**Because Jason was brave,** he battled the fierce dragon. [The clause does have a verb and its subject.]

Adverb clauses answer the following questions: *How? When? Where? Why? To what extent? How much? How long?* and *Under what condition?*

EXAMPLES   I feel **as though I will never catch up.** [The adverb clause tells *how* I feel.]

After I finish painting my bookcases, I will call you. [The adverb clause tells *when* I will call you.]

I paint **where there is plenty of fresh air.** [The adverb clause tells *where* I paint.]

I have more work to do today **because I didn't paint yesterday.** [The adverb clause tells *why* I have more work to do.]

Jennifer can paint better **than Victor can.** [The adverb clause tells *to what extent* Jennifer can paint better.]

I will paint **until Mom comes home;** then I will clean my brushes and set the table for supper. [The adverb clause tells *how long* I will paint.]

If I paint for two more hours, I should be able to finish. [The adverb clause tells *under what condition* I should be able to finish.]

Notice in the preceding examples that adverb clauses may be placed in various positions in sentences. When an adverb clause comes at the beginning, it is usually followed by a comma.

RESOURCES

The Adverb Clause
Practice
- *Language & Sentence Skills Practice,* pp. 119–123
- *Developmental Language & Sentence Skills,* pp. 51–52

Subordinating Conjunctions

Adverb clauses begin with *subordinating conjunctions*.

Common Subordinating Conjunctions		
after	because	though
although	before	unless
as	how	until
as if	if	when
as long as	in order that	whenever
as much as	since	where
as soon as	so that	wherever
as though	than	while

Some words that are used as subordinating conjunctions, such as *after, as, before, since,* and *until,* can also be used as prepositions.

PREPOSITION	**Before** sunrise, we left for the cabin.
SUBORDINATING CONJUNCTION	**Before** the sun had risen, we left for the cabin.
PREPOSITION	In the nineteenth century, buffalo skins were used **as** blankets and clothing.
SUBORDINATING CONJUNCTION	Around 1900, **as** the buffalo became nearly extinct, conservationists fought for its protection.

Exercise 5 Identifying Adverb Clauses

Identify the adverb clause in each of the following sentences.

EXAMPLE   1. As long as they have been a people, the Chinese have been making kites.

1. As long as they have been a people

1. Although the following story is only a legend, many people believe that a kite like the one pictured on the next page may have saved the people of China's Han dynasty.
2. The Chinese were about to be attacked by an enemy army when an advisor to the emperor came up with a plan.
3. As the advisor stood beside an open window, his hat was lifted off by a strong wind.
4. He immediately called for a number of kites to be made so that they might be used to frighten the enemy.

DIRECT TEACHING

Correcting Misconceptions

Prepositions and Subordinating Conjunctions. Students may misidentify prepositions as subordinating conjunctions. Write these sentences on a chalkboard or on a transparency.
*We slept until late in the morning.
We couldn't leave until we cleaned our rooms.*
Tell students that in the first sentence, *until* is used as a preposition. In the second sentence *until* is used as a subordinating conjunction in the clause *until we cleaned our rooms.* Ask students to explain in their own words how to tell the difference between a prepositional phrase and a subordinate clause. [*A prepositional phrase does not contain a subject or verb, but a subordinate clause does.*]

DIFFERENTIATING INSTRUCTION

Advanced Learners

To help students see how adverb clauses clarify relationships between ideas and give coherence to paragraphs, write the following paragraph on the chalkboard:

> Last year we visited several antique shops. We were looking for an old radio to use in the spring play. We came to a small shop. We were sure it didn't have what we wanted. It had one radio—just the radio we needed.

Ask students to revise the sentences, using adverb clauses to subordinate some of the ideas. [*Possible revision: Last year we visited several antique shops because we were looking for an old radio to use in the spring play. When we came to a small shop, although we were sure it didn't have what we wanted, it had just the radio we needed.*]

EXTENSION

Relating to Literature

If the Edgar Allan Poe poem "Annabel Lee" is in your literature textbook, you could use the poem to give students practice identifying subordinate clauses and the words they modify. As a class, discuss the effects of Poe's use of clauses in this poem. [*Poe's use of the word* that *and his placement of adjective clauses help sustain the poem's rhythm.*]

Exercise 6 Writing Adverb Clauses

ANSWERS

Clauses will vary. You may want students to label the subjects and verbs of their clauses and to draw arrows from the adverb clauses to the words they modify.

---

5. The kite makers had no trouble finding lightweight bamboo for their kite frames <u>because bamboo grows widely in China</u>.
6. <u>As each frame was completed</u>, silk was stretched over it.
7. The emperor's advisor attached noisemakers to the kites <u>so that they would produce an eerie sound</u>.
8. He ordered his men to fly the kites in the darkest hour of night <u>because then the enemy would hear the kites but would not be able to see them</u>.
9. <u>Unless the advisor was wrong</u>, the enemy would think that the kites were gods warning them to retreat.
10. According to the legend, the enemy retreated <u>as if they were being chased by a fire-breathing dragon</u>.

David F. Jue, *Chinese Kites, How to Make and Fly Them.* Charles E. Tuttle Co. Inc., of Tokyo, Japan.

─ HELP ─
Remember, a clause contains both a verb and its subject.

Exercise 6 Writing Adverb Clauses

Complete each of the following sentences with an adverb clause. Then, underline the subordinating conjunction.

EXAMPLE 1. ____, digital cameras will become quite popular.
          1. *If I'm right*, digital cameras will become quite popular.

1. ____, everything seemed fresh and new.
2. The gears jammed ____.
3. ____, the African dancers began their routine.

122 Chapter 6 The Clause

Learning for Life

Essay Questions. Throughout their school years (and possibly beyond), students will be asked to write essays, generally in testing situations. Ask students to respond to one of the following questions by writing a short one- or two-paragraph essay.

1. Describe what you see yourself doing ten years from now.
2. Explain how studying language arts helps you in other subjects.
3. Summarize your favorite movie.

122 The Clause

4. From the trees, a Bengal tiger watched the herd ____.
5. ____, maybe he'll help you clean your room.
6. Call us ____.
7. ____, the cement mixer backed up to the wooden frame.
8. The buses have been running on time ____.
9. ____, street sweepers rolled slowly next to the curb.
10. His map looked ____.

Review A Identifying and Classifying Subordinate Clauses

Identify the subordinate clause in each of the following sentences. Then, classify each clause as an *adjective clause* or an *adverb clause*.

EXAMPLES
1. American history is filled with stories of people who performed heroic deeds.
   1. who performed heroic deeds—adjective clause

2. As the American colonists struggled for independence, women played important roles.
   2. As the American colonists struggled for independence—adverb clause

1. When you study the American Revolution, you may learn about the adventures of a woman known as Molly Pitcher.
2. Molly Pitcher, whose real name was Mary, was the daughter of farmers.
3. Although she was born in New Jersey, she moved to the Pennsylvania colony.
4. There she married William Hays, who was a barber.
5. Hays joined the colonial army when the Revolution began.
6. Mary Hays went to be with her husband in Monmouth, New Jersey, which was the site of a battle on a hot June day in 1778.
7. At first, she carried water to the soldiers so that they would not be overcome by the intense heat.
8. The soldiers nicknamed her "Molly Pitcher" because she carried the water in pitchers.
9. Later, when her husband collapsed from the heat, she took over his cannon.
10. George Washington, who was the commander of the Continental Army, made Molly an honorary sergeant.

> **Review B** Writing Sentences with Subordinate Clauses
>
> **ANSWERS**
> Sentences will vary. You may want students to label the subjects and verbs of their clauses and to draw arrows to the words the clauses modify.

Review B Writing Sentences with Subordinate Clauses

Write twenty different sentences of your own. In each sentence, include a subordinate clause that begins with one of the following words or word groups. Underline the subordinate clause. After the sentence, classify the subordinate clause as an *adjective clause* or an *adverb clause*.

EXAMPLES
1. so that
    1. We hurried so that we wouldn't miss the bus going downtown.—adverb clause
2. whom
    2. Jim Nakamura, whom I met at summer camp, is now my pen pal.—adjective clause

1. which
2. before
3. since
4. who
5. than
6. whose
7. as though
8. although
9. that
10. if
11. because
12. unless
13. as soon as
14. whom
15. while
16. whenever
17. after
18. where
19. as much as
20. wherever

CHAPTER 6

Chapter Review

A. Identifying Independent and Subordinate Clauses

Identify the italicized clause in each of the following sentences as an *independent* or a *subordinate clause*.

1. As Jawan walked to school, *he saw a strange sight*.
2. *If you go to the library*, you should take a look at the young adult section.
3. The book *that I read last night* was very scary!
4. Long after the rain had stopped, *the ground was still wet*.
5. If the trip is cancelled, *we can play tennis*.
6. *When the spin cycle stops*, please take the laundry out of the washing machine.
7. The shells *that they found* are still in the closet.
8. *Most people are asleep* when the morning newspaper is delivered.
9. Was the movie *that the reviewers liked* sold out?
10. Since we moved here from Chile, *we have met many people*.

B. Identifying Adjective and Adverb Clauses

Identify each italicized clause in the following sentences as an *adjective clause* or an *adverb clause*. Then, write the word each clause modifies.

11. We camped near Lake Arrowhead *when we went fishing last year*.
12. *Because the weather was cold*, I wore a sweater under my jacket.
13. The coat *that my mother bought for me* was blue.
14. *As she left her office*, Cletha heard the phone.
15. Vince hit the home run *that won the game*!
16. Everyone *who signed up for the marathon* should meet at 8:00 A.M. tomorrow in the school parking lot.
17. On Tuesday the Chavez family went to the Rex parade, *which is held every year in New Orleans during Mardi Gras*.

18. adv. [6e]	18. Larry is a little <u>taller</u> *than Dana is.*
19. adj. [6d]	19. The <u>CD</u> *that Rita wanted to buy* was out of stock.
20. adv. [6e]	20. Louise <u>stayed</u> home today *because she has a bad case of the flu.*
21. adv. [6e]	21. <u>Play</u> soccer *if you need more exercise.*
22. adv. [6e]	22. The turtle moves <u>faster</u> *than I expected.*
23. adj. [6d]	23. My older <u>sister</u>, *who is on the varsity basketball team,* practices after school every day.
24. adv. [6e]	24. *Since it was such a beautiful evening,* we <u>decided</u> to take a long walk.
25. adj. [6d]	25. Will the <u>students</u> *whose families observe the Jewish Sabbath* be excused early on Friday?

C. Identifying Subordinate Clauses

Identify the subordinate clause in each sentence. Then, classify the clause as an *adjective clause* or an *adverb clause*. Write *none* if the sentence does not contain a subordinate clause.

26. [6c, d]	26. The denim blue jeans <u>that are known as Levi's</u> have an interesting history.
27. none [6b, c]	27. They were created in 1873 by Levi Strauss.
28. [6c, d]	28. Strauss, <u>who had immigrated to the United States from Bavaria,</u> founded a clothing company called Levi Strauss & Co.
29. [6c, e]	29. Six years after his arrival in the United States, he sailed to San Francisco <u>because his sister and brother-in-law had a dry goods business there.</u>
30. [6c, d]	30. In 1872, Strauss had received a letter from Jacob Davis, a tailor in Nevada <u>who was one of his regular customers.</u>
31. [6c, e]	31. Davis told Strauss about riveting the pocket corners of work pants <u>so that the pants would be more durable.</u>
32. [6c, e]	32. <u>Since Davis lacked the money to patent this invention,</u> he asked Strauss to be his partner.
33. none [6b, c]	33. Both men were named as patent holders in 1873.
34. [6c, d]	34. The copper-riveted overalls were popular with working people <u>who needed tough but comfortable pants.</u>
35. [6c, d]	35. In 1880, the company, <u>whose sales had reached $2.4 million,</u> was selling denim pants to retailers for about $1.50 a pair.

36. Strauss died in 1902, four years before an earthquake and fire in San Francisco destroyed his company's factories.
37. After the earthquake, the company built a new factory that is still operating today.
38. The company suffered financially, as did many other businesses, during the Great Depression of the 1930s.
39. Since the 1940s, the pants have become increasingly fashionable among young people.
40. In the 1950s, when actors such as James Dean wore them in film roles, the jeans skyrocketed in popularity.

36. [6c, e]
37. [6c, d]
38. [6c, e]
39. none [6b, c]
40. [6c, e]

Writing Application
Using Clauses in a Manual

Subordinate Clauses Your class project for National Safety Week is to write a safety manual. Each class member will write one page of instructions telling what to do in a particular emergency. Use subordinating conjunctions to show the relationships between your ideas.

Prewriting Think of a specific emergency that you know how to handle. List the steps that someone should follow in this emergency. Number the steps in order. If you aren't sure of the order or don't know a particular step, stop writing and get the information you need.

Writing Use your prewriting list to begin your first draft. As you write, make your instructions as clear as possible. Define or explain terms that might be unfamiliar to your readers. Be sure that your instructions are in the right order.

Revising Read over your instructions to be sure that you've included all necessary information. Add, cut, or rearrange steps to make the instructions easy to follow. Be sure to use appropriate subordinating conjunctions to make the order of the steps clear.

Publishing Check your work carefully for any errors in grammar, punctuation, and spelling. To publish your class safety manual, gather all the pages and make booklets out of printouts or photocopies. Organize your topics alphabetically, or group them by kinds of emergencies.

HELP
A health teacher, the school nurse, or an organization such as the Red Cross should be able to provide information.

Reference Note
For information about **punctuating introductory adverb clauses**, see page 305.

APPLICATION
Writing Application
Scoring Rubric. While you will want to pay particular attention to students' use of the subordinating conjunctions, you will also want to evaluate the students' overall writing performance. You may want to give a split score to indicate development and clarity of the composition as well as grammar skills.

EXTENSION
Critical Thinking
Synthesis. Ask students to design posters that highlight important safety tips based on their instructions. For example, if a student writes instructions explaining how to vacate one's home during a fire, the student's poster might illustrate the importance of each family's planning an evacuation route in advance. During the publishing stage of the writing process, students can present their posters with their instructions.

CHAPTER 7

Kinds of Sentence Structure
Simple, Compound, Complex, and Compound-Complex Sentences

INTRODUCING THE CHAPTER

- The chapter discusses the four types of sentences classified according to structure—simple, compound, complex, and compound-complex. The types are taught in terms of independent and subordinate clauses.

- The chapter closes with a **Chapter Review**, which includes a **Writing Application** that asks students to write a letter using a variety of sentence structures.

- For help in integrating this chapter with writing assignments, use the **Teaching Strands** chart on pp. T24–T25.

HELP

You may wish to review Chapter 6 before completing this part of the Diagnostic Preview.

Numerals in brackets refer to rules tested by the items in the Diagnostic Preview.

1.–10. [6a–c]

Diagnostic Preview

A. Identifying and Classifying Clauses

Identify each clause in the following sentences. Then, classify each clause as an *independent clause* or a *subordinate clause*.

EXAMPLE
1. Students who are interested in attending the science fair at the community college should sign up now.
1. *Students should sign up now—independent clause; who are interested in attending the science fair at the community college—subordinate clause*

1. We did warm-up exercises before we practiced the routine.
2. The musical *West Side Story* is a modern version of the story of Romeo and Juliet.
3. The first poem in the book is about spring, and the second one is about autumn.
4. Molasses, which is made from sugar cane, is a thick brown liquid used for human food and animal feed.
5. Before the test we studied the chapter and did the chapter review exercises.
6. While our teacher discussed the formation of the African nation of Liberia, we took notes.

CHAPTER RESOURCES

Internet
- Web resources: go.hrw.com

Practice & Review
- *Language & Sentence Skills Practice*, pp. 131–137; 138–140
- *Language & Sentence Skills Practice Answer Key*, pp. 60–64

Application & Enrichment
- *Language & Sentence Skills Practice*, pp. 130, 141–142, 143
- *Language & Sentence Skills Practice Answer Key*, pp. 60, 64–65

7. It rained Saturday morning, but the sun came out in time for the opening of the Special Olympics.
8. The player whose performance is judged the best receives the Most Valuable Player Award.
9. Not all stringed instruments sound alike, for their shapes and the number of their strings vary.
10. The tourists that we saw wandering up Esplanade Avenue went to the Japanese ceramics exhibit after they had reached the museum.

B. Identifying Simple, Compound, Complex, and Compound-Complex Sentences

Identify each of the following sentences as *simple*, *compound*, *complex*, or *compound-complex*.

EXAMPLE   1. The Museum of Science and Industry, which is in Chicago, features a German submarine captured during World War II.
   1. complex

11. Either Ana or Lee will sing the opening song for the fair.
12. We visit the Liberty Bell whenever we go to Philadelphia.
13. Have you chosen a topic for your report yet, or are you still making your decision?
14. When George Washington Carver was working on soil improvement and plant diseases, the South was recovering from the Civil War, and his discoveries gave planters a competitive edge.
15. *A Tree Grows in Brooklyn*, which was written by Betty Smith, is one of my favorite books.
16. The call of a peacock sounds very much like that of a person in distress.
17. Although it was warm enough to go swimming on Monday, snow fell the next day.
18. The student whose photographs of American Indian cliff dwellings won the contest was interviewed on the local news.
19. The house looked completely empty when I first saw it, yet a party was going on in the backyard.
20. The game was tied at the top of the ninth inning, but then Earlene hit a home run.

11. s. [7a]
12. cx. [7c]
13. cd. [7b]
14. cc. [7d]
15. cx. [7c]
16. s. [7a]
17. cx. [7c]
18. cx. [7c]
19. cc. [7d]
20. cd. [7b]

ASSESSING

Entry-Level Assessment

Diagnostic Preview. Part A of this informal **Diagnostic Preview** examines students' ability to identify clauses and to classify clauses as independent and subordinate. Part B requires students to classify sentences by structure. You may wish to use this preview to determine students' knowledge of the different types of sentences. You can also monitor students' writing to gauge how well they incorporate the different types of sentences into their compositions.

Differentiating Instruction

- *Developmental Language & Sentence Skills Guided Practice*, pp. 53–56
- *Developmental Language & Sentence Skills Guided Practice Teacher's Notes and Answer Key*, p. 14

Assessment

- *Holt Handbook Chapter Tests with Answer Key*, pp. 13–14, 46

PRETEACHING

Lesson Starter
Motivating. To demonstrate that using a variety of sentence types helps make writing interesting, read the following paragraph to students.

> I am nervous and excited. The championship game is tomorrow. Our team is ready. We have been practicing for months. The other team is good. We are better. We will win. I know it.

Explain to students that the repetitive use of short, simple sentences can make writing seem monotonous. Write the above paragraph on the chalkboard, and ask students to help you revise it. Upon completion, point out the use of different sentence types. [Possible revision: I am nervous and excited because the championship game is tomorrow. Our team is ready, as we have been practicing for months. The other team is good, but we are better. I know that we will win.]

The Simple Sentence
Rule 7a (pp. 130–131)

OBJECTIVE
- To identify subjects and verbs in simple sentences

HELP
Remember that an independent clause contains a subject and a verb, expresses a complete thought, and can stand by itself as a sentence. A subordinate clause also contains a subject and a verb, but it does not express a complete thought and cannot stand alone.

INDEPENDENT CLAUSE
Dr. Martin has a successful medical practice in Cedar Park.

SUBORDINATE CLAUSE
that she has built during the last ten years

Reference Note
For information on **independent and subordinate clauses,** see Chapter 6.

Reference Note
For information on the **understood subject,** see page 19.

HELP
Some sentences in Exercise 1 have a compound subject, a compound verb, or both.

The Simple Sentence

7a. A *simple sentence* contains one independent clause and no subordinate clauses.

EXAMPLES
         S   V
A good rain will help the farmers.

                 V   S
Up for the rebound leaped Reggie.

  V   S
Where are my keys?

     V
Please put that down near the table in the corner.
[The understood subject is *you*.]

A simple sentence may have a compound subject, a compound verb, or both.

EXAMPLES
    S   S   V
Chalupas and **fajitas are** two popular Mexican dishes.
[compound subject]

  S   V   V
Kelly read *The Planet of Junior Brown* and **reported** on it last week. [compound verb]

    S   S   V   V
The **dog** and the **kitten lay** there and **napped.**
[compound subject and compound verb]

Exercise 1 Identifying Subjects and Verbs in Simple Sentences

Identify the subjects and the verbs in each of the following sentences.

EXAMPLE 1. I enjoy urban life but need to escape from the city once in a while.
           1. *I—subject; enjoy, need—verbs*

1. My favorite escape from city life is the green world of Central Park in New York City.
2. Its beautiful woods and relaxing outdoor activities are just a few minutes from our apartment.

---

130 **Chapter 7** Kinds of Sentence Structure

RESOURCES

The Simple Sentence

Practice
- *Language & Sentence Skills Practice,* p. 131

3. The enormous size of the park, however, can sometimes be a problem.
4. Often, I take this map with me for guidance.
5. Using the map, I can easily find the zoo, the band shell, and the Lost Waterfall.
6. In the summertime my brothers and I row boats on the lake, climb huge rock slabs, and have picnics in the Sheep Meadow.
7. I also watch birds and often wander around the park in search of my favorite species.
8. Last month a pair of purple finches followed me along the pond.
9. Near Heckscher Playground, the birds tired of the game and flew off.
10. In Central Park my family and I can enjoy a little bit of nature in the middle of a bustling city.

The Compound Sentence

7b. A *compound sentence* contains two or more independent clauses and no subordinate clauses.

INDEPENDENT CLAUSE	Melvina wrote about her mother's aunt
INDEPENDENT CLAUSE	Leroy wrote about his cousin from Jamaica
COMPOUND SENTENCE	Melvina wrote about her mother's aunt, and Leroy wrote about his cousin from Jamaica.

The independent clauses of a compound sentence are usually joined by a comma and a coordinating conjunction (*and, but, for, nor, or, so,* or *yet*).

EXAMPLES A variety of fruits and vegetables should be a part of everyone's diet, **for** they supply many important vitamins.

Kathryn's scene is in the last act of the play, **so** she must wait in the wings for her cue.

No one was injured in the fire, **but** several homes were destroyed, **and** many trees burned down.

Reference Note
For more about using **commas in compound sentences,** see page 297.

The Compound Sentence   131

The Compound Sentence
Practice
- *Language & Sentence Skills Practice,* pp. 132–133
- *Developmental Language & Sentence Skills,* pp. 53–54

DIRECT TEACHING

Modeling and Demonstration

Identifying Compound Sentences. Model how to identify a compound sentence by using the example *Kathryn's scene is in the last act of the play, so she must wait in the wings for her cue.* First, ask students to identify the subject or subjects. [*scene, she*] Next, have them identify the verb or verbs. [*is, must wait*] Then, ask students whether the sentence has a comma and a coordinating conjunction. [*yes*] Next, ask students how many independent clauses the sentence has. [*two*] Then, ask students if the sentence has any subordinate clauses. [*no*] Explain to students that the sentence is a compound sentence. Now, have a volunteer use another example from this chapter to demonstrate how to identify a compound sentence.

DIFFERENTIATING INSTRUCTION

English-Language Learners

General Strategies. In many languages, the ordering of sentence elements is much less restricted than it is in English. Consequently, English-language learners may have problems identifying subjects and verbs in sentences. Start by having students identify subjects and verbs in simple sentences. Once students have mastered doing so, have them move on to compound sentences.

Reference Note

For more about using **semicolons in compound sentences,** see page 310.

The independent clauses of a compound sentence may be joined by a semicolon.

EXAMPLES Pedro Menéndez de Avilés founded St. Augustine, the first permanent European settlement in the United States; he also established six other colonies in the Southeast.

My favorite places are Miami, Florida, and Aspen, Colorado; Bernie's favorites are San Diego, California, and Seattle, Washington.

Exercise 2 Identifying Subjects and Verbs in Compound Sentences

Identify the subject and verb in each independent clause. Then, give the punctuation mark and coordinating conjunction (if there is one) that join the clauses.

EXAMPLE 1. A newspaper reporter will speak to our class next week, and we will learn about careers in journalism.
1. *reporter*—subject; *will speak*—verb; *we*—subject; *will learn*—verb; comma + *and*

1. Ruth Benedict was a respected anthropologist, and Margaret Mead was one of her students. **1.** comma + *and*
2. An area's weather may change rapidly, but its climate changes very slowly. **2.** comma + *but*
3. Linh Phan lived in Vietnam for many years, so he could tell us about Vietnamese foods such as *nuoc mam*. **3.** comma + *so*
4. Students may prepare their reports on the computer, or they may write them neatly. **4.** comma + *or*
5. Our apartment manager is kind, yet she will not allow pets in the building. **5.** comma + *yet*
6. Daniel Boone had no formal education, but he could read and write. **6.** comma + *but*
7. Sofia's favorite dance is the samba; Elena enjoys the merengue. **7.** semicolon
8. Benjamin Franklin is known for his inventions, and he should also be remembered for his work during the Constitutional Convention. **8.** comma + *and*
9. Sheena did not play soccer; she had sprained her ankle. **9.** semicolon
10. They did not watch the shuttle take off, nor did they watch it land. **10.** comma + *nor*

MINI-LESSON Mechanics

Commas in Compound Sentences. Correct comma usage depends upon students' ability to distinguish compound sentences from simple sentences with compound verbs. Write the following sentences on the chalkboard, and work with the class to punctuate them correctly.

1. Maureen stepped up to the plate[,] but she looked back at the bench for encouragement.
2. The ball soared through the air and

Chapter 7 Kinds of Sentence Structure

Simple Sentence or Compound Sentence?

A simple sentence has only one independent clause. It may have a compound subject or a compound verb or both.

A compound sentence has two or more independent clauses. Each independent clause has its own subject and verb. Any of the independent clauses in a compound sentence may have a compound subject, a compound verb, or both.

	S S V
SIMPLE SENTENCE	Kim and Maureen read each other's short stories
	V
	and made many suggestions for improvements. [compound subject and compound verb]

	S S V
COMPOUND SENTENCE	Kim and Maureen read each other's stories,
	S V
	and they gave each other suggestions for improvements. [The first independent clause has a compound subject and a single verb. The second independent clause has a single subject and a single verb.]

NOTE When a subject is repeated after a coordinating conjunction, the sentence is not simple.

	S V
SIMPLE SENTENCE	**We studied** the artist Romare Bearden **and**
	V
	went to an exhibit of his paintings.

	S V
COMPOUND SENTENCE	**We studied** the artist Romare Bearden, **and**
	S V
	we went to an exhibit of his paintings.

Exercise 3 Distinguishing Compound Sentences from Sentences with Compound Subjects or Compound Verbs

Identify the subjects and verbs in each of the sentences on the following page. Then, identify each sentence as either *simple* or *compound*.

The Compound Sentence **133**

DIRECT TEACHING

Correcting Misconceptions

Compound Sentences and Simple Sentences. Students may have problems telling the difference between compound sentences and simple sentences with compound subjects and verbs. Write these sentences on a chalkboard or on a transparency.

Delilah called her friend and invited him to a concert.

Delilah called her friend, and she invited him to a concert.

Tell students that although the first sentence has two verbs, it is a simple sentence, since it has only one subject: *Delilah.* The second sentence has two subjects—*Delilah* and *she*—each with its own verb, so it is a compound sentence. Tell students that if a subject is repeated after a comma and a coordinating conjunction, the sentence is not simple.

EXTENSION

Relating to Literature

The Emily Dickinson poem "I'm Nobody!" uses mainly simple sentences. If your literature book contains this poem, have students read it and discuss how the lack of variation in sentence types affects the poem. [*Students might say that the repetition of short, simple sentences gives the poem rhythm or creates a bold, strong feeling and a sense of immediacy.*]

---

landed just short of the fence.

Explain that the first sentence has two independent clauses and is a compound sentence; therefore, a comma is needed before the coordinating conjunction. The second sentence is not compound; the second verb has the same subject as the first. Therefore, no comma is needed.

Ask students to locate pieces of their own writing and to use this method to evaluate comma usage in any compound sentences.

The Compound Sentence **133**

GRAMMAR

TECHNOLOGY TIP

If possible, have students use a computer program designed to check for grammatical and stylistic errors. Such programs can identify such relevant errors as comma splices, run-on sentences, and sentence fragments. Common mistakes—for example, forgetting commas before coordinating conjunctions or joining two subordinate clauses to form a fragment—will be highlighted immediately for the student.

Some programs also evaluate students' ability to vary sentence types and, therefore, help to increase the readability of writing. If possible, have students run such a program on samples of their writing.

TEACHING TIP

Exercise 3 In many dictionaries, *rain forest* (sentence 8) and *raw materials* (sentence 10) are classified as compound nouns. You may want to remind students that a compound noun is two or more words used together as a single noun. Have students find *rain forest* and *raw material* in a dictionary.

EXAMPLES

1. A rain forest is a tropical evergreen forest and has heavy rains throughout the year.
   1. rain forest—subject; is, has—verbs; simple

2. The trees and other plants in a rain forest grow close together, and they rise to different heights.
   2. trees, plants—subjects; grow—verb; they—subject; rise—verb; compound

1. The Amazon River is located in South America and is one of the longest rivers in the world. **1. simp.**
2. The Amazon begins in Peru, and it flows across Brazil to the Atlantic Ocean. **2. comp.**
3. This river carries more water than any other river and drains about one fifth of the earth's entire freshwater supply. **3. simp.**
4. The Amazon is actually a network of several rivers, but most people think of these combined rivers as only one river. **4. comp.**
5. These rivers drain the largest rainy area in the world, and during the flood season, the main river often overflows its banks. **5. comp.**
6. In the photo at the left, the Amazon does twist and curve. **6. simp.**
7. Generally, it follows a fairly straight course and flows at an average rate of about one and one-half miles an hour during the dry season. **7. simp.**
8. The Amazon rain forest is only two hundred miles wide along the Atlantic, but it stretches to twelve hundred miles wide at the foot of the Andes Mountains in Peru. **8. comp.**
9. The variety of plant life in the Amazon rain forest is remarkable; in fact, of all rain forests in the world, this area may contain the greatest number of plant species. **9. comp.**
10. Raw materials are shipped directly from ports deep in the rain forest, for oceangoing ships can sail more than two thousand miles up the Amazon. **10. comp.**

134 Chapter 7 Kinds of Sentence Structure

CONTENT-AREA CONNECTIONS

Science

Compound Elements. Just as a compound sentence is formed by joining two or more independent clauses, most matter is made of two or more elements joined together to form a compound. For example, water is made of two parts hydrogen and one part oxygen (H_2O). Ask students whether they know of any other compounds. [salt—sodium and chlorine (NaCl); carbon dioxide—carbon and oxygen (CO_2)]

The Complex Sentence

7c. A *complex sentence* contains one independent clause and at least one subordinate clause.

Two kinds of subordinate clauses are adjective clauses and adverb clauses. Adjective clauses usually begin with relative pronouns such as *who, whom, whose, which,* and *that.* Adverb clauses begin with subordinating conjunctions such as *after, as, because, if, since,* and *when.*

EXAMPLES The boy **who left** is my cousin. [complex sentence with adjective clause]

When I hear classical music, I think of Aunt Sofia. [complex sentence with adverb clause]

One interesting annual event **that is held in the Southwest** is the Inter-Tribal Indian Ceremonial, **which involves many different American Indian peoples.** [complex sentence with two adjective clauses]

Oral Practice — Identifying Subordinate Clauses

Read each of the following sentences aloud, and identify the subordinate clause. Finally, identify the relative pronoun or subordinating conjunction that begins the subordinate clause.

EXAMPLES
1. Helen Keller, who overcame severe physical impairments, showed great determination.
   1. *who overcame severe physical impairments—who*
2. Keller was fortunate because she had such a skillful and loving teacher.
   2. *because she had such a skillful and loving teacher—because*

1. Helen Keller, who is shown in the photograph at right, became very ill as a small child.
2. After she recovered from the illness, she could no longer see or hear.
3. Because she could not hear, she also lost her ability to speak.

Reference Note
For more information about **adjective clauses**, see page 117. For more about **adverb clauses**, see page 120. For more about **relative pronouns**, see page 118. For more about **subordinating conjunctions**, see page 121.

Reference Note
For information on using **commas with subordinate clauses**, see page 299.

The Complex Sentence
Rule 7c *(pp. 135–137)*

OBJECTIVE
- To identify subordinate clauses, subordinating conjunctions, and relative pronouns

DIRECT TEACHING

Modeling and Demonstration

Identifying Complex Sentences. Model how to identify a complex sentence by using the example *The boy who left is my cousin.* First, ask students how many independent clauses the sentence has. [one] Then, ask students whether the sentence has any subordinate clauses. [yes—*who left*] Explain to students that the sentence is a complex sentence. Now, have a volunteer use another example from this chapter to demonstrate how to identify a complex sentence.

RESOURCES

The Complex Sentence
Practice
- *Language & Sentence Skills Practice,* pp. 134–135

RETEACHING

Complex Sentences

Activity. To help students understand the structure of a complex sentence, diagram on the chalkboard several of the example sentences on p. 135.

When I hear classical music, I think of Aunt Sofia.

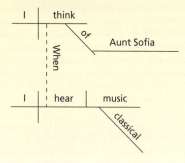

Have students diagram other sentences on this page. For additional instruction and practice in sentence diagramming, refer students to **Chapter 19: Sentence Diagramming**.

PRACTICE

Guided and Independent

Review A You may want to use the first five items in **Review A** as guided practice. Then, have students complete the exercise as independent practice. **HOMEWORK**

4. Helen's parents asked Alexander Graham Bell, who trained teachers of people with hearing impairments, for his advice about the child's education.
5. Upon Bell's suggestion, a special teacher, whose name was Anne Sullivan, stayed at the Kellers' home to teach Helen.
6. Sullivan spelled words into Helen's hand as the child touched the object represented by the word.
7. From this basic understanding of language, Helen went on to learn Braille, which is the alphabet used by people with visual impairments.
8. Sullivan, whose own vision had been partly restored by surgery, remained with Helen for many years.
9. Because she had triumphed over her impairments, Helen Keller was awarded the Medal of Freedom.
10. Keller's autobiography, which is titled *The Story of My Life*, tells about her remarkable achievements.

Review A Classifying Simple, Compound, and Complex Sentences

Classify each of the following sentences as *simple*, *compound*, or *complex*.

EXAMPLE 1. The Mississippi River, which begins in the town of Lake Itasca, Minnesota, is the setting for many of Mark Twain's stories.
    1. complex

1. I drew an illustration for a poem that was written by Robert Hayden. **1. cx.**
2. The Olympic skaters felt anxious, but they still performed their routine perfectly. **2. comp.**
3. Kamehameha Day is an American holiday that honors the king who united the islands of Hawaii. **3. cx.**
4. For the first time in his life, Luke saw the ocean. **4. simp.**
5. If you had a choice, would you rather visit China or Japan? **5. cx.**
6. The bull was donated to the children's zoo by the people who bought it at the auction. **6. cx.**
7. Lookout Mountain was the site of a battle during the Civil War. **7. simp.**
8. The guide led us through Mammoth Cave; she explained the difference between stalactites and stalagmites. **8. comp.**
9. Wilhelm Steinitz of Austria became famous after he was officially recognized as the first world champion of chess. **9. cx.**
10. Amy Tan is the author of the book *The Joy Luck Club*; it was published in 1989. **10. comp.**

The Compound-Complex Sentence

7d. A *compound-complex sentence* contains two or more independent clauses and at least one subordinate clause.

In the examples below, independent clauses are underlined once. Subordinate clauses are underlined twice.

EXAMPLES

        S   V   S   V
The band began to play, and Clarissa was pulled onto
                          S   V
the floor for a dance that was starting. [compound-complex sentence with adjective clause]

            S   V   S   V
Whenever we go on vacation, our neighbors mow our
     S   V
yard, and they collect our mail. [compound-complex sentence with adverb clause]

MEETING THE CHALLENGE

Simple sentences are best used to express single ideas. To describe more complicated ideas and to show how the ideas fit together, use compound and complex sentences.

Revise the sentences below to include at least one compound or complex sentence.

We went camping in the national park. Darla saw a snake. At first she was afraid. Then she looked more closely at it.

POSSIBLE ANSWER
When we went camping in the national park, Darla saw a snake. At first she was afraid, but then she looked more closely at it.

Reference Note
For more about **adjective and adverb clauses**, see pages 117 and 120.

EXTENSION

Simple, Compound, and Complex Sentences

Writers often adjust the complexity of their language and sentence structure so that it is appropriate to their audience. To illustrate, divide the class into small mixed-ability groups and ask each group to rewrite a simple children's story, gearing the revision to an audience of their peers. You may want to provide a stack of children's books for students or ask students to bring the books in advance. Because children's stories are often written in short, simple sentences, ask students to use a mixture of simple, compound, and complex sentences in their revisions. Then, ask volunteers from each group to read aloud both versions of their stories.

The Compound-Complex Sentence
Rule 7d (pp. 137–140)

OBJECTIVE
- To identify compound, complex, and compound-complex sentences

---

RESOURCES
The Compound-Complex Sentence
Practice
- *Language & Sentence Skills Practice,* pp. 136–137
- *Developmental Language & Sentence Skills,* pp. 55–56

Direct Teaching

Modeling and Demonstration

Identifying Compound-Complex Sentences. Model how to identify a compound-complex sentence by using the example *The band began to play, and Clarissa was pulled onto the floor for a dance that was starting.* First, ask students how many independent clauses the sentence has. [two—*The band began to play* and *Clarissa was pulled onto the floor for a dance*] Then, ask students whether the sentence has any subordinate clauses. [yes—*that was starting*] Explain to students that the sentence is a compound-complex sentence. Now, have a volunteer use another example from this chapter to demonstrate how to identify a compound-complex sentence.

COMPUTER TIP
A computer can help you focus on sentence length and structure in your writing. Programs are now available that can tell you the average number of words in your sentences. Such programs can also tell you how many different kinds of sentences you used. You can compare your numbers with the averages for students at your grade level. Using these programs, you can easily see which sentence structures you have mastered and which ones need work.

Exercise 4 **Identifying Compound, Complex, and Compound-Complex Sentences**

Identify each of the following sentences as either *compound*, *complex*, or *compound-complex*.

EXAMPLE 1. I'll sweep the porch, and Ben will start supper before Mom gets home.
 1. compound-complex

1. If you've never tried Indian curry, try some of Usha's. **1. cx.**
2. The disk drive light went on, and the drive motor whirred, but the computer would not read the disk. **2. cd.**
3. Although the river appeared calm, crocodiles lay motionless beneath the surface. **3. cx.**
4. Several small herds of mustangs roam these hills; we're going to find them. **4. cd.**
5. An antique wagon, whose wheels once rolled along the Chisholm Trail, stood next to the barn. **5. cx.**
6. You can talk to me whenever you have a problem, or you can talk to your mom. **6. cc.**
7. Since daylight saving time started, the sky doesn't get dark until late, and that just doesn't seem right to me. **7. cc.**
8. The plaster, which had been given a rough texture, cast shadows on itself. **8. cx.**
9. They don't have the book that we need, so let's go to the library. **9. cc.**
10. Did you really live in Nairobi, or are you just kidding? **10. cd.**

Review B **Classifying Simple, Compound, Complex, and Compound-Complex Sentences**

Classify each of the following sentences as *simple*, *compound*, *complex*, or *compound-complex*.

EXAMPLE 1. The Iroquois people traditionally held a Green Corn Festival in August when their crops were ready for harvesting.
 1. complex

1. For the early Iroquois, the Green Corn Festival was a celebration that included many events, so it often lasted several days. **1. cc.**
2. During the celebration, all children who had been born since midwinter received their names. **2. cx.**

138 Chapter 7 Kinds of Sentence Structure

Learning for Life

Continued on pp. 139–140

Anecdotes. This activity will focus on including a variety of sentence structures to add interest to anecdotes.

Explain to students that although anecdotes—brief, sometimes amusing retellings of events—are common to everyday conversation, they also play an important part in compositions and speeches. Anecdotes can catch an audience's attention in an introduction, elaborate on a main idea in the body of the speech or composition, or tie material together in the closing.

3. Iroquois leaders made speeches, and adults and children listened to them carefully. **3. cd.**
4. In one traditional speech, the leader would give thanks for the harvest. **4. s.**
5. After they had heard the speeches, the people sang and danced. **5. cx.**
6. On the second day of the festival, the people performed a special dance; during the dance they gave thanks for the sun, the moon, and the stars. **6. cd.**
7. On the third day, the Iroquois gave thanks for the helpfulness of their neighbors and for good luck. **7. s.**
8. The festival ended on the fourth day when teams of young people would play a bowling game. **8. cx.**
9. During the festival the people renewed their friendships, and they rejoiced in their harmony with nature. **9. cd.**
10. This Iroquois festival resembles the U.S. Thanksgiving holiday, which has its roots in similar American Indian celebrations. **10. cx.**

The Corn Dance

Review C — Writing Simple, Compound, Complex, and Compound-Complex Sentences

Write ten sentences of your own, following the guidelines given below.

EXAMPLE 1. Write a simple sentence with a compound subject.
   1. *Jorge and Pilar gave me their recipe for guacamole.*

1. Write a simple sentence with a compound verb.

The Compound-Complex Sentence   **139**

DIFFERENTIATING INSTRUCTION

Advanced Learners
To give students more practice with compound-complex sentences, divide the class into groups of three students each. One student will write a simple sentence, such as "My dog has fleas," and pass the piece of paper with this sentence to the next student. The second student will add a subordinate clause such as "because he sleeps outside." This student will pass the paper along to the third group member, who will add a comma, a coordinating conjunction, and another independent clause such as "he scratches all the time." The final compound-complex sentence would read "Because he sleeps outside, my dog has fleas, so he scratches all the time." Have the group work together to correct punctuation in the final sentence. Each group can repeat this exercise after switching roles.

Ask each student to write a brief anecdote that illustrates a point. You might want to provide the following topic sentences for students having trouble getting started.

1. Small acts of kindness can spread joy.
2. The traffic in the school halls is getting worse every day.
3. The ability to read can save lives.
4. My young cousin does the cutest things.

2. Write a simple sentence with a compound subject and a compound verb.
3. Write a compound sentence with two independent clauses joined by a comma and the coordinating conjunction *and*.
4. Write a compound sentence with two independent clauses joined by a comma and the coordinating conjunction *but*.
5. Write a compound sentence with two independent clauses joined by a semicolon.
6. Write a compound sentence with three independent clauses.
7. Write a complex sentence with an adjective clause.
8. Write a complex sentence with an adverb clause.
9. Write a compound-complex sentence with an adjective clause.
10. Write a compound-complex sentence with an adverb clause.

Answers
Review C
Sentences will vary. Here are some possibilities:
1. Emilia sang and danced at the talent show.
2. Juan and Kim went to the dance and met Steve.
3. Silvia found the scissors, and Lily searched for paper.
4. I wanted to go to the show, but he wanted to stay home.
5. Alex played tennis after school; Mia went to soccer practice.
6. Eric sliced tomatoes, Maria cut bell peppers, and Selena cleared the table.
7. Some of the sailors who took part in the mutiny on the British ship *Bounty* settled Pitcairn Island.
8. When I watch Martha Graham's performances, I feel like studying dance.
9. I have read several novels this month, and the one that I like best is *Animal Farm*.
10. When Bill left, he locked the door, but he forgot to turn off the lights.

Learning for Life

Continued from p. 139

Encourage students to include a variety of sentence structures in their anecdotes. You might want to share the following model.

The traffic in the school halls is getting worse every day. Just yesterday when I had an appointment to see the principal, I was running late. People were shoulder-to-shoulder in one hall, so I tried another to save time. What a mistake that was!

CHAPTER 7

Numerals in brackets refer to the rules tested by the items in the Chapter Review.

1.–10. [6a–c]

Chapter Review

A. Identifying Independent and Subordinate Clauses

Identify each clause in the following sentences. Then, classify each clause as an *independent clause* or a *subordinate clause*.

1. Yvette raked the leaves, and Tito mowed the lawn.
2. Lupe and Ben went to the park so that they could watch the fireworks display.
3. Carl and I chose enchiladas instead of sandwiches from the cafeteria's menu.
4. The new camp that offers instruction in computer programming will be in session from August 17 through August 28.
5. The rain changed to snow that was mixed with sleet.
6. Practice your tai chi exercises when you go to the beach.
7. My grandparents, who enjoy exciting vacations, visited Nepal last year.
8. Since last year Simone has grown three inches, but she still can't reach the top shelf in the kitchen.
9. Will Martin lend me this book by Jamaica Kincaid when he is through with it?
10. Aretha hopes to be a veterinarian because she likes to be around animals.

B. Identifying Simple and Compound Sentences

Classify each of the following sentences as *simple* or *compound*.

11. s. [7a]
12. cd. [7b]
13. cd. [7b]
14. s. [7a]
15. cd. [7b]

11. Do Nathan and Shenille read only science fiction or fantasy short stories?
12. My sister and brother-in-law live in Colorado, and they raise sheep and grow fruit trees.
13. Chai wants to walk to the theater, but I want to take the bus.
14. Aunt Evelyn and Uncle Michael are both surgeons and work at Riverside Hospital.
15. The good queen pardoned the jester, for he had meant no real harm.

ASSESSING

Monitoring Progress

Chapter Review. The **Chapter Review** asks students to identify simple, compound, complex, and compound-complex sentences. The results can be compared to those on the **Diagnostic Preview** (page 128) to assess student progress. You may want to work out specific goals for mastering essential information with individual students who are still having difficulty.

RESOURCES

Kinds of Sentence Structure

Review
- *Language & Sentence Skills Practice,* pp. 138–140

Assessment
- *Holt Handbook Chapter Tests with Answer Key,* pp. 13–14, 46

16. **s.** [7a]
17. **cd.** [7b]
18. **s.** [7a]
19. **s.** [7a]
20. **cd.** [7b]

16. Taking the train, Mei-Ling and her parents can be in Chicago in two hours.
17. Blair is interested in becoming an astronaut, so she wrote to NASA for information.
18. Tate laid out the patio and built it himself.
19. After eating, Marcia's cat Bartinka likes to take a long nap.
20. Mike designed and constructed the sets for the play, and Mary Anne designed the costumes and makeup.

C. Identifying Compound and Complex Sentences

Identify each of the following sentences as *compound* or *complex*. If the sentence is compound, write the comma and coordinating conjunction or the semicolon that joins the clauses. If the sentence is complex, write the relative pronoun or subordinating conjunction that joins the clauses.

21. **cx.**—which [7c]
22. **cx.**—who [7c]
23. **cd.**—comma + *and* [7b]
24. **cx.**—because [7c]
25. **cd.**—semicolon [7b]
26. **cd.**—comma + *and* [7b]
27. **cx.**—which [7c]
28. **cd.**—comma + *and* [7b]
29. **cx.**—since [7c]
30. **cd.**—comma + *so* [7b]

21. Nineteenth-century shopkeepers often attracted customers by placing a carved wooden figure, which was called a shop figure, outside their shops.
22. The shop figures were usually carved by ship carvers, who had learned to carve figures by creating ship figureheads.
23. The figures cost a great deal to make, and they were expensive to maintain.
24. Many shopkeepers were upset because the figures were so very costly.
25. Many of the wooden figures were of politicians and baseball players; others represented American Indians.
26. One surviving figure represents Father Time, and another one represents a New York City firefighter.
27. The firefighter, which commemorates Columbian Engine Company 14, now stands in the New York City Fire Museum.
28. The figures were popular between the 1840s and the 1890s, and during that time they actually became a fad.
29. By the end of the century, the carved shop figure was no longer widely used since new types of advertising had become available.
30. People saw shop figures as old-fashioned, so shopkeepers stopped using them.

D. Classifying Compound, Complex, and Compound-Complex Sentences

Classify each of the following sentences as *compound*, *complex*, or *compound-complex*.

31. Islam, which originated in Arabia, is the religion of the Muslims, and it is based on a belief in one God.
32. Most Muslims live in Africa, the Middle East, and Malaysia; in recent years many have come to the United States and have brought their religion with them.
33. Some American Muslims are members of the Nation of Islam, which was founded in the United States after World War II.
34. When a mosque was opened in New York in May 1991, religious leaders and other Muslims went there to pray.
35. Some worshipers wore the traditional clothing of their homelands; others were dressed in typical American clothes.
36. Muslims were particularly pleased that the new mosque opened in the spring.
37. The Muslim month of fasting, which is called Ramadan, had just ended, so the holiday after Ramadan could be celebrated in the new house of worship.
38. Although Muslims share a common religion, their languages differ.
39. Many Muslims speak Arabic, but those in Iran, Turkey, and neighboring countries, for example, speak other languages.
40. Of course, Muslims who were born in the United States generally speak English, and many Muslims who are recent immigrants are learning it as a new language.

31. cc. [7d]
32. cd. [7b]
33. cx. [7c]
34. cx. [7c]
35. cd. [7b]
36. cx. [7c]
37. cc. [7d]
38. cx. [7c]
39. cd. [7b]
40. cc. [7d]

E. Classifying Sentences by Structure

Classify each of the following sentences as *simple*, *compound*, *complex*, or *compound-complex*.

41. Easter Island, which is also known as Rapa Nui, is a small Polynesian island in the South Pacific.
42. The island is the most remote inhabited place on the planet.

41. cx. [7c]
42. s. [7a]

43. cd. [7b]
44. cd. [7b]
45. s. [7a]
46. cc. [7d]
47. cc. [7d]
48. cd. [7b]
49. cx. [7c]
50. cx. [7c]

43. The Polynesians were among the most accomplished sailors in the world; they are especially known for their skill at navigation.
44. The earliest evidence of people on Easter Island dates from around A.D. 700, but the island may have been inhabited earlier than that.
45. The island is best known for its giant stone statues with long noses and pursed lips.
46. The statues, which are called *moai*, were carved out of volcanic rock, and some of them were placed upright on platforms called *ahu*.
47. The *moai* that were set up on platforms were transported as far as six miles from the quarry, but no one knows for certain how.
48. Several theories have been proposed, yet no single theory explains all the evidence.
49. When the British explorer Captain Cook visited the island in 1774, he noticed that many of the statues had been overturned.
50. The oral tradition of the islanders speaks of a civil war that broke out between two peoples on the island, the Hanau Eepe and the Hanau Momko.

Writing Application
Writing a Letter

Using a Variety of Sentence Structures Anyone can enter the "Win Your Dream House" Contest. All you have to do is describe your ideal house. Write a letter to the contest judges, describing where your dream house would be and what it would look like. Use a variety of sentence structures to make your letter interesting for the judges to read.

Prewriting Make a list of the special features of the house you want to describe. To help you think of ideas, you may want to look through magazines or books to find pictures of interesting homes. You may also find it helpful to draw a rough diagram of the rooms, yard, and other features you would want to add. Take notes on the details you want to include.

Writing   As you write your first draft, use your notes to include vivid details that will give the contest judges a clear picture of your dream house.

Revising   Read your letter to make sure it is interesting and clear. Also, check to see whether you can combine similar ideas by using either compound or complex sentences. Ask an adult to read your letter. Does he or she think your description would impress the contest judges?

Publishing   Check the grammar and spelling in your letter. Also, make sure that you have used commas correctly in compound sentences and complex sentences. You and your classmates may want to create a bulletin board display of the pictures or diagrams you used in designing your dream house and to post your descriptions next to the display.

Reference Note
For information on **using commas,** see pages 297 and 299.

APPLICATION

Writing Application

Prewriting Tip. You could have students develop lists of things they dislike about houses as well as lists of things they like. Because their letters must be about the good things in their dream houses, tell them that they should identify the opposites of the things they dislike about houses.

Writing Tip. Have students list adjectives or short descriptions next to the features they identify in the prewriting stage. Then, have students look over their lists of adjectives to brainstorm about what kinds of images those adjectives or descriptions might give to a judge. [*Students might find that a bright, happy, open, and green house could be compared to an open field or a clear ocean.*] Encourage students to describe their houses in terms of these images.

Scoring Rubric. While you will want to pay particular attention to students' use of a variety of sentence structures, you will also want to evaluate overall writing performance. You may want to give a split score to indicate development and clarity of the composition as well as grammar skills.

Agreement
Subject and Verb, Pronoun and Antecedent

INTRODUCING THE CHAPTER

- The chapter reviews the concept of number and then moves to subject-verb agreement. Special problems in agreement, such as phrases between subjects and verbs, are discussed. Indefinite pronouns, compound subjects, and other agreement problems are presented. Additionally, an explanation of pronoun-antecedent agreement is given.

- The chapter closes with a **Chapter Review**, which includes a **Writing Application** that asks students to use correct subject-verb agreement in a short composition on a historical person.

- For help in integrating this chapter with writing assignments, use the **Teaching Strands** chart on pp. T24–T25.

Diagnostic Preview

A. Identifying Correct Subject-Verb Agreement and Pronoun-Antecedent Agreement

Choose the correct word or word group in parentheses in each of the following sentences.

EXAMPLE 1. Some of the paintings (*is, are*) dry now.
  1. are

Numerals in brackets refer to rules tested by the items in the Diagnostic Preview.

1. [8m]
2. [8p, q]
3. [8b(1), n]
4. [8p, t]
5. [8b(2), g]
6. [8p, q]
7. [8j]
8. [8m]
9. [8b(2), o, k]
10. [8p, q]

1. Three hours of work (*is, are*) needed to finish the charcoal drawing for art class.
2. Everybody has offered (*his or her, their*) advice.
3. *Harlem Shadows* (*is, are*) a collection of poems by the writer Claude McKay.
4. Either Stu or Ryan can volunteer (*his, their*) skill in the kitchen.
5. Black beans, rice, and onions (*tastes, taste*) good together.
6. Not one of them has offered (*his or her, their*) help.
7. Sometimes my family (*disagrees, disagree*) with one another, but usually we all get along fairly well.
8. Five dollars (*is, are*) all you will need for the matinee.
9. (*Doesn't, Don't*) too many cooks spoil the broth?
10. One of my aunts gave me (*her, their*) silk kimono.

CHAPTER RESOURCES

Internet
- Web resources: go.hrw.com

Practice & Review
- *Language & Sentence Skills Practice,* pp. 145–161; 162–165
- *Language & Sentence Skills Practice Answer Key,* pp. 66–73

Application & Enrichment
- *Language & Sentence Skills Practice,* pp. 144, 166, 167–168, 169
- *Language & Sentence Skills Practice Answer Key,* pp. 66, 73–74

B. Proofreading for Subject-Verb Agreement and Pronoun-Antecedent Agreement

Most of the following sentences contain an agreement error. Write the incorrect verb or pronoun. Then, write the correct form. If the sentence is already correct, write *C*.

EXAMPLE 1. Most stargazers has seen points of light shooting across the night sky.
   1. has—have

11. These points of light is commonly called shooting stars.
12. Scientists who study our solar system calls these points of light *meteors*.
13. Some meteors are pieces of asteroids that exploded long ago.
14. Each of these pieces are still flying through space on the path of the original asteroid.
15. Most nights, a person is lucky if they can see a single meteor now and then.
16. Throughout the year, however, there is meteor "showers."
17. None of these showers are as big as the ones that come each year in August and November.
18. Either Katie or Carla once saw a spectacular meteor shower on their birthday.
19. In November 1833, one of the largest meteor showers in history were recorded.
20. Two hundred forty thousand meteors observed in just a few hours are a record that has never been matched!

11. are [8b(2), c]
12. call [8b(2), c]
13. C [8b(2)]
14. is [8b(1), d]
15. he or she [8p]
16. are [8b(2), k]
17. C [8f]
18. her [8p, t]
19. was [8b(1), c]
20. is [8m, c]

Number

Number is the form a word takes to indicate whether the word is singular or plural.

8a. When a word refers to one person, place, thing, or idea, it is *singular* in number. When a word refers to more than one, it is *plural* in number.

Singular	igloo	she	one	child	class
Plural	igloos	they	many	children	classes

Reference Note
For more about **forming plurals**, see page 355.

ASSESSING

Entry-Level Assessment
Diagnostic Preview. You could use this informal **Diagnostic Preview** to evaluate your students' mastery of agreement. In **Part A,** students are asked to choose the correct word or word group for subject-verb and pronoun-antecedent agreement in sentences; in **Part B,** students are asked to proofread for subject-verb and pronoun-antecedent agreement. The results of this test will indicate whether students need extra practice.

Differentiating Instruction
- *Developmental Language & Sentence Skills Guided Practice,* pp. 57–66
- *Developmental Language & Sentence Skills Guided Practice Teacher's Notes and Answer Key,* pp. 15–16

Assessment
- *Holt Handbook Chapter Tests with Answer Key,* pp. 15–16, 46

PRETEACHING

Lesson Starter

Motivating. To introduce subject-verb agreement to students, write these two nonsense sentences on the chalkboard.

1. The shink (*grimp, grimps*) the vork.
2. The shinks (*grimp, grimps*) the vork.

Ask students to select the correct verb and to explain how they were able to make the correct choices. [Some students will probably say that they chose what sounded right.]

Ask volunteers to replace the nonsense words in each sentence with real words. Tell students to notice how the –s endings change in the two examples.

1. The horse jumps the fence.
   The girl drinks the milk.
2. The horses jump the fence.
   The girls drink the milk.

Number and Agreement of Subject and Verb

Rules 8a, b *(pp. 147–150)*

OBJECTIVES

- To classify nouns and pronouns by number
- To identify verbs that agree in number with their subjects
- To identify and correct errors in subject-verb agreement

PRACTICE

Guided and Independent

Exercise 1 You may want to use the first ten items in **Exercise 1** as guided practice. Then, have students complete the exercise as independent practice.

HOMEWORK

USAGE

1. s.	11. s.
2. p.	12. p.
3. p.	13. s.
4. s.	14. s.
5. p.	15. p.
6. p.	16. s.
7. p.	17. p.
8. p.	18. s.
9. s.	19. p.
10. p.	20. s.

TIPS & TRICKS

Most nouns ending in *s* are plural (*cheetahs, families*). Most verbs that end in *s* are singular (*fills, begins*). However, verbs used with the singular pronouns *I* and *you* do not end in *s*.

EXAMPLES
Ed takes the bus.
I take the train.
You ride your bike.

Reference Note

The plurals of some nouns do not end in *s* (*mice, teeth, deer*). For more about **irregularly formed plurals,** see page 356.

Exercise 1 Classifying Nouns and Pronouns by Number

Classify each of the following words as *singular* or *plural*.

EXAMPLES
1. girl   2. rivers
1. *singular*   2. *plural*

1. evening	6. teeth	11. hoof	16. magazine
2. wolves	7. tacos	12. mice	17. oxen
3. women	8. we	13. I	18. he
4. leaf	9. thief	14. shelf	19. cities
5. they	10. armies	15. geese	20. cargo

Agreement of Subject and Verb

8b. **A verb should agree in number with its subject.**

Two words *agree* when they have the same number. The number of a verb should agree with the number of its subject.

(1) Singular subjects take singular verbs.

EXAMPLES   The **lightning fills** the sky. [The singular verb *fills* agrees with the singular subject *lightning*.]

Jan **begins** her vacation today. [The singular verb *begins* agrees with the singular subject *Jan*.]

(2) Plural subjects take plural verbs.

EXAMPLES   **Cheetahs run** fast. [The plural verb *run* agrees with the plural subject *Cheetahs*.]

New **families move** into our neighborhood often. [The plural verb *move* agrees with the plural subject *families*.]

When a sentence contains a verb phrase, the first helping verb in the verb phrase agrees with the subject.

EXAMPLES   The **motor is** running.
The **motors are** running.

The **girl has** been delayed.
The **girls have** been delayed.

Is anyone filling the aquarium?
Are any **students** filling the aquarium?

RESOURCES

Number and Agreement of Subject and Verb Practice

- *Language & Sentence Skills Practice,* pp. 145–147, 162
- *Developmental Language & Sentence Skills,* pp. 57–58

Exercise 2 Identifying Verbs That Agree in Number with Their Subjects

Identify the form of the verb in parentheses that agrees with its subject.

EXAMPLE 1. wind (*howls, howl*)
1. howls

1. people (*talks, talk*)
2. rain (*splashes, splash*)
3. birds (*flies, fly*)
4. we (*helps, help*)
5. it (*appears, appear*)
6. geese (*hisses, hiss*)
7. night (*falls, fall*)
8. roofs (*leaks, leak*)
9. baby (*smiles, smile*)
10. tooth (*aches, ache*)

Exercise 3 Identifying Verbs That Agree in Number with Their Subjects

Identify the form of the verb in parentheses that agrees with its subject.

EXAMPLE 1. Special tours (*is, are*) offered at the National Air and Space Museum in Washington, D.C.
1. are

1. This museum (*has, have*) been called the best of all the Smithsonian museums.
2. This enormous building (*covers, cover*) three blocks.
3. Twenty-three galleries (*offers, offer*) visitors information and entertainment.
4. The different showrooms (*deals, deal*) with various aspects of air and space travel.
5. As you can see, the exhibits (*features, feature*) antique aircraft as well as modern spacecraft.
6. In another area, a theater (*shows, show*) films on a five-story-high screen.
7. A planetarium (*is, are*) located on the second floor.
8. Projectors (*casts, cast*) realistic images of stars on the ceiling.
9. Some tours (*is, are*) conducted by pilots.
10. In addition, the museum (*houses, house*) a large research library.

DIFFERENTIATING INSTRUCTION

English-Language Learners

Cantonese. The plural *s* may not appear in the speech or writing of Cantonese students for two reasons. First, Cantonese speakers do not generally use grammatical devices to express plurality. Second, Cantonese speakers find it difficult to pronounce final consonant clusters. Students may need some practice hearing and pronouncing final *s*.

Problems in Agreement

Rule 8c (pp. 150–151)

OBJECTIVE

- To choose verb forms that agree in number with subjects

DIRECT TEACHING

Modeling and Demonstration

Problems in Agreement. Using the example *The hero of those folk tales is Coyote,* model how a subject's number is not changed by the prepositional phrase following it. First, ask whether the subject *hero* is singular or plural. [singular] Then, ask what the verb's number is. [singular] Show that the phrase *of those folk tales* does not change the subject's number, even though *tales,* the object of the preposition, is plural. Explain, however, that the number of the indefinite pronouns *all, any, more, most, none,* and *some* may be determined by a prepositional phrase that follows. Now, have a volunteer use another example from this chapter to demonstrate how to choose a verb that agrees with its subject in number.

Exercise 4 **Proofreading for Errors in Subject-Verb Agreement**

Most of the following sentences contain errors in subject-verb agreement. If a verb does not agree with its subject, write the correct form of the verb. If a sentence is already correct, write *C*.

EXAMPLE 1. More than fifteen million people lives in and around Mexico's capital.

1. live

1. Located in an ancient lake bed, Mexico City have been built on Aztec ruins. **1. has**
2. Visitors admire the colorful paintings of Diego Rivera at the National Palace. **2. C**
3. In one of the city's many subway stations, an Aztec pyramid still stand. **3. stands**
4. Sculptures grace the Alameda, which is Mexico City's main park. **4. C**
5. Atop the Latin American Tower, an observatory offer a great view on a clear day. **5. offers**
6. At the National Autonomous University of Mexico, the library's outer walls is famous as works of art. **6. are**
7. Juan O'Gorman's huge mosaics shows the cultural history of Mexico. **7. show**
8. Usually, tourists is quite fascinated by the Great Temple of the Aztecs. **8. are**
9. Many fiestas fills Mexico City's social calendar. **9. fill**
10. In addition, the city has one of the largest soccer stadiums in the world. **10. C**

Problems in Agreement

Phrases Between Subject and Verb

8c. The number of a subject is not changed by a phrase following the subject.

EXAMPLES The **hero** of those folk tales **is** Coyote. [The verb *is* agrees with the subject *hero,* not with *tales.*]

The successful **candidate,** along with two of her aides, **has entered** the auditorium. [The helping verb *has* agrees with the subject *candidate,* not with *aides.*]

150 Chapter 8 Agreement

RESOURCES

Problems in Agreement
Practice
- *Language & Sentence Skills Practice,* pp. 148–150

Scientists from all over the world **have gathered** in Geneva. [The helping verb *have* agrees with the subject *Scientists,* not with *world.*]

The crystal **pitcher,** oozing water droplets, **was cracked** along the base. [The helping verb *was* agrees with the subject *pitcher,* not with *droplets.*]

NOTE If the subject is the indefinite pronoun *all, any, more, most, none,* or *some,* its number may be determined by the object of a prepositional phrase that follows it.

EXAMPLES **Most** of the essays **were** graded. [*Most* refers to the plural word *essays.*]

Most of this essay **is** illegible. [*Most* refers to the singular word *essay.*]

Reference Note
For more about **indefinite pronouns,** see Rules 8d–8f on page 152.

Exercise 5   Identifying Verbs That Agree in Number with Their Subjects

Identify the form of the verb in parentheses that agrees with its subject.

EXAMPLE   1. The water in the earth's oceans (*cover, covers*) much of the planet's surface.

   1. covers

1. A tidal wave, despite its name, (*is, are*) not caused by the tides.
2. Earthquakes beneath the sea (*causes, cause*) most tidal waves.
3. A network of warning signals (*alert, alerts*) people in coastal areas of an approaching tidal wave.
4. The tremendous force of tidal waves sometimes (*causes, cause*) great destruction.
5. Walls of earth and stone along the shore (*is, are*) often too weak to protect coastal villages.
6. Some tidal waves, according to this encyclopedia article, (*travel, travels*) more than five hundred miles an hour.
7. Tidal waves in the open ocean generally (*do, does*) not cause much interest.
8. The height of tidal waves there often (*remain, remains*) low.
9. However, waves up to one hundred feet high (*occur, occurs*) when tidal waves hit land.
10. The scientific name for tidal waves (*are, is*) tsunamis.

Problems in Agreement   **151**

DIFFERENTIATING INSTRUCTION

English-Language Learners

Japanese and Korean. In these languages, objects often appear before their verbs. For example, the English sentence "Mary sees the boys often" would have the order "Boys often Mary sees" or "Often Mary boys sees." Some English-language learners may try to write English sentences in one of these orders and, thus, try to make the verb agree with the object. Stress that students should concentrate primarily on writing English sentences in subject-verb-object order until they feel more comfortable with English. Remind them that the verb agrees with the subject, not the object.

RETEACHING

Prepositional Phrases

Some students may find diagramming helpful in understanding prepositional phrases as modifiers. Diagram several of the example sentences from **Rule 8c** (one is shown here). For more on diagramming sentences, see **Chapter 19: Sentence Diagramming.**

Most of this essay is illegible.

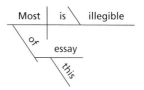

Indefinite Pronouns

Rules 8d–f (pp. 152–155)

OBJECTIVE

- To identify verb forms that agree in number with their subjects

DIRECT TEACHING

Modeling and Demonstration

Indefinite Pronouns. Model how to identify subject-verb agreement by using the example *Neither of these papayas is ripe*. First, ask whether the subject *Neither* is singular or plural. [*singular*] Then, ask what the verb's number is. [*singular*] Show that the phrase *of these papayas* does not change the subject's number. Explain that the indefinite pronoun *neither* and the other pronouns listed in Rule 8d are singular. Point out that the indefinite pronouns *both, few, many,* and *several* are always plural, while the number of *all, any, more, most, none,* and *some* may be singular or plural. Now, have a volunteer use another example from this chapter to demonstrate how to identify subject-verb agreement.

Indefinite Pronouns

You may recall that personal pronouns refer to specific people, places, things, or ideas. A pronoun that does not refer to a definite person, place, thing, or idea is called an *indefinite pronoun.*

Personal Pronouns	Indefinite Pronouns
she	anybody
them	both
we	either
you	everyone

HELP

The words *one*, *thing*, and *body* are singular. The indefinite pronouns that contain these words are singular, too.

EXAMPLES
Was [every]**one** there?
[No]**thing works** better.
[Some]**body has** answered.

8d. The following indefinite pronouns are singular: *anybody, anyone, anything, each, either, everybody, everyone, everything, neither, nobody, no one, nothing, one, somebody, someone,* and *something.*

EXAMPLES **Each** of the newcomers **was welcomed** to the city.

Neither of these papayas **is** ripe.

Does anybody on the bus **speak** Arabic?

Exercise 6 **Identify Verbs That Agree in Number with Their Subjects**

Choose the form of the verb in parentheses that agrees with its subject.

EXAMPLE 1. One of these books (*is, are*) yours.
1. *is*

HELP

Remember that the subject is never part of a prepositional phrase.

1. Neither of the movies (*were, was*) especially funny.
2. Everybody in those classes (*gets, get*) to research a historical person.
3. Someone among the store owners (*donates, donate*) the big trophy each year.
4. Each of the Jackson brothers (*study, studies*) dance.
5. No one on either team (*was, were*) ever in a playoff before.
6. Everyone with an interest in sports (*are, is*) at the tryouts.
7. Anybody with sewing skills (*are, is*) needed for the project.
8. Each of our neighbors (*have, has*) helped us plant the new community garden.

RESOURCES

Indefinite Pronouns

Practice

- *Language & Sentence Skills Practice,* pp. 149–150
- *Developmental Language & Sentence Skills,* pp. 61–62

9. One of the new Spanish teachers (*supervises*, *supervise*) the language lab.
10. Nobody in our family (*speak*, *speaks*) Greek well, but we all can speak a little bit.

8e. The following indefinite pronouns are plural: *both, few, many, several*.

EXAMPLES   **Few** of our neighbors **have** parakeets.

Many of them **keep** dogs as pets.

8f. The indefinite pronouns *all, any, more, most, none*, and *some* may be either singular or plural, depending on their meaning in a sentence.

The number of the pronouns *all*, *any*, *more*, *most*, *none*, and *some* is often determined by the number of the object in a prepositional phrase following the subject. These pronouns are singular when they refer to a singular word and are plural when they refer to a plural word.

EXAMPLES   **All** of the fruit **is** ripe. [*All* is singular because it refers to the singular word *fruit*. The verb *is* is singular to agree with the subject *All*.]

All of the pears **are** ripe. [*All* is plural because it refers to the plural word *pears*. The verb *are* is plural to agree with the subject *All*.]

Some of the harvest **has been sold**. [*Some* is singular because it refers to the singular word *harvest*. The helping verb *has* is singular to agree with the subject *Some*.]

Some of the apples **have been sold**. [*Some* is plural because it refers to the plural word *apples*. The helping verb *have* is plural to agree with the subject *Some*.]

NOTE   The pronouns listed in Rule 8f aren't always followed by prepositional phrases.

EXAMPLES   **All are** here.

Some has spilled.

In such cases you should look at the **context**—the sentences before and after the pronoun—to see if the pronoun refers to a singular or a plural word.

HELP
Some indefinite pronouns, such as *both*, *each*, and *some*, can also be used as adjectives. When an indefinite adjective comes before the subject of a sentence, the verb agrees with the subject as it normally would.

EXAMPLES
Children love playing in the park.
Both children love playing in the park.

The **child loves** playing in the park.
Each child loves playing in the park.

Problems in Agreement   153

DIRECT TEACHING

Correcting Misconceptions

Collective Nouns. Students may confuse collective nouns with plural nouns and so have problems with subject-verb agreement. Write the following nouns on a chalkboard or on a transparency:

mice, children, teeth, fleet, family, audience

Tell students that the first three words are plural nouns, while the last three words are collective nouns. Remind students that even in singular form, collective nouns refer to more than one, whereas plural nouns in singular form refer only to one.

USAGE

    Grammar   *Continued on p. 154*

Finding the Subject. To determine correct agreement of the subject and verb, students must be able to locate the subject of a sentence. Write the following sentences on the chalkboard, and have volunteers find the subjects by asking *Who?* or *What?* before the verbs. This exercise will be particularly helpful with sentences containing prepositional phrases between the subjects and verbs (see p. 150) and with sentences with inverted word order (see p. 160).

DIFFERENTIATING INSTRUCTION

Advanced Learners

Divide the class into groups of four. Give each group twenty-six index cards, and ask students to write on each card one of the twenty-six indefinite pronouns listed in **Rules 8d–f**. On the back of each card, students should indicate whether the pronoun is *singular*, *plural*, or *either singular or plural*.

Have students take turns being the card holder, holding up a card while the other members each write a sentence using the pronoun on the card as the subject of the sentence. Specify that the sentences must contain prepositional phrases modifying the subject. Ask the card holder to repeat the process several times with different cards, and then have the groups check all of the sentences for correct subject-verb agreement. The notations on the back of the cards should help with evaluation. Have students change roles until everyone in the group has had a chance to be the card holder.

Exercise 7 — Identifying Verbs That Agree in Number with Their Subjects

Identify the verb form in parentheses that agrees with its subject.

EXAMPLE 1. Somebody in the club (*want, wants*) the meetings held on a different day.

  1. wants

1. "Both of the songs (*sound, sounds*) good to me," Gregory said.
2. If anyone (*know, knows*) a better way to get to Washington Square, please tell me.
3. Each of the problems (*are, is*) easy to solve if you know the correct formulas.
4. Probably everyone in the class (*remember, remembers*) how to solve the equation.
5. All of the new research on dreams (*is, are*) fascinating.
6. Most of our dreams (*occur, occurs*) toward morning.
7. Few of us really (*understand, understands*) the four cycles of sleep.
8. Most of the research (*focus, focuses*) on the cycle known as rapid eye movement, or REM.
9. None of last night's dream (*is, are*) clear to me.
10. Many of our dreams at night (*is, are*) about that day's events.

Review A — Identifying Verbs That Agree in Number with Their Subjects

Identify the verb form in parentheses that agrees with its subject.

EXAMPLE 1. The flying object shown on the next page probably (*look, looks*) familiar to you.

  1. looks

1. Many people throughout the world (*claims, claim*) to have seen objects like this.
2. However, no one (*know, knows*) for sure what they are.
3. They (*resembles, resemble*) huge plates or saucers.
4. Not surprisingly, people (*call, calls*) them flying saucers.
5. Since 1947, they (*has, have*) been officially called unidentified flying objects, or UFOs.
6. The U.S. government (*has, have*) investigated many unusual UFO sightings.

MINI-LESSON Grammar — Continued from p. 153

1. The tired <u>campers</u> built a campfire.
2. <u>Leonie</u> enjoyed her hike through the canyon.
3. On the calm waters, the <u>boat</u> rocked gently.
4. The <u>cabin</u> in the valley offered shelter from the rain.

For additional information and practice, refer students to **Chapter 1: The Parts of a Sentence.**

7. The U.S. Air Force (*was*, *were*) responsible for conducting these investigations.
8. Government records (*shows*, *show*) that more than twelve thousand sightings were reported between 1948 and 1969.
9. Most reported sightings (*has*, *have*) turned out to be fakes, but others remain unexplained.
10. None of the official reports positively (*proves*, *prove*) that UFOs come from outer space.

Compound Subjects

8g. Subjects joined by *and* usually take a plural verb.

EXAMPLES   Our **dog and cat get** baths in the summer.

   Mr. Duffy and his **daughter have gone** fishing.

A compound subject that names only one person or thing takes a singular verb.

EXAMPLES   **A famous singer and dancer is going** to speak at our drama club meeting. [One person is meant.]

   Macaroni and cheese is my favorite pasta dish. [One dish is meant.]

Problems in Agreement   155

Compound Subjects
Practice
- *Language & Sentence Skills Practice,* p. 151
- *Developmental Language & Sentence Skills,* pp. 59–60

DIFFERENTIATING INSTRUCTION

English-Language Learners

Spanish. The rules for agreement with compound subjects in Spanish are complex. The number of the Spanish verb can be influenced by three things: the applicability of the verb to both elements of the compound subject, the relative distance of the subject and the object from the verb, and the importance of the predicate nominative, if there is one. You may want to emphasize the agreement rules for compound subjects in English and to give extra practice to any students who have trouble with agreement.

3. One person is meant.

8. One combination is meant.

STYLE TIP

Compound subjects that have both singular and plural parts can sound awkward even though they are correct. Whenever possible, revise sentences to avoid such constructions.

AWKWARD
Two small boards or one large one is what we need to patch that hole.

REVISED
We need two small boards or one large one to patch that hole.

156 Chapter 8 Agreement

Exercise 8 Identifying Verbs That Agree in Number with Their Subjects

Identify the correct form of the verb in parentheses. If you choose a singular verb with any of these compound subjects, be prepared to explain why.

EXAMPLE 1. Chris and her sister (*is, are*) in the school band.
 1. are

1. (*Is, Are*) the brown bear and the polar bear related?
2. Wind and water (*erodes, erode*) valuable farmland throughout the United States.
3. My guide and companion in Bolivia (*was, were*) Pilar.
4. New words and new meanings for old words (*is, are*) included in a good dictionary.
5. Mrs. Chang and her daughter (*rents, rent*) an apartment.
6. Iron and calcium (*needs, need*) to be included in a good diet.
7. Mr. Marley and his class (*has, have*) painted a wall-size map.
8. A horse and buggy (*was, were*) once a common way to travel.
9. Tornadoes and hurricanes (*is, are*) dangerous storms.
10. Fruit and cheese (*tastes, taste*) good together.

8h. Singular subjects joined by *or* or *nor* take a singular verb.

EXAMPLES The chief **geologist or** her **assistant is** due to arrive tonight. [Either one *is* due, not both.]

Neither a **rabbit nor** a **mole does** that kind of damage. [Neither one *does* the damage.]

Plural subjects joined by *or* or *nor* take a plural verb.

EXAMPLES Either **mice or squirrels are** living in our attic.

Neither the **senators nor** the **representatives want** the bill to be vetoed by the President.

8i. When a singular subject and a plural subject are joined by *or* or *nor*, the verb agrees with the subject nearer the verb.

EXAMPLES A **book or flowers** usually **make** an appropriate gift. [The verb agrees with the nearer subject, *flowers*.]

Flowers or a **book** usually **makes** an appropriate gift. [The verb agrees with the nearer subject, *book*.]

CONTENT-AREA CONNECTIONS

Math
Equations. You may want to use the concept of a math equation to help students determine correct subject-verb agreement with compound subjects. Write the following equations on the chalkboard or a transparency, and have students volunteer examples for each. If possible, keep the equations and examples on display as students work through the exercises in this segment.

Exercise 9 Identifying Verbs That Agree in Number with Their Subjects

Identify the correct form of the verb in parentheses in each of the following sentences. Be prepared to explain the reason for your choice.

EXAMPLE 1. The club president or the officers (*meets, meet*) regularly with the sponsors.

1. meet

—HELP—
In the example, the verb *meet* agrees with the nearer subject, *officers*.

1. Neither pens nor pencils (*is, are*) needed to mark the ballots.
2. Either my aunt or my uncle (*is, are*) going to drive us.
3. That table or this chair (*was, were*) made by hand in Portugal.
4. (*Has, Have*) the sandwiches or other refreshments been served yet?
5. Index cards or a small tablet (*is, are*) handy for taking notes.
6. Neither that clock nor my wristwatch (*shows, show*) the correct time.
7. One boy or girl (*takes, take*) the part of the narrator.
8. During our last visit to Jamaica, a map or a guidebook (*was, were*) my constant companion.
9. The dentist or her assistant (*checks, check*) my braces.
10. Either Japanese poetry or Inuit myths (*is, are*) going to be the focus of my report.

Review B Proofreading for Subject-Verb Agreement

Identify each verb that does not agree with its subject in the following sentences. Then, write the correct form of each verb.

EXAMPLE 1. The players in the photograph on the next page is competing in the most popular sport in the world—soccer.

1. is—are

1. One expert in the field of sports have described soccer as the world's favorite type of football. **1. has**
2. Some sports writers has estimated that there are over thirty million registered soccer players around the globe. **2. have**
3. Youth leagues and coaching clinics has helped make amateur soccer the fastest-growing team sport in the United States. **3. have**
4. In Dallas, Texas, neither baseball nor American football attract as many young players as soccer does. **4. attracts**

Problems in Agreement   **157**

---

1. subject + *and* + subject = plural verb
2. singular subject + *or/nor* + singular subject = singular verb
3. singular subject + *or/nor* + plural subject = plural verb
4. plural subject + *or/nor* + singular subject = singular verb

DIFFERENTIATING INSTRUCTION

Advanced Learners

Have your students write an expressive paragraph together using compound subjects. Have the first student at the head of each row or group write a topic sentence with a compound subject. If students have trouble getting started, suggest topics for paragraphs, such as snow, football, or summer vacation. As the first writer finishes writing, he or she will pass the paper to the next student in line, who will compose a sentence with another compound subject and verb and then pass the paper to the next student. Encourage students to use *or* and *nor* as well as *and* to connect their subjects. Encourage students who are having difficulty to ask questions. When all students have added their contributions, the students who began the writing will read the paragraphs aloud.

Other Problems in Subject-Verb Agreement

Rules 8j–o (pp. 158–164)

OBJECTIVES

- To identify subjects of sentences and the verbs that agree with them
- To choose correct verb forms in sentences
- To practice using correct forms of *don't* and *doesn't* orally

Reference Note
For more information about **collective nouns,** see page 29.

5. Also, more colleges now has varsity soccer teams than have football teams. **5.** have
6. This increase in soccer fans are a trend that started in 1967, when professional teams began playing in the United States. **6.** is
7. Additional interest were generated when the U.S. Youth Soccer Association was formed. **7.** was
8. Both males and females enjoys playing this sport. **8.** enjoy
9. In fact, by the 1980s, many of the soccer teams in the country was women's teams. **9.** were
10. In the past, professional soccer were more popular abroad, but the United States hosted the World Cup in 1994. **10.** was

Other Problems in Subject-Verb Agreement

8j. A collective noun may be either singular or plural, depending on its meaning in a sentence.

A **collective noun** is singular in form but names a group of persons, animals, or things.

RESOURCES

Other Problems in Subject-Verb Agreement Practice

- *Language & Sentence Skills Practice,* pp. 151–156

Common Collective Nouns		
People	**Animals**	**Things**
audience	brood	batch
chorus	flock	bundle
committee	gaggle	cluster
crew	herd	collection
faculty	litter	fleet
family	pack	set
jury	pod	squadron

A collective noun takes a singular verb when the noun refers to the group as a unit. A collective noun takes a plural verb when the noun refers to the individual parts or members of the group.

EXAMPLES The **class has decided** to have a science fair in November. [The class as a unit has decided.]

The **class were divided** in their opinions of the play. [The members of the class were divided in their opinions.]

My **family plans** to attend Beth's graduation. [The family as a unit plans to attend.]

My **family are coming** from all over the state for the reunion. [The members of the family are coming.]

8k. When the subject follows the verb, find the subject and make sure that the verb agrees with it.

The subject usually follows the verb in questions and in sentences beginning with *here* or *there*.

EXAMPLES Where **was** the **cat**?
Where **were** the **cats**?

Does Jim know the Chens?
Do the **Chens** know Jim?

Here **is** my **umbrella**.
Here **are** our **umbrellas**.

There **is** a scary **movie** on TV.
There **are** scary **movies** on TV.

MEETING THE CHALLENGE

Gaggle, pride, and *brood*—these words are examples of collective nouns. Choose five collective nouns, and look them up if you're not sure what they refer to. Then, for each word, write a pair of sentences. In the first sentence, use the collective noun as a singular subject that refers to the group as a unit. In the second sentence, use the collective noun as a plural subject that refers to the individual parts of the group. Be sure to check your sentences for correct subject-verb agreement.

DIRECT TEACHING

Modeling and Demonstration

Other Problems in Subject-Verb Agreement. Model how to identify and use correct subject-verb agreement by using the example *Has the class decided to have a science fair in November?* First, ask what the subject of the sentence is. [*class*] Then, ask whether this subject is singular or plural. [*singular*] Explain that although a class has more than one member, the collective noun *class* takes a singular verb when it refers to the group as a single unit. Next, ask whether the verb *has* is singular or plural. [*singular*] Point out that although the helping verb *Has* comes before the subject *class*, they still agree in number. Now, have a volunteer use another example from this chapter to demonstrate how to identify and use correct subject-verb agreement.

DIFFERENTIATING INSTRUCTION

English-Language Learners

General Strategies. Like English, many languages have rules for agreement between collective-noun subjects and verbs. For example, British English, which many European, African, and Asian students learn, uses the plural more frequently than American English, as in "The government have decided to . . ." In Spanish, collective-noun subjects generally take singular verbs. You may wish to give your English-language learners additional examples of sentences that use collective nouns and to explain whether each collective noun refers to a unit or to its members.

Reteaching

Collective Nouns

Helping students to picture the number of the subject may clarify collective nouns and words stating amounts. Write the following sentences on the chalkboard.

1. The herd of horses in the south pasture runs together.
2. The basketball team differ in their opinions of the new uniforms.
3. Ten dollars is the fee.

Ask volunteers to draw pictures illustrating these sentences. Then, ask students to label each subject as acting as *one group* or as *several individuals*. Finally, have the class tell whether the verbs are correct.

[1. subject—herd (one group), singular; verb—runs, singular; 2. subject—team (several individuals), plural; verb—differ, plural; 3. subject—dollars (one group), singular; verb—is, singular]

Reference Note

For more information about **contractions,** see page 333.

NOTE When the subject of a sentence follows part or all of the verb, the word order is said to be *inverted*. To find the subject of a sentence with inverted order, restate the sentence in normal subject-verb word order.

INVERTED	Here **are** your **gloves**.
NORMAL	Your **gloves are** here.
INVERTED	**Were** you **arriving** late, too?
NORMAL	**You were arriving** late, too.
INVERTED	In the pond **swim** large **goldfish**.
NORMAL	Large **goldfish swim** in the pond.

The contractions *here's*, *there's*, and *where's* contain the verb *is* and should be used only with singular subjects.

NONSTANDARD	There's our new neighbors.
STANDARD	There**'s** our new **neighbor**.
STANDARD	There **are** our new **neighbors**.

Exercise 10 Identifying Verbs That Agree in Number with Their Subjects

Identify the subject in each of the following sentences. Then, write the correct form of the verb in parentheses.

EXAMPLE 1. That flock of geese (*migrates, migrate*) each year.
 1. flock—migrates

1. There (*is, are*) at least two solutions to this complicated Chinese puzzle.
2. The soccer team (*was, were*) all getting on different buses.
3. (*Is, Are*) both of your parents from Korea?
4. Here (*comes, come*) the six members of the prom decorations committee.
5. Here (*is, are*) some apples and bananas for the picnic basket.
6. There (*is, are*) neither time nor money for that project.
7. (*Here's, Here are*) the social studies notes I took.
8. At the press conference, there (*was, were*) several candidates for mayor and two for governor.

9. The family (*has*, *have*) invited us over for a dinner to celebrate Grandma's promotion.
10. Here (*is*, *are*) some masks carved by the Haida people.

8l. Some nouns that are plural in form take singular verbs.

EXAMPLES **Electronics is** a branch of physics.

Civics is being taught by Ms. Gutierrez.

Gymnastics is my favorite Olympic sport.

The **news was** not encouraging.

8m. An expression of an amount (a measurement, a percentage, or a fraction, for example) may be singular or plural, depending on how it is used.

A word or phrase stating an amount is singular when the amount is thought of as a unit.

EXAMPLES Fifteen **dollars is** enough for that CD.

Sixteen **ounces equals** one pound.

Is two **weeks** long enough for a hiking trip?

Sometimes, however, the amount is thought of as individual pieces or parts. If so, a plural verb is used.

EXAMPLES **Ten** of the dollars **were borrowed.**

Two of the hours **were spent** at the theater.

A fraction or a percentage is singular when it refers to a singular word and plural when it refers to a plural word.

EXAMPLES **One fourth** of the salad **is** gone.

Forty percent of the students **are** new.

NOTE Expressions of measurement (such as length, weight, and area) are usually singular.

EXAMPLES Ten **feet is** the height of a regulation basketball hoop.

Seventy-five **pounds is** the maximum baggage weight for this airline.

Problems in Agreement

8n. Even when plural in form, the title of a creative work (such as a book, song, film, or painting), the name of an organization, or the name of a country or city generally takes a singular verb.

EXAMPLES **World Tales is** a collection of folk tales retold by Idries Shah. [one book]

Tonya's painting **Sunflowers was inspired** by the natural beauty of rural Iowa. [one painting]

Friends of the Earth was founded in 1969. [one organization]

The **Philippines is** an island country in the southwest Pacific Ocean. [one country]

Is Marble Falls a city in central Texas? [one city]

Exercise 11 Identifying Verbs That Agree in Number with Their Subjects

Identify the correct form of the verb in parentheses in each of the following sentences.

EXAMPLE 1. Three inches in height (*is, are*) a great deal to grow in one year.

  1. *is*

1. *The Friends* (*is, are*) a book about a girl from the West Indies and a girl from Harlem.
2. Two cups of broth (*seems, seem*) right for that recipe.
3. Fifteen feet (*was, were*) the length of the winning long jump.
4. Navarro and Company (*is, are*) selling those jackets.
5. The National Council of Teachers of English (*is, are*) holding its convention in our city this year.
6. Physics (*is, are*) the study of matter and energy.
7. Three hours of practice (*is, are*) not unusual for the band.
8. *Arctic Dreams* (*was, were*) written by Barry Lopez.
9. Two weeks of preparation (*has, have*) been enough.
10. A dollar and a half (*is, are*) the cost of a subway ride.

8o. *Don't* and *doesn't* should agree in number with their subjects.

The word *don't* is a contraction of *do not*. Use *don't* with plural subjects and with the pronouns *I* and *you*.

EXAMPLES   The **children don't** seem nervous.

I don't understand.

Don't you remember?

The word *doesn't* is a contraction of *does not*. Use *doesn't* with singular subjects except the pronouns *I* and *you*.

EXAMPLES   **Kim doesn't** ride the bus.

He doesn't play tennis.

It doesn't snow here.

Oral Practice Using *Don't* and *Doesn't*

Read the following sentences aloud, stressing the italicized words.

1. My friend *doesn't* understand the problem.
2. *Doesn't* she want to play soccer?
3. The tomatoes *don't* look ripe.
4. Our school *doesn't* have a gymnasium.
5. Italy *doesn't* border Germany.
6. The geese *don't* hiss at Mr. Waverly.
7. Our Muslim neighbors, the Nassers, *don't* eat pork.
8. He *doesn't* play chess.

Review C Identifying Verbs That Agree in Number with Their Subjects

Write the verb form in parentheses that agrees with its subject.

EXAMPLE   1. Wheelchairs with lifts (*help, helps*) many people.
   1. help

1. Twenty-five cents (*is, are*) not enough to buy the Sunday newspaper.
2. Everyone in her family (*prefers, prefer*) to drink water.
3. Allen and his parents (*enjoy, enjoys*) basketball.
4. Jan (*don't, doesn't*) know the rules of volleyball.
5. Neither the cassette player nor the speakers (*work, works*) as well as we had hoped.
6. There (*is, are*) 132 islands in the state of Hawaii.
7. Many California place names (*comes, come*) from Spanish.

8. The principal or her assistant (*is, are*) the one who can help you.
9. Home economics (*is, are*) a required course in many schools.
10. A flock of sheep (*was, were*) grazing on the hill.

Review D Proofreading for Subject-Verb Agreement

Most of the following sentences contain errors in subject-verb agreement. If a verb does not agree with its subject, write the correct form of the verb. If a sentence is already correct, write *C*.

EXAMPLE   1. Here is two pictures of Wang Yani and her artwork.
          1. *are*

1. There surely is few young artists as successful as Yani. 1. are
2. In fact, the People's Republic of China regard her as a national treasure. 2. regards
3. She has shown her paintings throughout the world. 3. C
4. Yani don't paint in just one style. 4. doesn't
5. Her ideas and her art naturally changes over the years. 5. change
6. The painting below shows one of Yani's favorite childhood subjects. 6. C
7. Many of her early paintings features monkeys. 7. feature
8. In fact, one of her large works portray 112 monkeys. 8. portrays
9. However, most of her later paintings is of landscapes, other animals, and people. 9. are
10. As her smile suggests, Yani fill her paintings with energy. 10. fills

Wang Yani, *Little Monkeys and Mummy.* © Byron Preiss Visual Publications, Inc. & New China Pictures Company. Photograph: Zheng Zhensun © 1991. All rights reserved. Published by Scholastic, Inc.

Wang Yani. © Byron Preiss Visual Publications, Inc. & New China Pictures Company. Photograph: Zheng Zhensun © 1991. All rights reserved. Published by Scholastic, Inc.

Agreement of Pronoun and Antecedent

A pronoun usually refers to a noun or another pronoun called its *antecedent.* Whenever you use a pronoun, make sure that it agrees with its antecedent.

8p. A pronoun should agree in number and gender with its antecedent.

Some singular pronouns have forms that indicate gender. Feminine pronouns refer to females. Masculine pronouns refer to males. Neuter pronouns refer to things (neither male nor female) and sometimes to animals.

Feminine	she	her	hers	herself
Masculine	he	him	his	himself
Neuter	it	it	its	itself

EXAMPLES **Carlotta** said that **she** found **her** book.

Aaron brought **his** skates with **him.**

The **plant** with mold on **it** is losing **its** leaves.

The antecedent of a pronoun can be another kind of pronoun. In such cases, you may need to look in a phrase that follows the antecedent to determine which personal pronoun to use.

EXAMPLES **Each** of the **girls** has offered **her** ideas. [*Each* is the antecedent of *her.* The word *girls* tells you to use the feminine pronoun *her* to refer to *Each.*]

One of the **men** lost **his** keys. [*One* is the antecedent of *his.* The word *men* tells you to use the masculine pronoun *his* to refer to *One.*]

Some antecedents may be either masculine or feminine. In such cases, use both the masculine and the feminine forms.

EXAMPLES Every **one** of the parents praised **his or her** child's efforts that day.

No one in the senior play forgot **his or her** lines on opening night.

Reference Note
For more information on **antecedents,** see page 30.

STYLE TIP

In conversation, people often use a plural personal pronoun to refer to a singular antecedent that may be either masculine or feminine. This nonstandard usage is becoming more common in writing, too.

NONSTANDARD Everybody brought their swimsuit.

For now, however, it is best to follow the rules of standard usage in formal situations.

STANDARD Everybody brought his or her swimsuit.

STYLE TIP

To avoid the awkward use of *his or her,* try to rephrase the sentence.

EXAMPLE Everybody brought his or her swimsuit.
Everybody brought **a** swimsuit.

Agreement of Pronoun and Antecedent **165**

RESOURCES

Agreement of Pronoun and Antecedent
Practice
- *Language & Sentence Skills Practice,* pp. 157–161, 163–165
- *Developmental Language & Sentence Skills,* pp. 63–66

DIFFERENTIATING INSTRUCTION

English-Language Learners

Asian Languages. English-language learners whose native languages use pronouns differently from the way English uses them may have difficulty with pronoun-antecedent agreement in English. In Korean, for example, pronouns do not refer to gender. Japanese has no number agreement, and the languages of Vietnam and Laos have no neuter pronouns. To prevent confusion, you can explain which personal pronouns refer to which sorts of antecedents, with special emphasis on the use of *he, she,* and *it.*

APPLICATION

Relating to Writing

Explain to students that using unclear pronouns can cause confusion in their writing. Write the following sentences on the chalkboard to show how sentences can be revised to correct unclear pronouns.

Unclear: Colleen called Alicia while she was doing her homework. [*The antecedent of* she *and* her *is unclear. Who was doing her homework, Colleen or Alicia?*]

Clear: While Colleen was doing her homework, she called Alicia.

Clear: While Alicia was doing her homework, Colleen called her.

Have students take out pieces of their own writing and work in pairs to revise any sentences that have unclear pronouns. Suggest that students highlight all pronouns and then identify the antecedents to which the pronouns refer. Remind students that pronouns often refer to antecedents in previous sentences.

STYLE TIP

Sentences with singular antecedents joined by *or* or *nor* can sound awkward if the antecedents are of different genders. If a sentence sounds awkward, revise it to avoid the problem.

AWKWARD
Odessa or Raymond will bring her or his road map.

REVISED
Odessa will bring **her** road map, or **Raymond** will bring **his**.

8q. Use a singular pronoun to refer to *anybody, anyone, anything, each, either, everybody, everyone, everything, neither, nobody, no one, nothing, one, somebody, someone,* or *something.*

EXAMPLES **Each** of the snakes escaped from **its** cage.

Someone in the class left behind **his or her** pencil.

8r. Use a plural pronoun to refer to *both, few, many,* or *several.*

EXAMPLES **Both** of the sailors asked **their** captain for shore leave.

Many among the others waiting below deck hoped that **they** could go, too.

8s. The indefinite pronouns *all, any, more, most, none,* and *some* may be singular or plural, depending on how they are used in a sentence.

EXAMPLES **All** of the book is interesting, isn't **it**?

All of the books are interesting, aren't **they**?

None of the casserole is left; **it** was terrific!

None of the casseroles are left; **they** were terrific!

8t. Use a singular pronoun to refer to two or more singular antecedents joined by *or* or *nor.*

EXAMPLES Either **Ralph or Carlos** will display **his** baseball cards.

Neither **Nina nor Mary** will bring **her** CD player.

8u. Use a plural pronoun to refer to two or more antecedents joined by *and.*

EXAMPLES **Isaac and Jerome** told me that **they** were coming.

Elena and Roberto sent letters to **their** cousin.

Exercise 12 Using Pronouns in Sentences

For each of the following sentences, write a pronoun or a pair of pronouns that will correctly complete the sentence.

EXAMPLE 1. David or Martin will show ____ slides.
　　　　　　1. *his*

Answers may vary.

1. A writer should proofread ____ work carefully. **1.** his or her
2. One of the boys had finished ____ homework. **2.** his
3. No, Joyce has not given me ____ answer. **3.** her
4. The store sent Paula and Eric the posters that ____ had ordered. **4.** they
5. Mark or Hector will arrive early so that ____ can help us. **5.** he
6. Everyone will read one of ____ poems aloud. **6.** his or her
7. One of the students raised ____ hand. **7.** his or her
8. ____ of the tennis rackets were damaged by the water leak. **8.** Many
9. The hamsters had eaten none of ____ food. **9.** their
10. Each of the dogs ate the scraps that we gave ____ . **10.** it
11. The principal and the Spanish teacher announced ____ plans for the Cinco de Mayo fiesta. **11.** their
12. All of the bowling pins were on ____ sides. **12.** their
13. The movie made sense to ____ of the audience members. **13.** none
14. Everyone in my class has ____ own writer's journal. **14.** his or her
15. Neither recalled the name of ____ first-grade teacher. **15.** his or her
16. ____ of the players, Sharon and P. J., agreed that the game was a draw. **16.** Each
17. Ms. Levine said ____ was proud of the students. **17.** she
18. Frank had tried on all of the hats before ____ chose one. **18.** he
19. Anyone may join if ____ collects stamps. **19.** he or she
20. Either Vanessa or Marilyn was honored for ____ design. **20.** her

8v. A pronoun that refers to a collective noun has the same number as the noun.

A collective noun is singular when it refers to the group as a unit and plural when it refers to the individual members of the group.

EXAMPLES The **cast** is giving **its** final performance tonight. [The cast as a unit is giving its final performance.]

The **cast** are trying on **their** costumes. [The members of the cast are trying on their individual costumes.]

The **faculty** has prepared **its** report. [The faculty as a unit has prepared its report.]

The **faculty** are returning to **their** classrooms. [The members of the faculty are returning to their separate classrooms.]

COMPUTER TIP

Using indefinite pronouns correctly can be tricky. To help yourself, you may want to create an indefinite pronoun guide. First, summarize the information in Rules 8d–8f and 8q–8s.

Then, choose several examples to illustrate the rules. If you use a computer, you can create a Help file in which to store this information.

Call up your Help file whenever you run into difficulty with indefinite pronouns in your writing. If you don't use a computer, you can keep your guide in a writing notebook.

EXTENSION

Relating to Literature

May Swenson uses many pronouns but only a few antecedents in her poem "Cat & the Weather." If the selection is in your literature book, ask students to read the poem carefully and to examine closely how all the pronouns and their antecedents are used.

Ask students to tell you how the poem uses gender and placement to avoid confusing the reader with so many pronouns. [*All pronouns referring to the cat are masculine; other pronouns are placed near their antecedents.*] The pronoun *it* in the contraction *it's* (line 26) does not have a stated antecedent. Ask students if they know what the pronoun refers to [*personal world, life*].

You may want to have students write short poems in which they use pronouns. Like Swenson, they may want to incorporate several pronouns and only a few antecedents. Ask for volunteers to read their poems in class.

8w. An expression of an amount may take a singular or plural pronoun, depending on how the expression is used.

EXAMPLES **Five dollars** is all I need. I hope my sister will lend **it** to me. [The amount is thought of as a unit.]

Two dollars are torn. The vending machine won't take **them.** [The amount is thought of as individual pieces or parts.]

8x. Even when plural in form, the title of a creative work (such as a book, song, film, or painting), the name of an organization, or the name of a country or city usually takes a singular pronoun.

EXAMPLES Have you read ***Great Expectations***? **It** is on our summer reading list.

The **United Nations,** which has **its** headquarters in New York, also has offices in Geneva and Vienna.

My grandmother, who is from the **Maldives,** told us of **its** coral reefs and lagoons.

Exercise 13 Choosing Pronouns That Agree with Their Antecedents

Choose the correct word or words in parentheses in the following sentences.

EXAMPLE 1. Even a trio can have a big sound if (*it, they*) can arrange the score properly.

1. it

1. They are asking two hundred dollars, but (*it, they*) should be a lower price because there is no chair with the desk.
2. Darla, *The Hero and the Crown* has been checked out; however, (*it, they*) should be back next Wednesday.
3. If the high school band doesn't show up soon, (*it, they*) won't lead the parade.
4. These plans call for ten feet of African ebony, and although (*it, they*) would look great, I have no idea where we could even find ebony.
5. Seven points may not seem like much, but in jai alai, (*it, they*) can be enough to decide the game.
6. The cavalry unit took up (*its, their*) position on the hill.

Learning for Life

Informal vs. Formal Language. Explain to students that in casual conversation, most people frequently use informal, sometimes even nonstandard, English. However, in formal writing and speaking situations, standard English—including correct agreement—is required.

Ask each student to imagine that he or she is applying for a summer scholarship to a camp or other summer program. In a let-

7. "Sixteen Tons" has always been one of my favorite songs, and (*it*, *they*) always will be.
8. Six of the sales teams exceeded (*its*, *their*) goals.
9. Will the board of directors alter (*its*, *their*) decision?
10. Try Harper Brothers Appliances first; if (*it*, *they*) happens to be closed, go up the street to Smith's Hardware.

Review E — Proofreading Sentences for Correct Pronoun-Antecedent Agreement

Most of the following sentences contain errors in pronoun-antecedent agreement. Identify each error, and write the correct pronoun or pronouns. If a sentence is already correct, write C.

EXAMPLE 1. At the meeting, each member of the Small Business Council spoke about their concerns.
1. their—his or her

1. Everybody had a chance to express their opinion about the new shopping mall. **1. his or her**
2. Mrs. Gomez and Mr. Franklin are happy about his or her new business locations at the mall. **2. their**
3. Both said that his or her profits have increased significantly. **3. their**
4. Neither Mr. Chen nor Mr. Cooper, however, feels that his or her customers can find convenient parking.
5. Anyone shopping at the mall has to park their car too far from the main shopping area. **5. his or her**
6. Several members of the council said that the mall has taken away many of their customers. **6. C**
7. One of the women on the council then presented their idea about creating a farmers' market on weekends. **7. her**

Review F   Writing Sentences That Demonstrate Correct Subject-Verb and Pronoun-Antecedent Agreement

POSSIBLE ANSWERS

1. Both Jed and Bob <u>found</u> <u>their</u> lost books in the office.
2. None of the puppies <u>has</u> eaten today.
3. Los Angeles <u>is</u> known as the "city of angels."
4. Fifty cents <u>is</u> not very much money these days.
5. *Anne of Green Gables* <u>is</u> my sister's favorite book; she has read <u>it</u> four times.
6. What good news <u>is</u> in today's paper?
7. Either the teacher or the students <u>need</u> to return the permission slips.
8. <u>Has</u> the litter of kittens <u>been fed</u>?
9. Neither Nancy nor Tim <u>remembers</u> who ate the last apple.
10. Everyone <u>wants</u> to help.
11. *The Adventures of Tom Sawyer* <u>was</u> written by Mark Twain, and <u>it</u> is still a very popular book.
12. The football team <u>hopes</u> to win the championship this year.
13. Each of the chairs <u>has</u> been repainted.
14. Athletics <u>is</u> her favorite activity, but I don't like <u>it</u> as much as I like singing in the choir.
15. The Masters tournament <u>becomes</u> more exciting every year.
16. Few armadillos <u>like</u> dogs.
17. Most of the apple <u>is</u> red.
18. Several days <u>is</u> too long to wait.
19. <u>Is</u> any of the orange juice left?
20. None of the pizza <u>is</u> left.

8. Many members said ~~he or she~~ favored the plan, and a proposal was discussed.   **8.** they
9. Each farmer could have ~~their~~ own spot near the town hall.   **9.** his or her
10. The Small Business Council then agreed to take ~~their~~ proposal to the mayor.   **10.** its

Review F   Writing Sentences That Demonstrate Correct Subject-Verb and Pronoun-Antecedent Agreement

Using the following words or word groups as subjects, write twenty sentences. In each sentence, underline the verb that agrees with the subject. Then, underline twice any pronoun that agrees with the subject.

EXAMPLE   1. all of the players
    1. All of the players <u>were</u> tired; <u>they</u> had had a long practice.

1. both Jed and Bob
2. none of the puppies
3. Los Angeles
4. fifty cents
5. *Anne of Green Gables*
6. news
7. either the teacher or the students
8. the litter of kittens
9. neither Nancy nor Tim
10. everyone
11. *The Adventures of Tom Sawyer*
12. the football team
13. each of the chairs
14. athletics
15. the Masters tournament
16. few armadillos
17. most of the apple
18. several days
19. any of the orange juice
20. none of the pizza

HELP
Not every sentence in Review F needs to have a pronoun that agrees with the subject.

CHAPTER

Numerals in brackets refer to rules tested by the items in the Chapter Review.

1. [8a, b(2)]
2. [8a, b(1)]
3. [8o, k]
4. [8a, c, b(1)]
5. [8l]
6. [8e, b(2)]
7. [8d, b(1)]
8. [8m]
9. [8g, b(1)]
10. [8k, b(2)]
11. [8d, b(1)]
12. [8k, a, b(2)]
13. [8f]
14. [8i]
15. [8k, e, b(2)]
16. [8g, b(2)]
17. [8n, b(1)]
18. [8k, b(2)]
19. [8j]
20. [8f]
21. [8l]
22. [8n]
23. [8d, b(1)]
24. [8f]
25. [8h, b(1)]

Chapter Review

A. Determining Subject and Verb Agreement

Identify the correct form of the verb given in parentheses in each of the following sentences. Base your answers on the rules of standard, formal usage.

1. Elephants (*has*, *have*) worked with people for centuries.
2. A blue vase (*is*, *are*) the only thing on the shelf.
3. (*Doesn't*, *Don't*) Midori come here every afternoon?
4. The exhibit of drawings by John James Audubon (*was*, *were*) fascinating, don't you think?
5. Civics (*was*, *were*) only one of the classes that challenged me.
6. Since Mom repaired them, both of the radios (*work*, *works*).
7. Everyone (*calls*, *call*) Latisha by her nickname, Tish.
8. Fifty cents (*was*, *were*) a lot of money in 1910!
9. Ms. Sakata's former neighbor and best friend, Ms. Chang, (*writes*, *write*) poetry.
10. (*Is*, *Are*) there any other blacksmiths in town?
11. I'm sorry, but somebody (*has*, *have*) checked out that book.
12. (*Was*, *Were*) the geese in the cornfield again?
13. All of the shells in my collection (*was*, *were*) displayed.
14. Neither Cindy nor her cousins (*knows*, *know*) how to sew.
15. Outside the back door (*is*, *are*) a few of your friends.
16. My brother and my uncles (*plays*, *play*) rugby.
17. The Netherlands (*has*, *have*) a coastline on the North Sea.
18. Here (*is*, *are*) several subjects for you to consider.
19. The team (*has*, *have*) all received their jerseys and hats.
20. Some of Ernest Hemingway's writings (*was*, *were*) autobiographical.
21. This news (*was*, *were*) just what Barb wanted to hear.
22. *Giants of Jazz* (*is*, *are*) an interesting book.
23. Everyone (*is*, *are*) expected to attend.
24. Most of our reading (*was*, *were*) done on weekends.
25. Either Gordon or Ruben (*knows*, *know*) the right answer.

ASSESSING

Monitoring Progress

Chapter Review. To assess student progress, you may want to compare the types of items missed on the **Diagnostic Preview** to those missed on the **Chapter Review.** If students have not made significant progress, you may want to refer them to **Exercises 8–13 of Chapter 17: Correcting Common Errors** for additional practice.

USAGE

RESOURCES

Agreement

Review
- *Language & Sentence Skills Practice*, pp. 162–165

Assessment
- *Holt Handbook Chapter Tests with Answer Key*, pp. 15–16, 46

B. Determining Pronoun and Antecedent Agreement

If the italicized pronoun in each of the following sentences does not agree with its antecedent, write the correct form of the pronoun. If the pronoun does agree with its antecedent, write C. Base your answers on the rules of standard, formal usage.

26. [8q, p]
27. [8t, p]
28. [8u, p]
29. [8r, p]
30. [8q, p]
31. [8x, p]
32. [8s, p]
33. [8t, p]
34. [8q, p]
35. [8p]
36. [8q, p]
37. [8w, p]
38. [8t, p]
39. [8q, p]
40. [8v, p]

26. Everyone put *their* suitcases on the bus. **26.** his or her
27. Either Marcia or Christina will bring *her* serving platter to the dinner party. **27.** C
28. Both Sarah and Sue agreed with *her* counselor. **28.** their
29. Several of my friends do *his or her* homework after school. **29.** their
30. One of the boys used *their* bat in the game. **30.** his
31. My grandfather's favorite television show is The Honeymooners. He watches *them* every night on cable. **31.** it
32. All of the horses received *its* vaccinations. **32.** their
33. Either Maria or Louise will receive *their* award today. **33.** her
34. Everybody should know *their* ZIP Code. **34.** his or her
35. Each student in the class has given *their* report on an African American folk tale. **35.** his or her
36. Every one of the dogs obeyed *its* owner. **36.** C
37. I found twenty dollars in my sock drawer. Do you think I should spend *them* on Christmas presents? **37.** it
38. Will either Hector or Tony read *his* paper aloud? **38.** C
39. Not one of the students had finished *their* science project on time this semester. **39.** his or her
40. After Celia finished her solo, the audience roared *their* approval for five minutes. **40.** its

Writing Application
Using Agreement in a Composition

Subject-Verb Agreement If you could be any person in history, who would you be? Why? Answer these questions in a short composition. Be sure to use correct subject-verb agreement in explaining your choice.

Prewriting First, decide what historical person you would like to be, and freewrite about that person. As you write, think about why the person is noteworthy and why you would want to be him or her.

Writing Use your freewriting ideas to write your first draft. Begin with a sentence that states the purpose of your composition and identifies your historical figure. Then, give your main reasons for wanting to be that person. Summarize your main points in a conclusion.

Revising Read through your composition, and then answer these questions: (1) Is it clear what person from history I want to be? If not, revise your main idea statement. (2) Is it clear why I want to be that person? If not, explain your reasons in more detail.

Publishing Make sure that all subjects and verbs agree in number. Check your composition for errors in spelling, capitalization, and punctuation. Your class may want to create a display using the compositions and pictures of the historical figures chosen.

APPLICATION

Writing Application

Prewriting Tip. Students may list more information in the prewriting stage than they can use in their essays. Suggest that students' main ideas focus on why they admire the individuals they have selected. Then, have students analyze the information they have listed and decide what supports their main ideas and what is irrelevant and should be left out.

Scoring Rubric. While you will want to pay particular attention to students' use of subject-verb and pronoun-antecedent agreement, you will also want to evaluate overall writing performance. You may want to give a split score to indicate development and clarity of the composition as well as usage skills.

CHAPTER 9

Using Verbs Correctly
Principal Parts, Regular and Irregular Verbs, Tense, Voice

INTRODUCING THE CHAPTER

- This chapter explains the use of regular and irregular verbs and emphasizes past and past participle forms. The chapter also discusses the use of active and passive voice. Also covered are tense and consistent use of tense as well as six verbs that are often used incorrectly.

- The chapter closes with a **Chapter Review**, which includes a **Writing Application** feature that asks students to write an exciting paragraph to serve as the cliffhanger opening of an adventure story. Students should use at least five verbs from the lists of **Common Irregular Verbs** on pp. 179–182.

- For help in integrating this chapter with writing assignments, use the **Teaching Strands** chart on pp. T24–25.

Diagnostic Preview

Proofreading Sentences for Correct Verb Forms

If a sentence contains an ~~incorrect past or past participle form~~ of a verb, write the correct form. If a sentence is already correct, write *C*.

EXAMPLE 1. Melissa drunk the medicine in one gulp.
   1. drank

1. We ~~swum~~ in the lake last weekend.
2. Carlos ~~come~~ from the Dominican Republic.
3. The crow just ~~set~~ there on the wire fence.
4. The balloon burst with a loud pop.
5. I ~~seen~~ that magician on television.
6. The leader raised his tambourine to begin the dance.
7. You should have ~~went~~ with Thomas to the game.
8. The ice cube has ~~shrinked~~ to half its original size.
9. Meanwhile, the water level has ~~rose~~.
10. I would have ~~wrote~~ to you much sooner, but I lost your new address.
11. Sandra ~~throwed~~ the ball to the shortstop.
12. Ms. Lopez has ~~spoke~~ before many civic groups.

Terms and numerals in brackets refer to concepts and rules tested by the items in the Diagnostic Preview.

1.–20. [9c]

1. swam
2. came
3. sat [*sit, set*]
4. C
5. saw
6. C [*rise, raise*]
7. gone
8. shrunk
9. risen [*rise, raise*]
10. written
11. threw
12. spoken

CHAPTER RESOURCES

Internet
- Web resources: go.hrw.com

Practice & Review
- *Language & Sentence Skills Practice*, pp. 171–184; 185–188
- *Language & Sentence Skills Practice Answer Key*, pp. 75–80

Application & Enrichment
- *Language & Sentence Skills Practice*, pp. 170, 189, 190–191, 192
- *Language & Sentence Skills Practice Answer Key*, pp. 75, 80–81

13. All of these photographs were taken in Florida's Everglades National Park.
14. The bell has ~~rang~~ for fourth period.
15. While visiting Los Angeles last August, I ~~run~~ into an old friend in the city's Little Tokyo district.
16. I ~~laid~~ down under a tree to rest.
17. I ~~done~~ everything asked of me.
18. It ~~begun~~ to rain shortly after dusk.
19. Some of the saucers were broken.
20. Sue ~~lay~~ her pen down and studied the question again.

13. C
14. rung
15. ran
16. lay [*lie, lay*]
17. did
18. began
19. C
20. laid [*lie, lay*]

Principal Parts of Verbs

The four basic forms of a verb are called the *principal parts* of the verb.

9a. The principal parts of a verb are the *base form*, the *present participle*, the *past*, and the *past participle*.

When they are used to form tenses, the present participle and the past participle forms require helping verbs (forms of *be* and *have*).

Base Form	Present Participle	Past	Past Participle
talk	[is] talking	talked	[have] talked
draw	[is] drawing	drew	[have] drawn

Because *talk* forms its past and past participle by adding *–ed*, it is called a *regular verb. Draw* forms its past and past participle differently, so it is called an *irregular verb.*

The principal parts of a verb are used to express time.

PRESENT TIME   He **draws** excellent pictures.
                Susan **is drawing** one now.

PAST TIME   Last week they **drew** two maps.
            She **has** often **drawn** cartoons.

FUTURE TIME   Perhaps she **will draw** one for you.
              By Thursday, we **will have drawn** two more.

HELP
Some teachers refer to the base form as the *infinitive*. Follow your teacher's directions when you are labeling this form.

Reference Note
For information on **participles used as adjectives,** see page 98. For information on **helping verbs,** see page 49.

ASSESSING

Entry-Level Assessment

Diagnostic Preview. This preview will show you which students have problems using correct verb forms. Some students may make errors because they do not recognize how helping verbs show tense. Others may have problems using the correct forms of irregular verbs and of the six troublesome verbs discussed in this chapter.

Differentiating Instruction
- *Developmental Language & Sentence Skills Guided Practice,* pp. 67–72
- *Developmental Language & Sentence Skills Guided Practice Teacher's Notes and Answer Key,* p. 17

Assessment
- *Holt Handbook Chapter Tests with Answer Key,* pp. 17–18, 46

PRETEACHING

Lesson Starter
Prior Knowledge. To help students practice using correct verb forms, prepare a set of flashcards with one of the following verbs on each card: *begun, done, eaten, gone, grown, known, lain, seen, swum,* and *sung*.

Ask students to write a sentence with each verb as you show a card. After all the cards have been used, let students work in groups of four to compare sentences. Students will probably discover that each of these verb forms needs a helping verb; clarify this point for groups who do not come to this realization. (Some students may find uses for the verbs as participial modifiers.)

Regular Verbs
Rule 9b (pp. 176–177)

OBJECTIVES

- To read aloud sentences containing the past tense forms of regular verbs
- To supply the present participle, past, and past participle forms of given regular verbs

DIFFERENTIATING INSTRUCTION

English-Language Learners
General Strategies. Adding the past tense suffix –*d* or –*ed* creates a final consonant sound that does not occur in many other languages. Speakers of these languages often simplify words ending in –*d* or –*ed* by omitting the last sound, a practice that might lead to omitting the final consonant in writing as well. You could model **Oral Practice 1** for students to emphasize the past tense suffix sound.

---

9 b

HELP—

Most regular verbs that end in *e* drop the *e* before adding –*ing*. Some regular verbs double the final consonant before adding –*ing* or –*ed*.

EXAMPLES
shake—shak**ing**
hug—hu**gged**

Reference Note
For more about **spelling rules**, see Chapter 16. For information on **standard and nonstandard English**, see page 245.

Regular Verbs

9b. A *regular verb* forms its past and past participle by adding –*d* or –*ed* to the base form.

Base Form	Present Participle	Past	Past Participle
clean	[is] cleaning	cleaned	[have] cleaned
hope	[is] hoping	hoped	[have] hoped
inspect	[is] inspecting	inspected	[have] inspected
slip	[is] slipping	slipped	[have] slipped

One common error in forming the past or the past participle of a regular verb is to leave off the –*d* or –*ed* ending.

NONSTANDARD   Our street use to be quieter.
STANDARD   Our street **used** to be quieter.

Another common error is to add unnecessary letters.

NONSTANDARD   The swimmer almost drownded in the riptide.
STANDARD   The swimmer almost **drowned** in the riptide.

NONSTANDARD   The kitten attackted that paper bag.
STANDARD   The kitten **attacked** that paper bag.

Oral Practice 1   Using Regular Verbs

Read each of the following sentences aloud, stressing the italicized verbs.

1. We are *supposed* to meet at the track after school.
2. The twins *happened* to buy the same shirt.
3. They have already *called* me about the party.
4. Do you know who *used* to live in this house?
5. I had *hoped* they could go to the concert with us.

176   Chapter 9   Using Verbs Correctly

RESOURCES

Regular Verbs
Practice

- *Language & Sentence Skills Practice,* pp. 171–172
- *Developmental Language & Sentence Skills,* p. 67

6. The chairs have been *moved* into the hall for the dance.
7. That salesclerk has *helped* my mother before.
8. Eli may not have *looked* under the table for the cat.

Exercise 1 — Writing the Forms of Regular Verbs

Write the correct present participle, past, or past participle form of the italicized verb given before each of the following sentences.

EXAMPLES
1. *learn* — Many people today are ____ folk dances from a variety of countries.
1. learning

2. *hope* — Dad and I had ____ to take lessons in folk dancing this summer.
2. hoped

1. *practice* — These Spanish folk dancers must have ____ for a long time.
2. *perform* — Notice that they are ____ in their colorful native costumes.
3. *wish* — Have you ever ____ that you knew how to do any folk dances?
4. *use* — Virginia reels ____ to be popular dances in the United States.
5. *promise* — Mrs. Stamos, who is from Greece, ____ to teach her daughter the Greek chain dance.
6. *lean* — The young Jamaican dancer ____ backward before he went under the pole during the limbo dance competition.
7. *start* — The group from Estonia is ____ a dance about a spinning wheel.
8. *request* — Someone in the audience has ____ an Irish square dance called "Sweets of May."
9. *dance* — During the Mexican hat dance, the woman ____ around the brim of the sombrero.
10. *fill* — The Jewish wedding dance ____ the room with both music and movement.

Principal Parts of Verbs   **177**

DIRECT TEACHING

Modeling and Demonstration

Regular Verbs. Model how to read aloud sentences and supply the principal parts of regular verbs by using the example *The kitten attacked that paper bag.* First, read the sentence aloud. Then, ask whether the verb in the sentence takes –d or –ed to form the past tense. [–ed] Ask whether *attacked* is a regular or an irregular verb. [regular] Next, ask what the principal parts of *attacked* are. [attack, [is] attacking, attacked, [have] attacked] Now, have a volunteer use another example from this chapter to demonstrate how to supply the principal parts of regular verbs.

Exercise 1 — Writing the Forms of Regular Verbs

ANSWERS

1. practiced
2. performing
3. wished
4. used
5. promised
6. leaned
7. starting
8. requested
9. danced
10. filled

DIFFERENTIATING INSTRUCTION

English-Language Learners

Spanish. Remind Spanish speakers that the English suffix –ing is equivalent to the Spanish –ando and –iendo. For example, *hablando* (speaking) comes from *hablar* (to speak), and *comiendo* (eating) comes from *comer* (to eat). Also, the English suffix –d or –ed is equivalent to the Spanish –ado and –ido, as in *abandonado* (abandoned) and *adquirido* (acquired). As in English, the past participle in Spanish may also function as an adjective.

Irregular Verbs

Rule 9c (pp. 178–186)

OBJECTIVES

- To read aloud sentences containing principal parts of irregular verbs
- To supply the past and past participle forms of given irregular verbs

DIRECT TEACHING

Modeling and Demonstration

Irregular Verbs. Model how to read aloud sentences and supply the principal parts of irregular verbs by using the example *Larry built an igloo out of blocks of ice.* First, read the sentence aloud. Next, ask when the verb's action takes place. [*in the past*] Ask whether the verb *built* takes *–d* or *–ed* to form the past tense. [*neither*] Then, ask whether *built* is regular or irregular. [*irregular*] Ask what the principal parts of *built* are. [*build, [is] building, built, [have] built*] Explain that irregular verbs form their past and past participles in other ways than adding *–d* or *–ed*. Now, have a volunteer use another example from this chapter to demonstrate how to supply the principal parts of irregular verbs.

HELP

If you are not sure about the principal parts of a verb, look in a dictionary. Entries for irregular verbs list the principal parts of the verb. If the principal parts are not given, the verb is a regular verb.

Irregular Verbs

9c. An *irregular verb* forms its past and past participle in some way other than by adding *–d* or *–ed* to the base form.

Irregular verbs form their past and past participle in various ways:

- by changing vowels

Base Form	Past	Past Participle
sing	sang	[have] sung
become	became	[have] become
drink	drank	[have] drunk

- by changing consonants

Base Form	Past	Past Participle
make	made	[have] made
build	built	[have] built
lend	lent	[have] lent

- by changing vowels *and* consonants

Base Form	Past	Past Participle
do	did	[have] done
go	went	[have] gone
buy	bought	[have] bought

- by making no changes

Base Form	Past	Past Participle
hurt	hurt	[have] hurt
put	put	[have] put
let	let	[have] let

RESOURCES

Irregular Verbs

Practice

- *Language & Sentence Skills Practice*, pp. 173–177
- *Developmental Language & Sentence Skills*, pp. 67–68

Common Irregular Verbs

Base Form	Present Participle	Past	Past Participle
begin	[is] beginning	began	[have] begun
bite	[is] biting	bit	[have] bitten *or* bit
blow	[is] blowing	blew	[have] blown
break	[is] breaking	broke	[have] broken
bring	[is] bringing	brought	[have] brought
build	[is] building	built	[have] built
burst	[is] bursting	burst	[have] burst
buy	[is] buying	bought	[have] bought
catch	[is] catching	caught	[have] caught
choose	[is] choosing	chose	[have] chosen
come	[is] coming	came	[have] come
cost	[is] costing	cost	[have] cost
cut	[is] cutting	cut	[have] cut
do	[is] doing	did	[have] done
draw	[is] drawing	drew	[have] drawn
drink	[is] drinking	drank	[have] drunk
drive	[is] driving	drove	[have] driven
eat	[is] eating	ate	[have] eaten
fall	[is] falling	fell	[have] fallen
feel	[is] feeling	felt	[have] felt
fight	[is] fighting	fought	[have] fought
find	[is] finding	found	[have] found
fly	[is] flying	flew	[have] flown
forgive	[is] forgiving	forgave	[have] forgiven
freeze	[is] freezing	froze	[have] frozen
get	[is] getting	got	[have] got *or* gotten
give	[is] giving	gave	[have] given
go	[is] going	went	[have] gone
grow	[is] growing	grew	[have] grown

(continued)

Differentiating Instruction

English-Language Learners

General Strategies. Some English-language learners might not understand the use of irregular verbs if their native languages have few or no irregular verbs. To give students practice using the base form, the past form, and the past participle form of irregular verbs, suggest that students read aloud the following sentences, filling in the blanks with verbs from the charts on pp. 179–182.

1. Today I _____.
2. Yesterday I _____.
3. Often I have _____.

Extension

Relating to Spelling

Using Dictionaries. Point out to students that when they have questions about the principal parts of irregular verbs, they can look up the verbs in a dictionary. Explain that the entry word in a dictionary is the base form and that the past, past participle, and present participle forms are listed following the entry word. For example, if they look up *sing*, they will also find *sang*, *sung*, and *singing* listed. Ask each student to look up two or three irregular verbs in a dictionary and to compare the principal parts listed in the dictionary with those on the chart in the textbook.

MINI-LESSON Usage *Continued on p. 180*

Participles as Modifiers. Use the following sentences to illustrate to students that the present participle and past participle forms of many verbs can be used as adjectives to modify nouns or pronouns. Point out that a participle used as a verb must have a helping verb (a form of *be* or *have*).

Verb: Snow <u>is falling</u> outside.
Adjective: The <u>falling</u> snow looks beautiful.
Verb: I <u>have broken</u> a saucer.
Adjective: That <u>broken</u> glass is sharp.

RETEACHING

Principal Parts of Verbs

Activity. Divide the class into groups of three. Give each group six index cards with the base form of one irregular verb written on each card.

Ask group members to take turns drawing cards. The student who draws the first card will confer with group members to write on the card four sentences—one using each of the four principal parts of that verb. For example, if the card says *eat,* the student might write the following:

1. I eat cereal for breakfast every day.
2. She is eating her lunch.
3. We ate at a new restaurant.
4. I have not eaten any fruit today.

If a group is unsure of a verb form, have the members use a dictionary rather than the charts in their textbooks. Groups should repeat the process until all students have had a turn writing sentences and all cards have been used. Then, have groups exchange their cards with other groups to check for sentence correctness.

PRACTICE

Guided and Independent

Exercise 2 You may want to use the first ten items in **Exercise 2** as guided practice. Then, have students complete the exercise as independent practice. **HOMEWORK**

(continued)

Common Irregular Verbs

Base Form	Present Participle	Past	Past Participle
have	[is] having	had	[have] had
hear	[is] hearing	heard	[have] heard
hide	[is] hiding	hid	[have] hid or hidden
hit	[is] hitting	hit	[have] hit
hold	[is] holding	held	[have] held
know	[is] knowing	knew	[have] known
lead	[is] leading	led	[have] led

Oral Practice 2 — Using Irregular Verbs

Read the following sentences aloud, stressing the italicized verbs.

1. Edward's sister *drove* him to the mall this afternoon.
2. My parents *came* to the spelling bee last year.
3. I should have *known* the test would be difficult.
4. He's *going* to Cape Canaveral this summer.
5. Maya has been *chosen* to play on our team.
6. The water pipe *burst* during the ice storm.
7. *Did* you see the northern lights last night?
8. Wyatt *brought* his new computer game to the party at Alexander's house.

Exercise 2 — Writing the Past and Past Participle Forms of Irregular Verbs

Write the correct past or past participle form of the italicized verb given before each of the following sentences.

EXAMPLE 1. *choose*   Sara has ____ her song for next month's piano recital.
         1. chosen

1. drove 1. *drive*   Last summer we ____ to Denver, where we visited the U.S. Mint.
2. began 2. *begin*   The concert ____ an hour ago.

MINI-LESSON Usage   Continued from p. 179

Have students work in pairs to write two sentences with each of the following words. As in the models, the word should first be used as a verb and then as an adjective. Have pairs exchange their sentences to check for correctness.

1. beginning
2. fallen
3. lost
4. written

For additional instruction and practice, refer students to **Chapter 5: The Phrase.**

3.	break	Mike Powell ___ the world long-jump record by jumping 29 feet 4½ inches.	3. broke
4.	blow	The wind has ___ the tent down.	4. blown
5.	get	We ___ tickets to ride *The Silverton*.	5. got
6.	fall	The leaves have ___ from the trees.	6. fallen
7.	do	Kate ___ her best, and she got a promotion.	7. did
8.	drink	According to legend, the Aztec emperor Montezuma ___ chocolate.	8. drank
9.	build	People in Africa ___ large cities hundreds, even thousands, of years ago.	9. built
10.	go	You've never ___ to Puerto Rico, have you?	10. gone
11.	bite	I think that Roseanne ___ into a green chile!	11. bit
12.	grow	Well, nephew, you surely have ___!	12. grown
13.	catch	You look like you just ___ the brass ring!	13. caught
14.	give	Mom had already ___ us a color copy of her grandmother's journal.	14. given
15.	eat	The Japanese have box lunches, too, but they call them *obentos*; we have ___ them several times.	15. eaten
16.	feel	They ___ better after taking a short nap.	16. felt
17.	cost	Those tickets shouldn't have ___ so much.	17. cost
18.	buy	Have you ever ___ a Greek sandwich called a *gyro*?	18. bought
19.	find	My cousin said that she has ___ a new canyon trail.	19. found
20.	freeze	The pond ___ last winter, and we went skating.	20. froze

More Common Irregular Verbs

Base Form	Present Participle	Past	Past Participle
leave	[is] leaving	left	[have] left
lend	[is] lending	lent	[have] lent
let	[is] letting	let	[have] let
light	[is] lighting	lighted *or* lit	[have] lighted *or* lit
lose	[is] losing	lost	[have] lost
make	[is] making	made	[have] made
meet	[is] meeting	met	[have] met
pay	[is] paying	paid	[have] paid

(continued)

HELP

Some verbs have two correct past or past participle forms. However, these forms are not always interchangeable.

EXAMPLES
I **shone** the flashlight into the woods. [*Shined* also would be correct in this usage.]

I **shined** my shoes. [*Shone* would be incorrect in this usage.]

If you are unsure about which past participle form to use, check an up-to-date dictionary.

Principal Parts of Verbs **181**

EXTENSION

Relating to Writing

Vivid Verbs. To help students improve their writing, explain that they should choose vivid verbs whenever possible. Offer the following sentences as examples of vivid verbs that could be used for *run*.

1. I <u>raced</u> down the street.
2. I <u>dashed</u> down the street.
3. I <u>sprinted</u> down the street.

Have the class work in groups of three to create a class word bank of vivid verbs. Ask each group to choose five common verbs and, using a thesaurus or dictionary, to list interesting synonyms for each verb. Then, have groups compile their lists on a poster or bulletin board to be displayed in the classroom.

To extend the activity or to challenge advanced students, suggest that students explore the shades of meaning of the synonymous verbs. For example, students might write the following definitions for the *run* example above.

1. race—to rush at top speed
2. dash—to move with sudden speed
3. sprint—to run at top speed for a short distance

EXTENSION

Critical Thinking

Metacognition. Ask students to think about the process that works best for them in trying to incorporate a new word or a new usage into their vocabulary. Is writing the word in a number of different sentences the best method? Does speaking it aloud repeatedly work best? Does hearing the word used correctly help? Encourage students to evaluate the effectiveness of their personal strategies and to consider more effective alternatives as needed.

(continued)

More Common Irregular Verbs

Base Form	Present Participle	Past	Past Participle
put	[is] putting	put	[have] put
read	[is] reading	read	[have] read
ride	[is] riding	rode	[have] ridden
ring	[is] ringing	rang	[have] rung
run	[is] running	ran	[have] run
say	[is] saying	said	[have] said
see	[is] seeing	saw	[have] seen
seek	[is] seeking	sought	[have] sought
sell	[is] selling	sold	[have] sold
send	[is] sending	sent	[have] sent
shrink	[is] shrinking	shrank *or* shrunk	[have] shrunk
sing	[is] singing	sang	[have] sung
sink	[is] sinking	sank *or* sunk	[have] sunk
speak	[is] speaking	spoke	[have] spoken
spend	[is] spending	spent	[have] spent
stand	[is] standing	stood	[have] stood
steal	[is] stealing	stole	[have] stolen
swim	[is] swimming	swam	[have] swum
swing	[is] swinging	swung	[have] swung
take	[is] taking	took	[have] taken
teach	[is] teaching	taught	[have] taught
tear	[is] tearing	tore	[have] torn
tell	[is] telling	told	[have] told
think	[is] thinking	thought	[have] thought
throw	[is] throwing	threw	[have] thrown
wear	[is] wearing	wore	[have] worn
win	[is] winning	won	[have] won
write	[is] writing	wrote	[have] written

Oral Practice 3 Using Irregular Verbs

Read the following sentences aloud, stressing the italicized verbs.
1. When the bell *rang*, we hurried out of the building.
2. The audience was quiet as the acrobats *swung* from the trapeze.
3. That dress had already *shrunk* before I washed it.
4. Otherwise, Lily would have *worn* it to the dance.
5. Have you *met* the new foreign exchange student?
6. We were late to the picnic because I *lost* the map.
7. My father *lent* me the money to buy a new watch.
8. Did you know that Rachel *took* singing lessons?

Exercise 3 Writing the Past and Past Participle Forms of Irregular Verbs

Write the correct past or past participle form of the italicized verb given before each of the following sentences.

EXAMPLE 1. *see*   I have ____ that movie twice already.
         1. seen

1. *run*   Michael ____ the 100-meter dash in excellent time. — 1. ran
2. *sell* My aunt has ____ more houses than any other real estate agent in the city. — 2. sold
3. *speak* The director of the state health department ____ to our class today. — 3. spoke
4. *win*   The Mexican poet Octavio Paz ____ the Nobel Prize in literature. — 4. won
5. *write* I have ____ some poems, but I am shy about showing them to anyone. — 5. written
6. *ride* Tamisha's whole family ____ mules to the bottom of the Grand Canyon. — 6. rode
7. *sing* At the concert, the group ____ my favorite song. — 7. sang
8. *throw* Someone must have ____ this trash from a car. — 8. thrown
9. *swim* Within minutes, the two beautiful swans had ____ across the lake. — 9. swum
10. *sink* King Arthur's sword Excalibur had ____ slowly to the bottom of the lake. — 10. sunk
11. *send* My aunt in South America ____ me a fabulous sweater made from the wool of an alpaca, which is an animal similar to a llama. — 11. sent

---

EXTENSION

Looking at Language
Explain to students that the English language is constantly changing as meanings, pronunciations, and usages are added or updated. For example, some verbs have alternate past tense forms such as *dived* or *dove*, *shone* or *shined*, *rang* or *rung*, and *shrank* or *shrunk*. Ask students to check a dictionary to see how these alternative verb forms are listed.

12. told	12. *tell*	Mr. Noguchi ____ us that *R.S.V.P.* at the bottom of an invitation means that you should let the host know whether you are coming or not.
13. lent	13. *lend*	Before the softball game, my friend Gabriela ____ me her glove.
14. worn	14. *wear*	Shouldn't you have ____ a warmer jacket for the hike this morning?
15. swam	15. *swim*	Soon-hee, who is training for a triathlon, ____ two miles on Saturday.
16. rung	16. *ring*	I have ____ the doorbell several times, but no one has come to the door.
17. lost	17. *lose*	The swan ____ many large feathers; Tony said it must be molting.
18. taken	18. *take*	It has ____ over ten minutes to locate the missing glasses.
19. sung	19. *sing*	Gerald, Annie, and Trish have ____ the national anthem at assembly.
20. said	20. *say*	The weather forecast this morning ____ to expect snow flurries.

Review A — Writing the Past and Past Participle Forms of Irregular Verbs

Write the correct past or past participle form of the italicized verb given before each of the following sentences.

EXAMPLE   1. *tell*   Has Alameda ____ you about the book *The Indian Tipi: Its History, Construction, and Use*?
          1. told

1. *write*   Reginald and Gladys Laubin ____ that book and others about American Indian culture.   **1.** wrote
2. *build*   The Laubins ____ their own tepee.   **2.** built
3. *stand*   Tepees of various sizes once ____ all across the Great Plains.   **3.** stood
4. *see*   I have ____ pictures of camps full of beautifully decorated tepees.   **4.** seen
5. *make*   For many years, American Indians have ____ tepees out of cloth rather than buffalo hides.   **5.** made
6. *come*   The word *tepee*, or *tipi*, has ____ into English from the Sioux language.   **6.** come

184   Chapter 9   Using Verbs Correctly

CONTENT-AREA CONNECTIONS

Multidisciplinary
Verbs. Use this activity to show students that correct verb usage carries over to subjects other than language arts. The activity will also give students additional practice with verb forms.

Divide the class into groups of three or four. Have each group list the subjects they take in school besides language arts. Next, have the groups brainstorm five verbs that could be associated with each of the listed subjects. For example, verbs used in art class might include *feel*, *make*, *teach*, *think*, and *draw*.

7. *draw* — On the outside of their tepees, the Sioux and Cheyenne peoples ____ designs like the ones shown on the previous page.   **7. drew**

8. *take* — Because the Plains Indians followed animal herds, they needed shelter that could be easily ____ from place to place.   **8. taken**

9. *know* — Even before reading the book, I ____ that the inside of a tepee cover was rarely painted.   **9. knew**

10. *do* — Traditionally, women ____ all the work of making tepees and putting them up.   **10. did**

Review B — Writing the Past and Past Participle Forms of Irregular Verbs

Write the correct past or past participle form of the italicized verb given before each of the following sentences.

EXAMPLE   1. *write*   I ____ a report on Jim Thorpe.
            1. wrote

1. *blow* — Yesterday the wind ____ the leaves into our yard.   **1. blew**
2. *break* — My pen pal from Australia has never ____ his promise to write once a week.   **2. broken**
3. *bring* — I ____ the wrong book to class.   **3. brought**
4. *burst* — The children almost ____ with excitement.   **4. burst**
5. *choose* — The director ____ James Earl Jones for the role.   **5. chose**
6. *come* — My aunt and her friend ____ to dinner last night.   **6. came**
7. *do* — I have always ____ my homework right after supper.   **7. done**
8. *drink* — The guests ____ fruit punch and lemonade.   **8. drank**
9. *fall* — One of Julian's Russian nesting dolls has ____ off the shelf.   **9. fallen**
10. *freeze* — Has the pond ____ yet?   **10. frozen**
11. *go* — We have never ____ to see the Parthenon in Nashville.   **11. gone**
12. *know* — Had I ____, I would have called you sooner.   **12. known**
13. *ring* — Suddenly the fire alarm ____.   **13. rang**
14. *run* — Joan Samuelson certainly ____ a good race.   **14. ran**
15. *see* — I ____ you in line at the movies.   **15. saw**
16. *shrink* — The apples we dried in the sun have ____.   **16. shrunk**
17. *speak* — After we had ____ to George and Marc, we decided to play dominoes.   **17. spoken**
18. *swim* — We ____ out to the float and back.   **18. swam**

Principal Parts of Verbs   185

Then, ask the groups to write sentences using the past or past participle forms of each of the verbs they listed, such as the following examples:

1. I have never <u>felt</u> such an interesting texture.
2. I have <u>made</u> a beautiful sculpture!
3. Mrs. Alt <u>taught</u> us about the color wheel.
4. I <u>thought</u> about using bright colors.
5. Have you ever <u>drawn</u> with charcoal?

If time permits, have each group read its sentences aloud.

USAGE

Tense
Rules 9d, e *(pp. 186–189)*

OBJECTIVE
- To revise a paragraph to make the tenses of verbs consistent

DIRECT TEACHING

Modeling and Demonstration

Tense. Model how to proofread for consistent verb tense by using the example *Randy has played bass guitar for the band, but now he plays drums.* First, ask what tense the verb *has played* is. [*present perfect*] Then, ask when this action occurs. [*sometime before now*] Next, ask what tense the verb *plays* is. [*present*] Ask when this action occurs. [*now*] Explain how this sentence displays consistent verb tense, since the verbs *has played* and *plays* correctly use different tenses to describe events that occur at different times. Now, have a volunteer use another example from this chapter to demonstrate how to proofread for consistent verb tense.

DIFFERENTIATING INSTRUCTION

English-Language Learners

General Strategies. Some languages do not use verb tenses to indicate time. The idea of specifying tense repeatedly in every sentence might seem redundant to some students; therefore, they might use only the present tense. Emphasize that in English the appropriate tense should be used in every sentence.

186 Using Verbs Correctly

---

9 d, e

19. written **19.** *write* She has ____ me several long letters.
20. thrown **20.** *throw* You shouldn't have ____ the ball to second base.

Tense

9d. The *tense* of a verb indicates the time of the action or of the state of being that is expressed by the verb.

EXAMPLES   Yesterday, Denise **served** lox and bagels for breakfast.

Randy **has played** bass guitar for the band, but now he **plays** drums.

Once they **have painted** the signs, Jill and Cody **will finish** the decorations for the dance.

Verbs in English have six tenses.

Present	Past	Future
Present Perfect	Past Perfect	Future Perfect

The following time line shows the relationship between the six tenses.

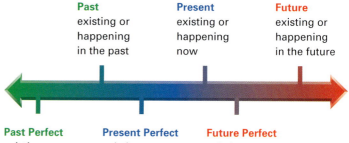

Past existing or happening in the past

Present existing or happening now

Future existing or happening in the future

Past Perfect existing or happening before a specific time in the past

Present Perfect existing or happening sometime before now; may be continuing now

Future Perfect existing or happening before a specific time in the future

Listing the different forms of a verb is called *conjugating* the verb.

186   Chapter 9   Using Verbs Correctly

RESOURCES

Tense

Practice
- *Language & Sentence Skills Practice,* pp. 178–179
- *Developmental Language & Sentence Skills,* pp. 69–70

Conjugation of the Verb *See*	
Present Tense	
Singular	**Plural**
I see	we see
you see	you see
he, she, *or* it sees	they see
Past Tense	
Singular	**Plural**
I saw	we saw
you saw	you saw
he, she, *or* it saw	they saw
Future Tense	
Singular	**Plural**
I will (shall) see	we will (shall) see
you will (shall) see	you will (shall) see
he, she, *or* it will (shall) see	they will (shall) see
Present Perfect Tense	
Singular	**Plural**
I have seen	we have seen
you have seen	you have seen
he, she, *or* it has seen	they have seen
Past Perfect Tense	
Singular	**Plural**
I had seen	we had seen
you had seen	you had seen
he, she, *or* it had seen	they had seen
Future Perfect Tense	
Singular	**Plural**
I will (shall) have seen	we will (shall) have seen
you will (shall) have seen	you will (shall) have seen
he, she, *or* it will (shall) have seen	they will (shall) have seen

STYLE TIP

Traditionally, the helping verbs *shall* and *will* were used to mean different things. Now, however, *shall* can be used almost interchangeably with *will*.

DIFFERENTIATING INSTRUCTION

English-Language Learners

Vietnamese. Vietnamese expresses time and tense differently from the ways English does. Therefore, verb tenses may cause much difficulty for Vietnamese students, particularly when an auxiliary verb is used to show tense: *John did not complete his work.* The Vietnamese student may rely on context clues, writing "I visit family last night" instead of "I visited family."

Help students practice verb tense forms through focused writing and speaking. For example, introduce the use of *–d* and *–ed* for regular past tense forms and give students base form verbs to change to the past tense. Then, have students respond orally to questions in which students use past tense, such as "Tell us something funny that happened to you this past week" or "Did you do something interesting this weekend?" Introduce the other tenses in the same way, but do so one at a time.

Spanish. Spanish speakers face a number of difficulties in conjugating verbs in English.

- Spanish makes a distinction between the past that is habitual or ongoing (imperfect tense) and the past that is completed (preterite tense).
- Spanish frequently uses the subjunctive mood.
- Spanish verb tenses usually have a different form for each combination of person and number.
- Two different verbs (*ser* and *estar*) split both the meanings and the duties of the English verb *be*.

Challenge your English-language learners to learn the listed English conjugations perfectly, encouraging them to look for patterns that will make the task easier.

Direct Teaching

Correcting Misconceptions

Progressive Forms. Students may misidentify progressive forms as passive voice. Write the following sentences on the chalkboard or on a transparency:

Joan will be seeing the movie.

The movie will be seen by me.

Inform students that in the first sentence, *will be seeing* is in the future progressive form. Tell them that in the second sentence, *will be seen* is in the passive voice. Remind students that although both the passive voice and the progressive form use forms of the verb *be* as helping verbs, the progressive forms always end in *–ing*, whereas passive voice forms end with a past participle.

Exercise 4 Making Tenses of Verbs Consistent

ANSWERS

Students can choose either present or past tense, but they must be consistent throughout their paragraphs. Verbs in direct quotations and in statements of general truth (an example of which is *what lightning is* in sentence 6) should not be changed. In the following answers, the present tense is given first and the past tense is in parentheses.

1. strikes, run (struck, ran)
2. exclaim (exclaimed)
3. is (was)

HELP
The progressive form is not a separate tense but an additional form of each of the six tenses.

NOTE Each tense has an additional form called the **progressive form,** which expresses continuing action or state of being. In each tense, the progressive form of a verb consists of the appropriate tense of *be* plus the verb's present participle.

Present Progressive	am, is, are seeing
Past Progressive	was, were seeing
Future Progressive	will (shall) be seeing
Present Perfect Progressive	has been seeing, have been seeing
Past Perfect Progressive	had been seeing
Future Perfect Progressive	will (shall) have been seeing

Consistency of Tense

9e. Do not change needlessly from one tense to another.

When writing about events that take place at the same time, use verbs that are in the same tense. When writing about events that occur at different times, use verbs that are in different tenses.

INCONSISTENT	When we go to the movies, we bought some popcorn. [The events occur at the same time, but *go* is in the present tense and *bought* is in the past tense.]
CONSISTENT	When we **go** to the movies, we **buy** some popcorn. [Both *go* and *buy* are in the present tense.]
CONSISTENT	When we **went** to the movies, we **bought** some popcorn. [Both *went* and *bought* are in the past tense.]

HELP
When you rewrite Exercise 4, either tense is correct, as long as you are consistent.

Exercise 4 Making Tenses of Verbs Consistent

Read the following sentences, and choose whether to rewrite them in the present or past tense. Then, rewrite the sentences, changing the verb forms to correct any needless changes.

EXAMPLE [1] I picked up the telephone receiver quickly, but the line is still dead.

1. I picked up the telephone receiver quickly, but the line was still dead.

or

I pick up the telephone receiver quickly, but the line is still dead.

[1] Lightning struck our house, and I run straight for cover. [2] "Oh, no!" I exclaim. [3] The electricity was out! [4] My parents get out the flashlights, and we played a game. [5] Later, since the stove, oven, and microwave didn't work without electricity, we have a cold supper in the living room—picnic style! [6] My younger brother asks me what lightning is. [7] "Lightning is a big spark of electricity from a thundercloud," I tell him. [8] He nods. [9] I started to tell him about positive and negative charges creating lightning, but he doesn't understand what I'm talking about and walks away. [10] In the morning, we were all glad when the sun shone and our electricity is on again.

Active and Passive Voice

A verb in the *active voice* expresses an action done *by* its subject. A verb in the *passive voice* expresses an action done *to* its subject. In passive voice, the verb phrase always includes a form of *be* and the past participle of the main verb. Other helping verbs may also be included. Compare the following sentences:

ACTIVE VOICE	The pilot **instructed** us. [The subject, *pilot,* performs the action.]
PASSIVE VOICE	We **were instructed** by the pilot. [The subject, *We,* receives the action.]
ACTIVE VOICE	Alice **caught** a fly ball. [The subject, *Alice,* performs the action.]
PASSIVE VOICE	A fly ball **was caught** by Alice. [The subject, *ball,* receives the action.]
ACTIVE VOICE	The firefighters **have put** out the blaze. [The subject, *firefighters,* performs the action.]
PASSIVE VOICE	The blaze **has been put** out by the firefighters. [The subject, *blaze,* receives the action.]

Exercise 5 Identifying Active and Passive Voice

Tell whether the verb is in the *active voice* or *passive voice* in each of the following sentences.

EXAMPLE 1. The 10K race was won by Mikki.
 1. passive voice

Reference Note
For more about **helping verbs,** see page 49.

STYLE TIP

In general, you should avoid using the passive voice because it can make your writing sound weak and awkward. Using the active voice helps make your writing direct and forceful.

PASSIVE VOICE
A no-hitter **was pitched** by Valerie, and the game **was won** by her team.

ACTIVE VOICE
Valerie **pitched** a no-hitter, and her team **won** the game.

RESOURCES

Active and Passive Voice
Practice
- *Language & Sentence Skills Practice,* p. 180

USAGE

Six Troublesome Verbs
(pp. 190–196)

OBJECTIVES

- To read aloud sentences containing six troublesome verbs
- To supply the correct forms of *sit* or *set* to complete sentences
- To choose the correct forms of *rise* or *raise* in sentences
- To choose the correct forms of *lie* or *lay* in sentences

DIRECT TEACHING

Modeling and Demonstration

Six Troublesome Verbs. Model how to read aloud and use the verbs *rise* and *raise* correctly by using the examples *The fans were rising to sing the national anthem* and *The fans were raising signs and banners*. First, ask whether a word or word group in the first sentence receives the action of the verb *were rising*. [no] The verb *rise* takes no direct object; therefore, *were rising* is used correctly here because there is no direct object in the sentence. Next, ask whether a word or word phrase in the second sentence receives the action of the verb *were raising*. [yes; signs and banners] *Raise* does take a direct object; therefore, *were raising* is correct here. Now, have a volunteer use other examples from this chapter to demonstrate the correct use of the problem verbs *sit, set, lie,* and *lay*.

1. active
2. passive
3. passive
4. active
5. passive
6. passive
7. active
8. active
9. passive
10. passive

1. On Sunday afternoon we painted the den.
2. Brianne was elected to the student council.
3. The CD has been misplaced by my cousin.
4. The new animation software creates vivid images.
5. Many of the yearbook photos were taken by Adrienne.
6. Shoddy work was done on the building.
7. Mike and I don't understand this algebra problem.
8. I am unloading the food and supplies at the campsite.
9. The tickets had been sold months before the concert.
10. Andre was awarded the certificate for his service to the community.

STYLE TIP

You may know that the word *set* has more meanings than the two given here. Check in a dictionary to see if the meaning you intend requires an object.

EXAMPLE
The sun **sets** in the West.
[Here, *sets* does not take an object.]

Six Troublesome Verbs

Sit and *Set*

The verb *sit* means "to be seated" or "to rest." *Sit* seldom takes an object. The verb *set* usually means "to place (something somewhere)" or "to put (something somewhere)." *Set* usually takes an object. Notice that *set* has the same form for the base form, past, and past participle.

Base Form	Present Participle	Past	Past Participle
sit	[is] sitting	sat	[have] sat
set	[is] setting	set	[have] set

EXAMPLES

Who **is sitting** on the blanket by the pool? [no object]

Theresa **is setting** the lawn chairs by the pool. [Theresa is setting what? *Chairs* is the object.]

Three boys **sat** on the platform. [no object]

The boys **set** the instruments on the platform. [The boys set what? *Instruments* is the object.]

We **had sat** on the pier for an hour before Suzanne arrived with the bait. [no object]

I **had set** the bucket of bait on the pier. [I had set what? *Bucket* is the object.]

190 Chapter 9 Using Verbs Correctly

Six Troublesome Verbs
Practice

- *Language & Sentence Skills Practice*, pp. 181–184, 188
- *Developmental Language & Sentence Skills*, pp. 71–72

190 Using Verbs Correctly

Oral Practice 4 **Using the Forms of *Sit* and *Set* Correctly**

Read each of the following sentences aloud, stressing the italicized verbs.

1. Darnell and I *sat* down to play a game of chess.
2. After we had been *sitting* for a while, he decided to make bread.
3. I *set* the pan on the table.
4. After Darnell had *set* out the ingredients, he mixed them.
5. We returned to our game but could not *sit* still for long.
6. We had not *set* the pan in the oven.
7. Then, we almost *sat* too long.
8. If the bread had *sat* in the oven much longer, it would have burned.

Exercise 6 **Writing the Forms of *Sit* and *Set* Correctly**

Write the correct form of *sit* or *set* for each blank in the following sentences.

EXAMPLE 1. I ____ my suitcase on the rack.
         1. set

1. On the train, I ____ next to a woman wearing a shawl. **1. sat**
2. She ____ a large covered basket on the floor by her feet. **2. set**
3. When the conductor asked her if she would like to ____ it in the baggage rack, she refused. **3. set**
4. She insisted that the basket must ____ by her feet. **4. sit**
5. As I ____ beside her, I wondered what was in the basket. **5. sat**
6. I ____ my book down and tried to see inside the tightly woven basket. **6. set**
7. Perhaps I was ____ next to a woman with a picnic lunch. **7. sitting**
8. Maybe she had ____ next to me because I looked hungry. **8. sat**
9. As the woman ____ her packages down, I watched the basket. **9. set**
10. A sudden movement of the train caused the basket to open, and inside it ____ a small, white rabbit. **10. sat**

Rise and *Raise*

The verb *rise* means "to move upward" or "to go up." *Rise* does not take an object. The verb *raise* means "to lift (something) up." *Raise* usually takes an object.

Six Troublesome Verbs **191**

DIFFERENTIATING INSTRUCTION

Learners Having Difficulty
Acting out the verbs might help students to differentiate between the troublesome verb pairs presented in this lesson. Have students work in pairs to act out the following sentences. Point out to students that the second verb in each pair requires a direct object that receives the action.

1. I <u>sit</u> in the chair.
2. I <u>set</u> the book on the table.
3. I <u>rise</u> from my chair.
4. I <u>raise</u> this book in the air.
5. I <u>lie</u> on the floor.
6. I <u>lay</u> this pencil on the desk.

Advanced Learners

Mnemonics. Place students in groups of four to create short poems that will help them remember the correct usage of the six troublesome verbs. An example follows:

> The bread has <u>risen</u>,
> And it's time to bake it.
> I <u>raised</u> my hand
> And asked to taste it.

Encourage students to recite their poems or to put them on posters.

USAGE

MINI-LESSON **Grammar**   *Continued on p. 192*

Direct Objects. You may want to review direct objects with students since one verb in each troublesome verb pair usually takes a direct object. Explain to students that a direct object is a noun or pronoun that receives the action of the verb; a direct object is never in a prepositional phrase. Write the following sentences on the chalkboard or on a transparency. Bracket the prepositional phrases, and circle the direct objects. Point out to students that remembering which verb in each pair takes a direct object will help them with

Six Troublesome Verbs **191**

DIFFERENTIATING INSTRUCTION

English-Language Learners

General Strategies. The vowel sounds in the six verbs in this section sound rather similar—especially to students who speak languages other than English. This similarity can cause confusion for students whose languages do not have these sounds. You could pronounce the words for any students who have difficulty, and students could write down these words to help with memorization. Be sure to emphasize the vowel sounds.

STYLE TIP

You may know that the verb *raise* has more meanings than the one given here.

EXAMPLE
The Nelsons **raise** geese.
[*Raise* does not mean "lift up" here, but it still takes an object.]

Base Form	Present Participle	Past	Past Participle
rise	[is] rising	rose	[have] risen
raise	[is] raising	raised	[have] raised

EXAMPLES The fans **were rising** to sing the national anthem. [no object]

Fans **were raising** signs and banners. [Fans were raising what? *Signs* and *banners* are the objects.]

The student **rose** to ask a question. [no object]

The student **raised** a good question. [The student raised what? *Question* is the object.]

Prices **had risen.** [no object]

The store **had raised** prices. [The store had raised what? *Prices* is the object.]

Oral Practice 5 Using Forms of *Rise* and *Raise* Correctly

Read the following sentences aloud, stressing the italicized verbs.

1. Mount Everest *rises* over 29,000 feet.
2. He *raises* the flag at sunrise.
3. The TV reporter *raised* her voice to be heard.
4. She *rose* from her seat and looked out the window.
5. The constellation Orion had not yet *risen* in the southern sky.
6. They had *raised* the piñata high in the tree.
7. I hope the bread is *rising*.
8. He will be *raising* the bucket from the well.

Exercise 7 Identifying the Correct Forms of *Rise* and *Raise*

Identify the correct verb of the two given in parentheses in each of the following sentences.

EXAMPLE   1. After the storm, Diana (*rose, raised*) the window.
           1. raised

1. The entire audience quickly (*rose*, *raised*) to their feet to sing the "Hallelujah Chorus."

MINI-LESSON Grammar Continued from p. 191

correct verb usage. For additional information and practice, refer students to **Chapter 4: Complements.**

1. The tourists <u>sat</u> [on benches].
2. We <u>set</u> the (dishes) [on the table].
3. The full moon <u>rose</u> [through the clouds].
4. The cheering crowd <u>raised</u> (banners).
5. The deer <u>lay</u> very still.
6. The senator <u>laid</u> her (notes) aside.

2. They used a jack to (*rise, raise*) the car so that they could change the tire.
3. The fire juggler is (*rising, raising*) two flaming batons over his head to signal the start of the show.
4. Some people have trouble remembering that the sun always (*rises, raises*) in the east.
5. He gently (*rose, raised*) the injured duckling from the lake.
6. Only half of Mauna Kea, a volcano on the island of Hawaii, (*rises, raises*) above the ocean.
7. The proud winner has (*risen, raised*) her trophy so that everyone can see it.
8. The wedding guests have (*risen, raised*) from their seats to see the bride enter.
9. Yeast makes the dough for pizza and other baked goods, such as bread and rolls, (*rise, raise*).
10. They will (*rise, raise*) the couch while I look under it.

Lie and Lay

The verb *lie* generally means "to recline," "to be in a place," or "to remain lying down." *Lie* does not take an object. The verb *lay* generally means "to put (something) down" or "to place (something somewhere)." *Lay* usually takes an object.

Base Form	Present Participle	Past	Past Participle
lie	[is] lying	lay	[have] lain
lay	[is] laying	laid	[have] laid

EXAMPLES The silverware **is lying** on the table. [no object]
The waiter **is laying** silverware beside each plate. [The waiter is laying what? *Silverware* is the object.]

The apple dolls **lay** drying in the sun. [no object]
Aunt Martha **laid** her apple dolls in the sun to dry. [Aunt Martha laid what? *Dolls* is the object.]

That bicycle **had lain** in the driveway for a week. [no object]
Bill **had laid** that bicycle in the driveway. [Bill had laid what? *Bicycle* is the object.]

MEETING THE CHALLENGE

Write a poem, correctly using each of the six troublesome verbs, *sit, set, rise, raise, lie,* and *lay*. Be sure to check your poem for correct usage of the troublesome verbs.

STYLE TIP

The verb *lie* can also mean "to tell an untruth." Used in this way, *lie* still does not take an object.

EXAMPLE
  Don't **lie** to her, Beth.

The past and past participle forms of this meaning of *lie* are *lied* and [*have*] *lied*.

Six Troublesome Verbs **193**

RETEACHING

Troublesome Verbs

Game. You may want to make the following tic-tac-toe game available to pairs of students who need help with troublesome verbs. To make the game, you will need nine one-inch squares of paper. On the front of five of the squares, write *lie, sit, rose, lain,* and *lay;* on the back of each of the squares, write *needs no object.* On the front of the remaining four squares, write *lay, set, raised,* and *laid;* on the back of each of these squares, write *needs an object.* Make a game board by dividing a nine-by-nine inch paper into one-inch squares.

To play the game, one student draws a square, reads the verb, and uses it in a sentence according to the description on the back of the square. If the sentence is correct, the player puts the square anywhere on the board, verb side down. If the sentence is wrong, the player returns the square to the pile. Then, the second player takes a turn. The winner is the first to get three *needs no object* cards or three *needs an object* cards in a row in any direction.

USAGE

Learning for Life

Continued on pp. 194–195

Telling a Story. Students will probably encounter times when they will be asked to describe a firsthand experience—to give an eyewitness report. For example, a friend might have missed the end of last night's game and wants to hear all about it, or a parent might ask how the vase in the living room *really* broke.

For this activity, tell students to imagine that they are reporters for the *Good News Gazette,* a local newspaper that reports on positive happenings. Their assignment is to

Six Troublesome Verbs **193**

Oral Practice 6 — Using Forms of *Lie* and *Lay* Correctly

Read the following sentences aloud, stressing the italicized verbs.

1. If you are tired, *lie* down for a while.
2. *Lay* your pencils down, please.
3. Two huge dogs *lay* by the fire last night.
4. The cat has been *lying* on the new bedspread.
5. Mr. Cortez *laid* the map of Puerto Rico on the table.
6. In our state, snow usually *lies* on the ground until late March or the first weeks of April.
7. He had *laid* your coats on the bed in my room.
8. After the baby had *lain* down for a nap, she still wanted to play with her new toy.

Exercise 8 — Identifying the Correct Forms of *Lie* and *Lay*

Identify the correct verb of the two in parentheses for each of the following sentences.

EXAMPLE 1. Marc (*lay, laid*) his new tennis shoes on the floor.
  1. laid

1. The islands of American Samoa (*lie, lay*) about 4,800 miles southwest of San Francisco.
2. Dad quickly (*lay, laid*) the hermit crab down when it began to pinch him.
3. I don't know where I have (*lain, laid*) my copy of *Chinese Proverbs* by Ruthanne Lum McCunn.
4. I have often (*lain, laid*) under the oak tree and napped.
5. Many visitors (*lie, lay*) flowers and wreaths at the Vietnam Veterans Memorial in Washington, D.C.
6. My brother, who is sick, has been (*lying, laying*) in bed all day.
7. The clerk (*lay, laid*) the small package on the scale.
8. (*Lie, Lay*) your backpack down, and come see the new comic books I bought yesterday.
9. Those clothes will (*lie, lay*) on the floor until you pick them up.
10. After he had circled several times, the puppy (*lay, laid*) down and slept.

COMPUTER TIP

Most word processors can help you check your writing to be sure that you've used verbs correctly. For example, a spellchecker will highlight misspelled verb forms such as *attackted* or *drownded*.

Grammar-checking software can point out inconsistent verb tense, and it may also highlight questionable uses of problem verb pairs such as *lie* and *lay* or *rise* and *raise*. Some programs can also identify verbs in the passive voice.

Remember, though, that the computer is just a tool. As a writer, you are responsible for making all the style and content choices that affect your writing.

Learning for Life

Continued from p. 193

write a brief eyewitness report about a true or imagined positive event in their school or neighborhood. Because proper sequence is necessary in the accurate retelling of an event, tell students to be particularly careful in their choice of tense and the use of verb forms.

You may want to share the following model with students.

Dog Returns Home
After several days of wandering, Zelda finally found her way back home early this

Review C **Identifying the Correct Forms of *Sit* and *Set*, *Rise* and *Raise*, and *Lie* and *Lay***

Identify the correct verb of the two given in parentheses in each of the following sentences.

EXAMPLE 1. The bricklayer (*rose, raised*) from the patio floor and dusted himself off.
1. rose

1. These rocks have (*lain, laid*) here for centuries.
2. Please (*sit, set*) there until your name is called.
3. The nurse (*lay, laid*) her cool hand on the sick child's brow and decided to take his temperature.
4. The horses are (*lying, laying*) in the pasture.
5. The senator and her advisors had (*sat, set*) around the huge conference table.
6. After the picnic, everyone (*lay, laid*) on blankets to rest in the shade of the oak tree.
7. Smoke (*rose, raised*) from the chimney.
8. The farmhands (*sat, set*) their lunch boxes under a tree to shade them from the sun.
9. Have you been (*sitting, setting*) there all afternoon?
10. The sun has already (*risen, raised*).
11. Why has the stage manager (*rose, raised*) the curtains before the second act has begun?
12. A gust of hot air caused the enormous balloon to (*rise, raise*) out of sight of the spectators.
13. Be sure to (*lie, lay*) these windowpanes down carefully.
14. When the queen enters, each guest should (*rise, raise*) from his or her chair.
15. Who (*sat, set*) these glasses on my chair?
16. "(*Lie, Lay*) down!" the trainer sharply ordered the puppy, but the puppy didn't obey.
17. If we had a pulley, we could (*rise, raise*) that stone.
18. Just (*sit, set*) those green beans by the sink; I'll get to them in a minute.
19. Mom and Aunt Linda must have been (*lying, laying*) tile in the kitchen all afternoon.
20. You (*rise, raise*) the garage door, and I'll bring the bikes in out of the rain.

Six Troublesome Verbs **195**

Review D **Proofreading Sentences for Correct Verb Forms**

Most of the following sentences contain incorrect verb forms. If a sentence contains the wrong form of a verb, write the correct form. If a sentence is already correct, write *C*.

EXAMPLE 1. During the 1800s, many German settlers choosed to live in the Hill Country of central Texas.
   1. chose

1. built
2. gone
3. lies
4. used
5. C
6. grew
7. rose
8. sat
9. spoken
10. C

1. These hardy, determined pioneers builded towns and cleared land for farming.
2. I have went to the town of Fredericksburg several times with my family.
3. This interesting town lays about 80 miles west of Austin.
4. Fredericksburg use to be in Comanche territory.
5. Early on, German settlers made peace with neighboring Comanche chiefs.
6. The town then growed rapidly.
7. German-style churches, public buildings, and houses like the one shown here raised along the town's central street.
8. On one of our visits, my family set and talked about the town with a woman who had been born there.
9. She said that she had spoke German all her life.
10. When we left, she raised a hand and said, *"Auf Wiedersehen"* (until we meet again).

196   Chapter 9   Using Verbs Correctly

CHAPTER 9

Chapter Review

A. Using Irregular Verbs

Write the correct past or past participle form of the italicized irregular verb provided before each sentence.

1. *break*   The thunder ___ the silence.
2. *ring*   Who ___ the fire alarm so quickly?
3. *shrink* This shirt must have ___ in the dryer.
4. *throw*   You've ___ the ball out of bounds!
5. *lead*   Julio ___ the parade last year, so now it's my turn.
6. *rise*   The sun ___ over the pyramids of Giza in Egypt.
7. *swim*   We have ___ only three laps.
8. *choose* Vera was ___ as captain of the volleyball team.
9. *go*   I have ___ to visit the Grand Canyon twice.
10. *sit*   The tiny tree frog ___ motionless.
11. *write* Joan has ___ a story about aliens from the Andromeda galaxy.
12. *do*   During class, Jorge ___ the first five problems of his homework assignment.
13. *steal* Three runners ___ bases during the first inning.
14. *break* This summer's heat wave has ___ all records.
15. *drink* Have you ___ all of the tomato juice?
16. *sink*   The log had slowly ___ into the quicksand.
17. *lie*   The old postcards have ___ in the box for years.
18. *drive* Have you ever ___ across the state of Texas?
19. *begin* Our local PBS station ___ its fund-raising drive.
20. *set*   Have you ___ the paper plates and napkins on the picnic table?
21. *throw* Who ___ the ball to first base?
22. *know*   I have ___ some of my classmates for six years.
23. *take*   Kadeem ___ the role of Frederick Douglass.
24. *tear*   My mother ___ the paper to make confetti.
25. *come*   We ___ close to winning the tournament.

Chapter Review 197

ASSESSING

Monitoring Progress

Chapter Review. To assess student progress, you may want to compare the types of items missed on the **Diagnostic Preview** to those missed on the **Chapter Review**. If students have not made significant progress, you may want to refer them to **Exercises 14–17** in **Chapter 17: Correcting Common Errors** for additional practice.

Terms and numerals in brackets refer to concepts and rules tested by the items in the Chapter Review.

1.–25. [9c]

1. broke
2. rang
3. shrunk
4. thrown
5. led
6. rose [*rise, raise*]
7. swum
8. chosen
9. gone
10. sat [*sit, set*]
11. written
12. did
13. stole
14. broken
15. drunk
16. sunk
17. lain [*lie, lay*]
18. driven
19. began
20. set [*sit, set*]
21. threw
22. known
23. took
24. tore
25. came

RESOURCES

Using Verbs Correctly

Review
- *Language & Sentence Skills Practice,* pp. 185–188

Assessment
- *Holt Handbook Chapter Tests with Answer Key,* pp. 17–18, 46

Chapter Review 197

26. has come/has brought [9d, a, c]
27. had slept [9d, a, c]
28. moves/hears [9d, a, b, c]
29. will have [9d, a, c]
30. knew/grew [9d, a, c]

31. comes/drives *or* came/drove [9e, d, c]
32. finishes/forgets *or* finished/forgot [9e, d, b, c]
33. drop/climbs *or* dropped/climbed [9e, d, b]
34. jumps/cheers/makes *or* jumped/cheered/made [9e, d, b, c]
35. presents/are *or* presented/were [9e, d, b, c]
36.–40. [active and passive voice]
36. passive
37. active

B. Changing Tenses of Verbs

Rewrite each of the following sentences to change the verb or verbs to the tense indicated in italics.

26. *present perfect*   Every time Roger ~~comes~~ to visit me, he ~~brings~~ his dog Zip with him.
27. *past perfect*   The dog ~~will sleep~~ on the kitchen floor for the entire visit.
28. *present*   Zip ~~moved~~ only if he ~~heard~~ the sounds of food being prepared.
29. *future perfect*   Zip ~~has~~ broken all records for a dog not moving a muscle.
30. *past*   We ~~had known~~ Zip before he ~~had grown~~ old.

C. Making Verb Tenses Consistent

Read the following sentences, and choose whether to rewrite them in the present or past tense. Then, rewrite the sentences, changing the verb forms to make the verb tense consistent.

31. My uncle ~~comes~~ back to Michigan for Christmas, and he ~~drove~~ his vintage sports car.
32. Ava ~~finished~~ her assignment, but she ~~forgets~~ to put a title page on it.
33. The stages of the booster rocket ~~dropped~~ away as the space shuttle ~~climbs~~ into the sky.
34. Aunt Maureen ~~jumped~~ to her feet and ~~cheers~~ when Mia ~~made~~ the winning basket.
35. When Barbara ~~presents~~ her science fair project, all the judges ~~were~~ very impressed.

D. Identifying Active and Passive Voice

Tell whether the italicized verb is in the *active voice* or the *passive voice* in each of the following sentences.

36. The grass clippings and the kitchen scraps *were placed* on the compost pile.
37. Most of the class *had* already *gone* to see that play.

38. All of the pencils *were sharpened* by Erica and Austin before the test began.
39. My father *was asked* for his advice on repairing the old playground equipment.
40. Every Friday night the Lopez family *invites* us to their house for dinner.

Writing Application
Using Verbs in a Story

Verb Forms and Tenses   A local writers' club is sponsoring a contest for the best "cliffhanger" opening of an adventure story. Write an exciting paragraph to enter in the contest. Your paragraph should leave readers wondering "What happens next?" In your paragraph, use at least five verbs from the lists of Common Irregular Verbs in this chapter.

Prewriting   First, you will need to imagine a suspenseful situation to describe. Jot down several ideas for your story opening. Then, choose the one you like best. With that situation in mind, scan the lists of irregular verbs. Note at least ten verbs you can use. Include some lively action verbs like *burst, swing,* and *throw*.

Writing   As you write your rough draft, think of your readers. Choose words that create a suspenseful, believable scene. Remember that you have only one paragraph to catch your readers' interest.

Revising   Ask a friend to read your paragraph. Does your friend find it interesting? Can he or she picture the scene clearly? If not, you may want to add, delete, or revise some details.

Publishing   Check your spelling, usage, punctuation, and grammar. Check to make sure the forms of verbs are correct and the tenses are consistent. You may want to exchange your cliffhanger with a partner, and complete each other's stories. With your teacher's permission, you can then read the completed stories aloud to the class.

CHAPTER

10 Using Pronouns Correctly

Nominative and Objective Case Forms, Other Pronoun Problems

Diagnostic Preview

A. Correcting Errors in Pronoun Forms

Most of the following sentences contain errors in the use of pronoun forms. Identify the ~~error~~, and give the correct pronoun form for each sentence. If a sentence is already correct, write *C*.

EXAMPLE 1. The Garcia children and them grew up together in East Texas.

  1. them—they

1. ~~Us~~ basketball players know the value of warming up.
2. The computer experts in our class are Rosalinda and ~~her~~.
3. Pablo and ~~me~~ are planning to visit the Andes Mountains.
4. At Passover, my grandparents make gefilte fish and other traditional foods for my cousins and ~~I~~.
5. Give Sue and him this invitation to the awards ceremony.
6. Josh made ~~hisself~~ a bookcase in industrial arts class.
7. Two angry hornets chased Earline and ~~she~~ all the way home.
8. The first actors on stage were Jesse and ~~him~~.
9. Mr. Mendez and ~~us~~ organized a debate about student rights.
10. Will you attend the rally with Scott and me?
11. Jeannette and ~~her~~ know a great deal about Greek myths.

12. The hickory smoke smelled good to we campers.
13. Liang was telling them and me about his home in Hong Kong.
14. Julia and them learned how to make batik patterns on cloth.
15. Tom asked Mark and he if they wanted to join a gospel band.

B. Revising for Clear Pronoun Reference

Revise each of the following sentences, correcting each unclear pronoun reference.

EXAMPLE 1. Brad informed Luke that his brother was late.
         1. Brad informed Luke that Luke's brother was late.

16. Liz called Gail while she was doing her Spanish homework.
17. Ryan spotted John in the crowded theater when he stood up.
18. As soon as Mom and Aunt Sue arrived in Denver, she e-mailed me.
19. Julie saw Louise while she was in Paris.
20. Before Chad met Kyle, he had never water-skied.

12. us [appositive, 10e]
13. C [10d]
14. they [10b]
15. him [10d]

HELP
Sentences in Part B of the Diagnostic Preview may have more than one possible answer.

16.–20. [clear reference] Answers may vary. Possible responses are given.
16. Liz/, she called Gail.
17. When John stood up,/him
18. Mom
19. Julie/, she saw Louise.
20. before he met Kyle.

Case

10a. *Case* is the form that a noun or pronoun takes to show its relationship to other words in a sentence.

English has three cases for nouns and pronouns:
- nominative
- objective
- possessive

The form of a noun is the same for both the nominative and the objective cases. For example, a noun used as a subject (nominative case) will have the same form when used as a direct object (objective case).

NOMINATIVE CASE   That Ming **vase** is very old. [subject]
OBJECTIVE CASE   Who bought the **vase**? [direct object]

A noun changes its form only in the possessive case, usually by adding an apostrophe and an *s*.

POSSESSIVE CASE   The Ming **vase's** new owner is pleased.

HELP
The nominative case is sometimes referred to as the subject form. The objective case is sometimes referred to as the object form. Follow your teacher's instructions when using these terms.

Reference Note
For more about **forming the possessive case of nouns,** see page 330.

DIRECT TEACHING

Modeling and Demonstration

Case. Model how to identify personal pronouns and their cases by using the example *He showed me his book.* First, ask which words are pronouns. [*He, me, his*] Next, ask how the pronoun *He* is used in this sentence. [*as the subject*] Then, ask how *me* is used. [*as the indirect object of the verb,* showed] Ask how *his* is used. [*to show possession*] Explain that the pronoun *He* is in nominative case, *me* is in objective case, and *his* is in possessive case. Point out that a pronoun takes one of these three cases depending on how it is used in a sentence. Now, have a volunteer use another example from this chapter to demonstrate how to identify pronouns and their cases.

DIFFERENTIATING INSTRUCTION

English-Language Learners

General Strategies. Languages vary in the number of cases they have; Korean has nine, Russian six, Arabic and English three, and Vietnamese none. Students who speak languages with cases different from those in English may struggle to adapt to the differences. Those who speak caseless languages may have trouble understanding what case is and why it is important. You may wish to hold individual or small group sessions with students to answer any questions they might have.

Unlike nouns, most personal pronouns have different forms for all three cases.

Personal Pronouns		
Nominative Case	Objective Case	Possessive Case
Singular		
I	me	my, mine
you	you	your, yours
he, she, it	him, her, it	his, her, hers, its
Plural		
we	us	our, ours
you	you	your, yours
they	them	their, theirs

NOTE The personal pronouns in the possessive case—*my, mine, your, yours, his, her, hers, its, our, ours, their, theirs*—are used to show ownership or relationship.

The possessive pronouns *mine, yours, his, hers, its, ours,* and *theirs* are used as parts of sentences in the same ways in which the pronouns in the nominative and the objective cases are used.

EXAMPLES His book and **mine** are overdue.

This desk is **his.**

We completed **ours** this morning.

The possessive pronouns *my, your, his, her, its, our,* and *their* are used as adjectives before nouns.

EXAMPLES **My** shoes need to be cleaned.

Have you proofread **her** report yet?

There goes **their** dog Rex.

NOTE Some authorities prefer to call these words adjectives. Follow your teacher's instructions regarding these possessive forms.

Chapter 10 Using Pronouns Correctly

RESOURCES

Case
Practice
- *Language & Sentence Skills Practice,* pp. 194–201, 207–208
- *Developmental Language & Sentence Skills,* pp. 73–78

The Nominative Case

10b. The *subject* of a verb should be in the nominative case.

EXAMPLES **He** and **I** mowed lawns. [*He* and *I* are used together as the compound subject of *mowed*.]

Did **they** craft candles from antique molds? [*They* is the subject of *Did craft*.]

She baked cranberry bread while **we** wrapped packages. [*She* is the subject of *baked*. *We* is the subject of *wrapped*.]

Oral Practice 1 Using Pronouns as Subjects

Read each of the following sentences aloud, stressing the italicized pronouns.

1. Dr. Chen and *they* discussed the usefulness of herbal medicines.
2. *He* and *I* live next door to each other.
3. *They* should try to get along better.
4. Yesterday *she* and *they* gave their reports on modern African American poets.
5. *You* and *she* left the party early.
6. Since the third grade, *we* have been friends.
7. *He* and his family are moving to Puerto Rico.
8. *I* will miss them.

Exercise 1 Identifying Correct Pronoun Forms

Choose the correct form of the pronoun in parentheses in each of the following sentences.

EXAMPLE 1. My friends and (*I, me*) like to spend time outdoors.
1. *I*

1. Lou and (*me, I*) asked my mother to drive us to a nearby state park.
2. There (*he and I, him and me*) set out on a marked trail through the woods.
3. Before long, (*he and I, him and me*) were exploring a snowy area off the beaten track.
4. At midday Lou and (*me, I*) reluctantly followed our tracks back to the path.
5. (*Us, We*) had had the best time of our lives.

Reference Note
For more about **subjects**, see page 5.

TIPS TRICKS

To help you choose the correct pronoun in a compound subject, try each form of the pronoun separately.

EXAMPLE
(*She, Her*) and (*I, me*) found them. [*She found* or *Her found*? *I found* or *Me found*?]

ANSWER
She and **I** found them.

DIFFERENTIATING INSTRUCTION

English-Language Learners

General Strategies. Before students try to determine when to use nominative or objective pronouns, make sure your English-language learners know how to distinguish between the two. You might want to provide simple template sentences to help students practice using the correct cases. For example: "____ will ask ____ about ____." [*Possible answer:* He *will* ask her *about* them.] If students need help with the basics of pronoun usage, refer them to **Chapter 2: Parts of Speech Overview.**

Cantonese. Cantonese uses fewer pronouns than English and drops them when they are understood: *The nurse put a thermometer in (my) mouth.* Also, there is no difference between the nominative and objective forms. Have students practice the forms of pronouns by relating personal information, such as likes and dislikes, in speech or writing.

Hmong. The objective and nominative cases of Hmong pronouns depend upon the pronouns' placement within the sentence rather than on the forms of the pronouns themselves, while the possessive case relies upon the use of a possessive classifier. Remind Hmong speakers that English pronouns change form to indicate their functions within sentences, and offer additional practice using pronouns in different cases.

USAGE

Case 203

CONTENT-AREA CONNECTIONS

Life Science

Classification. Explain to students that the **Personal Pronouns** chart on p. 202 classifies pronouns into three categories based on the way the pronouns are used in sentences. In science, items are also grouped according to their characteristics. For example, scientists classify all living things based on their characteristics, grouping them into five major groups called kingdoms. Ask students to think of other types of classification used in science. [*Living things are further classified by phylum, class, order, family, genus, and species. Elements are also classified.*]

Case 203

6. I told Mother that I thought (*she*, *her*) would enjoy the trail.
7. To my surprise, (*she*, *her*) wanted to walk part of the trail then.
8. Lou and (*she*, *her*) immediately started hiking down the trail.
9. (*They*, *Them*) knew that I would follow.
10. (*Us*, *We*) had fun but were ready to ride instead of walk home!

10c. A **predicate nominative** should be in the nominative case.

A **predicate nominative** is a word or word group that is in the predicate and that identifies or refers to the subject of the verb. A pronoun used as a predicate nominative completes the meaning of a linking verb, usually a form of the verb *be* (such as *am, are, is, was, were, be, been,* or *being*).

EXAMPLES The candidates should have been **he** and **she**. [*He* and *she* follow the linking verb *should have been* and identify the subject *candidates*.]

The members of the team are **they**. [*They* follows the linking verb *are* and identifies the subject *members*.]

Oral Practice 2 — Using Pronouns as Predicate Nominatives

Read each of the following sentences aloud, stressing the italicized pronouns.

1. Were the only Spanish-speaking people you and *they*?
2. The caller could have been *she*.
3. The leaders will be my mother and *he*.
4. The three candidates for class president are *she* and *we*.
5. That must be the pilot and *he* on the runway.
6. The three winners were Eduardo, Maya, and *I*.
7. The first ones on the scene were our neighbors and *they*.
8. The speakers at the rally were *she* and Jesse Jackson.

Exercise 2 — Identifying Correct Pronoun Forms

Choose the correct form of the pronoun in parentheses in each of the following sentences.

EXAMPLE   1. Were the ones who left early (*they*, *them*)?
          1. they

1. Two witnesses claimed that the burglar was (*him*, *he*).

STYLE TIP

Expressions such as *It's me* and *That's her* are acceptable in everyday speaking. However, these expressions contain the objective case pronouns *me* and *her* used incorrectly as predicate nominatives. Such expressions should be avoided in formal writing and speaking.

Reference Note

For more about **predicate nominatives**, see page 79.

TIPS TRICKS

To choose the correct form of a pronoun used as a predicate nominative, try reversing the order of the sentence.

EXAMPLE
The fastest runner is (*he*, *him*).
REVERSED
(*He*, *Him*) is the fastest runner.
ANSWER
The fastest runner is **he**.

DIRECT TEACHING

Correcting Misconceptions

Pronouns as Predicate Nominatives. Students may not know that it is correct to use nominative-case pronouns as predicate nominatives and may think that objective-case pronouns sound less awkward. Assure students that sentences such as "It is I" are correct, and encourage them to practice saying such sentences aloud to help make them more familiar. You can also tell students that they can rewrite sentences to make them sound more natural by using the predicate nominatives as subjects. For example, the second sentence in **Oral Practice 2** can be rephrased as "She could have been the caller."

MINI-LESSON — Mechanics

Contractions. You may want to discuss with students that pronouns in the nominative case can combine with helping or linking verbs to form contractions. Write the following sentences on the chalkboard to show that the apostrophe takes the place of omitted letters.

1. I've (I have) never eaten tofu.
2. They're (They are) arriving tomorrow.
3. We'll (We will) be home early.

2. The volunteers must be (*them*, *they*).
3. Is the last performer (*she*, *her*)?
4. The next speaker will be (*him*, *he*).
5. The guests of honor are Luther and (*us*, *we*).
6. I knew the one in red was (*she*, *her*), of course.
7. The hardest workers are Susan, Tranh, and (*me*, *I*).
8. Can that be (*she*, *her*) in the Indian sari?
9. The next batter should be (*she*, *her*).
10. Our newest neighbors are the Blumenthals and (*them*, *they*).

Review A — Writing Sentences That Contain Pronouns in the Nominative Case

The busy scene you see on the next page was painted by the Mexican American artist Carmen Lomas Garza. It shows one of her childhood birthday parties. The fish-shaped object is a piñata, full of treats for the children. Carmen is getting ready to take a swing at the piñata. Answer each of the following questions by writing a sentence. Follow the directions after each question.

EXAMPLE
1. What are the kneeling boys in the lower right-hand corner doing? (*Use a plural personal pronoun as the subject.*)
1. They are getting ready to play marbles.

1. What is Carmen using to hit the piñata? (*Use a singular personal pronoun as the subject.*)
2. For whom are the presents on the table? (*Use a plural personal pronoun as the subject.*)
3. Who will get the gifts and treats inside the piñata? (*Use a person's name and a plural personal pronoun as the compound subject.*)
4. Have you and your classmates ever played a game that requires a blindfold? (*Use a plural and a singular personal pronoun as the compound subject.*)
5. Why does the boy at the far left have presents in his hands? (*Use a singular personal pronoun as the subject.*)
6. What would Carmen say if you asked her, "Who's the birthday girl?" (*Use a singular personal pronoun as a predicate nominative.*)
7. Did Carmen's parents and her grandmother plan the party? (*Use a plural and a singular personal pronoun as a compound predicate nominative.*)

Review A Writing Sentences That Contain Pronouns in the Nominative Case

POSSIBLE ANSWERS
1. She is using a bat.
2. They are for Carmen.
3. Carmen and they will get the gifts and treats.
4. They and I have played a game that requires a blindfold.
5. He is going to give the presents to Carmen.
6. "The birthday girl is I."
7. Yes, it was they and she.

---

4. I'm (I am) happy to see you.

Have students work in pairs to use the following contractions in sentences: *I'm, I'd, you've, you're, he's, she'll, it's, they've, we're,* and *we've.* As in the models, have students identify the words that are combined to form the contractions.

Upon completion, have pairs exchange sentences to check for correctness. For additional information and practice, refer students to **Chapter 15: Punctuation,** p. 333.

Review A Writing Sentences That Contain Pronouns in the Nominative Case

ANSWERS continued

8. Yes, she and the baby are having a good time.
9. No, that is not he.
10. The one now looking at the picture of the birthday party is I.

EXTENSION

Relating to Literature

If the Edgar Allan Poe poem "Annabel Lee" is in your literature textbook, have students read it and discuss Poe's use of personal pronouns. Ask students why they think the poet repeated the pronoun *me* so often. [*Me* rhymes with *Annabel Lee; in the first four stanzas, every other line ends with the long e sound.*]

You may want to discuss the use of pronouns in comparisons, as in line 28, ". . . older than we," and line 29, ". . . wiser than we." Explain to students that the nominative case pronoun is used because *we* functions as a subject, but the verb has been omitted. With the missing verbs added, the lines would read "older than we were" and "wiser than we were."

Reference Note

For more about **direct and indirect objects,** see pages 74 and 76.

8. Are the baby and his mother near the table having a good time? (*Use* the baby *and a singular personal pronoun as the compound subject.*)
9. Is Carmen's father the man holding the piñata rope? (*Use a singular personal pronoun as a predicate nominative.*)
10. Who is the one now looking at the picture of Carmen Lomas Garza's birthday party? (*Use a singular personal pronoun as a predicate nominative.*)

The Objective Case

10d. *Direct objects* and ***indirect objects*** of verbs should be in the objective case.

A ***direct object*** is a noun, pronoun, or word group that tells *who* or *what* receives the action of the verb.

EXAMPLES   Mom called **me** to the phone. [*Me tells whom Mom called.*]

Julia bought sweet potatoes and used **them** to make filling for the empanadas. [*Them tells what she used.*]

An *indirect object* is a noun, pronoun, or word group that often appears in sentences containing direct objects. An indirect object tells *to whom* or *to what* or *for whom* or *for what* the action of the verb is done.

An indirect object generally comes between an action verb and its direct object.

EXAMPLES The hostess handed **her** a name tag. [*Her* tells *to whom* the hostess handed the name tag.]

Mr. Tanaka raises large goldfish; he often feeds **them** rice. [*Them* tells *to what* Mr. Tanaka feeds rice.]

NOTE Indirect objects do not follow prepositions. If *to* or *for* precedes a pronoun, the pronoun is an object of a preposition, not an indirect object.

OBJECT OF A PREPOSITION Send a letter to **me**.
INDIRECT OBJECT Send **me** a letter.

Oral Practice 3 — Using Pronouns as Direct Objects and Indirect Objects

Read each of the following sentences aloud, stressing the italicized pronouns.

1. I took Joe and *her* to a performance by French mimes.
2. The bus driver let Melba, Joe, and *me* off at the corner.
3. An usher gave *us* programs.
4. Another usher showed *them* and *me* our seats.
5. The performers fascinated Melba and *me*.
6. Their costumes delighted the crowd and *her*.
7. No one else impressed Joe and *me* as much as the youngest mime did.
8. We watched *her* exploring the walls of an invisible room.

Exercise 3 — Writing Pronouns Used as Direct Objects and Indirect Objects

Write an appropriate pronoun for each blank in the sentences on the following page. Use a variety of pronouns, but do not use *you* or *it*.

EXAMPLE 1. Have you seen Kim and _____ ?
1. her

TIPS & TRICKS

To help you choose the correct pronoun in a compound object, try each form of the pronoun separately in the sentence.

EXAMPLE
The teacher chose Luisa and (*I*, *me*). [The teacher chose *I* or The teacher chose *me*?]

ANSWER
The teacher chose Luisa and **me**.

RETEACHING

Pronouns

Activity. To help students with correct pronoun usage, suggest that they make a chart similar to the one on p. 202, eliminating the possessive-case pronouns. Then, have students highlight all the nominative-case pronouns in one color and all the objective-case pronouns in another color. Beneath the chart, have students write four sentences using one pronoun in each as

- a subject
- a predicate nominative
- a direct object
- an indirect object

Ask students to highlight the pronouns in sentences 1 and 2 in the same color as those in the nominative case on the chart. Have them highlight the pronouns in sentences 3 and 4 in the same color as the chart's objective case pronouns. Encourage students to keep the chart in their notebooks; they can refer to it as they complete the exercises in this chapter and expand it as they learn new rules.

Exercise 3

DISTRIBUTED REVIEW
In each of the sentences in **Exercise 3**, the added pronoun completes a compound object. Point out to students the similarities between this use of *compound* and other uses they may have already encountered: compound subjects and compound verbs **(Chapter 1: The Parts of a Sentence)**, compound nouns **(Chapter 2: Parts of Speech Overview)**, and compound sentences **(Chapter 7: Kinds of Sentence Structure).**

Responses will vary. Sample responses are given.
1. me
2. them/us
3. her
4. them/me
5. him
6. me
7. her/him
8. her/me
9. her
10. me

1. The manager hired Susana and ____.
2. Lana sent ____ and ____ invitations.
3. We gave Grandpa López and ____ round-trip tickets to Mexico City.
4. The firefighters rescued ____ and ____.
5. Aunt Coretta showed my cousins and ____ a carved mask from Nigeria.
6. The show entertained the children and ____.
7. The waiter served ____ and ____ a variety of dumplings.
8. Our team chose ____ and ____ as representatives.
9. The election committee nominated Gerry and ____.
10. The clerk gave Misako and ____ the receipt for the paper lanterns.

Review B Identifying Correct Pronoun Forms

Choose the correct form of each pronoun in parentheses in the following sentences.

EXAMPLE
1. Paul told Ms. Esteban that (*he, him*) and (*I, me*) need a topic for our report.

1. he, I

1. In our American history class, some of the other students and (*he, him*) thought that there should be more reports on women.
2. We were interested in Amelia Earhart and wanted to give (*she, her*) the recognition she deserves.
3. The picture on the left, showing Amelia Earhart looking relaxed and confident, interested Paul and (*I, me*).
4. Both (*he, him*) and (*I, me*) were eager to find out more about her contribution to aviation.
5. We learned that it was (*she, her*) who made the first solo flight by a woman across the Atlantic.
6. The fact that Amelia Earhart was the first pilot to fly from Hawaii to California surprised the rest of the class and (*we, us*), too.
7. In 1937, her navigator and (*she, her*) took off in a twin-engine plane for a trip around the world.
8. After (*they, them*) had completed two thirds of the trip, Earhart and her navigator lost contact with radio operators.

9. No one ever saw (*they, them*) or the airplane again.
10. Ms. Esteban and (*we, us*) are among the many people still puzzling over this mystery.

10e. The *object of a preposition* should be in the objective case.

A noun or pronoun that follows a preposition is called the *object of a preposition.* Together, the preposition, its object, and any modifiers of the object make a *prepositional phrase.*

EXAMPLES   Before **us** lay rows of green cornstalks. [*Us* is the object of the preposition *Before.*]

The secret is between **him** and **me**. [*Him* and *me* are the compound object of the preposition *between.*]

Please stand next to **her**. [*Her* is the object of the compound preposition *next to.*]

Oral Practice 4   Using Pronouns as Objects of Prepositions

Read each of the following sentences aloud, stressing the italicized prepositions and pronouns.

1. Mr. Torres divided the burritos *among them* and *us*.
2. At the game Maria sat *near him* and *her*.
3. Rose walked *toward* Nell and *me*.
4. Sam stood *between him* and *me*.
5. Mom ordered sandwiches *for* Hannah and *her*.
6. "*Without* Squanto and *me*, the Pilgrims won't last another winter," thought Samoset.
7. I have read biographies *about him* and Martin Luther.
8. David's parents gave a bar mitzvah party *for him*.

Exercise 4   Choosing Pronouns Used as Objects of Prepositions

Choose the correct form of the pronoun in parentheses in each of the sentences on the following page.

EXAMPLE   1. Of all the people who traveled with Lewis and Clark, Sacagawea was particularly helpful to (*them, they*).
          1. them

Reference Note

For a list of commonly used **prepositions**, see page 58. For more about **prepositional phrases**, see page 90.

To determine the correct pronoun form when the object of a preposition is compound, use each pronoun separately in the prepositional phrase.

EXAMPLE
Maria sent a postcard to (*she, her*) and (*I, me*). [*To she* or *to her*? *To I* or *to me*?]

ANSWER
Maria sent a postcard to **her** and **me**.

PRACTICE

Guided and Independent

Exercises You may wish to use Exercise 4 as guided practice and then have students complete Review C as independent practice.

HOMEWORK

EXTENSION

Critical Thinking

Metacognition. Ask students to think about the process they use to determine a pronoun's function in a sentence. Do they locate the verb first, find the subject, and then identify any complements? Do they draw a mental diagram to visualize the sentence parts? Do they first identify and eliminate prepositional phrases, since the skeleton of the sentence does not include prepositional phrases? Encourage students to evaluate the effectiveness of their personal strategies.

STYLE TIP

Sometimes pronouns such as *I, he, she, we,* and *they* sound awkward when used as parts of a compound subject. In such cases, it is a good idea to revise the sentence.

AWKWARD
She and we are going to the concert.
They and I will meet for lunch.

REVISED
We are going to the concert with her.
I will meet them for lunch.

STYLE TIP

Just as there are good manners in behavior, there are also good manners in language. In English it is considered polite to put first-person pronouns (*I, me, my, mine, we, us, our, ours*) last in compound constructions.

EXAMPLE
Please return the photos to **Bill, Ellen,** or **me** [not *me, Bill, or Ellen*].

---

1. Sacagawea's husband, a guide named Toussaint Charbonneau, joined the expedition with (*her, she*) and their newborn baby.
2. The Shoshone were Sacagawea's people, and she longed to return to (*them, they*).
3. Captain Clark soon realized how important she would be to Lewis and (*he, him*).
4. The land they were exploring was familiar to (*she, her*).
5. Luckily for (*she, her*) and the expedition, they met a group of friendly Shoshone.
6. From (*them, they*), Sacagawea obtained the ponies that Lewis and Clark needed.
7. Sacagawea's baby boy delighted the expedition's leaders, and they took good care of (*he, him*).
8. In fact, Captain Clark made a promise to (*she, her*) and Charbonneau that he would give the boy a good education.
9. At the age of eighteen, the boy befriended a prince and traveled with (*him, he*) in Europe.
10. Although sources disagree about when Sacagawea died, a gravestone for (*she, her*) in Wyoming bears the date April 9, 1884.

Review C Identifying Correct Pronoun Forms

Choose the correct form of the pronoun in parentheses in each of the following sentences. Then, tell what part of the sentence each pronoun is: *subject, predicate nominative, direct object, indirect object,* or *object of a preposition.*

EXAMPLE 1. My brother Pete and (*I, me*) wanted to know more about Elizabeth Blackwell.
   1. I—subject

1. Mom told Pete and (*I, me*) the story of Elizabeth Blackwell, the first woman to graduate from medical school in the United States. **1.** i.o.
2. Geneva College granted (*she, her*) a degree in 1849. **2.** i.o.
3. At first, because she was a woman, no male doctor would let her work for (*he, him*). **3.** o.p.
4. Pete and (*I, me*) admire Elizabeth Blackwell for not giving up. **4.** s.
5. She wanted to help the poor and opened her own clinic for (*they, them*). **5.** o.p.

6. Wealthy citizens were soon supporting (*she*, *her*) and the clinic with donations. **6.** d.o.
7. Before long, one of the most talked-about topics in medical circles was (*she*, *her*) and the excellent work she was doing for the poor. **7.** p.n.
8. Mom and (*we*, *us*) read more about Dr. Blackwell, and we learned that she opened a medical school just for women. **8.** s.
9. Dr. Blackwell set high standards for students and gave (*they*, *them*) hard courses of study to complete. **9.** i.o.
10. Her teaching prepared (*they*, *them*) well, and many went on to become successful physicians. **10.** d.o.

Special Pronoun Problems

Who and Whom

The pronoun *who* has different forms in the nominative and objective cases. *Who* is the nominative form; *whom* is the objective form.

When you need to decide whether to use *who* or *whom* in a question, follow these steps:

STEP 1 Rephrase the question as a statement.
STEP 2 Decide how the pronoun is used in the statement—as a subject, a predicate nominative, a direct or an indirect object, or an object of a preposition.
STEP 3 Determine the case of the pronoun according to the rules of formal, standard English.
STEP 4 Select the correct form of the pronoun.

EXAMPLE (*Who*, *Whom*) is she?
STEP 1 The statement is *She is* (*who*, *whom*).
STEP 2 The pronoun is a predicate nominative that refers to the subject *She*.
STEP 3 A pronoun used as a predicate nominative should be in the nominative case.
STEP 4 The nominative form is *who*.
ANSWER: **Who** is she?

STYLE TIP

In informal English, the use of *whom* is becoming less common. In fact, in informal situations, you may correctly begin a question with *who* regardless of the grammar of the sentence. In formal English, however, you should distinguish between *who* and *whom*.

RESOURCES

Special Pronoun Problems
Practice
- *Language & Sentence Skills Practice,* pp. 202–206, 209
- *Developmental Language & Sentence Skills,* pp. 75–80

USAGE

DIFFERENTIATING INSTRUCTION

English-Language Learners

Spanish. In Spanish, *who* does not change form when used as an object, so Spanish-speaking students may be confused by the pronoun *whom*. As a supplement to **Oral Practice 5,** have students work in pairs to create original sentences using *who* and *whom*. After you check for correct usage, suggest that students read the sentences aloud.

TEACHING TIP

Oral Practice 5 To help students decide when to use *who* or *whom* in their speaking and writing, share the following tip. Ask students to substitute other nominative case pronouns such as *I, she,* or *they* for the word *who* or *whom*. If the nominative case substitution is not correct, then the objective form *whom* is needed.

Use **Oral Practice 5** to demonstrate this process. Model the process for the first sentence. Then, have students work alone or in pairs to continue.

1. Can *She* correctly replace *Who?*
2. If so, the nominative case *Who* is correct. If not, *Whom* is needed.

EXAMPLE	(*Who, Whom*) will you invite to the dance?
STEP 1	The statement is *You will invite (who, whom) to the dance.*
STEP 2	The pronoun is the direct object of the verb *will invite*.
STEP 3	A pronoun used as a direct object should be in the objective case.
STEP 4	The objective form is *whom*.
ANSWER:	**Whom** will you invite to the dance?

Oral Practice 5 Using *Who* and *Whom*

Read each of the following sentences aloud, stressing the italicized pronouns.

1. *Who* is captain of the football team this year?
2. To *whom* did you give your old skateboard?
3. *Whom* will you call to come and pick us up after band practice?
4. *Who* were the first Americans?
5. In the last play of the game, *who* passed the ball to *whom*?
6. *Who's* that woman in the green sari?
7. For *whom* did you buy those flowers?
8. *Who* painted that beautiful picture?

Exercise 5 Choosing *Who* or *Whom*

Choose the correct form of the pronoun in parentheses in each of the following sentences.

EXAMPLE
1. (*Who, Whom*) helped load the hay on the wagon this morning?
1. Who

2. To (*who, whom*) are you going to give the award?
2. whom

1. (*Who*, **Whom**) will your brother invite to his birthday party?
2. (*Who*, **Whom**) will be our substitute teacher while Mr. Chen is away?
3. (*Who*, **Whom**) has Ms. Spears appointed?
4. Of the three candidates, in (*who*, **whom**) do you have the most confidence?
5. To (*who*, **whom**) do you wish these balloons sent?
6. For (*who*, **whom**) is the package that was delivered?

212 Chapter 10 Using Pronouns Correctly

Learning for Life

Continued on pp. 213–214

Speaking on the Telephone. Although most students have used a telephone since early childhood, they can always practice and improve telephone skills. The following activity will focus on skills that include correct pronoun usage.

Write on the chalkboard or on a transparency the following beginnings of telephone conversations. Ask volunteers to read aloud parts #1 and #2 of each scenario.

7. (*Who*, *Whom*) is the architect of the new library building?
8. With (*who*, *whom*) would you most like to talk?
9. Among your friends, (*who*, *whom*) is the tallest?
10. (*Who*, *Whom*) have the students elected class president?

Pronouns with Appositives

Sometimes a pronoun is followed directly by a noun that identifies the pronoun. Such a noun is called an ***appositive.*** To help you choose which pronoun to use before an appositive, omit the appositive and try each form of the pronoun separately.

Reference Note
For more about **appositives**, see page 301.

EXAMPLE   On Saturdays, (*we*, *us*) cyclists ride to Mount McCabe and back. [*Cyclists* is the appositive identifying the pronoun.]
We ride or *Us ride*?
ANSWER   On Saturdays, **we** cyclists ride to Mount McCabe and back.

EXAMPLE   The speaker praised (*we*, *us*) volunteers. [*Volunteers* is the appositive identifying the pronoun.]
The speaker praised we or *The speaker praised us*?
ANSWER   The speaker praised **us** volunteers.

Exercise 6 Choosing Correct Pronouns

Choose the correct form of the pronoun in parentheses in each of the following sentences.

EXAMPLE   1. Hanukkah is always an exciting holiday for (*we*, *us*) Feldmans.
1. us

1. Tiger Woods is a role model for (*we*, *us*) golfers.
2. Miss Jefferson, (*we*, *us*) students want to thank you for all your help.
3. (*We*, *Us*) contestants shook hands warmly.
4. The woman gave (*we*, *us*) girls five dollars for shoveling the snow.
5. The attorneys politely answered the questions from (*we*, *us*) reporters.
6. For (*we*, *us*) volunteers, service is its own reward.
7. Frank loaned (*we*, *us*) fans two classical tapes.

Special Pronoun Problems   213

---

1. #1 Hello.
   #2 Is Leah there?
   #1 This is she.

2. #1 Hello.
   #2 May I please speak with Paul?
   #1 Who is speaking, please?

3. #1 Hello.
   #2 Is Mrs. Tays there?
   #1 Yes, she is. May I say who is calling?

4. #1 Hello.
   #2 Congratulations! Are you ready to hear about a once-in-a-lifetime offer?

DIFFERENTIATING INSTRUCTION

English-Language Learners

Spanish. The English pronouns *yourself, himself, herself, itself,* and *themselves* can all be translated into Spanish as *se*. Watch for any difficulties students might have distinguishing among these pronouns, and offer guidance and feedback.

HELP

The pronouns *himself* and *themselves* can also be used as intensive pronouns.

EXAMPLES
Daniel **himself** will lead the parade.

They **themselves** traveled only twenty miles to get here.

Reference Note
For more about **reflexive and intensive pronouns,** see page 31.

---

8. The pilot flew (*we, us*) passengers to Chicago.
9. (*We, Us*) actors need to rehearse again before Friday night.
10. The new team members were (*we, us*) boys.

Reflexive Pronouns

Do not use the nonstandard forms *hisself* and *theirself* or *theirselves* in place of *himself* and *themselves*.

NONSTANDARD	The secretary voted for hisself in the last election.
STANDARD	The secretary voted for **himself** in the last election.
NONSTANDARD	The cooks served theirselves some of the hot won-ton soup.
STANDARD	The cooks served **themselves** some of the hot won-ton soup.

Exercise 7 Identifying Correct Pronoun Forms

Choose the correct form of the pronoun in parentheses in each of the following sentences.

EXAMPLE   1. The contestants promised (*theirselves, themselves*) it would be a friendly competition.
   1. themselves

1. Before he started to read, Zack asked (*hisself, himself*) three questions to set his purpose.
2. My little brother often falls down, but he never seems to hurt (*himself, hisself*).
3. The guests helped (*theirselves, themselves*) to the nuts and raisins.
4. John Yellowtail enjoys (*himself, hisself*) when he is making fine silver jewelry.
5. When the early settlers wanted cloth, they had to spin it (*theirselves, themselves*).
6. My brother was upset with (*hisself, himself*) for being rude.
7. Andrew gave (*himself, hisself*) an early birthday present— a new CD.
8. The Sartens talked (*theirselves, themselves*) out of buying a second vehicle.

214   Chapter 10   Using Pronouns Correctly

Learning for Life

#1 With whom would you like to speak?

Then, have students work in pairs to incorporate the following lines into imaginary telephone conversations.

Continued from p. 213

1. This is she (he).
2. Who is speaking, please?
3. May I say who is calling?
4. With whom would you like to speak?

9. Uncle Allen took the last potatoes for (*hisself, himself*) and passed the broccoli to me.
10. Bart and Ana consider (*theirself, themselves*) authorities on stamp collecting.

Review D   Identifying Correct Pronoun Forms

Choose the correct form of the pronoun in parentheses in each of the following sentences.

EXAMPLE   1. To me, the two most interesting explorers are (*he, him*) and Vasco da Gama.
   1. he

1. The team captains will be Jack and (*he, him*).
2. The finalists in our school talent contest are Alexandra, Tomás, and (*I, me*).
3. We were praised by our parents and (*they, them*).
4. The Washington twins and (*I, me*) belong to the same club.
5. Both (*he and she, her and him*) promised to mail us postcards from Buenos Aires.
6. Pelé and (*he, him*) both played soccer for the New York Cosmos.
7. "What do you think of (*he and I, him and me*)?" I asked.
8. "You and (*he, him*) are improving," they replied.
9. When Miriam Makeba and the troupe of African musicians arrived, we gave (*she and they, her and them*) a party.
10. Do you remember my sister and (*I, me*)?
11. The coach spoke to (*we, us*) players before the game.
12. Was the joke played on you and (*he, him*)?
13. Are you and (*she, her*) going to celebrate Kwanzaa this year?
14. Madame Durand taught my brother and (*I, me*) several phrases in French.

15. Mom, Andy gave (*himself, hisself*) the biggest piece of banana bread.
16. Who are (*they, them*), Travis?
17. They congratulated (*themselves, theirselves*) on a difficult job well done.
18. Don't leave without (*he and I, him and me*).
19. (*We, Us*) skiers had a beautiful view from the lift.
20. (*Who, Whom*) were you expecting?
21. When we met at the auditions for the school play last year, (*he and I, him and me*) got along very well right away.
22. (*Who, Whom*) recommended that book about the history of Ireland to you?
23. When Sharon and (*I, me*) work on homework together, we always get through it faster and remember it better.
24. (*Who, Whom*) will you be tutoring from the elementary school, Margaret Tanaka or Billy Worthington?
25. Everyone agreed that the science project designed by Shannon and (*him, he*) was the best one in the show.

Clear Reference

A pronoun should refer clearly to its **antecedent,** the word or word group the pronoun stands for. If a pronoun could refer to more than one antecedent, revise the sentence to make the meaning clear.

UNCLEAR	Jeremy promised to meet Sean in front of his house. [To whom does *his* refer? Are Jeremy and Sean meeting in front of Jeremy's house or in front of Sean's house?]
CLEAR	Jeremy promised to meet Sean in front of Sean's house.
	or
CLEAR	Jeremy promised to meet Sean in front of Jeremy's house.

UNCLEAR	Mr. Cassner asked Todd to file the memo after he had read it. [To whom does *he* refer? Is Todd filing the memo after Mr. Cassner has read it or after Todd has read it?]
CLEAR	After Mr. Cassner had read the memo, he asked Todd to file it.
	or
CLEAR	Mr. Cassner asked Todd to file the memo after Todd had read it.

Exercise 8   Revising for Clear Pronoun Reference

Revise each of the following sentences, correcting each unclear pronoun reference.

EXAMPLE 1. The dog and the cat were both eating out of its dish.

1. The dog and the cat were both eating out of the dog's dish.

1. Jessica waved to Betsy while she was riding the Ferris wheel.
2. Byron told Alec that his cousin was on the telephone.
3. After Tracey and Jen arrived home, their mom gave her a birthday bouquet.
4. Tabitha asked Jill whether she could help with the painting.
5. As soon as Brett saw Carlos, he said hello.
6. The beagle and the Dalmatian played with its old chew toy.
7. Jake helped Austin clean the kitchen after he had finished preparing the bread dough.
8. Mr. Lewis told Mr. Washington that he had won the award.
9. As soon as she completed the chores, Wendy and Lori left for the soccer game.
10. Kip didn't see Matt at the pep rally until he stood on the bleachers.

MEETING THE CHALLENGE

Unclear pronoun references may confuse your reader. Compose five sentences that each contain an unclear pronoun reference. Then, write a revision that clarifies the unclear reference for each sentence.

HELP

Sentences in Exercise 8 may have more than one correct answer.

1. Jessica/ , she waved to Betsy.
2. Alec's
3. Tracey
4. Jill
5. Brett said hello/he
6. the beagle's
7. After/had finished preparing the bread dough, he
8. Mr. Washington
9. Wendy/she
10. Matt

Meeting the Challenge
ANSWER
Sentences will vary but should contain unclear pronoun references that are corrected in the revisions.

HELP

Some sentences in Review E may have more than one correct answer.

Review E Revising Sentences for Correct Pronoun Forms and Clear Pronoun Reference

Revise each of the following sentences, correcting each incorrect pronoun form and unclear pronoun reference. If a sentence is already correct, write *C*.

EXAMPLE
1. The twins, Veronica and Caroline, were reading her Caldecott Honor Book together.

1. *The twins, Veronica and Caroline, were reading Veronica's Caldecott Honor Book together.*

Answers:
1. After/got off work, he
2. C
3. he
4. me
5. Whom
6. Joseph's
7. them
8. Terri
9. Theresa
10. C

1. Malcolm met Aaron at the branch library after he got off work.
2. Peter and she were leaving the art museum.
3. The winner of the race is him.
4. Carnell spoke to Ed and I before hockey practice.
5. Who should I ask?
6. Joseph asked Matthew to wash his dirty dishes before their mom came home from work.
7. Elizabeth gave miniature roses to Lee and they.
8. Lisa asked Terri whether she could bake bread for our fund-raiser.
9. Katherine informed Theresa that she needed to change the oil in the car.
10. He and Angela won trophies yesterday.

Chapter Review

A. Identifying Correct Pronoun Forms

Identify the correct form of the pronoun in parentheses in each of the following sentences.

1. The counselor chose (*we*, *us*) students to give the tour.
2. Don't worry; my stepmother will take you and (*I*, *me*) home.
3. Ms. Chavez sat between Kareem and (*I*, *me*) at the assembly.
4. It's a shame that the boys hurt (*themselves*, *theirselves*) last night.
5. Will you and (*I*, *me*) be able to reach them in time?
6. Mayor Petrakis asked my mom and (*she*, *her*) to help.
7. Is this (*she*, *her*) to whom we spoke yesterday?
8. Our coach e-mailed (*we*, *us*) sprinters about the next meet.
9. The fastest typists in class are Tamika and (*they*, *them*).
10. While we were at the store, we saw my cousin and (*she*, *her*).
11. Our dog Piper will bring the ball to (*he*, *him*) or (*she*, *her*).
12. Last night Dad told Carlyn and (*I*, *me*) a story.
13. (*Whom*, *Who*) wrote *The Wind in the Willows*?
14. (*We*, *Us*) students were not expecting the pop quiz.
15. The referee signaled (*we*, *us*) players to begin the game.
16. The best calligrapher in the school is (*she*, *her*).
17. (*Whom*, *Who*) is the better candidate?
18. To (*who*, *whom*) is the letter addressed?
19. Roger and (*I*, *me*) are studying for our lifeguard certificates.
20. Derek looked at (*hisself*, *himself*) in the mirror.

B. Correcting Errors in Pronoun Forms

Most of the following sentences contain an error in the use of pronoun forms. Identify the error, and give the correct form for each sentence. If a sentence is already correct, write *C*.

21. May us choir members leave science class early today?
22. To who are you sending the flowers?
23. The opening procession of the Olympics will be led by he.

24. C [10e]
25. He [10b]
26. himself [reflexive pronoun]
27. she [10c]
28. Whom [who, whom; 10d]
29. me [10d]
30. C [who, whom; 10d]
31. We [appositive, 10b]
32. Whom [who, whom; 10d]
33. us [10d]
34. he [10b]
35. C [10c]
36. C [10b]
37. Who [who, whom; 10c]
38. her [10e]
39. themselves [reflexive pronoun]
40. C [appositive, 10e]
41. I [10b]
42. me [10e]
43. C [10d]
44. he [10c]
45. C [appositive, 10d]

HELP
Sentences in Part C of the Chapter Review may have more than one possible answer.

24. Please give these copies of Consuela's report to her and the committee members.
25. ~~Him~~ and his best friend watched the World Cup finals.
26. Darnell enjoyed ~~hisself~~ at the African Heritage Festival.
27. The last tennis player to beat my sister in straight sets was ~~her~~.
28. ~~Who~~ have you asked for help with your math homework?
29. Tell Jennifer and ~~I~~ what your science project will be this year.
30. Whom did you invite to the awards ceremony?
31. ~~Us~~ science fiction fans are going to the book signing.
32. ~~Who~~ will we see at the mosque?
33. Mario's mother will be driving Elena and ~~we~~ to the stadium.
34. Emilio and ~~him~~ volunteered to decorate the cafeteria.
35. The perfect person to play Lady Macbeth is she.
36. Neither Kevin nor I can decide which of Ray Bradbury's stories we like best.
37. ~~Whom~~ are the most famous inventors in history?
38. Last year, the best piñata was designed by the twins and ~~she~~.
39. They really outdid ~~theirselves~~!
40. You should hear the fight song written by us four fans this year!
41. My father and ~~me~~ watched *Amadeus* on video last night.
42. Between you and ~~I~~, I think Ko will win the Web page contest.
43. The state trooper gave her a ticket for an illegal left turn.
44. The last people to arrive at the party were Cordelia and ~~him~~.
45. Mom, will you take us tired yard workers out for dinner?

C. Revising for Clear Pronoun Reference

Revise each of the following sentences, correcting each unclear pronoun reference. 46.–50. [clear reference]

46. When ~~she~~ arrived, Sonia asked Liz for a pen.   46. Sonia/she
47. As soon as Grant and Patrick paddled back to the dock, ~~he~~ lashed the boat securely.   47. Grant
48. The tabby cat and the beagle both curled up on ~~its~~ rug before the warm fireplace.   48. the dog's   49. As/, she waved to Juliet
49. Sheila ~~waved to Juliet as she~~ biked along the trail.
50. Before Sara met Jan, ~~she~~ had never been kayaking.   50. Sara

Writing Application
Using Pronouns in a Letter

Nominative and Objective Case Your favorite radio station is having a "Create a Radio Show" contest. Write a letter to the manager of the station explaining what you would like to include in a half-hour weekly radio show. In your letter, use a variety of pronouns in the nominative case and the objective case. Be sure to include enough nouns so that the meaning of all your pronouns is clear.

Prewriting Discuss your ideas for a radio program with a group of your classmates. List the kinds of entertainment and information you could present. Above all, think about what you would like to hear on the radio.

Writing As you write your first draft, follow the format for a business letter. Give specific examples of what you want to do on the show, and give reasons for your choices. Remember that even though your ideas may be very creative, your writing must be formal.

Revising Ask the other group members to read your letter to see if your ideas sound interesting and are clearly stated. Ask them if the relationship between each pronoun and its antecedent is clear. If your meaning is not clear, revise your letter.

Publishing Re-read your letter, and correct any remaining errors in usage, spelling, punctuation, or capitalization. Be sure that you have followed the correct format for a business letter. Also, make sure that you have used all pronouns according to the rules for standard written English. With your teacher's permission, the class might vote on the best idea for a show and then produce and tape the pilot episode.

APPLICATION

Writing Application

Prewriting Tip. A successful radio show must address the concerns and interests of its intended audience. Explain that to write proposals for radio shows that young people will enjoy, students will need to analyze the concerns and interests of young people.

Publishing Tip. Explain that every pronoun refers to or stands for a noun or pronoun that is called its antecedent. You may want to write on the chalkboard some sentences that contain pronouns and guide students through the process of identifying each pronoun's antecedent.

Scoring Rubric. While you will want to pay particular attention to students' use of nominative- and objective-case pronouns, you will also want to evaluate overall writing performance. You may want to give a split score to indicate development and clarity of the composition as well as usage skills.

CHAPTER 11

Using Modifiers Correctly
Comparison and Placement

Diagnostic Preview

Revising Sentences by Correcting Errors in the Use of Modifiers

Most of the following sentences contain errors in the use, form, or placement of modifiers. Revise each incorrect sentence to eliminate the error. If a sentence is already correct, write *C*.

EXAMPLE 1. There wasn't nothing missing.
　　　　　 1. There wasn't anything missing.
　　　　　　　　or
　　　　　　 There was nothing missing.

Some answers may vary.

1. Please weigh both packages to see which of them is ~~heaviest~~.
2. Alarmed, the wildfire started to spread quickly to our camp.
3. Did you read that Eduardo Mata received an award ~~in the newspaper~~?
4. The bean soup tasted good.
5. We pass my aunt and uncle's restaurant ~~walking to school~~.
6. I think the play *Fiddler on the Roof* is better than the movie.
7. Reading a magazine, my cat jumped up in my lap.
8. Jason tried to push the huge desk but could~~n't~~ scarcely move it.
9. ~~The balloons~~ startled the young children ~~when they burst~~.
10. A jet taking off can sound ~~more~~ noisier than a jackhammer.

HELP—

Although two possible answers are shown, you need to give only one answer for each item in the Diagnostic Preview.

Numerals in brackets refer to rules tested by the items in the Diagnostic Preview.

1. heavier [11c(2, 3)]
2. we watched as [11h]
3. in the newspaper [11h]
4. C [11e, a]
5. Walking to school, [11h]
6. C [11c(2)]
7. While I was [11h]
8. [11g]
9. When the balloons burst, they [11h]
10. [11f]

222　Chapter 11　Using Modifiers Correctly

11. ^Surprised,^ my coin collection interested a local coin dealer.
12. He examined two old Greek coins but couldn't see no date.
13. The shinier of those two coins looked newer.
14. That coin turned out to be the ^oldest^ of the two, however.
15. I showed ^one coin~~ to the dealer~~ valued at nearly twenty dollars.
16. He said he couldn't hardly pay more than fifteen dollars for it.
17. If I had bargained ^~~good~~, I might have gotten more for it.
18. Those two coins ~~come from Ireland~~ that have images of harps on them.
19. Collecting coins, my knowledge about other countries and peoples.~~increases.~~
20. I polished my Saudi Arabian fifty-halala piece ^~~careful~~ so that I could see the Arabic writing on it.

11. I was/that [11h]
12. [11g]
13. C [11c(2)]
14. older [11c(2, 3)]
15. the dealer [11h]
16. [11g]
17. well [11d, b]
18. come from Ireland [11h]
19. increases [11h]
20. carefully [11b]

What Is a Modifier?

A *modifier* is a word, a phrase, or a clause that makes the meaning of a word or word group more specific. The two kinds of modifiers are *adjectives* and *adverbs*.

One-Word Modifiers

Adjectives

11a. Adjectives make the meanings of nouns and pronouns more specific.

ADJECTIVES   Andy gave a **loud** cheer. [The adjective *loud* tells *what kind* of cheer.]

The one I made is **blue**. [The adjective *blue* tells *which one*.]

Adverbs

11b. Adverbs make the meanings of verbs, adjectives, and other adverbs more specific.

ADVERBS   Andy cheered **loudly**. [The adverb *loudly* makes the meaning of the verb *cheered* more specific.]

Reference Note
For more about **adjectives**, see page 34. For more about **adverbs**, see page 54.

TIPS & TRICKS

Many adverbs end in –*ly*, but many others do not. Furthermore, not all words with the –*ly* ending are adverbs. Some adjectives end in –*ly*.

ADVERBS
quickly   soon
calmly   not

ADJECTIVES
elderly   holy
curly   silly

To decide whether a word is an adjective or an adverb, look at how the word is used in the sentence.

The design is **very** modern. [The adverb *very* makes the meaning of the adjective *modern* more specific.]

The crocodile moved **surprisingly** quickly. [The adverb *surprisingly* makes the meaning of the adverb *quickly* more specific.]

Phrases Used as Modifiers

Like one-word modifiers, phrases can also be used as adjectives and adverbs.

EXAMPLES   **Leaping from the step,** the toddler flapped his arms in the air. [The participial phrase *Leaping from the step* acts as an adjective that modifies the noun *toddler*.]

The Greek salad is the one **to try.** [The infinitive phrase *to try* acts as an adjective that modifies the pronoun *one*.]

Ms. Elizondo planted rosebushes **along the fence.** [The prepositional phrase *along the fence* acts as an adverb that modifies the verb *planted*.]

Clauses Used as Modifiers

Like words and phrases, clauses can also be used as modifiers.

EXAMPLES   Italian is the language **that I like best.** [The adjective clause *that I like best* modifies the noun *language*.]

Before Albert went to school, he took the trash to the curb. [The adverb clause *Before Albert went to school* modifies the verb *took*.]

Comparison of Adjectives and Adverbs

When adjectives and adverbs are used in comparisons, they take different forms. The specific form they take depends upon how many things are being compared. The different forms of comparison are called ***degrees of comparison.***

Reference Note

For more about different kinds of **phrases,** see Chapter 5.

Reference Note

For more about **clauses,** see Chapter 6.

Chapter 11   Using Modifiers Correctly

PRETEACHING

Lesson Starter

Motivating. To help students understand how adjectives and adverbs are compared, divide the class into four groups and give each group one of the following lists of modifiers:

- tall, taller, tallest
- thick, thicker, thickest
- happily, more happily, most happily
- tasty, less tasty, least tasty

Have each group demonstrate its modifier list without using words. Groups can use objects in the classroom (including themselves), draw pictures, or act out the concepts. As each group presents its demonstration, the rest of the class can guess which words are being demonstrated by using words and phrases alone or using the words in complete sentences.

Comparison of Adjectives and Adverbs

Rule 11c *(pp. 224–228)*

OBJECTIVE

■ To form the degrees of comparison of modifiers correctly

RESOURCES

Comparison of Adjectives and Adverbs
Practice
■ *Language & Sentence Skills Practice,* pp. 215–226, 236–237
■ *Developmental Language & Sentence Skills,* pp. 81–86

Using Modifiers Correctly

11c. The three degrees of comparison of modifiers are the *positive*, the *comparative*, and the *superlative*.

(1) The *positive degree* is used when at least one thing is being described.

EXAMPLES   This suitcase is **heavy.**

Luís **cheerfully** began the job.

Those murals are **colorful.**

(2) The *comparative degree* is used when two things or groups of things are being compared.

EXAMPLES   My suitcase is **heavier** than yours.

Luís talked **more cheerfully** than Albert.

Those murals are **more colorful** than these.

(3) The *superlative degree* is used when three or more things or groups of things are being compared.

EXAMPLES   Sylvia's suitcase is the **heaviest** of all.

Of the four boys, Luís worked at the task **most cheerfully.**

Those murals are the **most colorful** ones I've seen.

Regular Comparison

Most one-syllable modifiers form the comparative degree by adding *–er* and the superlative degree by adding *–est*.

Positive	Comparative	Superlative
close	clos**er**	clos**est**
slow	slow**er**	slow**est**
soon	soon**er**	soon**est**
straight	straight**er**	straight**est**

Notice that both adjectives and adverbs form their degrees of comparison in the same way.

STYLE TIP

In conversation, you may hear and use expressions such as *Put your best foot forward* and *May the best team win.* Such uses of the superlative are acceptable in spoken English. However, in your writing for school and other formal occasions, you should generally use superlatives only when three or more things are compared.

Reference Note

For guidelines on how to spell words when **adding –er or –est,** see page 353.

HELP

Here is a way to remember which form of a modifier to use. When comparing two things, use *–er* (the two-letter ending). When comparing three or more things, use *–est* (the three-letter ending).

DIRECT TEACHING

Modeling and Demonstration

Comparison of Adjectives and Adverbs. Model how to identify degrees of comparison by using the following examples: *This suitcase is heavy, My suitcase is heavier than yours,* and *Sylvia's suitcase is the heaviest of all.* First, ask which word in the first sentence is an adjective. [*heavy*] Then, ask if a comparison is made. [*no*] Since no comparison is made, the adjective is in the positive degree. Next, ask whether a comparison is made in the second sentence. [*yes*] Ask how many things are compared. [*two—my suitcase, yours*] Since only two things are compared, the adjective *heavier* is in the comparative degree. Finally, ask what is compared in the third sentence. [*Sylvia's suitcase, all*] Three or more things are compared here, so *heaviest* is in the superlative degree. Now, have a volunteer use other examples from this chapter to demonstrate how to identify degrees of comparison.

DIFFERENTIATING INSTRUCTION

English-Language Learners

Spanish. Spanish speakers may need extra practice adding –*er* and –*est* to words to form comparatives and superlatives, because suffixes are not used to form most comparatives or superlatives in Spanish. For example, the English words *fast, faster, fastest* are translated in Spanish as *rápido* (fast), *más rápido* (more fast), and *el más rápido* (the most fast).

Vietnamese. The comparative forms used in English—*more than* or adjective + *er than* and the form *(not) as . . . as*—are expressed differently in Vietnamese and must be learned and practiced.

The comparison in Vietnamese follows the pattern noun + adjective + *more than* + noun being compared, as in *Mr. Nguyen old more than Mr. Tran*. Students may use such constructions in English and may prefer the *more* + adjective form to the adjective + *er* forms. Students need to practice making comparisons in formal and informal class situations.

Exercise 1 Forming the Degrees of Comparison of Modifiers

ANSWERS

1. nearer, nearest
2. prouder, proudest
3. more carefully, most carefully
4. more honestly, most honestly
5. smaller, smallest
6. tinier, tiniest (*or*) more tiny, most tiny
7. more timidly, most timidly
8. more loyal, most loyal (*or*) loyaller, loyallest
9. safer, safest
10. shadier, shadiest (*or*) more shady, most shady

USAGE

STYLE TIP

Many two-syllable modifiers can correctly form the comparative and superlative degrees using either the suffixes –*er* and –*est* or the words *more* and *most*. If adding –*er* or –*est* sounds awkward, use *more* or *most*.

AWKWARD
  bitterer
  comicest

BETTER
  more bitter
  most comic

Two-syllable modifiers form the comparative degree by adding –*er* or by using *more*. They form the superlative degree by adding –*est* or by using *most*.

Positive	Comparative	Superlative
simple	simp**ler**	simp**lest**
easy	eas**ier**	eas**iest**
jealous	**more** jealous	**most** jealous
swiftly	**more** swiftly	**most** swiftly

Modifiers that have three or more syllables form the comparative degree by using *more* and the superlative degree by using *most*.

Positive	Comparative	Superlative
powerful	**more** powerful	**most** powerful
illegible	**more** illegible	**most** illegible
joyfully	**more** joyfully	**most** joyfully
attractively	**more** attractively	**most** attractively

Exercise 1 Forming the Degrees of Comparison of Modifiers

Give the forms for the comparative and superlative degrees of the following modifiers.

EXAMPLE 1. light
          1. *lighter; lightest*

1. near
2. proud
3. carefully
4. honestly
5. small
6. tiny
7. timidly
8. loyal
9. safe
10. shady
11. healthy
12. tall
13. grateful
14. quick
15. easy
16. confident
17. enthusiastically
18. dry
19. tasty
20. generous

Decreasing Comparison

To show decreasing comparisons, modifiers form the comparative degree by using *less* and the superlative degree by using *least*.

Positive	Comparative	Superlative
sharp	**less** sharp	**least** sharp
costly	**less** costly	**least** costly
often	**less** often	**least** often
frequently	**less** frequently	**least** frequently

Irregular Comparison

The comparative and superlative degrees of some modifiers are irregular in form.

Positive	Comparative	Superlative
bad	worse	worst
far	farther *or* further	farthest *or* furthest
good	better	best
well	better	best
many	more	most
much	more	most

Review A — Writing Comparative and Superlative Forms of Modifiers

Correctly complete each of the following sentences with the comparative or superlative form of the italicized adjective or adverb given.

EXAMPLE 1. *unusual* The Corn Palace in Mitchell, South Dakota, is one of the ____ buildings in the United States.

1. most unusual

1. *big* The Corn Palace is ____ than I thought it would be.
2. *pretty* People in Mitchell try to make each year's Corn Palace decorations ____ than the ones before.
3. *fresh* The building looks the ____ in September after new corn and grasses are put on it.
4. *easy* Some workers find it ____ to saw and nail the corn to panels, while others prefer to hang the finished panels on the building.

1. bigger
2. prettier [*or* more pretty]
3. freshest
4. easier [*or* more easy]

Comparison of Adjectives and Adverbs **227**

Exercise 1 Forming the Degrees of Comparison of Modifiers

ANSWERS continued

11. healthier, healthiest (*or*) more healthy, most healthy
12. taller, tallest
13. more grateful, most grateful
14. quicker, quickest
15. easier, easiest (*or*) more easy, most easy
16. more confident, most confident
17. more enthusiastically, most enthusiastically
18. drier, driest
19. tastier, tastiest (*or*) more tasty, most tasty
20. more generous, most generous

DIFFERENTIATING INSTRUCTION

English-Language Learners

General Strategies. The practice of counting the syllables of an adjective in order to determine how to form its comparative and superlative degrees (see p. 226) is found in few, if any, other languages. Some of your English-language learners may be unaccustomed to thinking about syllables or may be unsure what syllables are. If students have trouble with the comparative forms of two- and three-syllable modifiers, be sure they know how to consult a dictionary to check syllabication.

11 d–g

5. best	5. *well*	I could not decide which of the many corn murals on the Corn Palace I liked ____.
6. most mysterious	6. *mysterious*	The mural of the dancing figure was the ____ one to me.
7. most famous	7. *famous*	Until his death in 1983, Mitchell's ____ artist, Oscar Howe, helped to design and paint these murals.
8. most interesting	8. *interesting*	The life of this Sioux artist is the ____ story I've ever heard.
9. more slowly	9. *slowly*	My parents walked ____ around the Corn Palace than I did and studied every design.
10. more often	10. *often*	I met a family from Mexico who had traveled ____ than we had to see the Corn Palace.

USAGE

Special Problems in Using Modifiers
Rules 11d–g *(pp. 228–232)*

OBJECTIVES

- To decide when to use adjectives and when to use adverbs in sentences
- To revise sentences to eliminate double comparisons
- To revise sentences to eliminate double negatives

DIRECT TEACHING

Modeling and Demonstration

Special Problems in Using Modifiers. Model how to use the modifiers *good* and *well* correctly by using the examples *If you want a pear, here is a good one,* and *The trees are producing well this fall.* First, ask what the modifier *good* describes in the first sentence. [*one*] Then, ask what part of speech *one* is. [*pronoun*] Explain that since *good* is an adjective, it modifies nouns or pronouns. Next, ask what the modifier *well* describes in the second sentence. [*are producing*] Then, ask what part of speech *are producing* is. [*verb*] Point out that since *well* is an adverb, it usually modifies verbs. Now, have a volunteer use another example from this chapter to demonstrate how to identify the correct use of *good* and *well.*

Special Problems in Using Modifiers

Reference Note
For more about **using good** and **well**, see page 249.

11d. Use *good* to modify a noun or a pronoun in most cases. Use *well* to modify a verb.

EXAMPLES The weather was **good** on the day of the match. [*Good* modifies the noun *weather.*]

If you want a pear, here is a **good** one. [*Good* modifies the pronoun *one.*]

The trees are producing **well** this fall. [*Well* modifies the verb phrase *are producing.*]

228 Chapter 11 Using Modifiers Correctly

RESOURCES

Special Problems in Using Modifiers
Practice
- *Language & Sentence Skills Practice,* pp. 227–230

228 Using Modifiers Correctly

Good should not be used to modify a verb.

NONSTANDARD   Both teams played good.
STANDARD   Both teams played **well**.

Although *well* is usually used as an adverb, *well* may also be used as an adjective meaning "in good health" or "in good condition."

EXAMPLE   Mom feels quite **well** today. [Meaning "in good health," *well* modifies *Mom*.]

11e. Use adjectives, not adverbs, after linking verbs.

Linking verbs are often followed by predicate adjectives modifying the subject.

EXAMPLES   Ingrid looked **sleepy** [not *sleepily*] this morning. [The predicate adjective *sleepy* modifies the subject *Ingrid*.]

Christina felt **uncertain** [not *uncertainly*] about running in the relay race. [The predicate adjective *uncertain* modifies the subject *Christina*.]

NOTE   Some verbs can be used as either linking or action verbs. As action verbs, they may be modified by adverbs.

EXAMPLES   Ingrid looked **sleepily** at the clock. [*Sleepily* modifies the action verb *looked*.]

Christina **uncertainly** felt her way along the hall. [*Uncertainly* modifies the action verb *felt*.]

Reference Note
For a discussion of **standard and nonstandard English,** see page 245.

Reference Note
For a list of **linking verbs,** see page 46.

Exercise 2   Using Adjectives and Adverbs Correctly

Choose the adjective or adverb that will make each sentence correct.

EXAMPLE   1. John seems (*nervous, nervously*) about his speech.
          1. nervous

1. When we came into the house after ice-skating, the fire felt (*good, well*).
2. The wind sounds (*fierce, fiercely*) at night.
3. Tino looked (*good, well*) after recovering from his operation.
4. After all, it doesn't taste (*bad, badly*).
5. Venus looks (*beautiful, beautifully*) tonight.
6. Liang cooked a (*good, well*) meal of vegetables and shrimp.

Special Problems in Using Modifiers   **229**

CONTENT-AREA CONNECTIONS

Social Studies
Comparison. Divide the class into groups of three. Ask students to consider the ways in which using comparative and superlative words is important in the area of social studies. [Comparisons might be made between the sizes of two countries, their populations, their gross national products.]

Each student could research one country; then, students could divide the tasks of defining categories for comparison, creating a chart, and presenting the group's findings to the class. Students could then compare the countries based on each group's findings.

EXTENSION

Relating to Literature
At the beginning of *Flowers for Algernon,* the main character, Charlie, mistakenly uses *good* to modify a verb. After the experiment begins to work, however, Charlie makes fewer and fewer mistakes in his writing. He even learns to use *well* rather than *good,* when appropriate. If *Flowers for Algernon* is in your literature textbook, have students read it (or selections from it) and discuss how the changes in Charlie's language arts skills contribute to plot and character development in the story.

DIRECT TEACHING

Correcting Misconceptions
Linking Verbs. Students may have difficulty choosing correct modifiers because they often mistakenly believe that a modifier after a linking verb modifies that verb. Make sure that students understand that a linking verb is followed by an adjective rather than an adverb because the adjective modifies the subject of the verb, not the the verb itself.

Linking verbs that are forms of the verb *be* are relatively easy to identify, but some others may not be. You can point out to your students that a verb is a linking verb if the word *seem* can be substituted for it without significantly changing the meaning of the sentence. For example, one could change *This milk tastes sour* to *This milk seems sour. Tastes* is therefore used as a linking verb in this sentence.

Special Problems in Using Modifiers   **229**

7. Is the sick child feeling (*good*, *well*) enough to eat something?
8. We looked (*close*, *closely*) at the fragile cocoon.
9. A cup of soup tastes (*good*, *well*) on a cold day.
10. Kudzu grows (*rapid*, *rapidly*) in the South.

11f. Avoid using double comparisons.

A **double comparison** is the incorrect use of both *–er* and *more* (or *less*) or *–est* and *most* (or *least*) to form a comparison. When you make a comparison, use only one form, not both.

NONSTANDARD	This is Kathleen Battle's most finest performance.
STANDARD	This is Kathleen Battle's **finest** performance.
NONSTANDARD	His hair is more curlier than his sister's.
STANDARD	His hair is **curlier** than his sister's.
NONSTANDARD	The baby is less fussier in the morning than in the evening.
STANDARD	The baby is **less fussy** in the morning than in the evening.

Exercise 3 Correcting Double Comparisons

Identify the incorrect modifier in each of the following sentences. Then, give the correct form of the modifier.

EXAMPLES
1. I have been studying more harder lately.
    1. more harder—harder

2. Frederick Douglass was one of the most brilliantest speakers against slavery.
    2. most brilliantest—most brilliant

1. Sunday was less ~~rainier~~ than Saturday.   1. rainy
2. That is the ~~most~~ saddest story I have ever heard.
3. Are you exercising more oft~~er~~ than you used to?
4. That evening was the least ~~cloudiest~~ one in weeks.   4. cloudy
5. Native arctic peoples have learned to survive in the ~~most~~ coldest weather.
6. Please show me the ~~most~~ finest tennis racket in the shop.
7. It is ~~more~~ farther from New York to Montreal than from New York to Boston.
8. Grumpkins was less ~~jollier~~ than the other elves.   8. jolly

9. Your suitcase is ~~more~~ lighter since you took out the boots.
10. Is Venus the ~~most~~ brightest object in the sky tonight?

Double Negatives

11g. Avoid using double negatives.

A *double negative* is the use of two or more negative words to express one negative idea. Most of the negative words in the chart below are adjectives or adverbs.

Common Negative Words			
barely	never	none	nothing
hardly	no	no one	nowhere
neither	nobody	not (–n't)	scarcely

NONSTANDARD	We couldn't hardly move in the subway car.
STANDARD	We **could hardly** move in the subway car.

NONSTANDARD	Yolanda didn't eat no breakfast this morning.
STANDARD	Yolanda **didn't** eat **any** breakfast this morning.
STANDARD	Yolanda **ate no** breakfast this morning.

NONSTANDARD	Didn't she get you nothing for your birthday?
STANDARD	**Didn't** she get you **anything** for your birthday?
STANDARD	Did she get you **nothing** for your birthday?

Oral Practice Correcting Double Negatives

Read each of the following sentences aloud. Then, say each sentence again, correcting the double negative. *Revisions may vary.*

EXAMPLE 1. I couldn't find no one to go camping with me.
   1. I couldn't find anyone to go camping with me.
         or
      I could find no one to go camping with me.

1. I didn't see ~~no one~~ I knew at the game.
2. Early Spanish explorers searched that area of Florida for gold, but they didn't find ~~none~~.

HELP
Although two possible answers are given for the example in the Oral Practice, you need to give only one revision for each item.

1. anyone
2. any

USAGE

Placement of Modifiers
Rule 11h (pp. 232–240)

OBJECTIVES

- To revise sentences to eliminate misplaced prepositional phrases
- To add participial phrases correctly to sentences
- To revise sentences to eliminate misplaced or dangling participial phrases
- To revise sentences to eliminate misplaced clause modifiers

---

4. anything

6. any
7. any

10. anywhere

3. We couldn't hardly hear the guest speaker.
4. The cafeteria didn't serve nothing I like today.
5. Double negatives don't have no place in standard English.
6. The bird-watchers saw scarcely no bald eagles this year.
7. The club officers never do none of the work themselves.
8. We wouldn't never need three tractors on our small farm.
9. Jesse couldn't barely see the top of the waterfalls.
10. The Paynes didn't go nowhere special during the three-day holiday weekend.

Review B Using Modifiers Correctly

Most of the following sentences contain errors in the use of modifiers. Revise each incorrect sentence to eliminate the error. If a sentence is already correct, write C.   Revisions may vary.

EXAMPLES
1. My cold is worst today than it was yesterday.
1. *My cold is worse today than it was yesterday.*

2. There wasn't nobody willing to go into that house alone.
2. *There wasn't anybody willing to go into that house alone.*

1. C
3. well
4. really
5. C [or well]
7. stronger
8. any
9. C
10. [or most simple]

1. She is the funnier of the two comedians.
2. Kendo, a Japanese martial art, is more gracefuller than many other sports.
3. No one in our class can play volleyball as good as Sylvia Yee.
4. Time passes real slowly during the summer.
5. After a long swim, she felt good.
6. I wasn't scarcely able to hear you.
7. Which of the Rogers twins is strongest?
8. Some people don't seem to have no control over their tempers.
9. He hardly ever visits us.
10. Of all the folk dances my grandfather taught me, the polka is the most simplest.

Placement of Modifiers

11h. Place modifying words, phrases, and clauses as close as possible to the words they modify.

232   Chapter 11   Using Modifiers Correctly

RESOURCES

Placement of Modifiers

Practice
- *Language & Sentence Skills Practice,* pp. 231–235, 238–239
- *Developmental Language & Sentence Skills,* pp. 87–90

Notice how the meaning of the following sentence changes when the position of the phrase *from Cincinnati* changes.

EXAMPLES   The basketball player **from Cincinnati** gave a TV interview for his fans. [The phrase modifies *player*.]

The basketball player gave a TV interview for his fans **from Cincinnati.** [The phrase modifies *fans*.]

From Cincinnati the basketball player gave a TV interview for his fans. [The phrase modifies *gave*.]

A modifier that seems to modify the wrong word in a sentence is called a *misplaced modifier.* A modifier that does not clearly modify another word in a sentence is called a *dangling modifier.*

MISPLACED   Ringing, everyone glared at the man with the cell phone.

CORRECT   Everyone glared at the man with the **ringing** cell phone.

DANGLING   Before moving to Philadelphia, Mexico City was their home.

CORRECT   **Before moving to Philadelphia,** they lived in Mexico City.

Prepositional Phrases

A *prepositional phrase* consists of a preposition, a noun or a pronoun called the *object of the preposition,* and any modifiers of that object.

A prepositional phrase used as an adjective generally should be placed directly after the word it modifies.

MISPLACED   The hat belongs to that girl with the feathers.
CLEAR   The hat **with the feathers** belongs to that girl.

A prepositional phrase used as an adverb should be placed near the word it modifies.

MISPLACED   She read that a new restaurant had opened in today's newspaper.
CLEAR   She read **in today's newspaper** that a new restaurant had opened.

STYLE TIP

Be sure to place modifiers correctly to show clearly the meaning you intend.

EXAMPLES
Only Mrs. Garza teaches Spanish. [Mrs. Garza, not anybody else, teaches Spanish.]

Mrs. Garza **only** teaches Spanish. [Mrs. Garza teaches Spanish; she does not research Spanish texts.]

Mrs. Garza teaches **only** Spanish. [Mrs. Garza does not teach any other subjects.]

Reference Note
For more about **prepositions,** see page 58. For more about **prepositional phrases,** see page 59.

DIRECT TEACHING

Modeling and Demonstration

Placement of Modifiers. Model how a modifier must be placed as close as possible to the word or words it modifies, using the example *The basketball player from Cincinnati gave a TV interview for his fans.* First, ask what the prepositional phrase *from Cincinnati* modifies. [*player*] Point out that *from Cincinnati* immediately follows the noun it describes, *player.* Also, point out that if this prepositional phrase were moved to the end of the sentence, it would modify *fans*, and the meaning of the sentence would be different. Now, have a volunteer use another example from this chapter to demonstrate how a modifier must be placed as close as possible to the word it modifies.

DIFFERENTIATING INSTRUCTION

English-Language Learners

Hmong. Hmong English-language learners might display a tendency to place adjectives after the nouns they modify. For example, a Hmong speaker might write "a jacket green" rather than "a green jacket." Be sure to remind your Hmong speakers that in English, single-word adjectives usually precede the words they modify. Then, offer additional practice in adjective use and placement.

RETEACHING

Modifying Phrases and Clauses

Activity. To reinforce the concept that modifying phrases and clauses need to be as close as possible to the words they modify, write sentences on strips of paper. Next, for each sentence, write a modifying phrase or clause that could be added without any rewording. Ask students to cut the sentence strips where appropriate and to insert the corresponding phrase and clause strips. Then, have students work with partners to check each other's work.

DIFFERENTIATING INSTRUCTION

Advanced Learners

Students might benefit from diagramming an example from **Exercise 4.** Have the class help you diagram the following sentence.

Incorrect: The poster caught my eye on the wall. *[The diagram for this sentence would be like the one below except that* on the wall *might descend from* caught *or even* eye.*]*
Correct: The poster on the wall caught my eye.

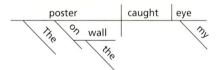

Explain to students that diagramming helps to clarify the relationship between modifiers and the words they modify. For further practice in diagramming to show the placement of modifiers, have students diagram more of the sentences in **Exercise 4,** or refer them to **Chapter 19: Sentence Diagramming.**

COMPUTER TIP
A computer can help you find and correct problems with modifiers. For example, a spellchecker can easily find nonstandard forms such as *baddest, expensiver,* and *mostest.* However, you will need to examine the placement of phrase and clause modifiers yourself.

HELP
Although some items in Exercise 4 can be revised in more than one way, you need to give only one revision for each. You may need to add, delete, or rearrange words.

Avoid placing a prepositional phrase so that it seems to modify either of two words. Place the phrase so that it clearly modifies the word you intend it to modify.

MISPLACED   Manuel said in the afternoon he would call Janet.
            [Does *in the afternoon* modify *said* or *would call*?]
CLEAR   Manuel said he would call Janet **in the afternoon.**
            [The phrase modifies *would call.*]
CLEAR   **In the afternoon** Manuel said he would call Janet.
            [The phrase modifies *said.*]

Exercise 4 Revising Sentences with Misplaced Prepositional Phrases

Each of the following sentences contains a misplaced prepositional phrase. Decide where the prepositional phrase belongs; then, revise the sentence.   Revisions will vary.

EXAMPLES 1. In the United States, Zora Neale Hurston grew up in the first self-governed black township.
          1. Zora Neale Hurston grew up in the first self-governed black township in the United States.

          2. The cat toy rolled down the hall with a clatter.
          2. With a clatter, the cat toy rolled down the hall.

1. Joshua and Reginald heard that there was a destructive hailstorm on the news.
2. The poster caught my eye on the wall.
3. In the tiny bird's nest, we thought there might be eggs.
4. Our teacher said on Monday the class would put on a play.
5. Don't forget to take the box to the store with the empty bottles.
6. We saw José Clemente Orozco's beautiful murals on vacation in Guadalajara.
7. Tranh read that a wasp larva spins a cocoon in the encyclopedia.
8. A beautiful Bolivian weaving hangs on our living room wall from the town of Trinidad.
9. Did you find the kimonos worn by your grandmother in that old trunk?
10. In confusion, they watched with amusement as the puppies scrambled all over each other.

MINI-LESSON   Mechanics   Continued on pp. 235–236

Comma Usage. If students are having trouble revising sentences due to uncertainty about comma usage, give them the following rules:

1. When a clause or phrase is not essential to the meaning of a sentence—that is, if the basic meaning of the sentence is the same without it—the clause or phrase should be set off by commas; for example, "My brother, who is a vegetarian, loves tofu."

Exercise 5 Placing Prepositional Phrases Correctly

Rewrite each of the following sentences, adding the prepositional phrase given in parentheses. Answers may vary.

EXAMPLE 1. Many paintings show strange, fantastical scenes. (*by Marc Chagall*)
1. Many paintings by Marc Chagall show strange, fantastical scenes.

HELP
Be careful to place each prepositional phrase in Exercise 5 near the word or words it modifies.

1. Chagall's *The Green Violinist* contains many delightful mysteries and surprises. (*for the eye and mind*)
2. As you can see in the painting, a gigantic violinist sits among the buildings of a small village. (*with a green face and hand*)
3. Dark windows look just like the windows of the houses. (*on the musician's pants*)
4. A man waves to the violinist, and a dog taller than a house seems to smile at the music it hears. (*above the clouds*)
5. As you look at the painting's bright colors, perhaps you can almost hear the enchanting music. (*of the green violinist*)
6. You may be surprised to learn that the fiddler is found in many of Chagall's other works. (*in this painting*)
7. Chagall enjoyed listening to his uncle play the violin. (*during his childhood*)
8. *The Green Violinist* and other paintings of the fiddler are tributes. (*to Chagall's uncle*)
9. In a painting titled *Violinist*, Chagall painted himself standing. (*beside the violinist*)
10. In that unusual painting, Chagall has three heads turned to show enjoyment of the music. (*toward the uncle*)

The Granger Collection, New York

Placement of Modifiers **235**

Reference Note

For more information about **participles**, see page 98. For more about **participial phrases**, see page 100.

MEETING THE CHALLENGE

A dangling modifier often occurs when a sentence is in the passive voice. Rewriting sentences in the active voice not only eliminates many dangling modifiers but also makes your writing more interesting and lively.

The following sentence contains a dangling modifier. Rewrite the sentence in the active voice to remove the dangling modifier.

Having just waxed the car, a trip to the fair was planned.

ANSWER
Student responses will vary. Here is one possibility.
Having just waxed the car, I planned a trip to the fair.

Reference Note

For more about **active voice and passive voice**, see page 189.

Reference Note

For more information on **using commas with participial phrases**, see pages 299 and 305.

Participial Phrases

A *participial phrase* consists of a present participle or a past participle and its modifiers and complements. A participial phrase is used as an adjective to modify a noun or a pronoun. Like a prepositional phrase, a participial phrase should be placed as close as possible to the word it modifies.

EXAMPLES **Walking to school,** Celia and James found a wallet. [The participial phrase modifies *Celia* and *James*.]

I. M. Pei, **born in China,** is a gifted architect. [The participial phrase modifies *I. M. Pei*.]

A participial phrase that is not placed near the noun or pronoun that it modifies is a *misplaced modifier.*

MISPLACED Stolen from the media center, the deputies found the videocassette recorder. [Were the deputies stolen from the media center?]

CLEAR The deputies found the videocassette recorder **stolen from the media center.**

MISPLACED Sleeping on the roof, I saw the neighbor's cat. [Was I sleeping on the roof?]

CLEAR I saw the neighbor's cat **sleeping on the roof.**

MISPLACED We're used to the noise living by the airport. [Is the noise living by the airport?]

CLEAR **Living by the airport,** we're used to the noise.

A participial phrase that does not clearly and logically modify a word in the sentence is a *dangling modifier.*

DANGLING Cleaning the attic, an old trunk was found. [Who was cleaning the attic?]

CLEAR **Cleaning the attic,** we found an old trunk.

Exercise 6 Placing Participial Phrases Correctly

Rewrite each of the following sentences, adding the participial phrases given in parentheses. Be sure to use commas to set off participial phrases that begin or interrupt your sentences.

Answers may vary.

 Mechanics Continued from p. 235

Walking home from school, we found a lost puppy.

For more information on comma usage, refer students to **Chapter 14: Punctuation.**

Using Modifiers Correctly

EXAMPLES
1. Finn and Darcy searched for their younger sister. (*scanning the crowd*)
1. Scanning the crowd, Finn and Darcy searched for their younger sister.

2. The sea turtle ducked back into its shell. (*startled by the sound of the boat's engine*)
2. Startled by the sound of the boat's engine, the sea turtle ducked back into its shell.

1. My older sister will be working at the garden center near my house. (*beginning next week*)
2. Our new kitten crawled under the sofa. (*exploring the house*)
3. By mistake, we sat on the swings. (*freshly painted*)
4. Lucy helped her brother find the books. (*lost somewhere in his messy room*)
5. Josie and Fred passed the playground. (*walking through the park*)
6. Ms. Surat told us about Sri Lanka and its people. (*pointing to the map*)
7. The two girls yelled loudly. (*surprised by their little brother*)
8. The horse likes to watch people. (*munching on grass*)
9. Andrea picked up her pencil and waited for the test to begin. (*sharpened moments earlier*)
10. On the beach this morning, the children found a mysterious note. (*folded in a blue bottle*)

Exercise 7 Revising Sentences to Correct Misplaced and Dangling Participial Phrases

Revise all of the sentences that contain misplaced or dangling participial phrases. If a sentence is already correct, write *C*.

EXAMPLE
1. Made from matzo meal, Rachel cooks tasty dumplings.
1. Rachel cooks tasty dumplings made from matzo meal.

1. Pacing in its cage, I watched the lion.
2. Talking on the telephone, Amanda did not hear the doorbell ringing.
3. Exploring the cave, a new tunnel was discovered.

HELP
Although some items in Exercise 6 can be revised in more than one way, you need to give only one revision for each.

HELP
You will need to add, delete, or rearrange some words in your revisions for Exercise 7.

Placement of Modifiers   237

Exercise 7 Revising Sentences to Correct Misplaced and Dangling Participial Phrases

ANSWERS continued

4. The circus featured a clown wearing a bright orange suit and floppy yellow shoes.
5. The two young girls walked slowly through the field filled with countless daisies.
6. While he was reading his part, his nervousness was hard to overcome.
7. The turkey, stuffed with sage and bread crumbs, was large enough for three families.
8. Tired from the long walk through the snow, we welcomed food and rest.
9. C
10. Selling the old farm, she felt sadness well up inside.

DIRECT TEACHING

Adjective Clauses

Write on the chalkboard four sentences containing adjective clauses. Have student volunteers go to the chalkboard, circle the adjective clauses, and draw arrows from the clauses to the words they modify. Possible sentences:

1. Akeem, (who is very good at math), helped me study.
2. I enjoyed the movie (that we saw).
3. The man (whose books you borrowed) wants them back.
4. The bicycle (that she rides to school) is broken.

---

4. Wearing a bright orange suit and floppy yellow shoes, the circus featured a clown.
5. Filled with countless daisies, the two young girls walked slowly through the field.
6. Reading his part, the nervousness was hard to overcome.
7. The turkey was large enough for three families stuffed with sage and bread crumbs.
8. Tired from the long walk through the snow, food and rest were welcomed.
9. Checking the shelves, Judy found all the reference books she needed.
10. Selling the old farm, sadness welled up inside.

Adjective Clauses

An *adjective clause* modifies a noun or a pronoun. Most adjective clauses begin with a relative pronoun—*that, which, who, whom,* or *whose.* Like an adjective phrase, an adjective clause should generally be placed directly after the word it modifies.

MISPLACED The Labor Day picnic in the park that we had was fun. [Did we have the park?]

CLEAR The Labor Day picnic **that we had** in the park was fun.

MISPLACED The girls thanked their coach who had won the relay race. [Did the coach win the relay race?]

CLEAR The girls **who had won the relay race** thanked their coach.

Reference Note
For more about **adjective clauses,** see page 117.

HELP
Be sure to use commas to set off nonessential adjective clauses.

Reference Note
For information on using commas to set off **nonessential adjective clauses,** see page 299.

Exercise 8 Revising Sentences with Misplaced Clause Modifiers

Revise each of the following sentences by placing the adjective clause near the word it should modify.

EXAMPLE 1. My friend Beverly visited me who lives in Sarasota, Florida.
1. My friend Beverly, who lives in Sarasota, Florida, visited me.

1. The students received an A who made the first presentation.
2. The kitten belongs to my neighbor that is on the branch.

238 Chapter 11 Using Modifiers Correctly

Learning for Life

Comparison Shopping. Every day, students are bombarded with advertisements claiming that some company's products are the best—or at least better than the competition's. Ask students to compare three

Continued on pp. 239–240

different brands of a product, such as a video game. Students should use a rating chart like the one on p. 239.

3. I showed the colorful cotton fabric that was made in Kenya to my sister.
4. The doctor who examined them said that the triplets were quite healthy.
5. The cleanup program that the president of the seventh-grade class suggested was supported by all of the students.
6. The flight attendant whose brother I know welcomed us aboard the plane.
7. The friend whom I called has a broken leg.
8. Donald's package, which came in the mail, is from his mother.
9. Quasars, which many astronomers throughout the world study, fascinate me.
10. The dog that has been running loose in the neighborhood barked at the letter carrier.

Review C Correcting Errors in the Use of Modifiers

Each of the following sentences contains an error in the use, form, or placement of a modifier. Revise each sentence by changing the form of a modifier or by adding, deleting, or rearranging words.   Answers may vary.

HELP

Although some sentences in Review C can be correctly revised in more than one way, you need to give only one revision for each sentence.

EXAMPLE 1. I have never been more happier in my life.
1. I have never been happier in my life.

1. My stepsister plays both soccer and softball, but she likes soccer best.   **1. better**
2. The waiter brought plates to Terrell and me piled high with spaghetti and meat sauce.   **2. to Terrell and me.**
3. Very frustrated, her locker just would not open!   **3. she just could not open**
4. Barking and growling loudly, the stranger was frightened by the dogs.   **4. the dogs frightened**
5. The antique German cuckoo clock still runs good after all these years.   **5. well**
6. I didn't do too bad on the geography quiz this morning.   **6. badly**
7. Our puppy is much more playfuller than our older dog is.
8. We walked slow past the duck pond to see if any new ducklings had hatched.   **8. slowly**
9. They never did find no sponsor for their team.   **9. a**
10. The CD is the soundtrack of my favorite movie that we heard.   **10. that we heard**

Placement of Modifiers 239

	PRICE	FEATURE 1	FEATURE 2	FEATURE 3
Brand A				
Brand B				
Brand C				

Review D Proofreading Sentences for Correct Use of Modifiers

Each of the following sentences contains an error in the use, form, or placement of a modifier. Revise each sentence by changing the form of a modifier or by adding, deleting, or rearranging words.

EXAMPLE 1. Of all the important women featured in this book, Dolores S. Atencio is the one I admire more.

1. *Of all the important women featured in this book, Dolores S. Atencio is the one I admire most.*

1. Her mother thought that a law career would offer her daughter the most brightest future.
2. Ms. Atencio always knew she would become a lawyer, but she didn't never expect to be so successful.
3. Looking ahead to college and law school, her grades in high school were excellent.
4. Along with two other Hispanic women, her efforts helped to launch Denver's first bilingual radio station in 1985.
5. Ms. Atencio felt quite proudly about helping to organize Colorado's first minority women lawyers' conference.
6. She decided to run for president of the Hispanic National Bar Association (HNBA) receiving encouragement from a friend.
7. Serving as president of HNBA, the legal rights of Hispanics were her main focus.
8. In 1991, she was named one of the most outstanding Hispanic women in *Hispanic Business Magazine*.
9. She also was given the Outstanding Young Woman Award from the city of Denver, which she received for all the time she had devoted to community service.
10. In addition to enjoying community service, Ms. Atencio feels really well when she is spending time with her family.

Learning for Life

Continued from p. 239

Then, have each student write a testimonial to the company that makes the best brand. Letters should list the good qualities of the favorite brand and provide specific comparisons with features of the other two brands. Have students pay particular attention to their use of comparative and superlative forms and to the placement of their phrase and clause modifiers. Students could post their letters in class or compile a consumer's guide using the charts and letters of the entire class.

CHAPTER 11

Numerals in brackets refer to rules tested by items in the Chapter Review.

1. [11e, a]
2. [11b]
3. [11e, a]
4. [11b]
5. [11d, b]
6. [11b]
7. [11b]
8. [11d, e, a]
9. [11e, a]
10. [11d, e, a]
11. [11c(3)]
12. [11d, b]
13. [11c(2)]
14. [11d, b]
15. [11c(2)]

16. drier [11c(2)]
17. more grateful [11c(2)]
18. smallest [11c(3)]
19. prouder [11c(2)]
20. slowest [11c(3)]

Chapter Review

A. Using the Correct Modifier

Identify the word in parentheses that will make each sentence correct.

1. I have to admit that this recording sounds (*bad, badly*).
2. Our Irish setter came (*shy, shyly*) toward the new puppy.
3. Yoki was anxious, but she appeared (*calm, calmly*).
4. Must the twins play so (*noisy, noisily*)?
5. We're pleased that you did so (*good, well*).
6. The storm ended as (*sudden, suddenly*) as it began.
7. With a little oil, the engine started (*easy, easily*).
8. Their performance is now (*good, well*) enough for any stage.
9. The kitchen counter looks (*clean, cleanly*).
10. It is (*good, well*) to be alive on a beautiful day like today.
11. Of the five designs, which one do you like (*better, best*)?
12. José Canseco played (*good, well*).
13. This ring is the (*more, most*) expensive of the two.
14. That striped tie would go (*good, well*) with your green shirt.
15. Choose the (*larger, largest*) of the two poodles.

B. Writing Comparative and Superlative Forms of Modifiers

Write the comparative or superlative form of the italicized adjective or adverb in each of the following sentences.

16. *dry* — The towels felt ____ after an afternoon on the clothesline than they had felt coming out of the washer.
17. *grateful* — We were ____ for Mr. Chang's advice than we could say.
18. *small* — The screwdriver my father used to repair my glasses was the ____ one he had.
19. *proud* — After the awards ceremony, Kerry seemed ____ of her son than she ever had before.
20. *slow* — The ____ horse of them all finished last in the race.

ASSESSING

Monitoring Progress

Chapter Review. The **Chapter Review** asks students to identify the correct use of modifiers in sentences. The results can be compared to those of the **Diagnostic Preview** to assess student progress. If students are still having difficulty, refer them to **Exercises 21–24** in **Chapter 17: Correcting Common Errors** for additional practice.

RESOURCES

Using Modifiers Correctly

Review
- *Language & Sentence Skills Practice,* pp. 236–239

Assessment
- *Holt Handbook Chapter Tests with Answer Key,* pp. 21–22, 46

21. enthusiastically [or most enthusiastically] [11c(1, 3)]
22. tastier [or more tasty] [11c(2)]
23. most loyal [11c(3)]
24. more easily [11c(2)]
25. tallest [11c(3)]

21. *enthusiastically* — Pleased by all the performances, the audience applauded ____ for the dancers.
22. *tasty* — Since Dad started taking cooking classes, each dinner is ____ than the previous one.
23. *loyal* — Tadger is the ____ of our three dogs.
24. *easily* — With more practice, we solved the second puzzle ____ than the first one.
25. *tall* — Which of the five Romine girls do you think is ____?

C. Correcting Double Comparisons and Double Negatives

Rewrite the following sentences to correct errors in the use of modifiers.   Revisions may vary.

26. any [11g]
27. [11f]
28. [11f]
29. [11g]
30. [11g]

26. These Hawaiian shirts don't have ~~no~~ pockets.
27. Pineapple juice tastes ~~more~~ sweeter than orange juice to me.
28. What is the ~~most~~ funniest thing that ever happened to you?
29. I can't hardly take another step.
30. Sakima couldn't barely catch her breath after running so far.

D. Correcting Misplaced and Dangling Modifiers

Each sentence below contains a misplaced or dangling modifier. Rewrite the sentences so that they are clear. You may need to add, delete, or rearrange words.   Revisions may vary.

31. bruised by the storm [11h]
32. that you heard [11h]
33. we left [11h]
34. When I opened [11h]
35. As my brother was / him [11h]
36. , born in Virginia, [11h]
37. While I was [11h]
38. , are using fish ladders [11h]

31. The fruit was marked for quick sale. ~~bruised by the storm.~~
32. Those tapes came from the library. ~~that you heard.~~
33. After ~~leaving~~ India, Singapore was the next destination.
34. ~~Opening~~ a savings account, a form of identification was required.
35. Skateboarding down the street, a large dog chased ~~my brother~~.
36. Black Hawk was a chief of the Sauk people. ~~born in Virginia.~~
37. Trying to study, the noise from the chainsaw was distracting.
38. These salmon ~~are using fish ladders~~, which are returning to spawn.

39. Sifting carefully through the sand, an old Spanish coin called a doubloon ~~was found~~.

40. I saw the gazelles jumping ~~through the binoculars~~.

39. she found [11h]
40. Through the binoculars, [11h]

Writing Application
Using Comparisons in a Letter

Comparative and Superlative Forms An anonymous donor has given a large sum of money for improvements to your school. Write a letter to the school administrators describing the improvements you would like to see made. Use at least three comparative and two superlative forms of adjectives and adverbs in your writing.

Prewriting What facilities, equipment, or supplies would make your school a better place? List your improvement ideas. You may want to discuss your ideas with a classmate or a teacher before you select the ones to include in your letter. Also, note why the improvements are needed.

Writing As you write your first draft, use your list to help you make clear and accurate comparisons. Keep your audience in mind. The administrators need practical suggestions for how to spend the money, so let them know exactly what improvements your school needs and why.

Revising Read your letter to a parent or other adult to see if your arguments are convincing. Add, delete, or rearrange details to make your letter more interesting and effective.

Publishing Be sure you have used the correct comparative and superlative forms of adjectives and adverbs. Check the form of your letter to make sure it follows the guidelines for business letters. Read through your letter a final time to catch any errors in spelling, grammar, usage, or punctuation. Share your ideas for improving the school with the rest of the class, and make a chart displaying the most popular suggestions.

APPLICATION

Writing Application

Writing Tip. This assignment gives students practice writing business letters. Students must consider their audience (the school administrators) and their purpose (to influence administrators' decisions about how the money given to the school should be spent).

Scoring Rubric. While you will want to pay particular attention to students' use of modifiers, you will also want to evaluate overall writing performance. You may want to give a split score to indicate development and clarity of the composition as well as usage skills.

CHAPTER 12

INTRODUCING THE CHAPTER

- This chapter discusses commonly misused words and expressions as well as certain nonstandard expressions. Guidelines and examples are given for understanding the differences between formal and informal speech and writing. Exercises cover many usages common in students' speaking and writing. The chapter also demonstrates the importance of precision in word choice.

- The chapter concludes with a **Chapter Review,** which includes a **Writing Application** feature that asks students to write a formal, persuasive speech for a fictional TV show.

- For help in integrating this chapter with writing assignments, use the **Teaching Strands** chart on pp. T24–T25.

CHAPTER 12

A Glossary of Usage
Common Usage Problems

Terms in brackets refer to rules tested by the items in the Diagnostic Preview.

1. all ready [*already, all ready*]
2. among [*between, among*]
3. bring [*bring, take*]
4. well [*good, well*]
5. [*he, she, they*]
6. teach [*learn, teach*]
7. [*this here, that there*]
8. have [*could of*]
9. used [*use to, used to*]
10. who [*who, which, that*]
11. all right [*all right*]
12. that [*where*]
13. They're [*their, there, they're*]
14. burst [*bust, busted*]
15. unless [*without, unless*]
16. than [*than, then*]

Diagnostic Preview

Correcting Errors in Usage

Each of the following sentences contains an error in the use of formal, standard English. Revise each sentence to correct the error.

EXAMPLE 1. They did they're best to help.
  1. They did their best to help.

1. We are ~~already~~ for our trip to Washington, D.C.
2. They divided the crackers equally ~~between~~ the four toddlers.
3. Please ~~take~~ those packages here to me.
4. Elena had a cold, but she is feeling ~~good~~ now.
5. Mr. Chang ~~he~~ is my tai chi instructor.
6. Will you ~~learn~~ me how to play chess?
7. May I borrow that ~~there~~ collection of Cheyenne folk tales?
8. Tara might ~~of~~ come with us, but she had to baby-sit.
9. We ~~use~~ to live in Karachi, Pakistan.
10. She is the woman ~~which~~ owns the Great Dane.
11. I dropped the pictures, but I think they're ~~alright~~.
12. I read ~~where~~ Mayor Alvarez will visit our school.
13. ~~Their~~ the best players on the team this season.
14. The pipes ~~busted~~ last winter during a hard freeze.
15. We cannot go sailing ~~without~~ we wear life jackets.
16. Her new apartment is bigger ~~then~~ her last one.

Chapter 12 A Glossary of Usage

CHAPTER RESOURCES

Internet
- Web resources: go.hrw.com

Practice & Review
- *Language & Sentence Skills Practice,* pp. 245–249; 250–252
- *Language & Sentence Skills Practice Answer Key,* pp. 101–104

Application & Enrichment
- *Language & Sentence Skills Practice,* pp. 244, 253, 254–255, 256
- *Language & Sentence Skills Practice Answer Key,* pp. 101, 104–105

17. The group went everywheres together.
18. Lydia acted like she was bored.
19. *Antonyms* are when words are opposite in meaning.
20. I hope that you will except my apology.

About the Glossary

This chapter contains an alphabetical list, or *glossary,* of many common problems in English usage. You will notice throughout the chapter that some examples are labeled *nonstandard, standard, formal,* or *informal.* **Nonstandard English** is language that does not follow the rules and guidelines of standard English. **Standard English** is language that is grammatically correct and appropriate in formal and informal situations. **Formal** identifies usage that is appropriate in serious speaking and writing situations (such as in speeches and compositions for school). The label **informal** indicates standard usage common in conversation and in everyday writing, such as personal letters.

The following are examples of formal and informal English.

Formal	Informal
angry	steamed
unpleasant	yucky
agreeable	cool
very impressive	totally awesome

a, an   Use *a* before words beginning with a consonant sound. Use *an* before words beginning with a vowel sound. Keep in mind that the sound, not the actual letter, that a word begins with determines whether *a* or *an* should be used.

EXAMPLES   They are building **a** hospital near our house.

I bought **a** one-way ticket. [Even though *o* is a vowel, the word *one* begins with a consonant sound.]

I would like **an** orange.

We worked for **an** hour. [Although *h* is a consonant, the word *hour* begins with a vowel sound. The *h* is not pronounced.]

17. everywhere [*anyways, anywheres, everywheres, nowheres, somewheres*]
18. as if [*like, as if, as though*]
19. that [*when, where*]
20. accept [*accept, except*]

Reference Note
For a list of **words often confused,** see page 358.

COMPUTER TIP

The spellchecker on a computer will help you catch misspelled words such as *anywheres* and *nowheres.* The grammar checker may help you catch errors such as double negatives. However, in the case of words that are often misused, such as *than* and *then* and *between* and *among,* you will have to check your work yourself for correct usage.

HELP

In doing the exercises in this chapter, be sure to use only standard English.

PRETEACHING

Lesson Starter

Motivating. Explain to students that while *of* is unnecessary and nonstandard following prepositions such as *outside, inside,* and *off,* some compound prepositions (such as *out of, because of,* and *in spite of*) do end in *of.*

Have pairs of students brainstorm a list of compound prepositions ending in *of.* Students may want to search literature books, magazines, or other sources. Ask students to devise a rule explaining when *of* is standard as part of a compound preposition and when it is unnecessary. [If the preposition makes sense or has the same meaning without *of,* as with *inside, of* is unnecessary. If the preposition does not make sense or does not have the same meaning without *of,* it is necessary. For example, "Get out here" has a different meaning from "Get out of here."]

USAGE

---

accept, except   *Accept* is a verb; it means "to receive." *Except* may be used as either a verb or a preposition. As a verb, it means "to leave out." As a preposition, *except* means "excluding."

EXAMPLES   Ann **accepted** the gift. [verb]

No one will be **excepted** from writing a research paper. [verb]

All my friends will be there **except** Jorge. [preposition]

ain't   Do not use this nonstandard word in formal situations.

all right   Used as an adjective, *all right* means "satisfactory" or "unhurt." Used as an adverb, *all right* means "well enough." *All right* should be written as two words.

EXAMPLES   Your science project looks **all right** to me. [adjective]

Judy cut her toe, but she is **all right** now. [adjective]

I did **all right** in the drama club tryouts. [adverb]

STYLE TIP

Many writers overuse *a lot.* Whenever you run across *a lot* as you revise your own writing, try to replace it with a more exact word or phrase.

ACCEPTABLE
Emily Dickinson wrote a lot of poems.

BETTER
Emily Dickinson wrote **hundreds** of poems.

a lot   *A lot* should be written as two words.

EXAMPLE   I have read **a lot** of American Indian folk tales.

already, all ready   *Already* means "previously." *All ready* means "completely prepared."

EXAMPLES   By 5:00 P.M., I had **already** cooked dinner.

The students were **all ready** for the trip.

among   See **between, among.**

anyways, anywheres, everywheres, nowheres, somewheres   These words should have no final *s.*

EXAMPLE   I looked **everywhere** [not *everywheres*] for it!

as   See **like, as.**

as if, as though   See **like, as if, as though.**

at   Do not use *at* after *where.*

NONSTANDARD   Where are the Persian miniatures at?
STANDARD   Where are the Persian miniatures?

bad, badly   *Bad* is an adjective. It modifies nouns and pronouns. *Badly* is an adverb. It modifies verbs, adjectives, and adverbs.

246   Chapter 12   A Glossary of Usage

RESOURCES

A, An—Had Ought, Hadn't Ought

Practice
- Language & Sentence Skills Practice, p. 245
- Developmental Language & Sentence Skills, pp. 91–92

EXAMPLES The fruit tastes **bad.** [The predicate adjective *bad* modifies *fruit.*]

Don't treat him **badly.** [The adverb *badly* modifies the verb *Do treat.*]

Exercise 1 Identifying Correct Usage

For each of the following sentences, choose the word or word group in parentheses that is correct according to the rules of formal, standard usage.

EXAMPLE 1. Navajo people came to the American Southwest from (*somewhere, somewheres*) in the North.
  1. somewhere

1. One group of Navajos settled in the region where the Pueblo people (*lived, lived at*).
2. The Pueblo people were (*already, all ready*) farming and living in permanent dwellings by the time the Navajos arrived.
3. The Navajos may have (*excepted, accepted*) the practice of sand painting from the Pueblos and adapted it to fit their own customs.
4. When the Navajo artists are (*all ready, already*) to begin a sand painting, they gather in a circle, as shown in the picture here.
5. When creating a sand painting, (*a, an*) artist receives directions from the singer, who leads the ceremony.
6. The painter might make a certain design when things are not (*all right, allright*) in the community.
7. The Navajo sand painter may also use this art to help someone who is injured or feeling (*badly, bad*).
8. Because sand paintings used in healing ceremonies are swept away at the end of each ceremony, the designs are recorded nowhere (*accept, except*) in the artist's imagination.
9. However, the patterns used in sand painting (*ain't, aren't*) limited to this art form.
10. Variations of the sacred designs can be found almost (*anywheres, anywhere*) on items that the Navajos make.

STYLE TIP

The expression *feel badly* has become acceptable in informal situations although it is not strictly grammatical English.

INFORMAL
Carl felt badly about losing the race.

FORMAL
Carl felt **bad** about losing the race.

DIRECT TEACHING

Modeling and Demonstration

A, An. Model how to identify correct usage of *a* and *an* by using the example *I would like an orange.* First, ask whether *orange* begins with a vowel or a consonant sound. [vowel sound] Next, ask if *an* is used correctly. [yes] Then, ask whether *an* could be replaced with *a* here. [no] *A* is used before words beginning with a consonant sound, and *an* is used before words beginning with a vowel sound. Point out that the sound that begins a word, not the actual letter, is what determines whether *a* or *an* should be used. Now, have a volunteer use another example from this chapter to demonstrate how to use *a* and *an* correctly.

DIFFERENTIATING INSTRUCTION

Advanced Learners

To inspire students to use alternatives for the overused *a lot,* bring in a copy of *An Exaltation of Larks* by James Lipton. This illustrated book lists traditional names for groups of animals, such as a "pride of lions." Lipton then coins a series of modern group names such as a "slouch of models" or a "wince of dentists." Have students work in small groups to come up with collective terms for numerous items or groupings in their world: books, teachers, homework, music videos, and so on.

CONTENT-AREA CONNECTIONS

Standard Usage. Have students create artworks illustrating words in this glossary. Assign pairs of students to brainstorm visual ways to teach one of the glossary entries. Students might create cartoon drawings, three-dimensional clay figures, or even a tableau or computer-graphics presentation to illustrate the concepts. Be sure that each important entry is covered, but allow more than one pair of students to work on a specific entry, if necessary. Assign a student to photograph any display that cannot be pasted directly into a book. Assign a volunteer to compile the materials into a book to be kept in the classroom.

DIRECT TEACHING

Correcting Misconceptions

Could of. Some students may not understand that the *of* sound in *could of* is the contraction *have,* not the preposition *of.* The standard construction *could have* is often spoken quickly or shortened to the contraction *could've;* to the ear it is virtually indistinguishable from *could of.* Ask students to consider what the expression means, and lead them to see that a helping verb makes sense there but that the preposition *of* does not. To reinforce the use of *have* instead of *of,* have students recite aloud sentences containing constructions that include *have* while dramatically exaggerating and emphasizing the *have*'s. You could write the following sentences on the chalkboard for students to recite in sequence three or four times.

> We should *have* stopped for gas.
>
> You could *have* told me you weren't going.
>
> She must *have* gone on that trip.
>
> They ought to *have* worn their costumes.
>
> He might *have* told you my secret.
>
> I would *have* been sad if they had stayed home.

Reference Note
For more about **double negatives,** see page 231.

between, among   Use *between* when referring to two items at a time, even when they are part of a group consisting of more than two.

EXAMPLES   Who was standing **between** you and Sue?

Between the season's track meets, I trained very hard. [Although there may have been more than two meets, the training occurred between any two of them.]

There isn't much difference **between** these three brands of juice. [Although there are more than two brands, each one is being compared with the others separately.]

Use *among* when referring to a group rather than to separate individuals.

EXAMPLES   We divided the burritos **among** the five of us.

There was much discussion **among** the governors about the new tax plan. [The governors are thought of as a group.]

bring, take   *Bring* means "to come carrying something." *Take* means "to go carrying something." Think of *bring* as related to *come* (*to*), *take* as related to *go* (*from*).

EXAMPLES   Please **bring** that chair here.

Now **take** this one over there.

bust, busted   Avoid using these words as verbs in formal English. Use a form of either *burst* or *break* or *catch* or *arrest.*

EXAMPLES   The pipe **burst** [not *busted*] after the storm.

The Japanese raku vase **broke** [not *busted*] when it fell.

Mom **caught** [not *busted*] our dog Pepper digging in the garden.

Did the police **arrest** [not *bust*] the burglar?

can't hardly, can't scarcely   The words *hardly* and *scarcely* are negative words. They should not be used with another negative word.

EXAMPLES   I **can** [not *can't*] **hardly** wait to hear your new CD.

We **had** [not *hadn't*] **scarcely** enough food for everyone at the Juneteenth picnic.

could of   Do not write *of* with the helping verb *could*. Write *could have*. Also avoid *ought to of, should of, would of, might of,* and *must of.*

EXAMPLES   Abdullah **could have** [not *could of*] helped us.

You **should have** [not *should of*] hung the piñata higher.

don't, doesn't   See page 162.

everywheres   See **anyways**, etc.

except   See **accept, except.**

fewer, less   *Fewer* is used with plural words. *Less* is used with singular words. *Fewer* tells "how many"; *less* tells "how much."

EXAMPLES   We had expected **fewer** guests.

Please use **less** salt.

good, well   *Good* is an adjective. Do not use *good* to modify a verb; use *well*, which can be used as an adverb.

NONSTANDARD   The steel-drum band played good.
STANDARD   The steel-drum band played **well.**

Although it is usually used as an adverb, *well* is also used as an adjective to mean "healthy."

EXAMPLE   I did not feel **well** yesterday.

had of   See **of.**

had ought, hadn't ought   The verb *ought* should not be used with *had*.

NONSTANDARD   You had ought to learn to dance the polka.
You hadn't ought to be late for class.
STANDARD   You **ought** to learn to dance the polka.
or
You **should** learn to dance the polka.
You **oughtn't** to be late for class.
or
You **shouldn't** be late for class.

HELP

Feel good and *feel well* mean different things. *Feel good* means "to feel happy or pleased." *Feel well* simply means "to feel healthy."

EXAMPLES
Helping others makes me feel **good.**

I went home because I didn't feel **well.**

Reference Note
For more information about **using *good* and *well*,** see page 228.

RETEACHING

Fewer, Less

Tell students that a simple way to know when to use *fewer* or *less* is to remember that *fewer* is used with things that can be counted.

For practice with this concept, have students work in groups of four. Have pairs of students within the groups work together to create a list of twenty nouns to be modified by *fewer* or *less*. Then, have each pair trade lists with the other pair and the individuals in each pair take turns adding *fewer* or *less* to each of the nouns on the list they have been given. Finally, have all four students go over the nouns together until they all agree on the standard usage of *fewer* or *less* with each noun from their lists.

DIFFERENTIATING INSTRUCTION

English-Language Learners

General Strategies. Korean and Russian do not have articles, and Arabic does not have indefinite articles. Few languages other than English have articles that vary in form depending on the following sound. You may need to remind students that in English the use of *a* or *an* is determined by the sound of the following word.

Cantonese. Cantonese does not use the equivalent of the English articles *a*, *an*, or *the*. Also, Cantonese-speaking students may find the concepts of countable/uncountable and definite/indefinite difficult to grasp. Students may sometimes omit articles (*I like book*), add articles unnecessarily (*She goes to the school every morning*), or confuse the two main types of articles (*Please lend me the pen and the piece of paper*).

Articles are unstressed in English and difficult to hear for those whose language does not use articles. When introducing nouns, use the article with the noun: *This is **a** noun, and this is **an** adjective.* Also, have students practice the definite *the* by using it to point to specific items.

Teacher: Which book do you want?
Student: **The** one with **the** red cover.

Exercise 2 Identifying Correct Usage

For each of the following sentences, choose the word or word group in parentheses that is correct according to the rules of formal, standard usage.

EXAMPLE 1. Bike riders (*had ought, ought*) to know some simple rules of safety.
      1. ought

1. Just about (*everywheres, everywhere*) you go these days, you see people riding bikes.
2. Riders who wear helmets have (*fewer, less*) major injuries than riders who don't.
3. When Aunt Shirley came for a visit, she (*brought, took*) her bicycle with her.
4. In choosing clothes, cyclists (*can hardly, can't hardly*) go wrong by wearing bright, easy-to-see colors.
5. On busy streets, groups of cyclists should ride in single file and leave space (*among, between*) their bikes in case of sudden stops.
6. Members of cycling clubs decide (*between, among*) themselves on special communication signals.
7. A cyclist who is involved in an accident should not try to ride home, even if he or she seems to feel (*well, good*).
8. The cyclist should call a family member or friend who can (*bring, take*) both the rider and the bike home.
9. A tire that is punctured can usually be patched, but you may not be able to fix one that has (*burst, busted*).
10. Many of the cycling accidents that have happened over the years (*could of, could have*) been avoided if cyclists and motorists had been more careful.

Review A Proofreading for Correct Usage

Each of the following sentences contains an error in formal, standard English usage. Identify each error. Then, write the correct word or words.

EXAMPLE 1. Don't almonds grow somewheres in Africa?
      1. somewheres—somewhere

1. burst
2. fewer

1. Check the hoses to see whether a seal has busted.
2. When rainfall is low here, there are less rabbits because there are not as many plants for them to eat.

250 Chapter 12 A Glossary of Usage

3. I didn't know you could program computers that ~~good~~ well.
4. Except for the spelling errors, you could ~~of~~ have gotten an A.
5. Tracy's new hamster has ~~all ready~~ already escaped.
6. Even a ten-ton truck ~~can't~~ can hardly haul a load this size.
7. That bull ~~ain't~~ isn't likely to appreciate anybody trespassing on his property.
8. ~~Bring~~ Take a glass of ice water outside to your father.
9. *Chutzpah* is a term applied to people who have ~~alot~~ a lot of nerve.
10. You really ~~had~~ ought to hear Thelonious Monk's music.

he, she, they Do not use a pronoun along with its antecedent as the subject of a verb. This error is called the *double subject*.

NONSTANDARD   Michael Jordan he was named Most Valuable Player.
STANDARD   Michael Jordan was named Most Valuable Player.

hisself, theirself, theirselves These words are nonstandard English. Use *himself* and *themselves*.

EXAMPLES   Bob hurt **himself** [not *hisself*] during the game.

They served **themselves** [not *theirselves*] last.

how come In informal English, *how come* is often used instead of *why*. In formal English, *why* is preferred.

INFORMAL   How come caribou migrate?
FORMAL   **Why** do caribou migrate?

its, it's *Its* is a personal pronoun in the possessive case. *It's* is a contraction of *it is* or *it has*.

EXAMPLES   The kitten likes **its** new home. [possessive pronoun]

We have Monday off because **it's** Rosh Hashana. [contraction of *it is*]

It's been a long day. [contraction of *It has*]

kind, sort, type The words *this*, *that*, *these*, and *those* should agree in number with the words *kind*, *sort*, and *type*. *This* and *that* are singular. *These* and *those* are plural.

EXAMPLES   **That kind** of watch is expensive. [singular]

Those kinds of jokes are silly. [plural]

A Glossary of Usage

DIFFERENTIATING INSTRUCTION

English-Language Learners

General Strategies. Many languages, such as Spanish and Portuguese, do not require a subject pronoun in a sentence when there is no noun subject. Languages such as Korean and Japanese make a point of avoiding the use of subject pronouns. Learning that subject pronouns are necessary in English, as in "He went there" instead of "Went there," students might think subject pronouns are necessary in all English sentences and try to use them when a subject noun is present, as in "That man he went there." Remind students that in English, a subject pronoun is used in place of, not in addition to, a noun subject.

Reference Note
For more information about **prepositional phrases**, see page 90. For more about **clauses**, see Chapter 6.

---

kind of, sort of   In informal English, *kind of* and *sort of* are often used to mean "somewhat" or "rather." In formal English, *somewhat* or *rather* is preferred.

INFORMAL   I feel **kind of** tired.
   FORMAL   I feel **somewhat** tired.

learn, teach   *Learn* means "to acquire knowledge." *Teach* means "to instruct" or "to show how."

EXAMPLES   My brother is **learning** how to drive.

   The driving instructor is **teaching** him.

leave, let   *Leave* means "to go away" or "to depart from." *Let* means "to allow" or "to permit."

NONSTANDARD   Leave her go to the movie.
   STANDARD   **Let** her go to the movie.
   STANDARD   Let's **leave** on time for the movie.

less   See **fewer, less**.

lie, lay   See page 193.

like, as   *Like* is used as a preposition to introduce a prepositional phrase. In informal English, *like* is often used before a clause as a conjunction meaning "as." In formal English, *as* is preferred.

EXAMPLES   Your uncle's hat looked **like** a sombrero. [*Like* introduces the phrase *like a sombrero*.]

   Marcia trained every day **as** the coach had suggested. [*As the coach had suggested* is a clause and needs the conjunction *as*, not the preposition *like*, to introduce it.]

like, as if, as though   In formal, standard English, *like* should not be used for the subordinating conjunction *as if* or *as though*.

EXAMPLES   The Swedish limpa bread looks **as if** [not *like*] it is ready.

   The car looks **as though** [not *like*] it needs to be washed.

might of, must of   See **could of**.

nowheres   See **anyways**, etc.

MINI-LESSON   Usage

Apostrophes. The use of *it's* instead of *its* as a possessive pronoun may stem from students' confusing possessive nouns, which do take an apostrophe [*the* dog's *toy*], with possessive personal pronouns, which do not [*its* toy].

Write on the chalkboard the following list of word groups. Do not include bracketed answers.

- the book that belongs to me [*my book*]
- the chair that belongs to you [*your chair*]

Exercise 3 Identifying Correct Usage

For each of the following sentences, choose the word or word group in parentheses that is correct according to the rules of formal, standard usage.

EXAMPLE 1. Young rattlesnakes (*learn, teach*) themselves to make a rattling noise by imitating their parents.

   1. teach

1. (*Its, It's*) a sound that most people have learned to dread.
2. The snake's rattle consists of "buttons" of flesh at the end of (*its, it's*) tail, which are shaken against rings of loose skin.
3. The rings of skin (*themselves, theirselves*) are fragile.
4. (*Like, As*) zookeepers have discovered, snakes that rattle at visitors all day may damage their rattles.
5. (*This kind, These kind*) of snake delivers a poisonous bite, but rattlesnakes do not attack unless threatened.
6. Not all scientists agree about (*how come, why*) certain snakes have rattles.
7. According to many scientists, rattlesnakes (*they use, use*) the rattling sound to frighten enemies.
8. Some scientists believe that snakes use the rattles (*as, like*) other animals use different sounds—to communicate with each other.
9. Snakes don't have ears; however, they are (*sort of, rather*) sensitive to sound vibrations.
10. When people hear a rattlesnake, they may react (*like, as if*) the situation is an emergency—and it often is.

Review B Proofreading for Correct Usage

Each of the following sentences contains an error in formal, standard English usage. Identify each error. Then, write the correct word or words.

EXAMPLE 1. I should of known that the painting on the next page was done by Grandma Moses.

   1. should of—should have

1. My art teacher gave me a assignment to write a report about any artist I chose.
2. ~~Between~~ all the artists that I considered, Grandma Moses appealed to me the most.

1. an

2. Among

A Glossary of Usage **253**

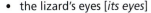

- the lizard's eyes [*its eyes*]
- Bob's shoes [*his shoes*]
- Karina's grades [*her grades*]
- the flowers we bought [*our flowers*]
- Lee's and Maria's project [*their project*]

Have students rewrite the phrases, using possessive pronouns to transform each of these word groups. For more about possessive pronouns, direct students to **Chapter 10: Using Pronouns Correctly.**

Grandma Moses, *Rockabye*. Copyright © 1987, Grandma Moses Properties Co., New York.

3. I went to the library and looked for a quiet place where I could do my research ~~at~~.
4. I learned that Anna Mary Robertson Moses didn't start painting until she was ~~all ready~~ in her seventies.
5. By then, her children were grown, and she had ~~less~~ responsibilities.
6. Grandma Moses had no art teacher ~~accept~~ herself.
7. As you can see in the self-portrait *Rockabye*, Grandma Moses felt ~~well~~ about her role as a grandmother.
8. You can't ~~hardly~~ help feeling that Grandma Moses really loves these children.
9. My sister Kim likes this painting ~~alot~~.
10. My report is ~~already~~ for class now, and I can't wait to tell my classmates about Grandma Moses.

4. already
5. fewer
6. except
7. good
9. a lot
10. all ready

of Do not use *of* with prepositions such as *inside, off,* and *outside*.

EXAMPLES We waited **outside** [not *outside of*] the theater for the ticket window to open.

The glass fell **off** [not *off of*] the table.

Only Muslims are allowed **inside** [not *inside of*] the city of Mecca in Saudi Arabia.

Of is also unnecessary with the verb *had*.

EXAMPLE If we **had** [not *had of*] tried harder, we would have won.

ought to of See **could of.**

real In informal English, the adjective *real* is often used as an adverb meaning "very" or "extremely." In formal English, *very, extremely,* or another adverb is preferred.

INFORMAL The new car is real quiet.
FORMAL The new car is **very** quiet.

254   Chapter 12   A Glossary of Usage

USAGE

Of—Type
(pp. 254–258)

OBJECTIVES

- To identify correct formal, standard usage of words in sentences
- To correct errors in usage by rewriting sentences

DIRECT TEACHING

Modeling and Demonstration

Of. Model how to identify and correct common errors in usage by using the incorrect example *The glass fell off of the table.* First, ask whether there are any prepositions in this sentence. [yes—*off, of*] Next, ask what the preposition *off* describes. [*from where the glass fell*] Then, ask if the preposition *of* is necessary to the meaning of the sentence. [no] Explain that *of* should not be used with prepositions such as *inside, off,* and *outside*. Now, have a volunteer use another example from the chapter to demonstrate how to identify and correct errors in using *of*.

RESOURCES
Of—Type
Practice
- *Language & Sentence Skills Practice,* p. 248
- *Developmental Language & Sentence Skills,* pp. 95–96

254   A Glossary of Usage

rise, raise See page 191.

she, he, they See **he,** etc.

should of See **could of.**

sit, set See page 190.

some, somewhat Do not use *some* for the adverb *somewhat*.

NONSTANDARD I like classical music some.
STANDARD I like classical music **somewhat.**

somewheres See **anyways,** etc.

sort See **kind,** etc.

sort of See **kind of,** etc.

take See **bring, take.**

teach See **learn, teach.**

than, then *Than* is a subordinating conjunction used in comparisons. *Then* is an adverb meaning "next" or "after that."

EXAMPLES I sing better **than** I act.
We'll eat first, and **then** we'll ride our bikes.

that See **who,** etc.

that there See **this here, that there.**

their, there, they're *Their* is the possessive form of *they*. *There* is used to mean "at that place" or to begin a sentence. *They're* is a contraction of *they are*.

EXAMPLES Do you have **their** CDs?

The lake is over **there.**

There are five movie theaters in town. [*There* begins the sentence but does not add to its meaning.]

They're writing a report on the poet Américo Paredes.

theirself, theirselves See **hisself,** etc.

them *Them* should not be used as an adjective. Use *these* or *those*.

EXAMPLE Where did you put **those** [not *them*] papers?

they See **he,** etc.

MEETING THE CHALLENGE

A **mnemonic** is a device, often a rhyme or visual aid, used as an aid to remembering. Choose two entries from this chapter (try to pick usage problems that you have trouble with). Create a mnemonic device of your own for each of the entries you picked.

Reference Note

For information about **subordinating conjunctions,** see page 121. For more about **adverbs,** see page 54.

A Glossary of Usage 255

this here, that there The words *here* and *there* are not needed after *this* and *that*.

EXAMPLE   I like **this** [not *this here*] Chinese dragon kite, but I like **that** [not *that there*] one better.

this kind, sort, type   See **kind,** etc.

try and   In informal English, *try and* is often used for *try to*. In formal English, *try to* is preferred.

INFORMAL   I will try and be there early.
FORMAL   I will **try to** be there early.

type   See **kind,** etc.

Exercise 4   Identifying Correct Usage

For each of the following sentences, choose the word or word group in parentheses that is correct according to the rules of formal, standard usage.

EXAMPLE   1. The Amish people (*try and, try to*) maintain a simple, traditional way of life.

    1. *try to*

1. In the early 1700s, the Amish were not allowed to practice (*their, they're, there*) religion in Germany and Switzerland.
2. Hearing that there was more freedom in the Americas (*than, then*) in Europe, the Amish left their homes and settled in North America.
3. Since that time, they have remained (*outside of, outside*) the mainstream of American life.
4. The Amish work (*real, very*) hard at producing organically grown crops.
5. In Amish communities such as (*this, this here*) one, modern conveniences such as telephones, cars, and televisions are not used.
6. The closeness of Amish family life is evident in the way (*these, them*) people build their homes.
7. (*They're, There, Their*) are often three generations—grandparents, parents, and children—living in a large residence made up of several houses.

256   Chapter 12   A Glossary of Usage

8. Pictures and photographs are not allowed (*inside of*, *inside*) Amish homes, but the Amish brighten their plain houses with colorful pillows, quilts, and rugs.
9. If an Amish person gets sick, he or she is almost always cared for by family members rather (*than*, *then*) by a doctor.
10. The Amish way of life might surprise you (*somewhat*, *some*), yet Amish communities have thrived in North America for nearly three hundred years.

Oral Practice Correcting Errors in Usage

Each of the following sentences contains an error in the use of formal, standard English. Read the sentences aloud, and identify each error. Then, say each sentence again, this time correcting the error.

EXAMPLE   1. It was real cold that spring!
          1. real—It was extremely cold that spring!

1. Few people commanded more respect and admiration then Mother Teresa did.
2. Nobody can dance like you do, Ariel.
3. These sort of questions can be found on every standardized test.
4. Oh, no! The baby's gotten oatmeal all over hisself.
5. The structure of molecules like these, it can most easily be understood by building a model.
6. What I want to know is how come we can't go to the concert.
7. Who learned your dog all those tricks?

1. than
2. as
3. sorts [*or* This sort of question]
4. himself
6. why
7. taught

A Glossary of Usage   **257**

Use to, Used to—Your, You're
(pp. 258–260)

OBJECTIVES

- To identify correct usage of words and expressions in sentences
- To correct errors in usage by rewriting sentences

DIRECT TEACHING

Modeling and Demonstration

Use to, Used to. Model how to identify and correct common errors in usage by using the incorrect example *Gail use to be on the softball team.* First, ask what word or word group makes up the verb in this sentence. [*use*] Next, ask whether this verb is in the correct past form. [*no*] Ask what the correct past form is. [*used*] Point out that the *–d* should not be left off the verb *used* in *used to*, just as the *–d* should not be left off the verb *supposed* in *supposed to*. Now, have a volunteer use another example from the chapter to demonstrate how to identify and correct errors in using *used to*.

---

8. those

10. to

8. A *howdah* is one of them seats that have a canopy and that sit on a camel or an elephant.
9. The RV campsite is just outside of town.
10. Mrs. Whitfield will try and explain how the European Economic Community is organized.

use to, used to Don't leave off the *d* when you write *used to*. The same advice applies to *supposed to*.

EXAMPLE Gail **used to** [not *use to*] be on the softball team.

way, ways Use *way*, not *ways*, in referring to a distance.

EXAMPLE Do we have a long **way** [not *ways*] to drive?

well See **good, well**.

when, where Do not use *when* or *where* incorrectly to begin a definition.

NONSTANDARD A *homophone* is when a word sounds like another word but has a different meaning and spelling.

STANDARD A *homophone* is a word that sounds like another word but has a different meaning and spelling.

where Do not use *where* for *that*.

EXAMPLE Did you read in the newsletter **that** [not *where*] the teen center is closing?

who, which, that The relative pronoun *who* refers to people only. *Which* refers to things only. *That* refers to either people or things.

EXAMPLES Jolene is the one **who** called. [person]

Here is the salad, **which** is my favorite part of the meal. [thing]

The book **that** you want is here. [thing]

This is the salesperson **that** helped me choose the gift. [person]

who, whom See page 211.

whose, who's *Whose* is used as the possessive form of *who* and as an interrogative pronoun. *Who's* is a contraction of *who is* or *who has*.

RESOURCES

Use to, Used to—Your, You're
Practice

- *Language & Sentence Skills Practice*, pp. 249–252
- *Developmental Language & Sentence Skills*, pp. 95–96

EXAMPLES **Whose** book is this? [possessive pronoun]

Whose is this? [interrogative pronoun]

Who's the new student? [contraction of *Who is*]

Who's read "A Walk to the Jetty"? [contraction of *Who has*]

without, unless Do not use the preposition *without* in place of the conjunction *unless*.

EXAMPLE I can't go **unless** [not *without*] I ask Dad.

would of See **could of**.

your, you're *Your* is the possessive form of *you*. *You're* is the contraction of *you are*.

EXAMPLES **Your** Saint Patrick's Day party was great!

You're a good friend.

Exercise 5 Identifying Correct Usage

For each of the following sentences, choose the word or word group in parentheses that is correct according to the rules of formal, standard usage.

EXAMPLE 1. Last week I received a letter from Sandra Joyce, (*who's, whose*) a good friend of mine.

1. who's

1. When I opened the envelope, I saw (*where, that*) she had sent me chopsticks and these instructions.
2. "I thought you'd like (*you're, your*) own pair of chopsticks, with instructions showing how to use them," Sandra wrote.
3. Instructions like the ones Sandra sent me are helpful because chopsticks can be hard to use (*unless, without*) you are shown how.
4. In the letter, Sandra told me (*that, where*) she and her family had been to New York.
5. Because Sandra lives in a small town, she wasn't (*use, used*) to the crowds.

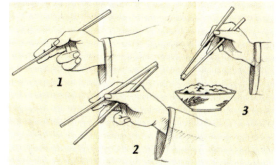

A Glossary of Usage **259**

DIFFERENTIATING INSTRUCTION

English-Language Learners

General Strategies. Many of the points of usage covered in this chapter are problems that native English speakers have, such as using *ways* for *way* or *like* for *as*. English-proficient speakers will be familiar with such usages, while English-language learners might wonder why certain points of usage are emphasized. Explain that many of the problems outlined in this chapter arise from the differences in usage between regional or ethnic dialects in the United States and standard English.

EXTENSION

Relating to Literature

If the Marjorie Kinnan Rawlings story "A Mother in Mannville" is in your literature textbook, have students read it and discuss the author's use of formal and informal English. Ask students to identify situations in which the author uses informal or nonstandard English. [*She does so when she is quoting the boy, Jerry.*] Ask students to cite passages in which she uses standard English. [*She does so when quoting the narrator and in the narrative portions of her story.*] Why did she not correct Jerry's usage in her story? [*His speech would have seemed stilted and unnatural.*]

1. your
2. there
3. unless
4. who [*or* that]
5. When a plane flies low and fast over the runway, it is "buzzing the runway."
6. that
7. why do I win every time I wear it?
8. used
9. to
10. it's

---

6. She enjoyed visiting her grandparents, (*who's*, *whose*) home is near Chinatown, on Manhattan Island.
7. While her family was eating in a Chinese restaurant, one of the servers, (*which*, *who*) was very helpful, showed her how to use chopsticks.
8. "(*Your*, *You're*) not going to believe this," she wrote, "but by the end of the meal, I was using chopsticks quite well."
9. Etiquette is (*when you use good manners*, *the use of good manners*); Sandra wondered whether using chopsticks to eat Chinese food was a matter of etiquette or of skill.
10. I'll write Sandra that I have a long (*ways*, *way*) to go before I'm an expert in using chopsticks.

Review C Proofreading for Correct Usage

Each of the following sentences contains an error in the use of formal, standard English. Rewrite each sentence to correct the error. Answers may vary.

EXAMPLE   1. If the quarterback can't play, whose the backup?
         1. If the quarterback can't play, who's the backup?

1. Are you selling you're old bike or one of theirs?
2. If they're not their, you can have their seats.
3. Don't go outside without you wear those galoshes!
4. Is Alfonso García Robles the man which was awarded the 1982 Nobel Peace Prize?
5. "Buzzing the runway" is when a plane flies low and fast over the runway.
6. I read where the word *Nippon* means "where the sun rises."
7. If this hat isn't lucky, then how come every time I wear it, I win?
8. Yes, I use to live in Madrid.
9. Please try and be ready on time tonight.
10. Listen to Lydia's new poem; its dedicated to Queen Liliuokalani.

CHAPTER 12

Chapter Review

A. Identifying Correct Usage

For each of the following sentences, choose the word or word group in parentheses that is correct according to the rules of formal, standard English usage.

1. Helene made (*fewer*, *less*) mistakes this time.
2. That restaurant looks (*as if*, *like*) it might be nice.
3. Those (*kind*, *kinds*) of games are easy to learn.
4. Terrance felt (*badly*, *bad*) about losing the house key.
5. Leticia practiced an hour every day (*like*, *as*) her teacher had recommended.
6. Divide the sheet music (*among*, *between*) the three musicians.
7. We brought the juice, but (*it's*, *its*) still in the car.
8. Both cars had pinstripes painted on (*their*, *there*) hoods.
9. The rice will feed more people (*then*, *than*) the bread will.
10. "(*Your*, *You're*) a polite young man," Aunt Henrietta told Jason.
11. There's the police officer (*which*, *who*) helped me yesterday.
12. Did you see in the newspaper (*that*, *where*) farmers are losing their crops because of the drought?
13. Chika is the woman (*whose*, *who's*) going to be my math tutor.
14. The child cried out when her balloon (*busted*, *burst*).
15. Vincent van Gogh did not receive (*a lot*, *alot*) of recognition during his lifetime.
16. Just do your best, and everything will be (*allright*, *all right*).
17. Will you (*take*, *bring*) that *National Geographic* to me?
18. Elyssa must (*of*, *have*) left her wallet here.
19. Petra likes salsa music (*somewhat*, *some*).
20. Can your brother (*learn*, *teach*) me how to play the drums?
21. Let the bread rise for (*a*, *an*) hour, and then put it in the oven.
22. Is Emily coming to the party, or (*ain't*, *isn't*) she?
23. (*Leave*, *Let*) me walk to the concert by myself.
24. We (*should not*, *hadn't ought to*) let the cat eat whatever it wants.
25. With contacts, I can see (*all right*, *alright*).

Terms in brackets refer to concepts tested by the items in the Chapter Review.

1. [*fewer, less*]
2. [*like, as if, as though*]
3. [*kind, sort, type*]
4. [*bad, badly*]
5. [*like, as*]
6. [*between, among*]
7. [*its, it's*]
8. [*their, there, they're*]
9. [*than, then*]
10. [*your, you're*]
11. [*who, which, that*]
12. [*where*]
13. [*whose, who's*]
14. [*bust, busted*]
15. [*a lot*]
16. [*all right*]
17. [*bring, take*]
18. [*could of*]
19. [*some, somewhat*]
20. [*learn, teach*]
21. [*a, an*]
22. [*ain't*]
23. [*leave, let*]
24. [*had ought, hadn't ought*]
25. [*all right*]

ASSESSING

Monitoring Progress

Chapter Review. The Chapter Review asks students to identify and correct common usage errors. The results of this review can be compared to the results of the Diagnostic Preview on pp. 244–245 to assess student progress.

If students need additional practice, refer them to Exercises 25–27 in Chapter 17: Correcting Common Errors.

USAGE

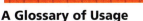

RESOURCES

A Glossary of Usage

Review
- *Language & Sentence Skills Practice,* pp. 250–252

Assessment
- *Holt Handbook Chapter Tests with Answer Key,* pp. 23–24, 46

26. very [real]
27. unless [without]
28. [of]
29. C [like, as if]
30. to [try and]
31. [at]
32. broken [bust, busted]
33. C [could of]
34. rather [kind of]
35. [this here]
36. used [use to]
37. [he, she, they]
38. why [how come]
39. somewhere [anyways]
40. C [had ought]
41. those [them]
42. There [their, there]
43. accept [accept]
44. that [when, where]
45. already [already]
46. can [can't hardly]
47. way [way, ways]
48. C [real; good, well]
49. himself [hisself]
50. C [its, it's; doesn't, don't]

B. Proofreading for Correct Usage

Read each sentence below, and decide whether it contains an error in the use of formal, standard English. If the sentence contains an error in usage, rewrite the sentence correctly. If the sentence is already correct, write C. Answers may vary.

26. Try to be real quiet while you are inside the library.
27. We cannot ride our bikes without it stops raining.
28. Be careful not to knock the lamp off of the table.
29. The cartoon page looks as if it got wet.
30. I told Gretchen to try and keep still.
31. Where's the salt shaker at?
32. Robbie said that the lock on the back door is busted.
33. Andrea thought we should have turned right at the stop sign.
34. Mr. Funicello seems kind of uncomfortable.
35. This here poem would be easier to memorize than that one.
36. Before 1920, farmers use to grow strawberries here.
37. My grandmother she worked in a factory when she was my age.
38. Sakura knows how come the play was canceled.
39. Those game tickets are somewheres in this drawer.
40. Before our trip, we ought to buy a map.
41. Where did Rory put them CDs?
42. Their are two bridges downriver.
43. The tollbooth will except quarters and dimes but not pennies.
44. A pronoun is when a word is used in place of a noun.
45. By noon we had all ready seen Mr. Kerr's film.
46. The class can't hardly wait to go on the field trip to the power plant.
47. The Immerguts have a long ways to drive to visit their grandparents.
48. My older sister is doing very well in law school.
49. In the final seconds of the game, Lee tripped hisself and missed the winning basket.
50. It's true: Mimi doesn't want to come to the New Year's Eve party.

Writing Application
Writing a Speech

Using Formal English A local television station has started a new program called *Sound-Off*. Each speaker on the program gets five minutes on the air to express an opinion about a community issue. Choose a topic that you think is important, and write a speech to submit to the TV station. Use only formal, standard English in your speech.

Prewriting First, choose a specific topic that interests you. List important facts and information about the issue. Do you have all the information you need? If not, do some research at your school or local library. Also, be sure to include your own feelings and opinions about your topic. Finally, make a rough outline of what you want to say.

Writing Use your notes and outline to help you write a draft of your speech. Try to write a lively introduction that will grab your listeners' attention. In your introduction, give a clear statement of opinion. Then, discuss each supporting point in a paragraph or two. Conclude your speech by restating your main point.

Revising Ask a friend to time you as you read your speech aloud. Then, ask your friend the following questions:
- Is the main idea clear?
- Does the speech give useful information?

Publishing Proofread your speech for errors in grammar or formal, standard usage. You and your classmates may want to present your speeches to the class. You might also want to investigate whether a local TV or radio program would allow you to give your speeches on the air.

CHAPTER 13

Capital Letters
Rules for Capitalization

INTRODUCING THE CHAPTER

- Basic rules of capitalization are outlined in this chapter. Students receive instruction for capitalizing the first words of sentences, the pronoun *I*, and school subjects. Detailed information is also given on capitalizing proper nouns, proper adjectives, and titles.

- The chapter concludes with a **Chapter Review,** which includes a **Writing Application** feature that asks students to apply their knowledge of correct capitalization to writing a personal letter.

- For help in integrating the chapter with writing assignments, see the **Teaching Strands** chart on pp. T24–T25.

Numerals in brackets refer to rules tested by the items in the Diagnostic Preview.

1. [13d(6), g(3)]
2. [13g(3), c]
3. [13d(1), g(1)]
4. [13d(1, 2)]
5. C [13d(2, 4)]
6. [13d(4)]
7. [13d(4), g(1), d(1)]
8. [*or* President] [13d(1, 6), g(1)]
9. [13d(1), f, d(2)]

Diagnostic Preview

Proofreading Sentences for Correct Capitalization

Write each word that requires capitalization in the following sentences. If a sentence is already correct, write *C*.

EXAMPLE   1. Next saturday rachel and i will get to watch the taping of our favorite TV show.
   1. Saturday, Rachel, I

1. The curtiss soap corporation sponsors the television show called three is two too many.
2. The show's theme song is "you and i might get by."
3. My favorite actor on the show is joe fontana, jr., who plays the lovable dr. mullins.
4. The female lead, janelle bledsoe, used to go to our junior high school right here in houston, texas.
5. The action is set in the West just after the Civil War.
6. The program is on monday nights, except during the summer.
7. One episode took place at a fourth of july picnic, at which dr. mullins challenged the sheriff to a grapefruit-eating contest.
8. Ms. Bledsoe plays a teacher who is married to Mr. reginald wilson foster II, president of the flintsville National bank.
9. Mrs. foster teaches latin, home economics, and arithmetic I at flintsville's one-room school.

264 Chapter 13   Capital Letters

CHAPTER RESOURCES

Internet

- Web resources: go.hrw.com

Practice & Review

- *Language & Sentence Skills Practice,* pp. 258–272; 273–275

- *Language & Sentence Skills Practice Answer Key,* pp. 106–115

Application & Enrichment

- *Language & Sentence Skills Practice,* pp. 257, 276, 277–278, 279

- *Language & Sentence Skills Practice Answer Key,* pp. 106, 116–117

10. One local character, uncle ramón, once played a practical joke on judge grimsby right outside the mayor's office.
11. Some people, including my mother, think that the program is silly, but my father enjoys watching it occasionally.
12. Even i don't think it will receive an emmy from the academy of television arts and sciences.
13. When grandma murray and aunt edna from mobile, alabama, visited us, they watched the program.
14. In that monday night's show, an alien named romax from the planet zarko stayed at the sidewinder hotel.
15. The alien, who looked like president zachary taylor, spoke english perfectly and could read people's minds.
16. He settled a dispute between the union pacific railroad and the flintsville ranchers' association.
17. In another show a united states senator and romax discussed their views of justice.
18. In the silliest show, the people in the next town, longview, thought that a sea monster was living in lake cranberry and reported it to the department of the interior.
19. A week later, mayor murdstone lost the only copy of his secret recipe for irish stew and saw the recipe in the next issue of the *flintsville weekly gazette*.
20. One time a mysterious stranger appeared, claiming he had sailed around cape horn on the ship *the gem of the ocean*.
21. Another time, the wealthy landowner mabel platt hired the law firm of crumbley, lockwood, and starr to sue mayor murdstone and threatened to take the case all the way to the united states supreme court.
22. In the next episode, a buddhist priest who just happened to be traveling through the west on his way back to china stopped off in flintsville.
23. Once, when someone mistakenly thought he had found gold down at cutter's creek, thousands of prospectors flocked to flintsville, including three bank-robbing members of the feared gumley Gang.
24. The programs are taped before a live audience in the metro theater in los angeles, california.
25. You can get tickets to be in the audience by writing to curtiss soap corporation, 151 holly avenue, deerfield, mi 49238.

10. [or Mayor's] [13g(1, 2), d(1)]
11. C [13g(2)]
12. [13c, d(9, 3)]
13. [13g(2), d(1, 2)]
14. [13d(4, 1, 11, 8)]
15. [13g(1), d(1, 5)]
16. [13d(6, 3)]
17. [or Senator] [13e, d(1), g(1)]
18. [13d(2, 3)]
19. [13g(1), d(1), e, g(3)]
20. [13d(2, 7)]
21. [13d(1, 6), g(1), e, d(3)]
22. [13d(10, 2)]
23. [13d(2, 3)]
24. [13d(8, 2)]
25. *MI* should be written with two capitals. [13d(6, 2)]

ASSESSING

Entry-Level Assessment
Diagnostic Preview. This **Diagnostic Preview** contains items testing rules in this chapter; therefore, you can use the **Diagnostic Preview** to determine which rules to focus on if you teach this chapter as a whole. You can also use the results of the **Diagnostic Preview** in conjunction with an assessment of students' writing.

PRETEACHING

Lesson Starter
Motivating. Make up categories based on the subrules of **Rule 13d**, such as names of singers, businesses, and holidays. Divide the class into two teams, and choose one of the categories. Then, tell one of the teams to select a specific, capitalized name to fit the category, and write that name on the chalkboard. The next team does the same, and play using that category continues until one team cannot give a name. The team with the last answer gets a point. Then, choose another category. The game can continue as long as time and categories permit; the team with the most points wins.

MECHANICS

Differentiating Instruction
- *Developmental Language & Sentence Skills Guided Practice,* pp. 97–108
- *Developmental Language & Sentence Skills Guided Practice Teacher's Notes and Answer Key,* pp. 23–25

Assessment
- *Holt Handbook Chapter Tests with Answer Key,* pp. 25–26, 46

First Words, Pronoun *I*, Proper Nouns

Rules 13a–d (pp. 266–276)

OBJECTIVES

- To write proper nouns from given common nouns
- To proofread and revise sentences for correct capitalization of the first words of sentences, quotations, and salutations in letters; the pronoun *I*; and proper nouns

DIRECT TEACHING

Modeling and Demonstration

First Words, Pronoun *I*, Proper Nouns. Model how to proofread sentences for correct capitalization by using the example *next tuesday david and i are flying to tennessee.* First, ask whether the first word in the sentence should be capitalized. [yes] Next, ask whether the pronoun *I* should be capitalized. [yes] Then, ask what proper nouns are in the sentence. [Tuesday, David, Tennessee] Ask whether these proper nouns should be capitalized. [yes] Point out that the first word in a sentence, the pronoun *I*, and all proper nouns should be capitalized. Now, have a volunteer use another example from this chapter to demonstrate how to proofread for correct capitalization.

MECHANICS

Reference Note
For more about using **capital letters in quotations**, see page 323.

Reference Note
For information on using **colons in letters**, see page 312. For information on using **commas in letters**, see page 307.

Reference Note
For more about **common nouns** and **proper nouns**, see page 26.

Using Capital Letters Correctly

13a. Capitalize the first word in every sentence.

EXAMPLES **M**y dog knows several tricks. **D**oes yours?

The first word of a directly quoted sentence should begin with a capital letter.

EXAMPLE Mrs. Hernandez said, "**D**on't forget to bring your contributions for the bake sale."

Traditionally, the first word of every line of poetry begins with a capital letter.

EXAMPLE
In the night
The rain comes down.
Yonder at the edge of the earth
There is a sound like cracking,
There is a sound like falling.
Down yonder it goes on slowly rumbling.
It goes on shaking.

A Papago poem, "In the Night"

NOTE Some modern poets do not follow this style. If you are using a quotation from a poem, be sure to use the capitalization that the poet uses.

13b. Capitalize the first word in both the salutation and the closing of a letter.

SALUTATIONS **D**ear Service Manager:
             Dear Emily,

CLOSINGS **S**incerely,
          Yours truly,

13c. Capitalize the pronoun *I*.

EXAMPLE This week **I** have to write two essays.

13d. Capitalize proper nouns.

A **proper noun** names a particular person, place, thing, or idea. Proper nouns are capitalized. A **common noun** names a kind or type of person, place, thing, or idea. A common noun generally is not capitalized unless it begins a sentence or is part of a title.

RESOURCES

First Words, Pronoun *I*, Proper Nouns
Practice

- *Language & Sentence Skills Practice*, pp. 258–265
- *Developmental Language & Sentence Skills*, pp. 97–104

Proper Nouns	Common Nouns
Central High School	high school
Saturday	day
Rigoberta Menchú	woman
Cambodia	country
USS Nautilus	submarine

Some proper nouns consist of more than one word. In these names, short words such as prepositions (those of fewer than five letters) and articles (*a, an, the*) are generally not capitalized.

EXAMPLES   House **o**f Representatives   Ivan **t**he Terrible

(1) Capitalize the names of persons and animals.

Be sure to capitalize initials in names.

Persons	Monica Sone	Aaron Neville
	Charlayne Hunter-Gault	Mohandas K. Gandhi
Animals	Shamu	Trigger
	Socks	Rikki-tikki-tavi

(2) Capitalize geographical names.

Type of Name	Examples	
Continents	Europe	South America
	Antarctica	Asia
Countries	Australia	Egypt
	El Salvador	Saudi Arabia
Cities, Towns	Miami	Indianapolis
	Los Angeles	Manila
States	Tennessee	Delaware
	Rhode Island	Wyoming

(continued)

Reference Note

Abbreviations of the names of states are capitalized. See page 291 for more about using and punctuating such abbreviations.

STYLE TIP

Some names consist of more than one part. The different parts may begin with capital letters only or with a combination of capital and lowercase letters. If you are not sure about the spelling of a name, ask the person with that name or check a reference source.

EXAMPLES
Van **d**en **A**kker,
van **G**ogh, **McE**nroe,
La **F**ontaine, **d**e **l**a **G**arza,
Ibn **S**aud

COMPUTER TIP

If you use a computer, you may be able to use a spellchecker to help you capitalize names correctly. Make a list of the names you write most often. Be sure that you have spelled and capitalized each name correctly. Then, add this list to your computer's dictionary or spellchecker.

Using Capital Letters Correctly   267

DIRECT TEACHING

Capitalizing Proper Nouns

Activity. To give students practice in capitalizing proper nouns, have them work in groups of four to brainstorm categories (such as holidays) that require items to be capitalized. Then, have each group write five categories on five slips of paper to be mixed in a cap or other type of container. Have each group in turn draw a slip and give a proper noun that exemplifies the category on the card [*for example,* Memorial Day *for the category* holidays]. While categories may be duplicated, the proper nouns must always be different from ones given previously. Continue passing the cap until all slips have been drawn and answered.

DIFFERENTIATING INSTRUCTION

English-Language Learners

Cantonese. Cantonese writers use ideographs, a graphic form of writing that does not use an alphabet—consequently, there is no need for capitalization. Therefore, the rules and conventions of English capitalization must be learned and practiced by students who write Cantonese.

MECHANICS

CONTENT-AREA CONNECTIONS

Geography

Geographical Names. To give students practice in capitalization of geographical names, provide them with state and local maps for your area. Have each student use the maps to write the name of one of each of the following items: a street, a river, a lake, a highway, a town or city, and a county. Then, ask a student to list the examples of each category on the chalkboard or a transparency as students give their answers aloud, noting which letters require capitalization.

Using Capital Letters Correctly   267

EXTENSION

Relating to Literature

Poetry. You may want to give students some examples of poems that begin every line with a capital letter and other poems that do not. You can find many suitable examples in literature anthologies. For example, Anna Lee Walters begins each line in "I Am of the Earth" with a capital letter, while Gogisgi/Carroll Arnett does not begin each line in "Early Song" with a capital letter. Ask students whether they think such a style difference matters, and discuss how the flow of a poem such as "Early Song" would be different if each line did begin with a capital letter. [*Capitalizing the first word in each line of a poem can give the poem a more formal tone. In "Early Song," not capitalizing the first word of each line focuses attention on the sentences in the poem rather than on the poem's structure.*]

DIRECT TEACHING

Correcting Misconceptions

Capitalizing Direction Words. Students may mistakenly capitalize words indicating direction, such as *north* and *south*. It may help students understand the difference between words used to indicate direction and the same words used to indicate a section of the country by telling them that an article (*a, an,* or *the*) will be used before a section of the country, such as *the Wild West*. If there is no article, there should be no capital letter.

STYLE TIP

A two-letter state abbreviation without periods is used only when it is followed by a ZIP Code. Both letters of the abbreviation are capitalized. No mark of punctuation is used between the abbreviation and the ZIP Code.

EXAMPLES
New Orleans, **LA** 70131-5140

New York, **NY** 10003-6981

Reference Note
In addresses, abbreviations such as *St., Blvd., Ave., Dr.,* and *Ln.* are capitalized. For more about abbreviations, see page 291.

(continued)

Type of Name	Examples	
Islands	**A**leutian **I**slands **C**rete	**L**ong **I**sland **I**sle of **P**ines
Bodies of Water	**A**mazon **R**iver **C**hesapeake **B**ay **S**uez **C**anal	**L**ake **O**ntario **J**ackson's **P**ond **I**ndian **O**cean
Streets, Highways	**M**ain **S**treet **E**ighth **A**venue	**C**anary **L**ane **H**ighway 71

NOTE In a hyphenated street number, the second part of the number is not capitalized.

EXAMPLE West Thirty-**f**ourth Street

Type of Name	Examples	
Parks and Forests	**S**herwood **F**orest **B**rechtel **P**ark	**E**verglades **N**ational **P**ark
Mountains	**C**atskills **M**ount **F**uji	**M**ount **E**verest the **A**lps
Regions	the **M**iddle **E**ast **N**ew **E**ngland the **W**est	the **S**outheast **C**orn **B**elt **S**outhern **H**emisphere
Other Geographical Names	**M**ayon **V**olcano **P**ainted **D**esert	**S**inai **P**eninsula **M**eteor **C**rater

NOTE Words such as *east, west, northern,* or *southerly* are not capitalized when the words merely indicate direction. However, they are capitalized when they name a particular region.

EXAMPLES A car was going **s**outh on Oak Street. [direction]

The **S**outh has produced some of America's great writers. [region of the country]

268 Chapter 13 Capital Letters

MINI-LESSON Mechanics

Capitalizing Direct Quotations. To help students capitalize dialogue correctly, explain that a direct quotation begins with a capital letter, but when the speaker tag (the expression identifying the speaker) interrupts a quoted sentence, the second part of the quotation begins with a lowercase letter. When the second part of a divided quotation is a complete sentence, however, it begins with a capital letter. Write the following sentences on the chalkboard:

Exercise 1 — Writing Proper Nouns

For each common noun given below, write two proper nouns. You may need to use a dictionary and an atlas. Be sure to use capital letters correctly.   Answers will vary.

EXAMPLE   1. country
           1. Canada, Japan

1. lake
2. continent
3. president
4. highway
5. teacher
6. athlete
7. park
8. ocean
9. city
10. region

Possible answers:
1. Lake Michigan, Town Lake
2. Asia, Africa
3. George Washington, John Tyler
4. Loop 410, Redwood Highway
5. Mr. Ferguson, Mrs. Longstreth
6. Mark McGwire, Randy Johnson
7. Zilker Park, Central Park
8. Indian Ocean, Pacific Ocean
9. Duluth, Memphis
10. Midwest, East Coast

Exercise 2 — Correcting Errors in Capitalization

Each of the following sentences contains at least one capitalization error. Correct these errors by writing the words that are incorrectly capitalized and either changing capital letters to lowercase letters or changing lowercase letters to capital letters.

EXAMPLE   1. The original Settlers of hawaii came from the marquesas islands and tahiti.
          1. settlers, Hawaii, Marquesas Islands, Tahiti

Words that should be capitalized or lowercased are underscored.
1. our Class is studying hawaii.
2. The Hawaiian islands are located in the pacific ocean, nearly twenty-four hundred miles West of san francisco, california.
3. Hawaii officially became the fiftieth State in the united states in 1959.
4. Our teacher, ms. Jackson, explained that the Capital City is honolulu; she said that it is located on the southeast Coast of oahu island.
5. The largest of the Islands is hawaii.
6. On the southeast shore of hawaii island is hawaii volcanoes national park.
7. Ms. Jackson asked, "can anyone name one of the Volcanoes there?"
8. Since i had been reading about National Parks, i raised my hand.
9. "The Park has two active volcanoes, mauna Loa and kilauea," I answered.

Using Capital Letters Correctly   **269**

DIFFERENTIATING INSTRUCTION

Learners Having Difficulty

Provide students with a questionnaire that personalizes the application of the capitalization rules for proper nouns. Here are some questions that you could include.

1. What is the name of your favorite television personality?
2. What high school will you attend?
3. In what city, county, and state do you live?
4. What is the full address of your current school?
5. What are the names of some shops, museums, parks, or restaurants that you like to visit?
6. What is your birth date?
7. What brands of cereal do you like?
8. What day of the week is today?

MECHANICS

---

10. "These pictures show how lava from kilauea's eruption threatened everything in its path in 1989," I added.
11. Its crater, halemaumau crater, is the largest active crater in the World.
12. "we'll go into much more detail about volcanoes tomorrow," ms. jackson said.
13. then ms. jackson told us that honolulu is probably the most important business center in the pacific ocean.
14. Ever since captain William Brown sailed into the harbor in 1794, Hawaii has played an increasingly important role in business.
15. It's easy to see why—Hawaii is midway between Continents.
16. hawaii's largest city has a fine seaport; it links japan, china, and even australia with North and south America.
17. Cultural and academic studies thrive there in places such as the university of hawaii and the east-west center.
18. You can even get a look at the iolani palace where the Rulers of hawaii once lived.
19. Perhaps best of all, hawaii offers Tourists a day in the sun at waikiki beach.
20. Suddenly, i blurted out, "wouldn't it be great if we could all go there now!"

270 Chapter 13 Capital Letters

(3) Capitalize names of organizations, teams, institutions, and government bodies.

Type of Name	Examples	
Organizations	Clark Drama Club Junior League	Modern Language Association
Teams	Boston Celtics Dallas Cowboys	Los Angeles Dodgers Hutto Hippos
Institutions	Westside Regional Hospital	Roosevelt Junior High School
Government Bodies	United Nations Peace Corps	Congress York City Council

(4) Capitalize the names of historical events and periods, special events, calendar items, and holidays.

Type of Name	Examples	
Historical Events and Periods	Revolutionary War Bronze Age Holocaust	United States Bicentennial Age of Reason
Special Events	Texas State Fair Special Olympics	Super Bowl Festival of States
Calendar Items and Holidays	Monday Memorial Day	February Thanksgiving Day

NOTE Do not capitalize the name of a season unless it is part of a proper name.

EXAMPLES   the winter holidays   the Quebec Winter Carnival

(5) Capitalize the names of nationalities, races, and peoples.

EXAMPLES   Mexican   Nigerian

African American   Iroquois

HELP

The names of organizations, businesses, and government bodies are often abbreviated to a series of capital letters.

EXAMPLES
National   NOW
Organization
for Women

American   AT&T
Telephone &
Telegraph

National   NSF
Science
Foundation

Usually the letters in such abbreviations are not followed by periods, but always check an up-to-date dictionary or other reliable source to be sure.

STYLE TIP

The words *black* and *white* may or may not be capitalized when they refer to races. Either way is correct.

EXAMPLE
In the 1960s, both Blacks and Whites [or blacks and whites] worked to end segregation.

Within each piece of writing, be sure to be consistent in your use of capitals or lowercase letters for these words.

Using Capital Letters Correctly   271

RETEACHING

Capitalization

Divide the class into eleven groups, and assign each group one of the eleven subrules of **Rule 13d**. Give each group a slip of paper with the subrule written on it. Then, have each group compile a list of at least five properly capitalized words that exemplify the subrule of **Rule 13d** that the group represents. Have each group choose a student to write down the words, while group members take turns supplying words. Circulate among the groups to observe and to offer support. Students may consult a dictionary or an encyclopedia if they run out of ideas. After the lists are completed, have a student from each group read the group's list to the rest of the class.

(6) Capitalize the names of businesses and the brand names of business products.

Type of Name	Examples	
Businesses	Sears, Roebuck and Co.	Fields Department Store
	Thrifty Dry Cleaners	First National Bank
Business Products	Schwinn Mesa	Apple Macintosh
	GMC Jimmy	Callaway Big Bertha

NOTE Names of types of products are not capitalized.

EXAMPLES Schwinn bicycle, Apple computer, Callaway golf club

(7) Capitalize the names of ships, trains, aircraft, and spacecraft.

Reference Note
For information on **using italics in names,** see page 320.

Type of Name	Examples	
Ships	Queen Elizabeth 2	Kon Tiki
Trains	City of New Orleans	Silver Meteor
Aircraft	Memphis Belle	Spruce Goose
Spacecraft	Voyager 2	Sputnik

(8) Capitalize the names of buildings and other structures.

EXAMPLES Sydney Opera House, St. Louis Cathedral, Aswan Dam, Eiffel Tower, Brooklyn Bridge

NOTE Do not capitalize such words as *hotel, theater,* or *high school* unless they are part of the name of a particular building or institution.

EXAMPLES
Capital Theater — a theater
Lane Hotel — the hotel
Taft High School — this high school

272 Chapter 13 Capital Letters

Learning for Life

Writing a Press Release. Correct use of capitalization is important in any formal writing that will be shared publicly. Have students write press releases about an event they want to advertise, such as a play, sports event, recital, dance performance, or fund-raiser. Information in the press release, which will go to all the area radio and television stations and newspapers, should include the following items:

- title and description of the event

(9) Capitalize the names of monuments, memorials, and awards.

Type of Name	Examples	
Monuments	Great Sphinx Navajo National Monument	Stonehenge Washington Monument
Memorials	Lincoln Memorial the Coronado Memorial	The Minute Man Tomb of the Unknown Soldier
Awards	Emmy Award Congressional Medal of Honor	Nobel Prize Pulitzer Prize

(10) Capitalize the names of religions and their followers, holy days and celebrations, sacred writings, and specific deities.

Type of Name	Examples	
Religions and Followers	Judaism Hinduism	Christian Muslim
Holy Days and Celebrations	Easter All Saints' Day	Yom Kippur Christmas Eve
Sacred Writings	Koran Bible	Dead Sea Scrolls Upanishads
Specific Deities	God Allah	Jehovah Krishna

NOTE The words *god* and *goddess* are not capitalized when they refer to a deity of ancient mythology. However, the names of specific gods and goddesses are capitalized.

EXAMPLES The king of the Norse gods was Odin.

Athena was the Greek goddess of wisdom and warfare.

DIFFERENTIATING INSTRUCTION

Advanced Learners

Students who have a firm grasp of **Rules 13a–13d** may want to analyze the effect of creative punctuation and capitalization. Students might analyze E. E. Cummings's use of capitalization or punctuation in a poem like "maggie and milly and molly and may" and that of Shel Silverstein in "Sarah Cynthia Sylvia Stout Would Not Take the Garbage Out." Tell students to write short analyses that give their opinions about the effects created by the creative uses of capitalization and punctuation.

- date, time, place, address
- names of five participants
- name of person writing the press release
- sponsoring organizations
- phone number to call for more information

Press releases should be written just as they are to be printed in newspapers and read aloud on the air. Have students pay special attention to their use of capitalization.

PRACTICE

Guided and Independent

Exercises You may wish to use Exercise 3 as guided practice, and then have students complete Review A as independent practice.

HOMEWORK

STYLE TIP

The word *earth* is not capitalized unless it is used along with the names of other heavenly bodies that are capitalized. The words *sun* and *moon* are generally not capitalized.

EXAMPLES
Oceans cover three fourths of the **e**arth's surface.

Which is larger—Saturn or **E**arth?

How many **m**oons does **J**upiter have?

(11) Capitalize the names of planets, stars, constellations, and other heavenly bodies.

Type of Name	Examples	
Planets	**M**ercury	**V**enus
Stars	**R**igel	**P**roxima **C**entauri
Constellations	**U**rsa **M**ajor	**A**ndromeda
Other Heavenly Bodies	**M**ilky **W**ay	**C**omet **K**ohoutek

Exercise 3 Proofreading Sentences for Correct Capitalization

Supply capital letters wherever they are needed in each of the following sentences. *Words that should be capitalized are underscored.*

EXAMPLE 1. Each arbor day the students at franklin junior high school plant a tree.

1. Arbor Day, Franklin Junior High School

1. The golden gate bridge spans the entrance of san francisco bay.
2. Our muslim neighbors, the Rashads, fast during the month of ramadan.
3. The peace corps became a government agency by an act of congress.
4. Do you think the henderson hornets will win the playoffs?
5. Thousands of cherokee people live in the Smoky Mountains in and around North Carolina.
6. To stop flooding in the South, the tennessee valley authority, a government agency, built thirty-nine dams on the Tennessee River and the streams that flow into it.
7. Which biographer won the pulitzer prize this year?
8. On new year's day, many fans crowd into football stadiums for annual bowl games such as the rose bowl.
9. Can you see neptune or any of its moons through your telescope?
10. Have you read any myths about apollo, a god once worshiped by the greeks?

274 Chapter 13 Capital Letters

Oral Practice **Proofreading Sentences for Correct Capitalization**

Read each of the following sentences aloud. Then, identify the words in each sentence that should be capitalized.

EXAMPLE 1. according to my sister, i'm a mall rat.

1. According to my sister, I'm a mall rat.

1. the branford mall is the largest in melville county.
2. It is on jefferson parkway, two miles north of duck lake state park and the big bridge that crosses duck lake.
3. Across the parkway from the mall is our new local high school with its parking lots, playing fields, and stadium, home of the branford panthers.
4. Near the mall are the american legion hall, bowlarama, and king skating rink.
5. The mall includes two jewelry stores, nicholson's department store, the palace cinema, and thirty-five other businesses.
6. They range from small stationery stores to one of the finest restaurants in the midwest.
7. The restaurant larue is run by marie and jean larue, who are from france.
8. Also in the mall is the american paper box company, which sells boxes for every packaging need.
9. My friends sharon and earl always shop at gene's jeans, which specializes in denim clothing.
10. An outlet store for northwestern leather goods of chicago sells uffizi purses and wallets.

STYLE TIP

Misusing a capital letter or a lowercase letter at the beginning of a word can confuse the meaning of a sentence.

EXAMPLE
I'd like to see inside the **w**hite **h**ouse. [The sentence means I'd like to see inside a particular house that is white.]

I'd like to see inside the **W**hite **H**ouse. [The sentence means I'd like to see inside the home of the president of the United States.]

You may be able to use double meanings effectively in poetry or in other creative writing. In formal writing, though, you should follow the rules of standard capitalization.

Review A **Correcting Errors in Capitalization**

Each of the following sentences contains errors in capitalization. Correct these errors by changing incorrect capital letters to lowercase letters and incorrect lowercase letters to capital letters.

EXAMPLE 1. African americans in massachusetts have played an important part in American history.

1. Americans, Massachusetts

1. In Boston, the Crispus attucks monument is a memorial to attucks and the other men who died in the boston Massacre.
2. According to many Historians, attucks was a former slave who fought against the british in the american Revolution.

Using Capital Letters Correctly 275

Proper Adjectives, Course Names

Rules 13e, f (pp. 276–278)

OBJECTIVE

- To proofread and revise sentences for correct capitalization of proper adjectives and the names of school subjects

DIRECT TEACHING

Modeling and Demonstration

Proper Adjectives, Course Names. Model how to proofread sentences for correct capitalization by using the example *My science teacher and my spanish teacher both like mexican food.* First, ask whether *science* should be capitalized. [*no*] Next, ask whether *spanish* should be capitalized. [*yes*] Point out that school subjects are not capitalized, except (1) course names followed by numbers and (2) language classes. Then, ask whether there are any proper adjectives that need to be capitalized. [*yes—Mexican*] Now, have a volunteer use another example from this chapter to demonstrate how to proofread for correct capitalization.

Jan Ernst Matzeliger

W.E.B. DuBois

Crispus Attucks

Reference Note

For more about **proper adjectives**, see page 37.

3. The department of the Interior has made the Home of maria baldwin a historic building in cambridge.
4. Baldwin was a Leader in the league for Community Service, an Organization to help the Needy.
5. One of the founders of the National association for the Advancement of colored people, w.e.b. DuBois, was born in great Barrington, Massachusetts.
6. A marker stands on the Spot where DuBois lived.
7. Jan ernst matzeliger, who lived in lynn, invented a machine that made Shoes easier and cheaper to manufacture.
8. The nantucket whaling Museum has information about Peter green, a Sailor on the ship john Adams.
9. During a storm at sea, Green saved the Ship and crew.
10. Use the Map of Massachusetts shown above to locate the Towns and Cities in which these notable african Americans lived.

13e. Capitalize proper adjectives.

A **proper adjective** is formed from a proper noun and is capitalized.

RESOURCES

Proper Adjectives, Course Names
Practice

- *Language & Sentence Skills Practice,* pp. 266–268
- *Developmental Language & Sentence Skills,* pp. 105–106

Proper Noun	Proper Adjective
Greece	**G**reek theater
Mars	**M**artian moons
Darwin	**D**arwinian theory
Japan	**J**apanese tea ceremony

13f. Do not capitalize the names of school subjects, except course names followed by numerals and names of language classes.

EXAMPLES **h**istory, **t**yping, **a**lgebra, **E**nglish, **S**panish, **L**atin, **H**istory 101, **M**usic III, **A**rt **A**ppreciation I

Exercise 4 — Proofreading Sentences for Correct Capitalization

Supply capital letters where they are needed in each of the following sentences. *Words that should be capitalized are underscored.*

EXAMPLE 1. Rosa said we were eating mexican bread.
 1. Mexican

1. The program featured russian ballet dancers.
2. The european Common Market improves international trade.
3. The scandinavian countries include both Norway and Sweden.
4. In geography, we learned about the platypus and the koala, two australian animals.
5. We read several english plays in my literature class.
6. I am planning to take computers I next year.
7. On the floor was a large persian rug.
8. England, France, Scotland, Russia, and the United States played important roles in canadian history.
9. The backyard was decorated with chinese lanterns.
10. Are you taking french or art II?

Review B — Correcting Errors in Capitalization

Each of the sentences on the following page contains errors in capitalization. Correct these errors by writing the words that are incorrectly capitalized and changing capital letters to lowercase letters or changing lowercase letters to capital letters.

MEETING THE CHALLENGE

Choose a country. Then, write a paragraph giving a short biographical sketch of a current or former leader of that country. In your paragraph, correctly use and capitalize at least five proper nouns and five proper adjectives.

DIFFERENTIATING INSTRUCTION

English-Language Learners

General Strategies. In many languages, adjectives derived from proper nouns are not capitalized. You may want to let students tell you about capitalization rules in their languages and how they differ from English rules. Discussion of this sort may help students remember English capitalization rules.

Meeting the Challenge

RESPONSES WILL VARY. A sample response follows.

Sir John Alexander Macdonald was the first prime minister of the Dominion of Canada. He was born in 1815 to a Scottish family that moved to North America in 1820. He studied and then practiced law, served in the Frontenac County militia, and in 1843 started his political career as a Kingston alderman. He served his country for many years. Macdonald held the office of prime minister for almost two decades, longer than any other Canadian prime minister except W. L. Mackenzie King. As prime minister, Macdonald helped create the dominion from a handful of British provinces. He was knighted by Queen Victoria, and he died in 1891.

Using Capital Letters Correctly 277

Titles
Rule 13g (pp. 278–284)

OBJECTIVE
- To proofread and revise sentences for correct capitalization of titles

DIRECT TEACHING

Modeling and Demonstration
Titles. Model how to proofread sentences for correct capitalization by using the example *The club secretary asked principal Simmons if we could have a retirement party for mrs. Bellini.* First, ask whether *secretary* should be capitalized. [*no*] Next, ask whether *principal* should be capitalized. [*yes*] Then, ask whether *mrs.* should be capitalized. [*yes*] Point out that the title of a person is capitalized when it comes before a name or is used in direct address, but generally a person's title is not capitalized if it is used alone or comes after a name. Now, have a volunteer use another example from this chapter to demonstrate how to proofread for correct capitalization.

DIFFERENTIATING INSTRUCTION

English-Language Learners
General Strategies. Some languages may vary from English in how the words in the title of a book, article, or movie are capitalized. Consequently, when using English, students might have difficulty determining which words in titles to capitalize. Help students by showing them a variety of titles so that they get a sense of which words in titles are capitalized in English.

MECHANICS

---

13 g

STYLE TIP

For special emphasis or clarity, writers sometimes capitalize a title used alone or following a person's name.

EXAMPLES
At the ceremony, the **Q**ueen honored the Royal Navy.

Mr. Biden, the **S**enator from Delaware, called for a committee vote.

278 Chapter 13 Capital Letters

EXAMPLE
1. "what do you know about Modern architecture at the beginning of the Century, sean?"

1. What, modern, century, Sean

Words that should be capitalized or lowercased are underscored.

1. In <u>S</u>ocial <u>S</u>tudies, <u>i</u> learned about the famous <u>A</u>rchitect Frank Lloyd Wright.
2. One of <u>w</u>right's best-known works is his house, <u>f</u>allingwater, in <u>b</u>ear <u>r</u>un, Pennsylvania.
3. "Yes, <u>w</u>right still may be the best-known <u>a</u>merican architect," Mrs. Lee said.
4. Louis <u>s</u>ullivan (1856–1924) was among the first <u>B</u>uilders in the <u>u</u>nited States to use a steel frame.
5. A <u>g</u>erman architect helped design the Seagram Building, an early <u>S</u>kyscraper in the <u>e</u>ast.
6. Both architects and the <u>P</u>ublic wanted new ideas after <u>w</u>orld <u>w</u>ar II, according to my <u>a</u>rchitecture 101 teacher.
7. <u>t</u>he use of reinforced <u>C</u>oncrete made possible large, thin roofs such as the one at the Massachusetts <u>i</u>nstitute of <u>t</u>echnology.
8. Next <u>t</u>uesday we will see a <u>F</u>ilm about inventive designs in the <u>b</u>razilian capital.
9. I imagine that <u>b</u>razilian <u>C</u>itizens are proud of the architect Oscar <u>n</u>iemeyer.
10. Hear my report on the <u>i</u>sraeli architect Moshe Safdie during <u>H</u>istory today.

13g. Capitalize titles.

(1) Capitalize the title of a person when the title comes before a name.

EXAMPLES   **P**resident Lincoln   **M**rs. Oliver Wendell

Mayor Bradley   **C**ommissioner Rodriguez

Generally, a title that is used alone or following a person's name is not capitalized, especially if the title is preceded by *a* or *the*.

EXAMPLES   The **s**ecretary of **d**efense held a news conference.

Lien Fong, our class **s**ecretary, read the minutes.

However, a title used by itself in direct address is usually capitalized.

RESOURCES

Titles
Practice
- *Language & Sentence Skills Practice*, pp. 269–275
- *Developmental Language & Sentence Skills*, pp. 107–108

EXAMPLES Is it very serious, **D**octor?

How do you do, **S**ir [or **s**ir]?

(2) Capitalize a word showing a family relationship when the word is used before or in place of a person's name.

EXAMPLES We expect **U**ncle Fred and **A**unt Helen soon.

Both **M**om and **D**ad work at the hospital.

However, do not capitalize a word showing a family relationship when a possessive comes before the word.

EXAMPLE We asked Pedro's **m**other and his **a**unt Celia to be chaperons.

(3) Capitalize the first and last words and all important words in titles and subtitles.

Unimportant words in titles include

- articles (*a, an, the*)
- coordinating conjunctions (*and, but, for, nor, or, so, yet*)
- prepositions of fewer than five letters (such as *by, for, on, with*)

Type of Name	Examples	
Books	*The Mask of Apollo* *Mules and Men*	*Long Claws: An Arctic Adventure*
Chapters and Other Parts of Books	"The Circulatory System" "Language Handbook"	"The Civil War Begins" "Epilogue"
Magazines	*Popular Mechanics* *Ebony*	*Seventeen* *Sports Illustrated*
Newspapers	*The Tennessean* the *Boston Globe*	*The Wall Street Journal*
Poems	"Season at the Shore"	*Evangeline* "Birches"

(continued)

Reference Note

For more information about **articles**, see page 35. For more about **coordinating conjunctions**, see page 62. For more about **prepositions**, see page 58.

Reference Note

For guidelines on **what titles are italicized**, see page 320. For guidelines on **what titles are enclosed in quotation marks**, see page 327.

DIFFERENTIATING INSTRUCTION

Advanced Learners

Have interested students interview at least five people to get answers to the following questions.

1. What is your favorite book?
2. What is your favorite magazine?
3. What is your favorite movie?
4. What is your least favorite CD?
5. What is your favorite television show?

Ask students to write short summaries of their findings, reminding them to capitalize titles correctly as they record responses and write their summaries. Then, ask volunteers to read their summaries to the class and post all the summaries on a bulletin board.

(continued)

Type of Name	Examples	
Short Stories	"The Purloined Letter"	"Zlateh the Goat" "Broken Chain"
Plays	The Three Sisters A Midsummer Night's Dream	A Doll's House I Never Sang for My Father
Movies and Videos	Fairy Tale: A True Story Babe	It's a Wonderful Life The Wizard of Oz
Television Series	Nova Kratt's Creatures	Star Trek: The Next Generation
Cartoons and Comic Strips	Jump Start Cathy	Scooby Doo Dilbert
Audiotapes and CDs	Butterfly Falling into You	Dos Mundos Spirit
Computer Games and Video Games	Sonic the Hedgehog Math Blaster Rockett's New School	Logical Journey SimCity Space Kids
Works of Art	Mona Lisa David	The Night Watch Mankind's Struggle
Musical Compositions	The Marriage of Figaro	"America the Beautiful"
Historical Documents	Magna Carta Treaty of Paris	The Declaration of Independence

HELP
The official title of a book is found on the title page. The official title of a newspaper or periodical is found on the masthead, which usually appears on the editorial page or the table of contents.

NOTE The article *the* at the beginning of a title is not capitalized unless it is the first word of the official title.

EXAMPLES My father reads *The Wall Street Journal*.

Does she work for **t**he *Texas Review*?

280   Chapter 13   Capital Letters

MINI-LESSON Mechanics

***The* in Titles.** Capitalizing and italicizing the word *the* when it is the first word in the title of a periodical or newspaper can be confusing. *The* is italicized and capitalized only when it is part of the official title. Ask students to refer to a reference work that contains titles of periodicals and newspapers and to make a list of five titles containing *the* and five titles that don't contain *the*. Students can ask at the reference desk of the library for help finding the appropriate reference books, or they could

280   Capital Letters

Exercise 5 — Correcting Sentences by Capitalizing Words

Most of the following sentences contain at least one word that should be capitalized but is not. Correctly write each incorrect word. If a sentence is already correct, write C.

EXAMPLE 1. Ms. Chang is meeting with principal Hodges.
1. Principal

1. Tom Hanks' career really took off after he starred in the movie *big*.
2. In 1998, John Glenn, a former senator, became the oldest person to travel in space.   **2. C [or Senator]**
3. The assignment is to compare and contrast Amy Tan's story "Two kinds" with Bernard Malamud's "The first seven years."
4. Rummaging through the pile of used books, Marcia found a copy of *the Complete Poems of Stephen Crane*.
5. Our English teacher, mrs. Fernandez, has a small sculpture of the globe theatre sitting on her desk.
6. Isn't it a coincidence that your aunt Jenny and my uncle Herbert work for the same company?   **6. C**
7. Which do you prefer, Bob Dylan's CD *Nashville skyline* or his son's *The wallflowers*?
8. Some of my friends claim that *The Empire strikes back* is the best movie of the series.
9. Did you remember to clip that article we read yesterday in *The Washington post*?
10. Mom and dad always chuckle when they read *Hagar the Horrible*.

Review C — Proofreading Sentences for Correct Capitalization

Write the sentences on the following page, using capital letters wherever they are needed.   **Words that should be capitalized are underscored.**

EXAMPLE 1. The series *all creatures great and small* is being rerun on public television.
1. The series *All Creatures Great and Small* is being rerun on public television.

Using Capital Letters Correctly   **281**

---

conduct a search on the Internet. Explain to students that whenever they are in doubt about whether *the* is part of the title of a periodical or newspaper, they can find the answer by consulting a reference work or a copy of the periodical or newspaper.

EXTENSION

Critical Thinking

Metacognition. After students have completed **Review D**, have them analyze the process they use to correct errors in capitalization. Do they check a word at a time, a sentence at a time, or read the entire exercise before starting to make corrections? Do they note areas of difficulty and go back to those after finishing the corrections for which they know the answers? Do they recheck their work to see if they may have overlooked a correction? How effective do they think their strategies are? What might they change to make their strategies more effective? Have students work in pairs to ask these questions and analyze their processes.

1. While waiting to interview mayor ward, I read an article in *newsweek*.
2. Have you read leslie marmon silko's poem "story from bear country"?
3. You have probably seen a picture of *the thinker*, one of rodin's best-known sculptures.
4. On television last night, we saw the movie *the return of the native*.
5. Every four years voters elect a president and several united states senators.
6. Uncle nick read aloud from francisco jiménez's short story "the circuit."
7. The reporter asked, "Can you tell us, senator inouye, when you plan to announce the committee's final decision?"
8. The main speaker was dr. andrew holt, a former president of the university of tennessee.
9. Besides uncle don, our visitors included aunt pat, aunt jean, both of my grandmothers, and my great-grandfather.
10. The soccer players listened to coach Daly as he outlined defensive strategy.

Review D — Proofreading Sentences for Correct Capitalization

The following sentences each contain at least one capitalization error. Correctly write the words that require capital letters.

EXAMPLE 1. The waters of the caribbean are pleasantly warm.
              1. Caribbean

1. The greeks believed that zeus, the king of the gods, lived on mount olympus.
2. The *titanic* sank after hitting an iceberg off the coast of newfoundland.
3. My cousin collects scandinavian pottery.
4. Stephanie is taking english, math II, and biology.
5. On friday we were cheered by the thought that monday, memorial day, would be a holiday.
6. My picture is in today's *austin American-Statesman*.
7. The quaker oats company has introduced a new corn cereal.
8. In *roots*, alex haley, a famous author, traces the history of his family.
9. She usually travels to boston on american airlines.

MINI-LESSON — Mechanics

Punctuating Titles. If students are confused about when to use underlining (italics) with titles and when to use quotation marks with titles, write the following titles on the chalkboard without punctuation. Have students add either underlining or quotation marks to each.

The Borrowers [The Borrowers]

Row, Row, Row Your Boat ["Row, Row, Row Your Boat"]

Jabberwocky ["Jabberwocky"]

Capital Letters

10. I wanted to name my persian cat after one of the justices on the supreme court.

Review E Proofreading a Paragraph for Correct Capitalization

Each sentence in the following paragraph contains at least one error in capitalization. Correctly write the words that require capital letters.

EXAMPLE [1] Before thanksgiving, i learned some interesting facts about africa in my history II class.

1. Thanksgiving, I, Africa, History II

[1] My teacher, mr. davidson, told us about the mighty kingdoms and empires that existed for hundreds of years in africa. [2] some of these kingdoms dated back to the time of the roman empire. [3] Others rose to power during the period known as the middle ages in europe. [4] For many years, the people in the kingdom of cush did ironwork and traded along the nile river. [5] Later, the cush were defeated by the people of axum, led by king ezana. [6] As you can see in the map below, several kingdoms in africa developed between lake chad and the atlantic ocean. [7] Three of these kingdoms were ghana, mali, and songhai. [8] These kingdoms established important trade routes across the sahara. [9] Tombouctou's famous university attracted egyptian and other arab students. [10] I read more about these african kingdoms and empires in our textbook, *world history: people and nations*.

Review F **Correcting Errors in Capitalization**

Each of the following sentences contains at least one error in capitalization. Correctly write each incorrect word, changing capital letters to lowercase letters or changing lowercase letters to capital letters.

EXAMPLE 1. On june 25, 1876, sioux and cheyenne warriors defeated general george a. Custer and his Troops.

1. June, Sioux, Cheyenne, General George A., troops

1. The Defeat of general custer occurred at the battle of the little bighorn.
2. In december of 1890, many Sioux were killed by Soldiers in a battle at wounded Knee creek in south Dakota.
3. Depicted by artists, writers, and filmmakers, both Battles have become part of american History.
4. In the late nineteenth century, the sioux Artist Kicking bear painted the *Battle Of the little Bighorn*.
5. The painting, done on muslin Cloth, is shown below.
6. Kicking bear, who himself fought in the Battle, painted at the pine Ridge agency in south Dakota, where he lived.
7. soldiers who fought against kicking Bear described him as courageous.
8. The well-known American Poet Stephen vincent benét wrote about the battle of wounded knee in a Poem called "american names."

Battle of Little Bighorn by Kicking Bear (Sioux), 1898. Courtesy of the Southwest Museum, Los Angeles

9. More recently, the author Dee brown wrote about the american indians of the west in his book *bury my Heart at Wounded knee*.
10. In 1970, the movie *Little big Man* told the story of a fictional 121-year-old character who had survived the Battle against general Custer.

CHAPTER 13

Chapter Review

A. Correcting Errors in Capitalization

Each of the following sentences contains at least one error in capitalization. Correct the errors either by changing capital letters to lowercase letters or by changing lowercase letters to capital letters. *Words that should be capitalized or lowercased are underscored.*

1. Please pick up a box of Tide <u>Detergent</u> at the store.
2. The "Battle Hymn <u>Of The</u> Republic" was written by Julia <u>ward</u> Howe.
3. Are we going to <u>uncle</u> Ted's house for Thanksgiving again?
4. Charing <u>cross book shop</u> is on Thirty-Second Street.
5. Ms. <u>wong</u> always stays at the Four Seasons <u>hotel</u> when she's in New York <u>city</u> on business.
6. Do you know if <u>professor</u> Ezekiel will be teaching <u>Creative Writing</u> during the spring semester?
7. In what year was the <u>battle</u> of <u>gettysburg</u> fought?
8. My aunt remembers when Mother Teresa won the Nobel Peace <u>prize</u>.
9. Every winter my <u>Grandparents</u> travel to the <u>southwest</u>.
10. My <u>Uncle</u> <u>sid</u> once met <u>sir</u> Winston Churchill.
11. Mr. Salter often remembers his old house on <u>vine street</u> in McAllen, Texas.
12. Father and <u>mother</u> traveled all over the <u>Earth</u> when they were buying furniture for their antique store.
13. The principal asked me, "<u>how</u> would you like to study <u>Geography</u> next semester?"
14. When Jim went back to New York for Christmas, he left his dog, <u>piper</u>, at the kennel.
15. Sometimes my <u>Mother</u> works at home on <u>friday</u>.
16. Grand Canyon National <u>park</u> was closed this weekend because of heavy snow.
17. Shall we renew our subscription to *national geographic*?
18. This <u>june</u> we plan to welcome a <u>swedish</u> exchange student to our home.

Chapter Review **285**

Numerals in brackets refer to rules tested by the items in the Chapter Review.

1. [13d(6)]
2. [13g(3), d(1)]
3. [13g(2)]
4. [13d(6, 2)]
5. [13d(1, 8, 2)]
6. [13g(1), f]
7. [13d(4)]
8. [13d(9)]
9. [13g(2), d(2)]
10. [13g(2), d(1), g(1)]
11. [13d(2)]
12. [13g(2), d(11)]
13. [13a, f]
14. [13d(1)]
15. [13g(2), d(4)]
16. [13d(2)]
17. [13g(3)]
18. [13d(4), e]

ASSESSING

Monitoring Progress

Chapter Review. To assess student progress, you may want to compare the types of items missed on the **Diagnostic Preview** to those missed on the **Chapter Review**. If students have not made significant progress, you may want to refer them to **Exercises 28, 29, 33, 34** and **Sections 1** and **2** of the **Mechanics Test** in **Chapter 17: Correcting Common Errors** for additional practice.

DIFFERENTIATING INSTRUCTION

Learners Having Difficulty

The twenty-five lengthy sentences in **Part A** of this **Chapter Review** might be overwhelming to some students. Here are some steps you can take to make the text more manageable.

1. Isolate each sentence so that students can focus on one sentence at a time.
2. Have helpers read the sentences aloud to students with visual-processing deficits.
3. Suggest that students first check for errors in the application of **Rule 13a** only. Next, students should look for errors in the application of **Rule 13b**, and so on.

MECHANICS

RESOURCES

Capital Letters

Review
■ *Language & Sentence Skills Practice,* pp. 273–275

Assessment
■ *Holt Handbook Chapter Tests with Answer Key,* pp. 25–26, 46

19. [13d(8)]
20. [13d(7, 2)]
21. [13c, d(6)]
22. [13g(2)]
23. [13d(8)]
24. [13b]
25. [13f, g(1)]

19. We're going to Washington, D.C., to see the *white* *house*.
20. At the Henry Ford Museum in Dearborn, Michigan, you can see a replica of the *spirit of st. louis*, the plane that Charles Lindbergh used to fly solo across the *atlantic*.
21. At the Crossbay Market, *i* bought a can of *progresso* soup.
22. My *Aunt* Janice visited Petrified Forest National Park.
23. The Rosenbach *museum* and *library* in Philadelphia is open Tuesday through Sunday.
24. *dear* Mr. Boylan:
    I enjoyed your book enormously.
    sincerely yours,
    Jimmy Connolly
25. In *History* class, we learned about *queen* Elizabeth I.

B. Proofreading Sentences for Correct Capitalization

Write the following sentences, and correct errors in capitalization either by changing capital letters to lowercase letters or by changing lowercase letters to capital letters.

Words that should be capitalized or lowercased are underscored.

26. [13e]
27. [13g(3, 2)]
28. [13d(6, 2)]
29. [13d(5, 2)]
30. [13g(3), d]
31. [13d(3)]
32. [13d(4)]
33. [13d(2)]
34. [13e]
35. [13d(2)]
36. [13d(10)]
37. [13f]

26. Mars, Venus, and Jupiter were *roman* gods.
27. *The wind in the willows* is my *Mother's* favorite book.
28. Davis Housewares *emporium* has moved to Fifth *street*.
29. The *lozi* people in Africa live near the Zambezi *river*.
30. "Stopping *By* Woods *On* a Snowy Evening" is by Robert Frost, a *Poet* from New England.
31. Do you know when David Souter was appointed to the *supreme* *court*?
32. Next Monday is *memorial* *day*.
33. When we traveled through the *south*, we visited the Antietam National Battlefield.
34. Ms. Ling is teaching us about *chinese* culture.
35. Cayuga *lake* stretches *North* from Ithaca, New York.
36. The main religion in Indonesia is *islam*, but there are also many Indonesian *buddhists*.
37. My older sister is taking Spanish, *Science*, Mathematics II, and *Art*.

38. Carlos and I had turkey sandwiches made with german mustard on french bread.
39. We turned west onto route 95 and stayed on it for five miles.
40. George Copway, who was born in Canada, wrote about his people, the ojibwa.

38. [13e]
39. [13d(2)]
40. [13d(5)]

Writing Application
Using Capital Letters in a Letter

Proper Nouns Students in your class have become pen pals with students in another country. You have been given the name of someone to write. Write your pen pal a letter introducing yourself and telling about your school and your community. In your letter, be sure to use capitalization correctly.

Prewriting Note the information you want to give in your letter. You may wish to include information such as your age; a description of yourself; your favorite books, movies, actors, or musicians; some clubs, organizations, or special activities you participate in; some special places, events, or attractions in your community or state.

Writing As you write your draft, keep in mind that your pen pal may not recognize names of some people, places, and things in the United States. For example, he or she may not recognize the names of your favorite movies or musical groups. Be sure to use correct capitalization to show which names are proper nouns.

Revising Read through your letter carefully. Have you left out any important information? Are any parts of your letter confusing? If so, you may want to add, cut, or revise some details. Is the tone of your letter friendly? Have you followed the correct form for a personal letter?

Publishing Read your letter carefully to check for any errors in grammar, spelling, and punctuation. Use the rules in this chapter to help you double-check your capitalization. With your teacher's permission, post a map of the world on the classroom wall and display the letters around the map.

APPLICATION

Writing Application

Scoring Rubric. While paying particular attention to students' use of correct capitalization, you will also want to evaluate overall writing performance. You may want to give a split score to indicate development and clarity of the composition as well as mechanics skills.

CHAPTER 14

INTRODUCING THE CHAPTER

- This chapter allows students to review and build on past knowledge of the four basic types of punctuation. First, the chapter discusses end marks and abbreviations. Then several rules about commas are presented, including how they are used in series; with compound sentences, interrupters, nonessential phrases and clauses, appositives, words of direct address, and introductory elements; and in conventional situations. Next, the chapter covers the use of semicolons and colons.

- The chapter concludes with a **Chapter Review,** which includes a **Writing Application** that asks students to write an announcement using correct punctuation.

- For help in integrating the chapter with writing assignments, use the **Teaching Strands** chart on pp. T24–T25.

CHAPTER 14 Punctuation
End Marks, Commas, Semicolons, and Colons

HELP

All of the punctuation marks that are already in the sentences in the Diagnostic Preview are correct.

Numerals in brackets refer to rules tested by the items in the Diagnostic Preview.

1. [14i(4), a]
2. [14l, f, a]
3. [14h, g, a]
4. [14h, a]
5. [14i(1), a]
6. [14j(2), f, a]
7. [14j(4), a]

Diagnostic Preview

Using End Marks, Commas, Semicolons, and Colons

The following sentences lack necessary periods, question marks, exclamation points, commas, semicolons, and colons. Rewrite each sentence, inserting the correct punctuation.

Optional commas are underlined.

EXAMPLE   1. Snakes lizards crocodiles and turtles are reptiles
          1. *Snakes, lizards, crocodiles, and turtles are reptiles.*

1. Toads and frogs on the other hand are amphibians
2. Some turtles live on land others live in lakes streams or oceans
3. Turtles have no teeth but you should watch out for their strong hard beaks
4. The words *turtle* and *tortoise* are similar in meaning but *tortoise* usually refers to a land dweller
5. The African pancake tortoise which has a flat flexible shell uses an unusual means of defense
6. Faced with a threat it crawls into a narrow crack in a rock takes a deep breath and wedges itself in tightly
7. Because some species of tortoises are endangered they cannot be sold as pets

288 Chapter 14   Punctuation

CHAPTER RESOURCES

Internet
- Web resources: go.hrw.com

Practice & Review
- *Language & Sentence Skills Practice,* pp. 281–296; 297–300
- *Language & Sentence Skills Practice Answer Key,* pp. 118–127

Application & Enrichment
- *Language & Sentence Skills Practice,* pp. 280, 301, 302–303, 304
- *Language & Sentence Skills Practice Answer Key,* pp. 118, 127–128

8. Three species of tortoises that can be found in the United States are as follows: the desert tortoise, the gopher tortoise, and the Texas tortoise.
9. The gopher tortoise lives in the Southeast, and the desert tortoise comes from the Southwest.
10. Is the Indian star tortoise, which is now an endangered species, very rare?
11. As this kind of tortoise grows older, its shell grows larger, the number of stars on the shell increases, and their pattern becomes more complex.
12. The Indian star tortoise requires warmth, sunlight, and a diet of green vegetables.
13. Living in fresh water, soft-shelled turtles have long, flexible beaks and fleshy lips.
14. Their shells are not really soft, however, but are covered by smooth skin.
15. Sea turtles are the fastest turtles; the green turtle can swim at speeds of almost twenty miles per hour.
16. Most turtles can pull their head, legs, and tail into their shell; however, sea turtles cannot do so.
17. Mr. Kim, my neighbor up the street, has several turtles in his backyard pond.
18. Come to my house at 4:30 in the afternoon, and I'll show you our turtle.
19. At 7:00 P.M., we can watch that new PBS documentary about sea turtles.
20. Wanda, may I introduce you to Pokey, my pet turtle?
21. Pokey, who has been part of our family for years, is a red-eared turtle.
22. The book *Turtles: A Complete Pet Owner's Manual* has helped me learn how to take care of Pokey.
23. Pokey has been in my family for fifteen years, and my parents say that he could easily live to be fifty if he is cared for properly.
24. What a great pet Pokey is! [or .]
25. Don't you agree with me, Wanda, that a turtle makes a good pet?

8. [14n, f, a]
9. [14h, a]
10. [14i(1), b]
11. [14j(4), f, a]
12. [14f, a]
13. [14j(2), g, a]
14. [14i(4), a]
15. [14l]
16. [14l, i(4)]
17. [14e, i(2)]
18. [14o]
19. [14e]
20. [14i(3, 2), b]
21. [14i(1)]
22. [14q]
23. [14h, a]
24. [14c or a]
25. [14i(3), b]

ASSESSING

Entry-Level Assessment

Diagnostic Preview. The **Diagnostic Preview** can help you analyze students' mastery of punctuation. You may choose to concentrate on the students' weakest areas and use the other areas as review.

The results of the **Diagnostic Preview** can help you decide which lessons to teach directly and which to assign to cooperative-learning groups.

Differentiating Instruction

- *Developmental Language & Sentence Skills Guided Practice,* pp. 109–114
- *Developmental Language & Sentence Skills Guided Practice Teacher's Notes and Answer Key,* pp. 26–27

Assessment

- *Holt Handbook Chapter Tests with Answer Key,* pp. 27–28, 46

PRETEACHING

Lesson Starter
Prior Knowledge. To give students practice in identifying sentence types and supplying appropriate end marks, have volunteers add end marks to the following nursery rhyme. Write the nursery rhyme on the chalkboard or on a transparency, or have students copy the nursery rhyme and work in groups to add one question mark, two exclamation points, and one period.

The north wind doth blow,
we soon shall have snow,
and what will poor robin do then [?]
Poor thing [!]
He'll sit in the barn
to keep himself warm,
and hide his head under his wing [.]
Poor thing [!]

MECHANICS

End Marks
Rules 14a–e *(pp. 290–293)*

OBJECTIVES
- To rewrite sentences by adding the appropriate end marks
- To punctuate abbreviations correctly

DIFFERENTIATING INSTRUCTION

Learners Having Difficulty
Point out to students that sentences beginning with *what* and *how* that are obviously not questions are usually exclamations, as in "What a beautiful day we're having!" or "How beautiful that flower is!" Then, work with students to write both exclamations and questions that begin with the words *what* or *how*. Have students illustrate the sentences. The illustrations could then be displayed on a bulletin board.

---

14 a–e

HELP

Periods (decimal points) are also used to separate dollars from cents and whole numbers from tenths, hundredths, and so forth.

EXAMPLES
$10.23 [ten dollars and twenty-three cents]
5.7 [five and seven tenths]

End Marks

An **end mark** is a mark of punctuation placed at the end of a sentence. *Periods, question marks,* and *exclamation points* are end marks.

14a. Use a period at the end of a statement.

EXAMPLE   Tea is grown in Sri Lanka.

14b. Use a question mark at the end of a question.

EXAMPLE   Did you see the exhibit about lightning?

14c. Use an exclamation point at the end of an exclamation.

EXAMPLE   Wow! What a high bridge that was!

14d. Use either a period or an exclamation point at the end of a request or a command.

When an imperative sentence makes a request, it is generally followed by a period. When an imperative sentence expresses a strong command, an exclamation point is generally used.

EXAMPLES   Please call the dog. [a request]
Call the dog! [a command]

Oral Practice   Adding End Marks to Sentences

Read each of the following sentences aloud, and indicate which end mark should be added.

EXAMPLE   1. Did you know that a choreographer is a person who creates dance steps

1. *Did you know that a choreographer is a person who creates dance steps?*

1. Why is Katherine Dunham called the mother of African American dance?
2. She studied anthropology in college and won a scholarship to visit the Caribbean.
3. How inspiring the dances she saw in Haiti were!
4. When Dunham returned to the United States, she toured the country with her own professional dance company.
5. How I admire such a talented person!
6. Ask me anything about Katherine Dunham.

290   Chapter 14   Punctuation

RESOURCES

End Marks
Practice
- *Language & Sentence Skills Practice,* pp. 281–283, 297

7. How many honors has Dunham's creativity won her?
8. She was named to the Hall of Fame of the National Museum of Dance in Saratoga, New York.
9. She was also given the National Medal of Arts for exploring Caribbean and African dance.
10. The editors of *Essence* magazine praised Dunham for helping to break down racial barriers.

14e. Many abbreviations are followed by a period.

Types of Abbreviations	Examples
Personal Names	A. B. Guthrie W.E.B. DuBois Livie I. Durán
Titles Used with Names	Mr. Mrs. Ms. Jr. Sr. Dr.
Organizations and Companies	Co. Inc. Corp. Assn.

NOTE Abbreviations for government agencies and other widely used abbreviations are written without periods. Each letter of the abbreviation is capitalized.

EXAMPLES FBI NAACP NIH NPR
          PTA TV   UN   YWCA

Types of Abbreviations	Examples
Addresses	Ave. St. Rd. Blvd. P.O. Box
States	Tex. Penn. Ariz. Wash. N.C.
Times	A.M. (*ante meridiem,* used with times from midnight to noon) P.M. (*post meridiem,* used with times from noon to midnight) B.C. (before Christ) A.D. (*anno Domini,* in the year of the Lord)

STYLE TIP

When writing the initials of someone's name, place a space between two initials (S. E. Hinton). Do not place spaces between three initials (M.F.K. Fisher).

STYLE TIP

An **acronym** is a word formed from the first (or first few) letters of a series of words. Acronyms are written without periods.

EXAMPLES
UNICEF (**U**nited **N**ations **I**nternational **C**hildren's **E**mergency **F**und)

VISTA (**V**olunteers **i**n **S**ervice **t**o **A**merica)

End Marks **291**

DIRECT TEACHING

Modeling and Demonstration

End Marks. Model how to add appropriate end marks by using the following examples: *Tea is grown in Sri Lanka, Did you see the exhibit about lightning,* and *Wow what a high bridge that was.* First, ask whether the first sentence is a statement, a question, or an exclamation. [*statement*] Explain that a period should be used at the end of a statement. Next, repeat this question for the second sentence. [*question*] A question mark should be used at the end of a question. Then, repeat the question for the third sentence. [*exclamation*] Explain that exclamation points should be used after the exclamation *Wow* and at the end of the sentence; also, point out that *what* should be capitalized since it begins a sentence. Now, have a volunteer use another example from this chapter to demonstrate how to add end marks.

MECHANICS

FAMILY/COMMUNITY ACTIVITY
Continued on pp. 292–293

Everyday Abbreviations. To demonstrate to students the common occurrence of abbreviations in daily life, write the following paragraph on the chalkboard or on a transparency.

Today I went to the store and bought 5 lbs of potatoes; then I stopped by the library to borrow a book of poems by E. E. Cummings. After that, I made it to the post office before it closed at 5:30 P.M. and mailed my tax forms

End Marks **291**

DIFFERENTIATING INSTRUCTION

Advanced Learners
Abbreviations. Tell students that some abbreviations commonly used in English have no periods. Ask students to consult a dictionary or reference book that deals specifically with abbreviations and to create a list of abbreviations that do not use periods. Ask students to suggest guidelines that explain when periods can be left out of abbreviations. [*Abbreviations used without periods are usually the names of government agencies (CIA), organizations (PTA), or job titles (CEO).*]

English-Language Learners
General Strategies. Discuss with students the kinds of end marks in various languages. A period is a vertical line in Hindi, a circle in Japanese, and four dots in Aramaic. In languages such as Greek and Korean, the period is slightly raised. The Greek question mark looks like an English semicolon, and Spanish interrogative and exclamatory sentences have end marks at both ends of the interrogative or exclamatory part of the sentence, with the first mark inverted.

Hmong. In Hmong, questions often are indicated by the inclusion of the word *puas*, meaning "what," within the body of a sentence rather than through the use of end punctuation. Therefore, some Hmong speakers will use periods where question marks are appropriate or will include the word *what* inappropriately within their sentences. Remind students of the differences between declarative, imperative, and interrogative sentences, and point out that written English in part relies on end punctuation to determine those sentence functions.

STYLE TIP

The abbreviations A.D. and B.C. need special attention. You should place A.D. before the numeral and B.C. after the numeral.

EXAMPLES
A.D. 760   54 B.C.

However, for centuries expressed in words, place both A.D. and B.C. after the century.

EXAMPLES
seventh century B.C.
fourth century A.D.

HELP

If you are not sure whether you should use a period with an abbreviation, look up the abbreviation in a dictionary.

NOTE A two-letter state abbreviation without periods is used only when it is followed by a ZIP Code. Both letters of such abbreviations are capitalized.

EXAMPLE   Orlando, **FL** 32819

Abbreviations for units of measure are usually written without periods and are not capitalized.

EXAMPLES   mm   kg   dl   oz   lb   ft   yd   mi

However, to avoid confusion with the word *in*, you should use a period with the abbreviation for *inch* (in.).

NOTE When an abbreviation with a period ends a sentence, another period is not needed. However, a question mark or an exclamation point is used as needed.

EXAMPLES   We will arrive by 3:00 P.M.
Can you meet us at 3:30 P.M.?
Oh no! It's already 3:30 P.M.!

Exercise 1 Punctuating Abbreviations

Some of the following sentences contain abbreviations that have not been correctly punctuated. Correct each error. If a sentence is already correct, write *C*. *Carets indicate where periods should be inserted.*

EXAMPLE   1. Of course, we watch P.B.S.; we love the science shows it broadcasts.
1. PBS

1. Not everyone knows that W^E^B^ DuBois eventually became a Ghanaian citizen.
2. The writing isn't clear, but I think it says *10 ft 6 in^* or *10 ft 5 in.*
3. Write me in care of Mrs. Audrey Coppola, 10 Watson Ave.^
4. Yes, that's in California—Novato, C^A^ 94949.
5. Were those clay statues made as far back as 500 B.C^?
6. Send your check or money order to Lester's Low-Cost Computer Chips, Inc^ Duluth, Minn^ and receive your new chips in two days!
7. Could you be there at 7:00 P.M.?   **7. C**

FAMILY/COMMUNITY ACTIVITY
Continued from p. 291

to the IRS office in Austin, Tex. Now I won't be panicking when the April 15 deadline comes. Finally, I drove home to my house on Harcourt Dr. for an evening of old movies on TV.

Ask a student volunteer to read the paragraph aloud, and then have another student underline all the abbreviations in the paragraph. Discuss with students which types of abbreviations are contained in the paragraph. Then, ask students to work in groups of three to list abbreviations they

8. I would never do business with a company whose only address was a P.O. box.
9. Miss Finch, Dr. Bledsoe will see you now.
10. His full name is Marvin French Little Hawk, Jr., but everyone calls him Junior. **10. C**

> **Review A** Adding Periods, Question Marks, and Exclamation Points to Sentences

Rewrite each of the following sentences, adding the necessary periods, question marks, and exclamation points.

EXAMPLE 1. Do you ever think about how electricity is produced

  1. *Do you ever think about how electricity is produced?*

1. Electricity can come from large hydroelectric power stations.
2. Wow, these stations certainly do create a lot of power!
3. How do hydroelectric power stations work?
4. Look at the diagram to gain a better understanding.
5. Falling water from natural falls or artificial dams provides the initial power in the process.
6. Have you ever been to Niagara Falls, New York, to see the famous falls?
7. From 12:00 A.M. to 12:00 A.M.—constantly, in other words—the falls are a tremendous power source.
8. As you can see, rushing water turns turbines, which then drive generators.
9. What exactly are generators, and what do they do?
10. J.D. explained that generators are the machines that turn the motion of the turbines into electricity.

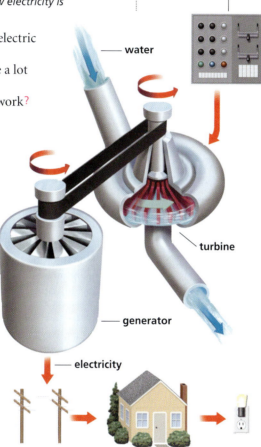

End Marks **293**

Commas

Rules 14f–k (pp. 294–309)

OBJECTIVES

- To proofread sentences for the correct use of commas
- To correct compound sentences by adding commas
- To add commas to sentences with nonessential phrases and clauses
- To proofread for the correct use of commas with appositives and appositive phrases
- To correct sentences by using commas with words of direct address
- To correct sentences by using commas to set off parenthetical expressions
- To edit sentences for the correct use of commas with introductory elements
- To edit sentences for the correct use of commas in conventional situations

MECHANICS

DIRECT TEACHING

Modeling and Demonstration

Commas. Model how to proofread sentences for correct use of commas by using the example *The baby was happy alert playful and active.* Ask whether there is a series of three or more items in the sentence. [yes—happy, alert, playful, active] Next, ask whether all the items in the series are joined by *and*, *or*, or *nor*. [no] Therefore, the items in the series *happy, alert, playful, and active* need to be separated by commas. Now, have a volunteer use another example from this chapter to demonstrate how to proofread sentences for correct use of commas.

Reference Note

For information about using **semicolons**, see page 310.

Commas

End marks are used to separate complete thoughts. *Commas,* however, are generally used to separate words or groups of words within a complete thought.

14f. Use commas to separate items in a series.

A *series* is a group of three or more items in a row. Words, phrases, and clauses may appear in a series.

Words in a Series
January, February, and March are all summer months in the Southern Hemisphere. [nouns]
The engine rattled, coughed, and stalled. [verbs]
The baby was happy, alert, playful, and active. [adjectives]

Phrases in a Series
There were fingerprints at the top, on the sides, and on the bottom. [prepositional phrases]
Cut into pieces, aged for a year, and well dried, the wood was ready to burn. [participial phrases]
To pitch in a World Series game, to practice medicine, and to run for mayor are all things I would like to do someday. [infinitive phrases]

Clauses in a Series
We sang, we danced, we ate dinner, and we played trivia games. [short independent clauses]
I knew that we were late, that the ice cream was melting, and that the car was nearly out of gas. [short subordinate clauses]

NOTE Only short independent clauses in a series may be separated by commas. A series of independent clauses that are long or that contain commas should be separated by semicolons.

EXAMPLE Yawning, Mother closed the curtains; Father, who had just come in, turned on the porch lights; and my little sister, Christina, put on her pajamas.

294 Chapter 14 Punctuation

RESOURCES

Commas

Practice

- *Language & Sentence Skills Practice,* pp. 284–293, 298
- *Developmental Language & Sentence Skills,* pp. 109–112

Always be sure that there are at least three items in the series; two items generally do not need a comma between them.

INCORRECT   You will need a pencil, and plenty of paper.
CORRECT   You will need a pencil and plenty of paper.

When all the items in the series are joined by *and* or *or*, do not use commas to separate them.

EXAMPLES   Take water **and** food **and** matches with you.

Stephen will take a class in karate **or** judo **or** aikido next year.

Exercise 2   Proofreading Sentences for the Correct Use of Commas

Some of the following sentences need commas; others do not. If a sentence needs any commas, write the word before each missing comma and add the comma. If a sentence is already correct, write *C*.   Optional commas are underlined.

EXAMPLES
1. Seal the envelope stamp it and mail the letter.
   1. envelope, it,
2. You should swing the club with your knees bent and your back straight and your elbows tucked.
   2. C

1. The mountains and valleys of southern Appalachia were once home to the Cherokee people.   1. C
2. Cleveland, Cincinnati, Toledo, and Dayton are four large cities in Ohio.
3. The captain entered the cockpit, checked the instruments, and prepared for takeoff.
4. Luisa bought mangos and papayas and oranges.   4. C
5. The speaker took a deep breath and read the report.   5. C
6. Rover can roll over, walk on his hind feet, and catch a tennis ball.
7. The neighbors searched behind the garages, in the bushes, and along the highway.
8. Rubén Blades is an attorney, an actor, and a singer.
9. Eleanor Roosevelt's courage, her humanity, and her service to the nation will always be remembered.
10. Tate dusted, I vacuumed, and Blair washed the dishes.

STYLE TIP

In your reading, you will find that some writers omit the comma before the conjunction joining the last two items of a series. Nevertheless, you should form the habit of including this comma. Sometimes a comma is necessary to make your meaning clear. Notice how the comma affects the meaning in the following examples.

EXAMPLES
Mom, Jody and I want to go to the movies. [Mom is being asked for her permission.]

Mom, Jody, and I want to go to the movies. [Three people want to go to the movies.]

DIFFERENTIATING INSTRUCTION

English-Language Learners

General Strategies. Discuss with students the uses of commas in various languages. In Japanese, Persian, and Arabic, for example, the comma is raised above the line of writing and reversed. If any of your students are native speakers and writers of these languages, perhaps they could share with the class some examples of what commas look like in sentences in their languages.

TIPS & TRICKS

To see whether a comma is needed between two adjectives, insert *and* between the adjectives. If *and* sounds awkward there, do not use a comma.

EXAMPLE
  unshaded electric light
TEST
  unshaded and electric light
ANSWER
  No comma is needed.

Another test you can use is to switch the order of the adjectives. If the sentence still makes sense when you switch them, use a comma.

EXAMPLE
  tiny, dense star
TEST
  dense, tiny star
ANSWER
  Use a comma.

Reference Note
For more information about **compound nouns,** see page 25.

14g. Use a comma to separate two or more adjectives that come before a noun.

EXAMPLES A white dwarf is a tiny, dense star.

Venus Williams played a powerful, brilliant game.

Do not place a comma between an adjective and the noun immediately following it.

INCORRECT My spaniel is a fat, sassy, puppy.
CORRECT My spaniel is a fat, sassy puppy.

Sometimes the final adjective in a series is thought of as part of the noun. When the adjective and the noun are linked in such a way, do not use a comma before the final adjective.

EXAMPLES A huge **horned owl** lives in those woods.
  [not *huge, horned owl*]

An unshaded **electric light** hung from the ceiling.
  [not *unshaded, electric light*]

NOTE When an adjective and a noun are closely linked, they may be thought of as a unit. Such a unit is called a **compound noun.**

EXAMPLES Persian cat Black Sea French bread

Review B Proofreading Sentences for the Correct Use of Commas

Most of the following sentences need commas. If a sentence needs any commas, write the word before each missing comma and add the comma. If a sentence is already correct, write *C*.

Optional commas are underlined.

EXAMPLE 1. Chen participated in debate volleyball and drama.
  1. debate, volleyball,

1. Carla sneaked in and left a huge, gorgeous, fragrant bouquet of flowers on the desk.
2. I chose the gift, Michael wrapped it, and Charley gave it to Gina and Kelly.
3. Smoking is a costly, dangerous habit.
4. In the human ear, the hammer, anvil, and stirrup carry sound waves to the brain.
5. Buffalo Bill was a Pony Express rider, a scout, and a touring stunt performer.

296 Chapter 14 Punctuation

MINI-LESSON Grammar   Continued on pp. 297–298

Punctuating Compound Nouns Preceded by Adjectives. Students may become confused about using commas when an adjective precedes a compound noun that is written as two words. To give students practice using commas with adjectives that precede compound nouns, write the following two columns of word sets on the chalkboard, leaving out the adjectives in brackets. Tell students that only one word set in each row is a compound noun.

6. "The Masque of the Red Death" is a famous horror story by Edgar Allan Poe.   6. C
7. According to Greek mythology, the three Fates spin the thread of life, measure it, and cut it.
8. LeVar Burton played the intelligent, likable character Geordi on *Star Trek: The Next Generation.*
9. The fluffy kitten with the brown, white, and black spots is my favorite.
10. Falstaff begged for mercy in a fight, ran away, and later bragged about his bravery in battle.

Compound Sentences

14h. Use a comma before *and, but, for, nor, or, so,* or *yet* when it joins independent clauses in a compound sentence.

EXAMPLES Tamisha offered me a ticket, and I accepted.

They had been working very hard, but they didn't seem especially tired.

The Mullaney twins were excited, for they were going to day care for the first time.

When the independent clauses are very short and there is no chance of misunderstanding, the comma before *and, but,* or *or* is sometimes omitted.

EXAMPLES It rained and it rained.

Come with us or meet us there.

NOTE Always use a comma before *for, nor, so,* or *yet* when joining independent clauses.

EXAMPLE I was tired, yet I stayed.

Do not be misled by a simple sentence that contains a compound verb. A simple sentence has only one independent clause.

SIMPLE SENTENCE WITH COMPOUND VERB Usually we **study** in the morning and **play** basketball in the afternoon.
COMPOUND SENTENCE Usually we study in the morning, and we play basketball in the afternoon. [two independent clauses]

STYLE TIP
The word *so* is often overused. If possible, try to reword a sentence to avoid using *so*.

EXAMPLE
  It was late, so we went home.
REVISED
  Because it was late, we went home.

Reference Note
For more information about **compound sentences,** see page 131. For more about **simple sentences** with **compound verbs,** see page 15.

RETEACHING

Compound Sentences
Using commas correctly will be easier if students can distinguish readily between a compound sentence, which requires a comma before the conjunction, and a simple sentence with a compound verb, which does not require a comma before the conjunction. To review the definitions of both types of sentences, refer to **Chapter 7: Kinds of Sentence Structure.**

Diagramming can be an effective way to help students understand the distinction between these two kinds of sentences. Guide students through diagramming the example sentences on this page, as shown below.

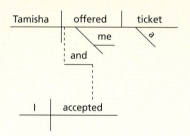

If students need help with diagramming, refer them to **Chapter 19: Sentence Diagramming.**

---

grand piano	new piano	[*beautiful*]
green tree	pecan tree	[*giant*]
lawn chair	white chair	[*new*]
cold juice	apple juice	[*refreshing*]

Guide students through placing adjectives before each word set and then punctuating each set. Help them to identify the sets of words that are compound nouns, which do not require a comma after the added adjective [*grand piano, pecan tree,*

Exercise 3 · Correcting Compound Sentences by Adding Commas

If a sentence needs a comma, write the word before the missing comma and add the comma. If an existing comma is unnecessary, write the words before and after the comma and omit the comma. If the sentence is already correct, write *C*.

EXAMPLE 1. American Indian artists have a heritage dating back thousands of years and many of them draw on this heritage, to create modern works.

1. years, heritage to

1. Today's artists sometimes work with nontraditional materials, but they often use traditional techniques.
2. In the photograph below, you can see the work of the Tohono O'odham artist Mary Thomas, and begin to appreciate this basket weaver's skill.
3. The baskets in the photograph are woven in the "friendship design" and show a circle of human figures in a traditional prayer ceremony.   3. C
4. Yucca and devil's claw are used to make these baskets, and each plant's leaves are a different color.
5. The Navajo artist Danny Randeau Tsosie listened to his grandmother's stories, and learned about his family's heritage.
6. Tsosie's works show her influence but also express his own point of view.   6. C
7. Christine Nofchissey McHorse learned the skill of pottery making from her grandmother, and now McHorse can make beautiful bowls.
8. McHorse has an unusual style, for her designs combine traditional Navajo and Pueblo images.

298   Chapter 14   Punctuation

MINI-LESSON Grammar   *Continued from p. 297*

lawn chair, and *apple juice*], and the sets that include a simple noun and adjective and therefore might require a comma between the adjectives [*new piano, green tree, white chair,* and *cold juice*]. If a word group is read aloud with the word *and* between the adjectives and *and* sounds awkward (for example, *giant and pecan tree*), no comma is needed.

For more information on compound nouns, refer students to **Chapter 2: Parts of Speech Overview.**

9. American Indian jewelry makers often use pieces of turquoise and coral found in North America,and they also use other stones from around the world.
10. American Indian art often looks very modern,yet some of its symbols and patterns are quite old.

Interrupters

14i. Use commas to set off an expression that interrupts a sentence.

Two commas are needed if the expression to be set off comes in the middle of the sentence. One comma is needed if the expression comes first or last.

EXAMPLES   Ann Myers**, our neighbor,** is a fine golfer.

Naturally, we expect to win.

My answer is correct**, I think.**

(1) Use commas to set off nonessential participial phrases and nonessential subordinate clauses.

A *nonessential* (or *nonrestrictive*) phrase or clause adds information that is not needed to understand the basic meaning of the sentence. Such a phrase or clause can be omitted without changing the main idea of the sentence.

NONESSENTIAL PHRASES
My sister**, listening to her radio,** did not hear me.

Paul**, thrilled by the applause,** took a bow.

NONESSENTIAL CLAUSES
*The Wizard of Oz***, which I saw again last week,** is my favorite movie.

I reported on *Secret of the Andes*, **which was written by Ann Nolan Clark.**

Each boldface clause or phrase above can be omitted because it is not essential to identify the word or phrase it modifies. Omitting such a clause or phrase will not change the meaning of the sentence.

EXAMPLES   Paul took a bow.

I reported on *Secret of the Andes*.

PEANUTS reprinted by permission of United Feature Syndicate, Inc.

EXTENSION

Relating to Writing

Adjective Clauses. Caution your students against overusing adjective clauses, as this tendency leads to wordiness. Here are two examples of sentences that overuse adjective clauses, along with revisions that make the sentences more concise. Write the sentences on the chalkboard, and guide students through the revisions.

1. The day, which was rainy and cold, dampened their spirits. [*The rainy, cold day dampened their spirits.*]
2. The girl, who was smart, helped the new boy in class. [*The smart girl helped the new boy in class.*]

Ask students to choose completed writing assignments from their notebooks or from another class and to proofread their writing for overuse of adjective clauses. Ask students to revise sentences containing wordy adjective clauses and to share their revisions with a partner. If some students don't find any sentences to revise, write the following sentences on the chalkboard and ask students to revise them.

1. The leaves, which were crimson, orange, and gold, caught the late afternoon fall sun and glowed radiantly. [*The crimson, orange, and gold leaves caught the late afternoon fall sun and glowed radiantly.*]
2. I lost my sweater, which is made of green wool. [*I lost my green wool sweater.*]

Reference Note

For more about **phrases,** see Chapter 5. For more about **subordinate clauses,** see page 114.

Do not set off an *essential* (or *restrictive*) phrase or clause. Since such a phrase or clause tells *which one(s)*, it cannot be omitted without changing the basic meaning of the sentence.

ESSENTIAL PHRASES   The people **waiting to see Michael Jordan** whistled and cheered. [Which people?]

A bowl **made by Maria Martínez** is a collector's item. [Which bowl?]

ESSENTIAL CLAUSES   The dress **that I liked** has been sold. [Which dress?]

The man **who tells Navajo folk tales** is Mr. Platero. [Which man?]

Notice how the meaning changes when an essential phrase or clause is omitted.

EXAMPLES   The people whistled and cheered.

A bowl is a collector's item.

The dress has been sold.

The man is Mr. Platero.

NOTE   A clause beginning with *that* is usually essential.

EXAMPLE   This is the birdhouse **that I made.**

Exercise 4   Adding Commas to Sentences with Nonessential Phrases and Clauses

Some of the following sentences need commas to set off nonessential phrases and clauses. Other sentences are correct without commas. If a sentence needs commas, write the word that comes before each missing comma and add the comma. If the sentence is already correct, write *C*.

EXAMPLE   1. My grandfather's favorite photograph which was taken near Ellis Island shows his family after their arrival from Eastern Europe.

1. photograph, Island,

1. Millions of immigrants who came to the United States between about 1892 and 1954 stopped at Ellis Island which is in Upper New York Bay.

300   Chapter 14   Punctuation

CONTENT-AREA CONNECTIONS

Math
Periods. Pose the following question to students: How does a decimal point function differently from a period in a sentence? You may want to have students in small groups brainstorm the possibilities or have them puzzle over the answers overnight and discuss the possibilities with family members

2. Families arriving from Europe were interviewed there.   **2. C**
3. The island and its buildings which were closed to the public for many years are now part of the Statue of Liberty National Monument.
4. In 1990, Ellis Island rebuilt as a museum was officially opened to the public.
5. Visitors who wish to see the museum can take a ferry ride from Manhattan Island.   **5. C**
6. The museum's lobby crowded with steamer trunks and other old baggage is the visitors' first sight.
7. One special attraction in the museum consists of audiotapes and videotapes that describe the immigrants' experiences.   **7. C**
8. The Registry Room which is on the second floor sometimes held as many as five thousand people.
9. The immigrants who came from many countries hoped to find freedom and a happier life in America.
10. Immigrants who came to the United States brought with them a strong work ethic and a variety of skills that helped to make our country great.   **10. C**

The Granger Collection, New York.

(2) Use commas to set off nonessential appositives and nonessential appositive phrases.

An *appositive* is a noun or a pronoun used to identify or describe another noun or pronoun.

NONESSENTIAL APPOSITIVE	My oldest sister, **Alicia,** will be at basketball practice until 6:00 P.M.
NONESSENTIAL APPOSITIVE PHRASES	Jamaica, **a popular island for tourists,** is in the Caribbean Sea.
	May I introduce you to Vernon, **my cousin from Jamaica**?

DIFFERENTIATING INSTRUCTION

Advanced Learners

Famous Appositives. In some historical cases, an appositive has become part of a proper name, as in *Attila the Hun*. In other cases, a phrase that may have started out as an appositive has come to stand alone as the name or title by which someone is known; for example, Elvis Presley is known as "the King" or "the King of Rock and Roll." Ask students to do some research to find more examples of these two kinds of appositives and to report their findings to the class. [*Possibilities include Catherine the Great, Erik the Red, and William the Conqueror.*]

Commas   **301**

or others. [*Students may conclude that in a sentence, the period signals a stop—the end of a sentence—while in a number, the decimal point means* and *(for example, 4.6 is interpreted as "four and six tenths"). Also, when reading amounts of money, the decimal point means* and *(for example, $1.98 is read as "one dollar and ninety-eight cents").*]

DIRECT TEACHING

Correcting Misconceptions

Rule 14i. Students may mistakenly generalize that appositive phrases should always be set off with commas and that appositives should never be set off with commas. Explain to students that whether or not an appositive or appositive phrase is set off with commas depends on the meaning of the sentence. Students may have particular difficulty when an appositive naming someone or something is preceded by a possessive and a noun signifying a relationship. Explain to students that they always have to ask in such cases, "Is this person or thing the only one?" For example, if Alicia is my only sister, her name is set off with commas and is nonessential. If, however, I have other sisters, Alicia's name is essential to identifying which sister I mean and is not set off with commas. Write on the chalkboard the following phrases:

Lilly's friend Elena
Mike's cousin Haman
my dog Pinta
your gerbil Fred
their sister Sara

Have students work in pairs to write two sentences with each phrase: one sentence with an essential appositive and one with a nonessential appositive. Have students explain the situation in each sentence. Then, have pairs trade sentences to check each other's identification of essential and nonessential appositives and correct use of commas.

MECHANICS

MEETING THE CHALLENGE

You can use appositives and appositive phrases to combine sentences.

ORIGINAL
Our old house is on Larchmont Street. That house is my favorite place.

COMBINED
Our old house, my favorite place, is on Larchmont Street.

Use appositive phrases to combine the following sentences.

1. Ms. Blewett asked me to help out after practice. She's our coach.
2. I play halfback. The halfback is the position between the forward and the fullback.

ANSWERS
1. Ms. Blewett, our coach, asked me to help out after practice.
2. I play halfback, the position between the forward and the fullback.

Do not use commas to set off an appositive that is essential to the meaning of a sentence.

ESSENTIAL APPOSITIVES   My sister **Alicia** is at basketball practice. [The speaker has more than one sister and must give a name to identify which sister.]

The planet **Mercury** is closer to the Sun than any other planet in our solar system. [The solar system contains more than one planet. The name is needed to identify which planet.]

Exercise 5 Proofreading for the Correct Use of Commas with Appositives and Appositive Phrases

Rewrite each of the following sentences, and underline the appositive or appositive phrase. Use commas to set off non-essential appositive phrases.

EXAMPLE
1. Mars one of the planets closest to Earth can be seen without a telescope.

1. Mars, *one of the planets closest to Earth*, can be seen without a telescope.

1. The whole class has read the novel *Old Yeller*.
2. Shana Alexander a former editor of a popular magazine was the main speaker at the conference.
3. The character Sabrina is Josie's favorite.
4. The Galápagos Islands a group of volcanic islands in the Pacific Ocean were named for the Spanish word that means "tortoise."
5. Rubber an elastic substance quickly restores itself to its original size and shape.
6. This bowl is made of clay found on Kilimanjaro the highest mountain in Africa.
7. The North Sea an arm of the Atlantic Ocean is rich in fish, natural gas, and oil.
8. Jamake Highwater a Blackfoot/Eastern Band Cherokee author writes about the history of his people.
9. At Gettysburg a town in Pennsylvania an important battle of the Civil War was fought.
10. My friend Imelda is teaching me how to make empanadas.

(3) Use commas to set off words that are used in direct address.

EXAMPLES   **Ben,** please answer the doorbell.

Mom needs you**, Francine.**

Would you show me**, ma'am,** where the craft store is?

Exercise 6   Correcting Sentences by Using Commas with Words of Direct Address

Identify the words used in direct address in the following sentences. Then, rewrite each sentence, inserting commas before, after, or both before and after the words, as needed.

EXAMPLE   1. Listen folks to this amazing announcement!

1. *folks—Listen, folks, to this amazing announcement!*

1. Andrea when are you leaving for Detroit?
2. Pay attention now class.
3. Let us my sisters and brothers give thanks.
4. Please Dad may I use your computer?
5. Senator please summarize your tax proposal.
6. Help me move this table Marlene.
7. "Tell me both of you what movie you want to see," Jo said.
8. Hurry William and give me the phone number!
9. Mrs. Larson where is Zion National Park?
10. I'm just not sure friends that I agree with you.

(4) Use commas to set off parenthetical expressions.

A *parenthetical expression* is a side remark that adds information or shows a relationship between ideas.

EXAMPLES   Carl**, on the contrary,** prefers soccer to baseball.

To tell the truth, Jan is one of my best friends.

Common Parenthetical Expressions		
by the way	in fact	of course
for example	in my opinion	on the contrary
however	I suppose	on the other hand
I believe	nevertheless	to tell the truth

Commas   303

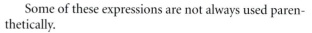

Some of these expressions are not always used parenthetically.

EXAMPLES **Of course** it is true. [not parenthetical]

That is**,** **of course,** an Indian teakwood screen. [parenthetical]

I suppose we ought to go home now. [not parenthetical]

He'll want a ride**,** **I suppose.** [parenthetical]

Exercise 7 Correcting Sentences by Using Commas to Set Off Parenthetical Expressions

The following sentences contain parenthetical expressions that require commas. Write the parenthetical expressions, inserting commas before, after, or both before and after the expressions, as needed.

EXAMPLES
1. Everyone I suppose has heard of the Hubble Space Telescope.
1. , I suppose,
2. As a matter of fact even a small refracting telescope gives a good view of Saturn's rings.
2. As a matter of fact,

1. You don't need a telescope, however, to see all the beautiful sights in the night sky.
2. For instance, on a summer night you might be able to view Scorpio, Serpens, and the Serpent Bearer.
3. By the way, you should not overlook the Milky Way.
4. The Milky Way, in fact, is more impressive in the summer than at any other time of year.
5. Hercules, of course, is an interesting constellation.
6. Studying the constellations is, in my opinion, a most interesting hobby.
7. It takes an active imagination, however, to spot some constellations.
8. Sagittarius, for example, is hard to see unless you're familiar with a constellation map.
9. Scorpio, on the other hand, is quite clearly outlined.
10. Astronomy is a fascinating science, I think.

304   Chapter 14   Punctuation

Introductory Words, Phrases, and Clauses

14j. Use a comma after certain introductory elements.

(1) Use a comma after *yes, no,* or any mild exclamation such as *well* or *why* at the beginning of a sentence.

EXAMPLES **Yes,** you may borrow my bicycle.

Why, it's Lena!

Well, I think you are wrong.

(2) Use a comma after an introductory participial phrase.

EXAMPLES **Beginning a new school year,** Zelda felt somewhat nervous.

Greeted with applause from the fans, Rashid ran out onto the field.

> **Reference Note**
> For information about **participial phrases,** see page 100.

(3) Use a comma after two or more introductory prepositional phrases.

EXAMPLES **At the bottom of the hill,** you will see the field.

Until the end of the song, just keep strumming that chord.

> **Reference Note**
> For information about **prepositional phrases,** see page 90.

Also, use a comma after a single introductory prepositional phrase if the phrase is long. If it is short, a comma may or may not be used. Be sure to use a comma when it is necessary to make the meaning of the sentence clear.

EXAMPLES In the morning they left. [clear without a comma]

In the morning, sunlight streamed through the window. [The comma is needed so that the reader does not read "morning sunlight."]

(4) Use a comma after an introductory adverb clause.

EXAMPLES **After I finish my homework,** I will go to the park.

When you go to the store, could you please pick up a gallon of milk?

> **Reference Note**
> For information about **adverb clauses,** see page 120.

> NOTE An adverb clause that comes at the end of a sentence does not usually need a comma.
>
> EXAMPLE I will go to the park **after I finish my homework.**

DIFFERENTIATING INSTRUCTION

Learners Having Difficulty

Introductory Phrases. To give students further instruction and practice in determining when to use a comma after a single introductory prepositional phrase, put the following sentences on the chalkboard:

- After eating my dog takes a nap.
- Before trimming trees should be well watered and healthy.
- In the winter twilight comes quickly.
- In our school regulations are enforced by hall monitors.

Have student volunteers read these sentences aloud. Then, discuss with students the confusion that arises when the word following the introductory phrase could be part of the phrase. Have student volunteers add commas to the sentences.

MECHANICS

Exercise 8 Using Commas with Introductory Elements

If a comma is needed in a sentence, write the word before the missing comma and add the comma.

EXAMPLE 1. Walking among the tigers and lions the trainer seemed unafraid.
 1. lions,

1. Because pemmican remained good to eat for several years, it was a practical food for many American Indians.
2. Although Jesse did not win the student council election, he raised many important issues.
3. On the desk in the den, you will find your book.
4. Yes, I enjoyed the fajitas that Ruben made.
5. Walking home from school, Rosa saw her brother.
6. When I go to bed late, I sometimes have trouble waking up in the morning.
7. Well, we can watch television or play checkers.
8. Attracted by the computer games in the store window, George decided to go in and buy one.
9. At the stoplight on the corner of the next block, they made a right turn.
10. After eating, the chickens settled down.

Conventional Situations

14k. Use commas in certain conventional situations.

(1) Use commas to separate items in dates and addresses.

EXAMPLES She was born on January 26, 1988, in Cheshire, Connecticut.

A letter dated November 26, 1888, was found in the old house at 980 West Street, Davenport, Iowa, yesterday.

Notice that a comma separates the last item in a date or in an address from the words that follow it. However, a comma does not separate a month from a day (*January 26*) or a house number from a street name (*980 West Street*).

Commas are also used in numbers over 999. Use a comma before every third digit to the left of the decimal point.

EXAMPLE
 3,147,425.00

NOTE Use the ZIP Code correctly on every piece of mail you address. The ZIP Code follows the two-letter state abbreviation; no punctuation separates the state abbreviation from the ZIP Code.

EXAMPLE   Fargo, ND 58102-2728

(2) Use a comma after the salutation of a personal letter and after the closing of any letter.

EXAMPLES   Dear Dad,   Dear Sharon,

With love,   Yours truly,

Reference Note
For information about using **colons for salutations in business letters,** see page 312.

Exercise 9 Using Commas Correctly

Rewrite the following sentences, inserting commas wherever they are needed.

EXAMPLE   1. I received a package from my friend who lives in Irving Texas.

1. I received a package from my friend who lives in Irving, Texas.

1. On May 25 1935 the runner Jesse Owens tied or broke six world track records.
2. The American Saddle Horse Museum is located at 4093 Iron Works Pike Lexington KY 40511-8462.
3. Marian Anderson was born on February 27 1902 in Philadelphia Pennsylvania.
4. Our new address will be 1808 Jackson Drive Ames IA 50010-4437.
5. Ocean City New Jersey is a popular seaside resort.
6. October 15 1988 is an important date because I was born then.
7. Have you ever been to Paisley Scotland?
8. We adopted our dog, King Barnabus IV, in Lee's Summit Missouri on May 9 1995.
9. The national headquarters of the Environmental Defense Fund is located at 257 Park Avenue South New York NY 10010-7304.
10. Dear Lynn
    I am fine. How are you and your family?

EXTENSION

Relating to Writing

Letters. Students may be interested in writing letters to pen pals. (You can get the names of appropriate pen-pal organizations from your school library.) Remind students to use the correct format for a personal letter—using a comma after the salutation and after the closing of the letter. Also, remind your students to use commas appropriately when addressing the envelopes to their pen pals.

> **HELP**
>
> Too much punctuation is just as confusing as not enough punctuation, especially where the use of commas is concerned.
>
> CONFUSING
> My uncle, Doug, said he would take me fishing, this weekend, but now, he tells me, he will be out of town.
>
> CLEAR
> My uncle Doug said he would take me fishing this weekend, but now he tells me he will be out of town.
>
> Have a reason for every comma or other mark of punctuation that you use. When there is no rule requiring punctuation and the meaning of the sentence is clear without it, do not use any punctuation mark.

Review C — Proofreading Sentences for the Correct Use of Commas

For the following sentences, write each word that should be followed by a comma and add the comma after the word. *Optional commas are underlined.*

EXAMPLE 1. The substitute's name is Mr. Fowler I think.
1. Fowler,

1. What time is your appointment, Kevin?
2. My aunt said to forward her mail to 302 Lancelot Drive, Simpsonville, SC 29681-5749.
3. George Washington Carver, a famous scientist, had to work hard to afford to go to school.
4. Quick, violent flashes of lightning cause an average of 14,300 forest fires a year in the United States.
5. My oldest sister, Kim, sent a postcard from Ewa, Hawaii.
6. A single branch stuck out of the water, and the beaver grasped it in its paws.
7. The beaver, by the way, is a rodent.
8. This hard-working mammal builds dams, lodges, and canals.
9. Built with their entrances underwater, the lodges of American beavers are marvels of engineering.
10. The beaver uses its large tail, which is flat, to steer.

Review D — Proofreading Sentences for the Correct Use of Commas

Each of the following sentences contains at least one error in the use of commas. Write each word that should be followed by a comma, and add the comma. *Optional commas are underlined.*

EXAMPLES
1. Kyoto's palaces shrines and temples remind visitors of this city's importance in Japanese history.
1. palaces, shrines,

2. In Japanese *Kyoto* means "capital city" which is what Emperor Kammu made Kyoto in A.D. 794.
2. Japanese, city,

1. Kyoto, a beautiful city, was Japan's capital for more than one thousand years.

2. It still may be called the cultural capital of Japan, for it contains many Shinto shrines, Buddhist temples, the Kyoto National Museum, and wonderful gardens.
3. Yes, Kyoto, which was called Heian-kyo during the ninth century, was so important that an entire period of Japanese history, the Heian period, is named for it.
4. Originating from the monasteries outside ancient Kyoto, the magnificent mandala paintings feature universal themes.
5. Oh, haven't you seen the wonderful *ukiyo-e* paintings of vast mountains and tiny people?
6. Believe it or not, readers, there are now more than twenty colleges and universities in this treasured city.
7. Its people, historic landmarks, and art are respected across the globe.
8. With attractions like these, it's no surprise that Kyoto is a popular tourist stop.
9. Used in industries around the world, the tools of fine crafts are made in Kyoto.
10. Kyoto manufactures silk for the fashion industry, copper for artists and electricians, and machines for businesses.
11. Fine, delicate porcelain from Kyoto graces many tables around the world.
12. The Procession of the Eras, celebrated every autumn, takes place in Kyoto.
13. The Procession of the Eras festival, which celebrates Kyoto's history, begins on October 22.
14. The beautiful, solemn procession is a remarkable sight.
15. At the beginning of the festival, priests offer special prayers.
16. Portable shrines are carried through the streets, and thousands of costumed marchers follow.
17. Elaborate headgear and armor, for example, are worn by marchers dressed as ancient warriors.
18. Because the marchers near the front represent recent history, they wear costumes from the nineteenth-century Royal Army Era.
19. Marching at the end of the procession, archers wear costumes from the eighth-century Warrior Era.
20. The procession is, in fact, a rich memorial to Kyoto's long and varied history.

Semicolons

Rules 14l, m (pp. 310–311)

OBJECTIVE

- To proofread sentences for correct semicolon use

DIRECT TEACHING

Modeling and Demonstration

Semicolons. Model how to proofread sentences for correct use of semicolons by using the incorrect example *Jimmy took my suitcase upstairs, he left his own travel bag in the car.* First, ask whether there are two independent clauses in this sentence. [*yes*] Next, ask whether the two clauses are joined by *and, but, for, nor, or, so,* or *yet.* [*no*] Then, ask whether the ideas in these two clauses are closely related. [*yes*] Point out that these two independent clauses should be joined by a semicolon, placed after *upstairs,* to form a compound sentence. Now, have a volunteer use another example from the chapter to demonstrate how to proofread sentences for correct use of semicolons.

MECHANICS

STYLE TIP

Semicolons are most effective when they are not overused. Sometimes it is better to separate a compound sentence or a heavily punctuated sentence into two sentences rather than to use a semicolon.

ACCEPTABLE
Garden visitors include butterflies, bats, and ladybugs; such creatures benefit gardens in various ways, some by adding color, some by controlling pests, and all by pollinating plants.

BETTER
Garden visitors include butterflies, bats, and ladybugs. Such creatures benefit gardens in various ways, some by adding color, some by controlling pests, and all by pollinating plants.

Semicolons

A *semicolon* looks like a combination of a period and a comma, and that is just what it is. A semicolon can separate complete thoughts much as a period does. A semicolon can also separate items within a sentence much as a comma does.

14l. Use a semicolon between independent clauses if they are not joined by *and, but, for, nor, or, so,* or *yet.*

EXAMPLES   Jimmy took my suitcase upstairs; he left his own travel bag in the car.

After school, I went to band practice; then I studied in the library for an hour.

Use a semicolon to link clauses only if the clauses are closely related in meaning.

INCORRECT   Uncle Ray likes sweet potatoes; Aunt Janie prefers the beach.

CORRECT   Uncle Ray likes sweet potatoes; Aunt Janie prefers peas and carrots.

or

Uncle Ray likes the mountains; Aunt Janie prefers the beach.

14m. Use a semicolon rather than a comma before a coordinating conjunction to join independent clauses that contain commas.

CONFUSING   I wrote to Ann, Ramona, and Mai, and Jean notified Charles, Latoya, and Sue.

CLEAR   I wrote to Ann, Ramona, and Mai; and Jean notified Charles, Latoya, and Sue.

NOTE Semicolons are also used between items in a series when the items contain commas.

EXAMPLES   They visited Phoenix, Arizona; Santa Fe, New Mexico; and San Antonio, Texas.

Mr. Schultz, my science teacher; Ms. O'Hara, my English teacher; Mrs. Gomez, my math teacher; and Mr. Kim, my social studies teacher, attended the seventh-grade picnic.

RESOURCES

Semicolons

Practice

- *Language & Sentence Skills Practice,* pp. 294–295
- *Developmental Language & Sentence Skills,* pp. 113–114

Exercise 10 Using Semicolons Correctly

Most of the following sentences have a comma where there should be a semicolon. If the sentence needs a semicolon, write the words before and after the missing semicolon and insert the punctuation mark. If the sentence does not need a semicolon, write *C*.

Carets indicate placement of semicolons.

EXAMPLE   1. Human beings have walked on the moon, they have not yet walked on any planet but earth.

1. *moon; they*

1. Miyoko finished her homework, then she decided to go to Sally's house.
2. Each January some people try to predict the major events of the upcoming year, but their predictions are seldom accurate.
3. Tie these newspapers together with string, put the aluminum cans in a bag.
4. I called Tom, Paul, and Francine, and Fred called Amy, Luis, Carlos, and Brad.
5. Reading is my favorite pastime, I love to begin a new book.
6. In 1991, Wellington Webb was elected mayor of Denver, he was the first African American to hold that office.
7. The two companies merged, and they became the largest consumer goods firm in the nation.
8. Your grades have definitely improved, you will easily pass the course.
9. Paris, France, Cairo, Egypt, and Copenhagen, Denmark, are all places that I would like to visit someday.
10. We haven't seen the movie, for it hasn't come to our town yet.

2. C
7. C
10. C

Colons

14n. Use a colon before a list of items, especially after expressions such as *the following* or *as follows*.

EXAMPLES   You will need these items for map work**:** a ruler, colored pencils, and tracing paper.

Jack's pocket contained the following items**:** a key, a note from a friend, a button, and two quarters.

The primary colors are as follows**:** red, blue, and yellow.

Colons   **311**

RESOURCES

Colons

Practice

- *Language & Sentence Skills Practice,* pp. 296, 299–300
- *Developmental Language & Sentence Skills,* pp. 113–114

Reference Note

For information about **objects of verbs,** see page 73. For information about **objects of prepositions,** see pages 59 and 90.

Do not use a colon between a verb and its object or between a preposition and its object. Omit the colon, or reword the sentence.

INCORRECT	Your heading should contain: your name, the date, and the title of your essay.
CORRECT	Your heading should contain your name, the date, and the title of your essay.
CORRECT	Your heading should contain the following information: your name, the date, and the title of your essay.
INCORRECT	This marinara sauce is made of: tomatoes, onions, oregano, and garlic.
CORRECT	This marinara sauce is made of tomatoes, onions, oregano, and garlic.
CORRECT	This marinara sauce is made of the following ingredients: tomatoes, onions, oregano, and garlic.

NOTE Colons are also often used before long formal statements or quotations.

EXAMPLE My opinion of beauty is clearly expressed by Margaret Wolfe Hungerford in *Molly Bawn*: "Beauty is in the eye of the beholder."

Conventional Situations

14o. Use a colon between the hour and the minute.

EXAMPLE 8:30 A.M.   10:00 P.M.

14p. Use a colon after the salutation of a business letter.

EXAMPLES Dear Sir or Madam: Dear Mrs. Foster:

To Whom It May Concern: Dear Dr. Christiano:

14q. Use a colon between chapter and verse in Biblical references and between all titles and subtitles.

EXAMPLES I Chronicles 22:6–19

"Oral Storytelling: Making the Winter Shorter"

Use a comma after the salutation of a personal letter.

EXAMPLES
Dear Kim,
Dear Uncle Remy,

Exercise 11 Using Colons and Commas Correctly

Make each of the following word groups into a complete sentence by supplying the item called for in the brackets. Insert colons and commas where they are needed.

EXAMPLE 1. The test will begin at *[time]*.
         1. The test will begin at 9:30 A.M.

1. So far, the class has studied the following topics *[list]*.
2. You will need these supplies for your science-fair experiment *[list]*.
3. If I were writing a book about my friends and me, I would call it *[title and subtitle]*.
4. Meet me at the mall at *[time]*.
5. My classes this year are the following *[list]*.
6. You should begin your business letter with *[salutation]*.
7. The concert begins at *[time]*.
8. I need the following from the hardware store *[list]*.
9. Three countries I would like to visit are *[list]*.
10. The alarm is set to go off at *[time]*.

Answers will vary. Optional commas are underlined.
1. : periods, commas, semicolons, and colons
2. : paper, glue, and scissors
3. *The Best Days: The Adventures of Kim, Eddie, Fran, and Julio*
4. 4:15 this afternoon
5. : geometry, biology, English, American history, and gym
6. *Dear Sir or Madam:*
7. 8:00 tonight
8. : nails, wood glue, and a c-clamp
9. Austria, India, and Argentina
10. 6:30 A.M.

Review E Using End Marks, Commas, Semicolons, and Colons Correctly

The sentences in the following paragraph lack necessary end marks, commas, semicolons, and colons. Write each sentence, inserting the correct punctuation. Optional commas are underlined.

EXAMPLE [1] What an unusual clever caring way to help animals that is
         1. What an unusual, clever, caring way to help animals that is!

[1] Animal lovers, have you heard about the Sanctuary for Animals? [2] Founded by Leonard and Bunny Brook, the sanctuary is a safe home for all kinds of animals. [3] Through the years, hundreds of stray, unwanted, and abused animals have found a home at the sanctuary. [4] It is located on the Brooks' land in Westtown, New York. [5] On their two hundred acres, the Brooks take care of the following animals: dogs, cats, camels, elephants, lions, and even an Australian kangaroo. [6] Of course, Mr. and

Mrs. Brook also raise chickens keep horses and look after their other farm animals [7] The Brooks their family and their friends care for animals like this young cougar they also let the animals work for themselves [8] How do the animals work [9] The Brooks formed the Dawn Animal Agency and their animals became actors and models [10] You may have seen a camel or some of the other animals in magazines movies television shows and commercials

CHAPTER 14

Chapter Review

A. Using End Marks, Commas, Semicolons, and Colons Correctly

The following sentences lack necessary periods, question marks, exclamation points, commas, semicolons, and colons. Write each sentence, inserting the correct punctuation.

Optional commas are underlined.

1. The following students gave reports: Carlos, Sue, and Alan.
2. Tanay carved this beautiful soapstone cooking pot.
3. Walter, this is Ellen, who has transferred to our school.
4. Calling Simon's name, I ran to the door.
5. The Wilsons' new address is 3100 DeSoto St., New Orleans, LA 70119-3251.
6. Have you listened to that Bill Cosby tape, Felix?
7. Let me know, of course, if you can't attend.
8. Joy, our club president, will conduct the meeting, and Gary, our recently elected secretary, will take notes.
9. Looking at the harsh, bright glare, Mai closed the blinds.
10. Carlos Montoya picked up the guitar, positioned his fingers, and strummed a few chords of a flamenco song.
11. If you hurry, you can get home before 9:00.
12. Help! This is an emergency!
13. By the way, Rosa, have you seen any of Alfred Hitchcock's movies?
14. Dave hit a long fly ball, but Phil was there to catch it.
15. Flooding rapidly, the gully quickly became a tremendous torrent.
16. *The Grapes of Wrath*, which is one of my favorite movies, is about a family's struggles during the Great Depression.
17. Nicaragua, Panama, and Honduras are in Central America; and Colombia, Peru, and Chile are in South America.
18. One of our cats, Gypsy, scooted through the door, across the room, and out the window.
19. The Lock Museum of America, a fascinating place in Terryville, Connecticut, has more than twenty thousand locks.
20. Could the surprise gift be in-line skates, a new football, or tickets to a concert?

Numerals in brackets refer to rules tested by the items in the Chapter Review.

1. [14n, f, a]
2. [14a]
3. [14i(3, 1)a]
4. [14j(2), a]
5. [14e, k(1), a]
6. [14i(3), b]
7. [14i(4), d]
8. [14i(2), m, a]
9. [14g, j(2), a]
10. [14f, a]
11. [14j(4), o, a]
12. [14d, c]
13. [14i(4, 3), b]
14. [14h, a]
15. [14j(2), a]
16. [14i(1), a]
17. [14f, m, a]
18. [14i(2), f, a]
19. [14i(2), k(1), a]
20. [14f, b]

ASSESSING

Monitoring Progress

Chapter Review. To assess student progress, you may want to compare the types of items missed on the **Diagnostic Preview** to those missed on the **Chapter Review.** If students have not made significant progress, you may want to refer them to **Exercises 30–32** in **Chapter 17: Correcting Common Errors** for additional practice.

RESOURCES

Punctuation: End Marks, Commas, Semicolons, Colons

Review
- *Language & Sentence Skills Practice*, pp. 297–300

Assessment
- *Holt Handbook Chapter Tests with Answer Key*, pp. 27–28, 46

B. Proofreading a Business Letter

The following business letter lacks periods, commas, semicolons, and colons. Correct each error.

```
                    Gable Books
                    387 Monocle Lane
                    Bozeman, MT  59715
                    June 28, 2003
```

21. [14e, p]
22. [14q, i(2), e]
23. [14h, a]
24. [14l]
25. [14k(2)]

[21] Dear Mr. Gable

[22] Please find enclosed a copy of *Edith Wharton A Biography* a book by R. W. B. Lewis. **[23]** I purchased this book recently at your book shop but I have since discovered that several pages are missing. **[24]** I am not happy with the book; please send me a new copy.

[25] Sincerely,

E. Frome

E. Frome

C. Proofreading for Correct Punctuation

Most of the following sentences lack at least one period, question mark, exclamation point, comma, semicolon, or colon. Correct each error. If a sentence is already correctly punctuated, write *C*.

Optional commas are underlined.

26. C [14f, a]
27. [14j(3), d]
28. [14e, i(2)]
29. [14i(3), b]
30. [14j(1), i(3)]
31. [14j(3)]
32. [14e, k(1)]
33. [14l, a]
34. [14l]
35. [14h]

26. C He went shopping, cooked dinner, and washed the dishes.
27. For the good of us all please think before you act next time.
28. Mr. T. E. Hawk a friend of my mother's helps me with math.
29. Caroline have your relatives arrived?
30. Yes Mario they came just last week.
31. At the center of a map of Texas you will find Brady.
32. Our new address is 72 Maple Ave. Rochester, NY 14612.
33. Inger designs the clothes her mother sews them.
34. We followed the trail it led around the garage.
35. The world record in the long jump was held by Jesse Owens for several years but the record is now held by another outstanding athlete.

Chapter 14 Punctuation

36. On June 15, 1983, my father opened his first florist shop.
37. Your use of materials, for example, is very artistic. 37. C
38. My hobbies are as follows: baseball, ballet, and magic tricks.
39. After I carry the groceries into the house, my sister puts them away.
40. Stop that now, Veronica!

36. [14k(1)]
37. C [14i(4), a]
38. [14n, f]
39. [14j(4)]
40. [14i(3), d]

Writing Application
Using Punctuation in an Announcement

Correct Punctuation   Your class is sponsoring a carwash to raise money for a special project or trip. You have been chosen to write an announcement about the carwash for publication in a community newsletter. Write a brief announcement telling when and where the carwash will be, how much it will cost, what the money will be used for, and any other important details. Be sure to use end marks, commas, semicolons, and colons correctly in your announcement.

Prewriting   List the information that you will include in your announcement. Make sure you have included all the facts people will need to know about the purpose, time, location, and cost of the carwash.

Writing   As you write, remember that the purpose of your announcement is to attract customers. Start with an attention-grabbing first sentence that explains the purpose of the carwash. Be sure to present all your information in clear, complete sentences. Add any important details that you did not list earlier.

Revising   Ask a friend to read your announcement. Is it clear and straightforward? Does it convince your friend that the carwash is for a good cause? If not, revise, rearrange, or add details.

Publishing   As you proofread your announcement, pay special attention to your use of punctuation. Remember to check the placement of colons in expressions of time. You may wish to offer your announcement-writing services to a club or service organization at your school.

APPLICATION

Writing Application

Writing Tip. Announcements must include enough information to be clear about the event. You may want to specify how many sentences students should write.

Scoring Rubric. While paying particular attention to students' use of punctuation, you will also want to evaluate overall writing performance. You may want to give a split score to indicate development and clarity of the composition as well as punctuation skills.

CHAPTER 15

Punctuation
Underlining (Italics), Quotation Marks, Apostrophes, Hyphens, Parentheses, Brackets, and Dashes

Diagnostic Preview

HELP—
Sentences in the Diagnostic Preview, Part A, may contain more than one error.

Numerals in brackets refer to rules tested by the items in the Diagnostic Preview.

1. [15x, a]
2. [15d, s, z]
3. [15d, y]
4. [15s, n]

A. Proofreading Sentences for the Correct Use of Underlining (Italics), Quotation Marks, Apostrophes, Hyphens, Parentheses, Brackets, and Dashes

Revise each of the following sentences so that underlining, quotation marks, apostrophes, hyphens, parentheses, brackets, and dashes are used correctly. Hyphens are indicated by the - symbol.

EXAMPLE 1. "May I borrow your copy of 'Life' magazine?" Phil asked Alan.
         1. "May I borrow your copy of <u>Life</u> magazine?" Phil asked Alan.

1. Boris Karloff (his real name was William Henry Pratt) played the monster in the original movie version of <u>Frankenstein</u>.
2. "I've never known—do you?—what the word *kith* means," Paul said.   2. dash
3. "It (the new version of the software) corrects that problem," said Steve.   3. brackets
4. I've heard that the program's announcer and interviewer will be Connie Chung.

318   Chapter 15   Punctuation

5. Anne said that "Norma couldn't understand why twenty-two people had voted against having the dance on a Friday night.
6. "A two-thirds majority said they didn't want to have it then," Shawn said.
7. Fred said, "This magazine article titled Luxury Liners of the Past is interesting."
8. "Does the public library have copies of The Seminole Tribune or any other American Indian newspapers"? Tanya asked.
9. My sisters' enjoy reading folk tales like the stories in Two Ways to Count to Ten by Ruby Dee.
10. "The Garcia's cat is I don't think they know living in our garage," Mary said.   **10.** dash/dash [*or* parentheses]

5. [15d, s, v]
6. [15d, v, s]
7. [15d, l, m]
8. [15d, a, i]
9. [15p note, a]
10. [15d, p, z or x, s]

B. Punctuating Quotations Correctly

Add quotation marks where they are needed in each of the following sentences.

EXAMPLE   1. I wonder why so many people enjoy collecting things, said J. D.

1. "I wonder why so many people enjoy collecting things," said J. D.

11. I know I do! Julia exclaimed.
12. Tomás said, My grandmother said, It's the thrill of the hunt.
13. Do you collect anything as a hobby? Josh asked Marsha.
14. No, Marsha answered, but I know a person who collects old cameras and antique costume jewelry.
15. My aunt collects John McCormack's records, Kevin said. Do you know who he is?
16. I'm not sure, Julia said, but I think that he was an Irish singer.
17. Yes, he sang in the opera; he also sang popular Irish songs such as The Rose of Tralee, Kevin said.
18. My stepbrother has a collection of arrowheads. He hasn't been collecting them very long, Sydney said.
19. You should see Mrs. Kominek's collection of Chinese jade carvings, J. D. said. It's great!
20. Some people—I'm sure you know—have odd collections, Josh said. For instance, my aunt collects old shoelaces.

11. [15d, i]
12. [15d, l, h]
13. [15d, i]
14. [15d, h, g, f]
15. [15d, h, i]
16. [15d, h, g, f]
17. [15d, l, h]
18. [15d, k, h]
19. [15d, h, i]
20. [15d, h]

Underlining (Italics)

Rules 15a–c (pp. 320–322)

OBJECTIVE

- To identify words that should be italicized and to underline them

DIRECT TEACHING

Modeling and Demonstration

Underlining (Italics). Model how to identify words that should be underlined (italicized) by using the example *Would you like to subscribe to the San Francisco Chronicle?* First, ask what the *San Francisco Chronicle* is. [*title of a newspaper*] Next, ask whether this title should be underlined (italicized). [*yes*] Then, ask whether the word *the* is part of the newspaper's title. [*no*] Point out that when *the* is part of the sentence and not part of the title, it should not be underlined (italicized). Now, have a volunteer use another example from this chapter to demonstrate how to use underlining (italics) correctly.

MECHANICS

RETEACHING

Titles

Remembering which titles require underlining (italics) and which require quotation marks can be confusing for students. It might be helpful to teach the rule for using quotation marks with titles **(15m)** with the rule for using underlining (italics) with titles **(15a).** Point out to students that titles requiring quotation marks are often titles of a work that is a part of a larger work—for example, a story or article in a magazine; a song on a CD; or an episode in a television series. Titles requiring italics are titles of things that stand alone or contain the smaller parts: the magazine itself, the CD, or the television series.

---

15 a–c

COMPUTER TIP

If you use a personal computer, you can probably set words in italics yourself. Most word-processing software and many printers can produce italic type.

Reference Note

For examples of **titles** that are not italicized but are **enclosed in quotation marks**, see page 327.

Underlining (Italics)

Italics are printed letters that lean to the right—*like this*. When you write or type, you show that a word should be italicized by underlining it. If your composition were printed, the typesetter would set the underlined words in italics. For example, if you typed

```
Gary Soto wrote Pacific Crossing.
```

the sentence would be printed like this:

Gary Soto wrote *Pacific Crossing*.

15a. Use underlining (italics) for titles and subtitles of books, plays, periodicals, films, television series, works of art, and long musical works.

Type of Name	Examples	
Books	*My Life and Hard Times*	*Life on the Mississippi*
	To Kill a Mockingbird	*Maud Martha*
Plays	*Our Town*	*I Never Sang for My Father*
	Hamlet	
Periodicals	the *Daily News*	*National Geographic*
	Essence	
Films	*The Maltese Falcon*	*Stand and Deliver*
Television Series	*Nova*	*Bill Nye the Science Guy*
	Sesame Street	
Works of Art	*Starry Night*	*The Dream*
	American Gothic	*View of Toledo*
Long Musical Works	*Carmen*	*Don Giovanni*
	An American in Paris	*Music for the Royal Fireworks*

RESOURCES

Underlining (Italics)

Practice

- *Language & Sentence Skills Practice,* pp. 306–308, 322
- *Developmental Language & Sentence Skills,* pp. 115–116

NOTE Underline (italicize) an article at the beginning of a title only if it is the first word of the official title. Check the table of contents or the masthead to find the preferred style for the title.

EXAMPLES   Would you like to subscribe to **the** San Francisco Chronicle?

The Seattle Times is a daily newspaper.

15b. Use underlining (italics) for the names of ships, trains, aircraft, and spacecraft.

Type of Name	Examples	
Ships	HMS Titanic	the USS Eisenhower
	the Pequod	
Trains	the City of New Orleans	the Orient Express Golden Arrow
Aircraft	the Silver Dart	the Hindenburg
Spacecraft	Soyuz XI	Atlantis

15c. Use underlining (italics) for words, letters, and numerals referred to as such.

EXAMPLES   Double the final **n** before you add **–ing** in words like **running.**

If your **Z's** look like **2's,** your reader may see **200** when you meant **zoo.**

Exercise 1 Using Underlining (Italics) Correctly

For each of the following sentences, write and underline each word or item that should be italicized.

EXAMPLE 1. Does Dave Barry write a humor column for The Miami Herald?
1. The Miami Herald

1. The British spell the word humor with a u after the o.
2. In Denmark, you might see the spelling triatlon for the word triathlon.

STYLE TIP

Writers sometimes use underlining (italics) for emphasis, especially in written dialogue. Read the following sentences aloud. Notice that by italicizing different words, the writer can change the meaning of the sentence.

EXAMPLES
"Are you going to buy the *green* shirt?" asked Ellen. [Will you buy the green shirt, not the blue one?]

"Are you going to buy the green *shirt*?" asked Ellen. [Will you buy the green shirt, not the green pants?]

"Are *you* going to buy the green shirt?" asked Ellen. [Will you, not your brother, buy it?]

"Are you going to *buy* the green shirt?" asked Ellen. [Will you buy it, or are you just trying it on?]

EXTENSION

Relating to Reading

You may want to point out that individual newspapers and magazines may have house styles for the punctuation of titles that differ from the rules presented here. For example, some publications use quotation marks rather than italics for the titles of films. Have students search newspapers and magazines for these differences.

Underlining (Italics) **321**

CONTENT-AREA CONNECTIONS

Science
Underlining. Point out to students that foreign words or phrases used in writing require underlining (italics). Therefore, the Latin names used in biological classification, such as Tyrannosaurus rex, should be underlined (italicized). If you team teach with a science teacher, you could check to see if there is a reference work in the science room that students could consult to look up the Latin names of animals or plants that interest them.

Quotation Marks

Rules 15d–m *(pp. 322–328)*

OBJECTIVES

- To proofread and revise sentences for the correct use of quotation marks, commas, end marks, and capital letters
- To revise indirect quotations to create direct quotations

DIRECT TEACHING

Modeling and Demonstration

Quotation Marks. Model how to proofread and revise sentences for correct use of quotation marks and capitalization by using the example *When the bell rings, said the teacher, leave the room quietly.* First, ask whether the example contains the speaker's exact words. [yes] Explain that this is a direct quotation, and therefore the teacher's words should be enclosed in quotation marks. Then, ask where the quotation marks should be placed. [*"When the bell rings" said the teacher, "leave the room quietly."*] Ask whether the first word in the quotation should be capitalized. [yes—When] Point out that the first word in the second half of the quotation, *leave,* should not be capitalized because it does not begin a new sentence. Now, have a volunteer use another example from this chapter to demonstrate how to use quotation marks and capitalization correctly.

---

3. The current Newsweek has an informative article on the famine in Africa.
4. Our school newspaper, the Norwalk Valley News, is published weekly.
5. Luis Valdez wrote and directed La Bamba, a movie about the life of the singer Ritchie Valens.
6. Mr. Weyer said that the Oceanic is one of the ocean liners that sail to the Caribbean.
7. I think the movie The Sound of Music has some of the most beautiful photography that I have ever seen and some of the most memorable songs.
8. Our local theater group is presenting The Time of Your Life, a comedy by William Saroyan.
9. Charles Lindbergh's Spirit of St. Louis is on display at the museum, along with the Wright brothers' Flyer and NASA's Gemini IV.
10. The best novel that I read during vacation was The Summer of the Swans.

Quotation Marks

15d. Use quotation marks to enclose a ***direct quotation***—a person's exact words.

Be sure to place quotation marks both before and after a person's exact words.

EXAMPLES   The sonnet containing the words "Give me your tired, your poor, /Your huddled masses/ . . ." is inscribed on the Statue of Liberty.

"When the bell rings," said the teacher, "leave the room quietly."

Do not use quotation marks for an ***indirect quotation***—a rewording of a direct quotation.

DIRECT QUOTATION   Tom predicted, "It will be a close game." [Tom's exact words]

INDIRECT QUOTATION   Tom predicted that it would be a close game. [not Tom's exact words]

RESOURCES

Quotation Marks

Practice

- *Language & Sentence Skills Practice,* pp. 309–313, 322
- *Developmental Language & Sentence Skills,* pp. 117–120

15e. A direct quotation generally begins with a capital letter.

EXAMPLES   Lisa said, "The *carne asada* isn't ready yet, but please help yourself to the guacamole."

While he was in prison, Richard Lovelace wrote a poem containing the well-known line "Stone walls do not a prison make."

15f. When an expression identifying the speaker interrupts a quoted sentence, the second part of the quotation begins with a lowercase letter.

EXAMPLE   "Lightning has always awed people," explained Mrs. Worthington, "and many of us are still quite frightened by it."

A quoted sentence that is divided in this way is called a *broken quotation.* Notice that each part of a broken quotation is enclosed in a set of quotation marks.

When the second part of a divided quotation is a complete sentence, it begins with a capital letter.

EXAMPLE   "I can't go today," I said. "Ask me tomorrow."

15g. A direct quotation can be set off from the rest of the sentence by one or more commas or by a question mark or an exclamation point, but not by a period.

If a quotation begins a sentence, a comma follows it. If a quotation ends a sentence, a comma comes before it. If a quoted sentence is interrupted, a comma follows the first part and comes before the second part.

EXAMPLES   "I think science is more interesting than history," said Bernie.

Velma commented, "I especially like to do the experiments."

"Yes," Juan added, "Bernie loves experiments, too."

When a quotation at the beginning of a sentence ends with a question mark or an exclamation point, no comma is needed.

EXAMPLES   "Is that a good video game?" Jane wanted to know.

"I'll say it is!" Debbie exclaimed.

HELP
To *set off* means "to separate."

EXTENSION

Relating to Writing

Direct quotations. Point out to students that using direct instead of indirect quotations can enliven their writing. Ask each student to pick a story from his or her notebook and to edit the story by changing some indirect quotations to direct quotations. If students have not written stories, they could edit the following paragraph:

> Peggy said she has to baby-sit her little brother tonight. I told her I was really upset because I wanted her to go to the concert with me. Peggy suggested that if we could come up with some money to pay her next-door neighbor to baby-sit, Peggy's mom would probably let her go to the concert. So we pooled our savings and gathered together ten dollars. We asked Peggy's mom if it would be okay, and she said our plan sounded fine to her. We asked the neighbor if he could baby-sit, and he said he could. I told Peggy I was so happy that now she could go with me to the concert.

Discuss with the class the different feelings the two versions convey, and ask students which version they find more interesting.

Differentiating Instruction

English-Language Learners

Vietnamese. Vietnamese uses a punctuation system inherited from the French. Instead of using quotation marks in direct speech, as English does, Vietnamese generally uses a dash in direct speech: —*I saw the game.* Quotation marks, when they are used, resemble marks used in French: << >>.

Students need to be able to identify quotation marks and explain their uses and be able to use those marks correctly in their own writing. Point out the use of quotation marks in books the students read in class, and provide students with exercises to reinforce the use of quotation marks.

MECHANICS

15h. A comma or a period should be placed inside the closing quotation marks.

EXAMPLES "The Ramses exhibit begins over there**.**" said the museum guide.

Darnell replied, "I'm ready to see some ancient Egyptian jewelry and artwork**.**"

15i. A question mark or an exclamation point should be placed inside the closing quotation marks when the quotation itself is a question or an exclamation. Otherwise, it should be placed outside.

EXAMPLES "How far have we come**?**" asked the exhausted man. [The quotation is a question.]

Who said, "Give me liberty or give me death"**?** [The sentence, not the quotation, is a question.]

"Jump**!**" ordered the firefighter. [The quotation is an exclamation.]

I couldn't believe it when he said, "No, thank you"**!** [The sentence, not the quotation, is an exclamation.]

When both the sentence and the quotation at the end of the sentence are questions (or exclamations), only one question mark (or exclamation point) is used. It is placed inside the closing quotation marks.

EXAMPLE Did Josh really say, "What's Cinco de Mayo**?**"

Exercise 2 Punctuating and Capitalizing Quotations

Use commas, quotation marks, and capital letters where they are needed in each of the following sentences. If a sentence is already correct, write *C.*

EXAMPLE 1. Let's go to a movie this afternoon, said Bob.
1. "Let's go to a movie this afternoon," said Bob.

1. When I shrieked in fear, the usher warned me to be quiet. **1. C**
2. At the same time, Bob whispered it's only a movie—calm down.
3. He pointed out that the people around us were getting annoyed. **3. C**

324 Chapter 15 Punctuation

Learning for Life

Continued on pp. 325–327

Testimonials in Advertising. Point out to students that testimonials used in advertising—whether on television or radio or in print—are direct quotations. Write the following example testimonials on the chalkboard.

"I laughed, I cried, and I was deeply moved by this play." —Fran Ellison, Centerville Junior High

Alan Whittle, a junior at Lincoln High School, says, "This is definitely the most

4. I quietly replied I'm sorry.
5. You shouldn't have screamed, he complained.
6. From now on I said to him I promise I'll try to be quiet.
7. When the lights came on, Bob said "it's time to go."
8. Outside the theater he muttered something about people who shouldn't go to scary movies.   8. C
9. I just couldn't help it I explained.
10. You were afraid Bob protested even during the credits!

Exercise 3   Punctuating and Capitalizing Quotations

Use capital letters, quotation marks, and other punctuation marks where they are needed in each of the following sentences.

EXAMPLE 1. Ashley Bryan wore traditional African clothes when he came to our school Elton said.

1. "Ashley Bryan wore traditional African clothes when he came to our school," Elton said.

1. Oh, like the clothes Mr. Johnson showed us in class Janell exclaimed.
2. Elton asked have you read any of Ashley Bryan's books about African culture?
3. I've read Janell quickly replied the one titled *Beat the Story-Drum, Pum-Pum*.
4. I'd like to read that again Elton said those African folk tales are wonderful.
5. Mrs. Ray thinks *Walk Together Children* is excellent Janell said.
6. Isn't that Elton asked about African American spirituals?
7. You're right Janell answered and Bryan wrote that spirituals are America's greatest contribution to world music.
8. She added he grew up in New York City and began writing stories and drawing when he was still in kindergarten.
9. Did you know Elton asked that he illustrated his own books?
10. Bryan made woodcuts to illustrate *Walk Together Children* he added.

Differentiating Instruction

Special Education Students

Some students may find it difficult to use quotation marks in conjunction with other punctuation marks. To give students modified practice in writing quotations, write visual cues on the chalkboard. For example, a cue for a statement could be presented like this.

___ said, "___."

Similarly, the cue for a question and exclamation could be presented like this.

___ asked, "___ ?" and ___ exclaimed, "___!"

Exercise 4 **Creating Direct Quotations**

ANSWERS
Answers may vary.

1. Mayor Alaniz announced, "I will lead the parade this year."
2. Ms. Feldman asked me, "What are your plans for the big parade?"
3. I answered, "My brother and I are building a float."
4. She exclaimed, "I think your float will look terrific!"
5. Ron remarked, "Your float probably has something to do with sports."
6. I told Ron, "You are exactly right."
7. Alinda asked me, "What sports will be represented on the float?"
8. I replied, "The float will salute swimming, soccer, and tennis."
9. Ron said excitedly, "I would love to help!"
10. Ms. Feldman said, "You and your brother would probably be glad to have help."

MECHANICS

Exercise 4 **Creating Direct Quotations**

Revise each of the following sentences by changing the indirect quotation to a direct quotation. Be sure to use capital letters and punctuation wherever necessary.

EXAMPLE 1. I asked my grandmother whether she would like to help us paint our float.
  1. "Grandma," I asked, "would you like to help us paint our float?"

1. Mayor Alaniz announced that he would lead the parade this year.
2. Ms. Feldman asked me what my plans for the big parade were.
3. I answered that my brother and I were building a float.
4. She exclaimed that she thought our float would look terrific.
5. Ron remarked that our float probably had something to do with sports.
6. I told Ron that he was exactly right.
7. Alinda asked me what sports will be represented on the float.
8. I replied that the float will salute swimming, soccer, and tennis.
9. Ron said excitedly that he would love to help.
10. Ms. Feldman said that my brother and I would probably be glad to have help.

15j. When you write dialogue (a conversation), begin a new paragraph every time the speaker changes.

EXAMPLE   The young man smiled, and said, "My old master, now let me tell you the truth. My home is not so far away. It is quite near your temple. We have been old neighbors for many years."
   The old monk was very surprised. "I don't believe it. You, young man, will have your joke. Where is there another house round here?"
   "My master, would I lie to you? I live right beside your temple. The Green Pond is my home."
   "You live in the pond?" The old monk was even more astonished.
   "That's right. In fact," said Li Aiqi, in a perfectly serious tone, "I'm not a man at all. I am a dragon."

"Green Dragon Pond," a Bai folk tale

326 Chapter 15 Punctuation

Learning for Life

Continued from p. 325

advertise: a performance they're involved in, a service they want to market (such as baby-sitting, mowing lawns, or computer work), or a speech or presentation on an issue that interests them. Ask the student pairs to take notes carefully during the interviews. If they have access to a tape recorder, they could tape the interviews and transcribe them later. (Students should get permission from the interviewees before taping.) They will want to choose the most enthusiastic testimonials for their ads.

15k. When a quotation consists of several sentences, put quotation marks only at the beginning and the end of the whole quotation.

EXAMPLE "Mary Elizabeth and I will wait for you at Robertson's Drugstore. Please try to get there as soon as you can. We don't want to be late for the concert," Jerome said.

15l. Use single quotation marks to enclose a quotation within a quotation.

EXAMPLES Brandon added, "My mom always says, 'Look before you leap.'"

"Did Ms. Neuman really say, 'It's all right to use your books and your notes during the test'?" asked Sakura.

15m. Use quotation marks to enclose the titles of short works such as short stories, poems, songs, episodes of television series, essays, articles, and chapters and other parts of books.

Type of Name	Examples
Short Stories	"A Day's Wait" "The Medicine Bag"
Poems	"In Time of Silver Rain" "Birdfoot's Grampa"
Songs	"The Star-Spangled Banner" "Swing Low, Sweet Chariot"
Episodes of Television Series	"This Side of Paradise" "Growing Up Hispanic"
Essays	"Self-Reliance" "The Creative Process"
Articles	"Rooting for the Home Team" "Annie Leibovitz: Behind the Images"
Chapters and Other Parts of Books	"The Natural World" "The Myths of Greece and Rome" "The Double Task of Language"

Reference Note
For examples of **titles that are italicized**, see page 320.

Quotation Marks   327

DIFFERENTIATING INSTRUCTION

Learners Having Difficulty

Titles. Have students create guides they can keep in their notebooks to use as references when punctuating titles in their writing. List on the chalkboard all the categories of titles in the examples for **Rules 15a** and **15m.** Have the class brainstorm other categories to add to the list.

Then, have students alphabetize their lists and designate beside each category whether it requires italics or quotation marks. Ask students to copy the list and to illustrate their guides with pictures or icons if they like.

MECHANICS

As students design their ads, have them pay particular attention to the use of quotation marks, commas, and end marks in their testimonials. Have each pair exchange ads with another pair to check for correct punctuation.

Quotation Marks   327

HELP

In general, the title of a work that can stand alone (for instance, a novel, a movie, or a newspaper) is in italics. The title of a work that is usually part of a collection or series (for instance, a short story, an episode of a television series, or a poem) is in quotation marks.

MEETING THE CHALLENGE

Correctly punctuate each of the following sentences with underlining (italics) and quotation marks.

1. My favorite poem is I Hear America Singing, which I read in the book Leaves of Grass.
2. Today's copy of the San Francisco Chronicle contains the article Moose on the Move.
3. I think the song Don't Touch My Hat is on the CD titled The Road to Ensenada.

NOTE Titles that are usually set in quotation marks are set in single quotation marks when they appear within a quotation.

EXAMPLE James said, "We learned 'The Star-Spangled Banner' in music class today."

Exercise 5 Using Quotation Marks

Insert quotation marks where they are needed in each of the following items. If a sentence is already correct, write *C*.

EXAMPLE 1. Let's sing 'The Ballad of Gregorio Cortez,' suggested Jim.

1. "Let's sing 'The Ballad of Gregorio Cortez,'" suggested Jim.

1. "Lani, have you seen my clarinet?" asked Rob. "It was on this table. I need it for my lesson this afternoon."
2. The most interesting chapter in *The Sea Around Us* is "The Birth of an Island."
3. "Didn't Benjamin Franklin once say, 'Time is money'?" asked Myra impatiently.
4. "I believe my favorite Langston Hughes poem is 'As I Grew Older,'" said Mom.
5. Lea Evans said, "One of the greatest changes in architecture has been in the design of churches. They no longer necessarily follow traditional forms. Churches have been built that are shaped like stars, fish, and ships."
6. The latest issue of *Discover* magazine has a fascinating picture of a shark that swallowed an anchor.   6. C
7. "Do you know which character asked 'What's in a name?' in *Romeo and Juliet*?" I asked.
8. "Yes, that was Juliet," answered Li. "My mother used to say that to me when I was a little girl. That's how I first heard of Shakespeare."
9. "A human hand has more than twenty-seven bones and thirty-five muscles!" exclaimed Marcus. "No wonder it can do so much."
10. There is an article titled "The Customers Always Write" in today's newspaper.

Review A Punctuating Paragraphs

Revise the following paragraphs, adding quotation marks and other marks of punctuation wherever necessary. Remember to begin a new paragraph each time the speaker changes. If a sentence is already correct, write C.

HELP
The marks of punctuation that are already included in Review A are correct.

EXAMPLES
[1] Mr. Brown asked Can you baby-sit tonight?
1. Mr. Brown asked, "Can you baby-sit tonight?"

[2] Sure I said I'd be happy to.
2. "Sure," I said. "I'd be happy to."

[1] Last night I baby-sat for the Browns, a new family on our block. [2] Come in Mrs. Brown greeted me. [3] You must be Lisa. [4] Hello, Mrs. Brown I replied. [5] I'm looking forward to meeting the children. [6] First Mrs. Brown explained I want you to meet Ludwig. [7] Is he a member of the family I asked. [8] In a way replied Mrs. Brown as she led me to the kitchen and pointed to an aging dachshund. [9] That is Ludwig. [10] He rules this house and everyone in it.

[11] Mr. Brown entered the kitchen and introduced himself. [12] I see that you've met Ludwig he said. [13] Yes Mrs. Brown answered for me. [14] Why don't you give Lisa her instructions while I go find the children?

[15] If Ludwig whines said Mr. Brown please give him a dog treat. [16] Should I take him for a walk I asked. [17] No replied Mr. Brown. [18] Just let him out into the yard.

[19] Mrs. Brown came back into the kitchen with the children. [20] Did my husband remind you to cover Ludwig when he falls asleep she asked. [21] I'll remember I promised. [22] Also, what should I do for the children? [23] Don't worry said Mr. Brown. [24] They'll behave themselves and go to bed when they're supposed to. [25] As I told you laughed Mrs. Brown Ludwig rules this house and everyone in it, even the sitter!

1. C
6. ∧ (before "First")
11. C
19. C

Quotation Marks 329

PRACTICE

Guided and Independent

Review A You may want to use the first ten items in **Review A** as guided practice. Then, have students complete the exercise as independent practice. **HOMEWORK**

Direct Quotations

To give students more practice with putting together the elements of sentences containing direct quotations, write on the chalkboard the following word groups.

Hurry up
What's for lunch today
I'm not in that class
What a great idea
Did you really write that
shouted Carla
Paul yelled
asked Nanong
Winton asked
Jeremy told me

Have students copy each of the word groups onto a separate strip of paper; also, have students write five strips each for opening and closing quotation marks, commas, and end marks. Then, have students arrange the strips and tape them together to form complete sentences. Some commas and end marks may be left over.

Have students work in pairs to check each other's sentences.

MECHANICS

Apostrophes

Rules 15n–t *(pp. 330–337)*

OBJECTIVES

- To add apostrophes to singular possessives
- To rewrite expressions using the possessive case
- To form possessives of personal and indefinite pronouns
- To add apostrophes to contractions
- To complete sentences by adding suitable contractions
- To create contractions from given pronouns and verbs

DIRECT TEACHING

Modeling and Demonstration

Apostrophes. Model how to use apostrophes correctly by using the examples *Kathleens desk, mens hats,* and *horses manes.* Ask what is being expressed in the phrase *Kathleens desk.* [*possession*] Ask where the apostrophe should be placed to show possession. [*before the s—Kathleen's*] Next, ask how to form the possessive of *men.* [*men's*] Then, ask how to form the possessive of the plural noun *horses.* [*horses'*] Point out that plural nouns that do not end in *s* form the possessive by adding an apostrophe and an *s,* and that plural nouns that end in *s* form the possessive by adding just an apostrophe. Now, have a volunteer use another example from this chapter to demonstrate how to use apostrophes to show possession.

Apostrophes

Possessive Case

The ***possessive case*** of a noun or a pronoun shows ownership or possession.

EXAMPLES	**Kathleen's** desk	**anybody's** guess
	his bat	an **hour's** time
	their car	those **horses'** manes

15n. To form the possessive case of a singular noun, add an apostrophe and an *s*.

EXAMPLES   a boy**'s** cap   Cleon**'s** pen

the baby**'s** toy   Charles**'s** opinion

> **NOTE**   A proper noun ending in *s* may take only an apostrophe to form the possessive case if the addition of an apostrophe and an *s* would make the name awkward to say.
>
> EXAMPLES   the Philippine**s'** government
>
> Ms. Rodger**s'** cat

Exercise 6   Using Apostrophes for Singular Possessives

Identify the word that needs an apostrophe in each of the following sentences. Then, write that word correctly punctuated.

EXAMPLE   1. The Prado in Madrid, Spain, is one of the worlds greatest museums.

1. worlds—world's

1. Shown on the next page is one of the Prados paintings by Diego Velázquez, *Las Meninas.*
2. Velázquezs painting is known in English as *The Maids of Honor.*
3. In the center of the canvas is Princess Margarita, the royal couples daughter.
4. To the princesss right, a kneeling maid of honor offers her something to drink.

RESOURCES

Apostrophes

Practice

- *Language & Sentence Skills Practice,* pp. 314–319, 323
- *Developmental Language & Sentence Skills,* pp. 121–122

5. To the royal child's left, another maid of honor curtsies.
6. On the far left of the canvas, you can see the artist's own image, for he has painted himself!
7. The palace's other important people, such as the chamberlain and a court jester, also appear.
8. The faces of Margarita's parents are reflected in the mirror on the back wall.
9. In the foreground, the royal dog ignores a young guest's invitation to play.
10. This painting's fame has grown since it was painted in 1656, and each year millions of people see it when they visit the Prado.

The Granger Collection, New York

15o. To form the possessive case of a plural noun that does not end in *s*, add an apostrophe and an *s*.

EXAMPLES   mice's tracks   men's hats

children's games   teeth's enamel

women's shoes   Sioux's land

15p. To form the possessive case of a plural noun ending in *s*, add only the apostrophe.

EXAMPLES   cats' basket   four days' delay

brushes' bristles   the Carsons' bungalow

NOTE In general, you should not use an apostrophe to form the plural of a noun.

INCORRECT   Three girl's lost their tickets.
CORRECT   Three **girls** lost their tickets. [plural]
CORRECT   Three **girls'** tickets were lost. [plural possessive]

Reference Note
For information on **using apostrophes to form the plurals of letters, numerals, and symbols and of words used as words,** see page 337.

Apostrophes **331**

Exercise 7 Writing Possessives

ANSWERS

1. the party's nominee
2. the babies' clothes
3. my sister's grades
4. the guests' name tags
5. the cat's dish
6. Mr. Granger's yard
7. my foot's muscles
8. the oxen's strength
9. James's computer
10. the teams' members

DIRECT TEACHING

Correcting Misconceptions

It's/Its. Because apostrophes are used to form many possessives, students may incorrectly believe that *it's* is a possessive form. Consequently, students may confuse *its* and *it's* in their writing. Draw students' attention to **Rule 15q**, and tell them that if they are having trouble deciding whether to use an apostrophe, they should try saying the word as two words (*it is*). If the sentence makes sense with the two words, the contraction is appropriate. If the sentence doesn't make sense, the possessive personal pronoun *its* is appropriate.

Exercise 7 Writing Possessives

Using the possessive case, rewrite each of the following word groups. Be sure to insert an apostrophe in the correct place.

EXAMPLE 1. food for the dog
1. the dog's food

1. the nominee of the party
2. the clothes of the babies
3. the grades of my sister
4. the name tags of the guests
5. the dish for the cat
6. the yard of Mr. Granger
7. the muscles of my foot
8. the strength of the oxen
9. the computer of James
10. the members of the teams

15q. Do not use an apostrophe with possessive personal pronouns.

EXAMPLES Is that sticker **yours** or **mine**?

Our cat is friendlier than **theirs**.

His report on Cherokee folk tales was as good as **hers**.

NOTE Do not confuse the possessive pronoun *its* with the contraction *it's*. The possessive pronoun *its* means *belonging to it*. The expression *it's* is a contraction of the words *it is* or *it has*.

POSSESSIVE PRONOUN Please give the cat **its** rubber ball.
CONTRACTIONS **It's** time for the soccer tournament.
It's taken three hours.

15r. To form the possessive case of some indefinite pronouns, add an apostrophe and an *s*.

EXAMPLES neither's homework   somebody's jacket

everyone's choice   anything's cost

Oral Practice Creating Possessives of Personal and Indefinite Pronouns

Read each of the following expressions aloud. Then, read it again, changing the expression so that it uses the possessive case. Finally, say whether the revised expression needs an apostrophe when written.

EXAMPLE 1. the park for everyone
1. everyone's park

Reference Note
For more information about **possessive personal pronouns**, see page 30.

Reference Note
For a list of **words that are often confused**, see Chapter 16.

Reference Note
For more information about **indefinite pronouns**, see page 32.

1. the opinion of them
2. the footprints of anyone
3. the fault of nobody
4. the turn of either
5. the stereo that belongs to you
6. the logo of it
7. the idea of neither
8. the backpack of someone
9. the guess of anybody
10. the land owned by no one

Contractions

15s. Use an apostrophe to show where letters, words, or numerals have been omitted (left out) in a contraction.

A *contraction* is a shortened form of a word, a numeral, or a word group. The apostrophe in a contraction shows where letters or numerals have been left out. Contractions are acceptable in informal writing, but in formal writing, you should generally avoid using them.

Common Contractions			
I am	I'm	they had	they'd
1999	'99	where is	where's
let us	let's	we are	we're
of the clock	o'clock	he is	he's
she would	she'd	you will	you'll
we have	we've	what is	what's
they are	they're	I would	I'd

The word *not* can be shortened to *n't* and added to a verb, usually without any change in the spelling of the verb.

EXAMPLES	is not	isn't	has not	hasn't
	are not	aren't	have not	haven't
	does not	doesn't	had not	hadn't
	do not	don't	should not	shouldn't
	was not	wasn't	would not	wouldn't
	were not	weren't	could not	couldn't
EXCEPTIONS	will not	won't	cannot	can't

STYLE TIP

In formal writing, avoid using a contraction of a year. In informal writing, if the reader cannot determine the time period from the context of the sentence, it is best to write out the year.

EXAMPLE
The famous tenor toured Europe in '01. [Did the tenor tour in 1801, 1901, or 2001?]

The famous tenor toured Europe in **2001**.

Apostrophes 333

EXTENSION

Relating to Writing

Contractions. Remind students that while contractions are handy in everyday speech and writing, they are generally not appropriate in formal writing. Ask each student to find a piece of formal nonfiction writing in his or her notebook and to edit the writing for the use of contractions. Any contractions they find should be changed to two words. If the contraction is used to form a question, some rearranging may be required.

DIRECT TEACHING

English-Language Learners

Hmong. Since written Hmong does not use apostrophes, Hmong speakers may find English contractions confusing. Remind students that English uses apostrophes in contractions to indicate missing vowels. Have students practice forming contractions: *Do not, don't; I am, I'm.*

MECHANICS

DIFFERENTIATING INSTRUCTION

Advanced Learners
Have students write on strips of paper word combinations that can be made into contractions, such as *cannot, have not, they would, we have,* and *who is.* Students should also write apostrophes on several strips. Have students cut and rearrange the strips to change the words and phrases into contractions. Then, have students consult a dictionary to check their contractions.

Be careful not to confuse contractions with possessive pronouns.

Contractions	Possessive Pronouns
It's Friday. [*It is*]	**Its** nest is over there.
It's been a pleasure. [*It has*]	
Who's your server? [*Who is*]	**Whose** is this backpack?
Who's been practicing the piano? [*Who has*]	
They're arriving soon. [*They are*]	**Their** parakeet is friendly.
There's the path. [*There is*]	That rosebush is **theirs**.

Exercise 8 Using Apostrophes Correctly

Correct each error in the use of possessive forms and contractions in the following sentences. If a sentence is already correct, write *C.*

HELP—
Some sentences in Exercise 8 contain more than one error.

EXAMPLE   1. Arent you going with us at one oclock?
            1. Aren't; o'clock

1. We'd better chain our bicycles to the rack.
2. You're old car's seen better days, hasn't it?   2. Your
3. She wasn't too happy to see us.
4. Whose ringing the doorbell?   4. Who's
5. We won't forget how helpful you've been.
6. I'm certain you'll be invited.
7. Whose turn is it to take attendance?   7. C
8. Ann's an excellent swimmer, but she can't dive.
9. They're turning in their's now.   9. theirs
10. She's sure they'll show up before it's over.

Exercise 9 Punctuating Contractions

For each of the following sentences, identify the <u>word that needs an apostrophe</u> to indicate a contraction. Then, write the word correctly.

EXAMPLE   1. Whats the best route from Lawrenceville, New Jersey, to Newtown, Pennsylvania?
            1. Whats—What's

334 Chapter 15 Punctuation

1. There's one especially pretty route you can take to get there.
2. I think you'll enjoy the drive.
3. You shouldn't go due west directly.
4. You've got to go north or south first.
5. It's easier to go south on Route 206 to Route U.S. 1, cross the Delaware River, and then go north on Route 32 to Yardley.
6. From Yardley, turn left on Route 322, and in a little while I'm sure you will find yourself in Newtown.
7. If you'd prefer a different route, go south on Route 206 to Route 546 and make a right turn to go west.
8. After you cross the Delaware River and the road becomes 532, don't turn until Linton Hill Road.
9. When you turn left onto Linton Hill Road, it won't be long before you arrive in Newtown.
10. Here's a map you can use to help you find your way.

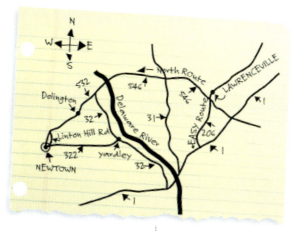

Exercise 10 Writing Contractions

Write a suitable contraction to correctly complete each of the following sentences.   Answers may vary.

EXAMPLE   1. Do you know _____ for supper?
          1. what's

1. _____ my sweater?   1. Where's
2. _____ lying on the beach.   2. It's
3. We _____ help you right now.   3. can't
4. _____ dinner ready?   4. Isn't
5. They _____ played that game before.   5. haven't
6. She was in the class of _____.   6. '01
7. _____ go to the museum.   7. Let's
8. I _____ know that game.   8. don't
9. _____ rather order the salad.   9. He'd
10. Is it nine _____ yet?   10. o'clock

Apostrophes   335

Exercise 11 Writing Contractions

Write the contraction of the underlined word or words in each of the following sentences.

EXAMPLE 1. If you think it <u>should have</u> been easy to visit the building shown below, guess again!

    1. should've

1. <u>It is</u> the Potala Palace in Lhasa, Tibet, which my parents and I visited last year.
2. The city of Lhasa is two miles high in the Himalaya Mountains, and we <u>could not</u> exercise much because the lack of oxygen made us tired.
3. The Potala Palace is the former residence of the Tibetan spiritual leader, <u>who has</u> been living in exile in India.
4. Because this palace is a holy shrine, pilgrims <u>do not</u> mind traveling on foot from all over the country to worship there.
5. After <u>they have</u> bought yak butter in the city square, they take it to the palace as an offering.
6. From the photograph, you <u>cannot</u> imagine how steep those stairs on the right are!
7. Because it <u>would have</u> taken a long time to climb them, our bus driver took us directly to the rear entrance on the left.
8. Once inside, we spent hours exploring the palace, but we <u>were not</u> able to visit most of its more than one thousand rooms!
9. <u>I am</u> sure we would never have found our way out without our guide, who led us to an exit on the right.
10. Walking down the stairs <u>was not</u> too hard, and soon we were in the beautiful central square in the Himalayan sunshine!

Answers:
1. It's
2. couldn't
3. who's
4. don't
5. they've
6. can't
7. would've
8. weren't
9. I'm
10. wasn't

CONTENT-AREA CONNECTIONS

Math

Apostrophes. To help students become more familiar with the correct use of apostrophes, have students find and graph the use of apostrophes in print material. Divide the class into groups of four. Have each group assemble some written sources—comics, newspapers, books, and magazines. Then, have each group designate two students to find examples of apostrophe use, one student to record each use, and one to match apostrophe rules in this chapter to the examples the group finds. Each entry should include the source, the page number, the word containing an apostrophe, and the rule number that applies. Have students switch tasks until each

Plurals

15t. Use an apostrophe and an *s* to form the plurals of letters, numerals, and symbols, and of words referred to as words.

EXAMPLES Your *o*'s look like *a*'s, and your *u*'s look like *n*'s.

There are three *5*'s and two *8*'s in his telephone number.

Place *$*'s before monetary amounts and *¢*'s after.

One sign of immature writing is too many *and*'s.

STYLE TIP

In your reading, you may notice that an apostrophe is not always used in forming the kinds of plurals in Rule 15t. Nowadays, many writers leave out the apostrophe if a plural meaning is clear without it. However, to make sure that your writing is clear, you should use an apostrophe.

Review B Using Underlining (Italics) and Apostrophes Correctly

For each of the following sentences, add underlining or apostrophes as necessary. The punctuation already supplied is correct.

EXAMPLE 1. One of my oldest brothers college textbooks is History of Art by H. W. Janson.

1. brother's; *History of Art*

1. Whos the painter who inspired the musical play Sunday in the Park with George?
2. Hes Georges Seurat, one of Frances greatest painters.
3. "The young childrens reactions to Jacob Lawrences paintings were surprising," Angie said.
4. Didnt you read the review in Entertainment Weekly of the movie Vincent & Theo?
5. Its about Vincent van Gogh and his brother, who often supported him.
6. "I like Jasper Johns," Rick said, "but I cant tell if that is one of Johnss paintings."
7. Have you ever tried counting all the 2s or 4s in his painting Numbers in Color?
8. On a class trip to Chicago, we saw a bronze statue titled Horse, by Duchamp-Villon.
9. In our group, everybodys favorite painting is Cow's Skull: Red, White and Blue, by Georgia O'Keeffe.
10. "On PBS, Ive seen an American Playhouse program about O'Keeffes life," Joyce said.

Apostrophes **337**

student has had a chance to complete each task, and encourage the groups to use a variety of sources. Have each group make a graph like this one to illustrate their findings.

Then, have each group present its graph to the rest of the class.

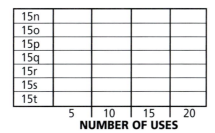

Hyphens

Rules 15u–w (pp. 338–339)

OBJECTIVE

- To use hyphens correctly when writing numbers

DIRECT TEACHING

Modeling and Demonstration

Hyphens. Model how to use hyphens correctly by using the example *My great grandfather is seventy seven years old.* First, ask whether any written numbers are in this sentence. [yes—seventy-seven] Explain that compound numbers from twenty-one to ninety-nine should be punctuated with hyphens. Next, ask whether any other words in this sentence need hyphens. [yes—great-grandfather] Point out that hyphens should be used with the prefixes *ex–*, *self–*, *all–*, and *great–* and with the suffixes *–elect* and *–free*. Now, have a volunteer use another example from this chapter to demonstrate how to use hyphens correctly.

MECHANICS

COMPUTER TIP

Some word-processing programs will automatically divide a word at the end of a line and insert a hyphen. Sometimes, such hyphenation will violate one of the rules given here.

Always check a printout of your writing to see how the computer has hyphenated words at the ends of lines. If a hyphen is used incorrectly, revise the line by moving the word or by dividing the word yourself and inserting a "hard" hyphen (one that the computer cannot move).

STYLE TIP

Hyphens are often used in compound names. In such cases, the hyphen is thought of as part of the name's spelling.

EXAMPLES
Jackie Joyner-Kersee [person]

Rikki-tikki-tavi [animal]

Wilkes-Barre [city]

If you are not sure whether a compound name is hyphenated, ask the person with that name, or look in a reference source.

338 Chapter 15 Punctuation

Hyphens

15u. Use a hyphen to divide a word at the end of a line.

EXAMPLE   Will you and Marguerite help me put the silver-ware on the table?

When dividing a word at the end of a line, remember the following rules:

(1) Divide a word only between syllables.

INCORRECT   The tall man in the pinstriped suit sat bes-ide the tree, looking bewildered.

CORRECT   The tall man in the pinstriped suit sat be-side the tree, looking bewildered.

(2) Do not divide a one-syllable word.

INCORRECT   Exercises like push-ups help to develop stren-gth of the arm muscles.

CORRECT   Exercises like push-ups help to develop strength of the arm muscles.

(3) Do not divide a word so that one letter stands alone.

INCORRECT   The seating capacity of the new stadium is e-normous.

CORRECT   The seating capacity of the new stadium is enor-mous.

15v. Use a hyphen with compound numbers from *twenty-one* to *ninety-nine* and with fractions used as modifiers.

EXAMPLES   During a leap year, there are twenty-nine days in February.

Thirty-two species of birds are known to live in the area.

Did you know that Congress may override a president's veto by a two-thirds majority? [*Two-thirds* is an adjective that modifies *majority*.]

The pumpkin pie was so good that only one sixth of it is left. [*One sixth* is not used as a modifier. Instead, *sixth* is a noun modified by the adjective *one*. Fractions used as nouns do not have hyphens.]

RESOURCES

Hyphens

Practice

- *Language & Sentence Skills Practice,* p. 320
- *Developmental Language & Sentence Skills,* pp. 123–124

---

338   Punctuation

15w. Use a hyphen with the prefixes *ex–, self–, all–,* and *great–* and with the suffixes *–elect* and *–free.*

EXAMPLES ex-coach   president-elect   all-star

great-uncle   self-propelled   fat-free

Exercise 12 Using Hyphens Correctly

Write an expression—using words, not numerals—to replace the blank in each of the following sentences. Use hyphens where they are needed with compound numbers and fractions.

EXAMPLE 1. The sum of ten and fifteen is ____.
1. twenty-five

1. January, March, May, July, August, October, and December are the months that have ____ days.
2. ____ of the moon is visible from the earth, but the other half can be seen only from outer space.
3. In twenty years I will be ____ years old.
4. I used ____ cup, which is 25 percent of the original one cup.
5. Our seventh-grade class has ____ students.
6. The train ride is short; the route is only ____ miles long.
7. The doctor said that the heel of my shoe needs to be raised ____ of an inch.
8. Who decided that there should be ____ hours in a day?
9. ____ teaspoon of vanilla is not enough in the cake batter.
10. Only about ____ of the expected people actually attended.

Review C Punctuating Sentences Correctly

Rewrite the following sentences, correcting any errors in the use of underlining, quotation marks, commas, apostrophes, and hyphens. *Hyphens are indicated by the - symbol.*

EXAMPLE 1. For the talent show, Leila is planning to reci-te Poes poem The Raven.
1. *For the talent show, Leila is planning to re-cite Poe's poem "The Raven."*

1. Queen Hatshepsut seized the throne of Egypt in 1503 B.C. and ruled for twenty-one years.
2. Whos borrowed my scissors? demanded Jean.
3. Its hard to decide which authors story I should read first.
4. A weeks vacation never seems long enough.

HELP

The prefix *half* often requires a hyphen, as in *half-life, half-moon,* and *half-truth.* However, sometimes it is used without a hyphen, either as a part of a single word (as in *halftone, halfway,* and *halfback*) or as a separate word (as in *half shell, half pint,* and *half note*). If you are not sure how to spell a word containing *half,* look up the word in a dictionary.

HELP

Hyphenate a compound adjective when it comes before the noun it modifies.

EXAMPLE
an event that is well organized

a **well-organized** event

Some compound adjectives are always hyphenated, whether they come before or after the nouns they modify.

EXAMPLE
a **full-scale** model

a model that is **full-scale**

If you are not sure whether a compound adjective is always hyphenated, look it up in an up-to-date dictionary.

Hyphens   339

DIRECT TEACHING

Hyphens

Using Dictionaries. To reinforce the practice of looking up words to check for syllable divisions, give each student a dictionary. (If there are not enough dictionaries available to give one to each student, divide the class into groups based on the number of available dictionaries.) Then, call out words one by one from the dictionary. As you call out a word, students should find the word in the dictionary and write the word with hyphens dividing the syllables. If there is a wide range of spelling and dictionary skills among your students, you may also want to write each word on the chalkboard as you call it out so that students can take longer to complete the exercise if needed.

After the class has completed the exercise, ask a student volunteer to rewrite the words on the chalkboard and to put hyphens between the syllables. (You may want to check the volunteer's work first.) Then, students can check their own lists.

Exercise 12 Using Hyphens Correctly

ANSWERS
Numbers will vary.

1. thirty-one
2. One half
3. thirty-two
4. one-quarter
5. twenty-seven
6. forty-five
7. one eighth
8. twenty-four
9. One-half
10. two thirds

5. After we'd eaten supper, we decided to watch an old episode of *Star Trek*.
6. The driver shouted, "Move to the rear of the bus!"
7. We didn't eat any salmon at all during our visit to O-regon.   7. Or-egon *or* Ore-gon *or* Oregon
8. "I wasn't very sorry," admitted the clerk, "to see those three picky customers leave."
9. "Very Short on *Law and Order*" is my favorite chapter in *Tough Trip Through Paradise*.   9. *Tough*
10. Our phone number has two 6's and two 4's.

Parentheses

15x. Use parentheses to enclose material that is added to a sentence but is not considered of major importance.

EXAMPLES   Emilio Aguinaldo (1869–1964) was a Filipino statesman.

Mom and Dad bought a kilim (pronounced ki • lēm') rug from our Turkish friend Ali.

Material enclosed in parentheses may be as short as a single word or as long as a short sentence. A short sentence in parentheses may stand alone or be contained within another sentence. Notice that a parenthetical sentence within a sentence is not capitalized and has no end mark.

EXAMPLES   Please be quiet during the performance. (Take crying babies to the lobby.)

Jack Echohawk (he's Ben's cousin) told us about growing up on a reservation.

Exercise 13 Correcting Sentences by Adding Parentheses

Insert parentheses where they are needed in the following sentences.

EXAMPLE   1. My bicycle I've had it for three years is a ten-speed.
   1. *My bicycle (I've had it for three years) is a ten-speed.*

1. At the age of fourteen, Martina Hingis began playing tennis (my favorite sport) professionally.

STYLE TIP

Too many parenthetical expressions in a piece of writing can keep readers from seeing the main idea. Keep your meaning clear by limiting the number of parenthetical expressions you use.

2. Elijah McCoy (1843–1929) invented a way to oil moving machinery.
3. I bought a new calculator (my old one stopped working) and a notebook.
4. Charlemagne (pronounced shär′lə • män′) was one of Europe's most famous rulers.
5. Lian Young (she's a friend of mine) told our class about China.
6. Jojoba (pronounced hō • hō′bə) is an evergreen desert shrub.
7. Albert Einstein (1879–1955) formulated the theory of relativity.
8. The soloist (he's my cousin) performed "Memory."
9. I read a book by the author E. M. Forster (1879–1970).
10. The relevant chart shows the election results. (See page 88.)

10. Item is also correct without parentheses.

Brackets

15y. Use brackets to enclose an explanation added to quoted or parenthetical material.

EXAMPLES Elena said in her acceptance speech, "I am honored by this [the award], and I would like to thank the students who volunteered this year." [The words are enclosed in brackets to show that they have been inserted into the quotation and are not the words of the speaker.]

By a vote of 6 to 1, the council approved the petition to build a nature preserve. (See next page for a map [Diagram A] of the proposed reserve.)

Dashes

A *parenthetical expression* is a word or phrase that breaks into the main thought of a sentence. Parenthetical expressions are usually set off by commas or parentheses.

EXAMPLES Grandma Moses**, for example,** started painting in her seventies.

In the first act of the play, the butler **(Theo Karras)** was the detective's prime suspect.

Some parenthetical elements need stronger emphasis. In such cases, a dash is used.

Reference Note

For more about using **commas with parenthetical expressions,** see page 303. For more about **using parentheses,** see page 340.

Dashes **341**

15z. Use a dash to indicate an abrupt break in thought or speech.

EXAMPLES   The right thing to do—I know it'll be hard—is to apologize.

"Do you think Ann will mind—mind very much—if I borrow her sunglasses?" asked Melody.

Exercise 14 Correcting Sentences by Adding Dashes and Brackets

Insert dashes or brackets where they are needed in the following sentences. Carets indicate placement of dashes.

EXAMPLE   1. The school lunchroom it was a dull green has been painted a cheery yellow.

1. The school lunchroom—it was a dull green—has been painted a cheery yellow.

1. Fireflies I can't remember where I read this make what is called cold light.
2. Roberto has always wanted to be can't you guess? an astronaut.
3. Shania Twain I really want to see her concert has a great new song out.
4. Do you mind I don't if Jill and Marcus go to the mall with us tomorrow?
5. The best way to learn how to swim that is, after you've learned the basic strokes is to practice.
6. (See page 8[Box A]of the school yearbook for a list of the drama club's best performers.)
7. Where is the computer game I've looked everywhere for it that I borrowed from Alex?
8. Please hand me if you don't mind the stack of magazines on the table behind you.
9. The newspaper quoted our principal as saying, "The girls' volleyball team took both the district[District 14–5A]and regional championships."
10. The class trip to Chicago I've never been there will include a visit to the Art Institute.

CHAPTER 15

Chapter Review

A. Using Underlining (Italics), Quotation Marks, Dashes, Parentheses, and Brackets

The following sentences contain errors in the use of underlining (italics), quotation marks, dashes, parentheses, and brackets. Rewrite the sentences correctly. *Carets indicate placement of dashes.*

1. The song "Amazing Grace" has been sung for many years.
2. Garth Brooks—I love his music—is giving a benefit concert.
3. Did you see the article titled "Yogamania" that appeared in last month's *Seventeen* magazine?
4. The poet Wallace Stevens (1879–1955) won a Pulitzer Prize.
5. (See the map of Normandy [Figure D] for the deployment of the German forces on June 6.)
6. The reading list included the novel *Great Expectations*.
7. Sharon—she's my youngest cousin—asked me to tell her a story.
8. The bearded man—you probably guessed this—is really the thief in disguise.
9. He misspelled the word *accommodate* by leaving out one *c*.
10. Aunt Rosie—the aunt I told you about—went to Mexico on the cruise ship *Princess*.

B. Proofreading for the Correct Use of Punctuation and Capitalization in Quotations

The following sentences contain errors in the use of punctuation and capitalization in quotations. Rewrite the sentences correctly. If a sentence is already correct, write *C*.

11. "Did you read Robert Hayden's poem "Those Winter Sundays"? asked Jorge.
12. "Who's your favorite baseball player." asked Don?
13. "Meet me at 2:30 sharp," my sister's note read.
14. Why did Ms. Redfeather say, "I need to see a doctor"?
15. Ms. Liu said, Turn to Chapter 7, 'Fractions,' now.
16. "Did you know," Katrina said, "That Robin Williams organizes fund-raisers for the homeless"?

Chapter Review 343

Chapter Review
B. Proofreading for the Correct Use of Punctuation and Capitalization in Quotations

ANSWERS continued

17. C
18. "Are the La Vernia Bears playing tomorrow?" Lorraine asked Ted.
19. Chang predicted that it would be a rainy summer.
20. "He can work ten hours a week," said Liang.

Chapter Review
C. Writing Dialogue Correctly

ANSWERS

21. "A few of us are starting a reading group," said Michael.
22. "Would you like to join us?"
23. ¶"That sounds like fun," replied Audra.
24. "Who is in the group?"
25. ¶"Well, I am, of course," Michael said, "and Stephanie, Jeff, and Kerry.
26. I've asked Megan to join, too, but she may be too busy.
27. She's going to let me know tomorrow."
28. ¶"What books are you going to read," asked Audra, "or haven't you decided that yet?"
29. ¶"I'm going to suggest that we start with <u>The Owl Service</u>, by Alan Garner," said Michael, "but only if it is everyone's choice."
30. ¶"I'd love to join!" said Audra.

---

17. [15d, e, i]
18. [15d, i]
19. [15d]
20. [15d, e, h]

HELP
Some sentences in Part C may not require additional punctuation.

21. [15d, h]
22. [15d, i]
23. [15j, d, h]
24. [15d, i]
25. [15j, d, h, f, k]
26. [15k]
27. [15k, s, h, d]
28. [15j, d, h, f, s, i]
29. [15j, d, s, a, h, f, r]
30. [15j, d, s, i]

31. [15v]
32. [15s, t]
33. [15v, o]
34. [15p, r, u(3), q]
35. [15s, n, u(2)]
36. [15s]
37. [15q, p]
38. [15s, n]

---

17. Akeem exclaimed, "Those giant redwoods are more than three hundred feet tall!"
18. "Are the La Vernia Bears playing tomorrow? Lorraine asked Ted.
19. Chang predicted that "it would be a rainy summer."
20. "he can work ten hours a week", said Liang.

C. Writing Dialogue Correctly

Revise the following paragraphs, adding quotation marks and other punctuation marks wherever necessary. Begin a new paragraph each time the speaker changes.

[21] A few of us are starting a reading group said Michael. [22] Would you like to join us? [23] That sounds like fun replied Audra. [24] Who is in the group? [25] Well, I am, of course Michael said and Stephanie, Jeff, and Kerry. [26] I've asked Megan to join, too, but she may be too busy. [27] She's going to let me know tomorrow.

[28] What books are you going to read asked Audra or haven't you decided that yet? [29] I'm going to suggest that we start with The Owl Service, by Alan Garner, said Michael but only if it is everyones choice. [30] I'd love to join! said Audra.

D. Using Apostrophes and Hyphens

The following sentences contain errors in the use of apostrophes and hyphens. Correctly write each incorrectly punctuated word. Hyphens are indicated by the - symbol.

31. The test includes twentytwo questions.
32. Its easy to see that you like to use &s instead of writing out the word *and* each time.
33. One fourth of the childrens toys were broken.
34. My two sisters bicycles are sporty, but neithers is as sporty as mine.   **34.** sporty
35. Isnt this play often considered one of Shakespeares best works, Stephanie?   **35.** works
36. Whats the lowest common denominator of these two numbers?
37. Are those lawn chairs our's or the Millers?   **37.** ours
38. Theyre drawings of Augusta Savages sculptures.

344 Chapter 15 Punctuation

39. My baby brother's a good sleeper; he should have a mobile made of Z's instead of airplanes over his crib.

40. Who's going to help repaint the club's float for the parade?

39. [15s, t]
40. [15s, n]

Writing Application
Using Quotations in Reports

Direct Quotations Your social studies class is taking a survey of people's attitudes toward recycling. Interview at least three people from different households in your community. Ask them specific questions to find out whether they think recycling is important; what items, if any, they recycle; and how they think recycling could be made easier for people in the community. Based on the information you gather, write a brief report about recycling in your community. In your report, quote several people's exact words.

Prewriting First, think of several questions to ask. Next, decide whom you want to interview. Begin each interview by recording the person's name, age, and occupation. When all your interviews are completed, compare your interviewees' responses. What conclusions can you draw about attitudes toward recycling in your community? Jot down some notes to help you organize your information.

Writing In the first paragraph of your draft, give a statement that sums up the main idea of your report. Then, use your interviewees' answers to support your main idea.

Revising Re-read your first draft. Does the body of your report support your main idea? If not, you may need to rethink and revise your main idea.

Publishing As you proofread your report, check your quotations against your notes. Make sure that you have put quotation marks around direct quotations and that you have capitalized and punctuated all quotations correctly. Your class may want to combine the information from all the reports and create a wall chart showing the community's attitudes toward recycling.

APPLICATION

Writing Application

Prewriting Tip. You may want to videotape a couple of sample television interviews to show to your class. After students have watched the interviews, use the question at the end of **Prewriting** to initiate discussion.

Publishing Tip. You could also allow students to videotape their own interviews and show them to the class. (Be sure students obtain permission from the interviewees before taping the interviews.) However, students who videotape interviews should still be required to complete written reports.

Scoring Rubric. While paying particular attention to students' use of quotation marks, you will also want to evaluate overall writing performance. You may want to give a split score to indicate development and clarity of the composition as well as punctuation skills.

CHAPTER

16 Spelling
Improving Your Spelling

INTRODUCING THE CHAPTER

- The chapter begins with an introduction to the basic rules and techniques of spelling. The exercises can help reinforce understanding of the spelling rules. The final segment of the chapter contains lists of homonyms and other confusing sets of words.

- The chapter features a **Chapter Review** including a **Writing Application** that asks students to write a one- or two-paragraph review, using at least five words often confused. The chapter ends with a list of spelling words.

- For help in integrating this chapter with writing assignments, use the **Teaching Strands** chart on pp. T24–T25.

Diagnostic Preview

Proofreading Sentences for Correct Spelling

Write correctly all of the misspelled words in the following sentences.

EXAMPLE 1. Andrew carefully lifted the massive lid and peekked inside the trunk.
1. carefully, peeked

Numerals and terms in brackets refer to rules and concepts tested by the items in the Diagnostic Preview.

1. tomatoes/strawberries [16i(7, 3)]
2. daily/training [16d, h]
3. led [lead, led]
4. laid/knives [16g, i(5)]
5. scissors [16i(1)]
6. two/nieces [to, too, two;16a]
7. benches/freezing [16i(2), e]
8. studies/swimming [16i(3), h]
9. Weaving [16e]
10. piece/proceed [16a, b]

1. Do you have any fresh tomatos or strawberrys?
2. Alex rides her bicycle forty miles dayly when she is in trainning.
3. The experienced tour guide lead the students to the base of the trail.
4. My sister made the salad while I layed the spoons and knifes on the table for dinner.
5. Would you please hand me the scissor's?
6. Mr. Escobar's too neices went to the annual family reunion.
7. Icicles formed on the park benchs when the temperature dropped below freezeing.
8. Angela's favorite classes are social studys and swiming.
9. On Wednesday our science class watched *Weavving Ants*, a film about the insect world.
10. Take out a peice of paper, and then prosede with the test.

CHAPTER RESOURCES

Internet
- Web resources: go.hrw.com

Practice & Review
- *Language & Sentence Skills Practice*, pp. 331–349; 350–353
- *Language & Sentence Skills Practice Answer Key*, pp. 140–146

Application & Enrichment
- *Language & Sentence Skills Practice*, pp. 330, 354, 355–356, 357
- *Language & Sentence Skills Practice Answer Key*, pp. 140, 146–147

Good Spelling Habits

Practicing the following techniques can help you spell words correctly.

1. **To learn the spelling of a word, pronounce it, study it, and write it.** Pronounce words carefully. Mispronunciation can lead to misspelling. For instance, if you say *ath•a•lete* instead of *ath•lete*, you will be more likely to spell the word incorrectly.

   - First, make sure that you know how to pronounce the word correctly, and then practice saying it.
   - Second, study the word. Notice especially any parts that might be hard to remember.
   - Third, write the word from memory. Check your spelling.
   - If you misspelled the word, repeat the three steps of this process.

2. **Use a dictionary.** When you find that you have misspelled a word, look it up in a dictionary. Do not guess about the correct spelling.

3. **Spell by syllables.** A *syllable* is a word part that is pronounced as one uninterrupted sound.

   EXAMPLES   thor•ough [two syllables]

                  sep•a•rate [three syllables]

   Instead of trying to learn how to pronounce and spell a whole word, break it up into its syllables whenever possible.

Exercise 1   Spelling by Syllables

Look up the following words in a dictionary, and divide each one into syllables. Pronounce each syllable correctly, and learn to spell the word by syllables.

1. legislature
2. perspire
3. modern
4. temperature
5. probably
6. similar
7. library
8. definition
9. recognize
10. awkward
11. accept
12. interest
13. temperament
14. conscious
15. separate
16. opportunity
17. eliminate
18. government
19. business
20. appreciation

HELP

If you are not sure how to pronounce a word, look it up in an up-to-date dictionary. In the dictionary, you will usually find the pronunciation given in parentheses after the word. The information in parentheses will show you the sounds used, the syllable breaks, and any accented syllables. A guide to the pronunciation symbols is usually found at the front of the dictionary.

STYLE TIP

In some names, marks that show how to pronounce a word are considered part of the spelling.

PEOPLE
Díaz   Rölvaag   Žižka

PLACES
Aswân   Cádiz

Compiègne

If you are not sure about the spelling of a name, ask the person with that name or look it up in a dictionary or other reference source.

Answers may vary according to the dictionary used. These answers are from Webster's New World College Dictionary, Third Edition.

Good Spelling Habits and Spelling Rules

Rules 16a–h (pp. 347–355)

OBJECTIVES

- To divide words correctly into syllables
- To spell correctly words that contain the letters *ie* or *ei*
- To proofread sentences to correct spelling errors
- To add prefixes and suffixes to words correctly

DIRECT TEACHING

Modeling and Demonstration

Spelling Words with e*i* and *ie*. Model how to spell correctly words that contain *ie* or *ei* by using the examples *brief, deceive, weight, foreign, neither,* and *pie*. First, ask what sound *ie* makes in *brief*. [long e] Point out that a word is spelled with *ie* when the sound is *long e*. Next, ask what sound *ei* makes in *deceive*. [long e] Explain that after *c* the *long e* sound is spelled *ei*. Point out that *ei* is also the correct spelling when the sound is not *long e*, or when the sound is *long a*. [*weight, foreign*] Show that *neither* and *pie* represent exceptions to these rules. Now, have a volunteer use another example from this chapter to demonstrate how to spell words with *ie* or *ei*.

COMPUTER TIP

A computer can help you catch spelling mistakes. Use the computer's spellchecker whenever you proofread your writing. Remember, though, that a computer's spellchecker points out misspellings but not misused homonyms. For example, if you use *their* when you should use *there*, a spellchecker won't catch the mistake. Always double-check your writing to make sure that your spelling is error-free.

4. **Proofread for careless spelling errors.** Re-read your writing carefully, and correct any mistakes and unclear letters. For example, make sure that your *i*'s are dotted, that your *t*'s are crossed, and that your *g*'s don't look like *q*'s.

5. **Keep a spelling notebook.** Divide each page into four columns:

   COLUMN 1   Correctly spell any word you missed. (Never enter a misspelling.)

   COLUMN 2   Write the word again, dividing it into syllables and indicating which syllables are accented or stressed.

   COLUMN 3   Write the word once more, circling the spot that gives you trouble.

   COLUMN 4   Jot down any comments that might help you remember the correct spelling.

Here is an example of how you might make entries for two words that are often misspelled.

Spelling Rules

ie and *ei*

16a. Write *ie* when the sound is long *e*, except after *c*.

EXAMPLES   ch**ie**f, br**ie**f, bel**ie**ve, y**ie**ld, rec**ei**ve, dec**ei**ve

EXCEPTIONS   s**ei**ze, l**ei**sure, **ei**ther, n**ei**ther, prot**ei**n

RESOURCES

Good Spelling Habits and Spelling Rules
Practice
- *Language & Sentence Skills Practice,* pp. 331–339, 350
- *Developmental Language & Sentence Skills,* pp. 125–128

Write *ei* when the sound is not long *e*, especially when the sound is long *a*.

EXAMPLES sl**ei**gh, v**ei**l, fr**ei**ght, w**ei**ght, h**ei**ght, for**ei**gn

EXCEPTIONS fr**ie**nd, misch**ie**f, anc**ie**nt, p**ie**

Exercise 2 Writing Words with *ie* and *ei*

Rewrite the following words, adding the letters *ie* or *ei*.

EXAMPLE 1. conc...t
1. conceit

1. dec..ei..ve
2. n..ei..ther
3. rec..ei..ve
4. h..ei..ght
5. fr..ie..nd
6. l..ei..sure
7. misch..ie..f
8. w..ei..ght
9. ..ei..ght
10. sl..ei..gh
11. fr..ei..ght
12. n..ei..ghbor
13. c..ei..ling
14. shr..ie..k
15. rec..ei..pt
16. p..ie..ce
17. r..ei..gn
18. th..ei..r
19. s..ei..ze
20. br..ie..f

Exercise 3 Proofreading Sentences to Correct Spelling Errors

Most of the following sentences contain a spelling error involving the use of *ie* or *ei*. Write each misspelled word correctly. If a sentence has no spelling error, write *C*.

EXAMPLE 1. Last summer I recieved an airline ticket as a birthday gift.
1. received

1. I used the ticket to fly to Puerto Rico with my freind Alicia to see my grandmother and other relatives.
2. We flew to San Juan, where my grandmother's nieghbor, Mr. Perez, met us and drove us to my grandmother's house.
3. When we got there, all of my relatives—aunts, uncles, cousins, neices, nephews—came to welcome us.
4. They couldn't believe that niether of us had ever been to Puerto Rico before, so they took us sightseeing the next day.

DIRECT TEACHING

Correcting Misconceptions

Spelling. Some students may have the misconception that correct spelling is unimportant in contemporary life. Ask students to jot down a list of reasons that correct spelling is important. Ask students whether correct spelling may be less important sometimes, such as when taking class notes or writing in personal diaries. Lead students to understand that using correct spelling is good practice. Doing so helps break bad spelling habits and prevents such poor habits from developing.

TIPS & TRICKS

You may find this time-tested verse a help in remembering the *ie* rule.

I before *e*
Except after *c*
Or when sounded like *a*,
As in *neighbor* and *weigh*.

If you use this rhyme, remember that "*i* before *e*" refers only to words in which these two letters are in the same syllable and stand for the sound of long *e*, as in the examples under Rule 16a.

1. ie
2. ei

3. ie
4. ei

Differentiating Instruction

Learners Having Difficulty

Spelling Bee. You may want to conduct a modified spelling bee for students by asking them to pronounce and spell the words below. Call out a word (enunciate normally), and ask a student to pronounce it syllable by syllable, pausing slightly after each syllable, and then to spell the word.

To continue this activity beyond the provided words, ask other students to use a dictionary to find challenging words. Give everyone in the class a chance to participate.

1. stripe [*stripe*]
2. clearance [*clear•ance*]
3. examination [*ex•am•i•na•tion*]
4. improbable [*im•prob•a•ble*]
5. characteristic [*char•ac•ter•is•tic*]
6. dilate [*di•late*]
7. powerful [*pow•er•ful*]

MECHANICS

5. C
6. ie
7. ei
8. ie
9. ie
10. ei

5. First, we walked through a field in Humacao, which is located on the Caribbean Sea.
6. Then, we drove along the coast to Ponce, the island's cheif city after San Juan.
7. Continuing north from Ponce, we thought that we'd take a liesurely drive on the mountain road *Ruta Panoramica*, which means "Panoramic Road."
8. However, the road turned and twisted so much that I was releived to get back on the main road.
9. After we had a breif rest that afternoon, we explored the western part of the island.
10. Within a week, Puerto Rico no longer seemed foriegn to us.

–cede, –ceed, and –sede

16b. The only English word ending in *–sede* is *supersede*. The only English words ending in *–ceed* are *exceed*, *proceed*, and *succeed*. Most other words with this sound end in *–cede*.

EXAMPLES   con**cede**   re**cede**

                   pre**cede**   se**cede**

Prefixes and Suffixes

A **prefix** is a letter or a group of letters added to the beginning of a word to change its meaning. A **suffix** is a letter or a group of letters added to the end of a word to change its meaning.

16c. When adding a prefix to a word, do not change the spelling of the word itself.

EXAMPLES il + legal = il**legal**

un + natural = un**natural**

dis + appear = dis**appear**

mis + spent = mis**spent**

Exercise 4 Spelling Words with Prefixes

Spell each of the following words, adding the given prefix.

EXAMPLE 1. semi + circle
1. *semicircle*

1. il + legible
2. un + necessary
3. im + partial
4. in + offensive
5. im + mortal
6. mis + spell
7. dis + satisfy
8. dis + approve
9. mis + understand
10. over + rule

1. illegible
2. unnecessary
3. impartial
4. inoffensive
5. immortal
6. misspell
7. dissatisfy
8. disapprove
9. misunderstand
10. overrule

16d. When adding the suffix *–ness* or *–ly* to a word, do not change the spelling of the word itself.

EXAMPLES sudden + ness = **sudden**ness

truthful + ly = **truthful**ly

EXCEPTION For most words that end in *y*, change the *y* to *i* before adding *–ly* or *–ness*.

kindly + ness = kindl**iness**   day + ly = da**ily**

16e. Drop the final silent *e* before adding a suffix beginning with a vowel.

EXAMPLES nice + est = **nic**est

love + ing = **lov**ing

EXCEPTION Keep the silent *e* in words ending in *ce* and *ge* before a suffix beginning with *a* or *o*.

notice + able = notic**eable**

courage + ous = courag**eous**

HELP

A ***derivative*** is a word formed by adding one or more prefixes or suffixes to the base form of a word.

EXAMPLES
warmth [*from* warm]
electricity [*from* electric]

HELP

Vowels are the letters *a, e, i, o, u,* and sometimes *y.* The other letters of the alphabet are consonants.

EXTENSION

Relating to Vocabulary Skills

Explain to students that base words (*part, take*) can stand alone or combine with other word parts (*partly, mistake*). Word roots (*–dict–, –vis–*), like prefixes and suffixes, cannot stand alone and are combined with other word parts to form words (*dictionary, visible*).

Write on the chalkboard or a transparency the following base words and word roots.

base words: *verse, cycle, graph, gram*

word roots: *–loc–, –gest–, –crit–, –fer–*

Ask students to take a base word or word root and add a prefix, a suffix, or both to form a word. They should continue until they have at least five words.

When the whole class has finished, ask a few student volunteers to read their words out loud while you write the words on the chalkboard or a transparency. If any students have additional words, add them to the list on the chalkboard. Then, students can check the spelling of their own words.

EXTENSION

Relating to Literature

If Shel Silverstein's poem "Sarah Cynthia Sylvia Stout Would Not Take the Garbage Out" is available in students' literature textbooks, ask students to read the poem aloud and to look at the word at the end of each line. Ask students whether any of these words conform to the spelling rules they have studied in this chapter [*ceilings, pie*]. Next, ask students to look at the words at the ends of lines 40 through 45; ask if a pronunciation rule could be derived from the spellings of these words. [*An a followed by a single consonant will usually have a long sound if that consonant is followed by an* e.]

To test the rule, divide the class into two teams and give each a dictionary. Ask one team to list as many words as it can find that follow the rule [*made, ace*], and ask the other to find as many exceptions as it can [*cadet, panel*]. If the team looking for exceptions finds as many or almost as many words as the other team, the rule must be declared invalid or must be further qualified.

Exercise 5 — Spelling Words with Suffixes

ANSWERS

1. awfully
2. careful
3. sincerely
4. writing
5. desirable
6. changeable
7. crossing
8. advancement
9. truly
10. courageous
11. noticeable
12. bravest
13. accidentally
14. pacing
15. valuable
16. hopeful
17. gratefully
18. pleasantness
19. sorest
20. finally

16f. Keep the final silent *e* before adding a suffix that begins with a consonant.

EXAMPLES   care + less = car**eless**

plate + ful = plat**eful**

false + hood = fals**ehood**

EXCEPTIONS   argue + ment = argu**ment**

true + ly = tru**ly**

Exercise 5 — Spelling Words with Suffixes

Spell each of the following words, adding the given suffix.

EXAMPLE   1. like + able

              1. likable

1. awful + ly
2. care + ful
3. sincere + ly
4. write + ing
5. desire + able
6. change + able
7. cross + ing
8. advance + ment
9. true + ly
10. courage + ous
11. notice + able
12. brave + est
13. accidental + ly
14. pace + ing
15. value + able
16. hope + ful
17. grateful + ly
18. pleasant + ness
19. sore + est
20. final + ly

16g. For words ending in *y* preceded by a consonant, change the *y* to *i* before any suffix that does not begin with *i*.

EXAMPLES   beauty + ful = beaut**iful**   mystery + ous = myster**ious**

carry + ing = carr**ying**   envy + able = env**iable**

EXCEPTIONS   dry + ness = dr**yness**   fry + er = fr**yer**

Words ending in *y* preceded by a vowel do not change their spelling before a suffix.

EXAMPLES	key + ed = ke**yed**	buy + er = bu**yer**
	pay + ment = pa**yment**	enjoy + ing = enjo**ying**

EXCEPTIONS	lay + ed = la**id**	say + ed = sa**id**	day + ly = da**ily**

16h. Double the final consonant before adding *–ing*, *–ed*, *–er*, or *–est* to a one-syllable word that ends in a single consonant preceded by a single vowel.

EXAMPLES	sit + ing = si**tt**ing	can + er = ca**nn**er
	hop + ed = ho**pp**ed	flat + est = fla**tt**est

EXCEPTIONS Do not double the final consonant in words ending in *w* or *x*.

  mow + ed = mo**w**ed   tax + ing = ta**x**ing

For a one-syllable word ending in a single consonant that is not preceded by a single vowel, do not double the consonant before adding *–ing*, *–ed*, *–er*, or *–est*.

EXAMPLES	reap + ed = rea**p**ed	neat + est = nea**t**est
	cold + er = col**d**er	hold + ing = hol**d**ing

In words of more than one syllable, the final consonant is usually not doubled before a suffix beginning with a vowel.

EXAMPLES   final + ist = fina**l**ist   center + ed = cente**r**ed

> **NOTE** In some cases, the final consonant may or may not be doubled.
>
> EXAMPLES cancel + ed = cance**l**ed *or* cance**ll**ed
>
>   travel + er = trave**l**er *or* trave**ll**er
>
> Most dictionaries list both spellings for each word as correct.

Exercise 6 Spelling Words with Suffixes

Spell each of the twenty words on the following page, adding the given suffix.

EXAMPLE   1. beauty + ful
       1. beautiful

HELP—
When you are not sure about the spelling of a word, it is best to look it up in an up-to-date dictionary.

Spelling Rules

DIFFERENTIATING INSTRUCTION

English-Language Learners

Vietnamese. Modern Vietnamese spelling uses a Roman alphabet (ABCs) and is phonetic. Vietnamese students may find English spelling complex because it lacks consistency. Since mispronunciation may hinder spelling ability, check students' pronunciation as they repeat new words orally.

Hmong. The Hmong language's Romanized Popular Alphabet uses unvoiced final consonants as tonal markers whose only purpose is to indicate a word's stress and pitch. Therefore, when reading, Hmong students may have a tendency to leave English end consonants unvoiced. Because pronunciation is so crucial to spelling, this tendency may result in dropped final consonants on the part of Hmong spellers. Have students practice reading aloud, emphasizing final consonants as they read, until they begin to voice end consonants with regularity.

Cantonese. Cantonese learners may find English spelling complex. Problems may arise from not applying spelling conventions (*letter* spelled *leter*), from the number of exceptions in English (including silent letters and various spellings of similar sounds), and from incorrect pronunciation (including not pronouncing all syllables). Write words on the chalkboard often, and have students pronounce them with you. Frequently point out unusual spellings (as in the word *Wednesday*).

MECHANICS

> **Exercise 6** Spelling Words with Suffixes
>
> ANSWERS
>
> 1. baying
> 2. showed
> 3. dropped
> 4. denying
> 5. pitiless
> 6. qualifier
> 7. tripped
> 8. employment
> 9. happiest
> 10. hitting
> 11. swimmer
> 12. tidier
> 13. hurried
> 14. tapping
> 15. cleaner
> 16. folded
> 17. daily
> 18. bountiful
> 19. fixing
> 20. helpful

DIFFERENTIATING INSTRUCTION

Special Education Students
Some students may benefit from three special techniques to identify spelling errors in their writing. The first strategy is to have students use rulers or pieces of paper to cover all but the sentences on which they are working. The second strategy is for the student to read through the selection, moving his or her fingers along under the words to check for words that do not sound or look right. A third strategy is for students to read passages backward to help them spot incorrect spellings.

MECHANICS

---

1. bay + ing
2. show + ed
3. drop + ed
4. deny + ing
5. pity + less
6. qualify + er
7. trip + ed
8. employ + ment
9. happy + est
10. hit + ing
11. swim + er
12. tidy + er
13. hurry + ed
14. tap + ing
15. clean + er
16. fold + ed
17. day + ly
18. bounty + ful
19. fix + ing
20. help + ful

Review A Proofreading Sentences for Correct Spelling

Most of the following sentences contain a word that has been misspelled. Write each misspelled word correctly. If a sentence is already correct, write *C*.

EXAMPLE
1. Have you seen the beautyful bonsai trees on display in the new garden center?
   1. beautiful

1. C
2. proceed
3. inexpensive
4. choosing
5. careful

1. These trees can live to be hundreds of years old, yet you can quickly create one of your own in an afternoon.
2. Simply use these pictures to help you as you procede through the following steps.
3. First, you will need an inxpensive plant (such as a juniper), some soil, some moss, and a shallow bowl.
4. When you are chooseing a plant, try to get one with a trunk that has some of its roots showing above the soil so that your tree will look old.
5. Make a curful study of your plant, and decide how you want the bonsai to look in the bowl.

354 Chapter 16 Spelling

CONTENT-AREA CONNECTIONS

Social Studies
Spelling. Point out to students that knowing how to spell correctly is important in any of their studies that involve writing. Ask the social studies teacher to provide you with a list of terms or place names that are frequently misspelled by students. Then, have students apply the spelling techniques they are learning to these words.

6. Then, cut or pinch away <u>undesireable</u> branches and leaves until the plant looks like a tree.
7. After <u>triming</u> your plant, remove most of the large roots so that the plant can stand in the bowl.
8. Cover the remaining roots with soil, and if the weather is mild, put your bonsai in a shaded place outside.
9. You don't have to water your plant <u>dayly</u>, but you should keep the soil moist.
10. After your plant has healed, you will have <u>succeded</u> in creating your very own bonsai.

6. undesirable
7. trimming
8. C
9. daily
10. succeeded

Forming the Plurals of Nouns

16i. Observe the following rules for spelling the plurals of nouns.

(1) To form the plurals of most nouns, add –s.

SINGULAR	girl	breeze	task	oat	banana
PLURAL	girl**s**	breeze**s**	task**s**	oat**s**	banana**s**

NOTE Make sure that you do not confuse the plural form of a noun with its possessive form. Generally, you should not use an apostrophe to form the plural of a word.

INCORRECT	The girl's raced to the stadium for soccer practice.
CORRECT	The **girls** raced to the stadium for soccer practice. [plural]
CORRECT	The **girls'** soccer team has practice today. [possessive]

Reference Note
For a discussion of the **possessive forms of nouns,** see page 330. For information about **using an apostrophe and an *s* to form the plural of a letter, a numeral, a symbol, or a word used as a word,** see page 337.

(2) Form the plurals of nouns ending in *s, x, z, ch,* or *sh* by adding –es.

SINGULAR	moss	wax	Sanchez	birch	dish
PLURAL	moss**es**	wax**es**	Sanchez**es**	birch**es**	dish**es**

NOTE Some one-syllable words ending in *z* double the final consonant when forming plurals.

EXAMPLES	quiz	fez
	qui**zz**es	fe**zz**es

Spelling Rules **355**

RESOURCES

Forming the Plurals of Nouns
Practice
■ *Language & Sentence Skills Practice,* pp. 340–344
■ *Developmental Language & Sentence Skills,* pp. 129–130

EXTENSION

Critical Thinking

Evaluation. Point out to students that in some situations—especially in product labeling and advertising—phonetic, nonstandard spellings of words are used. For example, in the names of many products, *lite* is substituted for *light* to make the name more catchy. Write on the chalkboard or a transparency the following list of words, and have students write possible phonetic spellings of the words: though, highway, tough, night, cheese, knight, rough, right [*tho, hiway, tuff, nite, cheez, nite, ruff, rite*]. Then, ask students if any of these phonetically spelled words would be confusing for the reader. [Ruff *for* rough *could be confusing because* ruff *is already a word.* Nite *for* knight *would be confusing because most people would think of* night *when they see* nite.]

MECHANICS

Oral Practice — Creating the Plurals of Nouns

Read each of the following nouns aloud. Then, say the plural form of the noun, and say whether the plural form has the *–s* or *–es* ending.

EXAMPLE   1. match
                       1. matches

1. box**es**
2. crash**es**
3. sneeze**s**
4. address**es**
5. church**es**
6. tax**es**
7. Gómez**es**
8. ditch**es**
9. miss**es**
10. mask**s**
11. mix**es**
12. clip**s**
13. gym**s**
14. coach**es**
15. dash**es**
16. plate**s**
17. key**s**
18. pass**es**
19. Walsh**es**
20. business**es**

(3) Form the plurals of nouns ending in *y* preceded by a consonant by changing the *y* to *i* and adding *–es.*

SINGULAR	lady	hobby	county	strawberry
PLURAL	lad**ies**	hobb**ies**	count**ies**	strawberr**ies**

EXCEPTION   With proper nouns, simply add *s.*
                          the Appleby**s**   the Trilby**s**

(4) Form the plurals of nouns ending in *y* preceded by a vowel by adding *–s.*

SINGULAR	toy	journey	highway	Wednesday
PLURAL	toy**s**	journey**s**	highway**s**	Wednesday**s**

(5) Form the plurals of most nouns ending in *f* by adding *–s.* The plural form of some nouns ending in *f* or *fe* is formed by changing the *f* to *v* and adding *–es.*

SINGULAR	gulf	belief	knife	loaf	wolf
PLURAL	gulf**s**	belief**s**	kni**ves**	loa**ves**	wol**ves**

HELP—
When you are not sure about how to spell the plural of a noun ending in *f* or *fe,* look up the word in a dictionary.

(6) Form the plurals of nouns ending in *o* preceded by a vowel by adding *–s.*

SINGULAR	video	ratio	patio	Romeo
PLURAL	video**s**	ratio**s**	patio**s**	Romeo**s**

(7) The plural form of many nouns ending in *o* preceded by a consonant is formed by adding *–es.*

SINGULAR	veto	hero	tomato	potato
PLURAL	veto**es**	hero**es**	tomato**es**	potato**es**

EXCEPTION   silo—silo**s**

356   Chapter 16   Spelling

MINI-LESSON   Usage

Spelling and Agreement. Remind students that when they make a subject noun plural in a sentence by adding an *s,* they often must remove an *s* from the verb to make the verb plural. For example, *The horse gallops* becomes *The horses gallop.*

Write the following sentences on the chalkboard or a transparency. Ask students to rewrite each sentence, making the subject noun plural and changing the form of

NOTE With proper nouns, simply add *–s*.

EXAMPLES   the Sato**s**   the Korolenko**s**

However, you should form the plural of most musical terms ending in *o* preceded by a consonant by adding *–s*.

SINGULAR	piano	alto	solo	trio
PLURAL	pianos	altos	solos	trios

NOTE To form the plural of some nouns ending in *o* preceded by a consonant, you may add either *–s* or *–es*.

SINGULAR	banjo	mosquito	flamingo
PLURAL	banjo**s**	mosquito**s**	flamingo**s**
	or	or	or
	banjo**es**	mosquito**es**	flamingo**es**

The best way to determine the plural forms of words ending in *o* preceded by a consonant is to check their spellings in an up-to-date dictionary.

(8) The plurals of some nouns are formed in irregular ways.

SINGULAR	man	mouse	foot	ox	child
PLURAL	m**e**n	m**i**ce	f**ee**t	ox**en**	child**ren**

Exercise 7   Spelling the Plurals of Nouns

Spell the plural form of each of the following nouns.

EXAMPLE   1. industry
           1. industries

1. turkeys
2. studios
3. chiefs
4. sopranos
5. puppies
6. selves
7. chimneys
8. babies
9. tomatoes
10. echoes
11. ferries
12. joys
13. lives
14. heroes
15. bluffs
16. radios
17. lobbies
18. wives
19. feet
20. Whitbys

STYLE TIP

When it refers to the computer device, the word *mouse* can form a plural in two ways: *mouses* or *mice.* Someday one form may be the preferred style. For now, either is correct.

RETEACHING

Spelling

Activity. Some students may be confused when they see long words written. Explain that many long words are made up of letter combinations that by themselves may also be words. Isolating syllables that are words in themselves may make longer words easier to spell. Write the following words on the chalkboard or a transparency, and ask students to copy them. Then, have the students find some small words in the longer words by isolating part of a longer word one syllable, or even one letter, at a time.

1. peppermint [*pep, pepper, mint*]
2. breakfast [*break, fast*]
3. another [*an, other*]
4. careless [*care, less*]

---

the verb to agree with the subject. Then, ask volunteers to provide answers.
  The thief has escaped. [*thieves have*]
  The kitty you found belongs to my sister. [*kitties belong*]
  The fax I sent you doesn't have all the information. [*faxes don't*]
  Our dog gets out of the yard often. [*dogs get*]

PRACTICE

Guided and Independent

Exercise 8 You may wish to use the first ten items in **Exercise 8** as guided practice. Then, have students complete the exercise as independent practice. **HOMEWORK**

Exercise 8 Spelling the Plurals of Nouns

ANSWERS

1. side-wheelers
2. deer *or* deers
3. mothers-in-law
4. A's
5. hello's
6. thirteen-year-olds
7. aircraft
8. governors-elect
9. O's
10. commanders in chief
11. maids of honor
12. runners-up
13. spoonfuls
14. vice-presidents
15. x's
16. lean-tos
17. Swiss
18. $'s
19. Japanese
20. M's

Words Often Confused
(pp. 358–370)

OBJECTIVE

- To choose between words often confused

Reference Note
For more information on **compound nouns**, see page 25.

STYLE TIP
In your reading you may notice that some writers do not use apostrophes to form the plurals of numerals, letters, symbols, and words referred to as words. However, an apostrophe is not wrong, and it may be needed for clarity. Therefore, it is best to use the apostrophe.

(9) For most compound nouns written as one word, form the plural by adding *–s* or *–es*.

| SINGULAR | textbook | grandfather | toothbrush |
| PLURAL | textbook**s** | grandfather**s** | toothbrush**es** |

(10) For many compound nouns in which one word is modified by the other word or words, form the plural of the word modified.

| SINGULAR | sister-in-law | coat of arms | editor in chief |
| PLURAL | sister**s**-in-law | coat**s** of arms | editor**s** in chief |

(11) Some nouns are the same in the singular and the plural.

| SINGULAR AND PLURAL | moose | sheep | salmon |
| | Sioux | Chinese | spacecraft |

(12) Form the plurals of numerals, letters, symbols, and words referred to as words by adding an apostrophe and *s*.

| SINGULAR | 1800 | B | i | & | that |
| PLURAL | 1800**'s** | B**'s** | i**'s** | &**'s** | that**'s** |

Exercise 8 Spelling the Plurals of Nouns

Spell the plural form of each of the following nouns.

EXAMPLE 1. push-up
1. push-ups

1. side-wheeler
2. deer
3. mother-in-law
4. *A*
5. *hello*
6. thirteen-year-old
7. aircraft
8. governor-elect
9. *0*
10. commander in chief
11. maid of honor
12. runner-up
13. spoonful
14. vice-president
15. *x*
16. lean-to
17. Swiss
18. *$*
19. Japanese
20. *M*

Words Often Confused

People often confuse the words in each of the following groups. Some of these words are **homonyms**—that is, their pronunciations are the same. However, these words have different meanings and spellings. Other words in the following groups have the same or similar spellings yet have different meanings.

RESOURCES

Words Often Confused

Practice
- *Language & Sentence Skills Practice,* pp. 345–349, 351
- *Developmental Language & Sentence Skills,* pp. 131–136

accept	[verb] to receive; to agree to The Lanfords would not *accept* our gift.
except	[preposition] with the exclusion of; but Everyone *except* Lauren agreed with Selena.
advice	[noun] a recommendation for action What is your mother's *advice*?
advise	[verb] to recommend a course of action She *advises* me to take the job.
affect	[verb] to act upon; to change Does bad weather *affect* your health?
effect	[noun] result; consequence What *effect* does the weather have on your health?
already	[adverb] previously We have *already* studied the customs of the Navajo people.
all ready	[adjective] all prepared; in readiness The crew is *all ready* to set sail.
all right	[adjective] correct; satisfactory; safe; [adverb] adequately Jesse will be *all right* when his injury heals. We did *all right*, didn't we?

—HELP—
All right is the only acceptable spelling. The spelling *alright* is not generally considered standard usage.

Exercise 9   Choosing Between Words Often Confused

From each pair in parentheses, choose the word or words that make the sentence correct.

EXAMPLE   1. All of us (*accept, except*) Josh forgot our tickets.
          1. except

1. By the time Melba arrived, Roscoe had (*already, all ready*) baked the sweet potatoes.
2. One duty of the Cabinet is to (*advice, advise*) the president.
3. The soft music had a soothing (*affect, effect*) on the child.
4. The girls were (*already, all ready*) for the sleigh ride.
5. The (*affect, effect*) of Buddhism on Japanese culture was huge.
6. By this time of year, the snow has melted everywhere (*accept, except*) in the mountains.

DIRECT TEACHING

Modeling and Demonstration

Words Often Confused. Model the correct use of often confused words with the examples *The Lanfords would not accept our gift* and *Everyone except Lauren agreed with Selena.* First, point out that correct use can often be determined by asking what the confusing word means in a sentence or by knowing its part of speech. Ask what *accept* means in the first example. [*to receive*] Since *accept* describes an action, it is a verb and should be used only as a verb. Next, ask what *except* means in the second example. [*with the exception of, but*] Explain that *except* is a preposition; in this sentence *Lauren* is the object of the preposition *except*. Now, have a volunteer use another example from this chapter to demonstrate the correct use of confusing words.

Differentiating Instruction

English-Language Learners

General Strategies. Homonyms, words that can be spelled differently yet have the same pronunciation, may seem strange to many English-language learners whose languages lack or have few homonyms. A game might help students become more confident in the use of homonyms.

Write on the chalkboard or transparency the following list of words without the bracketed homonyms: be [*bee*], loan [*lone*], sent [*cent, scent*], seller [*cellar*], choose [*chews*], duct [*ducked*], hay [*hey*], knead [*need*], leased [*least*], so [*sow, sew*]. Divide students into teams of four, and challenge the teams to find the homonyms of the words on the list. Allow students to use dictionaries. After the teams have finished, have members of the class give answers as a student volunteer writes the answers on the chalkboard. Then, teams can check their homonyms.

7. The doctor's (*advice, advise*) was to drink plenty of fluids and get a lot of rest.
8. Sarita was happy to (*accept, except*) the invitation to the party.
9. Reading the newspaper usually (*affects, effects*) my ideas about current events.
10. Do you think it would be (*alright, all right*) to leave before the end of the movie?

Reference Note
In the Glossary of Usage (Chapter 12), you can find many other words that are often confused or misused. You can also look up such words in a dictionary.

Here is a sentence to help you remember the difference between *capital* and *capitol:* There is a d**o**me on the capit**o**l.

altar	[noun] a table or stand at which religious rites are performed There was a bowl of flowers on the *altar*.
alter	[verb] to change Another hurricane may *alter* the shoreline near our town.
altogether	[adverb] entirely It is *altogether* too cold for swimming.
all together	[adjective] in the same place; [adverb] at the same time *All together,* the class looked bigger than it was. Sing *all together* now.
brake	[noun] a device to stop a machine I used the emergency *brake* to prevent the car from rolling downhill.
break	[verb] to fracture; to shatter Don't *break* that mirror!
capital	[noun] a city; the location of a government What is the *capital* of this state?
capitol	[noun] a building; statehouse The *capitol* is on Congress Avenue.
choose	[verb, rhymes with *lose*] to select We *choose* activities today in gym class.
chose	[verb, past tense of *choose*] We *chose* activities yesterday.
cloths	[noun] pieces of cloth I need some more cleaning *cloths*.
clothes	[noun] wearing apparel I decided to put on warm *clothes*.

Exercise 10 **Choosing Between Words Often Confused**

From each pair in parentheses, choose the word or words that will make the sentence correct.

EXAMPLE 1. If it rains, we will (*altar, alter*) our plans.
1. alter

1. My summer (*cloths, clothes*) are loose and light.
2. In England, you can still see remains of (*altars, alters*) built by ancient peoples.
3. A bicyclist can wear out a set of (*brakes, breaks*) quickly.
4. You should use soft (*cloths, clothes*) to clean silver.
5. The cold weather did not (*altar, alter*) Ling's plans for the Chinese New Year celebration.
6. Accra is the (*capital, capitol*) of Ghana.
7. Keep the pieces of the vase (*altogether, all together*), and I will try to repair it.
8. Did he (*choose, chose*) a partner during class yesterday?
9. On the dome of the (*capital, capitol*) stands a large statue.
10. The audience was (*altogether, all together*) charmed by the mime's performance.

coarse	[adjective] rough; crude; not fine The *coarse* sand acts as a filter.
course	[noun] path of action; series of studies; [also used in the expression *of course*] What is the best *course* for me to take? You may change your mind, of *course*.
complement	[verb] to make complete; [noun] something that completes The piano music *complemented* Ardene's violin solo. Red shoes are a good *complement* to that outfit.
compliment	[verb] to praise someone; [noun] praise from someone Mrs. Katz *complimented* Jean on her persuasive speech. Thank you for the *compliment*.

(continued)

DIFFERENTIATING INSTRUCTION

Learners Having Difficulty

Homonyms. Students might need extra help to become proficient with homonyms. Write the following pairs of words on the chalkboard, and ask volunteers to circle the letter or letters that differentiate each pair. Next, ask students to copy the words, circling the differentiating letter or letters, and to write the definitions of the words next to them. (Definitions are available in this chapter in alphabetical order.)

1. altar, alter [a, e]
2. stationary, stationery [a, e]
3. their, there [ir, re]
4. threw, through [ew, ough]
5. weak, week [a, e]
6. capital, capitol [a, o]

DIRECT TEACHING

Spelling

Students can sometimes improve their spelling skills and expand their vocabularies by building related words from a word they are learning. To model this process, ask the class to think of words related to *popular* and list the words on the chalkboard [*population, popularity, populous, populate, populace, unpopular, depopulate*]. If students run out of ideas, show them how to add prefixes and suffixes and to consult a dictionary to build and find more related words. Ask the class to tell you the word root and meaning that all these words have in common [–*popul*– from the Latin *popularis, populus,* "people"]. Have student volunteers tell in their own words the meanings of all the related words and how they relate to the root word.

Then, write on the chalkboard or a transparency the following list of words: *advice, alter, break, jury*. Ask students to work in groups of three to brainstorm related words and to write down each word's root or base word and its meaning. One member of the group should serve as scribe. Students may consult dictionaries. After the groups are finished, appoint a class member to record student responses on kraft paper. Then, read aloud a word from the list and have a student volunteer give the word root or base word and its meaning. Have each group in turn call out one of the words related to the base or root. Continue until all the related words are listed, and then post the list in the classroom.

MECHANICS

(continued)

council	[noun] *a group called together to accomplish a job* The mayor's *council* has seven members.
counsel	[noun] *advice;* [verb] *to give advice* He needs legal *counsel* on this matter. His attorney will *counsel* him before the hearing.
councilor	[noun] *a member of a council* The mayor appointed seven *councilors*.
counselor	[noun] *one who advises* Mr. Jackson is the guidance *counselor* for the seventh grade.
desert	[noun, pronounced des'•ert] *a dry, barren, sandy region; a wilderness* This cactus grows only in the *desert*.
desert	[verb, pronounced de•sert'] *to abandon; to leave* A good sport does not *desert* his or her teammates.
dessert	[noun, pronounced de•sert'] *a sweet, final course of a meal* Let's have fresh peaches for *dessert*.

Exercise 11 Choosing Between Words Often Confused

From each pair in parentheses, choose the word that makes the sentence correct.

EXAMPLE   1. At the end of dinner, we ate a (*desert, dessert*) made of fresh fruits and berries mixed with frozen yogurt.

   1. dessert

1. The city (*council, counsel*) will not meet unless seven of the ten (*councilors, counselors*) are present.
2. The patient received (*council, counsel*) from the doctor on the best (*coarse, course*) to a speedy recovery.
3. Chutney and yogurt (*complement, compliment*) an Indian meal very well.
4. When we were staying in Cairo last year, we saw the Nile River, of (*coarse, course*).

5. Edward is preparing the enchiladas, and I'm making empanadas for (*desert, dessert*) tonight.
6. Marilyn made a hand puppet out of (*coarse, course*) burlap, buttons, and felt.
7. We all know the major would not (*desert, dessert*) her regiment for any reason.
8. Please, I am asking for your (*council, counsel*), not your (*complements, compliments*).
9. My mother and father both took part in the (*dessert, desert*) hiking trip last week.
10. What did you think when our camp (*councilor, counselor*) (*complemented, complimented*) us on our endurance?

formally	[adverb] with dignity; following strict rules or procedures We must behave *formally* at the reception.
formerly	[adverb] previously; at an earlier date *Formerly*, people thought travel to the moon was impossible.
hear	[verb] to receive sounds through the ears You can *hear* a whisper through these walls.
here	[adverb] in this place How long have you lived *here*?
its	[possessive form of the pronoun *it*] belonging to it That book has lost *its* cover.
it's	[contraction of *it is* or *it has*] *It's* [It is] the coldest winter I can remember. *It's* [It has] been a long time.
lead	[verb, rhymes with *feed*] to go first; to be a leader Can she *lead* us out of this tunnel?
led	[verb, past tense of *lead*] went first Elizabeth Blackwell *led* the movement for hospital reform.
lead	[noun, rhymes with *red*] a heavy metal; graphite used in a pencil There is no longer any *lead* in *lead* pencils.

(continued)

PRACTICE

Words Often Confused

Game. The following exercise gives students an opportunity to create a game with often-confused words. Divide the class into groups of three students each, and assign each team confusing words from this chapter.

Among the groups, divide up the list of words often confused from pp. 359–369. Leave out any word that contains apostrophes. Make sure each group has at least eight words. Students in each group will work together to make a grid of one hundred squares, with ten squares going down and ten across. They will write their words in the grid, with one letter in each square, fill in the remaining squares with random letters, and write short clues for each hidden word. The words can be placed in any direction, including diagonally. Groups should check their words against the spelling in the textbook. Have each group make three copies of its puzzle, and then have groups exchange puzzles so that each student has a puzzle to work. Ask students to study the clues and to draw a circle around each word they find. After students have finished working the puzzles, you could post the original unworked puzzles with their clues on a bulletin board.

(continued)

loose	[adjective, rhymes with *moose*] *not tight* This belt is too *loose*.
lose	[verb, rhymes with the verb *use*] *to suffer loss* Fran will *lose* the race if she panics.
passed	[verb, past tense of *pass*] *went by* He *passed* us five minutes ago.
past	[noun] *time that has gone by;* [preposition] *beyond;* [adjective] *ended* Good historians make the *past* come alive. We rode *past* your house. That era is *past*.

Exercise 12 Choosing Between Words Often Confused

From each pair in parentheses, choose the word that makes the sentence correct.

EXAMPLE 1. Kaya (*lead, led*) us to the ceremonial lodge.
    1. led

1. The woman who (*formally, formerly*) (*lead, led*) the band now teaches music in Alaska.
2. We do not expect to (*loose, lose*) any of our backfield players this year.
3. We (*passed, past*) three stalled cars this morning on our way to school.
4. "Why did you (*lead, led*) us (*hear, here*)?" the bewildered tourist demanded.
5. Can you (*hear, here*) the difference between the CD and the digital audio tape?
6. The workers removed the (*lead, led*) pipes from the old house and replaced them with copper ones.
7. Has the (*loose, lose*) bolt lost (*its, it's*) washer and nut?
8. The guests are to dress (*formally, formerly*) for the governor's inauguration ball.
9. "I think (*it's, its*) time for a pop spelling quiz," announced Mrs. Ferrari.
10. Has the last school bus of the morning already gone (*passed, past*) our street, Tiffany?

364 Chapter 16 Spelling

peace	[noun] quiet order and security World *peace* is the goal of the United Nations.
piece	[noun] a part of something Lian bought that *piece* of silk in Hong Kong.
plain	[adjective] unadorned, simple, common; [noun] flat area of land Jeans were part of his *plain* appearance. A broad, treeless *plain* stretched before them.
plane	[noun] a flat surface; a tool; an airplane The movers pushed the couch up an inclined *plane* and into the truck. I have just used a carpenter's *plane*. Have you ever flown in a *plane*?
principal	[noun] the head of a school; [adjective] chief, main Our *principal* spoke of his *principal* duties. I outlined the *principal* ideas.
principle	[noun] a rule of conduct; a fundamental truth Action should be guided by *principles*.
quiet	[adjective] still and peaceful; without noise The forest was very *quiet*.
quite	[adverb] wholly or entirely; to a great extent Some students are already *quite* sure of their career plans.
shone	[verb, past tense of *shine*] gleamed; glowed The moon *shone* softly over the grass in the silent meadow.
shown	[verb, past participle of *show*] revealed; demonstrated Tamisha has *shown* me how to crochet.

NOTE *Shine* can mean "to direct the light of" or "to polish," but the preferred past tense form for these meanings is *shined*, not *shone*.

EXAMPLES The firefighters **shined** a light into the attic.

Elton **shined** his shoes before the dance.

Here is a way to remember the difference between *peace* and *piece*. You eat a p**ie**ce of p**ie**.

To remember the spelling of *principal*, use this sentence: The princi**pal** is your **pal**.

PRACTICE

Relating to Dictionary Skills

Game. The activity described here gives students an opportunity to practice their spelling techniques by playing a game with a dictionary. Model the game for students by opening a student dictionary to any page and picking a fairly common word. Tell students the guide words listed at the top of the page, and give some hints about the word, such as what part of speech it is or what it means. For example, for *suspect* you could say, "The guide words are *surprisedly* and *suspend*. A verb, this word means 'to believe without real proof that someone is bad, wrong, or guilty.' What's the word?" You can keep giving more clues, such as how many letters are in the word, until someone guesses the word and spells it. Then, have students pair up and play the game. They should switch roles with each new word, with one student presenting the clue and the other giving the answer.

Exercise 13 Choosing Between Words Often Confused

From each pair in parentheses, choose the word that will make the sentence correct.

EXAMPLE 1. Mr. Ramírez used a (*plain, plane*) to smooth the board.
         1. plane

1. Each drop of water (*shone, shown*) like crystal.
2. Motor vehicles are one of the (*principal, principle*) sources of air pollution in our cities.
3. If you don't hurry, you will miss your (*plain, plane*).
4. The (*principals, principles*) of justice and trust can lead to world (*peace, piece*).
5. Jan has (*shone, shown*) me how to change a tire.
6. It is clear that Luisa is acting on (*principal, principle*), not from a personal motive.
7. On Christmas Eve we each have a (*peace, piece*) of fruitcake.
8. "The bake sale was (*quiet, quite*) successful," said Gloria.
9. "For once," the (*principal, principle*) announced with a smile, "you do not have to be (*quiet, quite*)."
10. (*Plain, Plane*) fruits and vegetables can be delicious.

HELP

Some sentences in Review B contain more than one spelling error.

Review B Proofreading for Words Often Confused

Identify the incorrect words in the following sentences. Then, give the correct spelling of each word.

EXAMPLE 1. Portraits of people do not have to be plane.
         1. plane—plain

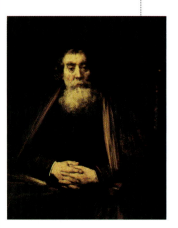

1. Some portraits have a striking affect. **1. effect**
2. A vivid portrait can often make people from the passed seem alive. **2. past**
3. The painting on the left is by Rembrandt, one of the principle painters of the seventeenth century. **3. principal**
4. The portrait, probably of a rabbi in the city of Amsterdam, is quiet lovely. **4. quite**
5. It's detail shows why Rembrandt was such a popular portrait artist. **5. Its**
6. The painting illustrates one of Rembrandt's main artistic principals, the strong contrast between light and dark. **6. principles**
7. Light has shown only on the rabbi's face, hands, and a peace of his clothing. **7. shone/piece**

366   Chapter 16   Spelling

8. The rest of the painting is quiet dark, highlighting these lighted features.   8. quite
9. The rabbi is shone in a state of piece, and the lack of detail in the painting gives an impression of quite elegance.
10. Rembrandt is excepted as a great artist because of his ability to give life to paintings of the human form.   10. accepted

9. shown, peace, quiet

stationary	[adjective] *in a fixed position* Is that chalkboard *stationary*?
stationery	[noun] *writing paper* Do you have any white *stationery*?
than	[conjunction used in comparisons] Alaska is bigger *than* Texas.
then	[adverb] *at that time* If we meet, we can talk about it *then*.
their	[possessive form of the pronoun *they*] *belonging to them* Can you understand *their* message?
there	[adverb] *at or to that place;* [also used to begin a sentence] Let's meet *there*. *There* are toys hidden inside the piñata.
they're	[contraction of *they are*] *They're* all from Guam.
threw	[verb, past tense of *throw*] *hurled; tossed* Ted *threw* me the mitt.
through	[preposition] *in one side and out the opposite side* I can't see *through* the lens.

TIPS & TRICKS

Here is an easy way to remember the difference between *stationary* and *stationery:* You write a lett**er** on station**er**y.

DIFFERENTIATING INSTRUCTION

Advanced Learners
Point out to students that although the words *through, cough, bough,* and *tough* all contain the letters *ough,* these letters are pronounced differently in each word. Have students consult a book on word origins, such as *The Story of English,* to find information on how words that at one time were pronounced similarly changed their pronunciations over time while the spellings stayed the same. Have students present their findings to the class in short oral reports.

Exercise 14   Choosing Between Words Often Confused

From each pair or group in parentheses, choose the word that makes the sentence correct.

EXAMPLE   1. (*Their, They're, There*) first rehearsal is after school.
1. Their

1. The stars appear to be (*stationary, stationery*), but we know that (*their, there, they're*) moving at very high speeds.
2. Thailand is much larger (*than, then*) South Korea.

Differentiating Instruction

English-Language Learners

General Strategies. English-language learners might be unsure of how to spell a word they hear or how to pronounce a word they see. English-proficient speakers who have not memorized spellings will make educated guesses based on the usual spellings of certain sounds or on similarities to other words they know. Some English-language learners, however, might not be able to distinguish subtle differences between some English sounds, know which spellings are more usual, or have the vocabularies to make analogies. Pointing out the various ways to spell certain sounds and giving practice with comparing similar words may help students minimize mistakes.

MECHANICS

3. That noise is from a jet plane going (*threw*, *through*) the sound barrier.
4. The pitcher (*threw*, *through*) a curveball.
5. A (*stationary*, *stationery*) store usually sells paper, pencils, and other writing supplies.
6. We started our trip in Barcelona and (*than*, *then*) traveled west to Madrid.
7. The girls completed (*their*, *there*, *they're*) displays for the science fair.
8. Is a moving target much harder to hit (*than*, *then*) a (*stationary*, *stationery*) one?
9. Each time Chris got a free throw, he lobbed the ball neatly (*threw*, *through*) the net to score one point.
10. The children in the back seat kept asking, "When will we get (*their*, *they're*, *there*)?"

to	[preposition] *in the direction of; toward* [*also used before the base form of a verb*] We are going *to* Mexico *to* visit Gabriel.
too	[adverb] *also; more than enough* Audrey is going, *too*. Kazuo used *too* much miso, so the soup was salty.
two	[adjective or noun] *one plus one* We bought *two* sets of chopsticks before we left the restaurant.
waist	[noun] *the midsection of the body* The anchor of the tug-of-war team wrapped the rope around her *waist*.
waste	[verb] *to use foolishly;* [noun] *a needless expense* Try not to *waste* all your film now. Rodney did not agree that golf is a *waste* of time.
weak	[adjective] *feeble; not strong* Melinda's illness has left her very *weak*.
week	[noun] *seven days* We'll wait for at least a *week*.

(continued)

(continued)

weather	[noun] the condition of the atmosphere The *weather* seems to be changing.
whether	[conjunction] *if* We do not know *whether* we should expect rain.
who's	[contraction of *who is* or *who has*] *Who's* [Who is] going to the museum? "*Who's* [Who has] been eating my porridge?" asked Papa Bear.
whose	[possessive form of the pronoun *who*] belonging to whom *Whose* report was the most original?
your	[possessive form of the pronoun *you*] belonging to you What is *your* middle name?
you're	[contraction of *you are*] *You're* my best friend.

MEETING THE CHALLENGE

A **mnemonic** is a device, often a rhyme or visual aid, used as an aid to remembering. The Tips and Tricks features on pages 360, 365, and 367 contain mnemonic devices. Create three mnemonic devices of your own for any of the Words Often Confused that do not already have mnemonics.

ANSWER
Mnemonics will vary.

Exercise 15   Choosing Between Words Often Confused

From each pair or group in parentheses, choose the word that makes the sentence correct.

EXAMPLE   1. What are (*your, you're*) plans for celebrating Juneteenth?

   1. your

1. (*Who's, Whose*) the present secretary of state of the United States, Elaine?
2. My stepsister and I built (*to, too, two*) snow forts on our front lawn yesterday.
3. "(*Your, You're*) late," my friend complained.
4. Would you be able to stand the (*weather, whether*) in Alaska?
5. That sounds like a (*weak, week*) excuse to me.
6. (*Your, You're*) dog is (*to, too, two*) sleepy to learn any new tricks today.
7. "(*Who's, Whose*) boots are these?" Mrs. Allen asked.
8. The pilot must decide very quickly (*weather, whether*) she should parachute to safety or try to land the crippled plane.

9. An obi is a sash that is worn around the (*waist, waste*).
10. My family is going (*to, too, two*) New Orleans.

Review C   Choosing Between Words Often Confused

From each pair or group in parentheses, choose the word that makes the sentence correct.

EXAMPLE   My parents asked my [1] (*advice, advise*) about where we should spend our vacation.
  1. advice

My family could not decide [1] (*weather, whether*) to visit Boston or Philadelphia. Finally, we all agreed on Boston, the [2] (*capital, capitol*) of Massachusetts. We drove [3] (*to, too, two*) the city one week later. Even my parents could not conceal [4] (*their, there, they're*) excitement. We did not [5] (*loose, lose*) a moment. Boston [6] (*formally, formerly*) was "the hub of the universe," and we discovered that [7] (*it's, its*) still a truly fascinating city.

Everyone in my family [8] (*accept, except*) me had eaten lobster, and I ate it for the first time there in Boston. I was not [9] (*altogether, all together*) certain how to eat the lobster, but my doubt did not [10] (*affect, effect*) my appetite. My parents insisted that pear yogurt was a strange [11] (*desert, dessert*) to follow lobster, but I would not [12] (*altar, alter*) my order. After the pear yogurt, I thought about ordering a small [13] (*peace, piece*) of pie, but I decided to keep [14] (*quiet, quite*).

While in Boston, we walked up and down the streets just to [15] (*hear, here*) the Bostonians' accents. [16] (*Their, There, They're*) especially noted for [17] (*their, there, they're*) pronunciation of *a*'s and *r*'s.

We had been in Boston for only a week or so when the [18] (*weather, whether*) bureau predicted a big snowstorm for the area. Since we had not taken the proper [19] (*cloths, clothes*) for snow, we decided to return home. On the way back, we were [20] (*already, all ready*) making plans for another visit to Boston.

CHAPTER 16

Chapter Review

A. Identifying Misspelled Words

Identify the misspelled word in each of the following groups of words. Then, write the correct spelling of the word.

1. height, weight, cheif
2. succeed, supercede, proceed
3. unecessary, unavailable, unusual
4. happyly, finally, truly
5. said, paid, keyd
6. cleaner, tapping, driped
7. taxes, buzzes, foxs
8. switches, mixs, keys
9. knifes, tomatoes, solos
10. mothers-in-law, father-in-laws, drive-ins
11. achieve, feirce, friend
12. mowwer, followed, staying
13. acquire, arguement, always
14. tired, trys, guesses
15. noticable, yield, daily
16. staying, priceless, easyer
17. halfs, coughs, princesses
18. heating, hiting, trying
19. changable, drinkable, smiling
20. misspell, ilegible, unnoticed

B. Writing the Correct Plural Form

Write the correct plural form of each of the following words.

21. boss es
22. thief ves
23. sheep [no change]
24. woman en
25. freeway s
26. ten-year-old s
27. Vietnamese [no change]
28. 3 's
29. city ies
30. soprano s

Numerals and terms in brackets refer to rules and concepts tested by the items in the Chapter Review.

1. chief [16a]
2. supersede [16b]
3. unnecessary [16c]
4. happily [16g]
5. keyed [16g]
6. dripped [16h]
7. foxes [16i(2)]
8. mixes [16i(2)]
9. knives [16i(5)]
10. fathers-in-law [16i(10)]
11. fierce [16a]
12. mower [16h]
13. argument [16f]
14. tries [16g]
15. noticeable [16e]
16. easier [16g]
17. halves [16i(5)]
18. hitting [16h]
19. changeable [16e]
20. illegible [16c]
21. [16i(2)]
22. [16i(5)]
23. [16i(11)]
24. [16i(8)]
25. [16i(4)]
26. [16i(10)]
27. [16i(11)]
28. [16i(12)]
29. [16i(3)]
30. [16i(7)]

ASSESSING

Monitoring Progress

Chapter Review. To assess student progress, you may want to compare the types of items missed on the **Diagnostic Preview** to those missed on the **Chapter Review.** If students have not made significant progress, you may want to refer them to **Exercises 36–37** in **Chapter 17: Correcting Common Errors** for additional practice.

RESOURCES

Spelling

Review
- *Language & Sentence Skills Practice,* pp. 350–353

Assessment
- *Holt Handbook Chapter Tests with Answer Key,* pp. 31–32, 46

C. Choosing Between Words Often Confused

In each of the following sentences, choose the correct word from the pair in parentheses.

31.–50. [Words Often Confused]

31. Have you (*already*, *all ready*) adopted a kitten from the animal shelter?
32. Although it's only July, the store already has a display of winter (*cloths*, *clothes*).
33. "I believe that both candidates for senator have very high (*principals*, *principles*)," my aunt said.
34. The sophomore (*councilor*, *counselor*) is working on next year's class schedules.
35. The moon is (*quiet*, *quite*) bright this evening.
36. Not getting enough exercise can (*effect*, *affect*) your health.
37. You must (*formally*, *formerly*) declare your interest in joining the club by filling out the membership card.
38. My (*advise*, *advice*) is that you buy a mountain bike.
39. (*Its*, *It's*) hard to believe that the leatherback turtle can grow to be seven feet long!
40. The fabric on the couch in Dr. Alexander's waiting room is (*course*, *coarse*) and scratchy.

D. Identifying Misused Words

In many of the following sentences, one word has been misused because it has been confused for another word. Write each incorrectly used word. Then, write the word that should have been used. If a sentence is already correct, write *C*.

41. alter
42. dessert
43. C
44. here
45. passed
46. C
47. than
48. weather
49. Who's
50. accept

41. An editor will altar this manuscript.
42. We had fruit and sherbet for desert.
43. I thanked Mr. Chu for the compliment.
44. While you are hear, use this towel.
45. Eventually, winter past and spring arrived.
46. Maria received a box of stationery for her birthday.
47. The blue chair is more comfortable then the green one.
48. The whether report comes on right after the news.
49. Whose the man speaking to Officer Grant?
50. The town voted to except the gift of a new library wing.

Writing Application
Using Correct Spelling in a Review

Spelling Words Correctly Write a one- or two-paragraph review of your favorite book or movie. Be sure to use at least five of the words listed as Words Often Confused in this chapter.

Prewriting Pick a favorite book or movie and make a list of the reasons that you prefer it over other books or movies. If you decide to write about a book, for example, you may want to compare it to a film that is based on that book.

Writing As you write your first draft, be sure to include information about the book or film, such as who wrote it, who directed it, and who stars in it. Remember to use a dictionary to help with correct spelling.

Revising Evaluate your draft and revise it to improve its content, organization, and style. Add sensory details that make the story come alive for the reader. Replace clichés and worn-out verbs and nouns with fresher, more precise words.

Publishing Check your paragraph for spelling mistakes. Use a computer spellchecker if one is available, but remember that spellcheckers will not recognize misused words (for example, *piece* for *peace*). Also, pay attention to the spelling of any words in languages other than English, and consult a dictionary if you have any doubt. Exchange your report with a partner, and check each other's spelling.

You and your classmates may want to gather the class's reviews and create a bulletin board display of favorite books and movies.

APPLICATION

Writing Application

Prewriting Tip. You may wish to have students make a list of the words they most often confuse and consider if those words would be appropriate to include in their reviews.

Scoring Rubric. While you will want to pay particular attention to students' use of words often confused, you will also want to evaluate overall writing performance. You may want to give a split score to indicate development and clarity of the review as well as spelling skills.

TEACHING TIP

The number of each word group in the **Spelling Words** list corresponds to a lesson number and objective below.

Lesson 1: OBJECTIVE
- To spell compound words

Lesson 2: OBJECTIVE
- To spell pairs of homophones

Lesson 3: OBJECTIVE
- To spell verb forms with –ed and –ing endings

Lesson 4: OBJECTIVE
- To spell English words that come from Spanish

Lesson 5: OBJECTIVE
- To spell words related to the field of music

Lesson 7: OBJECTIVE
- To spell words with the prefixes en– and ex–

Lesson 8: OBJECTIVE
- To spell words with the prefixes de– and dis–

Lesson 9: OBJECTIVE
- To spell the names of countries and continents and words derived from them

Lesson 10: OBJECTIVE
- To spell words that begin with forms of the prefix ad–

Lesson 11: OBJECTIVE
- To spell words with the adjective suffixes –some, –ish, –ine, and –ward

Lesson 12: OBJECTIVE
- To spell words that contain sounds often omitted in speech

Lesson 14: OBJECTIVE
- To spell words with the noun suffixes –ary, –ory, –ery, and –ury

Lesson 15: OBJECTIVE
- To spell multisyllabic words that include double consonants

Lesson 16: OBJECTIVE
- To spell word pairs that end with the suffixes –ar and –ation or –le and –ular

MECHANICS

Spelling Words

1.
- offshore
- strawberry
- daylight
- seaweed
- wildlife
- grandparents
- moonlight
- chairperson
- killer whale
- watermelon
- headache
- typewrite

2.
- shoot
- mist
- birth
- swayed
- shown
- tied
- pane
- shone
- reel
- berth
- chute
- suede

3.
- gathered
- hammered
- controlling
- bothering
- ruined
- listening
- studying
- swallowed
- permitting
- carrying
- compelled
- groaned

4.
- cafeteria
- alligator
- corral
- vanilla
- mosquito
- stampede
- guitar
- coyote
- jaguar
- chili

- cocoa
- tortillas

5.
- classical
- conductor
- concert
- instrument
- clarinet
- banjo
- bugle
- harmony
- pianist
- performance
- violin
- rehearsal

7.
- express
- envelope
- extend
- excitement
- exceed
- explode
- enthusiasm
- enclose
- expand
- exclaim
- exclude
- excel

8.
- defeat
- destroyed
- decline
- defects
- disabled
- disappeared
- disappointment
- dependent
- deduction
- disadvantages
- disguised
- dissolved

9.
- Spanish
- Greek
- England
- African
- French
- Spain
- Vietnam

- Australia
- Japanese
- Greece
- Australian
- Vietnamese

10.
- arrange
- accommodate
- announced
- approaching
- accepted
- appoint
- accompanying
- array
- arrangements
- accomplish
- accelerate
- annoy

11.
- selfish
- marine
- greenish
- awkward
- wholesome
- grayish
- childish
- masculine
- feminine
- reddish
- genuine
- awesome

12.
- temperature
- strength
- length
- vegetable
- arctic
- twelfth
- probably
- jewelry
- literature
- boundary
- reference
- beverage

14.
- machinery
- discovery
- nursery
- dictionary

- century
- injury
- missionary
- territory
- scenery
- revolutionary
- treasury
- luxury

15.
- barrier
- corridor
- umbrella
- buffalo
- gorilla
- pinnacle
- syllable
- tobacco
- massacre
- opossum
- moccasins
- cinnamon

16.
- muscular
- triangle
- muscle
- circular
- regulation
- particles
- particular
- rectangle
- vehicles
- rectangular
- triangular
- vehicular

17.
- doubtful
- specialist
- misfortune
- fortunate
- unfortunate
- especially
- specific
- specifications
- judicial
- judgment
- prejudice
- undoubtedly

374 Chapter 16 Spelling

Lesson 17: OBJECTIVE
- To spell words with the Latin roots –dub–/–doubt–, –jud–/–judg–, –fors–/–fort–, and –spec–

Lesson 18: OBJECTIVE
- To spell words with the verb-forming suffixes –ize, –ate, –yze, and –ise

Spelling

18
- organize
- cooperate
- congratulate
- exercise
- calculate
- illustrate
- recognize
- compromise
- memorize
- paralyze
- criticize
- inaugurate

20
- depositing
- recess
- televised
- revised
- position
- constructing
- composition
- opposite
- structures
- destruction
- vision
- necessary

21
- existence
- incident
- frequent
- endurance
- balance
- intelligent
- influence
- reluctant
- magnificent
- experience
- confidence
- elegant

22
- transmission
- contracted
- commitment
- attract
- submit
- references
- offered
- omit
- admits
- distract
- subtraction
- refer

23
- portrait
- buffet
- ballet
- bouquet
- dialogue
- antique
- unique
- vague
- fatigue
- technique
- plaque
- camouflage

24
- fantasy
- fantastic
- company
- companion
- editor
- editorial
- colony
- colonial
- strategy
- strategic
- diplomacy
- diplomatic

25
- hasten
- autumn
- autumnal
- softly
- heritage
- designated
- designed
- reception
- signature
- haste
- sign
- resign

27
- diameter
- graph
- meters
- astronomer
- barometer
- biography
- astronaut
- kilometers
- astronomy
- photography
- centimeters
- autograph

28
- trio
- monopoly
- quartet
- tricycle
- decade
- octopus
- decimal
- quarters
- triangles
- binoculars
- triple
- monotonous

29
- desperate
- lightning
- adjective
- penetrate
- aspirin
- athletes
- identity
- disastrous
- ecstatic
- platinum
- incidentally
- tentatively

30
- caravan
- luncheon
- champion
- gymnasium
- laboratory
- mathematics
- parachute
- submarine
- teenagers
- memorandum
- limousine
- examination

32
- logic
- biology
- monologue
- hydrant
- technology
- analogy
- mythology
- apologizing
- periscope
- telescope
- dehydrated
- psychology

33
- agricultural
- identification
- encyclopedia
- possibility
- exceptionally
- responsibilities
- characteristic
- recommendation
- rehabilitation
- acceleration
- simultaneously
- accumulation

34
- inspired
- convention
- formula
- adventure
- depends
- uniform
- inventor
- pending
- invention
- transformed
- perform
- suspended

35
- civilian
- historian
- guardian
- scientist
- biologist
- volunteer
- musician
- engineer
- physician
- technician
- politician
- psychiatrist

Spelling Words 375

Lesson 20: OBJECTIVE
- To spell words with the Latin roots –struct–, –vis–, –pos(i)t–, and –cess– or –ceed–

Lesson 21: OBJECTIVE
- To spell words with the unstressed endings –ant or –ent and –ance or –ence

Lesson 22: OBJECTIVE
- To spell words with the Latin roots –mit– or –miss–, –tract–, and –fer–

Lesson 23: OBJECTIVE
- To spell words of French derivation, especially those ending in –que, –gue, –et, and –age

Lesson 24: OBJECTIVE
- To spell related words in which a suffix is added to a base word, changing the vowel sound but not the vowel spelling near the end of the base word

Lesson 25: OBJECTIVE
- To spell related words with sounded and unsounded consonants

Lesson 27: OBJECTIVE
- To spell words that have the Greek word parts –ast(e)r–, –graph–, and –meter–

Lesson 28: OBJECTIVE
- To spell words that have the number prefixes and combining forms mon– or mono–, bi–, tri–, quadr– or quart–, oct–, and dec– or deci–

Lesson 29: OBJECTIVE
- To spell words that are commonly mispronounced

Lesson 30: OBJECTIVE
- To spell words that are often clipped to form shorter words

Lesson 32: OBJECTIVE
- To spell words with the Greek word parts –hydr–, –log–, –ology, and –scop–

Lesson 33: OBJECTIVE
- To spell words with five or six syllables

Lesson 34: OBJECTIVE
- To spell words with the Latin roots –ven–, –spir–, –form–, and –pend–

Lesson 35: OBJECTIVE
- To spell words with the suffixes –ian, –eer, –ist, and –ie

MECHANICS

CHAPTER 17

Correcting Common Errors

INTRODUCING THE CHAPTER

- This chapter provides additional application and review of some aspects of grammar, usage, and mechanics that cause students the greatest difficulty. Since this chapter concentrates on areas of greatest concern, you may find it useful in a variety of ways. You could use the exercises and tests in this chapter as diagnostic tests, judging by student scores which topics need greatest attention; you could use them as a resource for reteaching and remediation, providing extra practice for concepts you feel need extra emphasis; you could use them as a review of key concepts to help students prepare for standardized tests of language skills mastery; or you could use them in any combination of these ways.

Key Language Skills Review

This chapter reviews key skills and concepts that pose special problems for writers.

- Sentence Fragments and Run-on Sentences
- Subject-Verb and Pronoun-Antecedent Agreement
- Verb Forms and Pronoun Forms
- Comparison of Modifiers
- Misplaced Modifiers
- Standard Usage
- Capitalization
- Punctuation—End Marks, Commas, Semicolons, Colons, Quotation Marks, and Apostrophes
- Spelling

Most of the exercises in this chapter follow the same format as the exercises found throughout the grammar, usage, and mechanics sections of this book. You will notice, however, that two sets of review exercises are presented in standardized test formats. These exercises are designed to provide you with practice not only in solving usage and mechanics problems but also in dealing with these kinds of problems on standardized tests.

CHAPTER RESOURCES

Internet
- Web resources: go.hrw.com

Practice & Review
- *Language & Sentence Skills Practice,* pp. 359–390; 391–393
- *Language & Sentence Skills Practice Answer Key,* pp. 148–163

Application & Enrichment
- *Language & Sentence Skills Practice,* pp. 358, 394, 395–396, 397
- *Language & Sentence Skills Practice Answer Key,* pp. 148, 163–164

Exercise 1 Finding and Revising Sentence Fragments

Most of the following groups of words are sentence fragments. Revise each fragment by (1) adding a subject, (2) adding a verb, or (3) attaching the fragment to a complete sentence. You may need to change the punctuation and capitalization, too. If the word group is already a complete sentence, write S.

EXAMPLE
1. Because she likes Chihuahuas.
  1. My mother bought a book about dogs because she likes Chihuahuas.

1. Wanted to study the history of Chihuahuas.
2. Small dogs with big, pointed ears.
3. When my mother's Chihuahuas begin their shrill, high-pitched barking.
4. Chihuahuas lived in ancient Mexico.
5. Ancient stone carvings showing that the Toltecs raised Chihuahuas during the eighth or ninth century A.D.
6. Are related to dogs of the Middle East.
7. Travelers may have brought Chihuahuas to the Americas as companions.
8. That Chihuahuas score poorly on canine intelligence tests.
9. However, can be trained to assist people who have hearing impairments.
10. If you want a Chihuahua.

Exercise 2 Revising Sentence Fragments

Identify each of the following groups of words as a sentence fragment or a complete sentence. Write *F* if it is a sentence fragment and *S* if it is a sentence. Then, revise each sentence fragment by (1) adding a subject, (2) adding a verb, or (3) attaching the fragment to a complete sentence. You may need to change the punctuation and capitalization, too.

EXAMPLE
1. Juggling a fascinating hobby.
  1. F—Juggling is a fascinating hobby.

1. If you would like to be able to juggle.   1. F
2. You might start with a good, simple how-to book.   2. S
3. Most people can learn the basic moves.   3. S
4. Within a fairly short period of time.   4. F

Reference Note
For information about **correcting sentence fragments,** see page 414.

Reference Note
For information about **correcting sentence fragments,** see page 414.

Exercises 1–3

OBJECTIVE
- To identify complete sentences and sentence fragments and revise the sentence fragments to make complete sentences

Exercise 1 Finding and Revising Sentence Fragments

POSSIBLE ANSWERS

1. She wanted to study the history of Chihuahuas.
2. They are small dogs with big, pointed ears.
3. I cover my ears when my mother's Chihuahuas begin their shrill, high-pitched barking.
4. S
5. Ancient stone carvings show that the Toltecs raised Chihuahuas during the eighth or ninth century A.D.
6. Chihuahuas are related to dogs of the Middle East.
7. S
8. I was surprised to learn that Chihuahuas score poorly on canine intelligence tests.
9. However, Chihuahuas can be trained to assist people who have hearing impairments.
10. If you want a Chihuahua, I suggest that you read about the breed's history and characteristics.

Exercise 2 Revising Sentence Fragments

POSSIBLE ANSWERS

1. If you would like to be able to juggle, you might take a class.
4. Within a fairly short period of time, you may be entertaining your friends.

Differentiating Instruction
- *Developmental Language & Sentence Skills Guided Practice,* pp. 137–138
- *Developmental Language & Sentence Skills Guided Practice Teacher's Notes and Answer Key,* p. 33

Assessment
- *Holt Handbook Chapter Tests with Answer Key,* pp. 33–34, 47

Exercise 2 Revising Sentence Fragments

ANSWERS continued

5. While beginners first develop a sense of how to hold one juggling bag, they also practice tossing it up and letting it drop on the floor.
7. Next, the juggler must master the ability to toss one bag back and forth.
8. Then, the next step is learning the right way to throw two bags.
10. Before they move up to three bags, beginning jugglers must be competent juggling two bags.

Exercise 3 Finding and Revising Sentence Fragments

POSSIBLE ANSWERS

1. Eventually, the idea of dinosaurs started taking root in the imaginations of many people.
2. Considering this fascination, it is no wonder people flock to films about dinosaurs.
3. S
4. S
5. I saw a picture of the place where the first dinosaur eggs were found.
6. For example, people interested in dinosaurs can see magnificent, full skeletons in museums, lifelike animations, television documentaries, and even children's toys and cartoons.
7. What can explain the sudden disappearance of these mighty creatures?
8. The remarkable work of physicists Dr. Luis Alvarez and his son Walter sheds some light on this mystery.
9. Their theory is based on the idea of a meteor hitting the earth.
10. According to the theory, the meteor destroyed the dinosaurs by sending a huge, dark cloud around the earth, killing many plants and destroying the dinosaurs' food sources.

COMMON ERRORS

---

5. While beginners first develop a sense of how to hold one juggling bag. 5. F
6. They also practice standing in the proper, relaxed way. 6. S
7. Next, must master the ability to toss one bag back and forth. 7. F
8. Then learning the right way to throw two bags. 8. F
9. Beginners often need to practice juggling with two bags for some time. 9. S
10. Before they move up to three bags. 10. F

Reference Note
For information about **correcting sentence fragments,** see page 414.

HELP
Although the example for Exercise 3 shows two possible answers, you need to give only one for each item.

Exercise 3 Finding and Revising Sentence Fragments

Some of the following groups of words are sentence fragments. Revise each sentence fragment by (1) adding a subject, (2) adding a verb, or (3) attaching the sentence fragment to a complete sentence. You may need to change the punctuation and capitalization, too. If the word group is already a complete sentence, write *S*.

EXAMPLE 1. Could have been the source of the world's legends of dragons.

1. *Could dinosaur fossils have been the source of the world's legends of dragons?*

    or

    Large lizards, such as monitors, could have been the source of the world's legends of dragons.

1. Eventually, taking root in the imaginations of many people.
2. Considering this.
3. The word *dinosaur* was first used around one hundred and fifty years ago.
4. That fact surprises many people.
5. Where the first dinosaur eggs were found.
6. For example, magnificent, full skeletons in museums, lifelike animations, television documentaries, and even children's toys and cartoons.
7. Can explain the sudden disappearance of these mighty creatures.
8. The remarkable work of physicists Dr. Luis Alvarez and his son Walter on this mystery.
9. Their theory based on the idea of a meteor hitting the earth.
10. Sending a huge, dark cloud around the earth, killing many plants and destroying the dinosaurs' food sources.

Exercise 4 **Revising Run-on Sentences**

Each of the following items is a run-on sentence. Revise each sentence by following the italicized instructions in parentheses. Remember to use correct punctuation and capitalization.

EXAMPLE 1. The study of shells is called malacology, shell collections are particularly popular in Japan. (*Make two sentences.*)

1. The study of shells is called malacology. Shell collections are particularly popular in Japan.

Answers may vary. Sample responses are given.

1. At four feet in diameter, the shell of the giant clam is the largest shell today. during prehistoric times, the shell of the Nautiloidea sometimes grew to eight feet across. (*Make two sentences.*)
2. From the Mediterranean to Japan, shells have played an important part in everyday life. they have functioned as money, as decoration, and even as magic charms. (*Make two sentences.*)
3. American Indians used wampum, beads cut from shells, as money, West Africans and Arabs used the cowrie shell in the same way. (*Use a comma and a coordinating conjunction.*)
4. Africans prized the shell as jewelry, shells are still sold as jewelry. (*Use a comma and a coordinating conjunction.*)
5. Jewelry, buttons, figurines, and all kinds of decorative objects can be purchased at tourist shops along the coasts, shells are plentiful nearby. (*Make two sentences.*)
6. The ancient Greeks boiled mollusks and created a valuable purple dye. cloth treated with this dye may retain its color for hundreds of years. (*Make two sentences.*)
7. Perhaps because of their great beauty, shells have also played important parts in religious life. they may be found in several belief systems. (*Make two sentences.*)
8. Quetzalcoatl, god of the Mayans, Toltecs, and Aztecs, was born from a seashell. the chank shell is associated with the Hindu god Vishnu. (*Make two sentences.*)
9. Shells can be free for the taking, their rarity can make them quite valuable. (*Use a comma and a coordinating conjunction.*)
10. Shells are regularly exported from the United States to Europe, Japan and the United States also ship shells to each other. (*Make two sentences.*)

Reference Note

For information about **correcting run-on sentences,** see page 416.

3. , and
4. , and

9. , or

Exercise 4

OBJECTIVE

■ To revise run-on sentences

Exercise 5

OBJECTIVE
- To revise run-on sentences

Reference Note
For information about **correcting run-on sentences**, see page 416.

Exercise 5 Correcting Run-on Sentences

Correct each of the following run-on sentences by (1) making it into two separate sentences or (2) using a comma and a coordinating conjunction to make a compound sentence. Remember to use correct punctuation and capitalization.

EXAMPLE   1. Anthony uses chopsticks skillfully I have trouble with them.

   1. Anthony uses chopsticks skillfully, but I have trouble with them.

Answers may vary. Sample responses are given.

1. The large crane lifted the ten-ton boxes, it set them on the concrete deck.
2. My dad does not know much about computers he has learned to surf the Internet.   *2. , but*
3. Allen Say wrote *The Ink-Keeper's Apprentice* the events in the story are based on his boyhood in Japan.
4. Two robins landed on the ice in the birdbath one of them drank water from around the thawed edges.
5. Egyptian hieroglyphics may be written from left to right or from right to left, they may be written from top to bottom.   *5. or*
6. John is my youngest brother Levy is my oldest brother.   *6. , and*
7. The nature preserve was beautiful some people had littered.   *7. , but*
8. Grandma believes in keeping a positive attitude, she says that thinking positively is the key to a happy life.
9. Let's see that new movie from Korea. I have never seen a Korean movie.
10. All my friends like to shop for bargains at the downtown mall, I do, too.   *10. and*

Exercise 6

OBJECTIVE
- To revise run-on sentences

Reference Note
For information about **correcting run-on sentences**, see page 416.

Exercise 6 Revising Run-on Sentences

Revise each of the following run-on sentences by (1) making it into two separate sentences or (2) using a comma and a coordinating conjunction to make a compound sentence. Remember to use correct punctuation and capitalization.

Answers may vary. Sample responses are given.

EXAMPLE   1. James Earl Jones is a famous actor he has been in movies and plays.

   1. James Earl Jones is a famous actor. He has been in movies and plays.

1. You may not remember seeing James Earl Jones, you would probably recognize his voice.   **1. but**
2. Jones provided the voice of Darth Vader in the *Star Wars* movies. Jones's deep voice helped make the character forceful and frightening.
3. Jones has a distinctive voice he has even won a medal for his vocal delivery.   **3. . and**
4. The prize was given by the American Academy of Arts and Letters, is that the organization that gives the Academy Awards?
5. Jones's autobiography was published in 1993, it is, quite appropriately, titled *Voices and Silences*.
6. Jones was born in Mississippi in 1931, he was raised by his grandparents on a farm in Michigan.   **6. and**
7. His father was a prizefighter and an actor. Jones decided to be an actor, too, and studied in New York City.
8. He portrayed a boxing champion in *The Great White Hope*, he starred in both the Broadway production and the movie version of the play.
9. Jones won a Tony Award for his Broadway performance he was nominated for an Academy Award for his role in the movie.   **9. . and**
10. Another of Jones's movies is *The Man*, in that movie he plays the first African American to be elected president of the United States.

Exercise 7 Revising Sentence Fragments and Run-on Sentences

Identify each of the following word groups by writing *F* if it is a sentence fragment, *R* if it is a run-on sentence, and *S* if it is a complete sentence. Revise each fragment to make it into a complete sentence. Revise each run-on to make it into one or more complete sentences. Remember to use correct capitalization and punctuation.

Reference Note
For information on **correcting sentence fragments,** see page 414. For information about **correcting run-on sentences,** see page 416.

EXAMPLE
1. Because my ancestors were Scandinavian.
1. F—I have heard many stories about Vikings because my ancestors were Scandinavian.

1. The Viking Age lasted three centuries, it started at the end of the eighth century A.D.   **1. R**

Grammar and Usage   **381**

Exercise 7

OBJECTIVE

■ To identify and correct sentence fragments and run-on sentences

Exercise 7 Revising Sentence Fragments and Run-on Sentences

ANSWERS
Revisions will vary. Sample responses are given.
1. The Viking Age lasted three centuries. It started at the end of the eighth century A.D.

Exercise 7 Revising Sentence Fragments and Run-on Sentences

ANSWERS continued

2. Vikings came from Scandinavian countries known today as Sweden, Denmark, and Norway.
4. The range of influence of the Vikings was enormous. The Vikings developed trade routes in western Europe and in the Middle East.
5. Vikings also were skilled at fishing and farming.
6. All Vikings spoke the language called Old Norse, and they shared similar religious beliefs.
7. Odin was the chief god of the Vikings, but Odin's son Thor was worshiped more widely.
9. Viking society was divided into three main social classes—royal families, free citizens, and slaves.
10. Viking women held several important rights; they could own property and land, for example.

Exercise 8

OBJECTIVE

- To choose verbs that agree with their subjects

---

2. Vikings from Scandinavian countries known today as Sweden, Denmark, and Norway.   **2.** F
3. Since the Vikings lived along the sea, they often became boatbuilders, sailors, and explorers.   **3.** S
4. The range of influence of the Vikings was enormous the Vikings developed trade routes in western Europe and also in the Middle East.   **4.** R
5. Also were skilled at fishing and farming.   **5.** F
6. All Vikings spoke the language called Old Norse they shared similar religious beliefs.   **6.** R
7. Odin was the chief god of the Vikings, Odin's son Thor was worshiped more widely.   **7.** R
8. After they were converted to Christianity, the Vikings built many wooden churches.   **8.** S
9. Was divided into three main social classes—royal families, free citizens, and slaves.   **9.** F
10. Viking women held several important rights, they could own property and land, for example.   **10.** R

Reference Note
For information about **subject-verb agreement**, see page 148.

Exercise 8 Identifying Verbs That Agree in Number with Their Subjects

For each of the following sentences, choose the form of the verb in parentheses that agrees with the subject.

EXAMPLE   1. The band (*play, plays*) mostly reggae.
         1. *plays*

1. Samantha and Matthew (*take, takes*) art classes at the museum on weekends.
2. The card table or the folding chairs (*belong, belongs*) in that closet by the front door.
3. Earlene (*don't, doesn't*) know the exact time because her watch stopped working last week.
4. Both the stalagmites and the stalactites (*was, were*) casting eerie shadows on the cave walls.
5. Several of the exchange students at our school (*speak, speaks*) Portuguese.
6. Neither an emu nor an ostrich (*lay, lays*) eggs that look like that.

7. The members of the audience always (*clap, claps*) as soon as the star appears onstage.
8. Mike said that either the main herd or the stragglers (*is, are*) in the near canyon.
9. The coaches on the visiting team (*agree, agrees*) with the referee's decision.
10. Some of the fruit baskets (*sell, sells*) for less than three and a half dollars each.

Exercise 9 Identifying Verbs That Agree in Number with Their Subjects

For each of the following sentences, choose the form of the verb in parentheses that agrees with the subject.

EXAMPLE 1. (*Do, Does*) you know what a powwow is?
1. Do

1. Each of us in my class (*has, have*) given a report about powwows, which are ceremonies or gatherings of American Indians.
2. Dancing and feasting (*is, are*) very important activities at powwows.
3. People in my family (*come, comes*) from around the country to attend the Crow Fair, which is held every August in Montana.
4. Many of the people at the powwow (*has, have*) come here from Canada.
5. Everyone here (*know, knows*) that it is the largest powwow in North America.
6. Peoples represented at the fair (*include, includes*) the Crow, Lakota, Ojibwa, Blackfoot, and Cheyenne.
7. Only one of my relatives (*dance, dances*) all four of the main kinds of dances at powwows.
8. Both skill and practice (*go, goes*) into the Traditional, Fancy, Grass, and Jingle-dress dances.
9. Last year, all of the costumes of the Fancy dancers (*was, were*) extremely colorful.
10. Either a row of porcupine quills or a band of beads (*go, goes*) all the way around some of the dancers' headdresses.

Reference Note
For information about **subject-verb agreement**, see page 148.

Exercise 10

OBJECTIVE

- To correct errors in subject-verb agreement

Reference Note

For information about **subject-verb agreement,** see page 148.

Exercise 10 Correcting Errors in Subject-Verb Agreement

Most of the following sentences contain errors in subject-verb agreement. Identify each error, and give the correct form of the verb. If a sentence is already correct, write *C*.

EXAMPLE 1. All of us is very excited about our Drama Club's next play.
  1. is—are

1. *Six Friends and One Dog* are the title of the play we are performing this fall.   1. is
2. The director and producer of the play are Mark Taylor.   2. is
3. Neither our sponsor nor the actors have ever staged a production like this.   3. C
4. Most of the actors was chosen last week.   4. were
5. Of course, the cast don't know their lines yet.   5. C
6. Many of the costumes is still being made.   6. are
7. Either Lauren or Kawanda's older brother is painting the backdrops.   7. C
8. Are five dollars too much for a ticket?   8. Is
9. My friends and the crew hopes not, because the tickets are already printed!   9. hope
10. Channel 6 News have promised to cover our opening night, so we'll all be famous, at least for a little while.   10. has

Exercise 11

OBJECTIVE

- To select pronouns that agree in number with their antecedents

Reference Note

For information about **pronoun-antecedent agreement,** see page 165.

Exercise 11 Choosing Pronouns That Agree with Their Antecedents

Choose the correct pronoun or pronouns in parentheses in each of the following sentences.

EXAMPLE 1. Tell anyone with an idea to take (*their, his or her*) suggestion to the vice-principal.
  1. his or her

1. Everyone on the field trip must bring (*their, his or her*) own sack lunch.
2. When my sister or mother comes back from the bakery, (*they, she*) will bring fresh-baked bread.
3. No, neither of the cowboys ever takes off (*their, his*) hat.
4. The United States was proud when (*its, their*) astronauts landed on the moon.

COMMON ERRORS

Chapter 17 Correcting Common Errors

5. If Doug or Simon is in the clear downfield, pass (*them*, *him*) the ball.
6. Usually Rosita or Paula plays (*her*, *their*) guitar at our picnics.
7. If anybody is still in the gym, tell (*them*, *him or her*) to turn out the lights and shut the door.
8. The colonists and Governor William Bradford depended on Squanto as (*his or her*, *their*) interpreter.
9. This is a large company, but (*they*, *it*) treats the employees with respect.
10. Ask Jennie or Sara what (*her*, *their*) middle name is.

Exercise 12 Proofreading Sentences for Correct Pronoun-Antecedent Agreement

Most of the following sentences contain errors in pronoun-antecedent agreement. Identify each error, and give the correct form of the pronoun. If a sentence is already correct, write *C*.

EXAMPLE 1. Jesse and Michael enjoyed his Kwanzaa activities.
1. his—their

1. During Kwanzaa, which lasts from December 26 through January 1, several of our friends and neighbors celebrate his or her African heritage. **1. their**
2. African American families affirm traditional values and principles during their Kwanzaa activities. **2. C**
3. This year, both of my sisters made storybooks as her *zawadi*, or Kwanzaa gifts. **3. their**
4. Either Uncle Willis or Uncle Roland will bring their candles for the observance. **4. his**
5. One of them will bring their wooden candleholder, called a *kinara*. **5. his**
6. The joyful celebration of Kwanzaa has its origins in African harvest festivals. **6. C**
7. Each of my parents will discuss his or her own individual ideas about Kwanzaa. **7. C**
8. Either Lily or Charlotte mentioned in their speech that Kwanzaa was created in 1966. **8. her**
9. Nobody in our family likes to miss their turn to make up dances on the sixth day of Kwanzaa. **9. his or her**
10. Jerry and Charles will volunteer his time on the third day of Kwanzaa, when collective work is celebrated. **10. their**

Exercise 12

OBJECTIVE

- To identify and correct pronouns that do not agree with their antecedents in number

Reference Note
For information about **pronoun-antecedent agreement,** see page 165.

Exercise 13

OBJECTIVE

- To identify and correct errors in subject-verb and pronoun-antecedent agreement

Reference Note

For information about **subject-verb agreement**, see page 148. For information about **pronoun-antecedent agreement**, see page 165.

Reference Note

For information about **using verbs correctly**, see Chapter 9.

Exercise 13 Proofreading Sentences for Correct Subject-Verb and Pronoun-Antecedent Agreement

Most of the following sentences contain agreement errors. For each error, identify the incorrect verb or pronoun and supply the correct form. If a sentence is already correct, write *C*.

EXAMPLE   1. Every animal, including humans, need water to survive.
　　　　　1. need—needs

1. The human body consist mostly of water.   **1. consists**
2. You and I, along with everyone else, is about 65 percent water.   **2. are**
3. Everybody in my family tries to drink at least eight glasses of water a day.   **3. C**
4. "Don't Carlos usually drink more than that?" Janet asked.   **4. Doesn't**
5. Either Angie or Ramona said that their family usually drinks bottled water.   **5. her**
6. Evidence shows that drinking water helps our bodies keep its proper temperature.   **6. their**
7. Ian or Calinda have studied the mineral content of our local water supply.   **7. has**
8. Industry and agriculture depend on a good water supply for its success.   **8. their**
9. Most of the world's fresh water is frozen in polar icecaps and glaciers.   **9. C**
10. While more than 70 percent of the earth's surface are covered by water, only 3 percent of that water is not salty.   **10. is**

Exercise 14

OBJECTIVE

- To supply the correct forms of given regular and irregular verbs to complete sentences

Exercise 14 Writing the Forms of Regular and Irregular Verbs

Provide the correct present participle, past, or past participle form of the given verb to complete each of the following sentences.

EXAMPLE   1. eat   Angela has already ___ her serving of acorn squash.
　　　　　1. eaten

1. install   The shopping mall has ___ wheelchair ramps at all of the entrances.   **1. installed**

2. *send*   We have already ____ for a new crossword-puzzle magazine.   **2.** sent
3. *see*   Have you ____ the koalas at the Australian wildlife exhibit?   **3.** seen
4. *put*   Marianna is ____ together a colorful mobile.   **4.** putting
5. *grow*   My uncle ____ the largest pumpkin in the United States this year.   **5.** grew
6. *draw*   Anthony has ____ two different self-portraits.   **6.** drawn
7. *run*   Both of my stepbrothers have ____ in the Cowtown Marathon.   **7.** run
8. *jump*   Have the cats ____ out of the tree?   **8.** jumped
9. *write*   Murasaki Shikibu of Japan ____ what may be the world's first novel.   **9.** wrote
10. *go*   More than half of my friends ____ to the May Day parade.   **10.** went

Exercise 15 Proofreading Sentences for Correct Verb Forms

Identify any incorrect past or past participle verb forms in the following sentences, and write the correct forms. If a sentence is already correct, write *C*.

EXAMPLE   1. Many African American women maked names for themselves during the pioneer days.
   1. made

1. A friend of mine lended me a book called *Black Women of the Old West*.   **1.** lent
2. It contains many biographies of African American women who leaded difficult but exciting lives.   **2.** led
3. For example, May B. Mason gone to the Yukon to mine gold during the Klondike Gold Rush.   **3.** went
4. Journalist Era Bell Thompson writed articles about the West for a Chicago newspaper.   **4.** wrote
5. In *American Daughter* she telled about her youth in North Dakota.   **5.** told
6. Our teacher has spoke highly of Dr. Susan McKinney Stewart, a pioneer physician.   **6.** spoken
7. During the 1800s, Cathy Williams wore men's clothes and served under the name William Cathay as a Buffalo Soldier.   **7.** C
8. I seen a picture of Williams at work on her farm.   **8.** saw

Reference Note

For information about **using verbs correctly**, see Chapter 9.

Exercise 15

OBJECTIVE

- To identify and correct errors in the use of verb forms

COMMON ERRORS

Grammar and Usage   **387**

9. Mary Fields choosed an exciting but sometimes hard life in the West. **9.** chose
10. Nicknamed "Stagecoach Mary," she drived freight wagons and stagecoaches in Montana. **10.** drove

Exercise 16

OBJECTIVE

- To identify and correct errors in verb forms

Reference Note

For information about **using verbs correctly**, see Chapter 9.

Exercise 16 Proofreading Sentences for Correct Verb Forms

For each of the following sentences that contains an incorrect past or past participle form of a verb, write the correct form. If a sentence is already correct, write *C*.

EXAMPLE 1. When I was ten, I begun to collect stamps.
 1. began

1. Over the years, my collection has growed large enough to fill three binders. **1.** grown
2. I have went to several stamp shows. **2.** gone
3. At nearly every show, I seen many rare and valuable stamps. **3.** saw
4. I telled my friend Warren that I aim to own some of those stamps one day. **4.** told
5. I once saw a picture of a rare two-cent stamp that cost one collector $1.1 million in 1987. **5.** C
6. As you might imagine, that price setted a world record! **6.** set
7. Stamps have appear in many shapes. **7.** appeared
8. My uncle, a mail carrier, sended me a banana-shaped stamp. **8.** sent
9. He also has give me a book about the history of stamp collecting. **9.** given
10. It sayed that stamp collecting was already a popular hobby by the 1860s. **10.** said

Exercise 17

OBJECTIVE

- To select correct verb forms

Reference Note

For information about using *rise* and *raise*, *sit* and *set*, and *lie* and *lay*, see page 190.

Exercise 17 Choosing Correct Verb Forms

Choose the correct verb form in parentheses in each of the following sentences.

EXAMPLE 1. (*Set, Sit*) those packages down, and come help me catch these kittens.
 1. Set

1. Did Keefe (*rise, raise*) the flag for the ceremony?
2. The crowd roared when Sheila (*sit, set*) a new track record for the fifty-yard dash.
3. A giant lobster was (*laying, lying*) motionless on the seabed.

388 Chapter 17 Correcting Common Errors

COMMON ERRORS

388 Correcting Common Errors

4. The incoming tide (*rose, raised*) the boat that had been beached on the sandbar.
5. An heirloom quilt (*lays, lies*) neatly folded on the bed.
6. Why is the price of housing (*rising, raising*) in this area?
7. Someone had (*laid, lain*) a row of stones carefully on either side of the path.
8. Freshly washed and brushed, the mare walked out to the corral, (*lay, laid*) down in the dust, and rolled over three or four times.
9. By noon, the fog had (*risen, raised*) and the sun had come out.
10. In the old photograph, five Sioux warriors (*sat, set*) and stared with dignity into the camera.

Exercise 18 Identifying Correct Pronoun Forms

Choose the correct form of the pronoun in parentheses in each of the following sentences.

EXAMPLE 1. Doris and (*me, I*) are planning a trip to Vietnam.
   1. *I*

1. Will you take the first-aid class with (*we, us*)?
2. The principal gave (*he, him*) the key to the trophy case.
3. The minister gave (*they, them*) a wedding present.
4. Ulani and (*he, him*) greeted their guests with "Aloha!"
5. Mr. Galvez saved the comics especially for (*I, me*).
6. (*They, Them*) are learning how to draw with pastels.
7. R. J. asked (*she, her*) for a new CD.
8. Stan's jokes amused Martha and (*I, me*).
9. The person who called you last night was (*I, me*).
10. The captain of the debate team is (*she, her*).

Reference Note
For information on **using pronouns correctly,** see Chapter 10.

Exercise 19 Identifying Correct Pronoun Forms

Choose the correct form of the pronoun in parentheses in each of the following sentences.

EXAMPLE 1. The guest speaker told (*us, we*) students many facts about Hispanic Americans in the arts.
   1. *us*

1. Mrs. Ramirez picked out some poems by Jimmy Santiago Baca and read (*they, them*) to us.

Reference Note
For information on **using pronouns correctly,** see Chapter 10.

Exercises 18–19

OBJECTIVE
- To identify correct pronoun forms

Exercise 20

OBJECTIVE

- To identify and correct errors in the use of pronouns

Reference Note

For information about **using pronouns correctly,** see Chapter 10.

2. Jan and (*he, him*) agree that Barbara Carrasco's murals are outstanding.
3. Between you and (*I, me*), Gaspar Perez de Villagra's account of an early expedition to the American Southwest sounds interesting.
4. (*He, Him*) wrote the first book to have been written in what is now the United States.
5. Our teacher showed (*we, us*) pictures of the work of the Puerto Rican artist Arnaldo Roche.
6. (*Who, Whom*) is your favorite artist?
7. The writings of Christina Garcia appeal to (*we, us*).
8. In Luz's opinion, the best writer is (*she, her*).
9. Tito Puente recorded at least one hundred albums and appeared in several movies; we saw (*he, him*) in *Radio Days*.
10. (*Who, Whom*) did you research for your report?

Exercise 20 Proofreading for Correct Pronoun Usage

Most of the following sentences contain errors in pronoun usage. Identify each error, and give the correct pronoun. If a sentence is already correct, write *C*.

EXAMPLE   1. Who did the student council appoint?
　　　　　　1. Who—Whom

1. Let me know whom will be in charge of decorating.   **1.** who
2. Mr. Rodriguez gave Nicole and we shop students a handout on using the jigsaw safely.   **2.** us
3. Waiting for us at the door were Grandma and they.   **3.** C
4. For Ron and myself, geometry is easy.   **4.** me
5. Gina, us girls are going to the park to fly our kites; come along with us!   **5.** we
6. Mr. Chin, his wife, and me are going to the Mayan exhibit at the museum next weekend.   **6.** I
7. The big dog always keeps the bowl of food for hisself, so we feed the little dog on the porch.   **7.** himself
8. From who could we borrow a map?   **8.** whom
9. Yes, the team did all the planning and production of the video by theirselves.   **9.** themselves
10. The only ones who can speak French are us boys from Miss LaRouche's class.   **10.** we

Exercise 21 Choosing Correct Forms of Modifiers

Choose the correct form of the modifier in parentheses in each of the following sentences.

EXAMPLE 1. Many people think that of all pets, Siamese cats are the (*better, best*).
 1. best

1. The boys thought that they were (*stronger, strongest*), but the girls beat them in the tug of war.
2. The (*simplest, simpler*) way to attract birds to a yard is by having water available for them.
3. Jovita is the (*most intelligent, intelligentest*) student in the seventh grade.
4. I worry about my grades (*least often, less often*) now that I do my homework every night.
5. Kim Lee has traveled (*farthest, farther*) on her bicycle than anyone else in our class has.
6. Hasn't this year's quiz-bowl team won (*more, most*) local competitions than last year's team?
7. Grandfather says that this winter is the (*colder, coldest*) one he remembers.
8. Wynton Marsalis was born in the city (*more, most*) associated with jazz—New Orleans.
9. Bicyclists who wear helmets are injured (*least, less*) often than those who do not.
10. Louisiana has (*fewer, fewest*) wetlands than it once had.

Exercise 22 Proofreading for Correct Modifiers

Most of the following sentences contain errors in the use of modifiers. Identify each incorrect modifier, and supply the correct form. If the sentence is already correct, write *C*.

EXAMPLE 1. Low, green hills roll gentle in the dawn mist.
 1. gentle—gently

1. The tourists looked uncomfortably as they rode the elephant along the beach.   1. uncomfortable
2. An Indian elephant calmly carried a surfboard with its trunk and did the job good, too.   2. well
3. The white waves of the Bay of Bengal smell quite well to us.   3. good

Reference Note
For information on **using modifiers correctly**, see Chapter 11.

Reference Note
For information on **using modifiers correctly**, see Chapter 11.

Exercise 21
OBJECTIVE
- To select the correct comparative or superlative forms of modifiers

Exercise 22
OBJECTIVE
- To identify and correct misused modifiers

COMMON ERRORS

Grammar and Usage

4. The island of Sri Lanka was once known as Ceylon, and tea grows good there.   **4. well**
5. At first, I felt bad for the workers up to their waists in mud.   **5. C**
6. I thought they had the worstest job in the world.   **6. worst**
7. They were searching for rubies and garnets that might appear sudden in their muddy baskets.   **7. suddenly**
8. I couldn't recognize a raw gem very well; could you?   **8. C**
9. I thought the highlands, especially Sri Pada and World's End, looked beautifully.   **9. beautiful**
10. You can live simple when you are in Sri Lanka.   **10. simply**

Exercise 23

OBJECTIVE

- To revise sentences with double comparisons or double negatives

Reference Note
For information about **double comparisons,** see page 230. For information about **double negatives,** see page 231.

Exercise 23 Revising Sentences to Correct Double Comparisons and Double Negatives

Revise each of the following sentences to correct each double comparison or double negative.   **Answers may vary.**

EXAMPLES
1. Of the three games, the first was the least funnest.
1. *Of the three games, the first was the least fun.*

2. There are not hardly any stores near the ranch.
2. *There are hardly any stores near the ranch.*

1. The recycling center is much more busier than it used to be.
2. Sometimes even indoor water pipes freeze if they do not have no insulation around them.
3. I think that our dog Sammy is most happiest when the weather is cold.
4. I haven't received a birthday card from neither of my grandmothers yet.   **4. either**
5. Almost any circle that you draw by hand will be less rounder than one you draw with a compass.   **5. round**
6. Wearing sunscreen with a high sun-protection factor can make being in the sun more safer.
7. My second-oldest cousin, Giovanni, is not like nobody else I know.   **7. anybody**
8. We never went nowhere during spring vacation this year.   **8. anywhere**
9. That was probably the most cleverest chess move I've ever seen you use, Elise.   **9. clever**
10. When I'm old enough to vote, I'm not never going to miss a chance to do so.

392   Chapter 17   Correcting Common Errors

Exercise 24 — Revising Sentences by Correcting the Placement of Modifiers

The following sentences contain errors in the placement of modifiers. Revise each sentence by adding or rearranging words or by doing both to correct the placement of each modifier.

EXAMPLE 1. My grandmother and I saw a horse on the way to the movie.

1. On the way to the movie, my grandmother and I saw a horse.

1. The party was held in the park celebrating Mary's birthday.
2. With wind-filled sails, I saw a ship approaching the harbor.
3. The tree was struck by lightning that we had pruned.
4. The Yamamotos enjoyed planting the iris that arrived from their Japanese relatives in a box.
5. The softball team is from my hometown that won the district championship.
6. Trying to steal home, the catcher tagged the runner.
7. Jaime told Katya about the kitten playing in a happy voice.
8. Painted bright colors, Kamal saw many houses.
9. Hanging from a clothes rack, the drama students finally found the costumes.
10. Recently picked from the orchard, the bowl was full of fruit.

Exercise 25 — Identifying Correct Usage

From the word or words in parentheses in each of the following sentences, choose the answer that is correct according to the rules of formal, standard English.

EXAMPLE 1. The boys carried the new recycling containers (*themselves, theirselves*).

1. themselves

1. This orange marmalade smells (*bad, badly*).
2. In science class last week, we learned (*how come, why*) water expands when it freezes.
3. The dam (*busted, burst*) because of the rising floodwaters.
4. Mario should plant (*fewer, less*) bulbs in that small flower bed.
5. This button looks (*as if, like*) it will match the material.
6. Let's (*try and, try to*) arrive at the concert early so that we can get good seats.

Grammar and Usage   393

7. The defending champion played (*good, well*) during the chess tournament.
8. Yes, our nearest neighbor lives a long (*way, ways*) from us.
9. Those (*kind, kinds*) of fabrics are made in Madras, India.
10. Did you share the leftover chop suey (*among, between*) the three of you?

Exercise 26 Identifying Correct Usage

From the word or words in parentheses in each of the following sentences, choose the answer that is correct according to the rules of formal, standard English.

EXAMPLE 1. Mrs. Lawrence is (*learning, teaching*) us about the Hohokam culture.
  1. teaching

1. The Hohokam civilization (*might of, might have*) begun around 300 B.C.
2. Where did the Hohokam people (*live, live at*)?
3. The Hohokam (*use to, used to*) live in the American Southwest.
4. Hohokam farmers grew their crops in a climate that was (*real, extremely*) dry.
5. The Hohokam irrigated the land by using (*alot, a lot*) of canals—more than six hundred miles of them!
6. (*Them, These*) canals sometimes changed the courses of rivers.
7. The Hohokam were also skilled artisans (*who's, whose*) work included jewelry, bowls, and figurines.
8. I (*can, can't*) hardly imagine what caused the culture to change so much around A.D. 1450.
9. (*Their, They're*) descendants are the Papago and the Pima peoples.
10. We read (*that, where*) one Hohokam site is known as Snaketown.

Exercise 27 Proofreading Sentences for Correct Usage

Each of the following sentences contains an error in the use of formal, standard English. Identify each error. Then, write the correct usage.

EXAMPLE 1. If that ain't the proper first aid for heat exhaustion, what is?
  1. ain't—isn't

Exercise 26

OBJECTIVE
- To identify correct usage

Reference Note
For information about **common usage errors**, see Chapter 12. For information about **formal, standard English**, see page 245.

Exercise 27

OBJECTIVE
- To proofread sentences for correct usage

Reference Note
For information about **common usage errors**, see Chapter 12. For information about **formal, standard English**, see page 245.

1. During the track meet last Saturday, we used a American Red Cross guidebook for first aid. **1.** an
2. Fortunately, their was a handy section about treating heat exhaustion. **2.** there
3. The day of the meet, the temperature was hotter then it had been all summer. **3.** than
4. The athletes were all ready hot by the time that the track meet began. **4.** already
5. Some of the runners should of been drinking more water than they were. **5.** should have
6. Several of the athletes which were not used to running in such high temperatures needed medical treatment for heat exhaustion. **6.** who [or that]
7. We volunteers helped the runners like the first-aid guidebook instructed. **7.** as
8. They soon felt alright after we led them out of the heat and helped them cool down. **8.** all right
9. The doctor on duty at the meet examined them and checked they're vital signs. **9.** their
10. According to the doctor, even athletes in good condition must protect theirselves against heat exhaustion and heatstroke. **10.** themselves

TEACHING TIP

Using the Grammar and Usage Tests. A **Correcting Common Errors Test Answer Sheet** that students may use for these **Grammar and Usage Tests** is provided on p. 47 of the *Holt Handbook Chapter Tests* booklet.

Students may benefit from reading "Test Smarts" (pages 470–475 of their textbook) before they take the **Grammar and Usage Tests.**

Grammar and Usage Test: Section 1

DIRECTIONS Read the paragraph that follows. For each numbered blank, select the word or word group that best completes the sentence.

EXAMPLE 1. The platypus is one of __(1)__ mammals that lays eggs.

(A) to
(B) too
(C) two
(D) 2

ANSWER 1. Ⓐ Ⓑ ●C Ⓓ

The platypus is __(1)__ very unusual mammal. It __(2)__ external ears, __(3)__ feet are webbed, and it has thick fur. A broad tail and a fleshy bill __(4)__ to the platypus's odd appearance. Platypuses use __(5)__ bills to catch water worms and insects. Besides having a bill like a duck's, a platypus is __(6)__ like a bird than a mammal in another important way. Like a duck, the platypus __(7)__ eggs. The mother deposits __(8)__ in a nest, __(9)__ she has dug in a riverbank. If you get to Australia, you may see a platypus making its nest __(10)__ a burrow.

---

1. (A) an   1. B
   (B) a
   (C) the
   (D) some

2. (A) don't have no   2. D
   (B) doesn't have no
   (C) has any
   (D) has no

3. (A) its   3. A
   (B) it's
   (C) its'
   (D) their

4. (A) adds   4. B
   (B) add
   (C) added
   (D) adding

5. (A) its   5. D
   (B) it's
   (C) they're
   (D) their

6. (A) more   6. A
   (B) most
   (C) mostly
   (D) least

7. (A) lays   7. A
   (B) lies
   (C) is lying
   (D) has lain

8. (A) it   8. C
   (B) they
   (C) them
   (D) their

396 Chapter 17 Correcting Common Errors

9. (A) which 9. A
   (B) it
   (C) who
   (D) whom

10. (A) inside of 10. D
    (B) outside of
    (C) a ways from
    (D) inside

Grammar and Usage Test: Section 2

DIRECTIONS Part or all of each of the following items is underlined. Using the rules of formal, standard English, choose the revision that most clearly expresses the meaning of the item. If there is no error, choose A.

EXAMPLE 1. The chopsticks that my aunt sent us made of bamboo.

   (A) The chopsticks that my aunt sent us made of bamboo.
   (B) The chopsticks that my aunt sent us are made of bamboo.
   (C) The chopsticks are made of bamboo, that my aunt sent us.
   (D) That my aunt sent us chopsticks made of bamboo.

ANSWER 1.

1. Don't buy none of that ripe fruit if you don't plan to eat it soon. 1. D
   (A) Don't buy none of that ripe fruit if you don't plan to eat it soon.
   (B) Do buy none of that ripe fruit if you don't plan to eat it soon.
   (C) Don't buy none of that ripe fruit if you do plan to eat it soon.
   (D) Don't buy any of that ripe fruit if you don't plan to eat it soon.

2. The study group meeting in the library on Wednesday? 2. C
   (A) The study group meeting in the library on Wednesday?
   (B) The study group that will be meeting in the library on Wednesday?
   (C) Is the study group meeting in the library on Wednesday?
   (D) Will the study group meeting in the library on Wednesday?

3. Some visitors to the park enjoy rock <u>climbing others prefer kayaking</u>. 3. D
   - (A) climbing others prefer kayaking
   - (B) climbing, others prefer kayaking
   - (C) climbing, others, who prefer kayaking
   - (D) climbing, and others prefer kayaking

4. Martin <u>prepares the salad, Justine sets the table</u>. 4. B
   - (A) prepares the salad, Justine sets the table
   - (B) prepares the salad, and Justine sets the table
   - (C) prepares the salad Justine sets the table
   - (D) preparing the salad, and Justine sets the table

5. Many Cherokee now live in Oklahoma, but <u>this area were not their original home</u>. 5. B
   - (A) this area were not their original home
   - (B) this area was not their original home
   - (C) this area was not they're original home
   - (D) this area were not they're original home

6. <u>Pulling weeds in the garden, a tiny toad was discovered by Ernie.</u> 6. D
   - (A) Pulling weeds in the garden, a tiny toad was discovered by Ernie.
   - (B) A tiny toad was discovered pulling weeds in the garden by Ernie.
   - (C) While pulling weeds in the garden, a tiny toad was discovered by Ernie.
   - (D) Pulling weeds in the garden, Ernie discovered a tiny toad.

7. <u>Will rehearse together for the class play.</u> 7. C
   - (A) Will rehearse together for the class play.
   - (B) Will be rehearsing together for the class play.
   - (C) We will rehearse together for the class play.
   - (D) Because we will rehearse together for the class play.

8. Some people are more afraider of snakes than of any other kind of animal.   8. C
   (A) more afraider
   (B) afraid
   (C) more afraid
   (D) most afraid

9. Several important African kingdoms developed between Lake Chad and the Atlantic Ocean.   9. A
   (A) Several important African kingdoms developed between Lake Chad and the Atlantic Ocean.
   (B) Several important African kingdoms that developed between Lake Chad and the Atlantic Ocean.
   (C) Several important African kingdoms between Lake Chad and the Atlantic Ocean.
   (D) Several important African kingdoms developing between Lake Chad and the Atlantic Ocean.

10. The singer waved to some people he knew in the audience from the stage.   10. D
    (A) The singer waved to some people he knew in the audience from the stage.
    (B) The singer waved to some people from the stage he knew in the audience.
    (C) The singer waved to some people from the stage in the audience he knew.
    (D) The singer waved from the stage to some people he knew in the audience.

FRANK & ERNEST reprinted by permission of Newspaper Enterprise Association, Inc.

Grammar and Usage   399

Exercise 28

OBJECTIVE

- To correct errors in capitalization

Exercise 29

OBJECTIVE

- To correct sentences with errors in capitalization

HELP

Some capital letters in Exercise 28 are already used correctly.

Reference Note

For information on **capital letters**, see Chapter 13.

Reference Note

For information on **capital letters**, see Chapter 13.

Exercise 28 Correcting Errors in Capitalization

The following groups of words contain errors in capitalization. Correct the errors either by changing capital letters to lowercase letters or by changing lowercase letters to capital letters.

EXAMPLE   1. a buddhist temple
          1. a Buddhist temple

1. appalachian state university
2. world history and math 101
3. tuesday, May 1
4. senator williams
5. Summer In texas
6. Thirty-Fifth avenue
7. saturn and the moon
8. a korean Restaurant
9. empire state building
10. will rogers turnpike

Exercise 29 Proofreading Sentences for Correct Capitalization

For each of the following sentences, find the words that should be capitalized but are not. Then, write the words correctly.

EXAMPLE   1. American indians gave the name Buffalo Soldiers to African American troops who served in the West during the civil war.
          1. *Indians, Civil War*

1. Thirteen Buffalo Soldiers won the congressional medal of honor, which is the highest military award in the United States.
2. *Black frontiers: A history of African american heroes in the Old west,* by Lillian Schlissel, was published in 1995.
3. A chapter about mary fields tells the story of a woman known as Stagecoach Mary who drove freight wagons and stagecoaches in the west.
4. One of the museums listed in the back of the book is the great plains black museum in Omaha, Nebraska.
5. The book also tells about benjamin singleton, who was born into slavery.

400   Chapter 17   Correcting Common Errors

6. After the Civil War, he and some others bought land and founded the communities of Nicodemus and dunlap, kansas.
7. The exciting story of the cowboy Nat Love is told in his autobiography, *the life and adventures of Nat Love.*
8. bill pickett, who was of black, white, and American Indian ancestry, was one of the most famous rodeo competitors of all time. **8.** *or* Black, White
9. Pickett's biography was published by the university of oklahoma press in 1977.
10. The businessman and gold miner Barney Ford became very wealthy and built ford's hotel on fifteenth street in denver, Colorado.

Exercise 30   Proofreading Sentences for the Correct Use of Commas

For each of the following sentences, write each word or numeral that should be followed by a comma and then add the comma.

EXAMPLE   1. The colors of the French flag are red white and blue.
             1. red, white,   Optional commas are underscored.

1. No the mountain dulcimer is not the same as the hammered dulcimer but both of them are stringed instruments.
2. Abraham Lincoln who was the sixteenth president of the United States died on April 15 1865.
3. If you want to knit a sweater you will need to get knitting needles yarn and a pattern.
4. After oiling the wheels on his sister's wagon Tyrel oiled the wheels on his skates and on his bicycle.
5. Competing in the 10K race Nathan found that he could run faster than his friends.
6. In my opinion a person should be fined if loose trash in the back of his or her pickup truck blows out and litters the road.
7. Lupe please show us how to use the new computer program.
8. Although Cody is afraid of heights he rescued a cat that was stuck high in a tree.
9. I hope that Amy Tan my favorite author will write another book soon.
10. Many people want to conserve resources yet some of these people overlook simple ways to recycle.

Reference Note
For information about **using commas correctly,** see page 294.

Exercise 30

OBJECTIVE

- To correct sentences with errors in the use of commas

COMMON ERRORS

Exercise 31

OBJECTIVE

■ To correct sentences with errors in the use of end marks and commas

Reference Note

For information about **end marks,** see page 290. For information about **commas,** see page 294.

Exercise 31 — Using Periods, Question Marks, Exclamation Points, and Commas Correctly

The following sentences lack necessary periods, question marks, exclamation points, and commas. Write the word before each missing punctuation mark, and insert the correct punctuation.

EXAMPLE   1. When will Anita Luís Martina and Sam be back from the mall

   1. Anita, Luís, Martina, mall?

Answers may vary. Optional commas are underscored.

1. Wow, look at the size of that alligator! [or Wow! . . . alligator.]
2. Leaning against the mast, I could feel the sails catch the wind.
3. Won't these new, colorful curtains brighten this room?
4. By the way, that stack of newspapers should be recycled.
5. Oil paints, whether used for art projects or home improvement, should be used only in well-ventilated areas.
6. Hidiko, watch out for that cactus! [or . . . cactus.]
7. Was Uncle Jesse born in Cincinnati, Ohio, or Louisville, Kentucky?
8. As far as I am concerned, the most interesting parts of the lecture were about the life of W. E. B. DuBois.
9. Monday, Tuesday, or Wednesday will be fine for our next meeting.
10. Would you like to watch a movie tonight, or should I bring over the model-plane kit to work on together?

Exercise 32

OBJECTIVE

■ To correct sentences with errors in the use of semicolons and colons

Reference Note

For information about **semicolons and colons,** see page 310.

Exercise 32 — Using Semicolons and Colons Correctly

The following sentences lack necessary semicolons and colons. Write the words or numerals that come before and after the needed punctuation, and insert the correct punctuation.

EXAMPLE   1. Elena learned Spanish and English at home she learned French and German at school.

   1. home; she

1. They should be here before 9:30 this morning.
2. Our recycling center accepts the following materials: glass, newspaper, cardboard, and aluminum cans.
3. The landscape designer planted bushes around the school last fall; she will plant flowers this spring.
4. Please be at the station by 2:15 P.M.

5. The children wanted to see bears, lions, and elephants:but parrots, snakes, tortoises, and goats were the only animals there.
6. The sermon was based on Isaiah 61:1.
7. To refinish this dresser, we will need some supplies:varnish remover, sandpaper, steel wool, wood stain, and a clear polyurethane sealant.
8. Walking is terrific exercise:it improves both your stamina and your muscle tone.
9. Many children's books have beautiful illustrations:some are worth having just for the art.
10. Many palaces in Europe are spectacular:Linderhof in Bavaria is my favorite.

Exercise 33 Punctuating and Capitalizing Quotations and Titles

For each of the following sentences, correct any capitalization errors and add or change quotation marks and other marks of punctuation where needed.

Reference Note
For information about **punctuating and capitalizing quotations,** see page 322.

EXAMPLE
1. I learned how to play a new virtual-reality game today Pat said.
1. "I learned how to play a new virtual-reality game today," Pat said.

1. The most helpful chapter in my computer manual is "Search Tips" I explained to her.
2. Do Asian cobras look like African cobras Shawn asked.
3. I want to go to the fair after school Ivan said but my trumpet lesson is today.
4. The pilot said we are now beginning our descent into Orlando. Please fasten your seat belts, and return your seats to the upright position.
5. Goodness! what a surprise Taka exclaimed
6. Did some famous person say A smile is contagious
7. Cyclists should always wear helmets said the safety officer
8. Was it he who said a penny saved is a penny earned Troy asked
9. Carlos shouted, look at that dolphin near our boat!
10. During his speech at our school, the mayor said Our children are our future

Mechanics **403**

Exercise 33

OBJECTIVE

- To correctly punctuate and capitalize quotations and titles

Exercise 33 Punctuating and Capitalizing Quotations and Titles

ANSWERS
Answers may vary slightly. Accept reasonable responses.

1. "The most helpful chapter in my computer manual is 'Search Tips,'" I explained to her.
2. "Do Asian cobras look like African cobras?" Shawn asked.
3. "I want to go to the fair after school," Ivan said, "but my trumpet lesson is today."
4. The pilot said, "We are now beginning our descent into Orlando. Please fasten your seat belts, and return your seats to the upright position."
5. "Goodness! What a surprise!" Taka exclaimed.
6. Did some famous person say, "A smile is contagious"?
7. "Cyclists should always wear helmets," said the safety officer.
8. "Was it he who said, 'A penny saved is a penny earned'?" Troy asked.
9. Carlos shouted, "Look at that dolphin near our boat!"
10. During his speech at our school, the mayor said, "Our children are our future."

Exercise 34

OBJECTIVE

- To correctly punctuate and capitalize quotations and titles

Exercise 34 Punctuating and Capitalizing Quotations and Titles

ANSWERS

Answers may vary slightly. Accept reasonable responses.

1. "She has lived a remarkable life," Ernesto said, "and I admire her very much."
2. Angela exclaimed, "Yes, I know about Menchú!"
3. "Menchú is from Guatemala," said Mrs. Harper. "She won the Nobel Peace Prize in 1992."
4. "I once wrote about Menchú in a poem called 'The Heart of a Peacemaker,' " Gale said.
5. "I think Rigoberta Menchú is a great role model," Carla said.
6. "Menchú has tried to make life better for the laborers. Her own family is of Quiché heritage," explained Mark.
7. "Did Stephanie say, 'My dream is to meet Rigoberta Menchú'?" asked Ryan.
8. "Yes, and I'd like to meet her too!" exclaimed Emilio.
9. Mark continued, "Menchú worked long hours on cotton and coffee plantations when she was a child."
10. "Menchú's autobiography is *I . . . Rigoberta Menchú*," said Mrs. Harper.

Exercise 35

OBJECTIVE

- To use apostrophes correctly

Reference Note

For information about **using quotation marks**, see page 322.

Reference Note

For information on **using apostrophes**, see page 330.

Exercise 34 Punctuating and Capitalizing Quotations and Titles

For each of the following sentences, correct any capitalization errors and add or change quotation marks and other marks of punctuation where needed.

EXAMPLE 1. Sheila asked have you read about Rigoberta Menchú?

1. Sheila asked, "Have you read about Rigoberta Menchú?"

1. She has lived a remarkable life Ernesto said and I admire her very much
2. Angela exclaimed yes, I know about Menchú!
3. Menchú is from Guatemala said Mrs. Harper She won the Nobel Peace Prize in 1992.
4. I once wrote about Menchú in a poem called "The Heart of a Peacemaker" Gale said.
5. I think Rigoberta Menchú is a great role model Carla said.
6. Menchú has tried to make life better for the laborers. Her own family is of Quiché heritage explained Mark
7. Did Stephanie say My dream is to meet Rigoberta Menchú asked Ryan
8. Yes, and I'd like to meet her too exclaimed Emilio.
9. Mark continued Menchú worked long hours on cotton and coffee plantations when she was a child.
10. Menchú's autobiography is *I . . . Rigoberta Menchú* said Mrs. Harper.

Exercise 35 Using Apostrophes Correctly

Add, delete, or move apostrophes where needed in the following word groups. If a word group is already correct, write *C*.

EXAMPLE 1. both boys shoes

1. boys'

1. somebody's lunch
2. can't play
3. Neal's motorcycle
4. better than theirs   4. C
5. women's volleyball
6. too many letter u's
7. its engine   7. C
8. Betsy Ross's flag
9. no more if's
10. the bushes' branches

404 Chapter 17 Correcting Common Errors

Exercise 36 Correcting Spelling Errors

Most of the following words are misspelled. If a word is spelled incorrectly, write the correct spelling. If a word is already spelled correctly, write *C*.

EXAMPLE   1. succede
            1. succeed

1. taxs
2. neice
3. supercede
4. disallow
5. countrys
6. emptyness
7. tracable
8. stathood
9. lovelyer
10. clearest
11. wolfs
12. sheild
13. preceed
14. father-in-laws
15. improper
16. fancifuly
17. dryest
18. cluless
19. overjoied
20. skiping

Exercise 37 Choosing Between Words Often Confused

From each pair in parentheses, choose the word or words that make the sentence correct.

EXAMPLE   1. The school plans to (*except, accept*) the new computer company's offer.
            1. accept

1. Did Coach Jefferson (*advise, advice*) you to take the first-aid course at the community center?
2. My cousins and I are (*all ready, already*) to enter the marathon.
3. Sacramento became the (*capital, capitol*) of California in 1854.
4. When garden hoses (*brake, break*), they sometimes can be mended with waterproof tape.
5. Avoid wearing (*loose, lose*) clothing when operating that equipment.
6. Many people know Mr. Perez, but I think he should be (*formerly, formally*) introduced.
7. My grandfather threw the football (*passed, past*) the trees and over the creek.
8. (*Its, It's*) a good idea to test home smoke detectors frequently to make sure the batteries are still working.
9. One basic (*principle, principal*) of our Constitution is the right to free speech.
10. Some cats are called bobtails because of (*their, there*) very short tails.

TEACHING TIP

Using the Mechanics Tests.
A **Correcting Common Errors Test Answer Sheet** that students may use for these **Mechanics Tests** is provided on p. 47 of the *Holt Handbook Chapter Tests* booklet.

Students may benefit from reading "Test Smarts" (pages 470–475 of their textbook) before they take the **Mechanics Tests**.

Mechanics Test: Section 1

DIRECTIONS Each numbered item below consists of an underlined word or word group. Choose the answer that shows the correct capitalization, punctuation, and spelling of the underlined part. If there is no error, choose D (Correct as is).

EXAMPLE   [1] 29 South Maple street

  (A) 29 south Maple Street
  (B) 29 South Maple Street
  (C) Twenty Nine South Maple Street
  (D) Correct as is

ANSWER   1.

---

29 South Maple Street
Philadelphia, PA 19107

[1] January 15 2001

Mail-Order Sales Manager
[2] Direct Electronics, Inc.
214-C Billings Boulevard
[3] New Castle, Ken 40050

[4] Dear Sales Manager,

The modem that I ordered from your company arrived today in [5] peices. The package was [6] open, and appeared not to have been sealed properly. [7] In addition I have not yet received the computer game that I also ordered. Please send me a new [8] modem the broken modem is enclosed.

I appreciate [9] you're prompt attention to both of these matters.

[10] Sincerely yours,

Cameron Scott

Cameron Scott

---

406 Chapter 17 Correcting Common Errors

1. (A) January 15, 2001   1. A
   (B) January, 15 2001
   (C) January 15th 2001
   (D) Correct as is

2. (A) direct electronics, inc.   2. D
   (B) Direct electronics, inc.
   (C) Direct Electronics, inc.
   (D) Correct as is

3. (A) New Castle Ken. 40050   3. B
   (B) New Castle, KY 40050
   (C) New Castle KY, 40050
   (D) Correct as is

4. (A) Dear sales manager,   4. C
   (B) dear sales manager:
   (C) Dear Sales Manager:
   (D) Correct as is

5. (A) pieces   5. A
   (B) piece's
   (C) peaces
   (D) Correct as is

6. (A) open and appeared   6. A
   (B) open; and appeared
   (C) open, and, appeared
   (D) Correct as is

7. (A) In addition, I   7. A
   (B) In addition i
   (C) In addition, i
   (D) Correct as is

8. (A) modem, the   8. B
   (B) modem; the
   (C) modem: the
   (D) Correct as is

9. (A) youre   9. C
   (B) your,
   (C) your
   (D) Correct as is

10. (A) Sincerely Yours',   10. D
    (B) Sincerely your's,
    (C) Sincerely yours:
    (D) Correct as is

Mechanics Test: Section 2

DIRECTIONS Each of the following sentences contains an underlined word or word group. Choose the answer that shows the correct capitalization, punctuation, and spelling of the underlined part. If there is no error, choose D (Correct as is).

EXAMPLE   1. Rosie said that her cousin sent her that <u>soft colorful fabric</u> from Kenya.

   (A) soft, colorful, fabric
   (B) soft, colorful fabric
   (C) soft; colorful fabric
   (D) Correct as is

ANSWER   1.

1. C 1. The following people have volunteered to make <u>enchiladas, Manuel</u>, Shawn, and Anita.

   (A) enchiladas; Manuel
   (B) enchiladas. Manuel
   (C) enchiladas: Manuel
   (D) Correct as is

2. A 2. Our school's <u>recycling program which</u> is now three years old, has been quite successful.

   (A) recycling program, which
   (B) Recycling Program, which
   (C) recycling program; which
   (D) Correct as is

3. C 3. <u>Looking at the astronomical map in my science book</u> I spotted the constellations Orion, Taurus, and Pisces.

   (A) Looking at the astronomical map, in my science book I
   (B) Looking at the astronomical map, in my science book, I
   (C) Looking at the astronomical map in my science book, I
   (D) Correct as is

4. A 4. Donna <u>asked, "who</u> plans to work as a baby sitter over the summer?"

   (A) asked, "Who
   (B) asked "who
   (C) asked, Who
   (D) Correct as is

5. D 5. Angela and Wanda painted the <u>mural, and Jamal</u> attached it to the wall in the gym.

   (A) mural and Jamal
   (B) mural: and Jamal
   (C) mural, and jamal
   (D) Correct as is

6. C 6. Many television programs have closed captioning for <u>people who cant</u> hear.

   (A) people, who cant
   (B) people, who can't
   (C) people who can't
   (D) Correct as is

7. B 7. "What a great time we had at the <u>park"! Sandy</u> exclaimed as she got into the car.

   (A) Park"! Sandy
   (B) park!" Sandy
   (C) park", Sandy
   (D) Correct as is

8. D 8. "<u>Your aunt Helen</u> certainly is a fascinating person," Carla said.

   (A) "Your Aunt Helen
   (B) "Your aunt, Helen
   (C) Your aunt Helen
   (D) Correct as is

9. "Many of us would have gone to the picnic if we had known about it" Alan said.   9. B

   (A) it",
   (B) it,"
   (C) it,
   (D) Correct as is

10. The Zunigas have a new puppy; its a cocker spaniel.   10. B

    (A) puppy; Its
    (B) puppy; it's
    (C) puppy, its
    (D) Correct as is

11. The ants carried large leafs across John Henry's backyard.   11. C

    (A) carryed large leafs
    (B) carryed large leaves
    (C) carried large leaves
    (D) Correct as is

12. Has the guide all ready led the hikers to the top of the mesa?   12. C

    (A) all ready lead
    (B) already lead
    (C) already led
    (D) Correct as is

13. If Carlos wants to play the role of Eddie in the musical, he'll have too practice the solos.   13. A

    (A) musical, he'll have to practice
    (B) musical; he'll have to practice
    (C) musical he'll have too practice
    (D) Correct as is

14. Sara said that the big guppy in the class aquarium is going to have babies.   14. D

    (A) Sara said "That the big guppy in the class aquarium is going to have babies."
    (B) Sara said "that the big guppy in the class aquarium is going to have babies."
    (C) Sara said "That the big guppy in the class aquarium is going to have babies".
    (D) Correct as is

15. On October 1 1960 Nigeria became an independent nation.   15. B

    (A) October, 1 1960
    (B) October 1, 1960,
    (C) October 1, 1960
    (D) Correct as is

Mechanics   409

RESOURCES

Correcting Common Errors

Review
- *Language & Sentence Skills Practice,* pp. 391–393

Assessment
- *Holt Handbook Chapter Tests with Answer Key,* pp. 33–34, 47

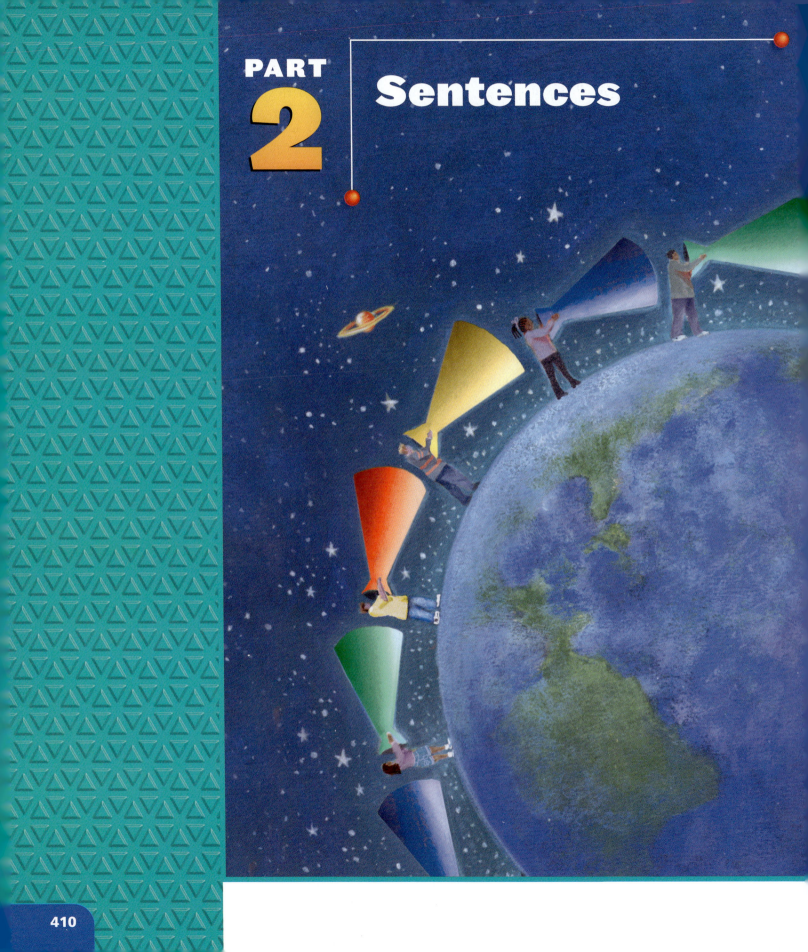

PART 2 | Sentences

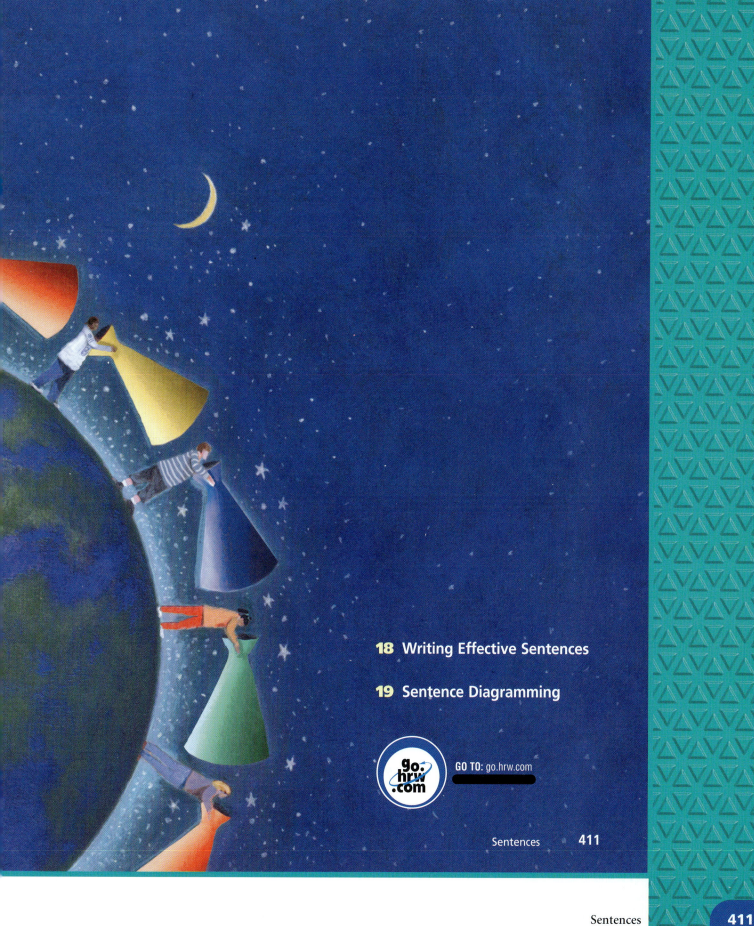

18 Writing Effective Sentences

19 Sentence Diagramming

CHAPTER 18

Writing Effective Sentences

INTRODUCING THE CHAPTER

- In this chapter, students will learn how to identify and correct sentence fragments and run-on sentences. They will also learn strategies for combining sentences, revising stringy and wordy sentences, and improving sentence style. Finally, they will cover varying sentence beginnings, varying sentence structures, and using transitions.
- For help in integrating this chapter with writing assignments, use the **Teaching Strands** chart on pp. T24–T25.

Terms in brackets refer to concepts tested by the items in the Diagnostic Preview.

1. The mouse makes a noise [fragment]
2. sentence [sentence]
3. ⊙ [run-on]
4. Tell me [fragment]
5. ∧ and [run-on]
6. ∧ so [compound sentence]
7. and [compound verb]
8. and butterflies [compound subject]

Diagnostic Preview

A. Identifying Sentences, Sentence Fragments, and Run-on Sentences

Identify each of the following word groups as a *sentence*, a *sentence fragment*, or a *run-on sentence*. Rewrite each fragment and run-on to make one or more complete sentences.

Here are possible answers.

EXAMPLE 1. After we left.
1. sentence fragment—After we left, I sighed.

1. ∧Like the sound of my pencil on paper.
2. Before we go, please pack the suitcases.
3. Lunch tasted great∧ we finished everything on our plates.
4. ∧If you think the answer is twenty-two or twenty-four.
5. At sunrise I climbed out of bed∧ then I brushed my teeth.

B. Combining Sentences

Combine the sentences in the following items.

EXAMPLE 1. Jon left early. He didn't feel well.
1. Jon left early because he didn't feel well.

Here are possible revisions.

6. I care about the environment∧ I recycle everything that I can.
7. He collects rocks∧ He keeps them in a special box.
8. Bees∧are flying insects that help pollinate flowers. Butterflies are flying insects that help pollinate flowers.

412 Chapter 18 Writing Effective Sentences

CHAPTER RESOURCES

Internet

- Web resources: go.hrw.com

Practice & Review
- *Language & Sentence Skills Practice,* pp. 399–404, 407–418, 421–428; 405–406, 419–420, 429–430

- *Language & Sentence Skills Practice Answer Key,* pp. 166–175

9. She sculpts paper clips into ∧pyramids. ~~The pyramids are tiny.~~
10. Ms. Merriam∧sometimes plays piano for our class. ~~She is one of our best teachers.~~

9. tiny [inserting words]
10. ∧one of our best teachers, [appositive phrase]

C. Revising Stringy and Wordy Sentences

Each of the following sentences is stringy, wordy, or both. Revise each sentence to make it simpler and clearer.

EXAMPLE 1. Robbie covered the floor with crackers, but his sitter walked in, and she gasped, and she picked Robbie up.
  1. *Robbie covered the floor with crackers. His sitter walked in, gasped, and picked Robbie up.*

Revisions will vary.
11. ∧Felicia and her family visited Carlsbad Caverns, ~~and~~ they spent the whole afternoon inside the cave, ~~but~~ they came out in the evening, and ~~they~~ watched the bats emerge.
12. Felicia's brother wanted to take a picture, but the ranger stopped him, and ~~she~~ told him to put his camera away.
13. He smiled at her, ~~and that was a polite thing for him to have done~~, but he still really wanted a picture.
14. ~~Due to the fact that~~ he had put his camera away, the ranger told him that she had a poster that she could give him.
15. The ranger walked to her bag, ~~and she~~ took out a poster ~~that was a poster~~ of a bat, and ~~she~~ gave the poster to him.

11. When/⊙/[stringy sentence]
12. [stringy sentence]
13. politely [stringy sentence, wordy sentence]
14. Because [wordy sentence]
15. it [stringy sentence, wordy sentence]

D. Creating Sentence Variety and Using Transitions

Revise the following paragraph to create sentences of different length and structure, vary sentence beginnings, and improve transitions between thoughts.

EXAMPLE   I like to watch storms. I especially like exciting storms.
   I especially like to watch exciting storms.

Revisions will vary.
   A storm rolled in after sunset last night. Lightning lit the sky. ~~It was on the horizon.~~ The warm wind cooled, ∧The breeze smelled like wet asphalt. The birds were silent. ∧We sat on the porch, ∧The storm got closer. We watched the lightning, ~~It flickered~~. The thunder rumbled, ~~It~~ shook the porch, ~~It~~ rumbled again, ∧The porch shook ~~again~~. I grew worried, ∧I imagined that I was a wilted tree, ~~I imagined that I was~~ a patch of dried grass, I felt better about the storm, ∧It looked like a welcome relief.

[sentence variety, transitions]

on the horizon
∧ and
As
∧/flicker
∧/∧ and
As/∧/Then
or/Then
and thought

Writing Complete Sentences

(pp. 414–418)

OBJECTIVES

- To identify and revise sentence fragments
- To identify and revise run-on sentences

DIRECT TEACHING

Modeling and Demonstration

Sentence Fragments. Model how to determine whether a group of words is a sentence or a sentence fragment and how to revise a fragment by using the incorrect example *The bird nest in the top of the oak tree.* First, ask students whether the group of words has a subject. [yes—*nest*] Then, ask whether the group of words has a verb. [no] Point out that we don't know about the nest—The bird nest *what*? Ask what verb would make the group of words a sentence. [*is*; answers may vary] Finally, ask whether the word group expresses a complete thought, now that a verb has been added. [yes] Now, have a volunteer use another example from this chapter to demonstrate how to identify and correct a sentence fragment.

HELP

A word group that has a subject and a verb and that expresses a complete thought is an **independent clause.** All complete sentences contain at least one independent clause.

Reference Note

For more information about **independent clauses,** see page 114.

Reference Note

For more information on **imperative sentences,** see page 18.

TIPS & TRICKS

Some words look like verbs but really aren't. These "fake" verbs can fool you into thinking a group of words is a sentence when it is really a fragment. A word that ends in *–ing* cannot stand as a verb unless it has a helping verb (such as *is, are,* or *were*) with it.

FRAGMENT
The children playing on the swings. [Without a helping verb, this is not a complete thought.]

SENTENCE
The children **were playing** on the swings.

Writing Complete Sentences

One of the best ways to make your writing clear is to use complete sentences. A **complete sentence**

- has a subject
- has a verb
- expresses a complete thought

SENTENCES Trees absorb excess carbon dioxide in the atmosphere. [The subject is *Trees.* The verb is *absorb.*]

Are some species in danger of extinction? [The subject is *species.* The verb is *Are.*]

The sentences above express complete thoughts. That is, each sentence has a topic (the subject) and tells you something about that topic.

NOTE **Imperative sentences** (sentences that express a command or direct request) have understood subjects. That is, the subject of the sentence is not expressed in the sentence but is understood to be *you.*

REQUEST Please tell me more. [The subject is understood to be *you.* The verb is *tell.*]

COMMAND Listen! [The subject is understood to be *you.* The verb is *Listen.*]

Sentence Fragments

Incomplete sentences are called sentence fragments. A **sentence fragment** is a word or word group that looks like a sentence but that has no subject, has no verb, or does not express a complete thought. Because it is incomplete, a sentence fragment can confuse your reader.

FRAGMENT Went to the grocery store yesterday. [This word group contains no subject. Who went to the grocery store yesterday?]

SENTENCE **We** went to the grocery store yesterday.

FRAGMENT The bird nest in the top of the oak tree. [This word group contains no verb. What about the bird nest in the top of the oak tree?]

414  Writing Effective Sentences

---

RESOURCES

Writing Complete Sentences

Practice

- *Language & Sentence Skills Practice,* pp. 399–406
- *Developmental Language & Sentence Skills,* pp. 139–142

SENTENCE	The bird nest **is** in the top of the oak tree.
FRAGMENT	Before the ice on the lake melts. [Although this word group contains a subject and a verb, it does not express a complete thought. What will happen before the ice on the lake melts?]
SENTENCE	**We will go skating** before the ice on the lake melts.
FRAGMENT	My friend Larry, who has a good voice. [This word group contains a subject, *friend,* but that subject doesn't have a verb. What about my friend Larry, who has a good voice?]
SENTENCE	My friend Larry, who has a good voice, **is singing.**

As you can see from the examples, you can correct some sentence fragments by adding a subject or a verb. Other fragments need to be attached to an independent clause to make a complete sentence.

Oral Practice — Identifying Sentence Fragments

Read each of the following groups of words aloud, and decide whether it is a sentence fragment or a complete sentence.

F 1. A flying squirrel a squirrel that can gracefully glide through the air.
F 2. Some Asian flying squirrels three feet long.
F 3. Skillfully leaps from one tree to another.
S 4. The squirrel glides downward, then straight, and finally upward.
F 5. Some flying squirrels more than fifty feet.
F 6. If they use a higher starting point.
S 7. Flying squirrels live in the forests of Asia, Europe, and North America.
F 8. To eat berries, birds' eggs, insects, and nuts.
F 9. Nesting in the hollows of trees.
S 10. Notice how this squirrel stretches out its legs to help it glide.

HELP
Remember that a complete sentence meets three requirements: It has a subject, it has a verb, and it expresses a complete thought.

EXTENSION

Relating to Literature

Fragments in Dialogue. Consider using a selection such as Anne McCaffrey's "The Smallest Dragonboy," in which the author intentionally uses sentence fragments in dialogue. Ask students to locate pieces of dialogue that are not complete sentences. Then, ask them why the author might have chosen to write these sentence fragments. [*The fragments reflect the way a person or character naturally speaks.*] Explain that while experienced writers, such as novelists or poets, may use fragments for effect, students should not use fragments in their formal writing for school.

MINI-LESSON — Usage — *Continued on pp. 416–417*

Cloze: Filling in the Missing Pieces. A cloze activity provides students with the opportunity to make meaning from sentences that lack essential pieces of information. Students use context and prior knowledge to fill in the gaps and make sense of the sentences. Because sentence fragments are word groups that are missing subjects or verbs or both, students may benefit from using a cloze activity. Work as a class or have students work in randomly assigned groups of two or three to complete

EXTENSION

Critical Thinking

Analysis. Before students analyze their own writing for examples of run-on sentences, write the following strategy on the chalkboard. Tell students to use the strategy as they look for run-on sentences.

- Look at the word count of your sentences. (If you are writing on a word processor, it probably has a function that can do this for you.) If your sentences have more than sixteen or seventeen words each, you should look at them more closely to see if they are run-ons.

Exercise 1   Finding and Revising Fragments

Some of the following groups of words are sentence fragments. Revise each fragment so that it contains a subject and a verb and expresses a complete thought. If an item is already a complete sentence, write S.

EXAMPLE   1. As soon as we finished eating breakfast.
1. *We left for our camping trip as soon as we finished eating breakfast.*

Possible revisions follow.

1. The storm began
2. S
3. , we unpacked
4. ran
5. We
6. S
7. We
8. S
9. was
10. , I cleaned the fish

1. As the whole family loaded into the car.
2. We traveled for hours.
3. When we arrived at the campground.
4. My sister and I down to the river.
5. Took our fishing gear with us.
6. We cast our lines the way our aunt had taught us.
7. Caught several trout in a few hours.
8. We headed back to the campsite at sunset.
9. Dad cooking bean soup over the fire.
10. While Mom and my sister pitched the tent.

Run-on Sentences

A **run-on sentence** is a word group made up of two complete sentences that have been run together with no punctuation between them or with only a comma between them. Run-on sentences make it hard for the reader to tell where one thought ends and another begins.

RUN-ON   Mockingbirds are great mimics they can imitate the songs of at least twenty other bird species.

CORRECT   Mockingbirds are great mimics**.** **T**hey can imitate the songs of at least twenty other bird species.

RUN-ON   People say that life is short, there are some redwoods more than 1,500 years old.

CORRECT   People say that life is short**, but** there are some redwoods more than 1,500 years old.

NOTE   A comma does mark a brief pause in a sentence, but it does not show the end of a sentence. If you use just a comma between two sentences, you create a run-on sentence.

416   Chapter 18   Writing Effective Sentences

 Usage   **Continued from p. 415**

the cloze activity that follows. After students complete the exercise, explain that only subjects and verbs are missing from the sentences and that each item is actually a sentence fragment. Possible answers appear in brackets.

1. This ____ a story about Claudia. [*is*]
2. ____ was walking to school one rainy day. [*Claudia*]
3. She ____ an amazing thing. [*saw*]
4. ____ unbelievable! [*It was*]

416   Writing Effective Sentences

Revising Run-on Sentences

Here are three ways you can revise run-on sentences.

1. You can make two sentences.

   RUN-ON Asteroids are tiny planets they are sometimes called planetoids.

   CORRECT Asteroids are tiny planets. They are sometimes called planetoids.

2. You can use a comma and a coordinating conjunction such as *and*, *but*, or *or*.

   RUN-ON Some asteroids shine with a steady light, others keep changing in brightness.

   CORRECT Some asteroids shine with a steady light, but others keep changing in brightness.

3. You can use a semicolon.

   RUN-ON Asteroids vary greatly in size, they range from about twenty feet across to about 600 miles in diameter.

   CORRECT Asteroids vary greatly in size; they range from about twenty feet across to about 600 miles in diameter.

Reference Note

For more information about **coordinating conjunctions,** see page 62. For information about **semicolons;** see page 310.

Exercise 2 Identifying and Revising Run-on Sentences

Decide which of the following groups of words are run-on sentences. Then, revise each run-on in one of the ways shown above. If the group of words is already correct, write *C*.
Sample revisions follow.

1. Saturn is a huge planet it is more than nine times larger than Earth. **1. ;**
2. Saturn is covered by clouds, it is circled by bands of color. **2. and**
3. Some of the clouds are yellow, others are off-white. **3. but**
4. Saturn has about twenty moons Titan is the largest. **4. ⊙**
5. Many of Saturn's moons have large craters the crater on Mimas covers one third of its diameter. **5. ⊙**
6. Saturn's most striking feature is a group of rings that circles the planet. **6. C**
7. The rings of Saturn are less than two miles thick, they spread out from the planet for a great distance. **7. and**
8. The rings are made up of billions of tiny particles. **8. C**
9. Some of the rings are dark, but others are brighter. **9. C**
10. You can use a telescope to view Saturn, you can visit a planetarium. **10. or**

DIFFERENTIATING INSTRUCTION

Advanced Learners

Some students might practice correcting run-on sentences in more sophisticated ways than those shown on p. 417. For example, if two independent clauses are joined by a conjunctive adverb, such as *however*, *therefore*, or *consequently*, the correct punctuation is a semicolon before the conjunctive adverb and a comma after it.

EXAMPLE:
I enjoyed the game; however, it was only the first time I had played it.

Encourage students to revise some of the sentences in **Exercise 2** by using semicolons and conjunctive adverbs.

---

5. Because her glasses were streaked with rain, ____ couldn't see clearly. [*Claudia*]
6. Then she ____ more closely. [*looked*]
7. ____ a dog wearing a red hat and carrying a basket of flowers. [*It was/Claudia saw*]
8. She ____ a friend, "What's going on?" [*asked*]
9. ____ was also confused. [*The friend*]
10. Actually, ____ the team mascot raising money for school. [*it was*]

SENTENCES

Combining Sentences
(pp. 418–428)

OBJECTIVES

- To combine sentences by inserting words and phrases
- To combine sentences by using *and*, *but*, and *or*
- To combine sentences by creating compound subjects and verbs and by forming compound sentences
- To combine sentences by using subordinate clauses

DIRECT TEACHING

Modeling and Demonstration

Combining Sentences. Model how to combine sentences by using the examples *Edison created a talking doll* and *He created the talking doll in 1894.* First, ask whether the two sentences are about the same subject. [yes—*Edison*] Next, ask whether the two sentences repeat any of the same information. [yes—*created a talking doll; created the talking doll*] Point out that when information is repeated in two sentences, it is often possible to move information from one sentence to the other sentence. Next, ask what information could be moved from the second sentence to the first sentence. [*when the talking doll was created*] Then, ask which word or words can be used to combine the sentences. [*in 1894*] Point out that the sentences could be combined in this way: *Edison created a talking doll in 1894.* Now, have a volunteer use another example from this chapter to demonstrate how to combine two sentences.

Review A Correcting Sentence Fragments and Run-on Sentences

Identify the sentence fragments and run-on sentences in the following paragraph. Then, revise each sentence fragment and run-on sentence to make the paragraph clearer.

Here is a possible revision.

EXAMPLE Visited the Mojave Desert.
I visited the Mojave Desert.

Many deserts have very little plant life,∧ some desert regions have a variety of plants. Many plants can survive, Where the climate is hot and dry. Cacti, Joshua trees, palm trees, and wildflowers grow in deserts∧ those plants do not grow close together. They are spread out,∧ each plant gets water and minerals from a large area.

but *so*

Combining Sentences

Although short sentences can sometimes express your ideas well, using only short sentences will make your writing sound choppy and dull. For example, read the following paragraph, which has only short sentences.

   Thomas Edison invented the phonograph. He also experimented with mechanical toys. Many people do not know this. Edison created a talking doll. He created the talking doll in 1894. The doll would recite a nursery rhyme or poem. It said the words when a crank in its back was turned. The talking doll was very popular. Edison opened a factory. The factory made five hundred of the dolls every day.

Now read the revised paragraph. Notice how the writer has combined some of the short sentences to make longer, smoother sentences.

418 Chapter 18   Writing Effective Sentences

RESOURCES

Combining Sentences

Practice

- *Language & Sentence Skills Practice*, pp. 407–420
- *Developmental Language & Sentence Skills*, pp. 143–148

418   Writing Effective Sentences

```
    Thomas Edison invented the phono-
graph. Many people do not know that
he also experimented with mechanical
toys. Edison created a talking doll
in 1894. When a crank in its back was
turned, the doll would recite a nurs-
ery rhyme or poem. The talking doll
was very popular, and Edison opened a
factory that made five hundred of the
dolls every day.
```

Sentence combining also helps to reduce the number of repeated words and ideas. The revised paragraph is clearer, shorter, and more interesting to read. The following pages contain strategies for combining sentences. Once you learn these strategies, you can apply them to your own writing.

Combining Sentences by Inserting Words

One way to combine short sentences is to take an important word from one sentence and insert it into another sentence. Sometimes you will need to change the form of the word before you can insert it. You can change some words into adjectives by adding an ending such as *–ed*, *–ing*, *–ful*, or *–ly*. The adjective can describe another word in the sentence.

ORIGINAL	Easter lily plants have leaves. The leaves have points.
COMBINED	Easter lily plants have **pointed** leaves.

Reference Note
For more information about **adjectives,** see page 34.

Exercise 3 Combining Sentences by Inserting Words

Each of the following items contains two sentences. To combine the two sentences, take the italicized word from the second sentence and insert it into the first sentence. The directions in parentheses will tell you how to change the form of the word if you need to do so.

EXAMPLE
1. Peanuts are the tiny fruit of the peanut plant. They have a good *taste*. (Change *taste* to *tasty*.)
1. Peanuts are the tiny, tasty fruit of the peanut plant.

RETEACHING

Combining Sentences

Point out to students that the repetition of words is an important clue that tells them sentences can be combined. Write the original example sentences at left on the chalkboard, using colored chalk for the repeated words. [*leaves, have*] Explain that the repeated words should appear only once in the combined sentence. Remind students to use this technique of identifying repeated or similar words as they complete Exercise 3.

EXTENSION

Relating to Mechanics

Combining sentences by inserting words often results in two or more adjectives preceding a noun. Remind students that if the word *and* would make sense between the adjectives, then a comma is needed between them. Write the following sentences on the chalkboard and have students determine if and where a comma is needed.

1. Poe was a great fiction writer. [*Using the* and *rule, the sentence reads "Poe was a great and fiction writer," which doesn't make sense, so no comma is necessary here.*]

2. Poe led a short tragic life. [*Here the sentence "Poe led a short and tragic life" does make sense, so a comma is needed between the words* short *and* tragic.]

 Learning for Life

Continued on p. 420

Students are probably at a stage in their lives when they have only vague ideas of what jobs or careers they might want to pursue when they are older, and they probably have no idea that many jobs have a writing component. Ask volunteers to name the careers that sound interesting to them. Then, take time to discuss whether

1. This picture shows peanuts ˰underground. ~~They grow underground.~~ (Add –*ing*.) **1. growing**
2. Peanuts are a ˰crop of many warm regions. ~~They are a *major* crop.~~ **2. major**
3. Peanuts are a ˰food for snacking. ~~Peanuts are good for your *health*.~~ (Add –*ful*.) **3. healthful**
4. The oil from peanuts is used in many ˰dressings. ~~The dressings are for *salad*.~~ **4. salad**
5. ˰Grades of peanut oil are used to make soap and shampoo. ~~The *low* grades are used for these products.~~ **5. Low**
6. Much of the world grows peanuts solely for their ˰oil. ~~This oil is *versatile*.~~ **6. versatile**
7. The ˰peanut-producing countries include China, India, and the United States. ~~These countries *lead* the world in peanut production.~~ (Add –*ing*.) **7. leading**
8. Some ˰soils will stain the peanut shells. ~~*Dark* soils are responsible for the stains.~~ **8. dark**
9. After peanuts are harvested, the plants are used for ˰feed. ~~The feed is for *livestock*.~~ **9. livestock**
10. Peanuts are a good source of ˰vitamins. ~~Peanuts contain *B* vitamins.~~ **10. B**

Combining Sentences by Inserting Phrases

A **phrase** is a group of words that acts as a single part of speech and that does not have both a subject and a verb. You can combine sentences by taking a phrase from one sentence and inserting it into another sentence.

ORIGINAL	Arachne is a famous figure. She is a figure in Greek mythology.
COMBINED	Arachne is a famous figure **in Greek mythology.** [The prepositional phrase *in Greek mythology* is inserted into the first sentence.]
ORIGINAL	Arachne was proud. She was proud of her weaving.
COMBINED	Arachne was proud **of her weaving.** [The prepositional phrase *of her weaving* is inserted into the first sentence.]

DIFFERENTIATING INSTRUCTION

English-Language Learners

General Strategies. To assist students with sentence combining, explain that the easiest phrases to use in sentence combining are prepositional phrases. Point out that students may find it helpful to identify prepositional phrases by first picking out the prepositions. Since English-language learners often have trouble identifying prepositions in English, you may want to take time to review with them a list of the most common ones. Refer students to **Chapter 3** for more information about prepositions.

Learning for Life

those jobs will require them to write effectively. Remind students that jobs in the fields of police work, journalism, medicine, consulting, business, social work, customer service, and law all demand good writing in the forms of formal reports, letters, memos, or public statements.

Continued from p. 419

NOTE Before you insert a phrase into a sentence, ask yourself whether the phrase renames or identifies a noun or pronoun. If it does, it is an **appositive phrase,** and you may need to set it off with one or more commas.

ORIGINAL Arachne challenged Athena to a weaving contest. Athena was the goddess of wisdom.

COMBINED Arachne challenged Athena**, the goddess of wisdom,** to a weaving contest. [The appositive phrase in boldface type renames the noun *Athena.*]

Reference Note

For more information and practice on using commas to set off **appositive phrases,** see page 301.

Another way to combine sentences is to change the verb and create a new phrase. Just add *–ing* or *–ed* to the verb, or put the word *to* in front of it. You can then use the new phrase to describe a noun, verb, or pronoun in a related sentence.

ORIGINAL The name *Inuit* refers to several groups of people. These people live in and near the Arctic.

COMBINED The name *Inuit* refers to several groups of people **living in and near the Arctic.** [The participial phrase *living in and near the Arctic* describes the noun *people.*]

ORIGINAL Early Inuit followed a special way of life. They did this so they could survive in a harsh environment.

COMBINED **To survive in a harsh environment,** early Inuit followed a special way of life. [The infinitive phrase *To survive in a harsh environment* modifies the verb *followed.*]

Reference Note

For more information about **prepositional, participial, infinitive, and appositive phrases,** see pages 89–106.

NOTE When you combine sentences by adding a word or phrase from one sentence to another sentence, the resulting sentence may contain a compound phrase. Be sure to keep the compound elements **parallel,** or matching in form. Otherwise, instead of making your writing smoother, combining may actually make it more awkward.

ORIGINAL Ana likes to hike. Ana also likes cycling.
NOT PARALLEL Ana likes to hike and cycling. [*To hike* is an infinitive; *cycling* is a gerund.]
PARALLEL Ana likes hiking and cycling. [*Hiking* and *cycling* are both gerunds.]

HELP

An **infinitive** is a verb form, often beginning with *to,* that can be used as a noun, an adjective, or an adverb. A **gerund** is a verb form ending in *–ing* that is used as a noun.

Combining Sentences

DIFFERENTIATING INSTRUCTION

Learners Having Difficulty

Students may need help understanding that a written sentence is not a rigid unit but a relatively flexible chain of words that may be grouped and regrouped. Have students write both example sentences in **Exercise 4** in large letters on a sheet of paper, using a different color ink for each sentence. Then, have them cut up the sentences into individual words. Now, demonstrate how words or phrases from one sentence can move into another by manipulating the cut pieces of paper. The colors will show more clearly how one sentence is combined with another. Challenge students to create other new sentences by moving the pieces of paper around on their desks.

Exercise 4 Combining Sentences by Inserting Phrases

Each of the following items contains two sentences. Combine the sentences by taking the italicized word group from the second sentence and inserting it into the first sentence. The hints in parentheses tell you how to change the forms of words if you need to do so. Remember to insert commas where they are needed.

EXAMPLE
1. The Inuit followed their traditional way of life. They followed this way of life *for thousands of years.*

1. The Inuit followed their traditional way of life for thousands of years.

1. The Inuit built winter shelters in a few hours. ~~They~~ *stacked blocks of snow.* (Change *stacked* to *Stacking.*)   **1. Stacking blocks of snow,**
2. They used harpoons. ~~This is how they~~ *hunted seals.* (Change *hunted* to *to hunt.*)   **2. to hunt seals.**
3. The Inuit also hunted and ate caribou. ~~Caribou are~~ *a type of deer.*   **3. , a type of deer.**
4. Whalers and fur traders came to the region and affected the Inuit way of life. ~~They arrived~~ *in the 1800s.*   **4. in the 1800s**
5. The Inuit often moved several times a year. ~~They moved so that they could~~ *find food.* (Change *find* to *to find.*)   **5. to find food.**   **6. made from animal skin.**
6. During the summer, traditional Inuit lived in tents. ~~The tents were~~ *made from animal skin.*
7. In the 1800s, many Inuit began to trap animals. ~~They trapped animals~~ *for European fur traders.*
8. Some Inuit worked on whaling ships. ~~They~~ *needed to find other ways to provide for their families.* (Change *need* to *Needing.*)
9. The Inuit have survived for thousands of years. ~~They have survived~~ *in the harsh Arctic climate.*
10. Most Inuit today follow a modern way of life. ~~They are~~ *like the Canadian Inuit seen in the photo on this page.*

7. for European fur traders.
8. Needing to find other ways to provide for their families,
9. in the harsh Arctic climate.
10. Like the Canadian Inuit seen in the photo on this page,

Combining Sentences Using *And, But,* or *Or*

You can also use the coordinating conjunctions *and*, *but*, and *or* to combine sentences. Doing so is called **coordination**. With these connecting words, you can make a *compound subject*, a *compound verb*, or a *compound sentence*.

Compound Subjects and Verbs

Sometimes two sentences have the same verb with different subjects. You can combine the sentences by linking the two subjects with *and* or *or* to make a **compound subject**.

ORIGINAL	Dolphins look a little like fish. Porpoises look a little like fish.
COMBINED	**Dolphins and porpoises** look a little like fish.

Two sentences can also have the same subject with different verbs. You can use *and*, *but*, or *or* to connect the two verbs. The result is a **compound verb**.

ORIGINAL	Dolphins live in water like fish. They breathe like other mammals.
COMBINED	Dolphins **live** in water like fish **but breathe** like other mammals.

Exercise 5 — Combining Sentences by Creating Compound Subjects and Verbs

Combine each of the following pairs of short, choppy sentences by using *and*, *but*, or *or*. If the two sentences have the same verb, make a compound subject. If they have the same subject, make a compound verb. Remember to keep the ideas in parallel form.

EXAMPLE
1. Dolphins belong to a group of mammals called cetaceans. Porpoises belong to a group of mammals called cetaceans.
    1. Dolphins and porpoises belong to a group of mammals called cetaceans.

Here are possible revisions. 1. and porpoises
1. Dolphins are warm-blooded. ~~Porpoises are warm-blooded.~~
2. Common dolphins live in warm waters. ~~Common dolphins swim in large schools.~~   2. and swim in large schools
3. Porpoises are similar to dolphins. ~~Porpoises~~ generally live in cooler water.   3. but

---

TIPS & TRICKS

When you use the coordinating conjunction *and* to link two subjects, your new compound subject will be a plural subject. Remember to make the verb agree with the subject in number.

ORIGINAL
Zach likes watching the sea mammals. Briana likes watching the sea mammals.

COMBINED
Zach and Briana like watching the sea mammals. [The plural verb *like* is needed with the plural subject *Zach and Briana*.]

For more information on **agreement of subjects and verbs,** see page 148.

HELP

When deciding whether to use *and*, *but*, or *or*, follow these rules.

- *And* shows equality. Use it if you mean *both*.
  Katie **and** Tyrone are my friends.

- *But* shows contrast. Use it to point out something *different*.
  Katie likes to play tennis, **but** Tyrone does not.

- *Or* shows a choice. Use it if you have *options*.
  Usually either Katie **or** Tyrone waits for me after school.

EXTENSION

Relating to Usage

Subject-Verb Agreement. One way that students can make sure that they have correctly used plural verbs with compound subjects joined by *and* is to substitute the word *they* for any compound subject. If the verb agrees in number with the subject *they*, then the verb is correct.

SENTENCES

DIRECT TEACHING

Correcting Misconceptions
Compound Verbs or Compound Sentences? Some students may incorrectly insert commas before conjunctions that link compound verbs. Remind students that a comma is used before a conjunction when two sentences are combined to create a compound sentence. Write the following sentences on the chalkboard and discuss them with students.

1. Zoe finished her lemonade and asked for another.
   [*Sentence 1 is a simple sentence with a compound verb.* Zoe finished and asked.]

2. Zoe finished her lemonade, and she asked for another.
   [*Sentence 2 is a compound sentence containing two independent clauses joined by a comma and the conjunction* and. Zoe finished her lemonade. She asked for another.]

Use colored chalk to highlight the compound verb in sentence 1 [*finished, asked*] and the two subjects and two verbs in sentence 2 [*Zoe finished; she asked*]. Now, ask students to write two compound sentences and two simple sentences with compound verbs. Then, have partners check one another's sentences.

EXTENSION

Relating to Grammar
Verb Tense. Remind students that when they combine two sentences into a compound sentence, they have to consider the tense of the verbs. For example, two sentences like "My cousins arrived" and "We go skating" cannot be easily combined, because the verb tenses differ. Point out that verb tense should be consistent.

---

4. Dolphins have beak-like snouts. Dolphins use sonar to locate objects under water.   4. and
5. Dolphins hunt fish. Dolphins eat fish.   5. and eat
6. Dolphins swim by moving their tails up and down. Porpoises swim by moving their tails up and down.   6. and porpoises
7. Porpoises can swim fast. Dolphins can swim fast.
8. A porpoise could outswim most sharks. A tuna could outswim most sharks.   7. and dolphins   8. or a tuna
9. Bottle-nosed dolphins can measure up to fifteen feet in length. Bottle-nosed dolphins can weigh over four hundred pounds.   9. and can weigh over four hundred pounds.
10. Sharks sometimes attack porpoises. Sharks sometimes kill porpoises.   10. and kill

Compound Sentences

Sometimes you will want to combine two sentences that express equally important ideas. You can connect two closely related, equally important sentences by using a comma plus the coordinating conjunction *and*, *but*, or *or*. Doing so creates a **compound sentence.**

ORIGINAL	My brother entered the Annual Chili Cook-off. His chili won a prize.
COMBINED	My brother entered the Annual Chili Cook-off**, and** his chili won a prize.
ORIGINAL	I did not help cook. I helped him clean the kitchen.
COMBINED	I did not help cook**, but** I helped him clean the kitchen.

NOTE A compound sentence tells the reader that the two ideas are closely related. If you combine two short sentences that are not closely related, you may confuse your reader.

UNRELATED	Fernando mowed the grass, and I had a broom.
RELATED	Fernando mowed the grass, and I swept the sidewalk.

Exercise 6 Combining Sentences by Forming a Compound Sentence

Each of the following pairs of sentences is closely related. Make each pair into a compound sentence by adding a comma and a coordinating conjunction such as *and* or *but*.

EXAMPLE 1. The Pueblos have lived in the same location for a long time. They have strong ties to their homeland.

1. *The Pueblos have lived in the same location for a long time, and they have strong ties to their homeland.*

Here are possible combinations.
1. Some Pueblos built villages in the valleys. Others settled in desert and mountain areas.   **1. , but**
2. Desert surrounded many of the valleys. The people grew crops with the help of irrigation systems.   **2. , but**
3. Women gathered berries and other foods. Men hunted game.   **3. , and**
4. Their adobe homes had several stories. The people used ladders to reach the upper levels.   **4. , and**
5. The Pueblos were generally peaceful. Some Pueblo tribes drove the Spanish from their territories.   **5. , but**
6. Today, each Pueblo village has its own government. The Pueblo people still share many customs.   **6. , but**
7. Long ago, women helped farm. Now only men cultivate Pueblo lands.   **7. , but**
8. Pueblo social life is still centered on the village. Native religion is important.   **8. , and**
9. Arts and crafts are part of the Pueblo economy. Pueblos also raise new kinds of crops.   **9. , but**
10. The Pueblos share many things with their ancestors. They enjoy much of modern life.   **10. , but**

Combining Sentences Using Subordinate Clauses

A *clause* is a group of words that contains a subject and a verb. *Independent clauses* can stand alone as a sentence. *Subordinate* (or *dependent*) *clauses* cannot stand alone because they do not express a complete thought.

| INDEPENDENT CLAUSE | Gertrude Ederle swam the English Channel. [This clause can stand alone.] |
| SUBORDINATE CLAUSE | when she was nineteen years old [This clause cannot stand alone.] |

You can combine related sentences by using a subordinate clause. Doing so is called *subordination.* The resulting sentence is called a *complex sentence.* The subordinate clause gives information about a word or idea in the independent clause.

Reference Note
For more information on **independent clauses** and **subordinate clauses,** see page 113.

Reference Note
For more information on **complex sentences,** see page 135.

Combining Sentences   425

DIFFERENTIATING INSTRUCTION

Learners Having Difficulty
You may wish to help students distinguish between independent and subordinate clauses. List a number of independent and subordinate clauses on the chalkboard. Then, ask volunteers to underline the subjects once and the verbs twice in both types of clauses. Finally, ask one volunteer to write an *I* next to the independent clauses. Ask another to write an *S* next to the subordinate clauses and to explain why these cannot be complete sentences.

DIRECT TEACHING

Complex Sentences

Relative Pronouns. As they create complex sentences by combining with subordinate clauses, students may benefit from your pointing out the distinctions between the relative pronouns *who, which,* and *that.* Explain that *who* refers to people only, *which* refers to things only, and *that* refers to people or things. Point out that the category *things* includes animals, organizations, and places. Write the following examples on the chalkboard and ask students to determine to what each underlined relative pronoun refers.

- Fernando is the man <u>who</u> installed the modem for our computer. [man]
- He had to move the computer, <u>which</u> needed to be connected to a cable line. [computer]
- Media Global, <u>which</u> is the local cable company, gave us the modem. [*Media Global*]
- Sue is the technician <u>that</u> trained my family to use the Internet. [technician]
- My mother designed a Web site <u>that</u> will help her at-home business grow. [*Web site*]

Reference Note
A clause that begins with *who, which,* or *that* and that modifies a noun or pronoun is an **adjective clause.** For more information on **adjective clauses,** see page 117.

Reference Note
A clause that is used to give information about time and place and that modifies a verb, adjective, or adverb is an **adverb clause.** For more information on **adverb clauses,** see page 120.

Reference Note
For more information on the use of **commas with introductory clauses,** see page 305.

| TWO SIMPLE SENTENCES | Theresa traveled to Rome. She saw the Sistine Chapel. |
| ONE COMPLEX SENTENCE | Theresa traveled to Rome, **where she saw the Sistine Chapel.** |

Making Clauses That Begin with *Who, Which,* or *That*

You can often make a short sentence into a subordinate clause by inserting *who, which,* or *that* in place of the subject.

ORIGINAL	The Everglades consist mainly of swamps. The Everglades cover the southern part of Florida.
COMBINED	The Everglades, **which consist mainly of swamps,** cover the southern part of Florida.
ORIGINAL	Everglades National Park is a large area. The area includes about one fifth of the Everglades' original land.
COMBINED	Everglades National Park is a large area **that includes about one fifth of the Everglades' original land.**

Making Clauses with Words of Time or Place

Another way to turn a sentence into a subordinate clause is to add a word that tells time or place. Words that begin this type of clause include *after, before, where, wherever, when, whenever,* and *while.* You may need to delete some words to insert the clause into another sentence.

ORIGINAL	The last ice age ended. Water from the melting ice flooded the area.
COMBINED	**After the last ice age ended,** water from the melting ice flooded the area.
ORIGINAL	No humans lived in the Everglades until 1842. In 1842, Seminoles fled to the area.
COMBINED	No humans lived in the Everglades until 1842, **when Seminoles fled to the area.**

> **NOTE** If you put your time or place clause at the beginning of the sentence, use a comma after the clause.

| ORIGINAL | People began draining the swamps to make farmland. The Everglades were in danger. |
| COMBINED | **When people began draining the swamps to make farmland,** the Everglades were in danger. |

Exercise 7 Combining Sentences by Using Subordinate Clauses

Combine each sentence pair by making one sentence into a subordinate clause and attaching it to the other sentence. You may need to cut a word or two from the second sentence.

EXAMPLE
1. Mother-of-pearl is a substance made by oysters and other mollusks. Mother-of-pearl is also called nacre (pronounced nā'kər). (Use *which*.)

   1. Mother-of-pearl, which is also called nacre (pronounced nā'kər), is a substance made by oysters and other mollusks.

Sample revisions follow.
1. The pearl is a gem. It is made by certain kinds of mollusks. (Use *that*.)
2. The finest pearls are produced by mollusks with special shells. Their shells are lined with mother-of-pearl. (Use *that*.)
3. Pearls are usually formed around particles of sand or dirt. The particles get inside the mollusk. (Use *when*.)
4. The mollusk's shell produces cells. The cells attach themselves to a particle. (Use *that*.)
5. A pearl is formed. The cells cover the particle with mother-of-pearl. (Use *as*.)
6. People culture certain types of pearls. These pearls can be as beautiful as natural pearls. (Use *that*.)
7. The first cultured pearls were grown in China. Chinese pearl divers discovered that they could put bits of mud, wood, bone, or metal inside a living mollusk. (Use *after*.)
8. Seed pearls form. It takes about three years for them to grow into full pearls. (Use *Once*.)
9. Cultured pearls often are grown on boats. Young oysters are raised in barrels. (Use *where*.)
10. A pearl producer puts spheres of polished mother-of-pearl inside the oysters. The oysters are ready to begin forming beautiful new gems. (Use *when*.)

Review B Revising a Paragraph by Combining Sentences

The following paragraph sounds choppy because it has too many short sentences. Use the methods you have learned in this section to combine sentences in the paragraph. A sample revision follows.

Improving Sentence Style
(pp. 428–431)

OBJECTIVES

- To identify and revise stringy sentences
- To identify and revise wordy sentences

EXAMPLE Basketball is an exciting team sport. It is also a popular form of recreation.

Basketball is an exciting team sport as well as a popular form of recreation.

⌃Dr. James Naismith invented the game **When** of basketball over one hundred years ago. ⌃He probably never guessed the sport would become so popular. He just wanted a new game that could be played indoors. The original basketball teams started in 1891. ⌃They had nine players instead **and** of five. The first basket was a peach basket. ⌃A player had to climb up and **and** retrieve the ball after each score. Some parts of the game have stayed the same. Players still cannot hold the ball while they run. ⌃They must dribble. Thousands **but** of teams across the world now play Dr. Naismith's game.

Improving Sentence Style

In addition to combining some sentences, you can also make your writing more effective by revising *stringy* and *wordy sentences* to make them shorter and clearer.

Revising Stringy Sentences

A **stringy sentence** is made up of several complete thoughts strung together with words like *and* or *but*. Stringy sentences just ramble on and on. They don't give the reader a chance to pause before new ideas.

To fix a stringy sentence, you can

- break the sentence into two or more sentences
- turn some of the complete thoughts into phrases or subordinate clauses

STRINGY Martina climbed the stairs of the haunted house, and she knocked on the door several times, but no one answered, and she braced herself, and then she opened the door.

RESOURCES

Improving Sentence Style
Practice

- Language & Sentence Skills Practice, pp. 421–424
- Developmental Language & Sentence Skills, pp. 149–152

REVISED Martina climbed the stairs of the haunted house. She knocked on the door several times, but no one answered. Bracing herself, she opened the door.

NOTE When you revise a stringy sentence, you may decide to keep *and* or *but* between two closely related independent clauses. If you do this, be sure to use a comma before the *and* or *but*.

EXAMPLE She knocked on the door**, but** no one answered.

Reference Note
For more information on **punctuating compound sentences,** see page 131.

Exercise 8 Revising Stringy Sentences

Some of the following sentences are stringy and need to be improved. First, identify the stringy sentences. Then, revise them by (1) breaking each sentence into two or more sentences or (2) turning some of the complete thoughts into phrases or subordinate clauses. If the sentence is effective and does not need to be improved, write *C* for *correct*.   Possible revisions follow.

EXAMPLE 1. I have a hero; and her name is Mercedes O. Cubría, and she had an interesting career.
1. *My hero, Mercedes O. Cubría, had an interesting career.*

1. Mercedes O. Cubría was born in Cuba, but her mother died, and she moved to the United States, and she moved with her two sisters.   1. When
2. She worked as a nurse, and then she joined the Women's Army Corps, and she soon became an officer in the army.   2. After working/
3. Cubría was the first Cuban-born woman to become an officer in the U.S. Army.   3. C
4. Her job during World War II was to translate important government papers into a secret code.   4. C
5. The war ended, and she was promoted to captain, and later her official rank rose to major.   5. After/
6. Then there was the Korean War, and she worked as an intelligence officer, and she studied information about the enemy.
7. Cubría retired from the army in 1953 but was called to duty again in 1962.   6. During/studying   7. C
8. After the Castro revolution, thousands of Cubans fled to the United States, and Cubría interviewed many of these refugees, and she also prepared reports on Cuba.   8.

HELP
As you revise these sentences, keep in mind that there is often more than one correct way to revise a sentence.

DIRECT TEACHING

Modeling and Demonstration

Revising Wordy Sentences. Model how to identify and revise wordy sentences by using the example *In a state of exhaustion, Tony slumped across the bus seat and fell asleep.* First, ask students whether the example includes any wordy expressions. [yes—*In a state of exhaustion*] Next, ask students how they would shorten the sentence. [*replace* in a state of exhaustion *with* exhausted] Explain to students that phrases can often be reduced to a single word. Now, have a volunteer use another example from this chapter to demonstrate how to identify and revise wordy sentences.

TECHNOLOGY TIP

Some word-processing programs offer a grammar-checking program that can assist students by identifying wordy sentences in their writing and suggesting alternatives. Encourage students to explore this feature but to be aware that it is not foolproof. Point out that while grammar-checking programs detect problems, students still have to make the decisions about necessary changes.

DIFFERENTIATING INSTRUCTION

Learners Having Difficulty

Identifying Wordy Sentences. As students learn to identify and revise wordy sentences, it may help them to have a list of words and phrases that can make sentences wordy. Start students with a list of items, such as *quite, really, a lot of,* and *in spite of the fact that.* Post the list in a prominent place as the class works on this section of the chapter, and encourage students to add other words and phrases to the list as they encounter more examples.

COMPUTER TIP

The grammar-checking option on a computer will often alert you if you have written a sentence that is too long. Review the sentence and see if you can break it into parts or edit out unnecessary words.

---

9. In her spare time, she helped people from Cuba find jobs and housing. **9. C**
10. She retired again in 1973, and she settled in Miami, Florida, and she was surrounded by friends and family there. **10. ⊙/where**

Revising Wordy Sentences

Sometimes you use more words in a sentence than you really need. Extra words do not make writing sound better, and, in fact, they can even interfere with your message. Revise **wordy sentences** in these three ways.

1. Replace a group of words with one word.

WORDY	In a state of exhaustion, Tony slumped across the bus seat and fell asleep.
REVISED	**Exhausted,** Tony slumped across the bus seat and fell asleep.

WORDY	As a result of what happened when the tire went flat, we were late.
REVISED	**Because** the tire went flat, we were late.

2. Take out *who is, which is,* or *that is.*

WORDY	Yesterday I went for a long hike with Sonya, who is my best friend.
REVISED	Yesterday I went for a long hike with Sonya, **my best friend.**

WORDY	Afterward, we drank some apple juice, which is a good thirst quencher.
REVISED	Afterward, we drank some apple juice, **a good thirst quencher.**

3. Take out a whole group of unnecessary words.

WORDY	I spent a lot of time writing this report because I really want people to learn about manatees so they can know all about them.
REVISED	I spent a lot of time writing this report because I want people to learn about manatees.

Exercise 9 Revising Wordy Sentences

Some of the following sentences are wordy and need improvement. To revise wordy sentences, you can (1) replace a group of words with one word, (2) take out *who is* or *which is*, or (3) take out a whole group of unnecessary words. If a sentence is effective as it is, write *C* for *correct*.

EXAMPLE 1. In order to be able to see the starfish better, I leaned toward the aquarium.

1. *To see the starfish better, I leaned toward the aquarium.*

Here is a sample revision.
1. Our science class has been learning about the starfish, ~~which is~~ a strange and beautiful animal.
2. ~~What I want to say is that~~ starfish are fascinating creatures.
3. A starfish has little feet tipped with suction cups ~~that are powerful~~. 3. powerful/⊙
4. At the end of each arm is a sensitive eyespot. 4. C
5. ~~In spite of the fact that~~ the eyespot cannot really see things, it can tell light from dark. 5. Although
6. The starfish's mouth is in the middle of its body. 6. C
7. ~~When it uses~~ its arms, it can pull at the shells of clams. 7. Using
8. ~~At the point at which~~ the clam's shell opens, the starfish can feed on the clam. 8. When
9. Starfish come in a variety of colors, shapes, and sizes, ~~and some are bigger than others~~. 9. ⊙
10. This photograph shows a blue sea star ~~that is~~ holding onto a soft coral.

Beyond Sentence Style

To make your writing the best it can be, you'll need to look at how your sentences go together. Good writers use a variety of sentence beginnings and a variety of sentence structures to keep readers interested. Good writers also use transitions to show the connections between ideas in a paragraph or other composition.

Beyond Sentence Style
(pp. 431–440)

OBJECTIVES

- To vary sentence beginnings
- To vary sentence structure
- To identify and use transitions in sentences

RESOURCES

Beyond Sentence Style

Practice
- *Language & Sentence Skills Practice,* pp. 425–430
- *Developmental Language & Sentence Skills,* pp. 153–156

SENTENCES

DIRECT TEACHING

Modeling and Demonstration

Varying Sentence Beginnings. Model how to vary sentence beginnings by using the example *They choose to visit places new to them.* First, ask students how the sentence begins. [*with a subject followed by a verb*] Next, explain to students that if they have too many sentences that begin with a subject followed by a verb, their writing may be dull. Then, ask students to add a modifier to the beginning of the sentence to make it more interesting. [*Occasionally; answers will vary*] Now, have a volunteer use another example from this chapter to demonstrate how to vary sentence beginnings.

STYLE TIP

When planning your own writing assignments, save time to edit your composition for style. Many writers revise first for content and organization; then they look at style elements like sentence variety.

Varying Sentence Beginnings

Basic English sentences begin with a subject followed by a verb, perhaps with a few adjectives and adverbs included. If you use too many basic sentences in a row, your sentences will sound too much the same, and you very likely will bore your reader—even if each separate sentence is itself interesting. Notice how dull the following paragraph sounds.

```
Long-distance bicycle tours can
be fun. Bicycle tours combine two
sports, camping and cycling, into one.
Cyclists study maps. The cyclists
decide where to go and what to see.
They choose to visit places new to
them. They load their bicycles with
food and equipment. Then they ride off
down the highways and back roads. They
meet interesting people. Cyclists on
bicycle tours may see wildlife such as
deer, birds, and even bears!
```

One good way to avoid boring your reader is to vary sentence beginnings. Instead of starting most sentences with the subject, you can begin some with one-word modifiers, with introductory phrases, or with subordinate clauses.

```
As with many other adventures,
long-distance bicycle tours can be
fun. Bicycle tours combine two sports,
camping and cycling, into one. To
decide where to go and what to see,
cyclists study maps. Often, they
choose to visit places new to them.
Happy with their choices, they load
their bicycles with food and equipment
and ride off down the highways and
back roads. On many occasions, they
meet interesting people. If they are
especially lucky, they see wildlife
such as deer, birds, and even bears!
```

	Varying Sentence Beginnings
One-Word Modifiers	**Suddenly,** a noise woke Gwen. [adverb] **Rustling,** some creature was in the underbrush of the woods. [adjective]
Phrases	**After a few minutes,** Gwen went back to sleep. [prepositional phrase] **Trotting away,** a raccoon left the campground with Gwen's favorite cap. [participial phrase] **To keep our caps safe,** we should zip them into our packs. [infinitive phrase]
Subordinate Clauses	**Since the raccoon took her cap,** Gwen thought she would have to buy a new one. [adverb clause] **When she went hiking the next day,** she found the cap in a nearby creek. [adverb clause]

TIPS & TRICKS

To check your writing for varied sentence beginnings, put parentheses around the first five words of each of your sentences. If most of your subjects and verbs fall within the parentheses, you need to begin more of your sentences with single-word modifiers, phrases, or subordinate clauses.

DIFFERENTIATING INSTRUCTION

English-Language Learners

Vietnamese. In Vietnamese, an introductory clause may be followed by a "balancing" word in the main clause.

English: *Because he runs fast, he is on the track team.*

Vietnamese: *Because he runs fast, therefore, he is on the track team.*

Some Vietnamese speakers may omit the subordinating conjunction and use just the balancing word. Others may use *also* as a balancing word with a range of uses: *Even if I had a bike, I would also not ride to school.*

Show students that when sentences combine with a subordinating conjunction, or connecting word, to form complex sentences, they do not need other connecting words. Have them locate connecting words in sample sentences, and check their writing for correct usage.

Cantonese. Cantonese sentences are sometimes patterned in ways that allow an adverb clause to act as a coordinating rather than a subordinating element: *Although I worked on homework, but I did not finish.*

Show students that sentences that begin with a connecting word to form complex sentences cannot also have *and* or *but* between clauses.

Exercise 10 Revising a Paragraph to Vary Sentence Beginnings

Rewrite the following paragraph to vary sentence beginnings so that the paragraph is more interesting. You can use one-word modifiers, introductory phrases, or subordinate clauses to begin the sentences, and you can rearrange other words as necessary.

EXAMPLE   I enjoy reading. I go to the library often to borrow books.

Because I enjoy reading, I go to the library often to borrow books.

Here is a sample revision.

Good books are full of great characters. ^Those characters are really just words on a page, ~~but~~ they certainly seem to be more than that. ^They can be wonderful friends. ~~These characters are~~ people who entertain us when we are bored. ^They show us exciting things that we might do with our time. ^They warn us about the foolish activities we should avoid. ^They say

Although

In fact,
or

Also,

Often,
Sometimes,

Beyond Sentence Style   **433**

, but/also
While/,
also/In short,

Ultimately,

and do things with which we might disagree. They say and do things that we
respect. We can get angry with them.
We can laugh with them. They share
all of the qualities of a good friend.
Characters in books sometimes help us
know that we are never really alone.

Varying Sentence Structure

An important way to keep your readers' attention is to mix sentences of different lengths and structures. Think like a movie director. If you were making a movie, you would include long, complex scenes; but you would mix those scenes with shorter, simpler scenes to keep your audience's attention. A movie made up entirely of long scenes or short scenes would be difficult for your audience to follow. Apply the same ideas to your writing.

For example, the writer of the following paragraph uses only short, simple sentences.

```
    Jim Knaub lost the use of his legs
in a motorcycle accident. He did not
let that slow him down. He started
racing wheelchairs. All the other
racers were using standard wheel-
chairs. Those wheelchairs were not
fast enough for Jim. He began to
design his own. Soon, his light-
weight, ultrafast wheelchair was
winning races. He became a well-known
wheelchair-racing champion. Jim now
designs wheelchairs for others.
```

Now read the revised paragraph. Notice how the writer has varied the sentence structure to include different sentence lengths and a mixture of simple, compound, and complex sentences.

434 Chapter 18 Writing Effective Sentences

CONTENT-AREA CONNECTIONS

Visual Arts

Varying Scenes. Discuss with students the idea of the writer as movie director. Ask students to think of scenes from movies or television programs that illustrate how directors use a variety of scenes. Students might mention typical science fiction films that have fast-paced scenes of wars between fighter pilots and space monsters, intercut with quiet, still scenes. Others might suggest specific musicals that alternate scenes of dancing and singing with scenes of dialogue. Ask students whether they agree that variety helps hold an audience's attention. Guide students to an awareness of this technique as it applies to writing.

When Jim Knaub lost the use of
his legs in a motorcycle accident, he
did not let that slow him down. He
started racing wheelchairs. All the
other racers were using standard wheelchairs, but those wheelchairs were not
fast enough for Jim. He began to design
his own. Soon, his lightweight, ultra-
fast wheelchair was winning races. He
became a well-known wheelchair-racing
champion and began to design wheelchairs for others.

Below is a chart that shows you the four sentence structures. Using a balance of these four structures will help you keep your reader interested in what you have to say.

Sentence Structure	Example
simple sentence contains one independent clause	Estivation is somewhat like hibernation.
compound sentence contains two or more independent clauses	Some animals hibernate to protect themselves during cold weather, and others estivate to protect themselves during hot, dry weather.
complex sentence contains one independent clause and at least one subordinate clause	When an animal estivates, its breathing and heartbeat slow down.
compound-complex sentence contains two or more independent clauses and at least one subordinate clause	Some animals, such as salamanders, form cocoons before they enter estivation; the cocoons help protect them from dehydration.

HELP

When adding variety to sentences in a paragraph, first look for words that are repeated. Sentences with repeated words can often be combined or rewritten to improve the paragraph.

Reference Note

For more help **identifying sentence structures**, see page 130.

Beyond Sentence Style   **435**

DIFFERENTIATING INSTRUCTION

Learners Having Difficulty

Students who have difficulty revising to improve sentence style may benefit from a review of some of the causes of wordy sentences. As students examine the paragraph in **Review C,** suggest that they also look for the conjunctions *and* or *but,* which may string together complete thoughts. Have students first try to revise the paragraph independently and then to consult with a peer editor for help.

Exercise 11 **Adding Variety to Sentences**

The following paragraph is uninteresting because it includes only compound sentences. Rewrite the paragraph to include a variety of sentence structures. Mix short, simple sentences; compound sentences; and longer sentences with subordinate clauses in your version. Use variety to keep your audience involved.

EXAMPLE   I have an idea, and I think it's a good one.
     I have a good idea.

Here is a sample revision.

My friends and I have ~~been talking, and we have made a decision.~~ decided that We would like a day off. ~~and~~ we could go on a class picnic. We ~~could do it~~ right before winter break, or ~~we could go~~ near the end of the school year. We could each bring a sack lunch, or ~~we could each bring~~ something to share with the rest of the class. The park near the school has picnic tables, ~~and it has~~ playing fields, and a pool. It might seem bad to take a free day, but we work hard the rest of the year. We would enjoy the picnic, and ~~we would~~ have a fun ~~day~~. We would return to school, ~~and we would with have~~ smiles on our faces.

Review C **Revising a Paragraph by Improving Sentence Style**

The following paragraph is hard to read because it contains stringy and wordy sentences. Use the methods you have learned to revise them. Try to use a mix of simple, compound, and complex sentences in your improved version.

EXAMPLE   One thing I would like to say is that I saw the movie *Anastasia*, and I very much enjoyed it.
     I saw the movie Anastasia, *which I very much enjoyed.*

A sample revision follows.

The movie *Anastasia* is based on a real story about ~~a real girl from history. Her name was~~ Anastasia Romanov, ~~and she~~ was born in 1901 and, who lived in Russia. ~~The movie is about~~ Although ~~some historical~~ events in Russia's history, ~~and~~ many things in the movie are not true. For example, the movie says that Anastasia was eight years old when the revolutionaries ~~came to~~ overthrew ~~overthrow and defeat~~ her father, ~~who was~~ the czar, but the real Anastasia was a teenager, ~~in real life~~. The movie shows Anastasia and her grandmother, ~~who was~~ the Grand Duchess Marie, escaping together, ~~but~~ in reality her grandmother was already safely in Denmark when the family was ~~seized and~~ captured. Unlike the character in the movie, the real Anastasia did not get away, her remains were found with her family's ~~remains when they were found~~ in 1991. Although *Anastasia* is an interesting movie, people who see it should also know the real story, ~~that happened~~.

Using Transitions

Imagine that you are reading a passage that is full of clear, complete sentences. Each sentence is itself interesting, and the writer has used a variety of sentence beginnings and a variety of kinds of sentences. However, you can't tell how the sentences are related to each other. You find yourself re-reading the passage and trying to puzzle out the connections between thoughts. What could be wrong? Chances are, the writer failed to include transitions. **Transitional words and phrases** help connect ideas. Acting as signposts, they lead readers along, pointing out the relationships between thoughts.

Transitional Words and Phrases		
also	first	meanwhile
another	for example	moreover
as a result	for instance	on the other hand
at last	furthermore	soon
besides	however	then
consequently	in fact	therefore
eventually	last	though
finally	mainly	thus

Read the following passage, which includes underlined transitional words and phrases. As you read, stop when you get to each underlined transition. Before you read the rest of the sentence, predict what kind of information will be in that sentence. For instance, will the sentence support the one before it? Will it present a contrast? Watch for transitional "signposts" that tell you that the passage is going to keep going straight and for those that tell you the writer is changing direction.

```
    Ed and I set out to hike to the peak of
the highest ridge. Soon, though, I real-
ized that the blister on my left heel was
getting worse. Furthermore, we had waited
until afternoon, and the highest ridge was
almost two miles away. However, my uncle
had told me that the view from the peak
was spectacular. I would be leaving on
Saturday and might not have this chance
again. In fact, Uncle Alex was planning to
sell his house and move inland, away from
the rocky shore. I decided, therefore, to
put a moleskin bandage on my heel and
hurry on.
```

Notice how the transitional words and phrases tell the reader what kind of ideas to expect. When you write, you should include words and phrases like these to guide your reader. Doing so will help you express your ideas more clearly and help you keep the interest of your reader.

Exercise 12 **Identifying Transitional Words and Phrases**

The transitional words and phrases in the following paragraph show how the ideas are related to one another. Make a list of the transitions in the paragraph.

EXAMPLE I found something that I thought was a fossil. Soon, though, I found out that it was just a rock with an unusual shape.
Soon, though

Sometimes we can be fooled by the way things look. For instance, earlier in this century, Charles Dawson found a few fossilized fragments of bone inside a gravel formation. The fragments seemed important. Consequently, Dawson took his discovery to a museum. Soon, a museum scientist announced that the fragments might be from a "missing link" between apes and people. As a result of his announcement, other scientists quickly believed that the missing link had been found. In fact, they even gave the new creature a fancy name, *Eoanthropus dawsoni*. However, they had been taken in by a hoax.

Exercise 13 **Revising a Paragraph to Show Transitions**

The sentences in the following paragraph do not clearly show how one idea is related to another. Rewrite the paragraph, adding appropriate transitions to show how the ideas are related.

EXAMPLE Eager for exciting discoveries, people can be taken in. Experts can be fooled.
Eager for exciting discoveries, people can be taken in. In fact, even experts can be fooled.

Here is a possible revision.
   Scientists discovered that the bones could not be as old as they seemed. Someone had stained the bones to make them look older than they were. People doubted *Of course,* whether a missing link had been found. Scientists discovered that the jaw *Then* and some of the teeth were those of an orangutan. One tooth was from a *Further,*

Beyond Sentence Style **439**

chimpanzee. Someone had filed the teeth to make them look human. No one knows who planned the hoax and hid the bones in the gravel. We do know that almost anyone may be fooled by the way things look.

[Editing marks insert: "Today," before "No one"; "However," before "We do know"]

Review D Revising a Passage to Improve Style

Rewrite the following passage to make it clearer and to improve its style.

Here are possible revisions.

EXAMPLE Carlie and Monica listened to the wind howl, and they wondered whether the storm would let up soon.

Wondering whether the storm would let up soon, Carlie and Monica listened to the wind howl.

The girls had been staying in the old house for nearly a week. They decided to explore some ~~of the rooms. The~~ rooms ~~were ones~~ that ~~Carlie and Monica~~ hadn't explored yet. These rooms ~~were~~ in the west wing. ~~They~~ were closed up. No one used them. The rooms were not empty. ~~They~~ contained ~~very old~~ furniture~~, which was ornate and old-fashioned~~. The day was dreary ~~and~~ it had been raining since dawn, and sometimes lightning flashed and thunder cracked ~~and~~ the rooms seemed spooky. The girls had a flashlight ~~with them, and it was good that they did because~~ the power went out when they were about to enter the big, dark study ~~that was~~ at the end of the hall. The room seemed very mysterious and ~~also to be~~ neglected. ~~Due to the fact that~~ the power ~~was~~ out and the room ~~was~~ dark, Carlie and Monica were nervous. They stood in the hallway and looked inside. The storm ~~outside~~ grew more fierce. Lightning flared and lit up the room. Thunder roared. The wind rattled the windows. ~~It also~~ howling ~~made a howling sound.~~ The girls looked at each other. ~~They each~~ took a deep breath. ~~They~~ stepped into the room.

[Editing marks insert: "when" after "decided"; "they" after "hadn't"; ", and" and "However,/but"; "ornate, old-fashioned" before "furniture"; "Fortunately,"; "With"; "As"; ", and"; "and"]

440 Chapter 18 Writing Effective Sentences

CHAPTER 18

Chapter Review

A. Identifying Sentences, Sentence Fragments, and Run-ons

Identify each of the following word groups as a *sentence*, a *sentence fragment*, or a *run-on sentence*. If a word group is a sentence fragment, rewrite it to make a complete sentence. If a word group is a run-on sentence, rewrite it to make it one or more complete sentences.   Here are possible revisions.

1. The morning‸spent at the dentist.
2. ‸Since sometime near the beginning of last week.
3. I should stay home and help with the yard work.
4. Turn left at the convenience store⁏ the library will be on your left.
5. ‸Said not to worry about the change to the schedule.
6. The goat‸ standing on top of John's car and chewing on your hat.
7. ~~Because~~ I want you to meet my cousin Ari.
8. The boat sailed at noon‸ however, the first mate was not aboard.
9. My computer was not working well, so I restarted it.
10. We cleaned the house,‸ we raked the yard.

B. Combining Sentences

Each of the following items contains two complete sentences. Combine these sentences to make a single sentence that is clear and interesting. To combine the sentences, you can add connecting words, insert words or phrases, or use compound or complex sentences.   Here are possible revisions.

11. I will send Terry a thank-you note‸ ~~I appreciated~~ her help last weekend.
12. The roses need to be pruned‸ ~~They~~ are overgrown and scraggly.
13. Aunt Sally‸ is my father's oldest sister‸ ~~She~~ visited us last September.

Chapter Review **441**

Terms in brackets refer to concepts tested by the items in the Chapter Review.

1. was [fragment]
2. I haven't seen her [fragment]
3. sentence [sentence]
4. [run-on]
5. Marcia [fragment]
6. is [fragment]
7. [fragment]
8. ; [run-on]
9. sentence [sentence]
10. and [run-on]

11. for [inserting phrases]
12. because [complex sentence]
13. [appositive phrase]

ASSESSING

Monitoring Progress

Chapter Review. To assess student progress, you may want to compare the types of items missed on the **Diagnostic Preview** to those missed on the **Chapter Review**. If students have not made significant progress, you may want to provide them with additional practice.

RESOURCES

Writing Effective Sentences
Review
- *Language & Sentence Skills Practice*, pp. 405–406, 419–420, 429–430

Assessment
- *Holt Handbook Chapter Tests with Answer Key*, pp. 35–38, 46

14. [inserting phrases]
15. and [compound verb]

14. Dr. Severson bought a bouquet of daisies. ~~They are~~ for his wife.
15. The horse that she was riding can run like the wind, ~~It can also~~ leap over fences and hedges.

C. Revising a Passage to Correct Errors and Improve Style

Using the skills you have learned throughout this chapter, revise the following paragraph. Be sure to correct sentence fragments and run-ons, to combine sentences where appropriate, to improve stringy and wordy sentences, and to vary your sentences.   A possible revision follows.

and
but

For instance,

of

a large circle

a mark

with

across the ice

, is worth a point
Again,

By sliding stones in front of the tee,

We know about hockey ~~and~~ ice-skating, ~~E~~ven about ice-fishing. They are fun. ~~There are~~ other sports people can play on ice ~~these sports~~ are just as enjoyable. ~~There is the game of curling.~~ ~~C~~urling is played on frozen lakes or ~~on~~ ice rinks. It is a little bit like lawn bowling, ~~and~~ there are two teams, ~~and each team has~~ four players. ~~There is a large circle~~ on the ice ~~and it~~ is called the "house", ~~and there is a mark~~ in the middle of the circle ~~and it~~ is called the "tee." The players slide round stones ~~across the ice the stones have~~ slightly curved bottoms and handles. The object of the game is ~~for players~~ to slide their stones into the house, ~~C~~lose to the tee. A player on each team slides two stones toward the tee. Only one of the stones ~~is worth a point~~, ~~it is~~ the stone closest to the tee. The next players on the two teams slide their stones toward the tee. ~~T~~he stone that is closest to the tee is worth one point. ~~P~~layers can use their stones to block their opponents from scoring. ~~Because they can slide stones in front of the tee.~~ They also use brushes or brooms ~~in order~~ to sweep away particles of ice or snow in the path of an oncoming stone ~~and also~~ so that the stone can slide across the ice more easily.

CHAPTER 19

Sentence Diagramming

INTRODUCING THE CHAPTER

- Diagramming gives students the opportunity to use their spatial skills to help them analyze language. You may find diagrams especially useful in helping students understand sentence structure and the relationships between parts of sentences.

- The system of diagramming used in this chapter is generally referred to as the Reed and Kellogg system; it was presented by Alonzo Reed and Brainerd Kellogg in their book *Higher Lessons in English*.

The Sentence Diagram

A ***sentence diagram*** is a picture of how the parts of a sentence fit together. It shows how the words in the sentence are related.

Subjects and Verbs

Reference Note
For information on **subjects and verbs,** see page 5.

To diagram a sentence, first find the simple subject and the simple predicate, or verb, and write them on a horizontal line. Then, separate the subject and verb with a vertical line. Keep the capital letters, but leave out the punctuation marks, except in cases such as *Mr.* and *July 1, 1999*.

EXAMPLE   Horses gallop.

```
Horses | gallop
```

Questions

Reference Note
For information on **questions,** see page 19.

To diagram a question, first make the question into a statement. Then, diagram the sentence. Remember that in a diagram the subject always comes first, even if it does not come first in the sentence.

EXAMPLE   Are you going?

```
you | Are going
```

The previous examples are easy because each sentence contains only a simple subject and a verb. Now, look at a longer sentence.

EXAMPLE   One quiet, always popular pet is the goldfish.

To diagram the simple subject and verb of this sentence, follow these steps.

Step 1:   Separate the complete subject from the complete predicate.

```
       complete subject      | complete predicate
One quiet, always popular pet | is the goldfish.
```

Step 2:   Find the simple subject and the verb.

```
simple subject | verb
     pet       |  is
```

Step 3:   Draw the diagram.

```
 pet | is
```

Understood Subjects

To diagram an imperative sentence, place the understood subject *you* in parentheses on the horizontal line.

EXAMPLE   Clean your room.

```
(you) | Clean
```

Reference Note
For information on **understood subjects**, see page 19.

Exercise 1   Diagramming Simple Subjects and Verbs

Diagram only the simple subject and verb in each of the following sentences.

EXAMPLE   1. Gwendolyn Brooks was the poet laureate of Illinois.

```
1. Gwendolyn Brooks | was
```

1. Angela just returned from Puerto Rico.
2. She was studying Spanish in San Juan.
3. Listen to her stories about her host family.

HELP
Remember that simple subjects and verbs may consist of more than one word.

Exercise 1   Diagramming Simple Subjects and Verbs

ANSWERS

1. Angela | returned

2. She | was studying

3. (you) | Listen

The Sentence Diagram   **445**

Exercise 1 Diagramming Simple Subjects and Verbs

ANSWERS continued

4. She | enjoyed

5. you | Have been

Reference Note

For information on **compound subjects,** see page 13. For information on **conjunctions,** see page 62.

4. She really enjoyed the year.
5. Have you ever been to Puerto Rico?

Compound Subjects

To diagram a compound subject, put the subjects on parallel lines. Then, put the connecting word (the conjunction) on a dotted line that joins the subject lines.

EXAMPLE   **Sharks** and **eels** can be dangerous.

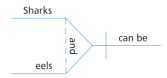

Compound Verbs

To diagram a compound verb, put the two verbs on parallel lines. Then, put the connecting word (the conjunction) on a dotted line that joins the verb lines.

EXAMPLE   The cowboy **swung** into the saddle and **rode** away.

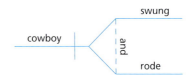

Reference Note

For information on **compound verbs,** see page 15.

This is how a compound verb is diagrammed when it has a helping verb that is not repeated.

EXAMPLE   Ray Bradbury **has written** many books and **received** several prizes for them.

446   Chapter 19   Sentence Diagramming

Compound Subjects and Compound Verbs

A sentence with both a compound subject and a compound verb combines the patterns for each.

EXAMPLE   **Rosa Parks** and **Dr. Martin Luther King, Jr., saw** a problem and **did** something about it.

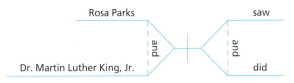

Sometimes parts of a compound subject or a compound verb are joined by correlative conjunctions, such as *both . . . and*. Correlatives are diagrammed like this:

EXAMPLE   **Both** Luisa **and** Miguel can sing.

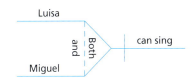

Reference Note
For information on **using compound subjects with compound verbs,** see page 15.

Exercise 2 Diagramming Compound Subjects and Compound Verbs

Diagram the simple subjects and the verbs in the following sentences. Include the conjunctions that join the compound subjects or the compound verbs.

EXAMPLE   1. Both LeAnn Rimes and Clint Black are going on tour and cutting new albums.

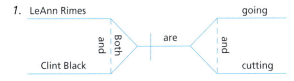

1. Everyone knows and likes Mr. Karras.
2. Hurricanes and tornadoes occur most often during the summer.
3. Julio and Rosa were cutting paper and tying string for the kites.

Exercise 2 Diagramming Compound Subjects and Compound Verbs

ANSWERS

1.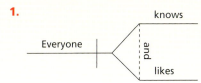

2.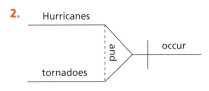

3.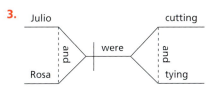

SENTENCES

Exercise 2 Diagramming Compound Subjects and Compound Verbs

ANSWERS continued

4.
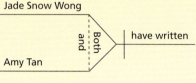

5.
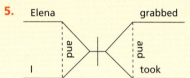

Exercise 3 Diagramming Sentences with Adjectives

ANSWERS

1.
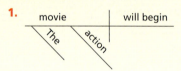

2.

3.
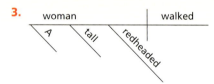

4.
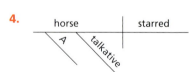

5.
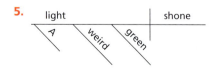

---

4. Both Jade Snow Wong and Amy Tan have written books about their childhoods in San Francisco's Chinatown.
5. Elena and I grabbed our jackets and took the bus to the mall.

Adjectives and Adverbs

Adjectives and adverbs are written on slanted lines connected to the words they modify. Notice that possessive pronouns are diagrammed in the same way adjectives are.

Adjectives

EXAMPLES   **dark** room   **a lively** fish   **my best** friend

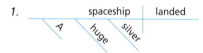

Reference Note
For information on **possessive pronouns,** see page 30.

Reference Note
For information on **adjectives,** see page 34.

Exercise 3 Diagramming Sentences with Adjectives

Diagram the subjects, the verbs, and the adjectives that modify the subjects in the following sentences.

EXAMPLE   1. A huge silver spaceship landed in the field.

1.

1. The action movie will soon begin.
2. The soft, silky kitten played with a shoelace.
3. A tall, redheaded woman walked into the room.
4. A talkative horse starred in that popular TV show.
5. A weird green light shone under the door.

Adverbs

EXAMPLES   walks **briskly**   arrived **here late**

Reference Note
For information on **adverbs,** see page 54.

When an adverb modifies an adjective or another adverb, it is placed on a line connected to the word it modifies.

EXAMPLES   a **very** happy child   drove **rather** slowly

This **extremely** rare record will **almost certainly** cost a great deal.

Conjunctions and Modifiers

When a modifier applies to only one part of a compound subject or compound verb, it is diagrammed like this:

EXAMPLE   Benjamin Davis, Sr., and **his** son worked **hard** and rose **quickly** through the military.

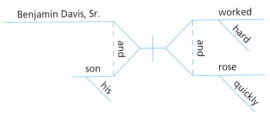

A conjunction joining two modifiers is diagrammed like this:

EXAMPLE   The **English and American** musicians played **slowly and** quite **beautifully.**

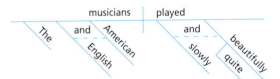

Reference Note
For information on **conjunctions,** see page 62. For information on **modifiers,** see Chapter 11.

Exercise 4 Diagramming Sentences with Adjectives and Adverbs

ANSWERS

1.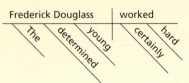

2.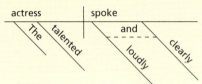

3.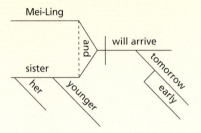

4.

5.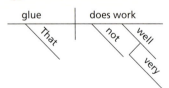

Reference Note

For information on **objects,** see Chapter 4.

Reference Note

For information on **direct objects,** see page 74.

Exercise 4 Diagramming Sentences with Adjectives and Adverbs

Diagram the subjects, verbs, adjectives, adverbs, and conjunctions in the following sentences.

EXAMPLE 1. A relatively unknown candidate won the election easily and rather cheaply.

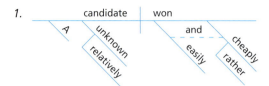

1. The determined young Frederick Douglass certainly worked hard.
2. The talented actress spoke loudly and clearly.
3. Mei-Ling and her younger sister will arrive early tomorrow.
4. The best musicians always play here.
5. That glue does not work very well.

Objects

Direct Objects

A direct object is diagrammed on the horizontal line with the subject and verb. A vertical line separates the direct object from the verb. Notice that this vertical line does not cross the horizontal line.

EXAMPLES We like **pizza.**

The robin caught a **worm.**

Compound Direct Objects

EXAMPLE   Lizards eat **flies** and **earthworms**.

> **Reference Note**
> For information on **compound direct objects,** see page 75.

Indirect Objects

An indirect object is diagrammed on a horizontal line beneath the verb. The verb and the indirect object are joined by a slanting line that extends past the lower horizontal line.

EXAMPLE   Marisol brought **me** a piñata.

> **Reference Note**
> For information on **indirect objects,** see page 76.

Compound Indirect Objects

EXAMPLE   Tanya gave the **singer** and the **dancer** cues.

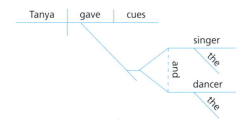

> **Reference Note**
> For information on **compound indirect objects,** see page 77.

Exercise 5 Diagramming Direct and Indirect Objects

Diagram the following sentences.

EXAMPLE   **1.** I gave the clerk a dollar.

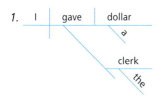

The Sentence Diagram

Exercise 5 Diagramming Direct and Indirect Objects

ANSWERS

1.
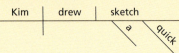

2.
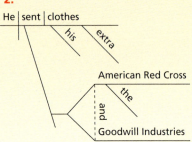

3.
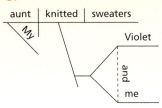

1. Kim drew a quick sketch.
2. He sent the American Red Cross and Goodwill Industries his extra clothes.
3. My aunt knitted Violet and me sweaters.
4. Gerardo and Wendie are organizing the play and the refreshments.
5. Several businesses bought our school new computers.

Subject Complements

A subject complement is diagrammed on the horizontal line with the subject and the verb. It comes after the verb. A line slanting toward the verb separates the subject complement from the verb.

Reference Note
For information on **subject complements,** see page 79.

Reference Note
For information on **predicate nominatives,** see page 79.

Predicate Nominatives

EXAMPLES   Mariah Carey is a famous **singer.**

That bird is a female **cardinal.**

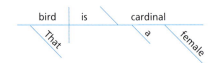

Compound Predicate Nominatives

EXAMPLE   Clara is a **student** and a volunteer **nurse.**

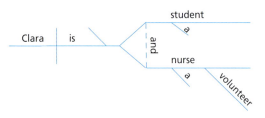

4.
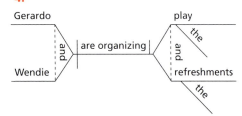

5.
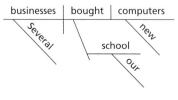

Predicate Adjectives

EXAMPLES She was extremely **nice**.

This juice tastes **great**.

Reference Note
For information on **predicate adjectives**, see page 81.

Compound Predicate Adjectives

EXAMPLE We were **tired** but very **happy**.

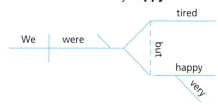

Exercise 6 Diagramming Sentences

Diagram the following sentences.

EXAMPLE **1.** The snake is large and shiny.

1. Turtles are reptiles.
2. Their tough beaks look sharp and strong.
3. Turtles may grow very old.
4. The alligator snapper is the largest freshwater turtle.
5. Few turtles are dangerous.

Exercise 6 Diagramming Sentences

ANSWERS

1.
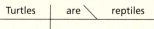

2.
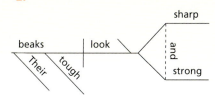

3.

4.
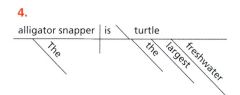

5.
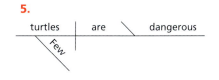

Phrases

Prepositional Phrases

A prepositional phrase is diagrammed below the word it modifies. Write the preposition on a slanting line below the modified word. Then, write the object of the preposition on a horizontal line connected to the slanting line.

Reference Note
For information on **prepositional phrases,** see page 90.

Adjective Phrases

EXAMPLES   traditions **of the Sioux**

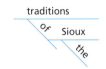

Reference Note
For information on **adjective phrases,** see page 92.

gifts **from Nadine and Chip**

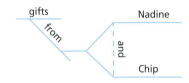

Adverb Phrases

EXAMPLES   a face bright **with good cheer**

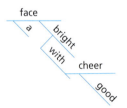

Reference Note
For information on **adverb phrases,** see page 94.

search **for the gerbil and the hamster**

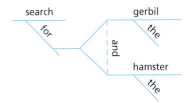

Two prepositional phrases may modify the same word.

EXAMPLE   The tour extends **across the country** and **around the world.**

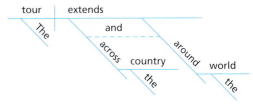

When a prepositional phrase modifies the object of another preposition, the diagram looks like this:

EXAMPLE   Richard Wright wrote one **of the books on that subject.**

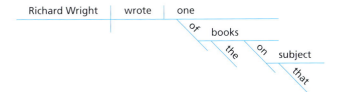

Exercise 7   Diagramming Sentences with Prepositional Phrases

Diagram the following sentences.

EXAMPLE   1. Our team practices **in the afternoon.**

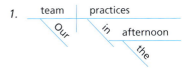

Exercise 7 Diagramming Sentences with Prepositional Phrases

ANSWERS

1.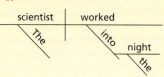

2.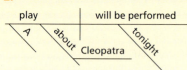

3.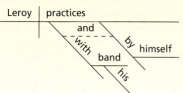

4.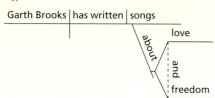

5.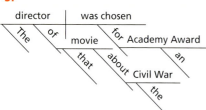

---

1. The scientist worked into the night.
2. A play about Cleopatra will be performed tonight.
3. Leroy practices with his band and by himself.
4. Garth Brooks has written songs about love and freedom.
5. The director of that movie about the Civil War was chosen for an Academy Award.

Verbals and Verbal Phrases

Participles and Participial Phrases

Participles are diagrammed much as other adjectives are, but the participle curves onto a horizontal line.

EXAMPLE Juan helped the **wailing** child.

Reference Note
For information on **verbals** and **verbal phrases,** see page 98.

Participial phrases are diagrammed as follows:

EXAMPLE **Seeing the new employee,** Sandy waved.

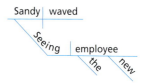

Reference Note
For information on **participles** and **participial phrases,** see pages 98 and 100.

Notice that the participle has a direct object (*the new employee*), which is diagrammed in the same way that the direct object of a verb is.

Infinitives and Infinitive Phrases

EXAMPLES **To act** is her dream. [infinitive used as subject]

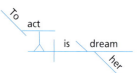

He was the first one **to finish the race.** [infinitive phrase used as adjective]

Would you like **to leave early**? [infinitive phrase used as direct object]

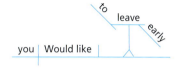

He hurried **to help us.** [infinitive phrase used as adverb]

Appositives and Appositive Phrases

To diagram an appositive or appositive phrase, write the appositive in parentheses after the word it identifies.

EXAMPLES My brother **Dan** is an accountant.

Samuel Johnson, **the British writer,** wrote an English dictionary.

Reference Note
For information on **appositives** and **appositive phrases,** see page 106.

Exercise 8 Diagramming Sentences That Contain Verbal and Appositive Phrases

Diagram the following sentences.

The Sentence Diagram   457

Exercise 8 Diagramming Sentences That Contain Verbal and Appositive Phrases

ANSWERS

1.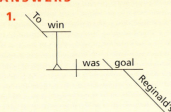

2.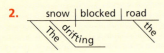

3.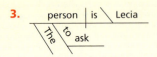

4.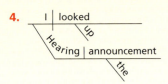

5.

EXAMPLE 1. She saw them riding bicycles.

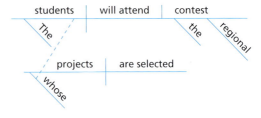

1. To win was Reginald's goal.
2. The drifting snow blocked the road.
3. The person to ask is Lecia.
4. Hearing the announcement, I looked up.
5. Kris, my good friend, will help.

Subordinate Clauses

Adjective Clauses

Diagram an adjective clause by connecting it with a broken line to the word it modifies. Draw the broken line between the relative pronoun and the word to which it relates.

NOTE The words *who*, *whom*, *whose*, *which*, and *that* are relative pronouns.

An adjective clause is diagrammed below the independent clause.

EXAMPLE The students **whose projects are selected** will attend the regional contest.

Reference Note
For information on **subordinate clauses**, see page 114.

Reference Note
For information on **adjective clauses**, see page 117.

Reference Note
For information on **relative pronouns**, see page 118.

Adverb Clauses

Diagram an adverb clause by using a broken line to connect the adverb clause to the word it modifies. Place the subordinating conjunction that introduces the adverb clause on the broken line.

Reference Note
For information on **adverb clauses**, see page 120.

NOTE The words *after, because, if, since, unless, when,* and *while* are common subordinating conjunctions.

The adverb clause is diagrammed below the independent clause.

EXAMPLE **If I study for two more hours,** I will finish my homework.

Reference Note
For information on **subordinating conjunctions,** see page 121.

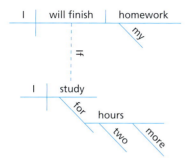

Exercise 9 Diagramming Sentences with Adjective Clauses and Adverb Clauses

Diagram the following sentences.

EXAMPLE   1. Will you stop by my house after you go to the library?

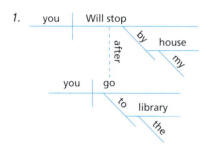

1. Most proverbs are sayings that give advice.
2. Because the day was very hot, the cool water felt good.
3. If it does not rain tomorrow, we will visit Crater Lake.
4. Janice and Linda found some empty seats as the movie started.
5. The problem that worries us now is the pollution of underground sources of water.

The Sentence Diagram   **459**

Exercise 9 Diagramming Sentences with Adjective Clauses and Adverb Clauses

ANSWERS

1.
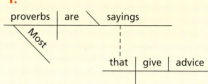

2.
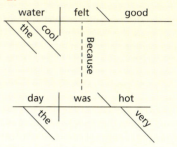

3.
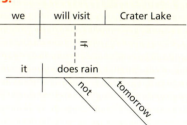

4.
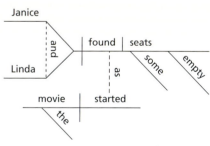

5.
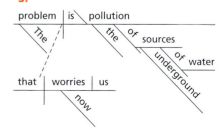

The Sentence Diagram   **459**

Exercise 10 Diagramming Compound Sentences

ANSWERS

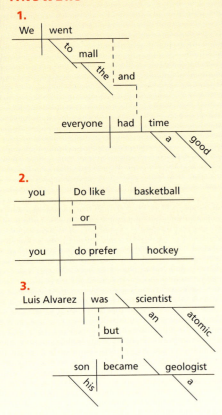

Reference Note
For information on the **kinds of sentence structure,** see Chapter 7.

Reference Note
For information on **simple sentences,** see page 130.

Reference Note
For information on **compound sentences,** see page 131.

The Kinds of Sentence Structure

Simple Sentences

EXAMPLE   Ray showed us his new bike. [one independent clause]

Compound Sentences

The second independent clause in a compound sentence is diagrammed below the first and usually is joined to it by a coordinating conjunction. A dotted line joins the clauses. The line is drawn between the verbs of the two clauses, and the conjunction is written on a solid horizontal line connecting the two parts of the dotted line.

EXAMPLE   Ossie Davis wrote the play, and Ruby Dee starred in it. [two independent clauses]

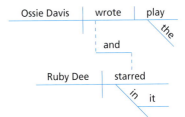

Exercise 10 Diagramming Compound Sentences

Diagram the following compound sentences.

EXAMPLE   1. Lucas likes that new CD, but I have not heard it.

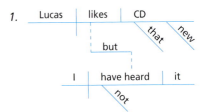

1. We went to the mall, and everyone had a good time.
2. Do you like basketball, or do you prefer hockey?

460   Chapter 19   Sentence Diagramming

3. Luis Alvarez was an atomic scientist, but his son became a geologist.
4. Miriam celebrates Hanukkah, and she told our class about the holiday.
5. Sammy Sosa is my baseball hero, but my sister prefers Randy Johnson.

Complex Sentences

EXAMPLE   Cheryl has a carving **that was made in Nigeria.**
[one independent clause and one subordinate clause]

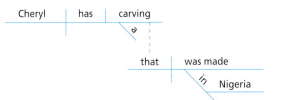

Reference Note
For information on **complex sentences,** see page 135.

Exercise 11 Diagramming Complex Sentences

Diagram the following complex sentences.

EXAMPLE   1. If you see Lola, you can give her this book.

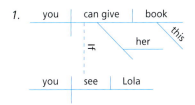

1. Valentina Tereshkova was the first woman who flew in space.
2. Because my cousins live in Toledo, they took a plane to the wedding.
3. Although Wilma Rudolph had been a very sick child, she became a top Olympic athlete.

The Sentence Diagram   461

Exercise 10 Diagramming Compound Sentences

ANSWERS continued

4. Miriam celebrates Hanukkah; and she told class about the holiday our

5. Sammy Sosa is hero my baseball but sister prefers Randy Johnson my

Exercise 11 Diagramming Complex Sentences

ANSWERS
(Answer to item 1 at bottom of page)

2.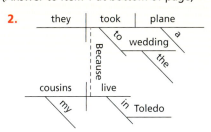

3.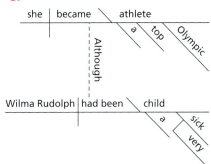

1.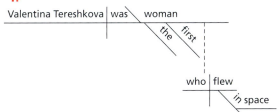

The Sentence Diagram   461

Exercise 11 Diagramming Complex Sentences

ANSWERS continued

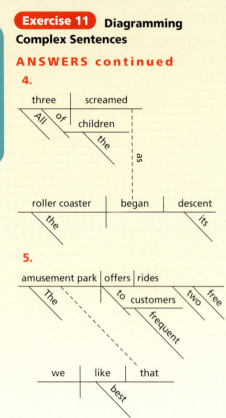

Reference Note
For information on **compound-complex sentences,** see page 137.

4. All three of the children screamed as the roller coaster began its descent.
5. The amusement park that we like best offers two free rides to frequent customers.

Compound-Complex Sentences

EXAMPLES Soon-Yee, whose father is a sculptor, studies art, but Mi-Kyung prefers the violin. [two independent clauses and one subordinate clause]

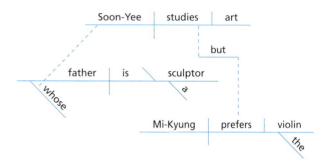

After the raccoon had fallen from the tree, it looked injured, so we called the Humane Society.

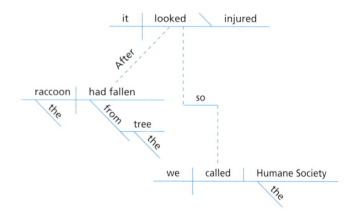

Exercise 12 Diagramming Compound-Complex Sentences

Diagram the following compound-complex sentences.

EXAMPLES 1. I smiled when I saw Wendell, and Mike waved.

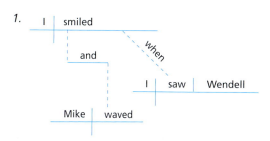

2. The room that Carla painted had been white, but she changed the color.

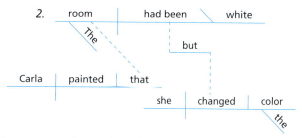

1. We have a game that we bought in Korea, but we do not understand the instructions.
2. Mariella wanted frozen yogurt after she won the tennis match, but Hector and I wanted sandwiches and milk.
3. When I returned to the store, the blue backpack had been sold, so I bought the green one.
4. The restaurant that we like best serves excellent seafood, and the chef has won many awards.
5. Before we conduct the experiment, we should ask for permission from the principal, and we should prepare the science lab.

The Sentence Diagram 463

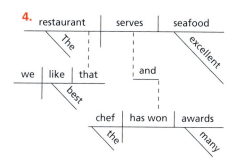

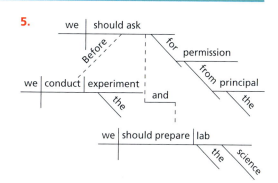

Exercise 12 Diagramming Compound-Complex Sentences

ANSWERS

1.

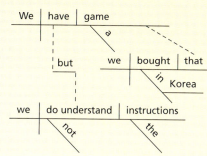

2.

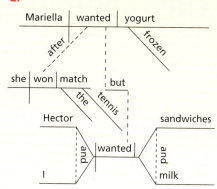

3.

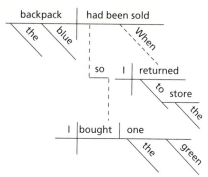

The Sentence Diagram 463

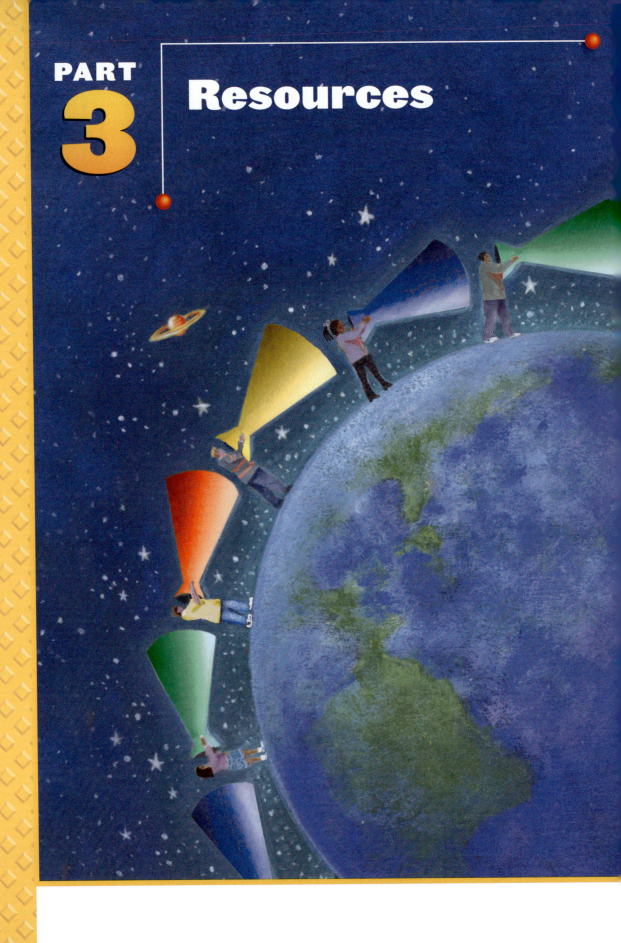

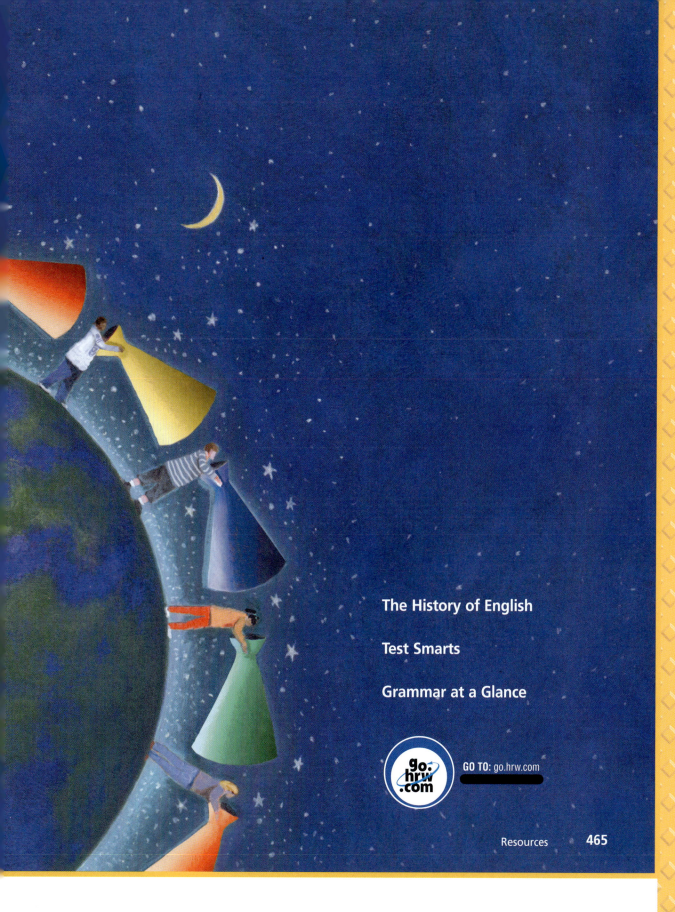

The History of English

Test Smarts

Grammar at a Glance

The History of English

Origins and Uses

A Changing Language

No one knows exactly when or how English got started. We do know that English and many other modern-day languages come from an early language that was spoken thousands of years ago. The related languages still resemble that parent language. For example, notice how similar the words for *mother* are in the following modern-day languages.

ENGLISH mother FRENCH mère
SPANISH madre   ITALIAN madre
SWEDISH moder

Over 1,500 years ago, a few small tribes of people invaded the island that is now Britain. These tribes, called the Angles and Saxons, spoke the earliest known form of English, called **Old English.** Old English was very different from the English we speak. English continued to evolve through a form known as **Middle English.** While the English language has always changed and grown, some of its most basic words have been around since the very beginning.

EARLY WORD
hand   dohtor   andswaru   hleapan

PRESENT-DAY WORD
hand   daughter   answer   leap

Changes in Meaning It may be hard to believe that the word *bead* once meant "prayer." Many English words have changed meaning over time. Some of these changes have been slight. Others have been more obvious. Below are a few examples of words that have changed their meanings.

naughty—In the 1300s, *naughty* meant "poor or needy." In the 1600s, the meaning changed to "poorly behaved."

lunch—In the 1500s, a *lunch* was a large chunk of something, such as bread or meat.

caboose—*Caboose* entered the English language in the 1700s when it meant "the kitchen of a ship."

Even today the meanings of words may vary depending on where they are used. For example, in the United States a *boot* is a type of shoe, but in Great Britain, a *boot* may refer to the trunk of a car.

Changes in Pronunciation and Spelling

If you traveled back in time a few hundred years, you would probably have a hard time understanding spoken and written English.

■ **Changes in pronunciation** English words used to be pronounced differently from the way they are pronounced today. For example, in the 1200s, people pronounced *bite* like *beet* and *feet* like *fate*. They also pronounced the vowel sound in the word *load* like the word *awe*.

You may have wondered why English words are not always spelled as they sound. Changes in pronunciation help account for many strange spellings in English. For example, the *w* that starts the word *write* was not always silent. Even after the *w* sound that started the word *write* was dropped, the spelling stayed the same. The *g* in *gnat* and the *k* in *knee* were once part of the pronunciations of the words, too.

■ **Changes in spelling** The spellings of many words have changed over time. Some changes in spelling have been accidental. For example, *apron* used to be spelled *napron*. People mistakenly attached the *n* to the article *a*, and *a napron* became *an apron*. Here are some more examples of present-day English words and their early spellings.

EARLY SPELLING
jaile   locian   slæp   tima

PRESENT-DAY SPELLING
jail   look   sleep   time

■ **British vs. American spelling and pronunciation** Pronunciations and spellings still vary today. For instance, the English used in Great Britain differs from the English used in the United States. In Great Britain, people pronounce *bath* with the vowel sound of *father* instead of the vowel sound of *cat*. The British also tend to drop the *r* sound at the end of words like *copper*. In addition, the British spell some words differently from the way people in the United States do.

AMERICAN SPELLING
theater   pajamas   labor

BRITISH SPELLING
theatre   pyjamas   labour

Word Origins

English grows and changes along with the people who use it. New words must be created for new inventions, places, or ideas. Sometimes, people borrow words from other languages to create a new English word. Other times, people use the names of people or places as new words.

■ **Borrowed words** As English-speaking people came into contact with people from other cultures and lands, they began to borrow words. English has borrowed hundreds of thousands of words from French, Hindi, Spanish, African languages, and many other

DIFFERENTIATING INSTRUCTION

Advanced Learners
Show students that the source language of a word can determine its spelling. Begin by pointing out other words from French that contain the pattern *ance* found in *dance,* including *romance* and *elegance.* Then, divide the class evenly into five groups and assign each group to research one of the following spelling patterns: *tio* (Latin) [relation, lotion], *ll* pronounced *y* (Spanish) [tortilla, llano], *ps/pt/pn* with silent *p* (Greek) [psychology, pteranodon, pneumonia], *gn* with a silent *g* (French) [campaign, gnome], and *sch* pronounced *sh* (German/Yiddish) [schnauzer, mensch]. Each group member should use a dictionary to search for three to five words from the source language. Then, group members should compile a list of all of the words found and try to identify two spelling patterns common to words from the source language. Finally, each group should present its findings in a poster that highlights the spelling patterns identified and lists all of the words found.

languages spoken around the world. In many cases, the borrowed words have taken new forms.

FRENCH ange
ENGLISH angel

HINDI champo
ENGLISH shampoo

KIMBUNDU mbanza
ENGLISH banjo

SPANISH patata
ENGLISH potato

- **Words from names** Many things get their names from the names of people or places. For example, in the 1920s, someone in Bridgeport, Connecticut, discovered a new use for the pie plates from the Frisbie Bakery. He turned one upside down and sent it floating through the air. The new game sparked the idea for the flying disk of today.

Dialects of American English

You probably know some people who speak English differently from the way you do. Different groups of people use different varieties of English. The kind of English we speak sounds most normal to us even though it may sound unusual to someone else. The form of English a particular group of people speaks is called a *dialect*. Everyone uses a dialect, and no dialect is better or worse than another.

Ethnic Dialects Your cultural background can make a difference in the way you speak. A dialect shared by people from the same cultural group is called an *ethnic dialect*. Because Americans come from many cultures, American English includes many ethnic dialects. One of the largest ethnic dialects is the Black English spoken by many African Americans. Another is the Hispanic English of many people whose families come from places such as Mexico, Central America, or Cuba.

Regional Dialects Do you *make* the bed or *make up* the bed? Would you order a *sub* with the *woiks* or a *hero* with the *werks*? In the evening, do you eat *supper* or *dinner*? How you answer these questions is probably influenced by where you live. A dialect shared by people from the same area is called a *regional dialect*. Your regional dialect helps determine what words you use, how you pronounce words, and how you put words together.

Not everyone from a particular group speaks that group's dialect. Also, an ethnic or regional dialect may vary depending on the speaker's individual background and place of origin.

Standard American English

Every dialect is useful and helps keep the English language colorful and interesting. However, sometimes it is confusing to try to communicate using two different dialects. Therefore, it is important to be familiar with **standard American English.** Standard English is the most commonly understood variety of English. You can find some of the rules for using standard English in this textbook. Language that does not follow these rules and guidelines is called **nonstandard English.** Nonstandard English is considered inappropriate in many formal situations.

NONSTANDARD   I don't want no more spinach.

STANDARD   I don't want **any** more spinach.

NONSTANDARD   Jimmy was fixing to go hiking with us.

STANDARD   Jimmy was **about** to go hiking with us.

Formal and Informal   Read the following sentences.

Many of my friends are excited about the game.

A bunch of my friends are psyched about the game.

Both sentences mean the same thing, but they have different effects. The first sentence is an example of *formal English,* and the second sentence is an example of *informal English.*

Formal and informal English are each appropriate for different situations. For instance, you would probably use the formal example if you were talking to a teacher about the game. If you were talking to a friend, however, the second sentence might sound natural. Formal English is frequently used in news reports and in schools and businesses.

- **Colloquialisms**   Informal English includes many words and expressions that are not appropriate in more formal situations. The most widely used informal expressions are *colloquialisms.* *Colloquialisms* are colorful words and phrases of everyday conversation. Many colloquialisms have meanings that are different from the basic meanings of words.

    EXAMPLES
    I wish Gerald would *get off my case.*
    Don't get *all bent out of shape* about it.
    We were about to *bust* with laughter.

- **Slang**   *Slang* words are made-up words or old words used in new ways. Slang is highly informal language. It is usually created by a particular group of people, such as students or people who hold a particular job, like computer technicians or artists. Often, slang is familiar only to the groups that invent it.

    Sometimes slang words become a lasting part of the English language. Usually, though, slang falls out of style quickly. The slang words in the sentences below will probably seem out of date to you.

    That was a really *far-out flick.*
    Those are some *groovy duds* you're wearing.
    I don't have enough *dough* to buy a movie ticket.

> **TEACHING TIP**
> You can reinforce the material in this section with practice tests found on pages 396, 397, 406, and 407 of the pupil's textbook and with tests found in the *Holt Handbook Chapter Tests* booklet.

Test Smarts
Taking Standardized Tests in Grammar, Usage, and Mechanics

Becoming "Test-Smart"

Standardized achievement tests, like other tests, measure your skills in specific areas. Standardized achievement tests also compare your performance to the performance of other students at your age or grade level. Some language arts standardized tests measure your skill in using correct capitalization, punctuation, sentence structure, and spelling. Such tests sometimes also measure your ability to evaluate sentence style.

The most important part of preparing for any test, including standardized tests, is learning the content on which you will be tested. To do this, you must

- listen in class
- complete homework assignments
- study to master the concepts and skills presented by your teacher

In addition, you also need to use effective strategies for taking a standardized test. The following pages will teach you how to become test-smart.

General Strategies for Taking Tests

1. **Understand how the test is scored.** If no points will be taken off for wrong answers, plan to answer every question. If wrong answers count against you, plan to answer only questions you know the answer to or questions you can answer with an educated guess.

2. **Stay focused.** Expect to be a little nervous, but focus your attention on doing the best job possible. Try not to be distracted with thoughts that aren't about the test questions.

3. **Get an overview.** Quickly skim the entire test to get an idea of how long the test is and what is on it.

4. **Pace yourself.** Based on your overview, figure out how much time to allow for each section of the test. If time limits are stated for each section, decide how much time to allow for each item. Pace yourself, and check every five to ten minutes to see if you need to work faster. Try to leave a few minutes at the end of the testing period to check your work.

5. **Read all instructions.** Read the instructions for each part of the test carefully. Also, answer the sample questions to be sure you understand how to answer the test questions.

6. **Read all answer choices.** Carefully read *all* of the possible answers before you choose an answer. Note how each possible answer differs from the others. You may want to make an *x* next to each answer choice that you rule out.

7. **Make educated guesses.** If you do not know the answer to a question, see if you can rule out one or more answers and make an educated guess. Don't spend too much time on any one item, though. If you want to think longer about a difficult item, make a light pencil mark next to the item number. You can go back to that question later.

8. **Mark your answers.** Mark the answer sheet carefully and completely. If you plan to go back to an item later, be sure to skip that number on the answer sheet.

9. **Check your work.** If you have time at the end of the test, go back to check your answers. This is also the time to try to answer any questions you skipped. Make sure your marks are complete, and erase any stray marks on the answer sheet.

Strategies for Answering Grammar, Usage, and Mechanics Questions

The questions in standardized tests can take different forms, but the most common form is the multiple-choice question. Here are some strategies for answering that kind of test question.

Correcting parts of sentences

One kind of question contains a sentence with an underlined part. The answer choices show several revised versions of that part. Your job is to decide which revised version makes the sentence correct or whether the underlined part is already correct. First, look at each answer carefully. Immediately rule out any answer in which you notice a grammatical error. If you are still unsure of the correct answer, try approaching the question in one of these two ways.

- **Think how you would rewrite the underlined part.** Look at the answer choices for one that matches your revision. Carefully read each possible answer before you make your final choice. Often, only tiny differences exist between the answers, and you want to choose the *best* answer.

- **Look carefully at the underlined part and at each answer choice, looking for one particular type of error, such as an error in capitalization or spelling.** The best way to look for a particular error is to compare the answer choices to see how they differ both from each other and from the underlined part of the question. For example, if there are differences in capitalization, look at each choice for capitalization errors.

After ruling out incorrect answers, choose the answer with no errors. If there are errors in each of the choices but no errors in the underlined part, your answer will be the "no error" or "correct as is" choice.

EXAMPLE

Directions: Choose the answer that is the **best** revision of the underlined words.

1. My neighbor is painting his <u>house and my brother helped him.</u>
   A. house; and my brother is helping him.
   B. house, and my brother had helped him.
   C. house, and my brother is helping him.
   D. Correct as is

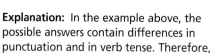

Explanation: In the example above, the possible answers contain differences in punctuation and in verb tense. Therefore, you should check each possible answer for errors in punctuation and verb tense.
   A. You can rule out this choice because it has incorrect punctuation.
   B. This choice creates inconsistent verb tenses, so you can rule out this answer.
   C. This choice has correct punctuation and creates consistent verb tenses.
   D. You can rule out this choice because the original sentence lacks correct punctuation between the clauses.

Answer: Choice C is the only one that contains no errors, so the oval for that answer choice is darkened.

Correcting whole sentences

This type of question is similar to the kind of question previously described. However, here you are looking for mistakes in the entire sentence instead of just an underlined part. The strategies for approaching this type of question are the same as for the other kind of sentence-correction questions. If you don't see the correct answer right away, compare the answer choices to see how they differ. When you find differences, check each choice for errors relating to that difference. Rule out choices with errors. Repeat the process until you find the correct answer.

EXAMPLE

Directions: Choose the answer that is the **best** revision of the following sentences.

1. After Brad mowed the lawn, he swept the sidewalk and driveway, then he took a shower. And washed his hair.
   A. After Brad mowed the lawn, he swept the sidewalk and driveway. Then he took a shower and washed his hair.
   B. After Brad mowed the lawn, he swept the sidewalk and driveway. Then he took a shower, and washed his hair.
   C. After Brad mowed the lawn. He swept the sidewalk and driveway; then he took a shower and washed his hair.
   D. Correct as is

Explanation: The original word groups and answer choices have differences in sentence structure and punctuation, so you should check each answer choice for errors in sentence structure and punctuation.

A. This choice contains two complete sentences and correct punctuation.
B. This choice contains two complete sentences and incorrect punctuation.
C. This choice begins with a sentence fragment, so you can rule it out.
D. You can rule out this choice because the original version contains a sentence fragment.

Answer: Choice A is the only one that contains no errors, so the oval for that answer choice is darkened.

Identifying kinds of errors

This type of question has at least one underlined part. Your job is to determine which part, if any, contains an error. Sometimes, you also may have to decide what type of error (capitalization, punctuation, or spelling) exists. The strategy is the same whether the question has one or several underlined parts. Try to identify an error, and check the answer choices for that type of error. If the original version is correct as written, choose "no error" or "correct as is."

EXAMPLE

Directions: Read the following sentences and decide which type of error, if any, is in the underlined part.

1. Marcia, Jim, and Leroy are participating in <u>Saturday's charity marathon. they</u> are hoping to raise one hundred dollars for the new children's museum.

A. Spelling error
B. Capitalization error
C. Punctuation error
D. Correct as is

Explanation: If you cannot tell right away what kind of error (if any) is in the original version, go through each answer choice in turn.

A. All the words are spelled correctly.
B. The sentences contain a capitalization error. The second sentence incorrectly begins with a lowercase letter.
C. The sentences are punctuated correctly.
D. The sentences contain a capitalization error, so you can rule out this choice.

Answer: Because the passage contains a capitalization error, the oval for answer choice B is darkened.

Revising sentence structure

Errors covered by this kind of question include sentence fragments, run-on sentences, repetitive wording, misplaced modifiers, and awkward construction. If you don't immediately spot the error, examine the question and each answer choice for specific types of errors, one type at a time. If you cannot find an error in the original version and if all of the other answer choices have errors, then choose "no error" or "correct as is."

EXAMPLE

Directions: Read the following word groups. If there is an error in sentence structure, choose the answer that best revises the word groups.

Test Smarts 473

1. Mary Lou arranged the mozzarella cheese and fresh tomatoes. On a platter covered with lettuce leaves.
   A. Mary Lou arranged the mozzarella cheese and fresh tomatoes on a platter covered with lettuce leaves.
   B. Mary Lou arranged the mozzarella cheese and fresh tomatoes, on a platter covered with lettuce leaves.
   C. Mary Lou arranged the mozzarella cheese and fresh tomatoes; on a platter covered with lettuce leaves.
   D. Correct as is

Explanation: The original sentence and answer choices have differences in sentence structure and punctuation.
   A. This choice is correctly punctuated and contains a correct, complete sentence.
   B. This choice contains an incorrect comma, so you can rule it out.
   C. This choice contains an incorrect semicolon, so you can rule it out.
   D. The original word groups contain a sentence fragment, so D cannot be correct.

Answer: Choice A is the only one that contains no errors, so the oval for that answer choice is darkened.

Questions about sentence style

These questions are often not about grammar, usage, or mechanics but about content and organization. They may ask about tone, purpose, topic sentences, supporting sentences, audience, sentence combining, appropriateness of content, or transitions. The questions may ask you which is the *best* way to revise the passage, or they may ask you to identify the *main* purpose of the passage. When you see words such as *best*, *main*, and *most likely* or *least likely*, you are not being asked to correct errors; you are being asked to make a judgment about style or meaning.

If the question asks for a particular kind of revision (for example, "What *transition* is needed between sentence 4 and sentence 5?"), analyze each answer choice to see how well it makes that particular revision. Many questions ask for a general revision (for example, "Which is the *best* way to revise the last sentence?"). In such situations, check each answer choice and rule out any choices that have mistakes in grammar, usage, or mechanics. Then, read each choice and use what you have learned in class to judge whether the revision improves the original sentence. If you are combining sentences, be sure to choose the answer that includes all important information, that demonstrates good style, *and* that is grammatically correct.

EXAMPLE

Directions: Choose the answer that shows the **best** way to combine the following sentences.

1. Jacques Cousteau was a filmmaker and author. Jacques Cousteau explored the ocean as a diver and marine scientist.
   A. Jacques Cousteau was a filmmaker and author; Jacques Cousteau explored the ocean as a marine scientist.
   B. Jacques Cousteau was a filmmaker and author, he explored the ocean as a diver and marine scientist.
   C. Jacques Cousteau was a filmmaker

and author who explored the ocean as a diver and marine scientist.
D. Jacques Cousteau was a filmmaker, author, diver, and scientist.

Explanation:
A. Answer choice A is grammatically correct but unnecessarily repeats the subject *Jacques Cousteau* and leaves out some information.
B. Choice B is a run-on sentence, so it cannot be the correct answer.
C. Choice C is grammatically correct, and it demonstrates effective sentence combining.
D. Choice D is grammatically correct but leaves out some information.

Answer: Because answer choice C shows the best way to combine the sentences, the oval for choice C is darkened.

Fill-in-the-blanks This type of question tests your ability to fill in blanks in sentences, giving answers that are logical and grammatically correct. A question of this kind might ask you to choose a verb in the appropriate tense. A different question might require a combination of adverbs (*first, next*) to show how parts of the sentence relate. Another question might require a vocabulary word to complete the sentence.

To approach a sentence-completion question, first look for clue words in the sentence. *But, however,* and *though* indicate a contrast; *therefore* and *as a result* indicate cause and effect. Using sentence clues, rule out obviously incorrect answer choices. Then, try filling in the blanks with the remaining choices to determine which answer choice makes the most sense. Finally, check to be sure your choice is grammatically correct.

EXAMPLE

Directions: Choose the words that **best** complete the sentence.
1. When Jack _____ the dog, the dog _____ water everywhere.
   A. washes, splashed
   B. washed, will be splashing
   C. will have washed, has splashed
   D. washed, splashed

Explanation:
A. The verb tenses (present and past) are inconsistent.
B. The verb tenses (past and future) are inconsistent.
C. The verb tenses (future perfect and present perfect) are inconsistent.
D. The verb tenses (past and past) are consistent.

Answer: The oval for choice D is darkened.

Using Your Test Smarts

Remember: Success on standardized tests comes partly from knowing strategies for taking such tests—from being test-smart. Knowing these strategies can help you approach standardized achievement tests more confidently. Do your best to learn your classroom subjects, take practice tests if they are available, and use the strategies outlined in this section. Good luck!

Grammar at a Glance

HELP

Grammar at a Glance is an alphabetical list of special terms and expressions with examples and references to further information. When you encounter a grammar or usage problem in the revising or proofreading stage of your writing, look for help in this section first. You may find all you need to know right here. If you need more information, **Grammar at a Glance** will show you where in the book to turn for a more complete explanation. If you do not find what you are looking for in **Grammar at a Glance,** turn to the index.

abbreviation An abbreviation is a shortened form of a word or a phrase.

- **capitalization of** (see page 267.)

TITLES USED WITH NAMES	**M**rs.	**C**apt.	**S**r.	**M.D.**
KINDS OF ORGANIZATIONS	**A**ssn.	**I**nc.	**D**ept.	**C**orp.
PARTS OF ADDRESSES	**A**ve.	**S**t.	**B**lvd.	**P.O. B**ox
NAMES OF STATES	[without ZIP Codes]	**V**a.		**A**rk.
			Mass.	**N. M**ex.
	[with ZIP Codes]	VA		AR
			MA	NM
TIMES	**A.M.**	**P.M.**	**B.C.**	**A.D.**

- **punctuation of** (See page 291.)

WITH PERIODS	(See preceding examples.)
WITHOUT PERIODS	CD-ROM NBC UFO FBI
	DC (D.C. without ZIP Code)
	mg qt tbsp cm yd
	[Exception: inch = in**.**]

action verb An action verb expresses physical or mental activity. (See page 45.)

EXAMPLE   Uncle Jim **drives** a school bus.

active voice Active voice is the voice a verb is in when it expresses an action done by its subject. (See page 189. See also **voice.**)

EXAMPLE   The dog **chased** the squirrel across the yard.

adjective An adjective modifies a noun or a pronoun. (See page 34.)

EXAMPLE   Do you see **that beautiful, old wood** house over there?

adjective clause An adjective clause is a subordinate clause that modifies a noun or a pronoun. (See page 117.)

EXAMPLE   We saw an advertisement for a car **that has aluminum wheels.** [The adjective clause modifies the noun *car.*]

adjective phrase A prepositional phrase that modifies a noun or a pronoun is called an adjective phrase. (See page 92.)

EXAMPLE   Dana prefers the backpack **with large pockets.** [The adjective phrase modifies the noun *backpack.*]

adverb An adverb modifies a verb, an adjective, or another adverb. (See page 54.)

EXAMPLE   Mom and Dad **often** drive us to the lake on weekends. [The adverb modifies the verb *drive.*]

adverb clause An adverb clause is a subordinate clause that modifies a verb, an adjective, or an adverb. (See page 120.)

EXAMPLE   Trudy's grades have improved **since she cut back her TV viewing.** [The adverb clause modifies the verb *have improved.*]

adverb phrase A prepositional phrase that modifies a verb, an adjective, or an adverb is called an adverb phrase. (See page 94.)

EXAMPLE   **After dark,** the carol singers went from house to house. [The adverb phrase modifies the verb *went.*]

affix An affix is a word part that is added before or after a base word or root. (See page 350. See also **prefix** and **suffix.**)

EXAMPLES   de + code = **de**code

im + polite = **im**polite

feel + ing = feel**ing**

serious + ly = serious**ly**

Grammar at a Glance   477

agreement Agreement is the correspondence, or match, between grammatical forms. Grammatical forms agree when they have the same number and gender.

- **of pronouns and antecedents** (See page 165.)

  SINGULAR **Desmond** often rides **his** bicycle to school.
  PLURAL Desmond's **classmates** ride **their** bicycles to school.

  SINGULAR Has **everyone** in the club paid **his** or **her** dues?
  PLURAL Have **all** of the club members paid **their** dues?

  SINGULAR **Neither Darleen nor Clarissa** was pleased with **her** audition.
  PLURAL **Darleen and Clarissa** were not pleased with **their** auditions.

- **of subjects and verbs** (See page 148.)

  SINGULAR The music **teacher is composing** an opera.

  The music **teacher,** with the help of her students, **is composing** an opera.

  PLURAL The music **students are composing** an opera.

  The music **students,** with the help of their teacher, **are composing** an opera.

  SINGULAR **Each** of the students **is looking** forward to seeing the dinosaur exhibit.
  PLURAL **All** of the students **are looking** forward to seeing the dinosaur exhibit.

  SINGULAR **Neither Kevin nor I was** able to go to band camp last summer.
  PLURAL Needless to say, both **Kevin and I were** disappointed.

  SINGULAR Here **is** a **list** of topics from which you can choose.
  PLURAL Here **are** the **topics** from which you can choose.

  SINGULAR The social studies **class is watching** a video about the space program.
  PLURAL The social studies **class are writing** their essays on the space program.

  SINGULAR **Six dollars is** the price of the kite.
  PLURAL From this stack of bills, **six dollars are** missing.

SINGULAR	***Parallel Journeys* was written** by Eleanor Ayer.
PLURAL	Early **journeys** to North America **were** risky.
SINGULAR	**Is gymnastics** an Olympic sport?
PLURAL	**Are** the **scissors** in your sewing basket?

antecedent An antecedent is the word or words that a pronoun stands for. (See page 30.)

EXAMPLE **Tim** doesn't know how long **his** essay will be.
[*His* refers to *Tim*.]

apostrophe
- to form contractions (See page 333.)
  EXAMPLES wouldn'␣t   I'll   o'clock   '99
- to form plurals of letters, numerals, and words used as words (See page 337.)
  EXAMPLES *A*'s and *B*'s   *and*'s instead of *&*'s   5's and 10's
- to show possession (See page 330.)
  EXAMPLES player's uniform

  players' uniforms

  children's literature

  someone's backpack

  Steven Spielberg's and George Lucas's movies

  Batman and Robin's first adventure

appositive An appositive is a noun or a pronoun placed beside another noun or pronoun to identify or describe it. (See page 106.)

EXAMPLE My friend **Désirée** recently moved to a new house.
[*Désirée* identifies *friend*.]

appositive phrase An appositive phrase consists of an appositive and its modifiers. (See page 106.)

EXAMPLE The first taxi in the line was driven by Stavros, **a gray-haired man with a mustache.**

article The articles, *a*, *an*, and *the*, are the most frequently used adjectives. (See page 35.)

EXAMPLES   **a** football   **a** uniform

                an antelope   **an** honor

                the answer   **the** farmhouse

bad, badly (See page 246.)

NONSTANDARD   This green apple tastes badly.

STANDARD   This green apple tastes **bad**.

base A base is a word that can stand alone or combine with other word parts. Prefixes and suffixes can be added to a base to create many different words. (See also **root**.)

EXAMPLES   false   cycle   graph

base form The base form, or infinitive, is one of the four principal parts of a verb. (See page 175.)

EXAMPLE   Can you help me to **find** this address?

brackets (See page 341.)

EXAMPLES   The movie critic wrote, "This actor's performance is a tour de force **[**an unusually skillful performance**]**."

                  Many of the Iroquois legends we know today might have been lost without the efforts of Kaiiontwa'ko (perhaps better known as Cornplanter **[**his Iroquois name means "by what one plants"**]**).

capitalization

- **of abbreviations** (See **abbreviation**.)
- **of first words** (See page 266.)

EXAMPLES   **M**y brother has started taking cello lessons.

                Nick asked, "**W**hat does the French phrase *déjà vu* mean?"

                Dear Ms. Neruda:

                Yours truly,

- **of proper nouns and proper adjectives** (See pages 266 and 276.)

Proper Noun	Common Noun
North America	continent
El Salvador	country
Staten Island	island
Chautauqua Lake	body of water
Jurassic Period	historical period
Mother's Day	holiday
Blue Ridge Mountains	mountain chain
Saguaro National Park	park
Bernheim Arboretum and Research Forest	forest
Mammoth Cave	cave
Kings Canyon	canyon
Southeast	region
Thirty-second Street	street
National Urban League	organization
San Diego Padres	team
Bowling Green State University	institution
Democratic Party (*or* party)	political party
Roth's Optical	business firm
Super Bowl	special event
February, May, August, November	calendar items
Yavapai-Apache	people
Christianity	religion
Buddhist	religious follower
God (*but* the god Zeus)	deity
Passover	holy day
Torah	sacred writing
Jupiter	planet
Alpha Centauri	star
Ursa Major	constellation
Andrea Doria	ship

(continued)

(continued)

Proper Noun	Common Noun
Enola **G**ay	aircraft
Atlantis	spacecraft
Biology **I** (*but* **b**iology)	school subject
Mandarin	language
Mount **R**ushmore **N**ational **M**emorial	monument
World **T**rade **C**enter	building
Heisman **T**rophy	award

- **of titles** (See page 278.)

    EXAMPLES   **S**enator Feinstein [preceding a name]

    Feinstein, a **s**enator from California [following a name]

    Thank you, **S**enator. [direct address]

    Uncle Alphonse (*but* my **u**ncle Alphonse)

    Anasazi: **A**ncient **P**eople of the **R**ock [book]

    Mythic **W**arriors: **G**uardians of the **L**egend [TV program]

    Arrangement in **B**lack and **G**ray: **T**he **A**rtist's **M**other [work of art]

    Rhapsody in **B**lue [musical composition]

    "**T**he **F**rog **W**ho **W**anted to **B**e a **S**inger" [short story]

    "**I A**m of the **E**arth" [poem]

    Reader's **D**igest [magazine]

    the **O**rlando **S**entinel [newspaper]

    Family **C**ircus [comic strip]

    Back to **T**itanic [audiotape or CD]

case of pronouns Case is the form a pronoun takes to show how it is used in a sentence. (See page 201.)

NOMINATIVE   **She** and **I** are taking tae kwon do lessons.

Two of the award winners are Erica and **he**.

	Neither baby sitter, Brigitte nor **she,** is available this evening.
	We students presented historical skits.
	Is David Alfaro Siqueiros the artist **who** painted this?
	We don't know **who** she is.
OBJECTIVE	Did you see Jamaal and **her** at the Juneteenth festival?
	Kristen invited **him** and **me** to the concert.
	Are you going with **them** to the video arcade?
	The Earth Day festivities are being organized by two teachers, Mr. Zapata and **her.**
	Our guide gave **us** spelunkers a map of the cave we would explore.
	Ms. Jennings, **whom** everyone at school admires, will retire this year.
	One of the candidates **whom** I will vote for is Tamisha.
POSSESSIVE	**Their** understanding of the rules differs from **ours.**
	Her making the jump shot in the final seconds sent the game into overtime.

clause A clause is a group of words that contains a subject and a verb and is used as part of a sentence. (See page 113. See also **independent clause** and **subordinate clause.**)

EXAMPLES   she arrives at work on time [independent clause]
unless the bus is late [subordinate clause]

She arrives at work on time unless the bus is late.

clear reference Clear reference occurs when a pronoun clearly refers to its antecedent. (See page 216.)

EXAMPLES   After **Ben** finished his homework, **he** walked to the library and checked out three books. [*He* refers to *Ben.*]

Although **Avery** and **Becca** arrived at the theater late, **they** were still able to find good seats. [*They* refers to *Avery* and *Becca.*]

colon (See page 311.)

■ **before lists**

EXAMPLES   To assemble the bookcase, you will need the following tools**:** a crescent wrench, a small hammer, and a Phillips screwdriver.

Grammar at a Glance

The Bookends Club is featuring books by these authors**:** A. A. Milne, Laura Ingalls Wilder, and Judy Blume.

- **in conventional situations**

EXAMPLES 7**:**30 P.M.

Exodus 20**:**3–17

*The Whole Internet***:** *User's Guide & Catalog*

Dear Sir**:**

comma (See page 294.)

- **in a series**

EXAMPLES Shandra**,** Seth**,** and I spent the summer working at the animal shelter.

Alonzo's hobbies include making wind chimes**,** working jigsaw puzzles**,** and writing short stories and poems.

- **in compound sentences**

EXAMPLES We seventh graders performed three plays this year**,** but my favorite was *Androcles and the Lion* by Bernard Shaw.

My friend Albert portrayed Androcles**,** and I played the part of the lion.

- **with nonessential phrases and clauses**

EXAMPLES Yu the Great**,** a mythical Chinese king**,** possessed superhuman powers. [nonessential phrase]

Yu the Great**,** who possessed superhuman powers**,** could transform himself into different animals. [nonessential clause]

- **with introductory elements**

EXAMPLES Sitting around the campfire**,** we sang songs and told silly stories.

If you like to read books in which animals are the main characters**,** you may enjoy *The Long Patrol.*

In one of the store windows**,** I saw an unusual silver trinket.

- **with interrupters**

  EXAMPLES The Gila monster, for example, is a poisonous lizard.

  Most other lizards, however, are harmless.

- **in conventional situations**

  EXAMPLES On Friday, July 17, 2000, we flew from Baltimore, Maryland, to Raleigh, North Carolina, to attend my brother's graduation.

  Isn't your address 728 Lakewood Boulevard, Grand Rapids, MI 49501-0827?

comma splice A comma splice is a run-on sentence in which only a comma separates two complete sentences. (See **run-on sentence**.)

COMMA SPLICE In 1962, John H. Glenn, Jr., became the first American to orbit the earth, then in 1998, at the age of 77, Glenn made history again by becoming the oldest person to travel in space.

REVISED In 1962, John H. Glenn, Jr., became the first American to orbit the earth**, and** then in 1998, at the age of 77, Glenn made history again by becoming the oldest person to travel in space.

REVISED In 1962, John H. Glenn, Jr., became the first American to orbit the earth**;** then in 1998, at the age of 77, Glenn made history again by becoming the oldest person to travel in space.

comparison of modifiers (See page 224.)

- **comparison of adjectives and adverbs**

Positive	Comparative	Superlative
short	short**er**	short**est**
heavy	heav**ier**	heav**iest**
generous	**more (less)** generous	**most (least)** generous
slowly	**more (less)** slowly	**most (least)** slowly
bad/ill	**worse**	**worst**

- **comparing two**

  EXAMPLES Of Mars and Venus, which planet is **closer** to Earth?

  In the balloon, we flew **higher** and **farther** than we had thought we would.

  China is **more populous** than **any other** country.

- **comparing more than two**

  EXAMPLES Lake Superior is the **largest** of the five Great Lakes.

  Of all of the figure skaters in the competition, I think that Michelle Kwan performed **most gracefully**.

complement A complement is a word or word group that completes the meaning of a verb. (See page 73. See also **direct object, indirect object, subject complement, predicate nominative,** and **predicate adjective**.)

EXAMPLES All of Ms. Lozano's students admire **her**.

Bring **us** the map, please.

Do you feel **thirsty**?

Angela, this is **Ramona**.

complex sentence A complex sentence has one independent clause and at least one subordinate clause. (See page 135.)

EXAMPLES My favorite animated film was *Cinderella* [independent clause] until I saw *The Jungle Book* [subordinate clause].

When my little sister wrote a letter to Santa Claus [subordinate clause], she used the address North Pole, AK 99705 [independent clause], which, by the way, is the correct address. [subordinate clause]

compound-complex sentence A compound-complex sentence has two or more independent clauses and at least one subordinate clause. (See page 137.)

EXAMPLES The Taj Mahal, which is located near Agra, India [subordinate clause], is a beautiful structure made almost entirely of white marble [independent clause]; it was built in the seventeenth century by Shah Jahan as a tomb for his wife [independent clause].

When they publish their works [subordinate clause], some writers use pseudonyms, or pen names, instead of their real names [independent clause]; for example, Theodor Geisel published most of his books for children under the pen name Dr. Seuss [independent clause].

The sweater that I bought last week [subordinate clause] was on sale [independent clause], and it fits well, too [independent clause].

compound sentence A compound sentence has two or more independent clauses but no subordinate clauses. (See page 131.)

EXAMPLES   Two of the kittens are gray [independent clause], but the third one is orange [independent clause].

Yuri was born on February 29 [independent clause]; consequently, each year, except in a leap year, he celebrates his birthday on February 28 [independent clause].

Last night, Dad and I made pizza primavera [independent clause]; he prepared the dough and the Parmesan-cheese sauce [independent clause], and I diced the green onions, red peppers, carrots, and broccoli [independent clause].

compound subject A compound subject is made up of two or more subjects that are connected by a conjunction and that have the same verb. (See page 13.)

EXAMPLES   **Leaves** and **branches** littered the yard after the hailstorm.

Apples, plums, and **blackberries** grow in my grandmother's orchard.

compound verb A compound verb consists of two or more verbs that are joined by a conjunction and that have the same subject. (See page 15.)

EXAMPLES   At the last track meet, Trevor **ran** the mile relay, **threw** the discus, and **participated** in the high jump.

Lauren **attended** soccer practice yesterday but **missed** today's game.

conjunction A conjunction joins words or groups of words. (See page 62.)

COORDINATING	fish **or** fowl
CORRELATIVE	**not only** fair **but also** firm
SUBORDINATING	**Although** Boris had a cold, he insisted on performing.

contraction A contraction is a shortened form of a word, a numeral, or a group of words. Apostrophes in contractions indicate where letters or numerals have been omitted. (See page 333. See also **apostrophe**.)

EXAMPLES	you're [you are]	there's [there is *or* there has]
	who's [who is *or* who has]	they're [they are]
	aren't [are not]	it's [it is *or* it has]
	'14–'18 war [1914–1918 war]	o'clock [of the clock]

coordinating conjunction (See **conjunction**.)

coordination Coordination is the use of a conjunction to link ideas of approximately equal importance. (See page 423. See also **conjunction**.)

EXAMPLES Kim **and** Ted volunteered to help. [*And* joins two nouns.]

The bird is in the tree **or** on the telephone wire. [*Or* joins two phrases.]

I enjoy the outdoors, **but** I have never liked camping. [*But* joins two clauses.]

correlative conjunction (See **conjunction**.)

dangling modifier A dangling modifier is a modifying word, phrase, or clause that does not clearly and sensibly modify a word or a word group in a sentence. (See page 233.)

DANGLING Digging a well near Xi'an, China, in 1974, thousands of ancient terra-cotta sculptures of warriors, horses, and chariots were uncovered. [Were thousands of sculptures digging a well?]

REVISED Digging a well near Xi'an, China, in 1974, **workers** uncovered thousands of ancient terra-cotta sculptures of warriors, horses, and chariots.

dash (See page 341.)

EXAMPLE   The marine biologist spent several days—ten, I think—recording the movements of the manatee and her calf.

declarative sentence A declarative sentence makes a statement and is followed by a period. (See page 18.)

EXAMPLE   Edinburgh is the capital of Scotland.

dependent clause (See **subordinate clause**.)

derivative Derivatives are words derived from other words.

EXAMPLES   earthling [from *earth*]

union [from the Latin word *unus*, meaning "one"]

direct object A direct object is a word or word group that receives the action of the verb or shows the result of the action. A direct object answers the question *Whom?* or *What?* after a transitive verb. (See page 74.)

EXAMPLE   Rashmi visited **them** Tuesday afternoon.

double comparison A double comparison is the nonstandard use of two comparative forms (usually *more* and *–er*) or two superlative forms (usually *most* and *–est*) to express comparison. In standard usage, the single comparative form is correct. (See page 230.)

NONSTANDARD   Olympus Mons, a volcano on Mars, is the most highest mountain in our solar system.

STANDARD   Olympus Mons, a volcano on Mars, is the **highest** mountain in our solar system.

double negative A double negative is the nonstandard use of two negative words when one is enough. (See page 231.)

NONSTANDARD   Alonzo is so very sleepy that he can't hardly keep his eyes open.

STANDARD   Alonzo is so very sleepy that he **can hardly** keep his eyes open.

NONSTANDARD   I haven't never ridden in an airplane.
STANDARD   I **have never** ridden in an airplane.
STANDARD   I **haven't ever** ridden in an airplane.

double subject A double subject occurs when an unnecessary pronoun is used after the subject of a sentence. (See page 251.)

NONSTANDARD   Abner Doubleday, contrary to popular belief, he did not create the game of baseball.
STANDARD   Abner Doubleday, contrary to popular belief, did not create the game of baseball.

end marks

- **with sentences** (See page 290.)

    EXAMPLES   In 1998, Mark McGwire broke Roger Maris's single-season home-run record. [declarative sentence]

    How many home runs did Mark McGwire hit in 1998? [interrogative sentence]

    Wow! [interjection] McGwire hit seventy home runs! [exclamatory sentence]

    Don't forget that in 1998 Sammy Sosa also surpassed Maris's record by hitting sixty-six home runs. [imperative sentence]

- **with abbreviations** (See page 291. See also **abbreviation**.)

    EXAMPLES   In 1964, the Nobel Peace Prize was awarded to Dr. Martin Luther King, Jr.

    In 1964, was the Nobel Peace Prize awarded to Dr. Martin Luther King, Jr.?

essential clause/essential phrase An essential, or restrictive, clause or phrase is necessary to the meaning of a sentence and is not set off by commas. (See page 300.)

EXAMPLES   The woman **who gives the lectures on Romanian art** is Ms. Antonescu. [essential clause]

The animals **drinking at the water hole** gave the elephants a wide berth. [essential phrase]

exclamation point (See **end marks**.)

exclamatory sentence An exclamatory sentence expresses strong feeling and is followed by an exclamation point. (See page 19.)

EXAMPLE   What a surprise this is!

fragment (See **sentence fragment**.)

fused sentence A fused sentence is a run-on sentence in which no punctuation separates complete sentences. (See **run-on sentence**.)

FUSED   Most totems, or images, carved into a totem pole are symbolic usually the totem at the top of the pole represents the family's guardian spirit.

REVISED   Most totems, or images, carved into a totem pole are symbolic; usually the totem at the top of the pole represents the family's guardian spirit.

REVISED   Most totems, or images, carved into a totem pole are symbolic. Usually the totem at the top of the pole represents the family's guardian spirit.

future perfect tense (See **tense of verbs**.)

future tense (See **tense of verbs**.)

good, well (See page 228.)

EXAMPLES   For a beginner, Julian is a **good** golfer.
Yes, for a beginner, Julian plays golf extremely **well** [*not* good].

hyphen (See page 338.)

- **to divide words**
  EXAMPLE   The Ecology Club at our school recently organ-ized a recycling campaign.
- **in compound numbers**
  EXAMPLE   The Ecology Club has ninety-seven members.
- **with prefixes**
  EXAMPLE   The Ecology Club began a recycling campaign in mid-September.

Grammar at a Glance

imperative sentence An imperative sentence gives a command or makes a request and is followed by either a period or an exclamation point. (See page 18.)

EXAMPLES   Please turn the TV off. [request]
            Turn that TV off! [command]

indefinite pronoun An indefinite pronoun does not refer to a definite person, place, thing, or idea. (See page 32.)

EXAMPLES   I have **many**, but he has **few**.
            Is **someone** calling for you?
            Both of the children wanted a drink of water.

independent clause An independent clause (also called a *main clause*) expresses a complete thought and can stand by itself as a sentence. (See page 114.)

EXAMPLE   Because Dad never has any spare time, **he hired a contractor to build the deck.**

indirect object An indirect object is a word or word group that often comes between a transitive verb and its direct object and tells to whom or to what or for whom or for what the action of the verb is done. (See page 76.)

EXAMPLE   Kathleen gave the **dog** a rubber toy. [The direct object is *toy*.]

infinitive An infinitive is a verb form, usually preceded by *to*, that is used as a noun, an adjective, or an adverb. (See page 102.)

EXAMPLE   We all wanted **to swim**, so Mom took us to the pool.

infinitive phrase An infinitive phrase consists of an infinitive and its modifiers and complements. (See page 103.)

EXAMPLE   **To help one's fellow human beings** is an admirable goal, Ronny.

interjection An interjection expresses emotion and has no grammatical relation to the rest of the sentence. (See page 65.)

EXAMPLE   **Wow!** Look at those fireworks!

interrogative sentence An interrogative sentence asks a question and is followed by a question mark. (See page 19.)

EXAMPLE   Have you ever seen the Rockies**?**

intransitive verb An intransitive verb is a verb that does not take an object. (See page 52.)

EXAMPLE   The wind **howls** fiercely.

irregular verb An irregular verb is a verb that forms its past and past participle in some way other than by adding –d or –ed to the base form. (See page 178. See also **regular verb.**)

Base Form	Present Participle	Past	Past Participle
be	[is] being	was, were	[have] been
bring	[is] bringing	brought	[have] brought
choose	[is] choosing	chose	[have] chosen
cost	[is] costing	cost	[have] cost
eat	[is] eating	ate	[have] eaten
grow	[is] growing	grew	[have] grown
pay	[is] paying	paid	[have] paid
spread	[is] spreading	spread	[have] spread

italics (See **underlining** [italics].)

its, it's (See page 251.)

EXAMPLES   **It's** [It is] your turn to clean **its** [the gerbil's] cage.

                It's [It has] been a long time since **it's** [it has] been cleaned.

lie, lay (See page 193.)

EXAMPLES   "You look tired, Mom. Perhaps you should **lay** your work aside and **lie** down for a while," I suggested.

                Agreeing with me, Mom **laid** her reading glasses on her desk and **lay** down on the sofa.

linking verb A linking verb connects the subject with a word that identifies or describes the subject. (See page 46.)

EXAMPLE   Starlings **are** determined nest-builders.

misplaced modifier A misplaced modifier is a word, phrase, or clause that seems to modify the wrong word or words in a sentence. (See page 233.)

MISPLACED   The pod of humpback whales entertained the passengers aboard the tour boat, leaping gracefully out of the gentle ocean waves. [Was the tour boat leaping gracefully?]

REVISED   **Leaping gracefully out of the gentle ocean waves,** the pod of humpback whales entertained the passengers aboard the tour boat.

modifier A modifier is a word or word group that makes the meaning of another word or word group more specific. (See page 223.)

EXAMPLES   Harriet is **happy.**

Laughing excitedly, the children burst the balloon.

nonessential clause/nonessential phrase A nonessential, or nonrestrictive, clause or phrase adds information not necessary to the main idea in the sentence and is set off by commas. (See page 299.)

EXAMPLES   Diana discussed her trip to Florida**, which took place last month.** [nonessential clause]

The twins**, sitting quietly for a change,** posed for the picture. [nonessential phrase]

noun A noun names a person, a place, a thing, or an idea. (See page 25.)

EXAMPLES   Elizabeth Peña   Paris   mountain   knowledge

number Number is the form a word takes to indicate whether the word is singular or plural. (See page 147.)

SINGULAR	child	man	leaf	town
PLURAL	children	men	leaves	towns

object of a preposition An object of a preposition is the noun or pronoun that ends a prepositional phrase. (See page 59.)

EXAMPLE She heard a composition on the **radio** by her **music teacher.** [*On the radio* and *by her music teacher* are prepositional phrases.]

parallelism Parallelism is the repetition of sentence patterns or of other grammatical structures. (See page 421.)

NOT PARALLEL Mark is a friendly person and kind. [a noun and an adjective]

PARALLEL Mark is **friendly** and **kind.** [two adjectives]

NOT PARALLEL He is in a hurry, anxious, and has run out of patience. [prepositional phrase, adjective, and predicate]

PARALLEL He is **hurried, anxious,** and **impatient.** [three adjectives]

parentheses (See page 340.)

EXAMPLES A praying mantis **(**see Illustration C**)** is the only insect that can turn its head from side to side.

A praying mantis is the only insect that can turn its head from side to side. **(**See Illustration C.**)**

participial phrase A participial phrase consists of a participle and any complements and modifiers it has. (See page 100.)

EXAMPLE **Admired for his courage,** my cousin George is an impressive young man.

participle A participle is a verb form that can be used as an adjective. (See page 98.)

EXAMPLE **Blushing,** Tina accepted the award.

passive voice The passive voice is the voice a verb is in when it expresses an action done to its subject. (See page 189. See also **voice**.)

EXAMPLE The treasurer **was re-elected** with 60 percent of the vote.

Grammar at a Glance   495

past perfect tense (See **tense of verbs.**)

past tense (See **tense of verbs.**)

period (See **end marks.**)

phrase A phrase is a group of related words that does not contain both a verb and its subject and that is used as a single part of speech. (See page 89.)

EXAMPLES   Steve, **our champion swimmer,** will represent King Junior High **at the meet in Kansas City.** [*Our champion swimmer* is an appositive phrase. *At the meet* and *in Kansas City* are prepositional phrases.]

To make her own quilt is Maya's goal. [*To make her own quilt* is an infinitive phrase.]

The leaves, **pressed thoroughly and laminated,** will make beautiful coasters. [*Pressed thoroughly and laminated* is a participial phrase.]

predicate The predicate is the part of a sentence that says something about the subject. (See page 8.)

EXAMPLES   **Will** she **perform a solo**?

Horace **may be responsible for that solution.**

predicate adjective A predicate adjective is an adjective that completes the meaning of a linking verb and modifies the subject of the verb. (See page 81.)

EXAMPLES   The trees looked **red** in the evening light.

This rose smells **beautiful.**

predicate nominative A predicate nominative is a noun or pronoun that completes the meaning of a linking verb and identifies or refers to the subject of the verb. (See page 79.)

EXAMPLES   A lizard is a **reptile.**

My sister will be a **lawyer** soon.

prefix A prefix is a word part that cannot stand alone and that is added before a base word or root to form a new word. (See page 350.)

EXAMPLES un + fair = **un**fair   il + legal = **il**legal

re + new = **re**new   pre + historic = **pre**historic

self + esteem = **self**-esteem   ex + governor = **ex**-governor

mid + April = **mid**-April   post + Holocaust = **post**-Holocaust

preposition A preposition shows the relationship of a noun or a pronoun to some other word in a sentence. (See page 58.)

EXAMPLE Berlin, the capital **of** Germany, is located **in** the east.

prepositional phrase A prepositional phrase is a group of words beginning with a preposition and ending with its object. (See page 59. See also **object of a preposition**.)

EXAMPLE **Before work,** Dan always feeds the birds.

present perfect tense (See **tense of verbs**.)

present tense (See **tense of verbs**.)

pronoun A pronoun is used in place of one or more nouns or pronouns. (See page 30.)

EXAMPLES **His** muscles ached, **she** was sunburned, and **their** feet were sore, but all in all **they** had had a wonderful day.

All of the guests helped **themselves** to **more** of the spinach salad.

question mark (See **end marks**.)

quotation marks (See page 322.)

- **for direct quotations**

EXAMPLE "Learning a few simple rules," said the teacher, "will help you avoid many common spelling errors."

Grammar at a Glance 497

- **with other marks of punctuation** (See also preceding example.)

  EXAMPLES "Through which South American countries does the Amazon River flow?" asked Enrique.

  Which poem begins with the line "The wind was a torrent of darkness among the gusty trees"?

  Cynthia asked, "Did Amy Tan write the short story 'Fish Cheeks'?"

- **for titles**

  EXAMPLES "Song of the Trees" [short story]

  "Mama Is a Sunrise" [short poem]

  "Many Rivers to Cross" [song]

regular verb A regular verb is a verb that forms its past and past participle by adding –d or –ed to the base form. (See page 176. See also **irregular verb**.)

Base Form	Present Participle	Past	Past Participle
ask	[is] asking	asked	[have] asked
attack	[is] attacking	attacked	[have] attacked
drown	[is] drowning	drowned	[have] drowned
suppose	[is] supposing	supposed	[have] supposed
use	[is] using	used	[have] used

rise, raise (See page 191.)

EXAMPLES The river **rose** rapidly.

The lieutenant **raised** a white flag to signal surrender.

root A root is a word part that cannot stand alone. It combines with other word parts to form words. Prefixes and suffixes can be added to a root to create new words. (See also **base**.)

EXAMPLES –loq–   –dict–   –lith–

e**loq**uent   pre**dict**   mono**lith**

run-on sentence A run-on sentence is two or more complete sentences run together as one. (See page 416. See also **comma splice** and **fused sentence.**)

RUN-ON   We were so impressed by the story that we said nothing he grew a little impatient.

REVISED   We were so impressed by the story that we said nothing. He grew a little impatient.

REVISED   We were so impressed by the story that we said nothing; he grew a little impatient.

semicolon (See page 310.)

- **in compound sentences with no conjunction**
    EXAMPLE   My sister plays violin in her school's symphony orchestra; her goal is to become first chair.

- **in compound sentences with conjunctive adverbs**
    EXAMPLE   I play that movie's soundtrack nearly every day; consequently, I know the lyrics of all of its songs.

- **between items in a series when the items contain commas**
    EXAMPLE   The band's cross-country tour includes concerts in Seattle, Washington; Albuquerque, New Mexico; Cincinnati, Ohio; and Miami, Florida.

sentence A sentence is a group of words that contains a subject and a verb and expresses a complete thought. (See page 4.)

                             S   V
EXAMPLE   Mr. Holland will give his presentation in the auditorium.

sentence fragment A sentence fragment is a group of words that is punctuated as if it were a complete sentence but that does not contain both a subject and a verb or that does not express a complete thought. (See pages 4 and 414.)

FRAGMENT   In 2002, the Winter Olympic Games in Salt Lake City.
SENTENCE   In 2002, the Winter Olympic Games will be held in Salt Lake City.

FRAGMENT   To find more information about the Zapotec culture.
SENTENCE   To find more information about the Zapotec culture, we searched the Internet.

Grammar at a Glance

simple sentence A simple sentence has one independent clause and no subordinate clauses. (See page 130.)

EXAMPLES Both the cheetah and the chimpanzee are endangered species.

How many other species of mammals are endangered?

sit, set (See page 190.)

EXAMPLES The science students **sat** quietly, watching the televised launch of the space shuttle *Atlantis*.

On top of the television, the science teacher **set** her model of the space shuttle *Atlantis*.

stringy sentence A stringy sentence is a sentence that has too many independent clauses. Usually, the clauses are strung together with coordinating conjunctions like *and* or *but*. (See page 428.)

STRINGY I remember that the first time I looked through binoculars at the night sky I was surprised that I could clearly see the craters of the moon and the satellites of Jupiter, but what amazed me most was a bright object shimmering with many different colors near the horizon, and I, of course, immediately thought that I had spotted a UFO, but I learned later that the colorful object was not a UFO but the planet Venus.

REVISED I remember the first time I looked through binoculars at the night sky. I was surprised that I could clearly see the craters of the moon and the satellites of Jupiter. What amazed me most, however, was a bright object shimmering with many different colors near the horizon. I, of course, immediately thought that I had spotted a UFO. I learned later, though, that the colorful object was not a UFO but the planet Venus.

subject The subject tells whom or what a sentence is about. (See page 5.)

EXAMPLE Finally, **the train** entered the station.

subject complement A subject complement is a word or word group that completes the meaning of a linking verb and identifies or describes the subject. (See page 79.)

EXAMPLE Linus was **impressive** in the play last night.

subordinate clause A subordinate clause (also called a *dependent clause*) does not express a complete thought and cannot stand alone as a sentence. (See page 114. See also **adjective clause** and **adverb clause**.)

EXAMPLE   Margaret and Melanie are two six-year-old girls **who live in San Marcos, Texas.**

subordinating conjunction (See **conjunction**.)

subordination Subordination is the use of a subordinate clause to show that an idea is not as important as the idea in an independent clause. (See page 425. See also **conjunction**.)

EXAMPLES   Until you called, I didn't know of your return. [*Until* connects the subordinate clause *Until you called* to the independent clause *I didn't know of your return.*]

Is the painting that Laura did on display? [*That* connects the subordinate clause *that Laura did* to the independent clause *Is the painting on display?*]

suffix A suffix is a word part that is added after a base word or root. (See page 350.)

EXAMPLES   safe + ly = safe**ly**   fair + ness = fair**ness**

busy + ly = busi**ly**   enjoy + ing = enjoy**ing**

active + ity = activ**ity**   knowledge + able = knowledge**able**

swim + er = swimm**er**   teach + er = teach**er**

syllable A syllable is a word part that can be pronounced as one uninterrupted sound. (See page 347.)

EXAMPLES   stretch [one syllable]

per • plex [two syllables]

un • der • stand [three syllables]

tense of verbs The tense of verbs indicates the time of the action or state of being expressed by the verb. (See page 186.)

Present

I write	we write
you write	you write
he, she, it writes	they write

Past

I wrote	we wrote
you wrote	you wrote
he, she, it wrote	they wrote

Future

I will (shall) write	we will (shall) write
you will (shall) write	you will (shall) write
he, she, it will (shall) write	they will (shall) write

Present Perfect

I have written	we have written
you have written	you have written
he, she, it has written	they have written

Past Perfect

I had written	we had written
you had written	you had written
he, she, it had written	they had written

Future Perfect

I will (shall) have written	we will (shall) have written
you will (shall) have written	you will (shall) have written
he, she, it will (shall) have written	they will (shall) have written

their, there, they're (See page 255.)

EXAMPLES   Did Mr. and Mrs. Wilson invite us to **their** Fourth of July party? [*Their* tells whose party.]

I hung the calendar **there** on the kitchen wall. [*There* tells where the calendar was hung.]

There is not much vegetable soup left. [*There* begins the sentence but does not add to the sentence's meaning.]

They're playing a new computer game. [*They're* is a contraction of *They are.*]

transitions Transitions are words or word groups that show how ideas are related. (See page 437.)

EXAMPLES   Sara and Adrian waded in the river; **however,** they decided not to swim.

Afterward, they had a picnic and **then** walked home.

transitive verb A transitive verb is an action verb that takes an object. (See page 52.)

EXAMPLE   Marcia **washed** her minivan yesterday.

underlining (italics) (See page 320.)

- **for titles**

  EXAMPLES   *Thurgood Marshall: American Revolutionary* [book]

  Sports Illustrated for Kids [periodical]

  American Gothic [work of art]

  The Water Carrier [long musical composition]

- **for words, letters, and symbols used as such and for foreign words**

  EXAMPLES   Notice that the word *Mississippi* has four *i*'s, four *s*'s, and two *p*'s.

  A *fait accompli* is anything that is done that cannot be undone.

verb A verb expresses an action or a state of being. (See page 45.)

EXAMPLES   We **walked** slowly down the steep hill.

The grasshopper **is** near the fence.

verbal A verbal is a form of a verb used as a noun, an adjective, or an adverb. (See page 98. See also **participle** and **infinitive.**)

EXAMPLES   The children were amazed by the **leaping** lemurs.

To leave was hard.

verbal phrase A verbal phrase consists of a verbal and any modifiers and complements it has. (See page 98. See also **participial phrase** and **infinitive phrase**.)

EXAMPLES **Running fast,** the squirrel reached the safety of the tree.

I don't want **to say goodbye.**

verb phrase A verb phrase consists of a main verb and at least one helping verb. (See page 11.)

EXAMPLES **Have** you **seen** Rich today?

I **would be going** tomorrow, otherwise.

voice Voice is the form a transitive verb takes to indicate whether the subject of the verb performs or receives the action. (See page 189.)

ACTIVE VOICE	Patricia MacLachlan **wrote** the book *Sarah, Plain and Tall.*
PASSIVE VOICE	The book *Sarah, Plain and Tall* **was written** by Patricia MacLachlan.

well (See *good, well*.)

who, whom (See page 211.)

EXAMPLES For two weeks last summer, I visited my pen pal Émile, **who** lives in Montreal, Quebec.

My pen pal Émile, **whom** I have known for five years, has taught me much about French Canadian traditions.

wordiness Wordiness is the use of more words than necessary or the use of fancy words where simple ones will do. (See page 430.)

WORDY	In the event that it rains, we will not cancel the party that we have planned in celebration of Cinco de Mayo but instead, as an alternative, will hold the party indoors, not outdoors.
REVISED	If it rains, we will hold our Cinco de Mayo party indoors.

INDEX

A, an
    as indefinite articles, 35
    usage of, 245
A, an, the, **capitalization of,** 267, 279
Abbreviations
    A.D., 292
    in addresses, 291
    B.C., 292
    capitalization of, 291–92, 476
    definition of, 476
    at end of sentence, 292
    exclamation points and, 292
    of governmental agencies, 291
    of organizations and companies, 291
    periods and, 291–92
    of personal names, 291
    punctuation of, 291–92, 476
    question marks and, 292
    state abbreviations with ZIP Codes, 268, 292
    of states, 291
    of times and dates, 291
    of titles used with names, 291
Abstract nouns, 28
Accept, except, 246, 359
Acronyms, definition of, 291
Action verbs, 47
    adverb modifiers and, 229
    definition of, 45, 476
    direct object and, 80
Active voice, 189, 236
    definition of, 476
A.D., 292
Addresses
    abbreviations in, 291
    capitalization in, 268
    hyphens in street numbers, 268
    punctuation of, 306–307
    ZIP Code, 292, 307
Adjective(s)
    adverbs distinguished from, 55
    definition of, 34, 477
    degree of comparison of, 224–27
    demonstrative adjectives, 31, 36
    diagramming and, 448
    ending in –*ly*, 55
    indefinite pronouns used as, 32
    infinitives used as, 102
    linking verbs and, 229
    as modifiers, 223
    nouns used as, 35, 37, 39
    participial phrases as, 100
    participles used as, 98
    personal pronouns as, 202
    placement of, 34
    pronouns used as, 36, 39
    proper adjectives, 37
    punctuation of a series of adjectives, 296
Adjective clauses
    adjective phrases distinguished from, 117
    in complex sentence, 135
    definition of, 117, 426, 477
    diagramming of, 458
    introductory words of, 135
    placement of, 117, 238
    relative pronouns and, 32, 118, 135, 238
Adjective phrases
    definition of, 92, 477
    diagramming and, 454
    identification of, 95
    as modifiers, 92
    placement of, 92, 95
Adverb(s)
    adjectives distinguished from, 55
    as defining verbs, 54
    definition of, 54, 477
    degree of comparison of, 224–27
    diagramming and, 448–49
    ending in –*ly*, 55
    formed from adjectives, 55
    infinitive used as, 102
    interrupting verb phrase, 50
    linking verbs and, 229
    list of, 54–55
    as modifiers, 223–24
    never, 12
    not, 12, 55
    placement of, 56–57
    prepositions distinguished from, 61
    questions answered by, 54
    very as overused adverb, 55
Adverb clauses
    adverb phrases distinguished from, 120
    definition of, 120, 426, 477
    diagramming of, 458–59
    introductory adverb clauses, 305
    placement of, 120
    punctuation of, 120, 305
    questions answered by, 120
    subordinating conjunctions and, 121, 135
Adverb phrases
    definition of, 94, 477
    diagramming and, 454–55
    as modifiers, 94–95
    placement of, 95
Advice, advise, 359
Affect, effect, 359
Affix, definition of, 477

Agreement (pronoun-antecedent)
   antecedents joined by *and,* 166
   antecedents joined by *or* or *nor,* 166
   in awkward-sounding sentence, 166
   collective noun as antecedent, 167
   definition of, 478
   expressions of amounts and, 168
   gender and, 165
   indefinite pronoun as antecedent, 151, 152–53, 166
   name of an organization, country, or city, 168
   number and, 165–68
   plural pronoun as antecedent, 166
   proper nouns in plural form, 168
   singular pronoun as antecedent, 166
   title of a creative work, 168

Agreement (subject-verb)
   in awkward-sounding sentences, 156
   collective nouns and, 158–59
   compound subject and, 155
   definition of, 478–79
   don't, doesn't, 162–63
   expressions of amounts and, 161
   here's, there's, where's, 160
   indefinite pronouns and, 151, 152–53
   inverted word order and, 160
   name of a country, city, or organization, 162
   number and, 150–51
   with phrase between subject and verb, 150–51
   plural nouns and, 161
   plural subjects and verbs, 148
   problems with, 150–63
   in questions, 159
   sentence revision and, 423
   in sentences beginning with *here* or *there,* 159
   singular subject and verb, 148, 156
   subjects following verbs, 159–60
   subjects joined by *and,* 155
   subjects joined by *or, nor,* 156
   title of a creative work and, 162

Ain't, 246
All right, 246, 359
A lot, 246
Already, all ready, 246, 359
Altar, alter, 360
Altogether, all together, 360
Among, between, 248

And
   agreement (subject-verb) and, 155
   antecedents joined by, 166
   independent clauses and, 428
   sentence combining and, 423–24

Antecedents
   clear references with pronouns, 216–17, 483
   definition of, 30, 479

Anyways, anywheres, everywheres, nowheres, somewheres, 246

Apostrophes
   with contractions, 332, 333–34, 479
   forming plurals of letters, numerals, words used as words and, 479
   personal pronoun possessives and, 330, 332
   plural possessive and, 331
   plurals of numerals, letters, symbols, and words and, 337, 358
   with possessives, 330–32, 479
   proper nouns and, 330
   singular possessive case and, 330

Appositive(s)
   definition of, 106, 213, 301, 479
   diagramming of, 457
   essential appositives, 302
   nonessential appositives, 301
   pronoun as, 213

Appositive phrases, 301
   definition of, 106, 479
   diagramming of, 457
   nonessential appositive phrases, 301
   punctuation of, 106, 421

Articles
   capitalization of, 267, 279
   definite articles, 35
   definition of, 35, 480
   indefinite articles, 35

As, if, as though, like, 252
As, like, 252
At, 246
Attractively, **comparison of,** 226
Auxiliary verbs. *See* Helping verbs.

Bad, **comparison of,** 227
Bad, badly, 246–47, 480
Base, **definition of,** 480
Base form of verbs, 175, 176, 178–82
   definition of, 480
Be
   forms of, 46, 493
   as helping verb, 50, 175
   as linking verb, 46–47
Become, **principal parts of,** 178
Begin, **principal parts of,** 179
Between, among, 248
B.C., 292
Bite, **principal parts of,** 179
Blow, **principal parts of,** 179
Borrowed words, 467–68
Brackets, 341, 480
Brake, break, 360
Break, **principal parts of,** 179
Bring, **principal parts of,** 179, 493
Bring, take, 248

British vs. American spelling and pronunciation, 467
Broken quotations, 323
Build, **principal parts of,** 178, 179
Burst, **principal parts of,** 179
Business letters, salutation in, 312
Bust, busted, 248
But
    independent clauses and, 297, 428
    sentence combining and, 423–24
Buy, **principal parts of,** 178, 179

Can't hardly, can't scarcely, 248
Capital, capitol, 360
Capitalization
    of abbreviations, 291–92, 476
    of aircraft, 272
    of animals, 267
    articles *a, an,* and *the,* 267, 279
    of awards, 273
    of brand names and business products, 272
    of businesses, 272
    of buildings and other structures, 272
    of calendar items and holidays, 271
    of common nouns, 266–67
    of constellations, 274
    coordinating conjunctions and, 279
    of deities (specific), 273
    of *earth, sun, moon,* 274
    of *east, west, north, south,* 268
    of family relationship words, 279
    of first word of direct quotation, 266
    of first word of sentence, 266, 480
    of geographical names, 267–68
    of *goddess, god,* 273
    of government bodies, 271
    of heavenly bodies, 274
    of historical events and periods, 271
    of holy days, 273
    of hyphenated street numbers, 268
    of institutions, 271
    of *I* pronoun, 266
    in letters (correspondence), 266
    of monuments and memorials, 273
    of names of persons, 267
    of nationalities, races, peoples, 271
    of organizations, 271
    of planets and celestial bodies, 274
    in poetry, 266
    of prepositions of fewer than five letters, 279
    of proper adjectives, 276–77, 481–82
    of proper nouns, 266–74, 481–82
    of proper nouns used as adjectives, 37
    in quoted sentences, 266, 323
    of religions, 273
    rules for, 266–80
    of sacred writings, 273
    of school subjects, 277
    of seasons, 271
    of sentence within sentence, 340
    of ships, 272
    of spacecraft, 272
    of special events, 271
    of teams, 271
    of titles and subtitles of works, 279–80, 482
    of titles of persons, 278–79, 482
    of trains, 272
Capitol, capital, 360
Case forms
    definition of, 201
    nominative case, 201, 202, 203–204, 482–83
    nouns and, 202
    objective case, 201, 202, 206–209, 483
    personal pronouns, 202
    possessive case, 201, 202, 330–32, 483
    pronouns and, 201–209, 482–83
Catch, **principal parts of,** 179
–cede, –ceed, –sede, **spelling rule for,** 350
Choose, chose, 360
Choose, **principal parts of,** 179, 493
Clauses. *See also* Adjective clauses; Adverb clauses; Subordinate clauses.
    adjective clauses, 117–18
    adverb clauses, 120–21
    beginning with *who, which,* or *that,* 426
    definition of, 113, 426, 483
    essential clauses, 300
    independent clauses, 114
    introductory clauses, 305
    kinds of, 114–21
    as modifiers, 224
    nonessential clauses, 299, 494
    phrases distinguished from, 89
    placement of, 232–38
    punctuation of, 294, 297, 299–300, 305, 426
    sentence fragments and, 113
    in a series, 294
    subordinate clauses, 114, 501
    with words of time or place, 426
Clean, **principal parts of,** 176
Clear reference of pronoun and antecedent, 216–17, 483
Close, **comparison of,** 225
Closing of a letter, punctuating with comma, 307
Cloths, clothes, 360
Coarse, course, 361
Collective nouns, 29, 158–59, 167
Colloquialisms, 469
Colons
    before a list of items, 311–12, 483–84
    between titles and subtitles, 312

in Biblical references, 312
in conventional situations, 484
in expressions of time, 312
following and *as follows,* 311
placement of, 311–12
in salutations of letters, 312
Combining sentences, 418–26
by using *and, but, or,* 423–24
phrase insertion and, 420–21
subordinate clauses and, 425–26
word insertion and, 419
***Come,* principal parts of,** 179
Commands, 18–19, 290
Commas
in addresses, 306–307
adverb clauses and, 120
appositive phrases and, 106
appositives and appositive phrases and, 301–302
in compound sentences, 131, 297, 484
in conventional situations, 306–307, 485
dates and, 306
direct address and, 303
independent clauses and, 294
interjections and, 65
with interrupters, 299–304, 485
introductory words, phrases, and clauses and, 305, 484
items in a series and, 294–95, 484
with multiple adjectives, 296
nonessential phrases and clauses and, 299, 484
parenthetical expressions and, 303–304
quotations and, 323–24
in salutations and closings of letters, 307
used before *and, but, or,* 297
used before *for, nor, so, yet,* 297
Comma splices, 485
Common nouns, 26, 266
Comparative degree, 225–27, 485
Comparison of modifiers
choosing form of, 225
comparative degree, 225–27, 485
comparing more than two, 486
comparing two, 225, 486
comparison of adjectives and adverbs, 224–27, 485
decreasing comparison, 226–27
double comparison, 230
irregular comparison, 227
positive degree, 225–27, 485
regular comparison, 225–27
superlative degree, 225–27, 485
Complement, compliment, 361
Complements
definition of, 73, 486
direct objects, 74–75
indirect objects, 76–77
recognizing complements, 73–74
subject complements, 79–81

Complete sentences, 414–17
requirements of, 414
Complete subjects, 6–7
Complex sentences
definition of, 135, 435, 486
diagramming of, 461
parts of, 135
and subordinate clauses, 425
Compound-complex sentences, 137, 435
definition of, 486–87
diagramming, 462
Compound direct object, 75
choosing the correct pronoun and, 207
diagramming and, 451
Compound indirect object, 77, 451
Compound nouns, 25, 296, 358
Compound numbers (numerals), hyphens with, 338, 491
Compound predicate adjectives, 453
Compound predicate nominatives, 80, 452
Compound sentences
compound subjects and verbs in, 133
definition of, 131, 435, 487
diagramming of, 460
independent clauses and, 131–32, 487
punctuation of, 131–32, 297
relationship of ideas in, 424
sentence combining and, 424
Compound subjects, 13, 133, 155, 423, 446, 447, 487
Compound verbs, 15, 133, 423, 446, 447, 487
Computers
creating a Help file, 167
correcting modifier problems, 234
editing on computer, 82, 138
grammar checker, 4, 194, 430
italicizing with, 320
proofreading and, 114
sentence structure and, 138
spellchecker and, 245, 267, 348
thesaurus program and, 34
Concrete nouns, 28
Conjugation of verbs, 186–88
Conjunctions. *See also* Coordinating conjunctions; Subordinating conjunctions.
with compound subjects, 13
with compound verbs, 15
correlative conjunctions, 63
definition of, 62, 488
diagramming and, 449
for as, 62
Consistency of tense, 188
Consonants, spelling rules for final consonant, 353
Context, definition of, 153
Contractions
apostrophes and, 332, 333–34, 488
definition of, 333, 488
don't, doesn't and agreement, 162–63

here's, there's, where's, 160
list of common contractions, 333
not in, 333
possessive pronouns distinguished from, 334
Coordinating conjunctions
    capitalization and, 279
    compound sentences and, 131, 133
    list of, 62
    punctuation of, 310
    run-on sentences and, 417
Coordination, definition of, 423, 488
Correlative conjunctions, 63, 488
Cost, **principal parts of,** 179, 493
Costly, **comparison of,** 227
Could of, 249
Council, councilor, counsel, counselor, 362
Course, coarse, 361
Cut, **principal parts of,** 179

–d, **ending,** 98
Dangling modifiers, 233, 236
    definition of, 488
Dashes, 489
    uses of, 341–42
Declarative sentences, 18
    definition of, 489
Definite articles, 35
Degrees of comparison, 224–27
Demonstrative adjectives, 31, 36
Demonstrative pronouns, 31, 36
Dependent clauses. *See* Subordinate clauses.
Derivatives, 489
Desert, dessert, 362
Diagrams. *See* Sentence diagrams.
Dialects, of English language, 468
Dialogue
    interjections in, 66
    new paragraphs and, 326
    punctuating dialogue, 326
    using underlining (italics) in, 321
Dictionary
    principal parts of verb and, 178
    as spelling aid, 347
Direct address
    capitalizing the title of person in, 278
    punctuation of, 303
Direct objects
    action verbs and, 80
    as compound, 75
    definition of, 74, 206, 489
    diagramming and, 450–51
    linking verbs and, 74
    objective case and, 206

    predicate nominative distinguished from, 80
    prepositional phrases and, 74
    pronouns as, 74
    questions answered by, 74
Direct quotations
    capitalization of, 266, 323
    punctuating with commas, 323–24
    punctuating with end marks, 324
    quotation marks and, 322–24
Dividing words, hyphens and, 338
Do
    as helping verb, 50
    principal parts of, 178, 179
Don't, doesn't, 162–63
Double comparison, 230
    definition of, 489
Double negatives, 231
    definition of, 489–90
Double subjects, definition of, 251, 490
Draw, **principal parts of,** 175, 179
Drink, **principal parts of,** 178, 179
Drive, **principal parts of,** 179

e (final silent), **spelling rules for,** 351–52
Easy, **comparison of,** 226
Eat, **principal parts of,** 179, 493
–ed **ending,** 98, 421
Editing, on computer, 82, 138
Effect, affect, 359
ei and *ie,* **spelling rule for,** 348–49
End marks, 290–92
    abbreviations and, 291–92, 490
    definition of, 290
    exclamation points, 290
    periods, 290
    question marks, 290
    with quotations marks, 324
    with sentences, 490
    sentence within sentence and, 340
English language
    borrowed words in, 467–68
    British vs. American spelling and pronunciation, 467
    changes in word meaning in, 466–67
    colloquialisms, 469
    dialects of, 468
    formal English, 245, 469
    good manners in use of, 210
    history of, 466–69
    informal English, 245, 469
    Middle English, 466
    nonstandard English, 245, 468–69
    Old English, 466
    pronunciation and spelling changes in, 467

slang, 469
standard American English, 468–69
standard English, 245
word origins in, 467–68
Essential phrases and clauses, 300, 490
Ethnic dialects of English language, 468
Everywheres, anywheres, anyways, nowheres, somewheres, 246
Except, accept, 246, 359
Exclamation points
abbreviations and, 292
as end marks, 4, 18–19, 290, 490
interjections and, 65
quotations and, 324
requests and commands and, 290
Exclamatory sentences
definition of, 19, 491
punctuation of, 4, 19, 290, 305

Fall, principal parts of, 179
Far, comparison of, 227
Feel, principal parts of, 179
Feel good, feel well, 249
Feminine pronouns, 165
Fewer, less, 249
Fight, principal parts of, 179
Final silent *e,* spelling rules for, 351–52
Find, principal parts of, 179
First-person pronouns, 30
Fly, principal parts of, 179
For, 62, 297
Forgive, principal parts of, 179
Formal English, 245, 469
Formally, formerly, 363
Fractions, hyphens and, 338
Freeze, principal parts of, 179
Frequently, comparison of, 227
Fused sentences, definition of, 491
Future perfect tense, 186, 187
Future tense, 186, 187

Geographical names, capitalization of, 267–68
Gerunds, 421
Get, principal parts of, 179
Give, principal parts of, 179
Glossary, definition of, 245
Go, principal parts of, 178, 179
Good, comparison of, 227
Good, well, 228–29, 249, 491

"Green Dragon Pond," 326
Grow, principal parts of, 179, 493

Had of, 254
Had ought, hadn't ought, 249
Have, as helping verb, 50, 175
Have, principal parts of, 180
He, she, they, 251
Hear, here, 363
Hear, principal parts of, 180
Helping verbs
definition of, 49
list of, 50
past participle and, 175
present participle and, 175
subject-verb agreement and, 148
Here's, 160
Hide, principal parts of, 180
Himself, hisself, 214
Himself, themselves, 214, 251
Hisself, theirself, theirselves, 214, 251
Hit, principal parts of, 180
Hold, principal parts of, 180
Homonyms
definition of, 358
words often confused, 358–69
Hope, principal parts of, 176
How come, 251
Hurt, principal parts of, 178
Hyphens
in addresses, 268
with compound numbers, 338, 491
dividing words with, 338
fractions and, 338
with prefixes, 339, 491
with suffixes, 339
syllables and, 338
word division and, 338

I pronoun, capitalization of, 266
ie and *ei,* spelling rule for, 348–49
Illegible, comparison of, 226
Imperative sentences, 492
definition of, 18, 414
punctuation of, 18–19
Indefinite articles, 35
Indefinite pronouns, 492
definition of, 32, 152
list of, 32

number and, 151, 152
possessive case, 332
singular and plural in numbers, 152–53
Independent clauses
    and or *but* with, 429
    in compound sentences, 131–32, 133, 487
    definition of, 114, 492
    punctuation of, 294, 310
    as sentences, 114, 425
Indirect objects
    as compound, 77
    definition of, 76, 207, 492
    diagramming and, 451
    nouns as, 76–77
    in objective case, 207
    placement of, 207
    prepositional phrases and, 77
    pronouns as, 76
Indirect quotations, 322
Infinitive phrases
    definition of, 103, 492
    diagramming of, 456–57
    example of, 89
Infinitives
    as adjectives, 102
    as adverbs, 102
    as base form of verbs, 175
    definition of, 102, 421, 492
    diagramming of, 456–57
    as nouns, 102
    prepositional phrases distinguished from, 60, 91, 102
Informal English, 245, 469
–*ing* ending, 98, 414, 421
Inside of, 254
***Inspect,* principal parts of,** 176
Instructions, using prepositional phrases in, 111
Intensive pronouns, 31
Interjections, 65, 66
    definition of, 492
Interrogative pronouns, 32
Interrogative sentences, 19
    definition of, 493
Interrupters, 299–304
"In the Night," 266
Intransitive verbs
    action verbs and, 45
    definition of, 52, 493
    linking verbs as, 46
Introductory words, phrases, clauses, 305, 484
Inverted word order, 160
Irregular verbs
    definition of, 175, 493
    list of, 493
    list of principal parts of specific verbs, 178–82
Italics. *See* Underlining (italics).
Items in a series
    commas and, 294–95, 484

semicolons and, 310, 499
It is I, 79
Its, it's, 251, 332, 363, 493
It's me, 79, 204

***Jealous,* comparison of,** 226
***Joyfully,* comparison of,** 226

Kind, sort, type, 251
Kind of, sort of, 252
***Know,* principal parts of,** 180

Lay, lie, 193, 493
***Lay,* principal parts of,** 193
Lead, led, 363
***Lead,* principal parts of,** 180
Learn, teach, 252
***Least, less,* in comparisons,** 226–27
Leave, let, 252
***Leave,* principal parts of,** 181
***Lend,* principal parts of,** 178, 181
Less, fewer, 249
Let, leave, 252
***Let,* principal parts of,** 178, 181
Letters (correspondence)
    capitalization in, 266
    closing of, 307
    punctuation of, 307, 312
Letters (grammar)
    plurals of, 337, 358
    spelling and, 358
    underlining (italics) and, 321, 503
Lie, lay, 193, 493
***Lie,* principal parts of,** 193
***Light,* principal parts of,** 181
Like, as, 252
Like, as if, as though, 252
Linking verbs
    action verbs used as, 229
    definition of, 46, 494
    direct object and, 74
    list of, 46–47
    predicate adjectives and, 229
    predicate nominatives and, 80

state of being and, 46
subject complements and, 79
Loose, lose, 364
Lose, loose, 364
Lose, principal parts of, 181
–ly ending, 55, 223
–ly or *–ness,* spelling rules for, 351

Main verbs, 49–50
Make, principal parts of, 178, 181
Many, comparison of, 227
Masculine pronouns, 165
Meet, principal parts of, 181
Middle English, 466
Might of, must of, 249
Misplaced modifiers, 233, 234, 236, 494
Mnemonic devices, 255, 369
Modifiers
    adjective clauses as, 238
    adjective phrases as, 92
    adjectives as, 34–37, 223
    adverb phrases as, 94–95
    adverbs as, 223–24
    clauses as, 224
    comparative degree, 225–27
    comparison of adjectives and adverbs, 224–27
    compound number used as, 338
    dangling modifiers, 233, 236
    decreasing comparison of, 226–27
    definition of, 223, 494
    degrees of comparison of, 224–27
    diagramming and, 449
    double comparisons and, 230
    double negatives and, 231
    fractions used as, 338
    irregular comparison, 227
    misplaced modifiers, 233, 234, 494
    one-word modifiers, 223–24, 433
    participial phrases as, 236
    phrases as, 224
    placement of, 232–38
    positive degree, 225–27
    in prepositional phrases, 90
    prepositional phrases as, 233–34
    problems with, 228–30
    regular comparison, 225–27
    superlative degree, 225–27
More, most, 226
Much, comparison of, 227
Must of, might of, 249

Negative words, 231
–ness, –ly, spelling rules for, 351
Neuter pronouns, 165
Newspapers, 320, 328
Nominative case, 201, 202, 203–204, 482–483
Nonessential appositive phrases, 301
Nonessential phrases and clauses, 299, 494
Nonrestrictive phrases and clauses, 299
Nonstandard English, 245, 468–69
Nor, 297
    antecedents joined by, 166
    subjects joined by, 156
Not
    as adverb, 12, 55
    contractions and, 333
Not, never, 12
Noun(s)
    abstract nouns, 28
    capitalization of nouns used as adjectives, 37
    case form, 201
    collective nouns, 29, 158–59, 167
    common nouns, 26
    compound nouns, 25, 296, 358
    concrete nouns, 28
    definition of, 25, 494
    as indirect objects, 76–77
    infinitives used as, 102
    irregular formation of plurals, 357
    plural nouns, 331, 355–58
    plural possessive case, 331
    possessive case, 201
    possessive form of, 330–31
    proper nouns, 26
    used as adjectives, 35, 37, 39
Nowheres, anyways, anywheres, everywheres, somewheres, 246
Number (grammar), definition of, 147, 494
Numbers (numerals)
    forming plurals of, 337, 358
    hyphens with compound numbers, 338
    underlining (italics) and, 321

Objective case, 201, 202, 206–209, 483
Object of preposition, 59–60, 90, 207, 209
    definition of, 495
Of, 254
Off of, 254
Often, comparison of, 227
Old English, 466

Or, 297
- antecedents joined by, 166
- sentence combining and, 423, 424
- subjects joined by, 156

Ought to of, 249
Outside of, 254

Parallelism, 421, 495
Parentheses
- overuse of, 340
- uses of, 495

Parenthetical expressions
- definition of, 303
- punctuation of, 303–304, 340, 341

Participial phrases
- as modifiers, 236
- definition of, 100, 495
- diagramming of, 456
- placement of, 100, 236
- punctuation of, 305

Participle(s)
- as adjectives, 98
- definition of, 98, 495
- diagramming of, 456
- kinds of, 98
- in verb phrases, 98

Parts of speech, 25–39, 45–67
- adjectives, 34–37
- adverbs, 54–57
- conjunctions, 62–63
- determining parts of speech, 39, 67
- interjections, 65, 66
- nouns, 25–29
- prepositions, 58–61
- pronouns, 30–32
- verbs, 45–52

Passed, past, 364
Passive voice, 189, 236
- definition of, 495

Past, passed, 364
Past participles
- definition of, 98
- dual forms of some verbs, 181
- of irregular verbs, 175, 178–82
- of regular verbs, 175, 176

Past perfect tense, 186, 187
Past tense, 186, 187
- of irregular verbs, 175, 178–82
- as principal part of verbs, 175
- of regular verbs, 175, 176

Pay, principal parts of, 181, 493
Peace, piece, 365

Periods
- abbreviations and, 291–92
- at end of statement, 4, 290
- quotations and, 324
- requests and commands and, 290

Personal pronouns
- as adjectives, 202
- case form of, 202
- definition of, 30
- plurals of, 30

Phrases. *See also* Adjective phrases; Adverb phrases; Prepositional phrases; Verbal phrases.
- adjective phrases, 92, 95
- adverb phrases, 94–95
- appositive phrases, 106, 302, 479
- combining sentences with, 420–21
- definition of, 89, 420, 496
- diagramming and, 454–57
- essential phrases, 300
- in a series, 294
- infinitive phrases, 103
- introductory phrases, 305
- as modifiers, 224
- nonessential appositive phrases, 301
- nonessential phrases, 299, 494
- participial phrases, 100, 305
- placement of, 232–38
- prepositional phrases, 90–91, 233–34
- punctuation of phrases in a series, 294
- varying sentence beginnings with, 432
- verbal phrases, 98–103, 504
- verb phrases, 11–12, 98, 504

Piece, peace, 365
Plain, plane, 365
Plural, definition of, 147
Plurals
- of compound nouns, 358
- irregular, 357
- of letters, 337, 358
- of nouns, 331, 355–58
- of nouns ending in *o* preceded by consonant, 356–57
- of nouns ending in *s, x, z, ch, sh*, 355
- of nouns ending in *y* preceded by vowel, 356
- of nouns ending in *f* or *fe*, 356
- of numerals, 337, 358
- possessive case and, 331
- punctuation of, 358
- of symbols, 337, 358
- of words referred to as words, 337, 358

Poetry, capitalization in, 266
Positive degree of comparison, 225–27, 485
Possessive case, 201–202, 483
- definition of, 330
- formation of, 330–32
- plurals nouns and, 331

Possessive pronouns

 513

apostrophes and, 330, 332
contractions distinguished from, 332, 334
Powerful, comparison of, 226
Predicate(s)
complete predicate, 10–11
definition of, 8, 496
placement of, 8–9
simple predicate, 10–11
Predicate adjectives
definition of, 81, 496
diagramming and, 453
linking verbs and, 229
Predicate nominatives
choosing correct form of pronoun and, 204
completing linking verbs, 80
compound predicate nominatives, 80
definition of, 79, 204, 496
diagramming and, 452
direct objects distinguished from, 80
nominative case pronouns and, 204
placement of, 80
pronouns as, 204
Prefixes
definition of, 350, 497
hyphens with, 339, 491, 497
spelling and, 350–51
Preposition(s)
adverbs distinguished from, 61
capitalization and, 279
definition of, 58, 497
for as, 62
list of, 58
Prepositional phrases, 209
as adjective phrases, 92, 95
as adjectives, 233
as adverb phrases, 94, 95
as adverbs, 233
definition of, 59, 90, 497
diagramming and, 454–55
direct object and, 74
example of, 89
indirect object and, 77
infinitives distinguished from, 60, 91, 102
as modifiers, 233–34
modifiers in, 90
placement of, 233–34
punctuation of, 305
subject-verb agreement and, 153
Present participles
definition of, 98
helping verbs and, 175
of irregular verbs, 178–82
as principal part of verbs, 175
of regular verbs, 176
Present perfect tense, 186, 187
Present tense, 186, 187
Principal, principle, 365

Principal parts of verbs
base form, 175
definition of, 175
dictionary and, 178
irregular verbs, 178–82
past participle, 175
past tense, 175
present participle, 175
regular verbs, 176
Progressive form, 188
Pronoun-antecedent agreement. *See* Agreement (pronoun-antecedent).
Pronouns
as adjectives, 36, 39
antecedents and, 30, 216–17, 479
apostrophes and, 330, 332
appositives and, 106, 213
case form of, 201–209, 482–83
clear reference and, 216–17, 483
as compound object, 207
definition of, 30, 497
demonstrative pronouns, 31, 36
as direct object, 74
feminine pronouns, 165
gender and, 165
himself, hisself, 214
indefinite pronouns, 32
intensive pronouns, 31
interrogative pronouns, 32
masculine pronouns, 165
neuter pronouns, 165
nominative case, 201, 202, 203–204, 482–83
number and, 165–68
objective case, 201, 202, 206–209, 483
as object of prepositions, 209
personal pronouns, 30, 202
possessive case, 201, 202, 483
possessive pronouns, 330, 332
as predicate nominative, 204
problems with, 211–17
reflexive pronouns, 31, 214
relative pronouns, 32, 118
theirselves, themselves, 214
types of, 30–32
uses of, 201–14
who, whom, 211–12
Pronunciation, spelling and, 347
Proper adjectives
capitalization of, 276–77
definition of, 37, 276
Proper nouns
abbreviation of, 291
apostrophes and, 330
capitalization of, 266–74
definition of, 26, 266
used as adjectives, 37
Punctuation

of abbreviations, 291–92
apostrophes, 330–37
brackets, 341
clauses, 294, 297, 299–300, 305, 426
colons, 311–12
commas, 294–307
of contractions, 333–34
in conventional situations, 306–307
dashes, 341–42
dialogue, 326
end marks, 290–92, 490
exclamation points, 18–19, 290
hyphens, 338–39
of interjections, 65
of interrupters, 299–304
of introductory words, phrases, clauses, 305
of items in a series, 294–95
overuse of, 308
parentheses, 340
of parenthetical expressions, 340, 341
periods, 290–92
of phrases, 294, 299–300, 305
of possessive case, 330–32
question marks, 19, 290
quotation marks, 322–28
of salutation of any letter, 307, 312
semicolons, 310
of short written works, 327
of titles, 327–28
underlining (italics), 320–21
of written works, 327
Put, **principal parts of,** 178, 182

Question marks
abbreviations and, 292
as end marks, 4, 19, 290
quotations and, 324
Questions, diagramming of, 444
Quiet, quite, 365
Quotation marks
broken quotations and, 323
in dialogue, 326
direct quotations and, 322–324, 497
indirect quotation and, 322
other punctuation marks preceding, 498
single quotation marks, 327, 328
titles and, 498
for titles of short works, 327–28
Quotations
broken quotations, 323
capitalization of, 266, 323
exclamation points and, 323, 324

question marks and, 323, 324
quotation within quotation, 327
several sentences and, 327

Raise, **principal parts of,** 192
Raise, rise, 191–92, 498
Read, **principal parts of,** 182
Real, 254
Reflexive pronouns, 31, 214
Regional dialects of English language, 468
Regular verbs, 175, 176
definition of, 498
list of, 498
Relative pronouns
adjective clauses and, 32, 135, 238
definition of, 32, 118
list of, 32, 118
Request, punctuation of, 290
Restrictive phrases and clauses, 300
Ride, **principal parts of,** 182
Ring, **principal parts of,** 182
Rise, **principal parts of,** 192
Rise, raise, 191–92, 498
Root words, 498
Run, **principal parts of,** 182
Run-on sentences, 416–17
definition of, 416, 499
punctuation and, 416
revision of, 417

Salutation
of business letter, 312
of personal letter, 307
punctuation of, 307, 312
Say, **principal parts of,** 182
School subjects, capitalization of, 277
Second-person pronouns, 30
–sede, –cede, –ceed, **spelling rule for,** 350
See
conjugation of, 187–88
principal parts of, 182
Seek, **principal parts of,** 182
Sell, **principal parts of,** 182
Semicolons
in compound sentences, 132, 499
with conjunctive adverbs, 499
definition of, 310
independent clauses and, 294, 310

items in a series and, 310, 499
overuse of, 310
run-on sentences and, 417
Send, principal parts of, 182
Sentence(s)
abbreviation at end of, 292
basic parts of, 5
combining sentences, 418–26
complete sentences, 414–17
complex sentences, 135, 137, 425, 435, 486
compound-complex sentences, 137, 435, 486–87
compound sentences, 131–32, 133, 137, 297, 424, 435, 487
declarative sentences, 18, 489
definition of, 4, 499
distinguishing between simple and compound, 133, 297
end marks and, 490
exclamatory sentences, 19, 491
fused sentences, 491
grammar checks and, 114
imperative sentences, 18–19, 414, 492
independent clauses used as, 114
interrogative sentences, 19, 493
inverted word order in, 160
kinds of, 130–37
punctuation of, 4, 18–19, 290
revision of, 116
run-on sentences, 416–17, 499
sentence fragments, 113, 414–15, 499
simple sentences, 4, 130, 133, 137, 297, 435, 500
stringy sentences, 428–29, 500
test-taking strategies and, 470–75
using transitions in, 437–38
wordy sentences, 430
Sentence diagrams, 444–62
Sentence fragments, 4, 113, 414–15, 499
Sentence structure
complex sentences, 135, 435
compound-complex sentences, 137, 435
compound sentences, 131–32, 133, 435
diagramming and, 460–62
simple sentences, 130, 133, 435
test-taking strategies and, 473–74
varying sentence structure, 434–35
Sentence style
combining sentences, 418–26
improvement of, 428–30
sentence length, 431–33
stringy sentence revision, 428–29
test-taking strategies and, 474–75
using transitions, 437–38
varying sentence beginnings, 432–33
wordy sentence revision, 430
Set, principal parts of, 190
Set, sit, 190, 500
Shall, will, 187

Sharp, **comparison of,** 227
She, he, they, 251
Shone, shown, 365
Should of, 249
Shrink, **principal parts of,** 182
Simple, **comparison of,** 226
Simple predicate, 10–11
Simple sentences
compound sentences distinguished from, 133, 297
definition of, 130, 435, 500
diagramming of, 460
Simple subjects, definition of, 6–7
Sing, **principal parts of,** 178, 182
Single quotation marks, 327, 328
Singular, definition of, 147
Sink, **principal parts of,** 182
Sit, **principal parts of,** 190
Sit, set, 190, 500
Slang, 469
Slip, **principal parts of,** 176
Slow, **comparison of,** 225
So, 297
Some, somewhat, 255
Somewheres, anyways, anywheres, everywheres, nowheres, 246
Soon, **comparison of,** 225
Sort, kind, type, 251
Sort of, kind of, 252
Speak, **principal parts of,** 182
Speech, parts of, 25–39, 45–67
Spelling, 347–75
–*cede,* –*ceed,* –*sede,* 350
computer use and, 245, 267, 348
of contractions, 333
dictionary use and, 347
final silent *e,* 351–52
good habits for, 347–48
homonyms, 358–69
ie and *ei,* 348–49
notebook used for, 348
one-syllable words, 353
pluralized compound nouns, 358
plurals of nouns, 355–58
plurals of numerals, letters, symbols, and words, 358
prefixes, 350, 351
proofreading for, 348
rules for, 348–58
suffixes, 350, 351–53
syllables and, 347
word list, 374–75
words often confused (homonyms), 358–69
Spend, **principal parts of,** 182
Spread, **principal parts of,** 493
Stand, **principal parts of,** 182
Standard American English, 468–69
Standard English, 245

State of being, linking verbs and, 46
Statements, punctuation of, 290
Stationary, stationery, 367
Steal, **principal parts of,** 182
Straight, **comparison of,** 225
Stringy sentences
    definition of, 428, 500
    revision of, 428–29
Style. *See* Sentence style.
Subject(s)
    complete subjects, 6–7
    compound subjects, 13, 133, 155–56
    definition of, 5, 500
    double subjects, 251, 490
    identification of, 13
    in nominative case, 202, 203
    placement of, 5
    sentence diagramming and, 444–47
    simple subject, 6–7
    understood subject, 19, 445
Subject complements
    definition of, 79, 500
    diagramming and, 452–53
    linking verbs and, 79
    predicate adjectives, 81
    predicate nominatives, 79–80
Subject-verb agreement. *See* Agreement (subject-verb).
Subordinate clauses
    adjective clauses, 117–18, 135
    adverb clauses, 120–21, 135
    combining sentences and, 425–26
    definition of, 114, 501
    diagramming of, 458–59
    introductory words of, 114
    relative pronouns and, 118
    subordinating conjunctions and, 121
    varying sentence beginnings with, 433
    and words of time or place, 426
Subordinating conjunctions, 63
    list of, 121, 459
    placement of, 121
Subordination, definition of, 425, 501
Suffixes
    definition of, 350, 501
    final consonant and, 353
    hyphens with, 339
    spelling changes of words ending in *y*, 351, 352
    spelling of, 350–53
Superlative degree of comparison, 225–27, 485
Swiftly, **comparison of,** 226
Swim, **principal parts of,** 182
Swing, **principal parts of,** 182
Syllables, 338, 501
    spelling and, 347
Symbols
    forming plurals of, 337, 358
    underlining (italics) and, 503

T

Take, bring, 248
Take, **principal parts of,** 182
Talk, **principal parts of,** 175
Teach, learn, 252
Teach, **principal parts of,** 182
Tear, **principal parts of,** 182
Tell, **principal parts of,** 182
Tense. *See also* Verb(s).
    consistency of, 188
    definition of, 186, 501–502
    list of, 186, 187
    progressive form, 188
Test-taking strategies, 470–75
    general strategies, 470–71
    strategies for answering grammar, usage, and mechanics questions, 471–75
Than, then, 255, 367
That, 118
    essential clauses and, 300
That, who, which, 258, 426
That's her, 204
That there, this here, 256
That was he, 79
That, which, **as relative pronouns,** 118
The
    capitalization of, 279, 280, 321
    as definite article, 35
    prepositional phrases and, 90
    underlining (italics) and, 321
Their, there, they're, 255, 367, 502–503
Theirself, theirselves, hisself, 214, 251
Them, 255
Themselves, himself, 214, 251
Themselves, theirselves, 214
Then, than, 255, 367
There's, 160
They, she, he, 251
They're, their, there, 255, 367, 502–503
Think, **principal parts of,** 182
Third-person pronouns, 30
This here, that there, 256
This kind, sort, type, 251
Threw, through, 367
Throw, **principal parts of,** 182
Time
    punctuating expressions of, 291, 312
    tense of verbs and, 175
Titles
    agreement of verbs with, 162, 168
    of books, magazines, newspapers, poems, short stories, 279–80, 320
    capitalization of, 278–80

of movies, television programs, works of art, musical compositions, 280, 320
official titles in published works, 279–80
of persons, 278–79
punctuation with subtitles, 312
of short works with quotation marks, 327
underlining (italics) and, 320, 503

To, too, two, 368
Transitional words and phrases, 437–38
    list of, 438
Transitions, 503
Transitive verbs, 45, 52
    definition of, 503
Try and, 256
Type, kind, sort, 251

Underlining (italics)
    artworks and, 320
    denoted by underlining, 320
    films and, 320
    foreign words and, 503
    musical works and, 320
    publications and, 320, 328
    television programs and, 320
    titles and, 320, 503
    the, 321
    transportation vehicles, 321
    word-processing software and, 320
    words, letters, and numerals, 321, 503
    in written dialogue, 321
Unless, without, 259
Understood subject, 19, 445
Units of measure, abbreviations for, 292
Use to, used to, 258

Verb(s)
    action verbs, 45, 47, 229
    active voice, 189
    adverbs as defining, 54
    base form of, 175, 176, 178–82
    compound verbs, 15, 133
    conjugation of, 186–88
    definition of, 45, 503
    direct objects and, 74
    helping verbs, 49–50
    intransitive verbs, 45, 46, 52, 493
    irregular verbs, 175, 178–82, 493
    lie, lay, 193

    linking verbs, 46–47, 229, 494
    main verbs, 49–50
    passive voice, 189
    principal parts of, 175–82
    regular verbs, 175, 176, 498
    rise, raise, 191–92
    sentence diagramming and, 444–47
    as simple predicate, 10–11
    sit, set, 190
    tenses of, 186–88, 501–502
    transitive verbs, 45, 52, 503
Verbal phrases, 98–103, 456–57
    definition of, 504
Verbals
    definition of, 98, 503
    diagramming of, 456–57
Verb phrases, 11–12
    definition of, 11, 49, 504
    example of, 89
    interrupted by another part of speech, 50
    participles and, 98
    subject-verb agreement and, 148
Very, 55
Vocabulary
    word origins, 467–68
    wordiness, 504
Voice
    active voice, 189, 236, 476
    passive voice, 189, 236, 495
    verbs and, 504

Waist, waste, 368
Way, ways, 258
Weak, week, 368
Wear, **principal parts of,** 182
Weather, whether, 369
Well, **comparison of,** 227
Well, good, 228–229, 249, 491
When, where, 258
Where, 258
Where's, 160
Which, that, **as relative pronouns,** 118
Which, who, that, 258, 426
Who, which, that, 258, 426
Who, whom, 211–12, 504
Who's, whose, 258–59, 369
Will, shall, 187
Win, **principal parts of,** 182
Without, unless, 259
Wordiness, definition of, 504
Word(s). See also English language.
    borrowed words, 467–68
    commonly confused (homonyms), 358–69

dividing words using hyphens, 338
root words, 498
in a series, 294

Words referred to as words
forming plural of, 337, 358
underlining (italics) of, 321, 503

Wordy sentences, definition of, 430

Would of, 249

Write, **principal parts of,** 182, 502

Writing application
capitalization in letter writing, 287
clear pronoun reference, 43
comparisons in a letter, 243
complete sentences, 23
correct spelling in written review, 373
formal English in speeches, 263
prepositional phrases, 71, 111
prepositional phrases in directions, 71
prepositional phrases in a note, 111
pronouns in letters, 221
punctuation in announcements, 317

quotations in reports, 345
sentence structures in letter writing, 144–45
subject complements and riddles, 87
subject-verb agreement, 172–73
subordinate clauses in manuals, 127
verb forms/tenses, 199

Yet, 297
You, **as understood subject,** 19
Your, you're, 259, 369

ZIP Codes, 268, 292, 307

ACKNOWLEDGMENTS

For permission to reprint copyrighted material, grateful acknowledgment is made to the following sources:

HarperCollins Publishers: From "Green Dragon Pond" from *The Spring of Butterflies,* translated by He Liyi. Copyright ©1986 by He Liyi.

University of California Press: From "In the Night" from *Singing for Power: The Song Magic of the Papago Indians of Southern Arizona* by Ruth Murray Underhill. Copyright ©1938, 1966 by Ruth Murray Underhill.

PHOTO CREDITS

Abbreviations used: (tl)top left, (tc)top center, (tr)top right, (l)left, (lc)left center, (c)center, (rc)right center, (r)right, (bl)bottom left, (bc)bottom center, (br)bottom right.

AUTHOR ESSAYS: Amy Benjamin (Dylan Griffin/HRW Photo), Brock Haussamen (Dylan Griffin/HRW Photo), Rei Noguchi (Henry Blackham/HRW Photo), Billy Boyar (John Langford/HRW Photo).

TABLE OF CONTENTS: Page v, Courtesy of Terry Dewald/Jerry Jacka Photography; vi, Tom Prettyman/Photo Edit; viii, John Elk, III/Bruce Coleman, Inc.; ix, Image Copyright ©1998 Photodisc, Inc.; xi, James Sugar/Black Star; xii, SuperStock; xv, Corbis Images (formerly Digital Stock Corp.); xvii (tl), Image Club Graphics ©1998 Adobe Systems; xviii, Gambell/SuperStock; xix, Ron Sefton/Bruce Coleman, Inc.

CHAPTER 1: Page 9, UPI/Bettmann/CORBIS; 12 (lc), Paul Chesley/Tony Stone Images; 12 (bl), John Elk, III/Bruce Coleman, Inc.; 14 (bc), Tony Arruza/Bruce Coleman, Inc.; 14 (bl), John Elk, III/Bruce Coleman, Inc.; 17, Corbis Images.

CHAPTER 2: Page 29, Chris Eden/Francine Seders Gallery; 39, Corbis Images.

CHAPTER 3: Page 53, Image Copyright ©1998 Photodisc, Inc.; 56, Tony Kirves/Southern Exposure; 60, Culver Pictures, Inc.; 67, Fred Bruemmer/Peter Arnold, Inc.

CHAPTER 4: Page 75, AllSport USA/Vandystadt Agence de Presse; 76, Nawrocki Stock Photo; 83, Image Copyright ©1998 Photodisc, Inc.; 84 (tl), Bob Daemmrich/Tony Stone Worldwide, Ltd.; 84 (lc), Jose Carrillo/Photo Edit; 84 (bl), Tom Prettyman/Photo Edit.

CHAPTER 5: Page 91, D.P. Hershkowitz/Bruce Coleman, Inc.; 93, Andrew Bernstein/Allsport; 99, Corbis Images; 101 (c), Fielder Kownslar/IBM Corporation; 101 (rc), The Granger Collection, New York; 104, Image Copyright ©1998 Photodisc, Inc.; 105, Bill Aron/PhotoEdit.

CHAPTER 6: Page 115, Michael Ochs Archives/Venice, CA; 116, Michael Ochs Archives/Venice, CA.

CHAPTER 7: Page 134, FPG International; 135, Corbis-Bettmann; 136, UPI/Bettmann/CORBIS; 139, Culver Pictures, Inc.

CHAPTER 8: Page 149 (br), Paul S. Conklin/Nawrocki Stock Photo; 149 (c), David R. Frazier Photolibrary; 150 (lc), Gerhard Gacheldle/HRW Photo; 150 (tl), Image Club Graphics ©1998 Adobe Systems; 155, SuperStock; 158, David Young Wolff/Tony Stone Images.

CHAPTER 9: Page 177, SuperStock; 189, Image Copyright ©2001 Photodisc, Inc.; 189, Image Copyright ©2001 Photodisc, Inc.; 196, Bob Daemmrich/The Image Works.

CHAPTER 10: Page 208, Bettmann/CORBIS; 211, Culver Pictures, Inc.

CHAPTER 11: Page 228 (rc, lc), Cameramann International; 235, The Granger Collection, New York; 240, H. Armstrong Roberts.

CHAPTER 12: Page 247, Paul Chesley/Tony Stone Images; 250, John Langford/HRW Photo; 253, HRW Photo Research Library; 257, Sylvain Grandadam/Tony Stone Images.

CHAPTER 13: Page 269, James Sugar/Black Star; 270, Richard Pasley/Viesti Collection; 276 (lc), Culver Pictures, Inc.; 276 (tl), The Granger Collection, New York; 276 (bl), Archive Photos.

CHAPTER 14: Page 290, Brian Lanker; 298, Courtesy of Terry Dewald/Jerry Jacka Photography; 301, The Granger Collection, New York; 304, Image Copyright ©2001 PhotoDisc, Inc.; 309, Corbis Images (formerly Digital Stock Corp.); 314, Sanctuary for Animals, Westtown, New York.

CHAPTER 15: Page 329, SuperStock; 331, The Granger Collection, New York; 336, James Montgomery/Bruce Coleman, Inc.

CHAPTER 16: Page 354 (all), Lightwave; 366, Scala/Art Resource, NY; 370, Image Copyright ©1998 Photodisc, Inc.

CHAPTER 17: Page 379, Image Copyright ©1998 Photodisc, Inc.; 383, John Kelly/HRW Photo; 386, Corbis Images; 388, Russel Dian/HRW Photo; 395, Tim Defrisco/Allsport; 400, Image Copyright ©2001 PhotoDisc, Inc.

CHAPTER 18: Page 415, Kim Taylor/Bruce Coleman, Inc.; 417, NASA/Nawrocki Stock Photo; 421, SuperStock; 422, Gambell/SuperStock; 425, SuperStock; 432, Ron Sefton/Bruce Coleman, Inc.; 435, Reuters/Mark Cardwell/Archive Photos; 418, Image Copyright ©2001 Photodisc, Inc.; 428, Image Copyright ©2001 Photodisc, Inc.

ILLUSTRATION CREDITS

All work, unless otherwise noted, contributed by Holt, Rinehart & Winston.

Page 20, Nancy Tucker; 97, Ortelius Design; 131, Ortelius Design; 184, Larry McEntire; 186, Leslie Kell; 259, Uhl Studios, Inc.; 276, Ortelius Design; 277, Brian Battles; 283, Ortelius Design; 293, Uhl Studios, Inc.; 335, Leslie Kell; 350, Ortelius Design.